# THE TWO U

**Alvin Jackson** is Sir Richard Lodge Professor of History and Head of the School of History, Classics, and Archaeology at the University of Edinburgh.

'In this distinguished book...Jackson sets out to provide a rigorous comparative treatment of the Irish and Scottish experience of union, and to explain why both have endured, if only partly in the Irish case. The result is richly textured work by a historian at the top of his game. Jackson's command of the historiographical debates pertaining to a daunting range of periods and issues in the history of the two unions, and his lucidly argued judgements and insights combine to put his book in pole position in the area of comparative historical studies concerning these islands. It is a book that could hardly have been timelier'

**Graham Walker**, *Irish Historical Studies*

'Why was the one union a success, while the other failed? Alvin Jackson brings the tools of modern historical scholarship to answer this question in his impressive book. *The Two Unions* offers welcome relief from the usual polemics'.

**Vernon Bogdanor**, *Literary Review*

'A superb run-through of 300 years of critical issues with lots of topical relevance and interest...highly recommended'

**Patrick Geoghegan**, 'Talking History', Newstalk Radio

'Alvin Jackson, the author of two excellent histories of Ireland in (and not in) the United Kingdom now broadens his canvas in a timely account of one [union's] death and the other's survival - so far'.

**Iain McLean**, *Times Literary Supplement*

'There could be no better moment to produce the first detailed scholarly history of the two unions. Its author Alvin Jackson spans them...tough-minded, unsentimental...With this new work he has performed an extraordinarily valuable service...Jackson is the first person to describe the strengths and achievements of the two unions over their entire lifetimes...perfect academic detachment is preserved...a superb book'

**A.B.Cooke, Lord Lexden**, *The House – Parliament's Magazine*

'For those interested in an excellent and up-to-date history of the relationship between the constituent parts of the United Kingdom, I would suggest Alvin Jackson's *The Two Unions*'

**Douglas Kanter**, American Historical Association, AHA Today

'enlightening and even fun...smart, wonderfully learned, and witty. [This] book would make a splendid present for anyone interested in Irish (or Scottish) history'

**Jude Collins**, 'Book Programme', Radio Ulster

'This superb book provides the first complete political and cultural history of the unions...highly recommended'

**D.R. Bisson**, *Choice*

'The study is based on a very wide range of sources, is elegantly written, and is filled with new insights. It is in every respect a triumph, managing to provoke historians of both Scotland and Ireland, while offering a fresh and timely perspective on the history of the Unions...the relationship of both Scotland and Ireland to the British Empire is also brilliantly delineated...the central achievement of this important book is that it can no longer be claimed that the Irish Union was doomed to failure from the start – or that the Scottish Union was destined to succeed'

**Thomas Bartlett**, *Annual Bulletin of Historical Literature*

# THE TWO UNIONS

## IRELAND, SCOTLAND, AND THE SURVIVAL OF THE UNITED KINGDOM, 1707–2007

ALVIN JACKSON

OXFORD
UNIVERSITY PRESS

# OXFORD

## UNIVERSITY PRESS

Great Clarendon Street, Oxford, OX2 6DP,
United Kingdom

Oxford University Press is a department of the University of Oxford.
It furthers the University's objective of excellence in research, scholarship,
and education by publishing worldwide. Oxford is a registered trade mark of
Oxford University Press in the UK and in certain other countries

British Library Cataloguing in Publication Data
Data available

ISBN 978–0–19–959399–6 (Hbk.)
ISBN 978–0–19–967537–1 (Pbk.)

Printed in Great Britain by
CPI Group (UK) Ltd, Croydon, CR0 4YY

2 4 6 8 10 9 7 5 3 1

For Alexander Thomas Jackson

# Contents

## IV. REFLECTIONS ON THE UNIONS

# Abbreviations

| | |
|---|---|
| ICS | Indian Civil Service |
| ILPU | Irish Loyal and Patriotic Union |
| IUA | Irish Unionist Alliance |
| NLS | National Library of Scotland |
| NUCA | National Union of Conservative Associations |
| PRONI | Public Record Office of Northern Ireland |
| RAMC | Royal Army Medical Corps |
| SCUA | Scottish Conservative and Unionist Association |
| SUA | Scottish Unionist Association |
| SUMC | Scottish Unionist Members' Committee |
| UAI | Unionist Associations of Ireland |
| UDL | Union Defence League |
| UUC | Ulster Unionist Council |

# List of maps / illustrations

# Acknowledgements

I am grateful to the British Academy for the award of a Senior Research Fellowship in 2008–2009, and to my colleagues in the School of History, Classics, and Archaeology at Edinburgh for facilitating some additional research leave. I am grateful, too, to the Carnegie Trust for the award of a Small Research Grant, which has permitted study in a range of archives and libraries. I also want to thank Marianne Elliott, the Institute of Irish Studies, and the School of History at the University of Liverpool for appointing me as the D.B. Quinn Lecturer in 2006 and for giving me an opportunity to test some of the ideas in Part III of the book. Versions of other parts were read to the Conference of British Historians at the University of Strathclyde in June 2007, the British Association of Irish Studies Conference, Liverpool, in September 2007, the American Conference of Irish Studies at Syracuse, New York, in October 2007, the Postgraduate Colloquium at Boston College, Massachusetts, in November 2007, the Beijing Forum and Postgraduate Seminars at the University of Peking in November 2008, the Irish History Seminar, Hertford College, Oxford, in December 2009, and the Modern British History seminar at Pembroke College, Cambridge, in November 2010. An early (and somewhat different) draft of Chapter 6 was published as 'The Survival of the Union' in Joseph Cleary and Claire Connolly (eds), *Companion to Irish Culture* (Cambridge: 2006).

I am grateful to the several scholars who have spent time and effort on my behalf. I must acknowledge once again the great influence and inspiration of Brian Harrison. Owen Dudley Edwards, the revered patriarch of Irish history in Scotland, has been an unfailingly generous source of ideas and comment. Other friends and colleagues at Edinburgh—Jay Brown, Ewen Cameron, and Jenny Wormald—have also kindly looked over the whole manuscript, and offered valuable suggestions for its improvement. The anonymous readers for Oxford University Press were similarly constructive and helpful. However, I alone am responsible for any errors of fact or interpretation which remain.

Christopher Wheeler at Oxford was a model of courtesy and efficiency. I am grateful, too, to the staff of the Bodleian Library, Oxford, Churchill College, Cambridge, the National Archives at Kew, the National Archives of Scotland, the National Library of Scotland, and Nuffield College, Oxford. In particular I should like to thank Peter Clapham at the Edinburgh City Archives, Jeremy McIlwaine of the Conservative Party Archive at the Bodleian, Oxford, Trevor Parkhill at the Ulster Museum, and Andrew Riley at Churchill College for their help. My thanks go, too, to Alima Bucciantini, now of Appalachian State University, for her help with the illustrations for the volume, and to Maura Pringle, Queen's University Belfast, for her work on the two maps.

A.J.

Edinburgh

**Map 1.** Ireland *c.* 1914: The Rail and Canal Networks, and Places mentioned in the Text.

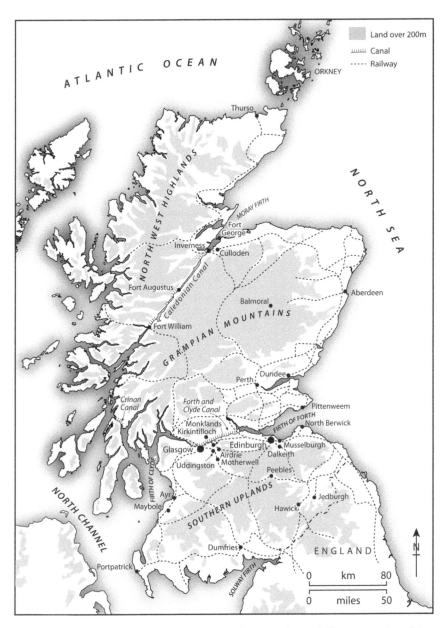

**Map 2.** Scotland *c.*1914: The Rail and Canal Networks, and Places mentioned in the Text.

# PART
# I

# The Measures and their Histories

# I

# Histories

## Historiography, comparability, complexity, longevity

To explain the success of the Union with Scotland (for in political operations so difficult as that of blending two separate, and not very friendly,
nations into one state it is success, not want of success, which needs explanation) is all but to unfold the grounds of the failure of the Union with
Ireland, since the shortest summary of the whole matter is that special
causes favoured or produced the incorporation of Scotland with England,
and that each one of these conditions was conspicuously wanting to the
attempt to unite Ireland with Great Britain. A.V. Dicey, 'The Two Acts of
Union: A Contrast', *Fortnightly Review*, 30, 176 (Aug. 1881)

You know that England, Ireland, Scotland and Wales are all joined together.
The first two to be joined together were England and Ireland. H.E.
Marshall, *Our Island Story* (1905).

[Mr Gladstone] is a Scotch member, a member for Midlothian, and yet,
though he may know all about the Greek islands and the Greek cities in
the time of Homer, he does not now know the geography between
Scotland and Ireland. Thomas MacKnight, *Ulster as It is* (1896), ii, p. 131

## The nature of union

The United Kingdom was in practice never truly a vision or an inspiration.
It was originally, and fundamentally, a bargain, concerned much less with
universal truths or aspirations or future possibilities, than with immediate
commercial and military realities. The union was about pragmatism, necessity and hybridity, the delicate negotiation of Scottish, Irish, and English
identities into new political and cultural formations; and while the attendant compromises ultimately illuminate some of the union's weaknesses, they

also go a long way to explaining the union's relative successes and longevity. The union succeeded, for a time, perhaps because there was so little (in terms of rigour or solidity) to fail.

The modern United Kingdom was created through the unions of (on the one hand) England, Wales, and Scotland in 1707, and (on the other) Great Britain and Ireland in 1801. There were many differences between these two contracts, but each was immediately rooted in the economic and military concerns of the day. Each was overwhelmingly concerned with the intricate details of trading relationships. Neither union was the fruit of pro-tracted, still less popular, campaigning. Neither union embodied any wide or mature consideration of future possibilities. Though each (particularly the Scots) had a lengthy prehistory, the two unions were swiftly (if shrewdly) formulated responses to immediate crises.

Indeed, it was perhaps precisely because each union had a complex and lengthy prehistory that their enactments were ultimately pursued with such speed and remorselessness. Though the union of 1800 drew upon that of 1707, in reality neither reflected any fundamentally shared conception. In fact the thoroughly contested nature of the union between the 17th and 19th centuries meant that its codification and enactment were always bound to create dispute and resentment even amongst those who were ostensibly committed to its principles. Religion and empire were certainly shared motifs in much of the early conceptualization of union from the mid 16th century onwards; but for later unionists military, economic, and other equally secular pressures became the main influences upon their thought. Throughout the 17th century union was variously envisioned as a shared religious and imperial enterprise (King James VI and I), a holy presbyterian confederation (the Scots Covenanters of the 1640s), an English political and military ascend-ancy (Oliver Cromwell), and as a confederal parliamentary structure (Andrew Fletcher of Saltoun). On the whole, the idea of the union as partnership, religious and material, was a Scots invention, with Caledonian thinkers such as Thomas Craig, John Gordon, David Hume, James Maxwell positing the idea of a shared and equal enterprise, and one in which Scots identity might be preserved and Scots interests sustained (in this sense Gordon Brown, strongly intellectual and unionist, stands in a tradition of Scots thought on the union which stretches back at least to the late 16th century)[1]. Conversely, however, opposition to union could be firmly rooted in religious principle, with some Irish Catholics associating Protestantism with British subjugation, and (equally) some Scottish Episcopalians linking Presbyterianism with the wiles and stratagems of the 'auld' enemy, England[2].

A critical motivation for the elaboration of Jacobean unionism was of course the elevation in 1603 of James VI of Scotland to the English throne. While a variety of religious and historical images informed his outlook, James cast himself as Constantine the Great, uniting his (British) empire under one ruler and (with luck) one agreed Christian faith (in a startling break from Tudor norms, James was sometimes depicted on his coinage in imperial or Constantinian mode, wearing the laurel wreath of an emperor and proclaiming 'faciam eos in gentem unam'—'I will make them into one people', drawn from Ezekiel 37:22). James, however, was distinctive in the passion and vitality of his unionism: subsequent monarchs (even Charles I, born in Dunfermline) were less actively interested or enthusiastic. Moreover, whether in 1603 or 1707 or 1800, the idea of a union partnership was looked upon with scepticism by the English generally, on the grounds that, as the richer and stronger power, more sacrifice would be required from them than from Scots. While, in the early 17th century, and through the Solemn League and Covenant of 1643, pious Scots wondered whether a shared Britain might be providentially ordained for the purpose of delivering a universal Presbyterianism, English parliamentarians feared for their markets and English antiquarians celebrated the distinctive (Anglo-Saxon) origins of their own nation[3]. One vigorously English definition of union was supplied by Oliver Cromwell after 1651, when Scotland and Ireland were effectively incorporated into what has been described as 'an English empire'[4]. Scots political thinkers, such as Andrew Fletcher of Saltoun, continued into the late 17th century to hold onto the possibility of a confederal union.[5] By the end of the century, therefore, there were at least three —religio-imperial, English and confederal—definitions of union. These were distinctive, largely discrete, and mutually incompatible; and while none individually or wholly supplied a precedent for the parliamentary unions of 1707 and 1800, it is hard to deny both that profound English scepticism and the Cromwellian notion of a greater England were significant and long-standing influences.

But in the event each union, British and Irish, was immediately rooted in international warfare, the threat (or reality) of internal subversion, and economic dislocation: each was the product of thinly rooted, ambivalent and contingent, English support. The creation of Great Britain in 1707 was pre-

cipitated by England's defence needs in the context of the War of the Spanish
Succession ('England sought union in the early 18th century mainly for
purposes of national security'), the mounting significance of Jacobite dissent, and by the parlous condition of the Scots economy (allowing that
some of its fundamentals were in a healthy if embryonic condition)[6]. The
creation of the United Kingdom in 1801 was precipitated by Britain's
defence needs in the context of the war with revolutionary France, the
challenge of republican subversion within Ireland itself, and by the uncertain condition of the Irish economy in the mid and late 1790s (even if,
again, some of the economic fundamentals were secure). In the case of both
the Anglo-Scots and the British-Irish unions, English support had matured
only relatively recently (the English parliament had opposed union with
Scotland through much of the 17th century, and with Ireland through much
of the 18th century), and was contingent upon perceptions of short-term
English needs.

The shape of union reflected, partly the economic and military supremacy of England, but (perhaps even more significantly than this) the divisions
and animosities within both Scotland and, later, Ireland: in so far as union
was first accepted in these polities, it was because of the needs and insecurities of local elites. The Anglo-Scots union dwelt lengthily on the concerns
of Scotland's landed, legal, and commercial classes, and gave solace (in particular) to those who had invested in the Company of Scotland and its
disastrous scheme for a trading colony at Darien in (what is now) Panama.
The British-Irish union offered enhanced security to the Anglican landed
(or 'Ascendancy') interest in Ireland, and lavish compensation to the (mostly
landed) proprietors of borough seats in the Irish parliament. Each union
offered a form of free trade, and the opportunity for gain to those in Scotland
and Ireland able to adapt to the rigours of the English industrial economy.
But of course many (small manufacturers, the industrial and agrarian under-
classes, Irish Catholics) lay wholly or partly beyond the blessed community
of those directly favoured by union.

On the whole the circumstances of these nativities illuminate the future
condition of the two unions. From the beginning the relationship of the
constituent kingdoms towards the union hinged upon perceptions of local
or national justice, or even advantage. If the unions were fundamentally
about local commercial prosperity and England's military security, then
they were vulnerable to economic downturn, to the revised calculation of
English military interest, or to the perception of inequity. It is clear that a

turning point in the British-Irish union occurred with the catastrophic Famine of 1845–1851, when the union state showed itself unable (or, in some arguments, unwilling) to rescue the lives and welfare of its Irish citizens. Equally, the security of the Anglo-Scots union was often shaky at times of economic downturn or in the context of perceived inequality: opposition to union remained deeply entrenched throughout most of the first half of the 18th century, when its economic costs (for example enhanced taxation) were not yet clearly offset by the benefits. Scottish nationalism was spurred during the recessions of the inter-war period, in the years of austerity immediately after 1945, in the 1970s, and indeed with the downturn in the British economy beginning in 2007. The British-Irish union has been revisited at times (such as in 1940, or in the context of paramilitary challenge) when it seemed to threaten rather than bolster England's wider security needs. In the mid 1880s Scottish home rule was born partly from the perception that Irish needs were commanding more attention and expenditure than those of Scotland.

The compromises and bargains embodied in the two unions also explain their subsequent condition and fate. Complex commercial and parliamentary unions are not necessarily the basis for ferocious emotion, sentiment or visceral loyalties. Union necessarily 'must be written up, spoken up, intrigued up, drunk up, sung up, and bribed up', Edward Cooke famously proclaimed in 1798; and there is a sense in which, more than for most political issues, support for the two unions (such as it was) was expensively and artificially induced. It is of course the case that a complex British identity arose in the wake of the Anglo-Scots union, drawing strength (it has been argued) from the monarchy, war, and Protestantism; but this always cohabited with persistent and more fundamental national and regional identities[7]. In any case, the crux was of course that the fashioning of British identity had begun before the consummation of union with the Act of 1801—and subsequent efforts to broaden this identity never really carried conviction, given its origins. Britishness had been defined against the Catholic 'Other'—yet after 1801 somehow had to accommodate this 'Other', at least in its Irish formulation. There was thus an ongoing tension between the United Kingdom state, and its supposedly unifying political identity. This tension was expressed in a variety of ways, but not least in the official silence accompanying the anniversaries of the creation of Britain and of the United Kingdom. The coronation, birthdays, and jubilees of the monarch, as head of the union state, might be celebrated; but not the birthday or anniversaries of the state itself. The centenary and bicentenary of the British-Irish union, and the bicentenary and tercentenary of the Anglo-Scots union passed largely in embarrassed passivity[8].

And yet, there were of course centenaries, bicentenaries, and tercentenaries to mark and commemorate. The two unions survived, and indeed are (in the case of Scotland and Northern Ireland) with us still. But there is little in the literature which directly seeks to explain the survival of the two constituent unions of the United Kingdom. This book is designed to address this lacuna, to provide a comparison of the origins and longevity of the two unions, and to identify the influences supporting and sustaining union in each polity. The work is not principally concerned with furthering the furious debates on why (or, more particularly, with what justice) the Scots and Irish unions were passed: nor is it concerned with the fairness (or otherwise) of the current union settlements. But it is interested in using a comparison between the origins and development of the two unions to illuminate their complexity, and their long-term condition and fate.

## Historiography

The history of the two unions has been melded and reshaped according to the needs, mood, and fashion of the times. One of the fundamental features of the literature on the unions has been that, from the beginning, it has been entangled with political dispute, national sentiment, and concomitant personal recrimination. In a sense (adapting the quip of the Irish historian, A.T.Q. Stewart), much of the history of the unions is 'applied' history: or, again—to deploy a favoured rebuke of the British historian Peter Jupp— much of the history of the unions is perhaps 'interventionist' history[9]. However, beyond these shared fundamentals, there are some significant historiographical distinctions between the two unions, Scots and Irish.

Although (what has been termed) 'the parcel of rogues' reading of 1707, beginning with the Jacobite parliamentarian and historian, George Lockhart of Carnwath, and popularized by Robert Burns—the idea that the Scots' union was forged in a welter of corruption—has had a significant purchase within Scotland (there is in fact an argument for locating the very origins of the idea of union in the context of Jacobean corruption), on the whole unionists have commanded the historiography of the Scots union[10]. The apparent economic benefits of union coincided with the high noon of the

Scottish Enlightenment, and while the origins of Enlightenment long pre-dated 1707, its luminaries were generally unionist in their sympathy. Colin Kidd has argued influentially that the Scots Enlightenment effectively served to subvert uncomplicated patriotic readings of the nation's history; and that this, in turn, helped to mothball any later historically or linguistically driven nationalism (such as that prevalent in 19th-century Ireland)[11]. In Ireland, in fact, Enlightenment tended to aid patriotic ideologies and causes; and (though there were significant, and still overlooked, unionist counter-responses) Irish historiography was a critical motor force behind the national and revolutionary movements which forwarded Home Rule and delivered independence. In essence, Scots history and historians mostly served the union in the 18th and 19th centuries, while 19th- and early 20th-century Irish history and historians mostly did not.

If Irish and Scots historiography had a differing impact upon politics, then from the beginning politics provided a shared stimulus for Irish and Scots historians or chroniclers: history, indeed, was a continuation, some-times an augmentation, of political conflict by other means. Daniel Defoe (1709), George Lockhart (1714), and John Clerk of Penicuik (c. 1724–1730) all provided contemporary histories of the Anglo-Scots union, stimulated by their own participation and subsequent ruminations (though Clerk's *Memoirs* and *De Imperio Britannico* were not published until long after his death). Similarly, the Irish union stimulated a frenzy of historiographical apologetic and indictment, supplied by antagonistic parliamentarians and participants such as Sir Jonah Barrington (*Historic Anecdotes and Secret Memoirs of the Legislative Union* (1810) and *The Rise and Fall of the Irish Nation* (1833)), former rebels such as Denis Taafe (*An Impartial History of Ireland*), angered Catholics like Francis Plowden (*An Historical Review of the State of Ireland* (1805–1806) and *The History of Ireland from its Union with Great Britain* (1811)), or Protestant supporters of union such as Sir Richard Musgrave (*Memoirs of the Different Rebellions in Ireland* (1801)).[12] To an extent, the terms and tenor of the subsequent historiography of the unions were defined by this con-temporary and polemical literature.

Irish historical polemic, primarily William Molyneux's *The Case of Ireland being bound by Acts of Parliament in England Stated* (1698), was reprinted and had an influence in Scotland in 1706. Equally, Scots literature widely informed Irish debate on the union, and events in Ireland sometimes pre-cipitated the revisiting or republication of Scottish history: Daniel Defoe's apologetic *History of the Union between England and Scotland*, which origi-

nally appeared in 1709, was reprinted in 1786 against the backdrop of con-
versations to effect a closer political and commercial relationship between
Britain and Ireland: in 1787 Jean Louis de Lolme contributed his *Essay
Containing a Few Strictures on Union of Scotland with England and on the Present
Situation of Ireland. Being An Introduction to Defoe's History of the Union*, a
work which was reprinted in 1799. Defoe's *History* itself was republished by
John Exshaw, of Grafton Street in Dublin, in 1799, on the eve of the union
between Britain and Ireland. Defoe's general advocacy clearly had a relevance for the unionists of 1799–1800, but some of his more detailed points
also had resonance—for example, his emphasis on the role of religion in the
failure of the union negotiations in 1702, or his argument that the association between the idea of union and Cromwellian tyranny was damaging to
the former project[13].

At the same time Revd Ebenezer Marshal of Cockpen produced his
*History of the Union of Scotland and England*, benefiting from the patronage of
the Lord Advocate, Robert Dundas ('encouraged by the recent steps which
have been taken for uniting Great Britain and the sister kingdom, I have
presumed to give to the Public the following brief history of the Union of
Scotland with England')[14]. Indeed, the Dundas clan was active elsewhere in
encouraging the application of Scottish historical experience to the facilitating of union with Ireland: John Bruce (a professor at the University of
Edinburgh, and a client of Henry Dundas, Pitt's Secretary of State for War
and Scottish 'fixer'), was commissioned to produce a history of the Anglo-
Scots union in order to inform conversation and debate (*Report on the Events
and Circumstances which produced the Union of the Kingdoms of England and
Scotland*)[15]. This provided a long-term pedigree to union, dating back at
least to Edward I's efforts to effect dynastic union; there were also more
directly didactic elements to the work, particularly evident in its harsh
reflections on the Cromwellian union and on the impact of 'the unprinci-
pled Republic of France, now sweeping all before it'[16]. Bruce delivered his
report to the Duke of Portland, who (as Secretary of the Home Department)
was one of the architects, indeed—as is now known—a key paymaster, of
the Irish union[17].

This historiographical stimulus was reciprocal: Scots literature informed
Irish political debate, but was also precipitated by it. The controversy over
Irish Home Rule, focused by the emergence of an Irish Parliamentary Party
in the 1870s, and the bills of 1886 and 1893, generated not only a parallel
interest in a restored Scots parliament, but also a flurry of historical writing

on the 1707 settlement, much of it (however grudgingly) unionist in tone or sympathy (as evinced in the work of—inter alia—John Hill Burton (1870, 1880), James Mackinnon (1896), R.S. Rait (1901), W.L. Mathieson (1905)). Charles Waddie's reflections on 1707 were relatively distinctive as a Home Rule perspective on the history of the union (*The Treaty of Union* (1883), *How Scotland Lost Her Parliament* (1891), *The Federation of Great Britain* (1895) and *The Bicentenary of the Union of the Scottish and English Parliaments* (1907))[18]. As is well known, the debate on Irish Home Rule, particularly given Gladstone's scholarly inclinations, was significantly historical in content, with the rival parties deploying historians as, if not the shock troops of their respective causes, then at least as auxiliaries. Gladstone's protracted spat with the Trinity College Dublin historian, Thomas Dunbar Ingram, is well known: but other Home Rulers such as James Bryce (1888), J.G. Swift MacNeill (1887, 1912), and T.M. Healy debated the historical minutiae and moral standing of the 1801 Act with Unionists such as W.E.H. Lecky (1892), Ingram (1887, 1900), and A.V. Dicey (1887)[19]. The architects of the Union, particularly William Pitt, were subjected to ever more intense and laudatory biographical appraisal[20]. In a more bantering historical vein, when Walter Long was appointed as Chief Secretary for Ireland in March 1905, the Irish Nationalist MP, J.G. Swift MacNeill, readily invoked Jonah Barrington's work on the union debates, recalling that in 1801 Long's maternal ancestor, William Hoare Hume, was a 'sturdy anti-Unionist and absolutely incorruptible'[21].

The centenary of the Irish union (which fell while the South African War was still being bloodily played out) stimulated little historical or wider interest, still less celebration. But the bicentenary of its Scots counterpart in 1907 brought reassessments of the Scots union, as evidenced by Messrs Oliphants' 'bicentenary edition' of G.W.T. Omond's *The Early History of the Scottish Union Question* (1906) (originally published in 1897) and the collection of articles published in the *Glasgow Herald*, and later collected by Peter Hume Brown, the William Fraser Professor of Scottish History at Edinburgh, as *The Union of 1707: A Survey of Events* (1907). In making his contribution to this bicentennial literature, Alexander MacRae offered a characteristic judgement in asserting that 'it is with the Union that the proudest and most instructive period of Scottish history begins, for it was then that Scotland began to assert her real influence as a nation on the affairs of the empire and of the world'[22]. And, the revival of Home Rule within British and Irish politics after 1910 brought a renewed flurry of historical activity, focusing on the origins primarily of the Irish Act (in work by Canon Ardill 1907, J.R. Fisher 1911), but also of the Scots.

Indeed, Oxford University's choice of Peter Hume Brown, an authority on the union, to deliver the Ford lectures in 1914, against the backdrop of the third Home Rule crisis, can hardly have been fortuitous. If there was any doubt, Hume Brown nailed the contemporary relevance of his theme ('The Legislative Union of England and Scotland') from the very outset, while conscientiously avoiding any historicist or tendentious reading of Godolphin and Harley's diplomacy towards the Scots:'at the present epoch, moreover, the Union of 1707 may be said to have a direct and special interest. The problem which the statesmen of the reign of Queen Anne had to solve has close analogies with the problem which has confronted their successors in recent years. I did not consider it within my scope to suggest these analogies, which, indeed, cannot be missed in any presentment of the circumstances in which the union of the English and Scottish peoples was effected'[23]. Some six years later Albert Venn Dicey and Robert Rait produced a celebration of the settlement of 1707 in their *Thoughts on the Union between England and Scotland*, published in 1920 (that 'high watermark of the appreciation of the Union')[24]. Dicey and Rait made little direct reference to the Irish, but (as with Hume Brown in 1914) Ireland has been seen as the critical backdrop to their musings:'the unstated implication was that this was a union in which the British could continue to have confidence, at a time when they faced a renewed threat of national secession in Ireland'[25].

Historians have been able to reinvent the unions according not only to the political but also the (often related) intellectual concerns and fashions of the time. In the 1960s and after those influenced by social science traditions of historical scholarship, like T.C. Smout or Rosalind Mitchison, tended to judge union in the light of long-term economic development, and were inclined, too, to see it (in almost Whiggish terms) as a logical and inevitable response to Scotland's fundamental needs.[26] Political, particularly high political, historians naturally tended to judge the events of 1703–1706 in the light of a different suite of evidence, and consequently exposed and emphasised some unlovely attitudes and actions. In 1978 P.W.J. Riley, influenced by the Namierite and Cambridge 'high political' schools, provided a portrait of the union characterized by individual aspiration, greed, and ambition, but stripped of much wider social, economic or intellectual contextualization.[27] In work which chimed in some respects with that of Riley, but anchored in a different array of traditions, William Ferguson provided a painstaking and learned, but also impassioned, denunciation of the corruption surrounding the manufacture of union: Riley drew inspiration from Namier and Cowling, while Ferguson provided a text which chimed with the mood of Scotland at the time of the Scottish National Party's first great efflorescence, in the early and mid 1970s.[28] The rise of the 'New British' and 'Atlantic' histories since the 1970s has encouraged a contextualization of (in particular the Scots) union within the wider confines of the first British Empire.[29]

More recently, the establishment of a devolved parliament, in 1999, together with the tercentenary of union in 2007, and the revival of the Scottish National Party, have stimulated a wide range of literature, particularly (though not exclusively) focused on the origins of union in 1707.[30] Contemporary debates on Scotland's national framework of reference have encouraged and complemented a scholarship on union which has looked beyond the Anglo-Scottish relationship towards Europe. There has, in fact, been a modest Europeanization of the Scots union (and the preceding Scots parliament) pursued by scholars keen to escape from English constrictions, and to recover something of the complexity of the old Scottish kingdom's international relationships.[31]

In the end, however, it is hard to escape the impression that, despite maturation and wider explorations, much Irish and Scots history on the union remains tied to, and influenced by, national sentiments and sensitivities. Indeed, there are some faint but telling historiographical parallels between the 'revisionist' debate within Irish history, and the conflicts amongst Scots historians on the origins and outcome of union. This is a matter of both style and substance: Irish revisionists and Scots 'Whigs' have each, strikingly, been accused by their more overtly patriotic colleagues of a lordly, ironic, or patronizing approach towards their respective subjects.[32] Discussion of the economic context and fall-out from union is linked to patriotic concerns in both the Scottish and Irish cases, the patriotic case being tied up with arguments for the relatively successful performance of the pre-union economy, with 'unionists' seeing 1707 as the facilitator of riches. In Ireland, nationalist historians have pointed to the blossoming of the late 18th-century Irish economy, in contrast with its post-union successor. Scholarly treatments of the action, or inaction, of the union government in Ireland and Scotland during calamitous episodes such as famine or land clearance remain (naturally enough) tinctured with passion and outrage. Scots and Irish patriotic critiques of the military subjugation, national stereotyping, and economic inequality perpetrated under the unions have much in common.

Less overtly nationalistic perspectives have also, arguably, affected the reading of each union. It is a central tenet of the critique of 'revisionism' within Irish historiography that liberal historians have tended to write violence and catastrophe out of the history of the union, and indeed out of the wider story of British intervention in Ireland.[33] It is also possibly the case that both liberal and left-leaning historians, interested in the construction and shape of an inclusive Scottish national identity, have tended to relegate the history of indigenous and imported sectarianism in the heyday of union, and to emphasize instead class and other forms of communal solidarity.[34]

In sum, from their respective beginnings, the Scots and Irish unions have been interpreted polemically, and in the light of the experience of the neighbouring polity. More particularly, the historiography of the Scots union has shaped the formation of its Irish successor; while debates upon the ending of the Irish union have precipitated an intense scholarship upon the origins of its Scots precursor. And yet, despite the intricate and entangled historical and historiographical interrelationship of the two unions, Scots and Irish, the literature combining and comparing the two is slight.

## Comparing the two unions

Just as at the end of the 19th century, so at the beginning of the 21st, the common experience of Ireland and Scotland under the union has become a matter of pressing political concern. Certainly before the onset of the Irish financial crisis in 2008, the nationalist government of Scotland regularly looked to Ireland as a polity which had also experienced union, but (unlike Scotland) had broken free, and had accordingly prospered while the Scots remained constricted and impoverished. Speaking at Trinity College Dublin on 13 February 2008, Alex Salmond, the First Minister of Scotland, approvingly quoted the great Irish Home Ruler, Charles Stewart Parnell ('no man has the right to fix the boundary of a nation'), while observing that 'Scotland has a different history and a different constitution. But our aspirations for our nation are no different from those that inspired generations of Irish people to independence and prosperity that you enjoy today'.[35] Indeed, Salmond himself has been occasionally cast as 'the Scottish Parnell'.[36]

Salmond's remarks simultaneously underlined the emotional and political charge of the shared Irish and Scots' experience of union, and a shared desire to escape the constraints of Union; but they also highlighted some of the difficulties in comparing the two national histories. Between 1801 and 1922 Scotland and Ireland were each constituent parts of the one country, the United Kingdom: the two unions have been closely interconnected, and have been distinguished by an intellectual and political cross-fertilization. Yet, despite this common ground, there has been little by way of sustained scholarly comparison of the two experiences of union. Of course, this is partly because the two nations have otherwise complex and distinct ancestries. But it is also the case that, from the passage of the Irish union through to current debate on the state of the United Kingdom, the comparison of the Irish and Scots union has been heavily infiltrated by political polemic. In 1799 British ministers cited the Scots union as a justification for the proposed union with Ireland, while their opponents denied the validity of the comparison: in the 1880s the Unionist deployment of Scottish analogies was questioned by Gladstone and his lieutenants; and in the new millennium Alex Salmond's invocation of Ireland has been interrogated by his unionist opponents, both before and particularly after the shrivelling of the Celtic Tiger.[37] Thus far, the task of comparison appears to have been largely (though by no means exclusively) in the hands of those politicians debating the utility of union.

While (as Conrad Russell has wisely observed) 'parallels are treacherous things', and while the distinctiveness of the two nations and their unions, Scots and Irish, should be recognized (and indeed has to be recognized, if the different fates of the two unions are to be fully understood), contemporaries and some later scholars were drawn to make comparisons, though rarely in a sustained and systematic way.[38] Albert Venn Dicey, the Victorian jurist and defender of union, writing in the *Fortnightly Review* in 1881, essayed a brief comparison of the making of the two unions; and in this he argued that a rigorous evaluation of the two measures had been effectively impeded by popular English characterizations of the Irish national character: 'the true lesson, they [the English] think, to be deduced from a comparison of Scotch and Irish history is that justice and wisdom and statesmanship, as understood, at least, by Englishmen, will not bear their proper fruit on Irish soil, and that at the time of the union, as at other times, the prudence and benevolence of England have been balked of their legitimate reward by the innate perversity or folly of Irish nature'.[39] Nevertheless, for Dicey, the evidently happy Scots' experience of union informed a read-ing of 'the failure or partial failure' of the union between Britain and Ireland: by identifying the keystones of Scottish success, the reasons for Irish failure would become self-evident.[40] With typically bold precision, Dicey ascribed the solidity and longevity of the Scots' union, not to any superiority of their national 'character' over that of the Irish, but rather to three cardinal 'facts'— that the Scots' union was a treaty negotiated between equal, consenting partners, that it embodied an unusually disinterested and strategic English statesmanship, and that it protected the central institutions of the Scottish nation. For Dicey, the Irish union of 1801, imposed by political and military fiat, bore a closer resemblance to the Cromwellian union in Scotland, than it did to the 'treaty or contract freely made between two independent states' in 1706'.[41] Writing in 1881, against the backdrop of the Land War in Ireland, and a tranquil and prosperous Scotland, Dicey believed that 'English policy has achieved no triumph so great as the union between England and Scotland' (a belief that he retained until the end of his life, and expressed at greater length in *Thoughts on the Union* (1920)).[42]

This judgement, inevitably, looks much less secure now, in the context of strengthened nationalist sentiment in Scotland (and, indeed, in terms of the vestigial survival of the union with Northern Ireland). Moreover, as with so much of his historical commentary (indeed, as with so much historical commentary on the unions more generally), Dicey was tacitly seeking to highlight a particular contemporary moral from his ruminations in 'The Two Acts of Union': just as Scots' animosity towards the English had been mitigated by creative statesmanship, so (even in the unpropitious circum-stances of 1881) Irish animosity and violence were susceptible to enlight-ened statesmanship. Dicey's stress on the 'fair and equal deal' of 1706, on the magnanimity of English statesmanship, and upon the sensitive treatment of Scottish national institutions were evidently designed as policy indicators for the 1880s; but they have informed interpretations of the survival of the Scots' union, and of the condition of its Irish counterpart, until effectively the present day.

It is clear, for example, that both Gladstone and the Conservative leader, the Marquess of Salisbury, read the Dicey article: both certainly shared much of the conceptual framework supplied by Dicey, viewing the Irish union in the comparative context supplied by Scotland (however much the genesis of 1801 was to be distinguished from that of 1707), and using some of the same language (as with, for example, the notion of 'moral union').[43] Salisbury accepted one of the central presumptions of Dicey's reasoning, namely that Scottish acquiescence in union legitimized the expectation that the Irish, too, could be eventually won to its cause.[44] Gladstone also accepted that, while both the unions were rooted in corruption, the level of immorality entombing the measure of 1801 was greater, and that the Scots union was at least the result of an equal bargain. Gladstone certainly read work which was critical of the Scots union, and of its origins (curiously, George Lockhart of Carnwath on the Scots union was absent from his reading, in contrast to Jonah Barrington on the Irish): but he was also clearly impressed and persuaded by the unionist scholarship of John Hill Burton, Scotland's 'latest and most authoritative historian', who 'denies that bribery has been proved'.[45]

Dicey's comparison of Ireland and Scotland was intended to prove that the Irish union, whatever its manifold failings, might yet attain the solidity of its Scottish counterpart. Gladstone accepted the legitimacy of making the comparison; yet he sought to turn the analogy on its head by emphasising not only that Scotland was no exemplar for Ireland, but also that Ireland might in fact prove to be a paradigm for the Scots. Scotland's debt to the Union of 1707 was, in Gladstone's argument, exaggerated; the independence of pre-union Scotland was infinitely greater than that characterizing pre-union Ireland, while the circumstances of union in each polity were thoroughly distinct. Comparison of the two unions was (by the definition of his own lines of argument) inevitable and proper, but frequently—at least in its unionist formulation— misconceived:'there was an Union in Scotland and an Union in Ireland, just as there was a river in Monmouth and a river in Macedon'.[46]

But an emphasis upon the distinctive national histories of Scotland and Ireland was not a Gladstonian preserve: the different social, cultural, and religious heritage of the two nations was explored and affirmed even within an emphatically unionist literature. Writing in 1893, the eighth Duke of Argyll, a Liberal Unionist, saw the divergence between Ireland and Scotland as being encapsulated in their different receptions of the Norman incursion. In the Lowlands of Scotland the Normans were (in Argyll's brisk and unforgiving analysis) embraced by a coherent indigenous political culture, whereas in Ireland they were overcome by native 'barbarism': 'in Scotland the Norman element was Scottified. In Ireland the Norman element was Ersefied. In Scotland the Norman element became assimilated by a germ of political civilisation which had been growing through stages of much obscurity for at least three hundred years before the Norman Conquest. In

Ireland it was still more assimilated with a barbarism which had been getting steadily worse and worse through history of a whole millennium.'[47]
Argyll's contribution can be seen as part of a strain within late 19th-century
Scottish unionist historiography which saw the lowlands of Scotland as
'sharing a common ethnic provenance' with England—that is to say, sharing
a similar anchorage in a Teutonic civilization.[48] It may be noted here that
racial theorizing of this kind was certainly present within some Ulster
unionist apologetic; but (unlike its Scottish equivalent) this served less as an
argument for union, than as part of the case for Ulster particularism—for
the separate treatment of the Protestant North.

Turning from Argyll's tendentious but influential unionist reading of the
Norman conquests, it was obvious—even to unionist polemicists—that
there were profound social and cultural differences separating the subsequent histories of Ireland and Scotland. In Scotland the Protestant
Reformation was successful, while in Ireland it was not: though the
Presbyterian form of church governance and Calvinist theology came to
distinguish most Scots Protestants from their English counterparts, and
though Catholicism became a powerful presence in the west of Scotland in
the 19th century, on the whole religion came to bind the Scots and English.
In Ireland, the effort to achieve Protestant reformation failed; and at the
time of union, in 1800, the island remained overwhelmingly Catholic in faith.
In 1706 it proved much easier to secure the rights of Scots Presbyterians
than it was in 1800 to secure the rights of Irish Catholics.

Scotland was (or rather claimed to be) independent, Protestant, and also
a more integrated society than Ireland. The effort to export British 'civilization' had involved recurrent efforts to colonize Ireland with English and
Scots migrants, the most famous and successful of these being in western
and southern Ulster in the years after 1608. The Cromwellian and Williamite
conquests of Ireland were also accompanied by extensive land seizure and
redistribution. While internal migration and colonization were not unknown
in Scotland, there was of course nothing to match the scale of the Irish
plantations.[49] Again, while there was Scots experience of expropriation (for
example after the 1745 Rising), however painful or violent, this was on a
slight scale compared with the Irish case. The consequence of these recurrent seizures in Ireland was that the land ownership became largely concentrated in the hands of Protestant newcomers. Landed proprietorship, and
therefore political authority, was the preserve of a religious minority in Irish
society (a highly unusual circumstance). In much of Scotland, landed pro-

prietorship emerged, by and large, from clan leadership. Scots landowners, no more selfless or magnanimous than their Irish counterparts, became figures of popular contempt in the context of the 18th- and 19th-century land clearances, and through the writings of labour polemicists such as Thomas Johnston (in *Our Scots Noble Families* (1909)); but they were nevertheless more completely bound to their tenants by history, culture, and faith than most of their Irish counterparts.[50]

Perhaps what all of this amounts to is the fact that Ireland was not only distinct from Scotland, but was unusual when viewed even in a wider European context. There has been much debate about Irish 'exceptionalism' in the 18th century and subsequently, stimulated in part by the highly influential notion that Ascendancy Ireland should be seen essentially as a Hibernian variant of the contemporary European *ancien régime*.[51] Ireland, it has been retorted, was (like England and Scotland and other European kingdoms) a confessional state, but it was one in which the 'confession', Anglicanism, was shared by as little as ten per cent of the population.[52] In England and Scotland (and elsewhere in Europe) religious minorities suffered discrimination; but in Ireland a highly complex legal code was enacted from the aftermath of the Williamite victories through to the death of George I, which subjected eighty per cent of the population, the Catholics, to an array of disabilities. These legal disabilities, it has been argued, laid the foundation for the demand for 'Catholic relief' in the later 18th century, through to the 'emancipation' of 1829; and they helped to ensure that the issue of Catholic civil rights fatally coincided with the wider constitutional realignment of the period, and in particular with union. In these senses, therefore, Ireland was distinctive; and its union was equally distinctive.

This was certainly the essence of the Gladstonian case in addressing the two unions; but it was not confined to Home Rulers, being shared by 'advanced' devolutionist Unionists such as W.T. Wyndham-Quin, the fourth Earl of Dunraven. In 1905 Dunraven produced a short, but cogent study (published originally in pamphlet form, but later revised and incorporated as the eighth chapter of his *The Outlook in Ireland* (1907)) which stood at the intersection of a polemical tradition of unionist historiography, and the more sceptical Gladstonian tradition of comparison. Dunraven's purpose here, as almost everywhere else in his prolific historical output, was to defend and evangelize his work with the Irish Reform Association, and in particular its devolutionist project within Ireland. One of the emergent unionist counter-arguments to the elaboration of devolved administration in Ireland was its

absence in Scotland, and indeed the wider prospect of prosperity which the
Scots experience of union appeared to promise the Irish: Dunraven was keen
to address not only this, but also the resurgent unionist sentiment in Scotland
(as revealed by the general election of 1900), which was intolerant of
constitutional concession to Ireland. These purposes necessitated an emphasis upon the differences in the Scots and Irish historical record, and resulted
in a somewhat emphatic narrative of Scottish independence and prosperity
in the prelude to union, and (equally) a somewhat rose-tinted portrayal of
Scotland's experience at the hands of its English neighbours. For Dunraven,
like Gladstone, Scotland did not hold out a meaningful paradigm of union to
the Irish, still less a vision of its happy potentialities—because Scotland's
national history and experience of the English were thoroughly distinctive.[53]
In essence, the logic of Dunraven's devolutionist politics compelled him to
compare the two unions in order to question the validity of making the
comparison; and to some extent (as has been indicated) this paradox characterized the Gladstonian perspective.

Notions of the divergent but interlinked Irish and Scots experience of
union became in fact a commonplace of the intellectual context against which
Home Rule was devised and debated in the 1880s, 1890s, and after. Writing in
1902 on *The Reign of Queen Anne*, the popular Irish nationalist historian (and
former parliamentary leader), Justin McCarthy, could not escape the evident
reality that the Scots union 'has proved thus far a complete success': but this
('one of the greatest and most successful events which mark with honour the
momentous history of that reign') necessarily precipitated McCarthy into a
lengthy diversion into the different circumstances and consequent 'injustice'
of the Irish Act of Union.[54] While in 1905 W.L. Mathieson certainly emphasised Scotland's traditions of independence, and Ireland's history of subjugation, by 1907 he was arguing that 'the two Unions have much in common, in
so far as they can be traced to constitutional causes': and indeed, in 1907
Mathieson essayed a brief scholarly comparison between the two unions.[55]

Equally, turning to more contemporary and less politicized scholarship,
the economic historian, Ron Weir, writing in 1999, has acknowledged that
'the unions of 1707 and 1801 are not at first sight the most promising bedfellows for comparative history'[56] Firstly, following Weir's exegesis, a century
of rapid industrial development separated the Scots and Irish unions; and
indeed Weir has opined that 'the economic gains from an earlier [Irish]
union would have been greater, and the risks less' (an Anglo-Irish union was
mooted at the time of the Anglo-Scots union).[57] Secondly, while the Scots

union was a deep and fundamental influence upon the Irish, the two Unions were (at the risk of stating the obvious) the products of very different historical eras—one launched in the complex aftermath of the English Revolution, the other in that of the French. Thirdly, in his analysis, 'there is the issue of the extent to which each country can be said to have been genuinely independent before union'.[58]

Although, as Weir suggests, the effective independence of Scotland before 1707 might well be questioned, Scots commentators have generally been keen, from the 17th century onwards, to distinguish their nation's proud tradition of sovereignty and independence from the allegedly less glorious Irish history of conquest and dependence: in 1905, for example, William Law Mathieson pointed out that Scotland 'retained the traditions and instincts of a separate kingdom' while 'Ireland had never been independent'.[59] And of course these arguments are not just a reflection of well-meaning patriotism, but have been vindicated in a more recent and disinterested scholarship: Brian Levack has emphasised that in the 17th and 18th centuries 'neither Ireland nor any of the American colonies...ever possessed Scotland's sovereign status', while for John Morrill Ireland was 'a dependent kingdom with no [legal or constitutional] existence apart from the crown of England'.[60] Union, clearly, in these circumstances, had potentially very different meanings for the Scots and Irish.

Contemporary scholars have acknowledged, like Gladstone, the difficulties of making comparisons, while accepting ultimately the desirability or need to overcome these. For Conrad Russell, parallels may indeed have been 'treacherous', but he went on to affirm that 'some comparative points stand out' in the shared experience of union, and that the successful aspects of 1707 might point to a completely different teleology of union.[61] Even for Ron Weir, the two unions may not have been 'the most promising bedfellows for comparative history', but this was emphatically 'at first sight'; and, having acknowledged the difficulties, he went on to compare in detail the economic arguments for and against the two measures of 1707 and 1801.[62]

Moreover, if there are recognized challenges in linking the Irish and Scots' experience of union, then there are yet more profound difficulties in comparing the experience of Scotland and Wales; and yet this comparison is central to the concerns of (for example) the last—posthumously published—work of the Oxford historian of empire, Sir Reginald Coupland (*Welsh and Scottish Nationalism: A Study* (1954)). And it may also be recalled that comparisons between the three kingdoms of the 'British' or 'These'

Isles have long informed early modern scholarship. Indeed, it is paradoxical that while early modern political historians, working within the framework of the New British History, have successfully broken down some of the overly rigid divisions separating the national histories of the Tudor and Stuart state systems, the frontier between them and late modernists (who are more completely confined within national borders) remains largely intact. Despite the continuing symmetries binding the histories of Ireland and Scotland from the 17th century and before to the 21st century, early modernists have on the whole been much more assiduous in identifying political links and shared political experience than their late modern counterparts (even allowing for the greater fluidity of political boundaries and the more modest dimensions of central government in the early modern era).[63]

Comparisons between the social and economic (in clear distinction to the political) history of modern Scotland and Ireland have certainly long informed scholarship, revived and systematized by Louis Cullen and T.C. Smout in the 1970s, and further elaborated by Tom Devine in the 1980s and 1990s.[64] But the pre-eminent social and economic concerns of Scottish historians, the comparative under-representation of 19th- and 20th-century Scottish political historiography within recent Scottish history, together with the (perhaps) disproportionate strength of Irish 'high' political historiography on the Home Rule and revolutionary periods within Irish history, have all given us two very different, and very differently contextualized, unions.[65] The historiography on the formation of the Scots union is distinctively rich, and emphasises its wider social, economic, intellectual, and international anchorage: the historiography on the formation of the Irish union has suffered from the countervailing emphasis on its unravelling and supersession, and has tended to be relatively narrowly focused.[66]

The fundamental challenge, therefore, in comparing the two unions has not been the divergent experience of the Scots and Irish, or the incompatible histories of the two countries, Scotland and Ireland. The problem has arisen, not from the history, but rather from the historians.

## The longevity of union

The shared experience of union is one of the central themes of this history: another of its themes is the longevity of union. If the literature on the internal dynamics and symmetries of the three kingdoms has been dominated by early modernists and others interested in the formation of the British state, then (while there are distinguished exceptions) late modernists have often been more preoccupied by the separate nationalisms of Ireland and Scotland or by 'declinology', the analysis of British retreat.[67] The British decline from global political and economic pre-eminence has a bearing on any consideration of the survival of the United Kingdom as a constitutional entity; but it is in essence a separate scholarly debate, with a separate agenda, concerns, and questions. An influential teleology within much modern British history, political science, and sociology (understandably) stems from the 'crisis' within Britishness and the 'imminent' break-up of the United Kingdom: this is linked to a scholarly emphasis on 'the differences and separate development of politics in Scotland, Wales and Northern Ireland'.[68] For example, the historical sociologist Michael Hechter, writing in the early 1970s, against the backdrop of a resurgence of 'Celtic' nationalism within the United Kingdom, sought to explain the 'relative failure of [a unifying] national development in the United Kingdom', together with the persistence of political and cultural distinctiveness in Ireland, Scotland, and Wales, through his influential 'internal colonialism' hypothesis: in particular he has sought to address the evident failure of earlier sociological theorists, who had been defined and damned by 'their substantial [but flawed] agreement in predicting the eventual demise of the culture of peripheral areas within the boundaries of the industrializing state'.[69] For Hechter, the notion of 'internal colonialism', with its focus and emphasis upon the cultural and political resilience of the 'periphery', explains the continuing fissiparousness of the United Kingdom state.

While the two unions have had lengthy, if highly controversial, gestations, and while much effort is focused on illuminating the unions' periodic vulnerability, the existing literature does not generally address the issue of their protracted survival. The historiography of the Scots union is predominantly the historiography of its creation: moreover, Scottish political historiography has been much more concerned with the development of Scottish nationalist politics than with Scottish unionism (it is striking that by far the most important scholar of modern Scottish unionism, David Torrance, is not a professional historian). Equally, Irish historians have been much more interested in chronicling and explaining the end of the union, in 1921–1922, than in illuminating its 120 year survival.[70] Though there is an extensive historiography on 1707, the literature on the origins of the Irish union is overshadowed by that on radical and republican politics in the 1790s, and on the great insurgency of 1798. In Ireland in 1998 and 2001 the popular and scholarly interest generated by the bicentenary of the 1798 rising far outshone any curiosity subsequently fired by the bicentenary of the union.

And yet, despite their periodic unpopularity and evident repressiveness, the two unions survived, and this history seeks to explain why this should have been so. Though there is little in Irish or Scottish historiography that foreshadows this endeavour, it is not altogether without parallel or precedent. Most Irish and Scots historians with an interest in the relationship between their respective nations and the union have tended to pursue this interest through focusing upon the challenge presented in the 19th century and after by nationalism.[71] But there are occasional exceptions to this rule, as evidenced (for example) by the University of Edinburgh historian, Gordon Donaldson's teasing lecture ('a kind of final entertainment') on 'The Anglicisation of Scotland' ('anglicisation of the country we now call Scotland started in the sixth century'). In pursuing his theme, Donaldson emphasised, inter alia, educational exchange, improved transport and communications, the labour movement, English immigration into Scotland, the empire, and soldiering and warfare; and his listing has been one of the influences determining the structure and concerns of Chapter 5.[72] His Edinburgh contemporary, Richard Pares', essay on 'A Quarter of a Millennium of Anglo-Scottish Union', originally delivered as a lecture in 1954, is also implicitly an exploration of some of the bolsters of this critical constitutional relationship. Pares, incidentally, also broaches the comparison with Ireland, arguing bluntly that (unlike the British-Irish union) the Anglo-Scots union was stable in the 19th century, and there was no Scots revolt against England at this time, because 'the English never treated the Scots nearly so badly as they treated the Irish'.[73]

Also, while historians have been highly reluctant to engage with the theme of the longevity of the union, scholars from other disciplines have sometimes been less timid. For example, David McCrone has considered the survival of the Anglo-Scots union both in his classic text, *Understanding Scotland: The Sociology of a Stateless Nation* (1992) and elsewhere in his writing (though the theme is certainly not a pre-eminent concern).[74] Likewise the political scientist, Iain McLean, has shed light on the survival of the Anglo-Scots union (and much else) through his painstaking scholarship on the Goschen and (in particular) the Barnett funding formulae. In general, the survival of the Scots union, though still underexplored across the disciplinary spectrum, has attracted relatively more attention than the ostensibly much less promising (indeed almost counterintuitive) notion of the survival of the Irish union.[75]

There is also cognate historical work on the stability of modern Scotland and of modern Britain—on the absence of sustained radical protest in 18th-century Scotland, and of revolution in 19th- and 20th-century Britain. Scottish historians such as Christopher Whatley, Tom Devine, and Callum Brown have examined (and indeed questioned) the relative tranquility of Scotland during the economic and political convulsions of the 18th century, emphasising the evidence for limited disturbance (with the significant exceptions of the two Jacobite rebellions), the strengths of the *ancien régime*, and the capacity of Scottish Presbyterianism to simultaneously stimulate, articulate, and contain social resentments.[76] British historians such as Brian Harrison have written on the centripetal tendencies within British politics, while others (Geoffrey Crossick, R.Q. Gray)—working from the theorization of labour aristocracy—have looked to divisions and gradations within the working classes in order to understand the relative social tranquility of the Victorian state.[77] Ross McKibbin has elaborated the case for understanding why there was no significant rejectionist political tradition in late 19th- and early 20th-century Britain.[78] McKibbin, for example, has identified 'a working class which was highly dispersed by occupation, having (appearances notwithstanding) a fairly low level of communitarian solidarity, following a number of competing associational activities, and highly conditioned by inherited ideologies which emphasised a common citizenship, the fairness of the rules of the game, and the class-neutrality of the major institutions of the state'.[79] He has also pointed out that 'these ideologies were themselves legitimated by an overwhelming public ceremonial'.[80]

Of course the stability of Britain depended not just upon the reconciliation of class, but also, critically, of nationality. However, it is certainly the case that some of the agencies and institutions which served to reconcile working-class opinion, and to ameliorate grievance, also help to illuminate the mediation of Irish and Scots national opinion within the supranational British state. Associational activity could work in 19th-century Scotland (admittedly much more than in Ireland) to dissipate communal identities, and to reconcile national feeling to the union state.[81] Monarchy could be seen not only as above class, but also as (in a sense) above nation—as simultaneously Scots, Irish, and English. Yet, while we know about the union's failures in this respect, we know less about its successes; and we have as yet only the crudest understanding of why some of these aspects of the union worked, and others did not. In fact, the literature on these themes may be said to be located at one or other of two poles: one is characterized by (what Michael Hechter has called) the 'diffusion model' which looks forward to the inevitable diffusion of metropolitan, core values to the 'periphery', while—at the other end of the spectrum—rest arguments designed to describe and explain the resistance of the British 'periphery' to assimilation.[82] In a sense this book is concerned in part to explore the distance or chasm between the 'diffusion model' and its 'internal colonial' antithesis, and to enquire—not why the diffusion of 'core' values to the 'periphery' was ultimately unsuccessful—but rather how and why the process got as far as it did.

# The book

How does this volume set about addressing these challenges? The work seeks (for the first time) to compare and combine national histories in an effort to illuminate the survival of union. It is divided into three parts, corresponding with the three governing themes of origins, longevity, and Unionism. The first of these explores, from a full comparative perspective, the origins and meaning of 'union' within both a Scottish and Irish context, together with the construction of the agreements enacted in 1707 and 1801. The second takes a range of Scots and Irish institutions, which for the most part have been identified as relevant by scholars (such as Gordon Donaldson) or contemporaries, and sketches their contribution to the longevity of the two unions (the section on the survival of the Irish union concludes with partition and Irish independence in 1920–1921, while the history of the vestigial union in Northern Ireland is considered in Chapter 8).[83] The third part of the book looks at the development of Scots and Irish Unionism, its linkages and divergences, and assesses the contribution of the two Unionisms to the survival of the two constitutional unions.

The volume is first and foremost a work of historical scholarship, though it does draw upon other cognate disciplines. However, it does not seek to be a full history of the United Kingdom, still less of the 'British Isles'.[84] It is not directly concerned with the Anglo-Welsh union: though the history of modern Wales has a relevance to much of the analysis that is offered here, the distinctiveness of the Welsh relationship with England precludes the possibility of the kind of comparison which is possible between Scotland

and Ireland (Reginald Coupland's work on Scotland and Wales is primarily
concerned with the parallel histories of the two nationalisms, Scots and
Welsh, rather than with the quality, integrity, and longevity of their unions
with England).[85] Though Owain Glyndwr held a parliament in Wales in
1404, there was no sustained parliamentary history such as characterized the
Scots and Irish before their respective parliamentary unions. The 'union' of
England and Wales was formalized, not by agreement or even by the manipulation of local political elites, but by English parliamentary fiat: the 'Laws
in Wales Acts' of 1536–1542, passed by the English parliament, secured the
legal and administrative union of England and Wales, as opposed to the parliamentary and political (and ecclesiastical) settlements envisioned by the
(much) later Scots and Irish unions. Wales at the beginning of the 18th century has been described as the 'nation most closely integrated with England',
on account of its assimilation at Westminster and within the English judicial
and fiscal structures, and (at this time) its 'substantially Anglican' religious
affiliation: symbolic interconnections such as the use of the 'Prince of Wales'
title by the eldest son of the monarch, and the links between the Welsh elite
and Oxford University have also been cited as evidence for this judgement.[86] Though the interrelationship between, particularly modern, Welsh
and Irish history is an underexplored and potentially important theme, and
indeed has been the focus of a recent research initiative, the interconnections between Scotland and Ireland for the period from the 17th century are
indisputably denser and more intimate than those binding Wales and
Ireland.[87]

The book strives to highlight and outline a range of approaches and
themes which are either partly or wholly fresh within the expansive literature on the constitutional relationships within these islands. Using a detailed
comparison of the origins and passage of the two unions (which, surprisingly has little precedent in existing modern scholarship), some effort is
made to shed light on their subsequent histories. The institutions which
helped to secure the longevity of union in Scotland are relevant to the story
of its survival in Ireland; and while there is a developing literature on some
of these individual institutions in their Irish and Scottish formulations (such
as the monarchy), no historian has yet sought to draw together analyses of
these different bodies, still less to meld them within a wider comparative
argument for the survival of union. Aside from the effort to craft fresh arguments from fresh approaches, a range of new evidence is presented on a
range of hitherto neglected issues (such as, for example, the cultural history

of union, Scots and Ulster parliamentary Unionism in the 20th century, or the honours system in its Irish and Scots applications). Similarly, while there is a solid historiography on Irish Unionism and (less so, surprisingly) on Scottish Unionism, the literature on comparative Unionism within the United Kingdom is extraordinarily slight; and no sustained comparison of Irish and Scots Unionism exists beyond the effort made in Part III of this volume.[88] In addition to providing a comparative perspective, the book offers some new insights into the survival and decline of Unionism in Scotland.[89] In contradistinction to the highly developed scholarly emphases upon 1707 and 1801, this book pivots on the late 19th century and early 20th century, a period that was critical to the evolution of both unions, Irish and Scots.

Previous histories of the two unions have concentrated upon the individual national stories of union, rather than upon the insights generated through comparison. Previous histories have focused upon institutional history and biography, rather than upon the cultural history of the politics of union and Unionism. Previous histories of the two unions have concentrated largely upon their beginnings and anticipated endings. This history is about the middle of the union story.

# 2

# Prehistories (1290–1690, 1300–1782)

## Scots and Irish

Blest revolution which creates
Divided hearts, united states
> Jonathan Swift, 'Verses said to be written on the Union' (1707)

## Historians and the two parliaments

The contours of the Scots and Irish relationship with the English and British states in the decades before union were ostensibly similar. For each, union (despite the currency of grander notions both in Scotland, and—to a lesser extent—in Ireland) was 'essentially' a parliamentary union, which was (in both 1707 and 1801) a radical, but certainly not an unanticipated, proposition: for each, union could be represented (and indeed was, in Whiggish interpretations) as a natural, indeed 'inevitable', denouement to the evolving connection with the neighbouring kingdom.[1] For each, parliamentary union succeeded forms of monarchical union (or 'union of the crowns'). Scotland and Ireland each shared a brief experience of enforced parliamentary union (under the Commonwealth, in the 1650s).[2] Parliamentarians in each kingdom periodically reverted to the thought of union in order to improve their political or economic circumstances. Moreover, when 'incorporating' union finally came to each kingdom, in 1707 and 1801, the constitutional, diplomatic, and economic contexts were similar: the birth of the United Kingdom in 1801 was apparently anticipated and accompanied by the same kinds of political turmoil that greeted the creation of Great Britain in 1707.

Union in the British Isles, therefore, may be said to have been conditioned by a particular conjunction of constitutional, diplomatic, and economic challenges and circumstances. There is a strong sense in which the two parliaments, Irish and Scottish, both lived as they died—that they were shaped and sustained by issues and relationships, and increasingly the needs of the English crown, which later precipitated their respective ends. In any event, the Scottish and Irish unions, as parliamentary unions, first need to be understood and defined in terms of the parliamentary history of the two nations. This is all the more pressing, because subsequent conflict over, in particular, the Scottish union has generally been conducted as a debate over the sovereign authority of the old Scottish parliament, and of its British successor.[3]

In comparing the two parliamentary traditions, it would certainly be wrong to overlook some critical distinctions: the Irish and Scots parliaments emerged contemporaneously, but the Irish (which first met at Castledermot, Kildare, in 1264) was a by-product of English circumstances in the shape of the provisions of Oxford, while the birth of the Scots parliament owed less to English than to Scottish, and wider developments (forms of representation were already becoming evident elsewhere in western Europe). The Irish parliament, reflecting its English ancestry, was bicameral: the Scottish parliament, reflecting continental European influences, emerged as a parliament of estates.[4] The Irish parliament, despite periods of relative autonomy, remained essentially subservient, and a tool of English royal government, while its Scots counterpart was from the start a comparatively more independent enterprise. These distinctions would also, inevitably, inform the nature of the two subsequent parliamentary unions, and indeed this is one of the central themes of what follows in this chapter: a comparatively independent Scottish parliament negotiated a comparatively more equitable settlement in 1706, while the relatively dependent Irish parliament accepted a settlement in 1800 which reflected its history of weakness.

On the other hand, there are clearly dangers in overly reductionist argument—and there is also clearly a basis for comparing the parliamentary histories of Scotland and Ireland. The early development of parliamentary representation in Scotland and Ireland was intimately connected both with the feudal relationships inside each kingdom, and also with the wider interconnections between the constituent kingdoms of the 'British Isles'. The Irish parliament evolved contemporaneously with the Anglo-Scottish (and

French and Welsh) wars of the late 12th- and early 13th-centuries, and Irish resources were used in full by the English monarchy (particularly Edward I) in the pursuit of its conquests in Scotland. Ireland was a critical base, and source of supply, for Edward I's and Edward II's Scottish campaigns. The imposition of taxation required the summoning of a parliament; and indeed many of the earliest recorded examples of such summonses in Ireland were concerned with the subsidizing of the king's campaigns in Scotland (as in 1300, for example, when knights and burgesses were called to parliament for the first time to vote monies for the Scottish wars). The early life of the Irish parliament was therefore bound up with the military ambitions of the English crown, and with the pursuit of an enhanced English realm.

Equally, the origins of the Scots' parliament were bound in with the military relationship between Scotland and England. As in Ireland, so in Scotland, there has been some discussion about the definition of 'parliament' and thus about the nativity of a national parliamentary tradition: as in Ireland, so in Scotland, a scholarly consensus accepts a date in the 13th century, with the term 'colloquium' being applied in royal documents from 1235 onwards in the Scots case, to be replaced in 1290 by 'parliamentum' (though some patriotic Scots claimed a greater antiquity for their legislature).[5] As in Ireland, so in Scotland, the business of many of the earliest 'parliaments' was dominated by the relationship with the English crown, and its military and territorial ambitions. For example, the 'parliament' held in July 1290 was for the purpose of settling a treaty with Edward I's England. Scottish parliaments—in the reign of King Robert I (Bruce) (1306–1329)—voted taxation supplies for the wars, or—in the reign of David II (1329–1371)—voted ransom monies in order to pay off the king's English captors (David had been seized in 1346, while on a raiding party into County Durham).[6] As in Ireland, so in Scotland, the cost of sustaining the Anglo-Scottish conflict eventually required the regular attendance in parliament of representatives of the 'third estate'—in Ireland knights and burgesses (from 1300), and in Scotland the representatives of the royal burghs (consulted on matters of taxation from the 1320s, and in regular attendance from the mid 14th century): recent scholarship has warned, however, against any reversion to a Stubbsian faith in the relentless consolidation of the burgess interest, which (it has been argued) in reality waxed and waned in the 14th and 15th centuries.[7] But the early life of the Scottish parliament was clearly interlinked with the independence and survival of the kingdom, and with national resistance to the military ambitions of the Plantagenet monarchy.

The history of these parliaments has attracted disproportionate attention from unionist scholars in both Ireland and Scotland; but the interpretative consequences of this allure have been different for the two nations and their historiographies. On the whole, Irish Protestant or unionist scholars of the medieval Irish parliament, such as Goddard Henry Orpen, or Maude Clarke, or May McKisack, have tended to emphasise the order and representativeness of the Anglo-Norman state and, critically, of its evolving parliamentary institutions, as distinct from the condition of Gaelic society.[8] In Scotland the distinctive national origins of parliament, together with the perceived success of the Anglo-Scots union, viewed certainly until the second half of the 20th century, have produced a different set of emphases. A.V. Dicey and Robert Rait, the doyens of early 20th-century Scottish unionist constitutional history, writing in the critical context of a stable union ('the success of the Act of Union is almost without a complete historical parallel'), argued that 'the parliament of Scotland, again, failed during the whole of its existence to become the centre of Scottish public life': Robert Rait further elaborated this motif of 'failure' or 'weakness' in his influential *The Parliaments of Scotland* of 1924.[9] However, the historiographical consensus at the beginning of the 21st century, in the context of devolution and of an unstable union, is that both the Scots and Irish parliaments could, and did, serve as centres for public life in their respective kingdoms: the new consensus is also impatient of narrow anglocentrism, and looks beyond Westminster to the wider history of European assemblies and parliaments.[10] But it is worth reiterating that at the height of union the historic Scots parliament was seen by most historians as a cypher, in sharp contradistinction to the reverence popularly applied (even by some unionists) at the same time to its Irish counterpart. As will become clear, it was not only parliamentary history which favoured unionism in modern Scotland.

In fact in the 15th century both parliaments acted to critique (and occasionally) oppose royal policies. In 1460 the Irish parliament challenged royal government by declaring that Ireland should only be governed by those laws which its parliament endorsed; and the parliament's later defiant support for the Yorkist cause precipitated royal intervention and the curtailing of its powers through Poynings' Law of 1494 (the parliament of 1487 had endorsed the coronation of the Yorkist pretender Lambert Simnel).[11] Indeed, the necessity for Poynings' Law reflected the wider augmentation of the Irish parliament's standing in the 15th century. The parliament of 1541–1543 has been seen by Brendan Bradshaw as being 'the chief instrument' in the redesign of Ireland's constitutional status, embodying the designation of Henry VIII as King of Ireland, and an increasing emphasis on Ireland as a united, sovereign state: Bradshaw has gone so far as to suggest that these shifts of the early 1540s 'mark the origins of Irish political nationalism'.[12]

In contemporary Scotland, parliament's success in monitoring the royal government of the Stewarts led the dynamic James IV (1488–1513) to bypass the estates in seeking cash, and the summoning of parliaments became much more sporadic in his reign than earlier in the century, when indeed parliament had been summoned annually (Keith Brown has called this stratagem the king's 'wisest decision of all').[13] But effective royal management and financial independence were temporary phenomena. Parliament emerged as a critical agent in the realization and enacting of the Scots Reformation (1560), and indeed the mid 16th century ('the Edwardian moment') has been identified more widely as an important seedbed of religious and political ideas which would later germinate as Jacobean unionism.[14] The large number of Scots parliaments in the late 16th century has been linked to 'the absence of strong royal government alongside deeply factional politics' as well as to James VI's irremediable impecuniousness.[15]

Parliament acted in other ways as a counter to the rule of the Stuart monarchy. James VI and I was both a principled absolutist as well as intellectually and strategically elusive —and far too slippery (and far too broke) a monarch to get locked for long into combat with his Scots parliament. But Charles I inherited his father's view of kingship without acquiring his father's intellectual dexterity, and conflict, famously and tragically, was the result. Relations between Charles and his parliament in Scotland weakened in the 1630s, with the parliament of 1633 now being seen as a high point of royal control and embodying 'a fundamental evaporation of trust': the stifling of parliamentary debate was a very short-term achievement for the crown, in so far as it encouraged the removal of dissent from beyond the formal structures of government.[16] The Scots parliament was intimately involved with the National Covenant (1638), the great ('justly famous if excessively turgid') popular protest against episcopacy and unfettered royal government, and in the subsequent Wars of the Covenant (1639–1651).[17] The Scots parliament of 1640, which met without Charles's consent, oversaw a constitutional revolution, which encompassed the doubling of the vote of the shires, the abolition of the clerical estate, the effective abolition of the Lords of the Articles, the inauguration of triennial parliaments, and the establishment of the 'committee of estates' to govern in the years between parliamentary sessions: 'here was a parliament free from royal control, with an inclusive committee structure, and free debate in which nobles could make use of rhetorical skills honed throughout a long education'.[18] Here, too, was a parliament where the 'Commons' were beginning to exercise a relatively great influence, and where precedents were being created for the later 17th century.[19]

The early 17th-century Irish parliament, like its Scots contemporary, but unlike its own (exclusively Protestant, and overwhelmingly Anglican) 18th-century successor, provided a platform for the range of religious interests within the kingdom, and was therefore briefly able to serve as a credible focus for political debate. As in Scotland, so in Ireland the high point of the royal manipulation of parliament was achieved in the early 1630s, and (in the Irish case) with the parliament of 1634: here the Lord Deputy, Wentworth, rode roughshod over a range of key interests and sensitivities in raising cash for his royal master. As in the 14th century, so in 1640, an Irish parliament was used to raising money for the pursuit of the King's Scottish enemies, on this occasion the Covenanters. But, as Aidan Clarke has argued, 'it was not until the breakdown of authority in the multiple Stuart kingship in the early 1640s, that the underlying assumptions of Irish politics were found to be in need of definition and justification, and it became necessary to defend the position that Ireland was a dependency, not of England, but of the English crown'. Indeed, if the Scots were asserting their religious and secular rights through the National Covenant, then the Irish parliament's protests against royal government were given intellectual coherence and force by Patrick Darcy's *Argument* (1643), a defence of Irish legislative independence, delivered originally as a speech in the Irish parliament in June 1641, that influenced subsequent generations of Irish patriot.[20] A form of parliamentary focus for Catholic Ireland was provided in the 1640s by the nine general assemblies of the Confederate Catholics of Ireland, an oath-bound union (technically not a parliament, since—though loyal to the king—it had not been summoned by him) formed in 1642 in order to govern those areas under Catholic control in the Ireland of the war years (1641–1653): Donal Cregan has called these Confederate Catholics 'seventeenth century Home Rulers', a view echoed in Tom Bartlett's judgement that 'the Confederation, as a whole, constituted both the last home rule parliament and independent government in Ireland until the 1920s'.[21] Drawing on Darcy's inspiration, the overwhelmingly Catholic Parliament of 1689 strove to assert Ireland's legislative independence by seeking the repeal of the restrictive Poynings' law of 1494.

The centrality of these 17th-century Irish parliaments and assemblies in the consciousness of subsequent generations, and particularly within an emergent mass nationalism in the 19th century, is illustrated by their importance in later popular and anti-union historiography. Patrick Darcy's *Argument* was reprinted on numerous occasions, while the Confederate Catholics of Ireland were rebranded as the 'Confederation of Kilkenny' in an eponymous book, written by Revd C.P. Meehan in 1846, and reprinted into the 20th century. The parliament of 1689 was also rebranded in the 19th century—as 'the Patriot Parliament'—and was the subject of a highly popular study by the 'Young Ireland' cultural nationalist, Thomas Davis.[22]

But the mythologization of individual parliaments, or particular acts of parliamentary defiance, while helping to underline the existence in both Scotland and Ireland of powerful national counterweights to the notion and tradition of union, also perhaps diverts from the ongoing realities of royal power: there is a danger, in interpreting both Scots and Irish parliamentary history in the 17th and (in the Irish case) 18th century of succumbing to the temptations of an overly Whiggish or patriotic narrative. In each case there was evidence for the gradual development of parliamentary sovereignty, but in each case, too, this development was by no means uninterrupted or linear. While recent scholarship in general underlines the strength and authority of the medieval and indeed wider Scots parliamentary tradition, and is suspicious of the strictures of an older, unionist, historiography, both the Scots and Irish parliaments were generally heavily subject to the influence of the royal government in the 17th and (for the Irish parliament) the 18th centuries.[23] For the most part this influence could be exercised through those within parliament who owed their position or fortunes in part or in full to the crown —the bishops, recently elevated noblemen, privy councillors: patronage was a necessary lubricant of royal government in both 17th-century Scotland and 17th- and 18th-century Ireland. However, there were more formal or structural mechanisms propagating royal influence. For Scotland the key parliamentary agencies in this respect were the Committee and Lords of Articles and the 'king's' or 'royal commissioner' (the *magnus commissionarius*).[24] The commissionership was created in 1604, and necessitated by James VI and I's removal to London: the first holder of this increasingly influential office was James's Treasurer since 1601, George Spot, soon to be ennobled as the Earl of Dunbar.[25] The Lords were originally and essentially a business committee for the Scots parliament, but their functions were adapted to the needs of the Stuart monarchy. The Lords comprised

representatives from the three estates of the Scots' parliament, although by
the reign of James VI and I it was the royally nominated (and restored) bishops who were the key players in shaping the membership and composi-
tion.[26] Their Committee of Articles vetted legislative proposals, killing off
those proposals which were not in tune with royal wishes, and presented
draft legislation to the full parliament for approval. The Lords waxed and
waned with the fortunes of the Stuart kings, peaking in significance under
James and Charles I, abolished with parliament's supremacy in the
Covenanting period, but restored with the monarchy after 1660. The revolution of 1689 brought with it the Scots parliament's definition of kingship
(enshrined within the Claim of Right and Articles of Grievances), a definition which encompassed Protestantism, regular parliaments, a limited monarchy, and a condemnation of the Lords of the Articles. The final flowering
of the Scottish parliament, in the years before union in 1707, occurred without the assistance of the Committee of Articles, William II and III having
traded these off against a grant of supply in 1690.

The autonomy of the Irish parliament was similarly circumscribed. Here
functions similar to those later exercised by the Scots Lords of the Articles
were legally enshrined in Poynings' Law of 1494, a measure which (as with
the Lords) effectively ensured the indirect exercise of royal influence over
the legislation of the Irish parliament. The conduit of this influence was the
Irish privy council (royally appointed, and chaired by the Lord Deputy, the
representative of the monarch) which vetted draft legislation ('heads of
bills'), approving, altering, delaying, or suppressing as it thought fit. The bills
which survived this scrutiny were transmitted to the (royally appointed)
English privy council where they were subjected to similar scrutiny, and
(again, if successful) returned to Ireland and to the Irish parliament. Here,
provided the two houses of the parliament accepted them without further
change, the bills became law. This mechanism, augmented by the Declaratory
Act of 1720, which asserted the right of the parliament in London to legislate for Ireland, long facilitated the reconciliation of British interests to the
existence of an Irish parliament.[27]

A second, informal, agency for royal authority within the Irish parliament
analogous in certain respects to the earlier Scots' Lords of the Articles were the
Undertakers. Just as in 17th-century Scotland the Lords functioned effectively
as a vehicle for royal policy-making, so in Ireland, from the 1690s onwards, the
crown and British government co-opted an array of influential parliamentarians, who 'undertook' to deliver majorities for government business in return

for a substantial share of official patronage.[28] The Scots parliament was eventually able (in 1690) to overthrow the Committee of Articles; but it was the British government which—with the appointment of Viscount Townshend as lord lieutenant of Ireland in 1767—finally dispensed with the Undertakers, replacing local subcontractors with an ostensibly more efficient managerial regime in the shape of a resident minister. But more efficient British management of the Irish parliament also meant more overt and unambiguous management, with the direct intervention of the lord lieutenant; and this in turn helped to pave the way for heightened parliamentary resentments and the assertion of Ireland's legislative independence by the late 1770s.[29]

## Uniting and marketing the three crowns

Despite patriotic interpretations of the two kingdom's parliamentary history, for both Scotland and Ireland the consideration, even the actuality, of union was by no means a novelty. Each kingdom had experienced a union of crowns, though—significantly, as will be argued—under very different circumstances and with very different implications. Each had direct experience of parliamentary union (under the Commonwealth), though again under different circumstances. However, patriotic readings and celebrations of the two national parliaments have a greater relevance to each of the periods immediately before the unions, for (again, significantly) the two parliaments grew in assertiveness in the years before the London government thought it expedient to negotiate their removal.

As has been seen, Ireland was designated as a kingdom in 1541, and incorporated within the titles of Henry VIII as joint monarch.[30] The significance of this form of 'union of crowns' was complex, however, and it certainly did not bring the co-equality of the Irish parliament, privy council, and other institutions of law and government with their English counterparts (the English parliament still claimed superiority, and legislated to that effect in 1720). John Morrill has described Ireland after 1541 as 'a dependent kingdom with no existence apart from the Crown of England'.[31] Moreover, the formal acknowledgement of the kingdom and of the united crowns took place in the aftermath of renewed English military conquest (the Geraldine rebellion, which looked to James V of Scotland as a replacement for Henry VIII as 'dominus' or lord of Ireland, had recently—1534—been suppressed). Ireland's status as a kingdom did not bring any heightened influence over

royal government—indeed rather the reverse, given that the unsettled circumstances of Ireland in the 1540s, and its rising strategic and geopolitical
significance, now demanded the presence of a royal 'chief governor'.[32] The
period circumscribed by the Geraldine rebellion and the Kingship Act also
saw the launch of a new and potent image of the supremacy of English royal
government in Ireland: the harp surmounted by a royal crown. This made
its first appearance on the coinage of Ireland in 1534 (on groats and half
groats), and has survived as a symbol of monarchical authority (in Northern
Ireland) into the 21st century.

In practice, therefore, while symbolically significant, this 'union of crowns'
was intimately connected with the exigencies of English policy at the time
(even if Henry VIII himself was highly ambivalent about its value); and it did
not bring any effective or equalizing union with England closer to realization. Indeed, as will be suggested, the outcome in some ways ran counter to
union: the promulgation of the 'new' kingdom, paradoxically, gave a patriotic focus and definition for later opponents of English ascendancy in
Ireland.

At the same time as Henry accepted the title of 'King of Ireland', an
opportunity arose to achieve a parallel regal union. Early theorists of a
British union, such as John Mair, the author of the *Historia Maioris Britanniae*
(1521) (and deemed by some to be 'the founding father of Scottish unionism') had seen an answer to the costly and bloody Anglo-Scots' rivalry in
the form of a dynastic alliance; but Mair (like generations of later Scottish
unionists) understood that, if a dynastic union were to be achieved, it could
not be on the basis of English ascendancy (as had been originally mooted in
the reign of the troubled David II), still less on the repudiation of Scotland's
standing and autonomy.[33] Though Mair was as much interested in providing
an historical corrective to English presumptions of sovereignty within
Scotland, in fact his hopes of a dynastic union seemed to gain substance
when, in December 1542, the infant Mary succeeded her father James V as
monarch of Scotland. James had died shortly after his defeat at the Solway
Moss, near Carlisle; and the peace settlement which Henry VIII imposed
upon Scotland, the Treaty of Greenwich, envisioned a union of the crowns
of England and Scotland, attained through the marriage of his son, Edward,
and the infant Queen of Scotland. In the event this did not take place: but
English (and some Scots) efforts to achieve this end have a clear significance
in terms of the history of unionism within the 'British' Isles. Dynastic union
would be sought both by military as well as propagandist means. James

Henrisoun's *Exhortacion to the Scottes* (1547) and the anonymous *Epistle or Exhortacion to unitie and peace* (1548) (possibly also by Henrisoun, according to Roger Mason) saw union and the royal marriage as a providential culmination to 'British' history. Henrisoun believed that the Scots and English possessed the same ethnic origins, he believed that they should sink their national distinctions into a shared Britishness, and he saw union as a divinely ordained opportunity to consolidate the true, reformed, faith: Henrisoun also saw the origins of a British monarchy as resting with Constantine the Great, the unifier of empire, and patron of True Faith. But, significantly, Henrisoun's work was also a form of polemical complement to the 'Rough Wooing' – to the Duke of Somerset's military campaign in Scotland, which (in turn) was effectively an effort to impose the notion of a dynastic (and Protestant) union on the Scots. Somerset won a bloody victory at Pinkie Heugh, near Musselburgh; but, when Mary was smuggled out of the country to France, he was compelled to remove his forces from Scotland, and to sue for peace. The Anglo-Scots union was born out of these hopes for a 'union of the crowns'; and it drew upon some of the polemic of what has been called 'the Edwardian moment.'[34] But it was also associated, alarmingly and significantly, with English military might, and with the English effort to impose a religious and constitutional settlement. It should be emphasised that the association between royal (and parliamentary) union and English military ascendancy has been long-standing, intimate, and influential.

Of course the 'union of the crowns' of Scotland and England was ultimately brought about by the wiles of fortune rather than any coherent political or military strategy.[35] The accession of James VI, Mary's son, to the throne of England in 1603 was achieved without any passage of arms, and by the consent (however muted) of all concerned. However, the union of 1603 raises a number of issues, and signals a range of themes, which have a lasting significance for any wider consideration of the unions of Britain and of the United Kingdom. James sought for a period to develop a full-blown union project, proclaiming himself King of Great Britain in 1604, and making provision, through Acts of Commission in the English and Scots parliaments, for the negotiation of closer relations (the repeal of statutes of enmity, the regularization of justice in what he rebranded as 'the Middle Shires', improvements in trade, the clarification of the legal status of Scots in England and English people in Scotland).[36] While it seems likely that James 'wanted ultimately the closest possible fusion', it is ultimately unclear whether this unfathomably crafty and cerebral king was genuinely seeking to enact deeply-laid plans for a thoroughgoing union or was merely pragmatically seeking peaceable Anglo-Scots relations, and enhanced Scots influence within the united monarchy.[37] Certainly increased numbers of Scots were appointed to the privy council and to the royal court, providing a critical medium of communication between Scotland and the crown: it has been said that James effectively created a Scots *noblesse de robe* to service the new union. Appointments to the royal Bedchamber tended to be Scots, a development which critically bolstered the new union ('for Scotland the Bedchamber was an essential mechanism for coming to terms with the problem of an absentee king…if Scots were to get a fair share of the patronage of an absent king, some such means were essential').[38]

James was also active in promoting the idea and symbolism of 'Great Britain': he was now King of this Great Britain, and he wanted appropriate trappings for this new realm, including a new, joint flag (combining the crosses of Saints George and Andrew) (see illustration B.1). Union was analogous to the sacrament of marriage, and enjoyed similar divine sanction: James famously asked and declared in 1604 'hath not God first united these two Kingdomes both in Language, Religion and similitude of maners?…what God hath conioyned then, let no man separate. I am the husband, and all the whole Isle is my lawfull wife'.[39] Indeed the scriptural tag 'quae deus coniunxit nemo separet' (drawn from Matthew 19:6) became a motto for union, adorning James's (and Charles I's) coinage (James himself seems to have taken a hand in the design of the new coins).[40] The shillings of James's second coinage bore this legend, while a gold 20 shilling coin (naturally dubbed the 'unite') broadcast another scriptural endorsement of union, 'faciam eos in gentem unam' ('I will make them into one nation'), drawn from Ezekiel 37:22. The successor to the unite was the 20 shilling gold laurel, which bore a portrait of James garlanded as a Roman emperor; and indeed the propaganda of union celebrated the King as a new Constantine, the unifier of the two halves of his empire within the embrace of the true faith.

Just as the later parliamentary and Anglo-Irish unions would have an architectural or spatial dimension, so James celebrated the union of the crowns in stone: for example, between 1618 and 1622 he added a soaring north wing to Linlithgow Palace, the retreat of his Stuart ancestors, and adorned it with 'I.R.6' (Iacobus Rex Sextus) and 'I.R.I' (Iacobus Rex Primus)—King James VI and I—together with the symbols of Scotland, England, and Ireland. Ben Jonson was responsible for the design of a more ephemeral structure—one of the triumphal arches erected for James's entry in London in March 1604, and bedecked with a figure representing the united monarchy, and a Latin motto trumpeting the new insular empire: 'orbis britannicus, divisus ab orbe'.[41] Jonson also celebrated the new union in his 'Hymenai' of 1606 (wherein the prevailing analogy between marriage and regal union was again deployed), and in a succession of later court masques: other, lesser, versifiers contributed their own celebratory doggerel.[42] While Keith Brown has rightly warned that 'it is very easy to exaggerate the effectiveness of cultural patronage by the crown in this era', still this broadly based royal effort to celebrate the 'union of crowns' is striking, and particularly the attempt to evoke classical (Constantinian) and biblical sanction and analogy, and to adapt Elizabethan national sentiment to the new, British cause.[43] It broaches the issue of the effort (more precisely, the relative lack of effort) subsequently invested in promoting and celebrating the complete realization of 'Great Britain' with the Union of 1707, and that of the United Kingdom in 1801.

From the start this Scottish 'union of crowns' also had a critical Irish aspect; and indeed Ulster has been seen a key locus for the realization of James's British ambitions. James interpreted the Plantation of Ulster as an opportunity to give effect to his vision of Britain, by uniting his English and Scots' subjects in a joint civilizing mission within the northern province of Ireland. The flight of the insurgent Gaelic earls in 1607, together with the suppression of Sir Cahir O'Doherty's rising in Donegal of 1608 (which Scots soldiers helped to defeat), coincided with legislation creating a joint citizenship for the kingdoms of England and Scotland.[44] Moreover, this effective removal of Gaelic lordship from Ulster created the opportunity for a scheme of colonization, which would bring these new 'Britons' and their civilization into those areas of central and western Ulster which had been hitherto largely resistant to the efforts of the English alone. But the Plantation was not only about extending, it was also concerned with stabilizing the boundaries of 'Britain'. The pacification of Ulster was a means of reducing the likelihood that the province would be used as a springboard for foreign invasion (a lasting motif within British statesmanship). Moreover, half of the Ulster planters were meant to be Scots (though this quota was not filled); and of these, most were to come from the south of Scotland, and in particular the economically and politically unsettled borderland with England (the 'Middle Shires'), whose people were also being used at this time to 'civilize' the Western Isles of Scotland.[45] In effect, James and his ministers were blurring and pacifying one border by creating another. But the project serves to underline the extent to which both the Scottish lowlands and Ireland helped to define Jacobean 'Britain'—and the extent to which Ireland remained central to the development of the Anglo-Scots relationship.[46]

It should also be said that, while plantation was about the consolidation of a British 'empire' and 'civilization', its long-term contribution (and that of the developing informal linkages between the North of Ireland and southern Scotland) to the stability of the multiple kingdom, and its Stuart monarchy, was highly ambiguous. Heightened communication across the 'North Channel World' was associated with the radicalization of Presbyterianism, and (looking ahead) with the growth of opposition to the personal rule of Charles I. The deployment of a Scottish army of occupation in the North of Ireland in the 1640s provided a significant bolster both to the covenanting movement in Ulster, as well as to the developing Presbyterian community in that province. Intellectual cross-fertilization in the later 17th century created strong synergies, but also bolstered the case for the rights of the two parliaments, Scots and Irish. So, paradoxically, while the consolidation of the multiple kingdom in the early 17th century may have created some of the preconditions for 19th-century Unionism in Ireland (and in Scotland), the Scots-Irish linkages of the 17th century tended to destabilize the (theoretically) single most important unifying institution of the three kingdoms, the Stuart monarchy. The Plantation, and the informal settlement of eastern Ulster, may have been widely seen as precursors to modern Unionism; but in reality the chain of causation was much more complex than its early 20th-century apologists cared to depict.[47]

Other details of the 'union of crowns' are suggestive. Even in this tentative format of 1603, union acquired an infrastructural dimension. Just as the Union of 1707 and that of 1801 were achieved by a range of improvements in communications and travel, so even in 1603 the 'union of the crowns' necessitated an improved postal service connecting James's two British capitals, London and Edinburgh.[48] Effective regal union, certainly under James, was associated with, indeed demanded, stable central government—'a government that could launch and in a measure implement long-term policies, rather than live frantically from day-to-day appeasing and balancing rival interests, hoping for the best and dreading, often with sufficient cause, the worst'.[49]

Equally telling and resonant, however, were the constraints upon James's project of union. The early 17th-century ideologues of union tended, much like their successors in the 18th and 19th centuries, to judge union as a matter of individual national advantage rather than as a full incorporating partnership. Writing in 1597, David Hume of Godscroft saw a union as essentially Scotland writ large, with (for example) the spread of Presbyterian church organization through a united realm. As noted, James himself may have been content merely to achieve enhanced Scottish influence within his new union. Equally, from the English perspective, union was often judged, less in terms of its potential to create a greater whole than of its local impact. Bruce Galloway has argued that, while there was no coherent opposition 'party' in the House of Commons, and while support for Union may have been underestimated, four key issues ultimately motivated a broad body of parliamentary opinion: anti-Scottish prejudice, English nationhood, economic self-interest, and institutional conservatism.[50] Intermingled with these were suspicions of Scots Calvinism. Sir Edwin Sandys ('by far the shrewdest of the English opponents of union'), opined that union could only be properly achieved in the context of a Scottish surrender of sovereignty.[51] By extension, it has been argued that 'the only union that [English parliamentarians] could understand was annexation', and that union jarred with the 'natural law of the nation' (that is the sovereign authority of the King-in-Parliament).[52]

Indeed, when the Scottish parliament accepted the principle of a full union of the kingdoms in 1607, conditional upon the parallel approval of the English parliament, no such sanction emanated from Westminster, and the idea withered. James's ambitions for union stalled in the context of English jealousies, Scottish claims and ambitions, and (in the end) mutual resentment; or (in the alternative and bracing assessment of John Morrill) they were scuppered 'by the English neurotic obsession about the sanctity of the Common Law, and by the Scots neurotic obsession of the purity of their Kirk within a perfect union'.[53] It was a striking premonition of the shape of things to come, that (the purity of the Kirk notwithstanding) advocates of union in the Jacobean period tended to be Scots, while the English (who felt that they had more to lose in the short-term) tended to be sceptical or uncomprehending. Much more than in Ireland, union was an indigenous and perennial Scottish flowering.[54]

Consideration of a full or 'incorporating' union did not of course die in the first decade of the 17th century only to reemerge, *ex silentio*, a century later. On the contrary, just as in the 19th and 20th centuries the recurrent debates upon Ireland's, and Northern Ireland's, position within the union generated a succession of influential and overlapping templates, so James VI and I's proposals for union were the starting point for discussion when the issue was subsequently excavated, and in particular at the beginning of the reign of Queen Anne.[55] Union was broached by the Marquess of Argyll and the covenanters in the 1640s, in the midst of the 'war of the three king-doms'—'a federal union which would limit the power of the royal execu-tive and thus produce all the advantages brought about by the great event of 1603 and mitigate its disadvantages': significantly, however, here, as in the future, it has been argued that union was 'not prized for its own sake, but as a weapon in the strife of parties'.[56] Union was enacted under Cromwell, after a form of negotiation between the Scots and English parliaments; and it was pursued in 1668 (when economic union was tabled), 1670 (an incor-porating, parliamentary, union), and again in 1688–1689, though (as John Robertson has pointed out) there remains 'a pressing need' for the thorough investigation of these still relatively murky Restoration episodes.[57] The 'murkiness' of these episodes notwithstanding, it should be noted that 'beginning in 1670, all union negotiations centred on proposals for an incor-porating or parliamentary union'.[58]

Sections of the Scottish political elite remained interested throughout the 17th century in the notion of a separate but intimate relationship with England, to a form of (in Allen Macinnes's definition) 'confederal' union of the two kingdoms. The idea of a universal British Presbyterianism contin-ued (despite recurrent setbacks) to have substantial traction in Scotland, and was embodied in a treaty between the Scots Covenanters and the Long Parliament in 1643—the Solemn League and Covenant.[59] The idea of a shared monarchy was also deeply grounded: though the Scots had revolted against the form of Stuart rule, and the exactions of the Stuart state, they remained bound to the Stuart dynasty; and, accordingly, when Charles I was executed in 1649, the Scots parliament proclaimed his son, Charles II, as King not just of Scotland but of Britain. By way of contrast (but fitting within a longer tradition of English nationalism and scepticism), the parlia-mentarians of the Rump Parliament, and of the early Commonwealth (1649–1653), like their Jacobean predecessors, conceived Scotland as a sepa-rate kingdom, Ireland as a subordinate and dependent polity, and union with each as being attainable only in the context of English military suprem-acy and conquest: Sarah Barber has emphasised that 'the dominant strain of English nationalism which characterised the early Commonwealth, includ-ing hatred of the Scots and ambivalence towards Irish reconquest, dictated that the Rump's reasons for union tended to be negative'.[60] It may also be observed that the early Commonwealth was characterized, not only by intense hostility to Irish Catholicism, but also by a desire to undermine the dominance of the Kirk in Scotland.[61]

For his part, Oliver Cromwell viewed Ireland as morally cankered, bloodied by the killings of the settler population in 1641, and was fired with a sense of mission in his military campaigning there in 1649–1650. But he felt no parallel vocation in Calvinist Scotland, professed no independent enthusiasm for union, and was otherwise content to let an English republic coexist with the kingdom of Scotland. Scotland's devotion to its monarchy and to the notion of a confederal British state brought Cromwell and his armies to Scotland in 1650, where he inflicted defeat on a Scots' army twice the size of his own at Dunbar. By December 1653, with Charles II of Great Britain and Scotland in exile, a new constitution for the 'British' Isles was promulgated, the Instrument of Government, and Cromwell was installed as Lord Protector of a unified Commonwealth: he now presided over a single Council of State for England, Scotland, and Ireland, made appointments to a single (generally English) judiciary, and answered to a single parliament, containing thirty representatives from Scotland and a further thirty from Ireland. Union had, indeed, been achieved, but—paradoxically—it followed the definition of English critics of James I's statecraft: union was encompassed through military conquest in Scotland and in Ireland, through the suppression of the Scottish and Irish parliaments, and the annihilation of Scottish sovereignty (Ireland, the Kingship Act notwithstanding, had always been affirmed as dependent and subservient). Moreover, it was a union which had only the most distant relationship with Britishness, and with the rhetoric of an imperial Britain: such notions were too thoroughly tainted by the Stuart monarchy to be of much use in Cromwell's functionalist 'Commonwealth of England'.

Critically, however, while Ireland and Scotland were each integrated along similar lines within the Commonwealth, the experience that each kingdom had of union was distinct. Taken in the round, it is clear that the notion of union now acquired quite different, and lasting, connotations within each of the two realms. Nicholas Canny has argued, influentially, that the Cromwellian revolution in Ireland reflected not just the religious and political zeal of the times, but drew upon some more fundamental themes and influences in the history of British colonization in Ireland—and in

particular the lasting impact of the poet-planter, Edmund Spenser, who, in
the context of half-hearted earlier British ventures, envisioned a comprehensive military subjugation and social reconstruction of Ireland and supplied a model to subsequent colonizers.[62] Cromwell's conquest of Ireland
was certainly marked by a ferocity which was not in evidence during his
campaigns in Scotland; and the killings, by his troops, of the defenders of
Drogheda and Wexford in September and October of 1649 were controversial (even by the sanguinary standards of the mid 17th century).[63] There was
no equivalent in Scotland of the Spenserian model of conquest and 'civilization'. This can be seen not least in that payment for the two campaigns
was exacted in wholly different ways. The bloody, protracted, and expensive
(£3.5 millions) war in Ireland, was paid for by the confiscation of rebel lands
which were turned over to those who had speculated their money in the parliamentary cause ('adventurers'), and to those who had served in Cromwell's
armies. The Cromwellian military presence in Scotland, by contrast, was
financed through regular imposts, which in fact were reduced in the later
1650s, when it became clear that the capacity of the country to pay was
constrained.

In both Ireland and Scotland union was imposed by military conquest,
but the tenor of government in each polity was distinct. It is clearly true that
there were some linkages between the Irish and Scots Cromwellian regimes,
embodied particularly in the form of Roger Boyle, Lord Broghill, the well-
connected Irish Calvinist who applied his Irish knowledge and experience
to the task of governing Scotland in 1655–1656: Patrick Little has emphasised the consequent parallels in the Scots and Irish experience of the
Cromwellian regime at this period, in the mid 1650s ('in Ireland and
Scotland the years 1655–6 saw the establishment of moderate government,
with the army's power reduced, radical religion discouraged, and more
influence placed in the hands of the local landowners, including former roy-
alists').[64] But in Ireland Catholic and royalist opposition was suppressed with
unparalleled ferocity, and accompanied by mass imprisonment, expropriation, and (for several thousand) transportation to the West Indies.

In Scotland, union was indeed a national humiliation, wrought as it was
in the aftermath of defeat and with scant consultation; but it was not without some benefits.[65] The Highlands were now brought under the rule of
law and of central government, though the treatment of the Highland
chieftains (as opposed to their Gaelic Irish equivalents) had a measure of
reason and imagination. If Catholicism in Ireland was being extirpated,

then Presbyterianism in Scotland was relatively untouched: David Daiches believed that 'the general Puritan tone of Cromwell's government was in itself far from uncongenial to the Scottish Presbyterians', while Scott Spurlock has argued more recently that 'the evidence from the Interregnum suggests an English policy of tolerating the Kirk so long as it did not attempt to oppress the consciences of those who chose "another gospel way"'.[66] In Scotland, after 1655, there was a nine-member Council of State, which (though chaired by Broghill) contained Scottish representation and sat in Edinburgh.[67] Cromwell's imposed parliamentary union was not popular; but his vision of a community of the godly had some meaning for the covenanting tradition, while his concern for 'the meaner sort', and for social justice, subsequently won the cautious respect of luminaries of the High Enlightenment such as David Hume and James Macpherson.[68] Thomas Carlyle is perhaps the supreme example of 19th century Scottish surrender to the allure of the Lord Protector, encapsulated most obviously through *Heroes and Hero Worship* (1841) and his work on *Oliver Cromwell's Letters and Speeches* (1845). For the later Edinburgh Presbyterian evangelist, James Black, preaching to Scottish recruits during the First World War, 'the best soldiers are always Christian men…without any doubt England's stoutest soldiers were Cromwell's Puritans, well called 'Ironsides', men who fought from conscience and a passion for justice. How they made Europe quake! And as surely our finest fighters in Scotland were the men of the Reformation and the Covenant, who by their valour made Scotland what it is today'.[69] Even those Scots not disposed to be sympathetic to English definitions of 'union' have occasionally relented in their judgement of Cromwellian rule.[70]

Even the symbolism of Cromwellian union was more obviously offensive to Irish, as distinct from Scottish, sensibilities. No separate Scottish coinage was struck during the Commonwealth, but the coins designed for circulation in England and Ireland bore shields with the two national symbols, St George's cross and the harp on one side, while the reverse carried only the English symbol together with the legend 'the Commonwealth of England'. Pattern bronze coins designed in the last years of the regime were certainly a rather more persuasive advertisement for union: these bore three interlinked 'pillars of wisdom', surmounted by the national symbols of England, Scotland, and Ireland, and circumscribed by the legend 'Thus United, Invincible'. But the design was never put into production, and the regime fell shortly afterwards.

Though widely unpopular, the Cromwellian union had had some overt support within Scotland. In 1660, amidst the wreckage of the Commonwealth, Cromwell's deputy in Scotland, General George Monck, was widely petitioned to sustain the union. This was not done, however: Monck's new, royal, master, Charles II was not prepared to uphold the architecture of the Cromwellian state. More significantly, perhaps, Charles wanted Scotland to remain in the position designed by his father, James VI and I—one of dependence on the crown. A union, and a united British parliament, were more powerful institutions, and more threatening for the monarchy, than their constituent parts. Certainly the restitution of an impoverished and biddable Scottish parliament, a parliament still loyal to the Stuarts, held few terrors for Charles. In 1660, therefore, as indeed before and after, union again became a tool rather than an ideal—a device to be taken up, or laid down, in the service of other English royal interests.

Gilbert Burnet, an opponent of the Commonwealth, which he saw as a 'usurpation', considered that in Scotland under Cromwell's union 'there was good justice done, and vice suppress'd and punished; so that we always reckon those eight years of usurpation a time of great peace and prosperity'.[71] The unionist Sir John Clerk observed that 'there are many to this day who swallow their pride and praise Cromwell's rule, saying that under it Scotland prospered as at no other time, with trade flourishing and justice firmly upheld'—though he also added with characteristic shrewdness that 'this view results from comparison with the next [Restoration] regime'.[72] In Ireland Cromwell may be said to have stimulated the first Irish unionism and unionists amongst the Protestant interest: by 1657, it has been observed, unionism 'lay at the very heart' of Broghill's political ambitions, as evidenced by the latter's advocacy of a united kingdom bound by a Cromwellian monarchy.[73] But if the first Irish unionists wanted Cromwell as a king, then in oral Gaelic culture he swiftly emerged as a bogeyman, a status subsequently confirmed and elaborated in print. Toby Barnard has argued that Cromwell's malign reputation in Ireland was finally established in the 19th century, in the context of a burgeoning popular historiography, and developing opposition to the Union of 1801 (and in fact even fervent Unionists, such as Edward Carson, were also antagonistic towards the Cromwellian record).[74]

In sum, the first experience of parliamentary union for Scotland was ambiguous, associated with military subjugation and with the killing of a Stuart king, but in some other respects benign. In Ireland union was identifiable with impoverishment, religious persecution, and slaughter—and with the birth of Irish unionism.

## The revolution and union

Scotland and Ireland had both an experience of union, under Cromwell, and a prehistory of discussions on the subject well in advance of the attainment of the Acts of 1707 and 1801. Indeed, the intermittent dialogue on the subject of a full Anglo-Scots union tended to stimulate a parallel interest in union amongst the Irish political elite, if only because this dialogue underlined the effectively dependent condition of the Irish kingdom and its parliament.

It has been suggested by several historians that 'the seeds for what would become the incorporating union of 1707 were sown late in 1688', when a call from Scotland came for 'ane entire and perpetuall union betwixt the two kingdoms'.[75] In January 1689, in the aftermath of the flight of James VII and II, William met with some of his Scottish supporters in London, and the idea of a parliamentary union was broached, with John Hay, second Earl (later first Marquess) of Tweeddale providing inspiration and a lead.[76] On 8 January Andrew Fletcher of Saltoun, later one of the most prominent opponents of the settlement of 1707, and a patriarch of modern Scottish nationalism, opined that 'we can never come to any trew setlement but by uniting with England in Parliaments and trade': union 'would redound to all sorts of people, and would be the only means to support an impoverished and sinking nation'.

Scottish historians have differed in their interpretations of this missive, and indeed of Tweeddale's initiative more broadly. T.C. Smout has suggested that at this stage Andrew Fletcher was disposed towards an incorporating union, William Ferguson has emphasised Fletcher's fundamental commitment to preserving the achievement of the Revolution, while Paul Henderson Scott has argued that Fletcher meant 'international cooperation' in the context of a separate Scottish parliament.[77] On the other hand, P.W.J. Riley, for example, has suggested that Tweeddale's motives were 'entirely political and religious. Likewise the attitudes of others to union were determined by its probable effect on their own aims, personal, political or religious. Trade was not mentioned'.[78]

The outlines of the episode are, in fact, clear enough: in April 1689 the Scots 'parliament' (or, strictly, Convention of Estates) passed legislation providing for commissioners to treat with the English on the issue of union. Scotland's commissioners were duly nominated, but in the context of renewed English indifference and disregard—'with the settlement of the

Scottish succession there was less immediate incentive for England to attempt a union'—they were never put to work.[79] Given the unsettled nature of the Anglo-Scots relationship, the dangers of religious division, and the prospect of wider reform and improvement, there had been some interest in union: and John Clerk resorted to a variant of a familiar argument in Scottish discourse on the Anglo-Scots relationship in lamenting that 'the Scots made prisoners of themselves to the English, and later duly paid for their lack of forethought. If they had restrained their revolutionary ardour for a few days only, kept the crown in their hands, and put first things first instead of shamefully doing what was expected of them, surely they would have won fair terms from the English and brought prosperity to their country long ago'.[80]

The broader observation—that the experience of James VII and II's rule and of the Revolution laid the foundations for a significant renewed interest in union—might be further widened to include the Irish case. Union was certainly a recurrent if muted motif within the political thought of Irish patriots and parliamentarians from the 1690s into the 18th century. The explanation for this apparent paradox was that these defenders of the Irish parliament and its rights were now, in the aftermath of the 'Glorious Revolution', exclusively Protestant, and they were looking fundamentally to the rights and the dignity of their own political interest. Challenges, or perceived challenges, to this dignity or to the influence of the Irish Protestant parliament at this time came from different sources—the English parliament, Irish Catholic resurgence, or—indirectly—from Scotland; but, whatever the origins of the ailment, union was increasingly the favoured, universally applicable, nostrum. In 1692 an Irish parliament was restored, after the years of Jacobite and Catholic ascendancy (1685–1688); and it now confronted the lingering possibility of Jacobite and Catholic resurgence, the dominance of Louis XIV's Catholic empire on the continent, and a hostile and threateningly mercantilist English parliament.[81] An additional dimension was supplied by Scotland, where (as noted) the notion of union had already been twice broached by the Scottish parliament. In these multiple contexts, the idea of parliamentary union surfaced amongst the Irish political elite, treated briefly but strikingly in William Molyneux's highly influential patriotic tract, Case of Ireland Stated, published in Dublin in 1698. For Molyneux, union was, famously, 'an Happiness we can hardly hope for'— that is to say, a preferred option, and worth highlighting as such, but one which (given the animosities of the English parliament on the subject) did not need to be further elaborated.[82] Other leaders of Irish Protestant opinion—Bishop William King of Derry, for example—shared the view that parliamentary union was the ideal solution to the problems of the Anglo-Irish relationship, and embraced, too, the central premise of this argument—that the Irish parliament represented the interests of a class which had helped to subdue and settle Ireland, to expand England's dominions, and which in no sense was subject or secondary to English claims. Classical republicans of the time such as Robert Molesworth or Henry Maxwell expatiated further upon the merits of the case, Molesworth (like Fletcher of Saltoun) favouring federative union.[83]

For Molyneux, King, and for other, sometimes republican, thinkers, union may well have reflected Irish Protestant vulnerability, but it certainly did not embody any acceptance of subordination. An Irish parliament which could not effectively protect the liberties and interests of the Protestant nation in Ireland was much less desirable than a union parliament, which was able to offer such protection. Moreover, these ideologues had a lasting impact on Irish (and indeed Scots and American) patriotic thought, with (for example) Molyneux's tract being reprinted in Edinburgh in 1705 and playing 'a part in the making of the Anglo-Scottish Union'.[84] The greatest of the mid-18th-century Irish patriot leaders, Charles Lucas, resurrected Molyneux's arguments in his own *Appeal to the Commons and Citizens of London* of 1756: for Lucas, like Molyneux, union and liberty were preferable to an effectively subject if separate parliament. Molyneux continued to be an influence in the late 18th century, for the generation of patriots succeeding Lucas; but (strikingly) reprints of his *Case of Ireland Stated* in the early 1780s omitted the allusion to the 'Happiness we can hardly hope for'. Support for union certainly remained an expression of relative political vulnerability; but by this time it was the British government, beset by domestic and imperial difficulty, which was quietly contemplating this end, and not the Irish Protestant elite.

The stimulus that Scotland's consideration of union provided for Ireland (and, indeed, an equally important consideration and theme—the reciprocal stimulus that Ireland's subservient condition had upon Scots debates on union) may be illustrated by other evidence. The debate over the future of the united crown of Scotland and England (and the dependent crown of Ireland) was fired by a succession of events in 1701–1702, and in particular the death of William III in March 1702, and the accession of his now heirless sister-in-law Anne (her last remaining child, William, Duke of Gloucester, had died in July 1700). English parliamentarians had ridden roughshod over Scots and Irish sensitivities through the Act of Succession (1701), which unilaterally asserted that the successor to Anne as future monarch of England, Scotland, and Ireland would be the Electress Sophia of Hanover. But Anne's accession coincided with a renewal of military conflict with France, with the War of the Spanish Succession—a struggle, which, given Louis XIV's renewed support for the Jacobite cause, 'was also the war of the English succession'.[85] War was declared with the sanction of the English parliament, but without that of the Scots. The question of the succession, and the war, lay behind a revisiting of the issue of union at the end of 1702, an enterprise driven by the new Queen, her representative in Scotland, the Duke of Queensberry, and the Court Party in the Scots parliament (the party most susceptible to the influence of the London government, and dubbed by 19th-century Scots patriots 'the English Party').[86] Two commissions, representing the Scots and English parliaments, met periodically in the three months after November 1702, trembling on the cusp of an agreement which would have secured the Hanoverian succession, a united kingdom, and a united parliament. The Scots commissioners fought vigorously for the economic interests of their homeland, wresting from their opposite numbers the concession of free trade with England, and—an even more notable success—free trade between Scotland and England's colonies. A Scots effort to secure a public bale-out for the spectacularly bankrupt Company of Scotland was at this stage, however, a claim too far for English pockets and sensibilities; and the negotiation broke down in February 1703.

These discussions, though abortive, had a complex significance, both in terms of the Anglo-Scots relationship as well as that connecting Scotland and Ireland. They precipitated a flurry of interest in Ireland on the question of union. In 1703 the Irish parliament agreed to submit a loyal address to Queen Anne requesting 'a more firm and strict Union with your Majesty's Subjects of England'; and in the following year the prominent Irish Whig, Henry Maxwell, published his 'Essay upon an Union of Ireland with England' in 1704, advocating union along the lines of the developing conversation between the Scottish and English parliamentary commissioners. In 1707, in the aftermath of the promulgation of the Anglo-Scots union, the subject of an Anglo-Irish union was briefly revisited. On each occasion the meek petitioning of the Irish parliament was dismissed contemptuously in London. The great 19th-century historian and Liberal Unionist, W.E.H. Lecky, believed that an historic opportunity had been wasted through this dismissal: if union had been accepted at this time, he argued, 'Ireland would have been at least saved from the evils that arose from the commercial restrictions and from the extreme jobbing that grew up around the local legislature, and she would, perhaps, have been saved from some parts of the penal code. But the golden opportunity was lost'.[87]

Numerous historians have commented upon the pliability and tranquility of early 18th-century Ireland, in contrast to the threatening nature of the Anglo-Scots relationship before 1707 (Dicey argued that 'an Englishman statesman of 1706 would, we suspect, have considered the Scotch at least as difficult to manage as the Irish. Oppression and interference produced in Scotland, as it produces everywhere, lawlessness and unreasonableness').[88] Scots national sensitivities had indeed been troubled by English claims to determine the occupancy of the throne of Scotland; and in 1705 they were further enflamed by the Alien Act, an English measure which now—when Scottish property, trade, and cash were at stake, as distinct from the stability of England's throne—treated Scots effectively as foreigners. Ireland, meanwhile, featured in the Scots patriotic consciousness (and indeed in English polemic) as a fearful example of constitutional subjugation: Fletcher of Saltoun held Ireland up as the impending fate for the Scots, were they not to resist English claims.[89] At a time when the Irish parliament (though disparaged by London) was respectfully petitioning for union, the Scots parliament began pursuing 'all-out constitutional warfare' with England, through the Act of Security (1703), the Act anent War and Peace (1703), and complicity in what has hitherto generally been deemed as 'the judicial assassination' in 1705 of three English sailors (Captain Thomas Green, First Mate John Madder, and Gunner James Simpson) on charges of piracy (a recent assessment asserts that while 'the charges were not without foundation', they were 'not proven').[90] It has been said that this legislative fusillade cannot simply be seen as 'bluff and counter-bluff'; but it is equally clear that, if bluff was not the whole story, then each parliament was defining and toughening its claims in advance of a renewed negotiation and anticipated bargain.[91] The Scots' parliament, secure in its national standing, had simultaneously the confidence to be bloody-minded and the shrewdness to retain some wriggle room in its legislative defiance. The Irish parliament, representing the minority Established Church, was overshadowed and unnerved by its Catholic and Presbyterian hinterlands, and by the recent memories of Jacobite ascendancy: meekness was the hallmark of its relationship with London in these years.

# Summary: vision and dole

For both the Scots and the Irish, notions of union were tied to English dynastic and military ambition, whether in terms of the Geraldine Rebellion, the 'Rough Wooing', the Cromwellian project, or the continental wars of the 18th century. For both the Scots in the 17th century and for the Irish in the late 17th and early 18th centuries the possibility of union had otherwise been smothered by English scepticism and opposition. Notions of union for both the Scots and Irish were shaped in quite different ways by their shared but distinctive experience of national parliaments. On the other hand, each parliament and political elite, Scots and Irish, was treated with a measure of disregard by English parliamentarians, conscious of their own historic, cultural, military, and economic pre-eminence, and suspicious of the apparently one-sided benefits of any possible union. For both the Scots and Irish, the forms and timing of union favoured within each nation were effectively set aside, to be replaced by definitions and timings favoured by the predominant partner, England.

But for (some) Scottish Protestants from the mid 16th century onwards union had at least a spiritual imperative and an ostensibly imperial ancestry: for them, union was sometimes (not always) associated with the possibility of religious reformation, and with evocations of a united imperial monarchy, whose origins stretched back to Constantine the Great. For the Irish, even Irish Protestants, union was not sanctified by religious idealism or historical legitimacy in the same ways. Henry VIII unwillingly created a nominally united, or joint, monarchy by annexing Irish kingship: the Scots willingly realized a 'union of the crowns' by supplying a monarch, and ruling dynasty, to the throne of England and of Great Britain. Scots unionism (arguably) emerged out of the intellectual and political ferment generated by this accession: Irish unionism (arguably) emerged out of the expropriations, blood-letting, and civil war of the Cromwellian union in the 1650s. As ever, ostensibly shared political and constitutional experience produced very different flowerings in the loam of Scotland and Ireland.

For the Scots of the early 18th century, union was emerging as a complex and delicately balanced bargain: for the Irish, union was (and to some extent remained) at best a sectional dole, a last resort, for the Protestant landed elite. Each polity learned from the other in terms of the definition of its relationship with the English parliament and government. For all of the parties union could be a tool or a pretext: for few was it ever, or did it ever fully become, a coherent inspiration or vision.

# A. Memorializing the Union

**Illustration A.1.** James Barry, Study for 'The Act of Union between Great Britain and Ireland' (1801). Copyright with the Trustees of the British Museum: all rights reserved.

**Illustration A.2.** Walter Thomas Monnington, 'The Parliamentary Union of England & Scotland, 1707' (1925). Courtesy of the Palace of Westminster Collection.

# 3

# Contexts (1689–1703, 1782–1798)

## Economic, military, and parliamentary

How did they pass the Union?
By perjury and fraud.
By slaves who sold their land for gold
As Judas sold his God. (John O'Hagan)

The political jobbing of this country gets the better of me: it has ever been the wish of my life to avoid all this dirty business...how I long to kick those whom my public duty obliges me to court. (Marquess Cornwallis to General Ross, 20 May 1800)

## Introduction

Writing in 1907, and in the contexts of the bicentenary of the Treaty of 1707, and of the smouldering Home Rule debate in Ireland, the distinguished Scottish historian William Law Mathieson was struck by the similarities in the origins and shape of the Anglo-Scots and British-Irish unions. Mathieson was interested in sketching an argument rather than in detailed exposition, and his concerns were primarily political and constitutional: 'the two unions have certainly much in common, in so far as they can be traced to constitutional causes'.[1] But his pioneering essay, though suggestive rather than comprehensive, still provides a helpful starting point for a wider investigation of the origins and contexts of the two unions. And it remains true that a comparison of the two acts reveals much about their purpose, strength, and limitations. Such comparisons, therefore, provide the central purpose of this chapter, which focuses on the contexts to the passage of the two measures, and of its successor, which looks at their respective contents and fall-out.

As has already been suggested, parliamentary union was an established motif, with very different resonances, in the politics of both 17th-century Ireland and 17th-century Scotland. Moreover, 'incorporating' union was not merely an airy ideal (or, equally, a threat): for both the Irish and the Scots it had been a Cromwellian reality, however bloody and transient, and however different the resonances in the two nations.[2] Later, the Scots and the Irish Acts of Union were launched against a shared background of European war, political and religious threat, and economic dislocation. Though each union was sanctioned by parliamentarians who were subsequently damned as corrupt in their respective national demonologies, the 'parcel' of Scottish and Irish 'rogues' in 1707 and 1801 had each exercised a much greater measure of legislative independence in the eighteen years preceding union than any earlier generation of representative. For the English, Scots, and Irish, union was tied up with history, religion, war, political stability, and economic opportunity. But the relative strength and truculence of the national parliaments before 1707 and 1801, particularly in the context of bloody and threatening European conflicts, meant that union was more desirable, indeed necessary, than hitherto for the English government: this strength also meant that the Scots and (to a lesser extent) the Irish now had forms of bargaining position where once there had only been the unanswerable eloquence of English economic and military dominion. This chapter is concerned with comparing this array of contexts, with a view to assessing their impact upon the forms of union inaugurated in 1707 and 1801.

## The Scottish economic 'crisis'

Union always promised the Scots and Irish not just parliamentary, but also economic union—that lodestar of much 17th-century Scottish political ambition, 'ane union of traid'.[3] The condition of the Scots economy on the eve of union has generated some scholarly dispute, with traditional estimates of the general impoverishment of the country before 1707 giving rise to suspicions of unionist determinism, still worse condescension, as evidenced by William Ferguson's vigorous assault in 1977 on T.C. Smout's *Scottish Trade on the Eve of Union* (1963).[4] There has certainly long been evidence of a scholarly backlash against assessments (endemic in Victorian historiography) which give credence to the notion of 'inevitability'—assessments of Scotland's condition which overemphasised the seemingly relentless convergence between Scotland and England, the dire state of the Scots economy, and the irresistible pull of parliamentary and economic union.[5] While traditionally, and widely, the union of the crowns was held to blame for many of Scotland's woes at the end of the 17th century, patriotic (and not only overtly patriotic) historians have simultaneously been keen to recognize that, under a resurgent national parliament, there were more positive features of the state of the Scots nation. In broad terms, the picture of the Scots and Irish economies on the eve of the two unions that historians are settling upon is now strikingly symmetrical: portraits of long-term success and vibrancy, coupled with short-term disruption and crisis. Though aspects of Smout's pioneering work—particularly his emphasis upon the convergence of Scottish trade with England, and downplaying of the theme of corruption—have been vigorously interrogated, on the whole his suspicions of Victorian Whiggery and unwillingness to write off the Scottish economy of the 'Union of the Crowns' era have found wide (if sometimes grudging) scholarly acceptance.

The Scottish population in 1690, before the crises of the 1690s, was around 1.2 million, of whom approximately eight-eight per cent were rural dwelling. Scotland's agriculture was the predominant element of the economy, and there was some evidence of growth, refinement, diversification, and commercialization throughout the 17th century. Black cattle and salmon were the most significant agricultural exports on the eve of union, and the sector was carefully monitored and tended by the Scots parliament: grain exports, for example, were encouraged by bounties in 1663 and 1695 (a premonition of stimulating measures taken by the Irish parliament in the era of legislative independence, at the end of the 18th century). The consolidation and enclosure of holdings was promoted by numerous measures in the late 17th century, while there was a rapid growth in the number of new markets sanctioned by parliament.

Scotland's towns grew slowly in the course of the century, but Edinburgh and Glasgow represented significant exceptions to this dilatory pattern. Edinburgh was the second largest city in Britain and a key centre for government, law, manufacturing and, increasingly, finance. Glasgow exploded (like Belfast in a later period) from a position of relative provincial obscurity in the sixteenth century, to real, international commercial pre-eminence by 1700: the town's population had virtually doubled between 1610 and 1660, and it was strategically well-placed to participate in the growing Atlantic trade (by 1680 a regular commerce between Glasgow and the tobacco plantations in North America had been established).[6] Scholars stress increasingly the energy and skill of Scotland's manufacturers and merchants. Manufacturing and foreign trade were certainly growing: by 1700 linen yarn and cloth were the country's main exports, with thirty-six times the quantity of material being shipped as compared with 1600. Scots traders were establishing, or consolidating, links with traditional destinations such as Ulster or the Baltic and North Sea ports, but also, now, with America and the West Indies. Tom Devine has suggested that 'the changes in patterns of overseas trade suggest a merchant class able to adapt, take risks and take advantage of new opportunities'.[7]

There can be no question, therefore, of any interpretation which renders the Scots economy before 1707 in drab monochromatic terms, as compared with the polychromatic bliss of union. But while there has been an understandable patriotic emphasis, or sensitivity, in much of the recent historiography, and while there is evidence of courage, entrepreneurship, and some economic advance in the decades before union, Scotland in 1700 was indisputably in turmoil. The late 1690s were characterized by bad weather, disastrous harvests, agricultural downturn, and general rural impoverishment. These were 'King William's ill years', when the state of the elements and of the Scots agrarian economy mirrored, in pathetic fallacy, and in Jacobite propaganda, the neglect and disregard of the King himself. The harvest failures of 1695–1699 (there was a geographically patchy respite in 1697) brought famine, and starvation-related disease, and enhanced migration, with the consequence that the Scots population may have fallen by around thirteen per cent between the Revolution and the renewal of the debate on union.[8]

This agricultural disaster has a manifold significance. The London parliament, dealing with a paler version of the crisis, banned the export of grain from England in 1698, including grain destined for the relief of the Scots. This evident disregard fed into Scots resentments, but it also may have underpinned a renewed interest in a commercial or trade union. It is also very striking that the Scots famine of the 1690s simultaneously exacerbated patriotic anger, while undermining confidence in the existing constitutional settlement, and stimulating interest in 'ane union of traid'. For the Scots, famine demonstrated the perfidy of the English, but it may also, paradoxically, if indirectly, have made a case for union. For the Irish, the

Great Famine of 1845–1851 (with which the Scots crisis of 1695–1699 has been compared) underlined the perfidy of the English, but also clinched the case against union.[9]

The Scots crisis of the 1690s was also interlinked in another striking, if admittedly attenuated, way with the politics of union and with Ireland. The crisis forced perhaps 50,000 impoverished Scots Presbyterians from the South West of the country into migration, and towards a new life in Ulster. This was a significant augmentation of the 'British' and Protestant presence in the north of Ireland; and the new migrants gravitated towards existing areas of Presbyterian settlement and influence. Some of these migrants, or their descendants, would later return to Scotland, or move on to the British colonies in North America. Some of their descendants would, in the 1780s and 1790s, be persuaded by the revolutionary achievement in America and France, and seek to emulate that effort in Ireland. But, with these caveats, it is still possible to see the Scots famine of the 1690s as effectively reinforcing those communities and cultures that would later, at the end of the 19th century, take shape as Ulster Unionism. Certainly the late 19th-century historian, James Mackinnon, saw these migrants as creating 'the foundation, by their thrift and energy, of modern Ulster'.[10]

If Scots agriculture was in a desperate condition, then the nation's trade (allowing for the evidence of earlier growth and entrepreneurship) was also suffering in the 1690s. In 1689 the English and the Scots had acquired not only a new king, but also his conflict with France. The course of this—the Nine Years War or War of the Grand Alliance—dominated the politics of the 1690s, creating tensions within the Anglo-Scots relationship, and disrupting Scotland's trade with continental Europe. By 1692 the Allies—Britain, the Dutch Republic, the Holy Roman Empire, and Spain—had succeeded in overpowering the French navy, but French privateers and overzealous English naval captains continued to pose a threat to Scottish vessels. Trade with France was now of course illegal, and those suspected of dealing with the enemy were likely to have their vessels and cargo seized by the Royal Navy. But the war also brought the ever more intrusive presence of English naval vessels in Scottish waters.

Scotland's trade had been curtailed by the English Navigation Act of 1660, and the related Staple Act of 1663, which essentially sought to restrict England's trade to English vessels. Though there were wheezes and dodges through which this legislation could be circumvented, on the whole it con-

strained Scots' access to England's colonial markets, and thus represented a
brake upon Scots commercial growth. Scots could surreptitiously use
English vessels, or otherwise blatantly defy these English impositions. But
there was a more radical and ambitious means of addressing exclusion from
the trade of England's colonies—and this was to create a separate Scots
colonial trade by creating a separate Scots trading empire. Various relatively
modest attempts to create colonies were essayed in Jamaica and South
Carolina in the 1680s.[11] This goal of a Scots commercial empire lay behind
the creation, in 1695, of the Company of Scotland (or, more fully, the
Company of Scotland Trading to Africa and the Indies); and one of the key
visionaries behind the Company, William Paterson, sought to resurrect
Scotland's trade and national dignity (and, incidentally, to make a fortune for
himself) by establishing a Scots colony at Darien, on the isthmus of Panama
in Central America.

It has been sometimes said that the fateful Darien Scheme 'was not quite
as wild as it is usually made out to be', or that 'it cannot be viewed simply
as a catastrophic eccentricity'.[12] It has also been argued forcefully that
Darien 'has to be seen not as an isolated and over-ambitious adventure, but
as an integral part of a general drive to the west'.[13] It is certainly the case
that Darien illustrates with brutal clarity the parlous condition of the
Anglo-Scots relationship, and indeed of the Scots economy. The Company
of Scotland initially attracted (and was designed to attract) both English
and Scots capital, but the English investors soon withdrew. The existing
chartered companies (such as the East India) were unsettled by the prospect of Scots competition (as they had been earlier in the 17th century
with previous Scots' efforts), and particularly now in the light of the legal
privileges which the new Company of Scotland enjoyed; these established
enterprises succeeded in creating a political controversy, and in persuading
English investors that their capital might be more securely placed elsewhere.[14] The Company of Scotland tried to raise alternative funding on
the continent, in the Amsterdam and Hamburg markets, but failed: the
'scotophobic' English resident in Hamburg, Sir Paul Rycaut (perhaps
deploying experience and prejudice acquired as Chief Secretary of Ireland
between 1686–1687), has traditionally been blamed for this blight, although
the most recent scholarship emphasises that the Company's difficulties
owed more to its own disordered affairs than to Rycaut.[15] Certainly, by
1697, King William and his servants viewed the Company as a potential
challenge to vital English commercial and diplomatic interests.

Confronted with opposition in England and on the continent, the directors of the Company of Scotland reluctantly chose to gamble on Paterson's scheme for a Scots colony at Darien. A first expedition, comprising five vessels, set out for Central America in July 1698, and was followed by a second in 1699. The results were soon seen to be disastrous: already by June 1699 the first desertions had taken place from 'Caledonia' (as the Darien colony was called). By April 1700 the remaining colonizers had given up; and later in that year three vessels (from an original total of thirteen) returned to Scotland with the bedraggled survivors of the Scots experiment at empire. Douglas Watt's work on the Company of Scotland's cash books indicates that by the early summer of 1701, in the immediate aftermath of the final return from Darien, 'the Company was basically moribund in financial terms'.[16]

The causes of the debacle have been much discussed: disease was rife at Darien, the Spaniards and indigenous peoples were antagonistic, and the colonists were simply unlucky in a variety of circumstances. But the ships (which had been built at too high a cost) were woefully victualled and prepared; and the leadership of the expeditions (though not without courage—there was a Scots victory over the Spanish in a skirmish at Toubacanti) also seems to have been wanting. There seems to have been a lack of foresight or detailed planning. The Company of Scotland (though famously absorbing much of the available liquid assets of Scotland) was under-capitalized: cash was successfully raised on the first call in 1696, but much of this was very rapidly dispersed, and indeed it has been calculated that ten per cent of the initial capital was swiftly lost owing to the actions and convoluted personal finances of one of its directors, James Smyth ('the greatest vilan and most notorious lyer in Nature').[17] While sober contemporaries were prepared to recognize that the causes of the disaster lay close to home, a more general reaction (stimulated by the Company itself, in conjunction with opposition politicians, some of whom— such as the ducal Hamiltons—had invested heavily) was to focus the blame on King William and the English.[18] It was English mercantilism which had stimulated Scottish action. It was established jealous English corporate interests which had denuded the Company of Scotland of capital. It was King William, who wanting to keep English commercial allies and Spanish diplomatic allies on side, had—through the likes of Sir William Beeston, Governor of Jamaica—denied the Darien colonists any succour.[19] On the whole, however, the most recent scholarly investigations have emphasised the 'financial mania' which afflicted very large numbers of Scots investors, and the inexperience, mismanagement, and excessive risk-taking of the Company's directors, rather than the chauvinism and mendacity of their southern neighbours.[20]

Darien was 'the final straw' in Scotland's economic ill-fortune at the end of the 17th century.[21] It was perhaps a measure of the desperate condition of the Scots economy that the need was felt to speculate in so rash a venture as Darien. Darien may indeed have fallen short of 'catastrophic eccentricity' or 'fatuosity'; but the investment of so much patriotic hope in (initially) five ill-provisioned vessels, filled with courageous but underprepared and squabbling colonists, suggests national desperation.[22] Equally, the fact that a total of thirteen vessels and their unimpressive cargoes represented perhaps one quarter of the available capital of Scotland says much about (the limits of) contemporary Scots wealth and liquidity.

The affair also says much about the Anglo-Scots relationship: Scots wanted, and expected, the united monarchy to work for them; but in reality their concerns were regularly overwhelmed by English commercial and military interests. From the Commonwealth until the 1690s the united monarchy triumphantly served England's needs—in so far as it delivered a largely quiescent and subjugated Scotland, stable borderlands, and ensured Scots military support for England's many wars. Investment in Darien and the Company of Scotland did not (it has now been established) directly influence votes for union in the Scottish parliament of 1705–1706.[23] But, given that Scotland and England's king had had to choose between Scottish and English interests, Darien underscored a lesson in the realpolitik of the regal union that should, perhaps, have been learned by the Scots many decades before.[24]

# War

Darien, like the wider economic crisis, demonstrated the problems with Scotland's constitution. Both, however, were tied to international conditions, and to the more or less continuous warfare that embroiled the English crown between 1689 and 1713. War brought the imposition of taxes and the curtailing of Scotland's trade. War also brought new diplomatic imperatives: one critical reason for King William's failure to bail out the Darien colonists in 1699 was that they were interfering in an area of Spanish influence at a time when he, William, was seeking Spain's cooperation in his grand diplomatic and military stratagems. The condition of Europe, in particular European war, were critical contexts for union, both in 1707 and, for the Irish, in 1801.

The War of the Spanish Succession, which broke out in 1701, was in some senses a renewal of the conflict of 1689–1697, with some of the same combatants, and the same Allied ambition to constrain the territorial ambition of Louis XIV's France (it was the threat of French control of the Spanish crown, of a united Franco-Spanish monarchy, which was one of the spurs to war). The War of the Spanish Succession 'was also the war of the English succession', in so far as any decisive defeat for William or Anne's forces on the continent would in all likelihood have undermined the newly determined (1701) Hanoverian succession, and augmented the chances of a second Stuart restoration.[25] The war underpinned a general English desire to secure the succession, and also (more patchily or inconsistently) a desire to secure Scotland through a revised union. The war, therefore, created constitutional uncertainty (just as a century later, in the 1790s, the victories of the French republic augmented republicanism and constitutional instability in Ireland).

The debate on the union in Scotland was played out against the backdrop of this European conflict. The implications for the Scots were complex, but clearly discernible. This was a war which brought higher taxation, and the further disruption of Scotland's already ailing trade networks. It was also a conflict which underlined the effectively secondary condition of the formally co-equal Scots parliament, in so far as the decision to go to war was taken without consultation in London, and only later rubber-stamped in Edinburgh. War, in other words, vindicated the arguments against the union of the crowns, and (at the very least) for a revision of the commercial relationships between Scotland and England.[26]

On the other hand, by virtue of the united monarchy, the war involved substantial numbers of Scots troops. The Royal Scots (The Royal Regiment of Foot, and the premier infantry regiment of the army) served throughout the war, as did (in terms of cavalry) the Royal Scots Dragoon Guards. It has been calculated that one third of the Duke of Marlborough's regimental commanders at Blenheim were Scots.[27] Leading protagonists of the debate on union between 1703 and 1707 were significantly connected, directly or otherwise, to the British army on the continent. Queen Anne's Lord High Commissioner in the Scots Parliament (1705–1706), John Campbell, second Duke of Argyll, intermixed politics and military service throughout his long career, being absent 'in Flanders' during a critical juncture of the union debate, and serving under Marlborough (despite their mutual loathing) at Oudenarde in July 1708 and Malplaquet in September 1709.[28] The Earl of Orkney, brother of James Douglas Hamilton, fourth Duke of Hamilton (leader of the Country Party in the union parliament, and notorious as one of the most erratic and elusive politicians of the era) was a key lieutenant to Marlborough at the battles of Blenheim (August 1704) and Ramillies (May 1706). Lord John Hay, son of the second Marquess of Tweeddale (Lord High Commissioner, 1704–1705), was a brigadier general in Marlborough's army, commander of the Scots Dragoon Guards, fought at Ramillies, and died on campaign at Courtrai in August 1706.

Given this Scots prominence in some of the most celebrated military victories of the age, it is unsurprising that the British campaign was keenly followed in Scotland, even by opponents of incorporating union like the sceptical George Lockhart of Carnwath.[29] As with the Irish in the Revolutionary and Napoleonic Wars, so for the Scots in the Wars of the Grand Alliance and Spanish Succession, widespread military service reinforced bonds with union and empire, though it would certainly be a mistake to oversimplify either connection (as Andrew MacKillop's work on a later generation of Scots' recruit to the British army eloquently warns).[30] For many Scots, service under Marlborough may have helped to underpin a sense of British Protestant communion in the face of Louis XIV's Catholic empire (though of course this was not primarily a war of religion, and Anglicans, Calvinists, and Catholics were united against French ambition at Blenheim, as elsewhere). Equally, such service may have served to bring some Scots into closer dealings with Englishmen, and into a greater familiarity with the trappings and iconography of the English state. Certainly Scots success in the War of the Spanish Succession, and the celebration of Scots heroes and victories, helped to mitigate the political and economic burdens that the conflict imposed at home. Moreover, the fact that Scots success was achieved effectively as (in the argument of the Earl of Stair in 1706) a 'troop of mercenaries behind England's triumphal chariot'—that is, as paid help within English-led armies—served to bolster the case for an incorporating union ('After great victories won with much Scottish bloodshed, our only role is to join the troop of mercenaries behind England's triumphal chariot. Theirs are the rewards of war and the promises of prosperity; ours is the lot of the broken-down stipendiary: wounds, scars, hunger poverty').[31] The union of the crowns meant, in effect, Scots service in

English armies and English appropriation of Scots glory and bloodshed: an incorporating union promised service as a co-equal partner in the armies of Great Britain, and the fair attribution of Scotland's military successes and sacrifices.

The considerable Scots' involvement in Marlborough's armies raises the issue of English military supremacy in the reign of Anne, and the perennial question of whether English ministers got their way (once they had irrevocably decided on union, in 17051706) by virtue of armed threat. There is some evidence to support this proposition. Sidney, Lord Godolphin, Lord High Treasurer of England, talked about the possibility of invasion in early 1705, though was careful not to threaten.[32] Sir John Clerk of Penicuik, the unionist author of a famous memoir of the period and of the tract 'De Imperio Britannico', remembered the national humiliation experienced at the hands of Cromwell and his English armies, and clearly continued to be impressed by the possibility of a renewed English subjugation of Scotland: England 'wou'd have fund little or no difficulty in subdueing us...and in treating us ignominiously and cruelly as a conquered province'.[33] Some military deployments were considered in the context of armed protests in Scotland and the north of Ireland against union (the idea of moving troops into Ulster to suppress Scots settler unrest on the union question was an intriguing premonition of the Liberal government's similar planned troop movements against Ulster Unionist protest in 1914, though in 1914 the protest was of course on behalf of the union).[34]

But there is surely a danger in pushing these arguments and evidence too far. Godolphin mused on, but did not pursue, the issue of armed intervention. Clerk of Penicuik was impressed by English military strength, but was principally concerned with the possibility of armed conflict were the Scots parliament to unilaterally break the union of the crowns. Moreover, the very fact that England was pursuing a continental war surely militated against action over the union in Scotland.[35] Opening up a second front, and the real possibility of renewed civil war, in the context of the titanic struggle with France, would have been madness.[36] Pursuing conflict in Scotland at a time when England depended upon Scots troops in fighting the French would have been equal madness. Some of these issues were, as noted, a shadowy premonition of Ireland in 1914. Then the Liberal ministers of King George V's government moved troops, but recognized the pitfalls of military intervention in defence of constitutional change; and in 1705 the ministers of Queen Anne had done likewise. The legacy of Cromwell and of Dunbar certainly continued to resonate; but overt English force does not make sense as a primary argument for union (indeed, rather the reverse in some ways, given the patriotic defensiveness of the Scots parliament). Indeed, in this latter respect, T.C. Smout's teasing observation 'that history does not record many instances of the Scots doing anything against their wills for fear of an English army' should be regarded as more than mere irony.[37] The most, therefore, that might be said is that in the critical years 1705–1706 the Scots parliament 'met against a background of coercive persuasion generated by the English ministry', though the 'persuasiveness' of this 'coerciveness' remains unclear.[38]

If the European war served to underline the limitations of the regal union, to encourage Scots' thought of a commercial union, and to connect some Scots to the British Protestant project, then the instability which it generated brought some English statesmen to union. There was little that was 'inevitable' in this development: again union, in 1707 and in 1801, was mostly about gritty practicalities, rather than luminous ideals. The successive monarchs, William and Anne, were supportive of union, and indeed Anne's commitment was one of the relatively few constants throughout the debates on the issue. However, while Anne had high Tory and unionist sympathies, the strengthening Tory interest in the House of Commons was often unenthused by union. There were unionist influences among, or connected to, Anne's ministers: those chiefly concerned with prosecuting the war tended to be unionist such as John Churchill, 1st Duke of Marlborough, Captain General and Commander in Chief of the Army, and the financier of war, Lord Godolphin, while Robert Harley, Speaker of the Commons (1701–1705) and Northern Secretary (1704–1708), a new force in English politics, was also an advocate of union. The Whig and moderate Tory interest tended to be more sympathetic to the prosecution of the war, and to union, than the high Tories, who were less interested in war and union. But these were, admittedly, no more than tendencies. Older antipathies to union died hard, English interest in 1702–1703 (when the issue was first discussed in commission) was cool, and the overall standing of union in the years 1702 to 1705 was relatively uncertain, caught as it was in the intricacies of parliamentary power play. The determinism of an older historiography has now rightly been replaced by interpretations which emphasise fluidity and contingency: as William Ferguson has argued, attitudes 'varied as expedience dictated, and were not determined by conviction of the merits or demerits of union, but by tactical considerations'.[39]

## Legislative independence

Both the Scottish and Irish parliaments grew assertive in the last years of their existence, and it is clear that this shared muscularity contributed to the desirability of union from the perspective of the crown and of Westminster. P.W.J. Riley has argued that 'the union of 1707 arose from a crisis of security for England...[what was at stake] was the governability of Scotland'.[40] Equally, the union of 1801 arose from 'a crisis of security for England': what was at stake in the late 1790s was the 'governability' of Ireland.

For most of the 17th century, the Scots parliament was thoroughly under royal control, broken, as it was, by the Lords of the Articles.[41] With the Revolution of 1688–1689 came the abolition of these Lords, and an augmentation of Scottish legislative independence. The crown was thrown onto the defensive, the management of parliament became much more challenging, and some of the central problems of Scottish government—a broken economy, an untrammelled, grasping, and competitive nobility, and religious tensions—were revealed in their full unloveliness. Equally, the winning of legislative independence by the Irish parliament in 1782–1783 brought greater patriotic chest-beating, and deeper problems of management for the crown. Equally, too, greater parliamentary licence exposed some of the central problems in Irish politics and society—pre-eminently religious division, and the exclusion (regardless of wealth or standing) of some eighty per cent of the Irish population from much of public life.

It has been observed that for both Ireland and Scotland the lifespan of legislative 'independence' was approximately eighteen years'.[42] In these eighteen years (1690–1707) the Scots parliament did some work of lasting value for the Scots people, while (certainly in the years 1702–1705) persistently demonstrating its unwillingness to work quietly within the 'union of the crowns'. Part of the revolution settlement involved an Act of Patronage, which vested in parish landowners and kirk elders the right to present ministers to a vacancy, and abolished the rights of individual patrons in this respect: when this legislation was overturned by the union parliament in 1712, destructive in-fighting within the Kirk was the (doubtless intended) outcome (this, and a related Toleration Act, were pursued in 1711–1712 by the fiercely anti-Presbyterian George Lockhart of Carnwath and his English Tory allies).[43] The cultivation of waste land, and enclosure were eased by the amended Act anent Lands lying in Runrig and the Act for the Division of Commonties. The financing of parish schools was elucidated in the Act for

Settling Schools. Through these measures the (temporary) unity of the Kirk was assured, agricultural improvement facilitated, and a broadly accessible and national education system anchored.

This was not the whole story of the augmented post-Revolution parliament. As in Ireland, so in Scotland the influence of the crown was exercised by royal representatives or ministers, and by a related Court party. But, as P.W.J. Riley has argued, 'Scotland had been ungovernable for much of the time since 1688', with matters coming to a head at the time of William III's death, when royal 'management of Scotland was seen to be on the point of collapse'.[44] This collapse was partly related to insecurities in England itself, where (as has been noted) there was, in 1701–1702, an inelegant struggle not only to determine the royal succession and to relaunch the European war, but also to bind Scotland to these endeavours. The Scots parliament, as is well known, retaliated with its Act anent Peace and War (1703), a measure which effectively challenged the decision to take Scotland to war, by providing, in the event of the death of the Queen, for the reestablishment of an independent national foreign policy. The Act of Security (1704), similarly, was designed to challenge the presumption that the Scottish royal succession would be determined by English act of parliament: the Act of Security determined that Queen Anne's successor as monarch of Scotland would be Protestant, descended from the Scots royal line, and—unless concessions were forthcoming from London—would not be Hanoverian. The passage of these measures was accompanied by turmoil within the government, with the royal representative and manager of crown business in the Scots parliament—the Lord High Commissioner —changing hands in rapid succession from the Duke of Queensberry (1700–1703) through the Marquess of Tweeddale (1703–1705) to the Duke of Argyll (1705–1706), before returning to the grasp of Queensberry in 1706. It was Argyll and Queensberry who were eventually able to re-establish a degree of managerial authority within the parliament; but by now, 1705, the decision had been taken in London to move towards a full parliamentary union.

Divisions among Scottish historians concerning the roots of the Union of 1707 have, to some extent, reflected not just arguments over evidence, but also differences of approach, and even (perhaps) of disciplinary emphasis. High political historians, influenced by Namier or by Cowling, have stressed the ways in which individual interest and contingency characterized the debate on union between 1702 and 1707: those grounded within social science approaches have looked to wider, or longer term, political and economic contexts. It is possible, indeed necessary, to have the best of both these approaches. An incorporating union was clearly not an inevitability in 1707, given Scots opposition, the existence of rival possibilities (such as some form of confederal arrangement), and the complexities and fluidities of English conviction. Equally, however, full union was not invented in these years, but was rather the product of a more ancient history. Moreover, the economic, diplomatic, and parliamentary histories of Scotland and England in the decade before 1707 tended to underpin the argument for, at the very least, a revision of the existing constitutional relationship. Ireland's economic, diplomatic, and parliamentary circumstances in the 1790s tended to underpin a similar argument.

## The Irish economy in crisis

Like the Scots, indeed partly because of the Scots, union was a recurrent motif in the relationship between Ireland and England long before the Act of 1801. As has been seen (and as Allan Macinnes amongst others has detailed) an Anglo-Irish union was broached in 1703, at the time of the first, abortive, Anglo-Scots commission on union.[45] Just as the discussion of an Anglo-Scots union had long antecedents, so the roots of British advocacy of an Irish union have been traced back to the mid 18th century—to clusters of ideologues, court and scientific Whigs (including many Scots, such as Adam Smith, Adam Ferguson, and Josiah Tucker), concerned by the challenges of political and commercial relationships within Britain's wider possessions, and advocating an imperial union.[46] But these early imperial unionists were, until the last quarter of the 18th century, 'a small minority on the fringes rather than at the centre of power'.[47] Just as war and Scots' patriotic defensiveness encouraged an increasing English receptivity towards union between 1702 and 1705, so by the 1770s, in the contexts of Irish parliamentary assertiveness, and of the protracted war in North America, English ministerial thoughts turned towards union.[48] Adam Smith, writing in *Wealth of Nations* (1776) against the backdrop of Britain's growing embroilment in North America, famously came out in favour of a union between Ireland and Great Britain.[49] Later in the 1770s the Irish parliament began to exploit Britain's North American crisis to press a claim for 'free trade' (by which was meant enhanced access to British imperial markets); and in October 1777 this prompted the Prime Minister, Lord North, to raise the subject of union with the Earl of Buckinghamshire, the Lord Lieutenant of Ireland (and the crown's manager in Ireland). Other ministerialists were attracted to the notion in the late 1770s, including the newly elected MP for Midlothian, Henry Dundas, who spelt out (to Adam Smith) in characteristic style the alternative methods of controlling Irish politics: 'I believe an union would be the best if it can be accomplished, if not the Irish Parliament must be managed by the proper distribution of loaves and fishes, so that the legislators of the two countries may act in union together'.[50]

Ireland won 'free trade' in 1779 through a combination of British vulnerability, poor parliamentary management by the crown (the inefficient 'distribution of loaves and fishes'), and by a distinctive fusion of constitutional patriotism and armed threat (in the shape of the aggressively patriotic Volunteer movement).[51] Thereafter the Irish parliament proceeded to agitate for the repeal of some of the legislative constraints under which it laboured. As in 1779, a combination of intense parliamentary and extra-parliamentary campaigning carried the day, and in 1782–1783 the British government was forced to concede 'legislative independence': the label 'legislative independence' (like 'free trade') was propagandist hyperbole, but the British certainly renounced their claims of superior jurisdiction and the right to legislate for Ireland, while the Irish parliament now had the sole authority to initiate Irish legislation. This new constitution again reflected British military weakness (the commander in North America, Cornwallis, had surrendered at Yorktown in 1781, while the new army commander holding Ireland in 1782 was the discredited and unthreatening John Burgoyne, humiliated at Saratoga in 1777). Moreover, the new constitution ran contrary to the hitherto predominant British interpretations of the relationship with Ireland—interpretations which stressed the need for metropolitan ascendancy, and which linked its dilution to the threat of separation. After 1782–1783 London was forced to 'reconceptualize' the British-Irish relationship; and this reconfiguring focused increasingly on union.[52]

As in 17th- and early 18th-century Scotland, so in Ireland in the mid 1780s, political and commercial union were separate goals, with often separate support, but which could be, and were, conflated in the interests of political brokerage. Scottish economic conditions (even if more buoyant than was once thought) had long encouraged Scots' interest in greater commercial union with England; Scottish political conditions eventually encouraged a greater English interest in a parliamentary union. The advantages of a united parliament were hard to discern for most Scots; while the advantages of a unified economy were lost on the English, the stronger partner. Each had little to gain in isolation; but each could derive some benefit from a union which incorporated both commercial and political dimensions.

This was also broadly, or potentially, true for Ireland in 1784–1785. William Pitt, the new British Prime Minister, recognized the dangers of drift inherent in the newly established Irish constitution; and he sought to tempt the Irish parliament back from the precipice of separation through the lure of a commercial union (and, in his thinking, an implicit federal union).[53] 'Free trade' had facilitated Irish access to British imperial markets, but there remained (tariff) barriers to free commerce between Ireland and Britain, and in 1784 Pitt proposed that these should be removed or reduced. As with similar, Anglo-Scots, conversations eighty years before, untrammelled access to the riches of the English market carried a price: in return for this access, Pitt proposed that the Irish should contribute to imperial defence, and that the Irish parliament should automatically enact all Westminster legislation relating to trade and navigation.[54] Pitt's commercial propositions eventually failed (in 1785), partly because of the opposition of English manufacturing interests (as over earlier experiments at Scots or Irish union), and partly because Irish patriots (though not immune themselves from some creeping unionism) saw the propositions for what they were—a form of 'creeping' union (Stephen Small refers to 'the staunch Protestantism and even unionism of early Patriotism').[55] But, more fundamentally, the propositions failed because (unlike the Scots in 1705), the Irish economy in the 1780s and 1790s was in a relatively vibrant condition. There is certainly an economic context to the British-Irish union which demands exploration; but that context is one of disruptive and dislocating growth rather than (as in Scotland) downturn and impoverishment.

Scotland approached union with a falling population (a result of famine and disease) and with trade networks broken (as a result of war). But Ireland in the late 18th century was booming: the population in the prelude to union exploded from perhaps 4 millions in 1790 to 5 millions in 1800, reaching a total of 6.8 millions by the time of the (admittedly vitiated) census of 1821: Cormac Ó Gráda has called this 'the great Irish population spurt...sensational by the standards of the day'.[56] There was wage and price inflation, but the ambiguous surviving evidence suggests at least the maintenance, if not the consolidation of living standards (though the early years of the war may have seen some difficult adjustments). Agricultural wages increased by some sixty to eighty per cent between 1780 and 1815, while agricultural prices doubled in the same period: farmers were therefore generally prospering. The Irish parliament used its 'independence' to promote native agriculture, particularly tillage, and industry (grain production was sustained by tariffs and bounties such as those offered by the Corn Law of 1784); and this encouragement and protection was compounded by the impact of the European war after 1793. Unlike Scotland at the time of the Wars of the Grand Alliance and of the Spanish Succession, the Irish of the 1790s *had* access to British colonial markets, and were able to take advantage of British naval ascendancy and protection in the Napoleonic era. British domestic and military consumption of Irish agricultural goods soared during the war. Famine had racked Scotland in the late 1690s, and was a recurrent threat in 18th-century Ireland; but, unlike the Scottish case, Ireland's subsistence crises of this era were (without minimizing the mortality or wider suffering) containable. There was a famine in 1800–1801, exactly contemporaneous with union—but its impact was short-lived, and easily accommodated within the rising tide of agricultural prosperity. There was, of course, no Irish 'Darien'.

This was also an age of relative industrialization in Ireland. It has been pointed out, strikingly, that (despite the common preconceptions of the early 19th-century Irish economy) Ireland in 1821 was a nation with a significant (over forty per cent) workforce engaged in 'trades, manufactures, or handicraft'.[57] In Ireland, as elsewhere at the end of the 18th century, the mechanization of textile, particularly cotton, production proceeded apace, with the adoption in the late 1770s and onwards of Arkwright's spinning jennies. The industry was protected by the Irish parliament and grew in scale in the last quarter of the 18th century, and into the post-Union period, only succumbing to the commercial crisis of the mid 1820s (when, amongst other buffeting factors, tariff protection was removed). The North of Ireland provided a particular haven for cotton, as it did for the other great Irish textile of the 18th and 19th centuries, linen. Linen (like wool) was longer established, but—certainly in the North—was briefly eclipsed by cotton, boosted as the latter was by technological advance. However, linen too benefited from manufacturing improvements, and in particular the adoption of the wet-spinning process in the 1820s. If the spinning of linen yarn was being refined, and concentrated within factories, then weaving (though occasionally concentrated into factory-style operations) remained on a domestic scale, the domain of the handloom operator.

How did these different developments shape the context for union? Unlike Scotland in 1707, it was in fact the *growth* of the Irish economy which helped (however indirectly) to deliver political instability and thus union. Thomas Malthus suggested, in his *Essay on the Principle of Population*, that the social and political unrest, Catholic and republican, of the 1790s, which culminated in the 1798 Rising against British rule, was located in the expanding population of that era.[58] The suggestion was not developed and is unprovable; but it rests on the reasonable assumption that the very rapid population growth of the 1790s (even if, in the mid term, supportable), created temporary pressures on resources, temporary social and economic dislocations, and so fed into political resentments. It is an argument which has been complemented by the work of present-day scholars such as David Miller and Thomas Bartlett. Miller has famously suggested that the growth of the linen industry in south Ulster at the end of the 18th century facilitated some limited Catholic economic mobility, in particular the adoption of the hitherto Protestant-dominated trade of handloom weaving. Competition between Catholic and Protestant weavers was occurring at a time when population growth in south Ulster, particularly in Armagh, was heightening demand for land. More generally, the spread of handloom weaving tended to destabilize long-established family structures within every confessional tradition. The profitability of weaving permitted young men to establish their independence much earlier than was usual within small farmer society, and freed them from the constraints and discipline of the patriarchal family. In this way rising population and new economic opportunities helped to rock the existing social order, to enflame religious rivalries (focused particularly within two rival secret societies, the Catholic Defenders and Protestant Peep O'Day Boys), and to stimulate protest and insurgency.[59] Bartlett, on the other hand, has argued that in the third quarter of the 18th century prosperity was generating a new moral economy: agricultural growth stimulated trade, the creation of more markets, and the gradual commercialization of rural economic life. Commercialization was linked with socialization; and this provided, in turn, ever greater opportunities for communal mobilization and protest.[60]

Demographic and economic growth helped to create some of the mechanisms, structures, and contexts for politicization and protest: in particular growth, which was centred on the agrarian economy and the predominantly Catholic farmer class, served to highlight the sectarian inequalities within Irish society. Sections of Catholic Ireland were beginning to grow prosperous and to cut a figure within the Anglican state in Ireland; but for much of the later 18th century they laboured amidst the residue of discriminatory legislation passed after the Glorious Revolution, including (between 1727 and 1793) exclusion from the parliamentary franchise. Economic growth created Catholic prosperity: but, in giving some Catholics economic influence, it also simultaneously underlined the community's near total exclusion from political authority, and (in the Bartlett thesis) provided new means of combination and protest. The American revolution, refracted in Ireland through the campaigns for 'free trade' and 'legislative independence', together with the French revolution, provided a republican vocabulary and grammar of protest; and (as will be shown) the French revolutionary war (from 1793) created the immediate conditions for rebellion in 1798. Without the 1798 Rising, the political elites of British and Irish society would not have been panicked into union in 1800.

There is a paradox in all this. Even though the nature of growth was undermining the stability of 'legislative independence', and feeding into revolutionary politics, Irish economic historians now generally accept that there were developing convergences between the English and the Irish economies in the years before the union (as evidenced, for example, by the increasingly anglocentric focus of Irish trade, and by the dependence of the Irish administration upon English financial subvention after 1796): there is a (limited) symmetry here with the arguments of an older generation of Scots economic historian, such as T.C. Smout, for the convergence of the Scots and English economies in the prelude to union.[61] So, from one narrow perspective, parliamentary union in 1801 was simultaneously a reflection of socio-economic turmoil, and a complement to protracted economic coalescence. It is also now accepted that, even with the (modest) tariff protection of an 'independent' parliament, and despite short-term successes, Irish industry stood little long-term chance of survival against its neighbour, the 'Workshop of the World'.[62] On the other hand, this is not how it looked to patriotic contemporaries, and to those (like the nationally minded economic historian, George O'Brien) viewing the union from a separatist political perspective in the Home Rule and revolutionary era: these saw an Irish economic efflorescence which was apparently tied to the boon of an independent legislature.[63] Ireland did not therefore need to trade its legislative independence for economic success, since (unlike the Scots in 1706–1707) it apparently had this already: in particular, Ireland did not need to trade its legislative independence for access to imperial markets, since (again, unlike the Scots in 1706–1707) it had already won this access. Union looked (and in some respects was) a much rougher deal for the Irish in 1801, than for the Scots a century before. If each union was essentially a bargain, and if (as has been suggested in a recent study) Scotland's bargainers were not up to the mark, then the Irish proponents of union appeared to have been in a wholly different league of ineptitude or, worse, corruption.[64]

## Ireland and the French wars

The war of the 1790s, it has been commonly suggested, determined much of the shape of modern Irish national politics, generating loyalism, republicanism, and union.[65] In the 1790s, as in the 1690s, France's desire to remodel the European order helped to make the argument for union and centralization within the British Isles. Just as the Wars of the Grand Alliance and of the Spanish Succession had implications for English political stability, and for union with Scotland, so the 'titanic struggle for dominance' in Europe between revolutionary France and its enemies (1793–1815) had implications for English political stability, and for union with Ireland.

France in the early 18th century posed both a military as well as an ideological threat to the English state, in so far as Louis XIV (despite the Treaty of Ryswick of 1697) remained the patron of Jacobitism. Equally, France in the late 18th century posed both a military as well as an ideological threat to the British state, in so far as the new French republic (of 1792), at war with Britain after 1793, was keen to disseminate its revolutionary gospel throughout Europe, including within the British Isles. The rationalist, rights-centred, and libertarian ideals of the revolution (or, at any rate, its ideologues) struck a chord with reformers in Ireland, and (as is well known) precipitated the formation of the United Irish Society in Belfast in October 1791 (with a branch in Dublin emerging in November 1791). The United Irishmen mixed the inspiration of America and France with patriotic and Whig reformism: they were initially interested in parliamentary reform, which they defined in 1794 in terms of universal male suffrage (this at a time when Catholic forty shilling freeholders had only just been enfranchised). They had some links with protest politics in Scotland, and in particular with the Scottish Friends of the People and with one of its leading spirits, the admiring but ineffectual young Glasgow advocate, Thomas Muir, (the admiration was not reciprocated—'of all the vain blockheads that I ever

met I never saw his equal', declared Theobald Wolfe Tone).[66] However, war
with France encouraged the more advanced (or reckless) spirits within the
United Irish Society to begin looking in that direction for support, while it
also made the authorities, in Dublin Castle as in Britain, less tolerant of radical or even reformist politics. The Dublin United Irishmen were suppressed
in 1794; and this action, in combination with other official repression, gave
credibility to those within the Society advocating armed insurgency and a
republic. By 1795 the Society had gone underground, adopted a new constitution, embraced the goal, not merely of a reformed House of Commons,
but rather of a republic. By 1796 Wolfe Tone had successfully solicited French
naval and military support for the vision of an Irish republic (although the
resultant expedition, led by General Lazare Hoche, was smashed by storms
off Bantry in County Cork in December 1796, and did not attempt a
landing).

Defenderism, the rural Catholic protest movement, was rooted partly in
sectarian and economic competition in south Ulster in the late 18th century—the desire for cheap land, better paid labour, the overturning of
ancient land confiscations. The Defenders spread from their Armagh birthplace in the late 1780s and 1790s, and (certainly in the assessment of Nancy
Curtin) gained in political sophistication the further they moved from their
original sectarian origins.[67] They, too, were inspired by the French revolution, as their membership oaths and catechisms attest. Moreover, there is
some evidence to suggest contact between the Defenders and French emissaries as early as 1792. War brought mixed messages from the Castle for
Catholic Ireland—a desire to copper-fasten Catholics to the war effort
combined with the same kind of murderous suspicion of Catholic conspiracy that had been applied to the United Irish Society. Influenced by the
revolution, harried by government, corresponding with the French—
Defenderism was developing in separate but similar ways to the United
Irishmen; and it was unsurprising that, despite the very different origins of
the two movements, they drifted into communication, and by 1796, into a
formal alliance. This marriage provided the strategic foundation for the
great and bloody Rising of May-June 1798.

War also created economic arguments for union. Although the panoramic context for union in the late 18th century was (as outlined earlier)
economic and demographic growth, and enhanced market and trading
opportunities, there were downsides. The war may have brought a dangerous acceleration of the pre-existing trends within the economy. Inflationary

pressures generated by growth were probably accommodated by some sections of the economy in the mid term; but it seems likely that inflation, and higher levels of taxation, were a particular problem for the poor in the first years of the war. Tom Bartlett has pointed to the probability that taxes and inflation made the poor 'more receptive to the message of subversives':[68] indeed, in some senses, the argument here has been that war also shaped both the subversives and their message. Moreover, if the poor were struggling, then so, too, was government itself: one striking context for the union was that the Castle had been virtually bankrupted by the cost of the war against France. Military costs soared after 1793 to a point (in 1799) where they were consuming seventy-eight per cent of government expenditure. In 1796 the attempted French landing at Bantry Bay caused a financial panic and 'credit crunch' bringing (in one informed contemporary assessment) 'the stoppage of the banks, the annihilation of all credit, trade and commerce, in short I might call it a general bankruptcy'.[69] Indeed it has been argued that the economic and other insecurities generated by the appearance of the French at Bantry 'marked a significant turning-point in Anglo-Irish relations', after which—with the Irish parliament dependent upon the British for financial support—'the much vaunted independence the Irish Protestant elite once possessed...now vanished'.[70] In 1896 Sir Edward Hamilton, the Permanent Secretary to the Treasury, calculated that if military expenditure by the Irish parliament had been conducted at the normal rate between 1793 and 1801, then there would have been an outlay of £4.53 millions: the actual expenditure was £20.8 millions, of which (Hamilton surmised) £10 millions arose from the cost of the war with France, and £6 millions arose out of the disturbed condition of Ireland itself.[71] Here alone, while the overall economic patterns stand in contrast, there seems some shadowy resemblance to the condition of Scotland on the eve of union, one hundred years before: in Scotland in 1707 'state finances...were in a parlous condition, with the cost of funding the civil list, the military and government being estimated to be some £14,311 sterling more than Scotland's total annual revenues of around £113,194'.[72]

Consideration of the war and union also demands some initial discussion of the complex relationship between the Irish and the crown forces, a relationship mirrored (in some ways) by that binding the Scots and the crown forces. The Scots and the Irish were embittered by English military might, and each had been on the receiving end of English conquest: each nation had a history of military contribution to continental powers, and sometimes

to England's enemies. But in each case the colonial-style relationship linking the weaker nation with the imperial power created ambiguous and
complex connections, a form of hybridity.

The Scots and the Irish were simultaneously victims of, and complicit in
English military ascendancy. Scots soldiers were (as has been indicated) a
powerful presence in Marlborough's armies during the War of the Spanish
Succession; and the Scots public appear to have taken pride in their compatriots' martial prowess. Scots commanders such as Argyll and Orkney were,
equally, a prominent feature of the 'English' and allied struggle against Louis
XIV. The British government had traditionally taken a sceptical view of
the recruitment of Irishmen (of whatever religion) to the army; but by the
end of the 18th century even Catholic Irishmen, judged of course to be
more of a political threat than Protestants, were being sought as recruits.
The exigencies of Britain's wars had overcome political and religious convictions in both Ireland and Scotland. In Scotland in 1778–1779, at the nadir
of the British campaign in North America, Henry Dundas sought to enact
a bill for the relief of Scots Catholics in order to win their recruitment, and
particularly that of Catholic Highlanders, to the army.[73] Irish Catholics were
serving in the crown forces overseas from the 1750s, during the Seven
Years War (1756–1763), and at home in Ireland from at least 1793. The
Revolutionary and Napoleonic war (1793–1815) involved (it has been calculated) perhaps twenty per cent of the adult male population of Ireland,
with attendant celebrity for the gamut of Irish regiments and various Irish
commanders: the doyen of the British struggle against France was, of course,
an Irishman, Arthur Wellesley, Duke of Wellington.[74]

It would be overly simplistic to link Scots or Irish service in the crown
forces in any uncomplicated way with unionism, or even political tranquility. Such service might as easily generate political resentments as attachments, arising from the ways in which soldiers might be impressed into
service, or indeed the shabby ways in which they might be treated on com-
pletion of service: equally, for Presbyterian Scots and Catholic Irish alike,
service in the crown forces might bring some grating contact with the realities of the Anglican state. Military service certainly did not diminish national
pride, and indeed rather the reverse in both Scots and Irish cases. However,
it might tentatively be suggested (the evidence is still unsatisfactory) that
service in the crown forces familiarized Scots and Irish soldiers with their
English colleagues-in-arms; it might also be suggested that such service
acclimatized the Scots and Irish to the symbolism and iconography and

propaganda of the British state. Monarchy, in particular, was at the heart of this iconography; and the fact that senior members of the British royal family continued to serve on the battlefield throughout the 18th century may have underpinned any nascent respect.[75] The effects of the French wars on Irish soldiery are thus layered and complex; the most that might be ventured is that wartime service was enormously significant for Irish male society, and that on balance this service acted as a cement for union (although there were clearly many significant exceptions).

If the 18th-century army brought Scots and Irish soldiers into new forms of contact with the Anglican and Protestant state, then the war of 1793 impacted upon Ireland's precarious sectarian frontiers, sensitivities, and imbalances: it demanded a re-imagining of community rights and relationships in Ireland. The upturn within the Irish agrarian economy, combined with the (interrelated) patriot effort to enhance the Irish parliament, had inevitably broached the issue of Catholic civil rights, or 'relief'. But the full recognition of these rights threatened the Protestant constitution in Ireland, and the domination of Irish society and politics by what was called after the late 1780s 'the Protestant Ascendancy' (the Anglican or Church of Ireland landed elite). Protestant political opinion, even patriot opinion, was divided on this Catholic question, with many Protestant patriots (like Henry Flood, an opponent of Catholic relief) being more Protestant than patriot.[76] Most, however, recognized that 'Protestant Ascendancy' could not be sustained in an Irish parliament where Catholics exercised full civil rights, and a proportionate measure of political authority. For these, fear of the traditional enemy, Catholicism, was becoming more persuasive than the case for the retention of a catholicized Irish parliament; and this in turn meant that, as the Catholic question gained momentum between 1791 and 1793, so too did a resigned acceptance of the possibility of a parliamentary union with Protestant Britain.[77]

The war did not of course create the Catholic question, but it did forefront its significance, together (indirectly) with that of union. When war was declared in January 1793, the British government needed the military and financial support of all Ireland, and not just of the Ascendancy elite. Middle class Catholics, businessmen and professionals, together with the vestigial Catholic gentry and aristocracy, were represented by the Catholic Committee, a body which had been in existence since 1760, but which was assuming a larger public profile in the early 1790s with the mounting demand for 'emancipation' (this label, meaning a full equalization of civil rights, was taken from the debate on slavery, and gained currency from this time on). However, some within the Committee were prepared to settle for less than full 'emancipation'; and a deal was struck with the Castle administration which delivered a reform act, passed in April 1793, granting Catholics limited enfranchisement, access to the upper professions and the officer class of the army, and (no less critically) the right to bear arms. The opening of the ranks of the army and the right to carry arms were highly charged concessions, and reflected wartime pressures as well as the long-standing strategies and vision of Henry Dundas, now William Pitt's Home Secretary, and the author of the 'main heads' of the relief legislation.[78] The British government not only needed Catholic political acquiescence at this time of war; they also needed Catholic military support, particularly given that the Irish garrison was being denuded of troops required for service in the struggle against France: Pitt and Dundas's arguments for a broadly based Irish militia, their desire 'to connect all lovers of order and good government in an union of resistors to all the abettors of anarchy and misrule' is in fact a premonition of their vision of parliamentary union at the end of the decade.[79] The Militia Act of April 1793 created, in effect, and for the first time since the late 17th century, an official Catholic army within the Protestant state.

The formation of the militia, combined with the arrival in January 1795 of a lord lieutenant, Earl Fitzwilliam, determined to overturn the great Ascendancy office holders and to achieve rapid progress on the 'emancipation' question, served to stimulate further frightened interest in the possibility of union within the Protestant political classes. War had effectively delivered Catholic enfranchisement, a Catholic army, and now, with Fitzwilliam, a pro-Catholic viceroy and the threatened constitutional overturning of the Ascendancy interest. By the time of Fitzwilliam's abrupt removal, on 21 February 1795, it was calculated that, in a parliament where talk of union had only recently been regarded as political blasphemy, some eighty MPs were now unionist in sympathy—even if 'there was no serious unionist dimension in Irish political debate until after the rebellion of 1798'.[80]

Moreover, the disappointed expectations that the Fitzwilliam viceroyalty (or 'episode') generated, fed into a cycle of political unrest and official repression, and generated further support for the evolving United Irish and Defender conspiracy against British rule. The Hoche expedition of December 1796, though a failure, was at least a tangible demonstration of French support for this conspiracy, and underlined the potential seriousness of the Irish plotters. This looming threat of a French-aided rebellion, perceptible to all in 1796–1797, gave further credence to the cause of union amongst the Protestant elite, although the necessary harmony of Irish and British opinion had not yet been achieved (William Pitt, amongst the British sponsors of the idea, remained cautious, not yet convinced that the timing was right).[81] When rebellion finally came, in Leinster and Ulster in May and June 1798, and with a half-cocked French landing in Mayo in August, the issue of timing was resolved; and Pitt moved swiftly to realize his long-cherished vision of union. For its part, the Protestant political elite emerged from the Rising initially more preoccupied with revenge than with constitutional change; but the recognition soon dawned that their cherished social order had very nearly given way to a Catholic and Presbyterian republic, and that the best available defence for Ascendancy now lay with union. In Ireland at the end of the 1790s, as in Scotland in 1707, union was simultaneously about apparently sweeping political change, but also emphatically about social continuities—whether in terms of the Irish ascendancy interest, or the semi-feudal powers and heritable jurisdictions of the Scottish nobility.

## Shared freedom and its implications

The chapter opened with an allusion to Mathieson's observations that 'in Ireland, as in Scotland, the span of legislative freedom was eighteen years', and that from the times these freedoms were secured (1782 and 1689), 'the two legislatures developed on almost parallel lines'.[82] Like the Scots between 1689 and 1707, the Irish parliament after 1782 was locked into a protracted and acrimonious contest with the London government, operating from a settlement which had been secured in the context of English weakness, and systematically asserting patriotic rights at the expense of any harmonious working relationship. The essential features of Irish government in the 1780s and 1790s were that Britain could not control the Irish parliament, and the parliament could not control Ireland. The potential ungovernability of Ireland, particularly in the context of war with France and the related collapse of the state's finances, ultimately stimulated thoughts of union, just as the ungovernability of Scotland, together with its financial condition, in the years before 1707 had inspired similar cogitation. There was, however, a critical distinction: it should be emphasised that union played a proportionately much more considerable role in Scottish political discourse before 1707, than in Irish discourse in the years before 1801—whatever the shared antiquity of the notion within each polity.[83]

Despite the abolition of the Lords of the Articles in Scotland in 1689–1690, and the achievement of the constitution of 1782–1783 in Ireland, the influence of the crown continued to be felt within each legislature through the executive, or officers of state. In Ireland these officers were led by the Lord Lieutenant, the representative of the monarch, who was served in the Irish House of Commons by his Chief Secretary: the Chief Secretary was primarily responsible for the management of government business, the distribution of official patronage, and the maintenance of some form of court party. The achievement of 'legislative independence' in 1782–1783 did not overturn the influence of the government; it simply made it more difficult and expensive to sustain.

These difficulties mounted in the 1780s and 1790s, and fed into senior English ministerial support for union. In Scotland, as in Ireland, the bate of commercial union was offered as a means of drawing the parliaments into closer union with Westminster. But as has been seen, given the distinctive economic contexts, this was a more appetizing prospect for the Scots than for the Irish: William Pitt was affronted by the dismissive Irish reaction to his 'Commercial Propositions', and the affair stimulated English interest in the possibilities of union in the mid and late 1780s.

In Scotland, as in Ireland, the parliaments demonstrated their independence from London by jealously asserting their respective rights to influence the royal succession. This occurred in Scotland over the Act of Security (of 1704), which (as has been outlined) underlined Scotland's right to decide upon the succession to the heirless Queen Anne, and which eventually brought down the Duke of Queensberry as the Lord High Commissioner in the Scots parliament. Similarly, the Irish in 1788–1789 asserted their right to decide the timing and conditions under which George Prince of Wales would act as Regent in the place of his porphyriac father, King George III. In this instance the Whig and patriot interest in the Irish House of Commons was proportionately stronger than in the British Commons; with the result that there was relatively greater parliamentary sympathy in Ireland for the Whiggish Prince of Wales than in Britain. Irish parliamentarians voted in February 1789 in favour of the Prince assuming the powers of regent (ahead of their British counterparts); and a loyal delegation was duly sent from Dublin to attend the Prince. In the event, George III recovered, and 'the

Regency crisis' evaporated; but the affair had demonstrated the party political disparities separating the Irish and British parliaments, and the wider gulf in Anglo-Irish relations.

This gulf continued to be a feature of the Anglo-Irish relationship in the 1790s. The patriot interest in the Irish parliament jealously guarded its dignity and autonomy, and remained keen to throw off any English ministerial intrusion. The ruling Ascendancy interest, representing the established Anglican landed order, remained unpersuaded by the need for reform, and were fully capable (as with Earl Fitzwilliam) of seeing off a minister of the crown who did not chime with their requirements. The patriots were ideologically resistant to English ministerial influence and advice; the Ascendancy was strategically resistant to pressing English calls for reform. The default position of government, particularly after 1793, was repression; and as constitutional radicalism and reformism was driven underground and criminalized in the mid 1790s, repression and revolutionary conspiracy together grew. After the reforming Fitzwilliam's recall in February 1795, the whole defiant and obdurate edifice of Irish government looked increasingly vulnerable; and, with the 1798 Rising, it came close to collapse. The Ascendancy parliament, with its independence and exclusivity, its jealousies and its blindness, had ultimately proved to be both ungovernable and ungoverning.

Before the war, in 1792, Pitt lamented that royal administration in Ireland 'must yet continue a government of expedients': much the same verdict has been applied to royal government in Scotland in the 1690s.[84] Royal government in Ireland, as in Scotland before union, was sustained only with great difficulty and great expense in the midst of often treacherous tides of parliamentary opinion. British ministers like Pitt and Dundas were increasingly persuaded of the necessity to expand the embrace of politics in Ireland to include Catholics; but their governing allies in Ireland, the Ascendancy interest, were prepared to move on this only with the greatest reluctance, while those most interested in Catholic relief (like Henry Grattan) also tended, regrettably, to be those most interested in the 'independence' of the Irish parliament. In sum, the Gordian bind of Irish politics for British government was that the constitution needed reform, its closest allies generally would not accept reform, while the reformers in Ireland generally would not accept the British government.[85] Little wonder that Pitt and his lieutenants sought to cut through this knot with the surgical steel of union.[86]

# B. Commodifying the Union

**Illustration B.1.** John de Critz, 'James VI and I' (1604) wearing the 'Mirror of Great Britain' jewel in his hat (created to commemorate the Union of the Crowns). Courtesy of the Scottish National Portrait Gallery.

**Illustration B.2.** Bronze medal commemorating the Act of Union (1801) by Conrad Kuechler. Copyright with the Birmingham Assay Office.

**Illustration B.3.** Tobacco tin: 'Dr. White's Glasgow Presbyterian Mixture, as smoked by the Rt. Hon. Stanley Baldwin' (*c.* 1936). Private Possession.

# 4

# Debates and terms (1705–1707, 1799–1801)

I never saw so much trick, sham, pride, jealousy, and cutting of friends' throats as there is among the noble men. In short money will do anything here. Daniel Defoe (1707)

You all committed a great mistake. You should have made terms as the Scotch did, and you could have got any terms. George IV (1821)

## The shock of union

Patriotically minded Scots and Irish historians return masochistically to their respective parliamentary unions, picking at the scab of the court victories, and wondering how the healthy flesh of independent legislatures could have become so thoroughly and so swiftly scarred. Both the Scots and Irish parliaments had enjoyed sustained periods of relative freedom, with the Scots throwing off the Lords of the Articles in 1690, and the Irish gaining their 'legislative independence' in 1782. Each parliament had defied the British crown over matters of money, with the Scots making (from the English perspective) exorbitant demands in the union negotiations of 1703, and the Irish spurning William Pitt's offer of commercial union in 1784–1785. Both had asserted their autonomy with regard to the crown itself—the Scots with their Act of Security in 1704, and the Irish during the Regency Crisis of 1788–1789. Both parliaments had substantial patriotic groupings, at best sceptical of English influence: the Country Party within the Scottish parliament was protective of its independence, while the Irish Whigs and Patriots were a periodic scourge of royal government in Ireland. Each parliament—in the years immediately preceding the two unions—had energetically defended its autonomy: the Act of Security asserted that the Scots would not accept the Hanoverian succession unless the independence of the Edinburgh parliament was underwritten, while as late as January 1799 the Irish parliament voted down a royal address which made provision for union. And yet, to the consternation of patriots in the succeeding generations, each parliament ultimately voted itself into oblivion.

In neither Scotland nor Ireland was 'union' a novelty or surprise. As has been shown, for the Scots the deep-seated problems created by the regal union allied with a range of commercial considerations meant that (at the very least) a revision in the constitutional relationship with England had long been on the cards: the refinement of union was considered by virtually every generation of Scottish politician in the 17th century, and even archetypal patriots such as Fletcher of Saltoun professed support for (in his case) 'federative', or confederal, union. The constitutional, economic, and military consequences of sustained warfare, allied with famine and the Darien venture in the 1690s, gave the issue a particular urgency for both the English and the Scots after 1702–1703. For contemporary Irish patriots, union was, indeed, 'an happiness we can hardly hope for': interest in union was ignited by the Scots case, but just as swiftly dampened, on the realization that, while English interests involved treating on broadly equitable terms with the Scots, they did not require any significant alteration of Ireland's subordinate status.[1] But union remained part of Irish political vocabulary throughout much of the 18th century, and particularly after the grant of 'free trade' and 'legislative independence' between 1779 and 1783, when the crown began to experience ever greater difficulties in its management of Irish government.

Thus, the shock of union in 1706–1707 and 1800–1801 arose, not from its conceptual novelty, because it was an established (if not always welcome) element of political discourse in the two kingdoms. The shock of union arose rather from the apparent revolution which had occurred in the convictions of the two parliaments in the months immediately preceding their demise. Contemporaries were dazed by the ostensibly rapid metamorphosis of patriots into lickspittles of royal government: historians have sometimes shared this disorientation. Of course, part of the interpretative challenge in all of this arose from the imperatives of a patriotic Scottish and Irish historiography which stressed the economic and other dividends bestowed by native parliaments, and which played down or wrote off the ubiquity of the union idea *avant la lettre*. With apparently burgeoning economies, and patriotic energy and achievement, union could only make sense, not in terms of context or precedent, still less of vision or ideals, but rather in terms of fundamental human weakness. Even for those literary patriots who ultimately reconciled themselves to the British state, like Robert Burns (an exciseman and member of the Dumfriesshire Volunteers) or (in the Irish case) W.E.H. Lecky (ultimately a Liberal Unionist Member of the United Kingdom House of Commons), union was to be explained primarily in terms of corruption. For both the Scots and Irish unions, then, were not about human virtue and aspiration: they were primarily about treachery, venality, and (even in some analyses) ineptitude. The focuses of this chapter, therefore, are upon the immediate explanations for the passage and shape of the two union measures.

## Scottish ineptitude?

In 1703 the Scots parliament, reacting to the provocation of the English Act of Settlement (1701) and the lack of consultation over the declaration of war with France in May 1702, demonstrated its righteous and patriotic anger by passing the Act of Security and the Act anent Peace and War, the consequences of which have been outlined earlier. By 1 September 1705, however, the Queen's ministers in Scotland had won parliament's acceptance for the principle of a treaty of union; and later on that same day the Duke of Hamilton, the schizoid leader of the opposition Country Party, moved, fatefully, that the Queen herself, rather than parliament, should appoint the Scots negotiators or commissioners for union (as the Earl of Seafield recorded in understated language, he, Hamilton 'said he was sorry there were so great division and animosities among us as that he was certain wee could make no good nomination in Parliament, and he had a great deal of trust and confidence in her Ma[jes]ty our soveraign, and yrfore he proposed the nomination be left to he Ma[jes]ty…His party was surprysed').[2] This has been widely viewed as the beginning of the end for the Scots parliament: on 16 April 1706 the Scots and English commissioners, meeting separately at the Council Chamber of the Cockpit at Whitehall, convened for the first time; and by 22 July the draft of a treaty of union had been successfully concluded between the two parties. On 4 November 1706, though there was still significant opposition from the Kirk, the once-defiant Scots parliament passed, by a majority of 116 votes to 83, the first and critical clause of the Treaty of Union, affirming 'that the two kingdoms of Scotland and

England shall…be united into One Kingdom by the name of Great Britain'.[3] In January 1707 the last parliamentary stand against union collapsed. The popular view, not without scholarly sanction, has been that human weakness was a critical factor in determining this apparent surrender; and the prevalence and tenacity of this emphasis has been of great significance in subverting the legitimacy of union. But, while (what has been deemed) the 'parcel of rogues' paradigm has attained an independent stature and significance, its accuracy remains open to question.[4]

In both the Scots and Irish cases, there is certainly much to be said (and indeed much has been said) for interpretations which lay emphasis on ministerial cynicism, and upon the treachery and venality of the political classes. These interpretations have deep roots, and are anchored in the readings of contemporary players. George Lockhart of Carnwath, the Jacobite who (benefiting, ironically, from 'exactly the kind of pernicious English interference in Scottish affairs that so outraged him in other circumstances') served as one of the Scots parliamentary commissioners, and who was therefore at the heart of the negotiation, defined the union largely in terms of corruption and surrender in his influential *Memoirs concerning the Affairs of Scotland*, published at a time of popular disillusionment, in 1714.[5] Jonah Barrington, a member of the Irish parliament and (inconsistent) proponents of its rights, popularized a similar reading of the Irish union in his equally influential (and equally problematic) *Rise and Fall of the Irish Nation*, published in 1833. Both of these commentators had axes to grind; but neither was answered by contemporary unionist axe-grinders of comparable skill or resonance. In the Scots case, the closest approximation to a unionist answer to George Lockhart's accusations came with Sir John Clerk of Penicuik, who was indeed partly inspired to put pen to paper through reading a (pirated) copy of Lockhart's *Memoirs*: but Clerk of Penicuik's rebuttal was written in Latin, remained buried at the time of his death, in 1755, and only saw the light of day, in translated and published form, in 1993.[6]

Lockhart's case emphasised corruption and venality, and there is some evidence to support his proposition. When John Campbell, second Duke of Argyll, and chief of the Clan Campbell, was appointed as the Lord High Commissioner to the Scots parliament in 1705, his brief was to settle the critical matter of the royal succession, and to win a majority for union; and this he proceeded to do with a precision worthy of his military background. Reliable allies within the old Court Party were advanced, unreliable allies (as in the New Party) were spurned, and enemies harried and crushed. But

Argyll's energetic services came at a price. Argyll (writing 'to Godolphin, and even to the Queen herself, as if he were addressing his chamberlain at Inverary') demanded, and won, an English peerage (the earldom of Greenwich) for himself, a Scots earldom (Islay) for his younger brother, and cash for his parliamentary campaigns.[7] Having demitted office in 1706, Argyll's English earldom was converted into a British dukedom: moreover, 'it was only after receiving the commission of a Major General that Argyle consented to appear in Parliament and support the Union'.[8] It is also worth noting, in judging Argyll's claims and rewards, that he had inherited his Scottish dukedom from his father, Archibald Campbell, one of William III's closest allies, who had himself been promoted from a marquessate as recently as 1701.

Argyll's work for union was conditional upon the advancement both of himself and his family, and his supporters. More common were the titles distributed, not for the promise of union service, but rather for its fulfilment (though here, admittedly, it remains difficult to distinguish between reward-ing loyalty which would have been forthcoming in any event, holding out the promise of reward to those backbones which needed strengthening, and simply buying loyalty from those not otherwise disposed to give it).[9] James Douglas, second Duke of Queensberry, succeeded Argyll as Lord High Commissioner, and oversaw the attainment of union in 1706–1707: in 1708 he received a British dukedom (Dover) and appointment to the British privy council. Other magnates central to the union cause received similar advancement. John Ker, fifth Earl of Roxburghe, and a leading member of the Squadrone Volante, was influential in nudging these critical floating vot-ers in the Scots parliament towards union; and in 1707 he too emerged with a newly minted dukedom. James Douglas Hamilton, fourth Duke of Hamilton, and (from the ministerial perspective) a helpfully disastrous leader of the opposition in the Scots parliament, won the British dukedom of Brandon in 1711, shortly after the passage of the union.

The great Scots magnates might also expect, or covet, enrolment to one of the highly exclusive orders of chivalry—the knights of the Thistle (an order revived by Queen Anne in 1703 at the time of the first negotiation over union), or even the order of the Garter, founded by Edward III of England in the mid 14th century.[10] Queensberry, for example, was given the Garter in 1701, while John Murray, second Marquess of Atholl, was given a dukedom in 1703 and the Thistle in 1704 in an (in fact unwarranted) antici-pation of his loyal services. John Erskine, sixth Earl of Mar (deemed 'Bobbing

John' on account of the volatility of his convictions) was given the Thistle in 1706 as a reward of loyalty. By way of comparison, Irish peers were appointed to the Order of Saint Patrick, created in 1783 in the wake of 'legislative independence' as a means of encouraging political cooperation and loyalty.

Lesser lordlings were given junior peerages, or other, more minor, disbursements. Sir John Clerk, for example, became in 1708 a baron of the exchequer for Scotland, while another unionist, Archibald Primrose, first Earl of Rosebery, was placated with the chamberlainship of Fife. David Boyle, first Earl of Glasgow was appointed to the strategically crucial office of Treasurer Depute in 1706: writing to Godolphin he cloyingly affirmed that his loyalties were secure—'now...that your Lo[rdshi]p hath been instrumentall in procuring me this mark of her Majesties favor in naming me her Treasurer-Deputt...I beg leave to give your Lo[rdshi]p all the assurances of a man of honor that I eve will faithfully ad sincerely serve her Majesty to the uttmost of my power and, whatever measures the Queen pleaseth to goe in to, either in this or any other session of Parliament, I shall heartily comply with without reserve or in the least disputing her commands'.[11] He later recorded that he had been rewarded with the office of Register for Scotland, and 'a settlement of 1200 l [pounds] yearly for my service in the Union Parliament'.[12] It is worth noting, as well, that both the Rosebery and Glasgow earldoms had been created as recently as 1703 in recognition of services past, present, and to come. The army, in common with these other branches of royal service, was part of the patronage of union. It has been calculated that nineteen members of the Scots parliament were serving army officers, and that a number of army commissions were strategically placed in the spring and summer of 1706 to coincide with the mustering of support for union (Argyll's commission as Major General has already been mentioned in this regard).[13]

Money was evidently a critical lubricant of union for the Scots in 1705–1706, as indeed for the Irish in 1799–1800. One noteworthy distinction between the two, however, seems to have been that the opponents of the Irish union had a fighting fund, amounting (allegedly) to £100,000, and that in February 1800 they were able to offer £5000 for every vote against union: in Scotland the opposition had no such resources, and indeed only a noble few held out against the crown's offers of title, office, or cash.[14] The financial resources of the crown and of the unionists were, of course, formidable. Argyll asked for, but was denied £12,000 to service the cause of union in the parliament and beyond (he calculated that, inter alia, this cash would secure twenty votes). Queensberry, on the other hand, asked for, and received £20,000 for the same broad purpose—to pay arrears of official salaries, and thereby to secure wavering unionist loyalties. No accounts were kept of the disposal of this huge sum of money, and the whole business was (and remains) murky. George Lockhart, who (though politically skewed) had detailed knowledge of treasury affairs, saw the £20,000 essentially as a bribe for union. But the overall picture was more complicated than this. Arrears were indeed owed, and the money was evidently intended to service these official debts. Of the claimants, Queensberry himself was the greatest; and he appears to have accounted for no less than £12,000 of the total. This in itself was highly suspect; but, again, it may well have been a legitimate account, given that he had served as Lord High Commissioner from 1700–1704, and probably subsidized the vast expenses of office from his own pocket (his recorded arrears at this time were £26,756).[15]

On the other hand, if the claims were broadly genuine, then the manner in which they were addressed remains undiscoverable. Furthermore, those who had responsibility for these funds—the Treasurer Depute, the Earl of Glasgow, and the Lord Chancellor of Scotland (James Ogilvy, first Earl of Seafield) subsequently demonstrated considerable anxiety about the detailed arrangements for the disbursement ('the discovering of it would be of no use, unless it were to bring discredit upon the manadgment of that [union] parliament').[16] Thus, there were legitimate claims on government, and payments were made: but serious doubts remain over the relationship between the amount of the claim and the amount paid out, and the nature of the transactions involved—doubts which were the more telling because they were fired by the anxieties of those responsible for the disbursements. When all is said, however, a rigorous modern investigation has been able to uncover only one clear example of a commissioner, or MP, who voted 'against his natural inclinations' as a result of official payment—Alexander Murray, fourth Lord Elibank whose 'natural inclinations' (it seems) were worth £50.[17]

The Darien failure was clearly central to the union settlement, and the suspicion has long been entertained that the desire to recoup losses overwhelmed any more disinterested, patriotic instincts in the minds of those speculators who sat in the Scots parliament. Again, there is some evidence for this proposition. Approximately 99 members of the parliament (1702–1706) were investors in Darien, with their subscriptions totalling just under

£63,000 or some sixteen per cent of the total capital ventured.[18] They, and other Scots, blamed the Darien disaster partly on English ministerial action (or rather inaction); and in 1702–1703 their representatives, or commissioners, in the first round of negotiations on union demanded compensation from England for the losses sustained (calculated at this time to be some £200,000). This proved to be a deal-breaker, and indeed some historians have suspected that it was designed so to be, and that neither side was committed to an agreement.[19]

In any event, having been placed on the agenda for union in 1702, Darien did not go away; and in this, as in so much else, the negotiations of 1702–1703 provided a blueprint for the discussions and deal of 1706–1707. Under the terms of Article 15 of the Treaty agreed in 1707, the Scots would receive a sum, termed the 'Equivalent', just short of £400,000, which was partly designed to offset the higher levels of taxation that union necessitated, partly to pay outstanding arrears to officeholders (notwithstanding the earlier £20,000), but also to compensate the Darien shareholders for the losses that they had sustained at (so the Scots argument went) English hands.[20] It has been convincingly demonstrated that there was 'surprisingly little relationship' between holding Darien shares and voting behaviour in the last Scottish parliament.[21] But at the very least Scots parliamentarians had invested heavily in Darien; and compensation was at the heart of the definition of union that they eventually approved. Moreover, the Darien investors were amongst the first and fullest of those compensated through the Equivalent.[22]

Recent interpretations of the debate on union have emphasised, not so much Lockhart's case for venality (he called the Equivalent 'a clear bribe'), as the perceived 'ineptness' of the Scots negotiators.[23] To some extent this case hinges upon readings of the Equivalent. This sum was not, indeed, an *ex gratia* payment from the English Treasury, but was instead a form of advance or compensation for the Scots, calculated on the basis that they, as new partners within the British state, would have to assume a proportion of the hefty war debt. This debt was of course serviced through taxation, and the union brought the regularization of customs and excise and other impositions. In practice this meant, for the Scots, a significant hike in the taxes which they paid to central government. Thus, the Equivalent, far from being an English subvention, was in fact ultimately generated by the Scots themselves: as Allan Macinnes has remarked, 'the Scots were effectively paying for their own compensation'.[24] Moreover, this paradox, in combination with other damning features of the union settlement (such as the low level of

Scottish representation in the 'new' British parliament) ultimately reflected on the competence of the Scots negotiators: the Equivalent, for example, was not so 'much a union dividend as a testimony to inept Scottish negotiation'.[25]

This is a compelling case; but several comments are still worth making. Whether or not the union passed because of the ineptness of its supporters remains to be seen, but the competence of the opposition must surely be seen as a factor. The Country Party, the main source of opposition to the crown, was 'essentially an umbrella movement', a fissiparous coalition of the principled, the discontented, and the worried: it 'had nothing like' the cohesion of the Court Party.[26] Its leaders were wanting. A great and thoughtful patriot like Fletcher of Saltoun sought to uphold parliament and limit the monarchy, produced his famous 'Limitations' on this theme, wrote and argued copiously, but alienated potential supporters through his vitriolic temper. Much learned effort has been invested in trying to make sense of the actions of the Country Party's leader, the Duke of Hamilton—but whatever method has been discerned in the madness of his leadership, it was surely mad nonetheless. His critical proposal, on 1 September 1705, that the Queen should nominate the Scottish commissioners for union is incomprehensible except in terms of his own hopelessly entangled private affairs. In January 1707 he was due to lead a critical final assault on the union, by organizing a withdrawal from parliament and an appeal to the country: infamously, a toothache prevented him turning up to save his nation.

There are also striking analogies between this kind of argument (emphasising the competence or courage of those negotiating with the English) and that made by disappointed republicans in reviewing the Anglo-Irish Treaty of December 1921. The Anglo-Irish Treaty, which effectively ended (most of) the Union of 1801, has had mixed historiographical fortunes; but its opponents have consistently (from the time of negotiation onwards) laid stress upon a combination of Irish susceptibility or ineptitude and upon the threat of British military coercion in 1921–1922: as the republican leader, Cathal Brugha, famously said of the Irish negotiators, 'the English selected their men'.[27] Such critiques are rooted in the regret-laden view that a different set of patriots, distinguished by somewhat less pliable vertebrae, could have secured a more advantageous settlement. Both the themes of English military threat and Celtic negotiating ineptitude are now central to the analysis of the Anglo-Scots union of 1707.

Were the Scots negotiators or parliamentarians 'inept'? Could a different team, a different set of hagglers, have improved upon the terms achieved? Contemporary criticisms of those responsible for the deal, such as those emanating from Lockhart, tended to emphasise scullduggery or venality (Lockhart, for example, 'allwayes was of opinion that a scheme of union was concerted and woud be agreet to here').[28] Given that virtually the entire Scottish political class was either involved with the negotiation or endorsement of the Treaty of Union, it is hard to see where more substantial backbones or greater cerebral power might have been found to wrest a better deal from English hands. Moreover, while later critics have energetically and comprehensively tackled the personalities and politics associated with the debates in 1706–1707, their focus has tended to linger upon both the inevitability and morality of the union rather than the competence of those Scots involved. For example, William Ferguson, no friend to the union, or to its architects, has said (in dealing with the Equivalent) that 'on the whole the fiscal and financial provisions of the treaty were fair, in some respects generous, and were calculated, in both senses of the word, to recommend the treaty to the Scottish parliament'.[29]

It is true, as apparent evidence of Scots' 'ineptitude', that there was both no detailed scheme laying out a plan of instalments for the delivery of the Equivalent, and that some creditors remained unpaid twenty years after the enactment of union. It is also true that a large portion of the first payment of the Equivalent came in the form of exchequer bills (totalling £298,000), which were looked upon with understandable suspicion by many in Scotland.[30] Against this, however, are the facts that an effort was made speedily to pay the first instalment of the Equivalent, and that (famously) a caravan of horse-drawn wagons, guarded by armed soldiers, was sent north from London in July 1707. Moreover, when it was grasped that exchequer bills were unlikely to impress the Scots, £50,000 in gold was speedily despatched as a substitute. As has been noted, the Darien shareholders were paid off with commendable alacrity, with most of their claims settled by December 1707.[31] In a country where specie and liquidity had hitherto been in short supply, these injections of cash, speedily administered, were disproportionately beneficial.

The reality was surely, not that Scots were politically inept, but rather that Scotland was poor and politically divided, and that the treaty of Union reflected this relative poverty and division. The Equivalent was not so much a case study in Scots incompetence, as an example of sectional advantage

and profiteering, since various Scots creditor interests, including pre-eminently the Darien speculators, effectively benefited from the burdens carried by the whole tax-paying community in Scotland. This did not mean,
however, that the union as a whole was a particularly egregious example of
political venality or spinelessness. The union passed in 1707, but not because
the patriotic parliamentarians of 1703 had been thoroughly 'bought and
sold': the reality was that few of them (nineteen only) moved from opposing
to supporting the union (those few centred on the Squadrone Volante), and
the evidence suggests that (while there was certainly very little accountability) any English cash distributed was for broadly legitimate purposes.[32] The
honours system was of course lavishly deployed as an instrument of government and of union in the run-up to 1707 (and indeed ever since); although
titles tended, conventionally, to be rewards for the loyal rather than the currency of vote gathering.

The union passed then, not because of overt venality, but rather because
the patriots of the 1703 parliament were subject, after 1705, to sterner and
more vigorous political management ('I am for al measurs [that can] stren-
then us in the carying the Union', declared Seafield in October 1706), and
because there was greater and more insistent interest in London.[33] In addition, as will be seen, the Scots were now getting more of what they wanted
from the deal. In 1703 union failed largely because the English would not
deliver compensation for Darien, and this recalcitrance fired those Scottish
national resentments and sensitivities which were never far below the surface even of active unionists. It was in fact this national pride of 1703 which
helped to deliver both the treaty of 1707 (in so far as it increased the price
that the English were willing to pay for Scots cooperation) and the patriotic
unionism which helped to ensure its long-term survival. As William Law
Mathieson wrote in 1905, 'the real power of Scottish nationality... is seen
most conspicuously in the apparent paradox that a sentiment, which had
proved its efficacy as a motive of separation, was to be equally efficacious as
an incentive to union'.[34]

## Irish venality?

Much of this explanatory framework is relevant, and has been applied, to
the debate on the Irish union of 1799–1800. The same transition from patriotic assertion and defiance towards an acceptance of union is perceptible in

the Irish parliament as in the Scots. As in Scotland, so in Ireland, the trans-formation of patriotic fortunes has been often explained in terms of venal-ity and corruption. As in Scotland, so in Ireland, the competence of Irish patriotic politicians has been deemed as relevant to the union debates. As in Scotland, so in Ireland, union was about management and brokerage, not about vision: union was primarily a deal, rather than an ideal. The difference between the two nations and their respective unions lay partly in the fact that the political class in Scotland was in a stronger position to negotiate than their Irish counterparts—and the two Unions, of 1707 and 1800, clearly reflected this.

In Ireland, as in Scotland, the years before union were generally charac-terized by a nervousness about English intervention, and by a determina-tion to express national self-determination. As has been seen, Irish patriots wrested legislative independence from the British parliament in 1782–1783, successfully fought off William Pitt's desire for closer commercial and politi-cal relations in 1784–1785, and asserted an independent right to make provi-sion for the regency of Ireland during George III's illness in 1788–1789. Irish parliamentarians either diluted (the legislation of 1792–1793) or sty-mied (as with the Fitzwilliam episode in 1795) British ministerial efforts to advance the question of Catholic relief. Only in the aftermath of the 1798 Rising did Pitt dare to raise his long-cherished project of parliamentary union, defining his plans at first largely (and significantly) in terms of the arrangements struck in 1706–1707; but even then his lot was initially humil-iation.[35] On 24 January 1799 the Irish parliament voted by 111 votes to 106 to excise a reference to union from the loyal address. By 15 January 1800, however, and despite the rhetoric of the great Irish patriot, Henry Grattan, the mood of parliament had changed, and union was endorsed by a vote of 138 to 96. On 5 February 1800 'in what was probably the best attended House hitherto known', the Irish Commons registered their approval of union by an even greater majority, 158 votes to 115.[36] By early June 1800 a bill for union had successfully cleared all of its parliamentary readings and was poised to take effect: it duly did so on 1 January 1801.

How, then, given this sustained history of resistance, and the initial defeat of union, did the Irish parliament ultimately succumb to British ministerial pressure? Contemporary assessments (such as those of Jonah Barrington—'a full account of the bribery and corruption by which the Union was car-ried') stressed venality, the lavish distribution of cash, of office, and of noble title.[37] The ubiquity of 'union peerages' meant that they became a byword for the inflation and devaluation of nobility, and doubtless further assisted in the undermining of the social structure of Ascendancy Ireland through the 19th century (in 1894, in the context of the second Irish Home Rule Bill, Swift MacNeill wrote a book called—expressively—*Titled Corruption: The Sordid Origins of Some Irish Peerages*, with these union creations partly in mind).[38] Here and elsewhere the minister immediately responsible for the union within the Dublin parliament, Lord Castlereagh, was interpreted as a bloodless aristocratic corrupter, and his Irish career was woven seamlessly within a wider radical, romantic, and patriotic reading of his iniquities.[39] These emphases were themselves incorporated within, and popularized by, nationalist readings of Irish history (written by the likes of A.M. Sullivan), which achieved a mass readership from the Fenian era, the 1860s, onwards.[40] Such assessments chimed with critiques of the overall British administration in Ireland during the Home Rule and revolutionary period, when the main agencies of British rule—Dublin Castle, the viceregal court, the army— were deemed in popular nationalist exegesis to be cankered by financial corruption, and sexual vice. But they also had a more scholarly vindication, supplied by (amongst others) W.E.H. Lecky, who (despite himself emerging as a unionist) agreed that corruption was a vital agent in the passage of the union in 1800 ('it would be idle to dispute the essentially corrupt character by which the union was carried').[41]

Indeed, the Home Rule era, when Lecky was active, saw a remarkable efflorescence of scholarly and popular interest in the two unions, Irish and Scots, and their mode of passage. In Scotland the vulnerability of the Irish union at this time, and the rise of a small Scots Home Rule movement, helped to stimulate a diverse literature on 1707 by (inter alia) Mackinnon (1896), Omond (1897), Rait (1901), Mathieson (1905), and Hume Brown (1907, 1914).[42] Significantly, however, this literature was broadly unionist in so far as (whatever the patriotism of its authors) it claimed to recognize that the union was widely beneficial, and was inclined towards a relaxed view of the means used to obtain its acceptance. On the issue of corruption in 1705–1706, Hume Brown (for example) asked directly 'did bribery carry the union?', and answered in the negative: he stressed the ubiquity of venality in the politics of the time, the Jacobitism (and thus bias) of the chief accuser, Lockhart, the arrears owed, and the evident sincerity of those in Scotland ultimately responsible for the union.[43] William Law Mathieson, writing in 1905, did not directly tackle the use of corruption in the securing the union; but he did emphasise that in Scotland after 1690, as in Ireland after 1782, political venality was not only endemic but necessary 'in order to secure a working agreement between an executive and a legislature which were always independent and frequently antagonistic'.[44] Corruption, by implication, was not essentially a problem connected with the passage of the two unions, but rather a problem endemic in the flawed arrangements existing before 1707 and 1800.

In Ireland, however, there was no such unionist historiographical consensus by the end of the 19th century, though a unionist case was occasionally proffered in the literature. Indeed, it appeared as if history was merely a continuation of politics by other means, with nationalists and unionists deploying rival historical interpretations of the debate on union as adjuncts to the political battlefield. Unionists like Ingram (1887 and 1900), Falkiner (1902), Fisher (1911) all sought to address the issue of corruption by placing it squarely within the context of contemporary usage.[45] But, unlike in Scotland, interpretations such as these were thoroughly outgunned by a coalition of Liberal and Home Rule politicians and scholars (led by Gladstone, Bryce, A.M. Sullivan, Swift MacNeill), informing a wider Irish public already susceptible to notions of the corrupting power of English government and of its money.[46] The war over (essentially) the righteousness of the union had probably long since been lost, or indeed never been winnable; but its scholarly defeat, and associated lack of moral and historical credibility, were fully confirmed in these years.

These historiographical distinctions, of vital importance in determining the legitimacy of the two unions, were linked to a range of other contrasts between the stories of the union's passage in Scotland and in Ireland. Speaking on the Irish union in February 1799, Henry Dundas (Pitt's Secretary of State for War, and the pre-eminent Scots unionist of the time) declared that 'when gentlemen pretend to think lightly of the sacrifices of Scotland compared with those of Ireland, let them recollect that Ireland has not for many centuries been free or independent of England, but that Scotland never was completely subdued or under the control of England; that Scotland gave up what Ireland cannot give up, an independent Parliament of King, Lords and Commons; and that Scotland gave up, what Ireland cannot give up, an independent and separate Crown'.[47] This was of course an exaggeration, which magnified the reality of Scots sovereignty at the time of union, and conveniently forgot both the Cromwellian conquest of Scotland in 1651 and the institution of Irish legislative independence in 1782–1783. But it did rightly point to the dependent condition of the Irish under the crown; and elsewhere Dundas, again looking back to 1707 for guidance, underlined another critical distinction between the Irish and Scots cases, in pointing to the peculiarly limited and confessional nature of the Irish parliament ('the plainest of all political truths [is] that a country where a Parliament and a free constitution is allowed to exist never can submit to the practice of three-fourths of the country being sacrificed to the whims, prejudices or opinions of the other fourth').[48] However, union between Britain and Ireland would (in Dundas's calculation) permit greater religious freedom for these 'three-fourths', just as greater toleration had been one of the many blessed outcomes of the Union of 1707.[49]

Other distinctions between the Irish and Scots cases also point up the importance of the Scots union (and Dundas himself) to the evolving union of 1799–1800. For example, the original intention of Pitt's inner circle was that the terms of union should be settled, as in the Scots case, by two commissions representing each of the national parliaments, British and Irish: this was Dundas's view, as it was that of the formidable Lord Chancellor of Ireland, John Fitzgibbon, Earl of Clare.[50] But with the shock defeat of union in January 1799 this idea was set aside, and the government concentrated instead upon more defensive and prescriptive policies. Union would not, as in the Anglo-Scots paradigm, be defined by parliamentary commissioners, but would instead be decided by ministers: Irish parliamentarians had of course the right to debate ministerial proposals, but effectively the initiative lay elsewhere. This is an important point, because (whatever the grounds for suspicion concerning the constitution, integrity, or competence of the Scots commissioners in 1705–1706), the Scots union was the outcome of a negotiating process, and indeed has been widely accepted as a compromise and a bargain, however flawed.[51] But for the Irish, union was (to borrow the language of the later land question) not so much about a negotiated 'free sale' as about 'compulsory purchase'. The view that union was thrust by English ministers upon corrupted legislators was common to both Scotland and Ireland; but it had deeper roots, and deeper justification, in the Irish case than in the Scots.

However, returning to an earlier point, the same broad interpretative framework which is generally applied to the passage of the Scots' union, is relevant to the Irish case in 1799–1800. Coercion, propaganda, patronage, and cash were all applied in Ireland in 1799–1800, as they had been in Scotland in 1705–1706. Allegations concerning, not only the venality, but also the competence of legislators have been made in the Irish case, as they have been made in the Scots.

A firm managerial regime characterized (in particular) both the Duke of Argyll's tenure as Lord High Commissioner in 1705, and that of Charles Cornwallis, first Marquess Cornwallis, Lord Lieutenant of Ireland (1798–1801). The sacking of those anti-unionists in crown office gathered pace as ministers sought to bolster votes in the Irish parliament in January 1799: Sir John Parnell, Chancellor of the Irish Exchequer (and Charles Stewart Parnell's grandfather), and James FitzGerald, Prime Sergeant of Ireland were both dismissed at this time, the first casualties of a more sustained campaign. This targeted not only comparatively small fry such as three anti-unionist commissioners of revenue (Wolfe, Foster, and Knox), sacked in May 1799, but also ultimately no less a magnate than Arthur Hill, second Marquess of Downshire, and one of the largest landowners and borough patrons in the country: in February 1800 he was stripped of his privy councillorship, his governorship of county Down, and removed from his position as registrar in the court of chancery.[52]

The corollary of sacking opponents was rewarding allies. As with Scotland, so with Ireland, elevations to, and promotions within, the peerage were used to bolster the support of the most wealthy parliamentarians (those with a rent roll of over £5000).[53] In December 1798 Cornwallis had obtained from the Home Secretary, William Cavendish Bentinck, third Duke of Portland, a free hand to enter into 'any engagements deemed necessary or expedient to carry the Union'.[54] It should be stressed that Cornwallis used this freedom within particular constraints. Only two peerages were granted when the government was building support for union in the winter of 1798–1799. Moreover, the great historian of the Irish union, G.C. Bolton, has been able to uncover only two examples of peerages given to those who had turned from opposing to supporting the union.[55] On the other hand, the peerage was liberally deployed (as in Scotland in the run-up to union) to strengthen the resolve, or to reward the loyalty of supporters. On 9 June 1800 Cornwallis forwarded to London a list of no less than sixteen individuals whom (on account of their services to the union) he was recommending for peerages. In addition, he recommended fifteen promotions in the peerage (nine new viscountcies, three earldoms, and three marquessates).[56] Though Bolton has pointed out that mass ennoblements of this kind were not without precedent, Cornwallis's liberality was sufficiently unusual for Pitt and other ministers to be unsettled, and initially to think of disowning the promises which had been made on this score since 1798.[57]

Indeed, until the late 1990s the settled historiographical consensus was that the government's wider methods of securing the passage of the Irish Act of Union had precedents, and differed little from the norms of contemporary parliamentary management: much the same, 'normalizing', or contextual, argument has been used by Scots historians in dealing with 1707. As has been seen, while some Scots historians have viewed the £20,000 sent north by the English government in 1705 as critical to the shift of mood within the Edinburgh parliament, the prevailing consensus has long been that this money represented legitimately accrued arrears, and that it mostly ended up in the pockets of the Duke of Queensberry, who (in any event) was owed much more.[58] Payment of official arrears may have shocked the government's creditors into endorsing the union; but it cannot credibly be construed as venal or illegal.

The Irish case is somewhat different. In 1997 David Wilkinson, of the History of Parliament, published an article, drawing upon newly released materials in the (then) Public Record Office at Kew, which revealed the true extent of the official expenditure on the campaign for the Irish union.[59] This totalled some £32,556, money which was fed through the secret service funds and (as in the Scots case) was without full and proper accounts. The funds were serviced by a functionary at the Home Office, John King, and were part of the empire of money and influence controlled by Pitt's spymaster, William Wickham, Under Secretary at the Home Office (1798–1801) and subsequently (appropriately enough) Chief Secretary for Ireland (1802–1804).[60] Wilkinson and other scholars have surmised that the money was spent on subventing the union's supporters, and paying for the campaign's other expenses (such as entertainment and propaganda).[61] As in Scotland, so in Ireland the government paid pamphleteers to promote the cause (no hack of the distinction of Daniel Defoe, apologist of the Scots union in 1705–1707, was available to Dublin Castle—although Defoe's work on 1707 was reprinted in 1799 to inform debate on the Irish union). Unlike Scots ministers, the Irish government spent lavishly on hospitality during the parliamentary session of 1800, organizing grand dinners with a view to maintaining the morale (and indeed the presence) of its support. These bibulous affairs also helped to smooth the negotiation of place and pension which was important, not so much in securing fresh support for union, as in bolstering or rewarding existing support.[62]

Critically, the money was also used to pay for the purchase of parliamentary seats for unionists. In the Irish parliament, like the Scots, the absolute number of parliamentarians who shifted from opposing to supporting the union was surprisingly small: in the Irish case perhaps twelve MPs moved in this way between January 1799 and January 1800, when the union majority was consolidated. But this relatively modest figure disguises some more fundamental (and expensive) shifts within Irish parliamentary representation. In the Irish parliament, unlike the Scots, borough seats were effectively a form of property, and could be bought and sold much like any other commodity of the time. With the stakes so high, and with both the Castle and the opposition striving for parliamentary advantage, the turnover in borough representation in 1800 was immense, affecting thirty-three boroughs and sixty-six seats.[63] Here, in part, was where the secret service's £32,556 was spent.

The trade in borough representation was unseemly but legal; but overall the secret service fund (as with other aspects of the Irish union) was an illegality. Here, again, there are distinctions to be made with the Scots case. Judgements on the Scots union have focused on morality and competence, but the issue of legality has rarely been raised (if at all). With the Irish union, the secret service funding was in contravention of the Civil List Act of 1782, which limited the amount of money to be spent in this way to £5000. It has been argued that similar contraventions were taking place regarding the secret service fund and the war against France, and that there were thus contemporary precedents for the Irish case.[64] But the Irish money was not being spent to bring confusion to the King's enemies; it was being spent to bolster a policy which was about the achievement of massive constitutional change rather than (as elsewhere) to subvert it. Moreover this rested alongside other, technical, illegalities such as (astonishingly) the parliamentary standing of the Chief Secretary himself, Lord Castlereagh. In January 1799 the opposition leader in the Irish House of Commons, George Ponsonby, pointed out that, under the rules of the Place Act of 1793 and an amending act in 1798, Castlereagh should have resigned his County Down seat, and sought reelection, when his appointment as Chief Secretary was confirmed in November 1798.[65] This had not happened; and the Castle seems either to have been ignorant of its own legislation, or (more probably) willing to break the rules for fear of creating a political crisis through an inevitably contentious by-election.

If the illegalities were distinctively Irish, then the level of competence displayed by the Irish opposition was as questionable as that characterizing the Scots opposition in 1705–1706. As in Scotland, so in Ireland the opposition to union was a relatively incoherent body, spanning those allegedly tainted by association with the 1798 Rising (like Henry Grattan) through to upholders of Ascendancy and opponents of Catholic relief, like the Speaker of the Irish Commons, John Foster. As in Scotland, so in Ireland opposition to union peaked too early, and was characterized by planned grand assaults which either misfired or were not followed through. For example, Ponsonby's assault on Castlereagh might well have seriously rocked the Castle administration, had the opposition leader done more thorough homework in preparing his case. The opposition victory over the government in January 1799 was immediately followed by miscalculation and retreat over a motion reaffirming the independent Irish parliament.[66] Lack of effort characterized the opposition more generally through the crucial remaining months of 1799: 'the most striking features of the opposition to an Anglo-Irish union in the summer of 1799 are its langour and effeteness'.[67]

Indeed, the failure of union in both Scotland and Ireland may be ascribed to a wider failure of opposition. In a sense, while the interpretative challenge of the Scots and Irish union is often cast in terms of a sudden and therefore surprising collapse of patriotic resistance, this (arguably) involves a useful but illusory image of total transformation. Of course the Scots and Irish parliaments did indeed move from patriotic assertiveness to unionist acquiescence relatively quickly; but to frame the problem in this way (a natural course within, in particular, nationally minded historiography) is to ignore the longer history of opposition failure in both legislatures. James Kelly has remarked that 'the opposition in the 18th century Irish parliament had seldom been able to sustain successfully a campaign of resistance against the combined interests of the British government and Dublin Castle'.[68] A similar judgement might be applied to Scotland: the opposition in the late 17th Scots parliament had seldom been able to sustain a campaign of resistance against the combined interests of the crown and its ministers. Judged in these contexts, the success of union appears much less surprising than that (occasionally) of the opposition.

But aside from the qualities shared by the opponents of union in 1705–1706 and 1799–1800, it is the distinctions between the passage of the two measures which ultimately resonates. The financial scullduggery which accompanied each of these stages in the creation of the United Kingdom state left the architects of union fearful of discovery and exposure for years afterwards: Castlereagh suffered the first of his several nervous breakdowns (in 1801) as a consequence of his anxieties on this score. There is no record of any of the Scots patriarchs of union suffering similar levels of apprehension (though there were certainly qualms and—by 1712–1713—some second thoughts); but then there is no clear record of the kind of illegality that existed in the Irish case. Each political elite, Scots and Irish, was certainly characterized by a greed and self-interest which ostensibly shocked the sensibilities of delicate English observers in 1707 and 1800; but the Irish elite—the Ascendancy, or Church of Ireland landed class—was of course more vulnerable than its Scots counterpart, as a propertied minority within a confessional minority. The Ascendancy's sale of its patrimony, legislative independence, in 1800 was shocking; but in the circumstances its right to conduct this sale was widely regarded as even more tenuous than that of the Scots parliamentarians in 1706–1707. The Scots union was primarily the product, however flawed or skewed, of a diplomatic negotiation between the emissaries of the two parliaments. The Irish union was fundamentally about salesmanship, with secret backhanders, inducements and penalties, the purchase of seats, and the epic dispensation of hospitality.

No wonder, then, that the 'parcel of rogues' have been a consistent, but often muted and contested presence in Scots historiography. But no wonder, too, that those more egregious 'rogues', the unionists of 1800, have thoroughly dominated the narrative of the Irish union. The survival of the Anglo-Scots union has been shaped in part, and reflected through, often complex and ambiguous readings of its nativity. For most Irish people in the 19th century there was no call for complexity or ambiguity in reading the events of 1800 and their aftermath: the Irish union appeared to have been born in squalor, raised in squalor, and killed off in squalor.

## The practice of union

While issues of management and corruption have dominated the popular perspective on union, both in Scotland but particularly in Ireland, the architecture of the two measures was also carefully crafted with a view to attracting support. Debate on the unions has tended to be interpreted patriotically and retrospectively as a zero-sum game; but of course it mattered to contemporaries not only whether a union was passed, but also what type of union emerged. It is all too easy to forget that in 1706 some of the most advanced Scots parliamentary opponents of English policy wanted a 'federative' union, and that in 1800 the most trenchant Irish opponents of Pitt and Castlereagh wanted both to retain and eat their constitutional cake by maintaining legislative independence and a strong connection to the British crown and its ministers. The practice of union was therefore as important as its principle (in some respects rather more so); and the shape and content of the two measures was of course vital to contemporaries, and vital, too, in influencing the fate of union in these islands.

The Acts of Union achieved in 1707 and 1801 were in practice (as opposed to the theory of the treaties and legislation) not so much about the union of parliaments, as about the incorporation of the Scots and Irish legislatures within those of England and Great Britain. Moreover, not only did Scots have to abandon the traditions of their 500 year old parliament, and adapt to English parliamentary procedures, it was also the case that there were comparatively few Scots in the new union legislature. In 1707 Scots representation was reduced from the 336 members, nobles, shire, and burgh representatives, serving in the old Edinburgh parliament to a mere 16 peers and 45 MPs (out of a total of 558) at Westminster. These proportions followed a formula based upon the relative taxable capacity of England and Scotland (38 to 1), rather than population (5 to 1), but generated accusations then (and later) that Scotland had been disfranchised. And, indeed, given that current wealth was not the principle governing the distribution of seats in the unreformed Commons of 1707, and that some relatively poor areas of England were well represented, the accusations had some apparent force.

Irish representation in 1801 was reduced to 28 representative temporal peers, 4 bishops of the Church of Ireland (serving on a rotation), and 100 members of the House of Commons—all this at a time when the Irish population numbered around 5 millions, and the Scots population some 1.6 millions.[69] By these standards the Scots did not, in fact, look particularly badly off, though with the fall in the Irish population after the Famine, and the booming of the Scots population in the 19th century, the disparities evident in 1800 faded. However, the Scots presence at Westminster was bolstered by those compatriots who had parliamentary seats outside Scotland, and by those who were given British peerages after 1707: though the Irish in the 19th century benefited similarly from compatriots holding United Kingdom peerages or English seats, these exiles were often southern unionists relatively distant politically (and geographically) from mainstream Catholic and Nationalist opinion. The massive disfranchisement of constituencies implicit in the Irish union project meant that Castlereagh had to mollify existing political interests, by both retaining the two-member county seats of the old parliament, and by offering lavish compensation to those patrons or owners of parliamentary boroughs set for the axe. The compensation amounted to no less than £15,000 a seat; and, though there were manifold complaints about official 'bribery', all borough owners (including the opponents of union) availed themselves of the government's offer.[70]

Each union passed because each carefully addressed, whether in terms of presentation or substance, the concerns of some key existing interests, and indeed this has given rise to the charge that, whatever their ostensible novelty or radicalism, the unions were fundamentally 'reactionary' enterprises. William Ferguson has expressed this point (in relation to Scotland) with characteristic directness: 'in many respects the Treaty and Act of Union of 1707 was demonstrably a triumph of reaction, granting as it did a fresh lease of life to the sinister heritable jurisdictions and oppressive feudal superiorities in Scotland. In the making of the Treaty of Union in 1707 the "meaner sort" were not considered'.[71] Heritable jurisdictions, the traditional rights of legal jurisdiction exercised by some landowners and clan chiefs, were explicitly protected by the Scots union, and survived until 1746 (clause 20). The rights of the royal boroughs were protected (clause 21). As has been discussed, the claims of the many creditors of the Company of Scotland were explicitly recognized with the definition of the Equivalent (clause 15). The rights and interests of the increasingly powerful Scots legal community were effectively underwritten by the continuity of Scots law (particularly relating to private right) and the Scots judiciary (clauses 18 and 19). It need hardly be said that this, Ferguson's, view of the Scots Union is reflected in popular Irish nationalist readings of the union of 1801.

Established or vested interests included, pre-eminently, the Church.[72] In 1907 Mathieson argued that 'the Irish and Scottish Churches were treated alike—both were to have been excluded from the union, and both insisted that their continuance should be made a positive condition'.[73] But in fact the Crown's varied handling of this critical issue highlights a classic distinction between the success of the two Unions. In Scotland the Kirk was essentially an opponent of union ('if the Union fail, it is owing to them', wrote the Earl of Mar of the Kirk), until its established status and Presbyterian government were guaranteed by an act of parliament, which was passed

alongside the union itself.[74] The 'Act for the Security of the Protestant
Religion and the Government of the Church', promoted by William
Carstares, William III's chaplain and Principal of the University of Edinburgh,
effectively silenced, if it did not remove, opposition to union within the
Church. In essence, the Church of Scotland was one of the key interest
groups which was successfully squared in the prelude to the enactment of
the Scots union. But, while the Crown dealt well (in this instance) with the
sensitivities of the Kirk, and while this provided the foundations on which
the Kirk would be successfully accommodated within the institutions of the
British state, including (by the 19th century) the monarchy, it handled the
challenge of other majority faiths with much less dexterity.[75]

The success of union in 1707, and afterwards, owed much to Carstares
and the 'Act for the Security of the Protestant Religion'. In Ireland, the
central architects of union—Pitt, Dundas, Castlereagh (all of whom, but in
particular Dundas, were influenced by their readings of 1707) —sought a
related accommodation between the new United Kingdom state and the
predominant faith community in Ireland, the Catholics. Dundas had a long
history of commitment to the easing of Catholic legal disabilities in Scotland,
and was keen to combine (what was now becoming known as) 'Catholic
emancipation' and union. In Scotland the support of the Kirk for union had
been an essential stabilizing force; and it was expected that interlinking
Catholic interests and union would promote a similar constitutional stability in Ireland. This was not the universal view of the form or purpose of
union, however; and the supporters of relief encountered entrenched hostility—with George III, famously, but also with some elements of the British
cabinet (in particular the Scottish-born Lord Chancellor, Alexander
Wedderburn, first Lord Loughborough) and much of the Irish administration (where John FitzGibbon, first Earl of Clare, Lord Chancellor of Ireland,
and the grandson of a Catholic cottier, was an especially able and vitriolic
opponent of the emancipationist cause). It seems reasonably clear that Pitt
and Dundas in London and Cornwallis and Castlereagh in Dublin gave
encouraging hints to the Catholic interest of the legal blessings that might
accompany union, while at the same time concealing their intentions from
useful Ascendancy magnates such as Clare. As a short-term expedient these
sleights of hand worked well enough, and indeed unquestionably helped to
deliver the union in 1800. But as a long-term policy, seeking to balance the
support of both the Catholic interest and its opponents, it was disastrous,
and led to profound distrust and disillusionment. For, though the union was

delivered on the strength (partly) of Catholic acquiescence, the price of that passivity—relief or emancipation—was not paid. Union entered the statute books, not (as in Scotland) as part of a complex and controversial but basically honest deal with a range of interest groups, including the Kirk, but instead on the back of popular Catholic disappointment and betrayal.[76]

In fact, not only was the Irish union unaccompanied by concessions to the majority faith, it vigorously underpinned the Protestant nature of the British constitution. Both the measures of 1707 and 1801 were centrally concerned with preserving a united Protestant monarchy; but the measure of 1801 went further than this, creating, through the union of the Church of England and the episcopal Church of Ireland, a united state church to minister to the needs of the newly united kingdoms. As noted, the Irish branch of the church had guaranteed representation and a guaranteed voice in the Lords. Indeed, the union of 1801 evinced rather more concern with the standing of Scots Presbyterians than with that of Irish Catholics: article five, in making provision for (as it was called) 'the United Church of England and Ireland' deliberately reaffirmed the legal and constitutional position of the Church of Scotland ('and that in like manner the doctrine, worship, discipline and government of the Church of Scotland shall remain and be preserved as the same are now preserved by law and by the acts of union for the two kingdoms of England and Scotland'). Presbyterians in Scotland had the dominance and government of their Kirk confirmed and protected; Irish Catholics were simultaneously denied emancipation (partly at the hands of a Scot), and presented with an augmented Protestant religious establishment.[77]

Moreover, the concerns of the Irish union were with established interests such as the Ascendancy landowning class rather than the faith communities on the island. In a sense this was wholly unremarkable, since the principal concerns of the legislators were with property right: religious sensibilities featured only in so far as they were related to the necessary interconnections between the church and Protestant state. Thus, Ascendancy borough owners were the principal beneficiaries from the compensation offered for disfranchisement, while there was no Scots-style 'Equivalent' paid to the mercantile or business communities. If (as has been remarked) the unionists of 1707 had little time for 'the meaner sort', then the architects of the Irish union were not only preoccupied with the condition of the established interests, but were also actively concerned to stop these interests finding common cause with the 'meaner sort' of the island (as had been the case with patriot leaders such as Grattan).[78]

As in Scotland, so in Ireland a central concern of union was with the creation of a free trade area within the British Isles: as in Scotland, so in Ireland a substantial element in each union measure was devoted to the issue of cushioning the commercial and industrial impact of union through assigning timetables or relief on taxation. However, unlike Scotland and England in 1707, full fiscal union between Britain and Ireland was delayed for over 20 years after 1801 in order to allow a lengthy period of adjustment (the dangerously swift fiscal incorporation of Scotland may well have provided lessons for the architects of union in 1801): where the English and Scottish exchequers were aligned by legislation in 1707, the Irish and British exchequers were only united in 1817, and protective tariffs on a range of Irish manufactures only finally removed in 1826. Essentially, though, the taxation regimes in Scotland and Ireland were to be reconciled, through union, with the rest of the kingdom. In Scotland, compensation for higher burdens of taxation was provided through the 'Equivalent' which went (as has been seen) mostly to the shareholders and creditors of the Company of Scotland. In Ireland, the imposition of union meant higher taxation and also the acquisition of two seventeenths of the new United Kingdom's huge (and rising) burden of debt. But there was no compensatory 'Equivalent', unless a comparison is sought (as well it might be) between this and the compensation doled out to borough owners. It has been argued eloquently that the Scots effectively paid for their own compensation, the Equivalent, through raised taxes: it might equally be argued that the Irish effectively paid for the compensation of others, the landed interest, through raised taxes.[79] But the subsequent industrial and commercial growth of Scotland meant that these impositions appeared much less painful than in Ireland, where the Great Famine occupied the place of the Industrial Revolution: and in Scotland there was no sustained complaint about over-taxation such as characterized the British-Irish relationship for most of the 19th century, and certainly after the 1850s.

Each, of course, was an incomplete or imperfect union. The Scots and Irish parliaments were dissolved, a common Protestant monarchy guaranteed, tax regimes were (in the case of the Irish, eventually) reconciled. But separate Scots and Irish judiciaries remained, as did the Scots system of private law, derived from Roman roots (Irish practice followed English common law precedents). The argument is sometimes made in Scotland that the incompleteness of the union made (paradoxically) for its success and survival, since Scots had local focuses for their patriotism, while being able to retain participation in the union state.[80] This is probably true; but the argument needs to be modified in an Irish context. The incompleteness of the Irish union arose partly because of the compromises between the old Ascendancy elite, which had dominated the Irish parliament, and the new United Kingdom state: the relics of Irish autonomy which survived tended, therefore, to be the preserve of the Ascendancy interest. For example, unlike its Scots counterpart, the Irish peerage enjoyed an afterlife beyond 1801, with numerous creations being made until 1898: one duke, three marquesses, ten earls, two viscounts, and nine barons were created in the peerage of Ireland, mostly for the benefit of Ascendancy lordlings, after the union (George Nathaniel Curzon, created baron Curzon of Kedleston in the peerage of Ireland in 1898, was the last of these and, as an Englishman, an exception which illustrated the wider rule). Elaborate procedures were laid out in the Act of Union which provided for the continued survival of the Irish peerage alongside the new United Kingdom peerage—and also detailing strict rules concerning the ratio of noble extinctions to creations, so that (while being continually renewed) the dignity of the honour would be upheld. In addition, the separate Irish administration, centred on Dublin Castle, and the separate judiciary, focused on the Four Courts, tended to be peopled by members of the Ascendancy, or their sympathizers (Catholics were not admitted to the legal profession until 1793): recent scholarly arguments assert that the highest levels of the union state in Ireland remained largely impermeable to Catholic ambition even in the last years of British rule.[81] So, unlike in Scotland, the incompleteness of union ultimately militated against its survival in Ireland; for the survival of Irish institutions tended to mean the survival of Ascendancy institutions.

They were also, structurally, different forms of union. The Scots union preserved Scottish institutions at the cost, initially, of administrative incorporation; the Irish union preserved Irish institutions at the cost of administrative devolution: after 1707, and particularly with the abolition of the Scottish privy council, 'there was not much of an executive centre in Scotland'.[82] Until 1726, and from 1742 to 1746, there was a London-based Secretary of State for Scotland: but, as Joanna Innes has remarked, 'this office never amounted to much'.[83] From 1782 until 1885 Scotland was administered through the Home Department and the Secretary of State for Home Affairs, where between 1801 and 1922 Ireland was overseen through an Irish Office, a Chief Secretary for Ireland, and a Lord Lieutenant: where the Scottish privy council was swiftly axed, the Irish privy council survived until 1922, and indeed enjoyed a form of afterlife in the shape of the privy council of Northern Ireland.[84] London was the administrative focal point for Scottish affairs until the reforms of the 1920s and 1930s, and the creation of St Andrew's House: Dublin, and in particular the Castle, were the administrative focuses of British rule in Ireland. But here again the survival of distinctively Irish forms of rule and administration served, not as a safety valve for patriotic resentments, but often rather as catalysts to this separatist ardour. For here, too, were institutions which were in the hands, not of Irish Catholics, but rather Irish Protestants, or (worse) Englishmen. No Irish Catholic, and only one English Catholic (Viscount Fitzalan) held the Lord Lieutenancy under the union: no Catholic, Irish or otherwise, held the Chief Secretaryship in the same period. Barry O'Brien wrote in 1909 that 'the choice of an "Irish" Secretary has, for a hundred years, helped to a great extent to perpetuate the sentiment of international hostility. As a rule, he came among the people—a stranger and an enemy. He was ignorant of Irish history, Irish character, and Irish wants. He was indifferent to Irish claims. He had not a thought in common with the nation which he was sent to rule. In race, in religion, in interest, in feeling, in point of view, political aims and national aspirations, he was anti-Irish.'[85] Here again, therefore, distinctive Irish institutions which might have worked to ease the shock of Union were continuously in the hands of the 'enemy'.[86]

Nevertheless, the critical distinction between the two unions was not simply one of inclusivity: both unions were exclusive in particular ways, for both primarily addressed the needs of existing vested interests in their respective societies. The distinction between the Unions arose rather from the fact that the Scots combined social and economic exclusivity with a degree of spiritual and confessional embrace. The Scots union, from the start, was tied to the faith of the people.[87]

The Irish union could, in 1801, have been inclusive in this sense.[88] But it was ultimately the remorseless Protestant vision of Lord Clare which prevailed, rather than the more daring and imaginative statesmanship of Pitt and his key lieutenants. In practice, unionism and Ascendancy went hand-in-hand in 1801, and perhaps this was always likely to be the case, given the all-consuming fears generated by the 1798 Rising amongst parts of the governing elite. The Scots union had pointed to other possibilities, however; and Henry Dundas, as the leading Scots practitioner of union, had sought to bring (as he saw it) the happy experience of his homeland to the task of incorporating Ireland. But he and his 'Scotch metaphysics' were unable to persuade a truculent monarch and a terrified Ascendancy; and the consequences of this failure are with us still.

## C. Monarchy, union, and unionism

**Illustration C.1.** Sir William Allan, The visit of Queen Victoria and Prince Albert to Hawthornden, 14 September 1842. Courtesy of the Scottish National Portrait Gallery.

**Illustration C.2.** Victor Albert Prout, 'Mar Lodge: group in the doorway of the Smoking Room, including the Prince and Princess of Wales' (1863). Courtesy of the Scottish National Portrait Gallery.

HER MAJESTY WITH VISCOUNT BROOKEBOROUGH AT WHITLA HALL, BELFAST.

**Illustration C.3.** Elizabeth II and Viscount Brookeborough, c.1960 (postcard image). Private possession.

# PART II

# The survival of the Unions: overviews

# 5

# The survival of the Scots union, 1707–1997

The assimilation of our two countries has been achieved fairly completely in those spheres which affect all citizens of the United Kingdom in much the same way—defence, social services and insurance, assistance and pensions, the Post Office, transport, aviation, trade and supply. In these activities and the legislation of these departments there is no such distinction as Scots or English—to them we are all citizens of the United Kingdom. Arthur Woodburn, former Secretary of State for Scotland (*Evening News*, 16 January 1952)

I have known a member of the House of Commons speak with great energy and precision, without being able to engage attention, because his observations were made in the Scotch dialect, which…certainly gives a clownish air even to sentiments of the greatest dignity and decorum. Tobias Smollett, *Humphry Clinker* (1771)

We can never be by instinct as tolerant as the English, as fair as the English, as forbearing as the English. We must make our special contribution from our special qualities—industry, fury, romance…change and crisis have formed our people. Walter Elliot, Rectorial Address, University of Aberdeen (1934)

## Introduction: the paradox of survival

The constitutional Union of 1707 was greeted with little popular ardour, and it remained unloved for many decades to come. The immediate consequences of the Treaty varied immensely throughout the regions and social structure of Scotland, but on the whole there was little to cheer: what boons there were tended to be socially and geographically constricted.[1] Established interests—landlords, others with capital such as the Darien investors—generally did well out of union, while (in the short-term, at any rate) many others suffered. On the whole, the union acted as a catalyst to forces which were already active in the Scots economy, rather than as the progenitor of the nation's subsequent economic woes. But for those struggling at the bottom of the social pyramid, this was an analytical distinction which made little real difference to the pain of everyday life in the new British state.

Union created a new British market place, new internal and colonial trading opportunities for Scots, and a shared currency, but it also brought heightened competition in certain sectors, and heightened taxation. The old, lightly taxed, lightly administered and impecunious Scottish administration was replaced with a relatively large and more vigorous and more burdensome (though also highly tight-fisted) British and Hanoverian successor; and amongst the immediate consequences was a plague of excisemen seeking to enforce heavier levies on a greater range of goods. A new level of malt tax (applicable with the end of the War) threatened the brewing industry, and the supply of cheap ale to the poor (the threat was activated in 1713, and again in 1724–1725). The impact of these higher taxes and a more energetic enforcement was immense: it helped to undermine a wide range of Scottish endeavours, as well as entrench a culture of evasion. Smuggling flourished, promoted frequently by otherwise regular merchants for whom the new impositions never acquired legitimacy; and indeed frequently the excisemen themselves were complicit in this scullduggery. The ubiquity of smuggling and of collusion was impressive, and economically significant, while of course undermining the authority of the new union state.[2]

The union state faced, indeed was threatened by, some fundamental problems in terms of its political culture. If one popular method of dealing with its impositions was smuggling and evasion, then another, related, form of expression lay with violent, head-on, confrontation; and indeed since the 1980s historians have increasingly moved away from characterizations of 18th-century Scotland as socially tranquil to emphasise the evidence for ongoing, if often low-level, disturbance.[3] In the 1720s and 1730s some sixty deaths occurred as a result of conflict over taxes: the most important and resonant of these episodes were the Malt Tax Riots, beginning in Hamilton and Glasgow in June 1725, and the Porteous Riot, which took place in Edinburgh's Grassmarket in April 1736. Both highly threatening affrays were related to popular contempt for the state's taxation policies, but each had a wider resonance. In 1725 popular protest was directed against a proposal to further raise the tax on malt, and quickly spread from Lanarkshire throughout much of the rest of Scotland (though the worst of the violence was in Glasgow). In 1736 disturbance was largely confined to Edinburgh, arose partly from the popular sympathy accorded to three convicted smugglers or tax evaders, and culminated in the lynching of John Porteous, the Captain of the Edinburgh City Guard.[4] One of the three popular convict heroes of 1736 was an Edinburgh merchant, Andrew Wilson, who—significantly—had robbed the customs house at Pittenweem in Fife. The Malt Tax Riots, and even the later Porteous lynching, illustrate the tenuous hold that the union state exercised at this time in 'North Britain'.[5] The Porteous affray exposed the weaknesses, not just of the Walpole government, but in particular of the Earl of Islay's regime in Scotland: Walpole moved, with Islay's effective acquiescence, to punish the City of Edinburgh, but was forced to climb down in the face of widespread opposition in Scotland—including from Islay's brother, the second Duke of Argyll.[6]

The other obvious popular challenge to the political culture, indeed survival, of the union state came from Jacobitism, and with the residual loyalties in Scotland to the old monarchy. Support for the deposed James VII and II, and his son, notionally James VIII and III after 1701, of course predated the attainment of the union; but the mounting unpopularity of the Treaty in the years immediately after its enactment fed into the Stuart cause. Jacobitism was concentrated in the Episcopalian clans and vestigial Catholicism of the Highlands; but immediately following the union it attracted considerable support in the Lowlands, and those areas economically damaged (or feeling themselves to be) by the Treaty. It has been calculated that, when the Jacobites rose in revolt in 1715, between thirty and forty per cent of their number were recruited from the Lowlands, and that—though Lowland Jacobitism was related to Episcopalian loyalties—economic distress and consequent antipathy for the union were also significant motivating factors:'the circumstances suggest that the decision of many Lowland Scots to take up arms in 1715 was a protest against the "unhappy union"'.[7] Jacobitism, the parallel monarchy, would remain a source of latent instability for the union and Hanoverian state until the mid 18th century, with a popular culture of defiance and opposition thriving in both Scotland and Ireland (indeed more thriving than that upholding the state—the Devil, in the form of the Stuarts, did in this case have the best tunes). As will be later outlined, one of the ultimate achievements of the Union state was its ability to embrace, tame, and neutralize the romance and culture of Jacobitism (by the 1990s the Secretary of State for Scotland worked from a desk in Dover House, Whitehall, which was overshadowed by a portrait of the Old Pretender).[8] But, for the moment, the compound of anti-unionist protest and Jacobitism represented a highly significant and combustible threat; and the extent of its potential seriousness is all too easy to miss, given the general fecklessness of its military command in 1715–1716.[9]

Part of the appeal of Jacobitism was, of course, that the Stuarts (their anglicized or continental manners and Catholicism notwithstanding) appeared authentically Scottish, while the union continued to cut across Scottish national sensitivities. It was not just that the Scots were slow to learn to be 'British', and that (to begin with) this process of education seemed to be more beset by penalties than inducements: it was also emphatically the case that the British parliament had not yet fully outgrown its immediate English ancestry. The problem from the beginning with the British, and (later) the United Kingdom state, not only lay with the tenacious influence of the Celtic nationalities, Scots, Irish, and Welsh, it also lay with the residual strength of English national feeling, particularly with regard to economic interest. Union had become, by 1707, an object of English policy because it promised to bring improved constitutional and military stability in the first instance for England (just as would be the case in 1801); but the price (granting equality to Scots economic interests), though fully understood, often proved difficult to pay. For years after 1707 Westminster's economic strategies and taxation policies recognized, not British, but rather English needs; and in the early years of union this was as much a threat to the stability of the new state as popular Scots patriotism or Jacobitism. Indeed, perhaps the fundamental problem with the union has been, not ineluctable Celtic patriotism, but rather the longevity of English national sensitivity: the English failure to fully buy into union has, because of their economic and demographic predominance, been a much more significant weakness for Britain and the United Kingdom than the complementary resistance of the Scots and Irish.

It was not just the passage of the union, then, but also its early formulation which deeply undermined or antagonized broad sections of Scots opinion. Little wonder, then, that (regardless of the complex realities), its architects entered popular historical mythology as Judas-like reprobates who had sold their patrimony for peerage, place, or pension. Indeed, like Judas, some of these planners of union swiftly and dismally recanted: in 1713

James Ogilvy, fourth Earl of Findlater and first Earl of Seafield, and recently a staunch supporter of the union enterprise was one of those Scottish peers who narrowly failed (by four votes) to obtain a repeal of the union in the British House of Lords.[10] Guilt or apprehension hung over others: Sir John Clerk of Penicuik, one of the Scots commissioners for union in 1706, famously wrote a memoir of the union in 1730, but as an act of catharsis or expiation, and in defensive rather than celebratory vein.[11] Yet others, disappointed both in personal as well as national terms, rediscovered the allure of the Stuarts: John Erskine, 22nd Earl of Mar, like Clerk of Penicuik a commissioner for union, and an initial supporter of the settlement, graduated into Jacobitism and rebellion in 1715.[12]

There can also be no great surprise that, given the early history of union, there was popular anger, physical violence, and popular revolt: nor, given this history, can there be much surprise that there was dismay, guilt, and recantation amongst the original supporters of union. The surprise is rather that, given these unpropitious origins, and given the tenacity of Jacobite readings of the politics of 1705–1707, the Anglo-Scots union, and its offspring, Great Britain, should have lasted: both of course, in however shaky a condition, are with us still. It is no less remarkable that, with all of this, Scotland should have remained tied to Westminster and without a national parliament from the time of union to the restoration of 1997.

As has been observed, the political historiography of modern Scotland, like its Irish counterpart, often seems much more concerned with illuminating the making of the union, as well as those national forces tending towards its unmaking, than with its obvious longevity. This appears to be particularly true now, in the early 21st century, when a combination of the Blair government's devolution settlement and the bicentenary of union appear to have stimulated ever greater scholarly interest in the loss of the original Scots parliament, in 1706–1707: monographs by Michael Fry (2006), Iain McLean and Alastair McMillan (2005), Allan Macinnes (2007), Christopher Whatley (2001, 2006), and edited collections by Tom Devine (2008) and Andrew Mackillop and Mícheál Ó Siochrú (2008) are amongst the most important expressions of this concern.[13] Indeed, it might further be argued that, just as there has been a significant recent efflorescence, so the wider historiography of the origins of the union is loosely related to the state of that great constitutional relationship, with periods of challenge or threat (however muted) tending to promote scholarly reassessment. Thus, the rapid rise in support for the Scottish National Party in the 1970s, and the debate around the devolution referendum (of 1979) were contemporaneous with important work on the origins of union by P.W.J. Riley (1978, 1979) and by William Ferguson (1977).[14] And, as has been outlined in an earlier chapter, the debate over the union associated with Irish Home Rule (and with the birth of the Scottish Home Rule cause) helped to stimulate critical work by (inter alia) James McKinnon (1896), G.W.T. Omond (1897), Robert Rait (1901), William Law Mathieson (1905), Peter Hume Brown (1907, 1914), A.V. Dicey and Robert Rait (1920).[15]

It is certainly true that this 'origins' literature (like its equivalent within Irish historiography) is coloured by different readings of the subsequent history of the union. There have, for example, been both essentially patriotic and unionist strains within the historiography: the former (increasingly influential and evident in the work of Fry (2006), Henderson Scott (1992, 1999, 2006), and Macinnes (2007)) has seen Union as a botched, imposed, and unequal deal, which reflected English national interests, and which ignored the vitality and complexity of Scotland's wider international connections and relationships.[16] Unionist, or Whig, readings (on the whole dominant in an older historiography) have seen the Union of 1707 as the inevitable and triumphant denouement to the economic and political coalescence of the two nations, and the necessary foundation for Scotland's subsequent successes: some of this scholarship, dating back to the 19th and early 20th centuries, has seen union as the constitutional complement to the supposedly profound racial and ethnic affinities connecting the English and Scottish peoples.[17] But neither celebrants nor critics have been principally concerned to explain the longevity of union (though there are admittedly rare exceptions to this broad rule, such as the work of Christopher Harvie).[18]

In sum, the history of 'British' Scotland has tended to be obscured by that of 'Scots' Scotland, just as the history of 'British' Ireland has little of the appeal of 'Irish' Ireland: the history of the Scots' repudiation of the British state (whether through Jacobitism, working class mobilization, or nationalism) has tended to overshadow the story of those Scots who ultimately bought into the union and British identity. Michael Fry has called the view that nationalism has been the most important 'thread' in modern Scots historiography 'misleading': he has argued that while Scotland's 'sense of identity persisted with surprising strength it was for nearly all that time [the past two centuries] quite overshadowed by British nationalism, the necessary consequence of a successful union'.[19] Richard Finlay has observed recently that 'it is well known that the Scots were said to have a "holy trinity" of education, law and church which acted as the main props of Scottish national identity. Yet it can also be said that monarchy, the armed forces and parliament acted as a [comparable] base of British identity in Scotland'. 'The former trinity', he has observed, 'has been studied more intensely...than the latter'.[20] In fact the same point might be applied to Irish historiography—namely that an emphasis on the evolution of nationalism and national consciousness has obscured the ways in which the British state embedded itself in 19th-century Irish society and culture.

The early history of union in both Scotland and Ireland was deeply unpropitious; yet in each nation (despite the omens of disaster) the union survived. In neither country does the historiography supply either adequate illumination on this apparent paradox, or adequate explanations for this survival. This chapter, and the next, seek to begin the task of explaining the longevity of the union state in Scotland and Ireland, by outlining some of the agencies, forces, and institutions which temporarily succeeded in upholding British rule and British identity.

## Terms of union (1): faith, money, and empire

The details of the 1707 union settlement partly explain its longevity, particularly in the light of the Irish experience in 1801. Though the Whig and unionist views of the Treaty were (in their extreme formulations) narrowly celebratory and historicist, and are now commonly dismissed, the commercial aspects of union certainly did help to fuel Scotland's economic growth from the middle of the 18th century. The origins of this growth are much debated, and multifaceted; but union retains a part (however diminished) in the explanatory argument. Moreover, as will be seen, while contemporary historians are now understandably contemptuous of Whiggish determinism, it would be a mistake to ignore the popularity and importance of such views for Victorian and later Scots (just as Irish historical revisionists are sometimes accused of mistakenly neglecting the independent force and significance of popular nationalist mythologies). Whig unionists may well have failed to recognize the stirrings of economic greatness in the years before 1707, or to value the breadth of Scotland's continental European cultural and economic connections, but (whatever its limitations) their creed was for a time ubiquitous and influential.

As outlined in the previous chapter, the Union of 1707 addressed the needs of critical established elements within Scots society, including landed and commercial interests, the Darien investors, those exercising heritable jurisdiction, and the royal burghs. However, there was no substantial cultural or religious tension between these privileged classes and the rest of society, such as characterized the gulf between the Irish Ascendancy interest and popular Catholic society in Ireland. The Union of 1707, therefore, may have favoured certain elites, but their legitimacy and Scottishness were not under sustained popular scrutiny. On the other hand, the Union of 1801 favoured elites, whose landed title was already being questioned at the time within popular Catholic historiography, and whose very Irishness would soon be repudiated (in the context of the fashioning of a primarily Catholic nationalism in the mid 19th century).

The Union of 1707 also effectively addressed (through the related 'Act for the Security of the Protestant Religion') the needs of the Kirk, in particular underwriting the Presbyterian governance of the Church of Scotland.[21] This mitigated some of the looming hostility to union which was emerging within the Church ('lykways the Prebiterian clergie discover themselves every day more and more to be against it', observed Viscount Dupplin in October 1706); and while it did not immediately convert Scots Presbyterians into enthusiastic unionists (some within the Covenanting tradition, particularly in the South West, remained bitterly opposed to the moral compromises implicit in union, and because it was apparently a breach of the Solemn League and Covenant), in the long-term the Kirk was won over.[22] The relationship between Presbyterianism and the new British state certainly continued to be uneasy: the Toleration Act of 1712 extended some (for many Presbyterians, unwanted) benefits to Scots Episcopalians, while the Patronage Act of the same year restored the rights of major landowners, or heritors, over the nomination of parish ministers (where formerly the wishes of the congregation had taken precedence). The patronage issue was particularly dangerous, since it effectively reopened that most difficult of the questions besetting the Kirk through the 17th century, namely the relationship between it and secular authority. However, the controversies and divisions surrounding patronage did not prevent the Kirk roundly welcoming the Hanoverian succession and the arrival of King George I in 1714. Indeed, it might even be ventured that the patronage question indirectly and unexpectedly bolstered the Kirk's connection to union, in so far as it long directed Scottish argument and energy into questions of Church rather than national governance: Scotsmen fought over the nature of their Presbyterianism for much longer than for their choice of monarch and royal house, although it is certainly true that much of the disputation concerned the relationship between the Church and the union state.[23] The late 19th-century Edinburgh historian, James Mackinnon, offered a version of this point in arguing that, certainly after the suppression of the 1745 Rising, 'the attention of Scotsmen centred in the contentions of ecclesiastical champions on the floor of the General Assembly rather than in the debates at Westminster. The displays of popular ecclesiastical orators took the place, in the estimation of the Scottish people, of those of the warring parties in the old national parliament'.[24] Moreover, as Callum Brown and others have argued, the influence of evangelical religion, felt in the Kirk from at least the 1740s, created critical inter-linkages between Scottish and English Protestantism, which in turn cemented notions of Britishness.[25] This, combined with the efforts of those (in the Scottish Society for the Promotion of Christian Knowledge, founded in 1709, and elsewhere) allied with the Kirk, evangelizing in the Highlands, and effectively countering both Rome and Jacobitism, served as bolsters to the union.

The contrast with the Irish union, and with Irish Catholicism, is clear. Irish Catholics were not incorporated within the Union of 1801, and indeed had been quietly encouraged to expect relief policies which, in the end, failed to materialize. Whatever else this signified, it did not mean that there was any inevitable or monolithic tension between the Catholic Church in Ireland and the British state: on the contrary, successive British governments in the 19th century were keen to co-opt the Church and its leaders in a range of policies, and primarily (from the 1860s) the war against Fenian 'terror', and the Church (for its part) was not unresponsive.[26] But the failure to tie union and Catholic interests together in 1801 unquestionably helped to destabilize the British state in Ireland, and to create a more unified and hostile Irish Catholic identity than would otherwise have been the case. While (to an extent) Scots Presbyterians were embraced by union, and then divided by some of its consequences, Irish Catholics were excluded and united. As with the Kirk, so with Irish Catholics, the question of outside secular influences on church government threatened to divide; but when versions of the patronage question arose in Ireland (there were repeated and controversial efforts to link Catholic 'emancipation' either to a royal veto over Episcopal nominations or to the official payment of clergy) Catholic Ireland united to keep the British state at bay. Indeed, Tom Bartlett has persuasively argued that 'in the [1808] veto controversy the [Irish] Catholic nation of the early 19th century found its voice'.[27] If the Treaty of 1707 ultimately strengthened the Scots union, by helping to divide acquiescent Presbyterians, then the Acts of 1801 weakened the Irish union, by helping to unify antagonistic Catholics.

Whatever the realities, whatever the complexities, the terms of union appeared to be critical to Scotland's economic success. The short-term economic impact of the Scots union was (as has been seen) on balance detrimental, with improvements in some trades (black cattle, grain) off-set by generally heavier taxation and competition. But from the mid 18th century onwards there was a massive surge towards industrialization and urban growth, focused primarily (but by no means exclusively) in the Central Belt and in Fife. In explaining this dramatic growth Tom Devine has emphasised Scotland's long traditions of developing overseas (as opposed to British and domestic) markets, the benefits of geology and geography (large scale coal and metal ore deposits), the availability of capital, a skilled and mobile labour force (for long acclimatized to economic migration), as well as a high standard of entrepreneurship. In this, influential, characterization, union was helpful and catalytic, but not the whole story: newly eased access to colonial markets unquestionably bolstered the developing re-export trades in tobacco and sugar, which were focused on Glasgow, and which also necessitated the development of new financial institutions, procedures, and techniques in that city.[28] The union delivered military and naval protection for Scots trade (in the shape of the new standing armies and the Royal Navy); and it made the spread and transfer of capital and technological innovation from the South easier than hitherto. But it did not create Scotland's international trading connections: nor did it create Scotland's transatlantic commerce, or Scottish entrepreneurial zeal, still less endow North Lanarkshire with iron-stone, or Ayrshire and the Lothians with coal streams. Moreover, as in Ireland, there was a real danger that a combination of union and the different histories of economic development in England and Scotland would have had blighting consequences for the latter: 'the new political integration might well have doomed Scotland to the status of an English economic satellite; a supplier of foods, raw materials and cheap labour for the more sophisticated southern economy, but with little possibility of achieving manufacturing growth and diversification in her own right'.[29]

For a short time after 1707, this looked set to be the legacy of union; but other influences intervened, and union became part of the meta-narrative of Scotland's success, rather than an explanation for subjugation and failure. Indeed, from the Victorian perspective, Scotland's economic efflorescence looked as if it was wholly founded upon union; and to some extent the subsequent economic health (or otherwise) of the nation has played a role in determining the balance of support for the union, as against the range of alternatives. Equally, from the Victorian perspective, eastern Ulster's economic growth looked as if it was wholly founded upon union; and the disaster of the Great Famine (1845–1851) played a decisive role in determining the spread of militant opposition to the connection with Britain.

If economic success was associated with union, then it was also promoted by the amalgamation of the Scottish and English currencies which occurred under the terms of the Treaty of 1707. As in Ireland, so in Scotland, one feature of the free trade associated with union was the elimination of the national currency and its supersession by a standardized British or United Kingdom equivalent. In both Ireland and Scotland distinctive local banknotes were retained, though not without a fight—led, for the Scots, in 1826 by Sir Walter Scott, writing in the *Edinburgh Weekly Journal* as Malachi Malagrowther. In Ireland the local pound (valued at slightly less than a pound sterling) was abandoned in 1826, and the last coins (before independence) prominently bearing the harp were struck in 1823. In Scotland the distinctive (if complex) local coinage was abandoned in 1707—turners, bodles, bawbees, merks, and pistoles—thereby often losing from everyday exchange coins which proudly bore the thistle, or the saltire, or the Thistle legend 'nemo me impune lacessit'. Some very limited and temporary compensation came with the respite granted to the Scottish mint at Edinburgh, which was briefly adapted to produce the new British coinage, and whose products were often proudly marked by an 'E', for its place of origin; but within two years of the union the Edinburgh mint had stopped functioning. Looking ahead, it was only with the accession of Edward VIII and II in 1936 that a distinctively Scottish coin was planned, and only with the accession of George VI that a distinctively Scottish coin was actually reintroduced, perhaps as a compliment to his Scots consort, Queen Elizabeth: between 1937 and 1970 half of the shillings in circulation in Britain bore the lion rampant of the Scottish royal crest.[30] On a related matter, the survival of the silver threepenny piece (until 1945) was credited to the particular enthusiasm of the Scots for this coin—although the Labour statesman, Thomas Johnston, also noted that the last (1937–1945) version of the coin, whose reverse bore a St George's shield and a Tudor rose, 'distressed' some patriots who wanted Scottish symbolism (Johnston 'personally was more interested in securing an added number of these silver pieces in Scots' pockets').[31]

This discussion of the economic terms of union might be briefly extended to suggest that, for the Scots (again, whatever the complex realities) union was linked with, and supported by, notions of economic modernization and Enlightenment. Aside from industrial and technological advance in the later 18th century, the union coincided with, and perhaps encouraged, a sometimes brutal agrarian 'modernization'—with the improvement and consolidation of lowland farms and the spread of sheep and clearances in the highlands. The union was also associated with (though it emphatically did not deliver) the Scots Enlightenment, with its greatest ornaments (including Adam Smith) defending the economic and cultural advances evidently guaranteed in 1707. These doyens of Enlightenment, in common with other compatriots, were content to see the retreat of the Gaelic and Scots tongues (and indeed the 'refinement' of Scots-English) in the interests of an economically advantageous standard English. Elocution was one of the minor growth industries of union, widely undertaken by Scots on the make under the tutelage of the likes of Thomas Sheridan (in 1761 Sheridan lectured on the English language to 300 eager Edinburgh students, after which an elocution society was formed).[32] Union was complemented by a single, increasingly standardized, national language (even if 'the vernacular was a long time a-dying').[33]

Intimately bound with the developing health of the Scots economy, and with the longevity of the union, was the issue of empire and imperial access. Union opened up opportunities for imperial service and the acquisition of colonial wealth; and it has been rightly said that 'war and empire ... were the means by which the union between Scotland and the rest of Great Britain was made real'.[34] In the early and mid 18th century a crisis has been detected within the fortunes of the middling gentry in Scotland, who had been buffeted by the ambitions of the major landowning interests as well as by the closure of various traditional roots for professional and financial advancement (such as service in continental European armies).[35] This crisis in the fortunes of the Scots' lairds was occurring at a time when the British East India Company was beginning an exponential growth, both in terms of its administrative as well as military needs. Moreover, a handful of strategically well-placed (and clannish) Scots within the ranks of the Company (notably one of its Directors between 1725 and 1742, John Drummond of Quarrell) served to facilitate the appointment and advance of their fellow-countrymen in India. Traditionally, Henry Dundas, 1st Viscount Melville, and the predominant figure in Scots politics (the 'King of Scotland') in the last quarter of the 18th century, has long been seen as the great patron of Scots within the empire; the Revd Sydney Smith remarked drily of Dundas that 'as long as he is in office, the Scotch may beget younger sons with perfect impunity. He sends them by loads to the East Indies, and all over the world'.[36] In fact recent arguments and evidence suggest that Warren Hastings, the first Governor General of British India (1773–1785), was at least as significant an upholder of the Scots interest there as Dundas.[37]

Either way, a combination of social pressures in Scotland, new opportunities for gain within the expanding British empire, and well-placed patrons, drove Scots recruitment to, particularly, the Indian empire. By the last quarter of the 18th century, it has been calculated that, though Scots numbered less than twenty per cent of the British population, they accounted for one third of the East India Company's officer corps, just under half of the elite 'writer' administrative class, and fully half of the Company's surgeons.[38] Warren Hastings' patronage of the Scots is suggested by the fact that, in the decade after his own appointment, forty-seven per cent of the 249 writers appointed to Bengal and sixty per cent of those permitted to practice in Bengal as free merchants were North Britons, albeit it 'almost all of them had Jacobite relations lurking in some cupboard'.[39] This disproportionate military, medical, administrative, and indeed mercantile influence was replicated within British North America and the Caribbean in the mid and late 18th century, and to some extent within southern Africa in the late 18th and 19th centuries.[40] The massive riches generated by many of these overseas, particularly Indian, Scots, were exported back to their homeland: here they facilitated the availability of capital, particularly (but not only) within the agrarian economy, where the purchase and improvement of estates was becoming *de rigueur* for returning and socially aspirant colonial administrators and traders. The profits of trade and industry in the Caribbean were substantially repatriated to Scotland, where recent research has pointed to a widespread and complex set of consequences: here, it is suggested, the profits of empire fed into the upward social mobility of the gentry class, the increasing 'coalescence' of the landed, industrial, and mercantile elites, and heightened Scottish influence within the politics of union and empire.[41] And, as John MacKenzie has emphasised, 'it was not just Indian nabobs who reinvested fortunes: South African money also came back'.[42]

Ireland participated in empire in the 18th century, but not at the same level of professional and political influence as the Scots. The explanations for this remain elusive, but some suggestions may be hazarded. Though Ireland is generally seen as the most restless of the three kingdoms of the British Isles, in the 18th century, certainly before the mid 1790s, it was Scotland which, by virtue of the Jacobite threat, was by far the greatest source of instability within the archipelago.[43] Tom Bartlett has pointed out that the migration of Scots to the north of Ireland in the early 18th century indicates the better prospects apparently offered by the Irish economy at that time.[44] Ireland was relatively settled after 1691, and (partly as a consequence) its economy was beginning to strengthen well before that of the Scots: Irish agricultural growth appears to have taken off after about 1740, pre-dating the consolidation of the Scots agrarian economy by around a quarter of a century. Perhaps in consequence no 'crisis' has yet been identified in the fortunes of the Irish gentry classes: this was certainly an age when the upkeep of landed status in both Ireland and Scotland was becoming ever more expensive, but it seems that the strength of the domestic agrarian economy may have supported the Irish, without recourse to the wealth of empire.

For most of the 18th century Ireland (unlike the Scots after 1707) did not have direct access to British colonial markets; and indeed between 1696 and 1731 'no goods of any kind could be landed in Ireland from the American plantations', though there was some subsequent relaxation in these legislative strictures, and one should not discount the impact of illicit trade.[45] Revisionist scholarship has demonstrated that Ireland was never wholly excluded from the Atlantic trade, but it is also clear that this trade generated only a relatively modest surplus in the forty years before the American War of Independence, and that it 'was dominated by English merchant houses, English intermediaries and English capital'.[46] Full, unfettered access to colonial markets was only acquired with the grant of 'free trade' to the Irish parliament in the settlement of 1779–1780, but did not result in any great commercial boom or redirection of Irish mercantile energy.[47]

The implications of all of this were dramatic. For the Scots, empire was simultaneously a benefit and a bulwark of the union: imperial access was facilitated by union, and in turn helped to underpin its popularity with the Scots elite. For the Irish, however, the picture was quite different. It was certainly the case that in the 18th century the Irish had some limited colonial trading linkages, which benefited in particular the linen and provisions trades; equally, the Irish had some access to lucrative colonial careers. The Derry man, Robert Cowan, Governor of Bombay (1729–1734), provides a rare example of the way in which the spoils of empire could fuel the upward trajectory into British and imperial politics of an ambitious Irish clan: Cowan left a fortune acquired in the service of the East India Company to his sister, Mary Cowan, who married into the rising Stewart family, ultimately Marquesses of Londonderry, and a force in British Conservative and Unionist politics for much of the 19th and early 20th centuries.

But, Cowan was the exception which demonstrated the broader rule— that despite spectacular individual careers, and despite some trading and professional opportunities, empire did not effect any wider sea-change in the Irish economy, still less in the social and political structure of 18th-century Ireland; and when Ireland was at last admitted to full trading rights within the empire (1779), and ultimately to the union (1801), its English and Scots rivals were far ahead in the race for imperial profit. As will be shown, the Irish (including Irish Catholics) exploited the professional and military opportunities presented by the expanding empire of the late 19th century with marked success; and some branches of the Irish economy, in particular Ulster shipbuilding and engineering, benefited from imperial access. But by the time that the socially aspirant gentry and middle classes of Ireland discovered the possibilities of imperial careers, they had lost some competitive advantage to the British. There is at present no evidence to suggest (despite individual cases, and whatever the impact upon Belfast) that the effect of repatriated imperial profits was anything like so profound or widespread in Ireland as in Scotland. Moreover, by the second half of the 19th century—it was too late for empire to act as the same kind of political or imaginative bolster for union as was the case in Scotland.

Ireland's comparative failure in the 18th century Empire, whatever its origins, helped to curtail (but not eliminate) the advance of popular imperial and unionist sympathies on the island, and not least because the Irish soon blamed their failure on the British themselves.[48] Moreover, Ireland's comparative failure in the 18th century empire helped to curtail social and economic opportunities for key social groupings—the younger sons of gentry and middlemen—who would eventually (by the 1790s) find an out-let for their ambitions and aspirations in revolutionary politics (there is a comparison to be made here between the redirection of thwarted ambitions into revolution in the 1790s and after 1916).[49] Scotland's success in the 18th and 19th century empire was such an important prop of union that the eventual disappearance of empire in the late 20th century was commonly seen as an inevitable precursor to the death of union itself.[50]

# Terms of union (2): political flexibility and accommodation

The terms of union also permitted an essential degree of malleability and flexibility within the new constitutional relationships: 'one of the most important characteristics of the Union is its inherent flexibility'.[51] This malleability stemmed in part from the incompleteness, indeed the patchwork quality, of union: (as has been seen) Scotland preserved its legal system, its royal burghs and their privileges, its heritable jurisdictions (until 1747), and (beyond the terms of the Treaty) its Presbyterian Church, its banking system, and its universities. This, allied with a relative English indifference towards not only the assimilation of the Scots (what the Edinburgh historian Richard Lodge called a 'contempt for symmetry'), but also (certainly for much of the 18th and 19th centuries) the government of Scotland more generally, gave plenty of scope for the survival of Scottish patriotic feeling.[52] The inconsistencies or ambiguities of union occasionally gave rise to crises (as over the appellate jurisdiction of the House of Lords in Scotland with the Greenshields case of 1711), but on the whole the looseness of the enterprise, and the relative subtlety and incremental quality of the attendant acculturation, may be seen as aiding its longevity.[53] As Lodge argued in 1907, the Scots' union was 'at its origin illogical, and will probably be illogical at the end. It may be well be that this is the secret of its success...[for] the Union has satisfied Scotland only because it has permitted the conservation of Scottish nationality'.[54]

In the 18th century, patriotic Scots generally defended their national institutions, not as part of an embryonic or nostalgic counter-state, but rather as levers by which— as individuals—they might enjoy full equality within the union: indeed James Livesey has gone further than this, locating the origins of civil society itself in the efforts of those within the 18th-century British Atlantic empire to accommodate their 'loss of citizenship' (and he has highlighted the distinction between the success of Scottish civil society in the later 18th century and the collapse of its Irish counterpart).[55] As in the 18th century, so in the 19th century, patriotic Scots were preoccupied by the issues of equity and justice within the union, and generally did not interpret their local or national institutions as being incompatible with ever greater commitment to the union.[56] By the midVictorian era (in contradistinction to Ireland), Scotland's 'historic' national institutions (the Law, the Kirk, the universities) were complemented by a distinctive Scottish civic culture, with a gamut of patriotically inclined voluntary associations, spanning philanthrophy, religion, science, literature, and commerce.[57] Mediating between this vibrant local culture and the relatively weak (though expanding) British state, were the politics of 'unionist nationalism'. 'Unionist nationalism'—the neologism has been coined by the urban historian, Graeme Morton—embodied a commitment to the union, and indeed an interest in closer union; but this was contingent upon patriotic fulfilment within local institutions and the continuing benefits (and 'light touch') of the union government.[58] The intrusion of the state, or perceived inequalities within the governance of the union, could give rise to patriotic protest, as with the National Association for theVindication of Scottish Rights in 1853; but the principal goal of such protest was not the repeal of the union, still less independence, but rather the more effective functioning of the union in the Scottish national interest. Scottish patriotic protest in the 19th century, therefore accepted the principle of union; but it was often opposed to innovations within its practice.

The Irish experience of union in the 19th century is relevant to the Scottish condition in several respects. Treated with appropriate caution, the phenomenon of 'unionist nationalism' is meaningful for the Irish, and perhaps more meaningful than has generally been understood within Irish historiography. Certainly before the Great Famine, mainstream Irish national politics, as defined (for instance) within the O'Connellite campaigns, were primarily about, not breaking with Great Britain, but rather making the union with Britain work more equitably for Catholic Ireland: this point will be explored at greater length in the next chapter. Moreover, if there were some symmetries between the priorities of patriotic politics in Scotland and Ireland, then the two were linked in another, more fundamental, way. Irish Catholic patriotism was partly driven by the recognition that the union of the early 19th century was skewed in the interests of the Ascendancy class. Scots patriotism in the 19th century, on the other hand, was driven partly by the view that the union was skewed in the interests of the Irish. Bodies such as the National Association, or the Scottish Home Rule Association (1886), were fired partly by discontent at the massive investment of legislative effort (and often cash) which was directed by the union government towards the settlement of Irish grievance and unrest. 'Unionist nationalism', therefore, was both shaped and energized by Irish protest.

The arguments surrounding 'unionist nationalism' have at least one further Irish resonance. A thriving civic culture in Scotland and a non-intrusive state helped to bolster the Anglo-Scots union, while state growth, intervention, and intrusion provided a spur to devolutionist sympathies. Applying this insight to Ireland, it might be suggested that the growth of the British state in late 19th-century Ireland, while partly accommodating ever greater numbers of Irish people, also tended to define and sharpen the divide between Irish patriotism and the Union of 1801.[59] As in Scotland, so in 19th-century Ireland, the growth and intrusiveness of the state tended (inter alia) to focus and mobilize popular patriotic protest—the difference between the two being that the Scots sought remedies in an improved union, where the post-Famine Irish increasingly looked to legislative (and eventually full) independence.

The terms of union were also, of course, fundamentally about the incorporation of Scots of all classes within a British (in reality a modified English) parliament, and what would eventually emerge as British politics: this was emphatically not a 'federative' union, such as had been favoured by the likes of Fletcher of Saltoun, but rather an 'incorporating' union. One aspect of the reconciliation of Scottish patriotism within the union state, and one further explanation for its longevity, was the gradual enmeshing and acculturation of Scots within its institutions and slowly evolving political culture. This was not, of course an immediate phenomenon; and indeed the instant imposition of 'British' politics in the aftermath of union would doubtless have provided an even greater revolutionary shock to the Scots than in fact was the case.

It has been said that 'Scotland enjoyed a state of "semi-independence" in the 18th century', part of this autonomy stemming from the range of national institutions guaranteed by the union.[60] This 'semi-independence', the separate and sometimes local management of much Scottish business, was possible because of the comparative lack of interest exhibited by Westminster in Scots affairs: English ministers possessed ultimate authority, but were prepared to delegate much of this to favoured Scots (there is an Irish, indeed an ongoing imperial, parallel here with the delegation of power from London to the great 'undertakers' of the mid 18th century).[61] After the axing of the Scottish Privy Council in 1708, and a period of (in every sense) indifferent government, from the mid 1720s Westminster ruled Scotland effectively by subcontracting power to a succession of magnates, the most prominent of whom where Archibald Campbell, first Earl of Islay and (after 1743) third Duke of Argyll (1682–1761) and Henry Dundas, first Viscount Melville (1742–1811). Argyll and Dundas dominated Scots politics for most of the 18th century (there was a hiatus between 1765 and 1780, when there was no Scottish 'manager' of the government's business): they were well integrated within the British political elite, and used their position to advance Scots interests, whether nationally or individually.[62] In the aftermath of the 1745 Rising, for example, when (despite the divisions within Scotland itself) English political opinion was in a recriminatory mood, 'Argyll's political clout and instinctive diplomacy prevented some [vindictive] excesses and modified others'.[63] After his appointment as Lord Advocate in 1775, Dundas famously built up an empire of patronage and politics which spanned Scotland, and was based on a firm control over the tiny Scottish electorate (2605 voters at the time of his death): Dundas subsequently used his Scottish base to launch himself upon a British and imperial career.[64] Each Scot had powerful English patrons—Sir Robert Walpole, in the case of Argyll, and William Pitt the Younger, in the case of Dundas.

Equally, Scottish representatives at Westminster were beginning to be embraced within the patronage networks of the British state in the aftermath of the 1745 Rising. Linda Colley has calculated that by 1780 more than half of Scottish members of parliament held official posts and salaries; and she has argued that even this striking figure omits those who benefited in other ways from the largesse of the state, whether through official pensions or supply contracts. In addition, there was an increasing army of Scots who were being recruited to sit for English constituencies, from where they could bid for official recognition with equal, or enhanced, persuasiveness.[65]

Of course there is a distinction to be made between the successful assimilation of individual Scots within the political elite, and popular English acceptance that this assimilation was a reasonable price to pay for the stability of the British state. The accession of John Stuart, third Earl of Bute, to the premiership in May 1762 illustrated the political possibilities opening up for ambitious Scotsmen, however 'elegant and ineffectual'; but, equally, the obloquy which Bute's short career generated, much of it directed against his Scottishness, and orchestrated by the populist English patriot, John Wilkes, indicated that the theory of union was not yet matched by adjustments in some popular English attitudes or practice.[66] Bute's career suggests the continuing limits to an inclusive 'British' politics, not least in terms of the sexual nature of much of the satire to which he was subjected: he was reputed to be bedding the Princess Dowager, George III's mother, much as Scots in general were held to be penetrating the British body politic.[67] Bute owed something of his political advance to royal patronage (he has been deemed the last prime minister who was advanced as a royal favourite, although Rosebery is also a contender for this accolade); and the popular antipathy which he inspired perhaps reflected wider popular suspicions of calculating Scottish servility. Indeed, much mid- and late-18th-century English satire and caricature was directed against, not just Bute, but the generically impecunious, thrusting, and grasping Scot, and the uncouth and servile Highlander. This satirical fury eventually eased when the Scots were finally accepted within the union, at the end of the 18th century, but they were swiftly succeeded by new recruits to union, the Irish, in English satirical thought and representation: 'the micks on the make' of mid-19th-century London superseded the 'jocks on the make' of a previous generation.[68] Linda Colley has argued that the virulence of mid-18th-century Scotophobia was at root 'testimony to the fact that the barriers between England and Scotland were coming down, savage proof that Scots were acquiring power and influence within Great Britain to a degree previously unknown': the later, mid-19th-century, virulence of anti-Irish comment may reflect popular English animus against Ireland's increasing dominance of the British political agenda, a case now of the Hibernian (rather than Caledonian) tail wagging the British dog.[69]

It has been suggested that the developing interlinkage of English and Scots politics in the 19th and 20th centuries should be contrasted with the 'otherness' of the Irish: 'from certain perspectives, English and Scottish politics in the 19th century were pretty fully meshed together—certainly compared to Ireland'.[70] One measure of this 'meshing' was the gradual incursion of Scots like Bute and Dundas into government, though this was certainly an incremental advance: in the half century after the death of Dundas (1811–1868), there were relatively few Scottish cabinet ministers, and only one Scottish prime minister (George Hamilton-Gordon, fourth Earl of Aberdeen, premier between 1852 and 1855). The argument has been made that, certainly in terms of elite politics, the apogee of Scottish domination came at the end of the 19th century and the early 20th century, between 1868 and 1935, when (for example) six of the eleven British prime ministers were Scottish by birth or origin (Gladstone, Rosebery, Balfour,

Campbell-Bannerman, Bonar Law, MacDonald): a seventh, Baldwin, was descended from highland stock through his mother, and identified strongly with a romanticized Scottish Toryism.[71] After the destruction in 1832 of the tiny electorates once manipulated by Dundas's Tory 'despotism', Liberalism dominated Victorian and Edwardian Scotland (though there was a temporary slump at the general elections of 1895 and 1900); and Scots Liberals, or Liberals representing Scottish constituencies, came to exercise a disproportionate influence, particularly evident in the years after 1906 with Sir Henry Campbell-Bannerman (MP for Stirling Burghs) as Prime Minister (1906–1908), and with H.H. Asquith (MP for East Fife) as his Chancellor and then successor (1908–1916): one third of Campbell-Bannerman's cabinet were Scots. Similarly, with the electoral consolidation of Scottish Unionism and Scottish Labour in the interwar years, Scots were well represented in government at this time: for example, contemporaries were impressed by the heavy Scottish presence in the reconstructed National Government of 1932, and some saw it indeed as an effective answer to the mounting call for Home Rule.[72]

Moreover, if Scots were coming to prominence within British government and politics at this time, then (as in the early years of union) Scots were also tasked with the challenge of administering their own country: Roland Quinault has observed that nine out of the ten Secretaries for Scotland appointed between 1886 and 1914 were Scottish, and the odd-man-out was Sir George Trevelyan who hailed from Northumberland, and who represented Hawick Burghs.[73] Indeed, with this Scots presence, and with David Lloyd George representing an effective conduit for Welsh influence within the British political elite, these years immediately before and after the First World War might be seen (perhaps counter-intuitively, given the Irish crisis) as the heyday of a particular, inclusive, type of British politics, and (more broadly) of the union itself.[74]

Scottish, certainly Scottish Unionist, representation at Westminster was strong, and seemingly well integrated within metropolitan political structures. The records of the Scottish Unionist Members' Committee survive, covering the years between 1932 and 1967; and they depict a well-disciplined body, which was taken seriously by ministers, and which served as a buffer between government and a wide range of Scottish interests.[75] When the Conservatives were in office, the Scottish Unionist Members' Committee was regularly briefed by the Secretary of State for Scotland or (at the very least) by one of the (increasingly numerous) Under Secretaries of State; and it regularly entertained deputations from a gamut of Scottish lobbying groups with interests in forthcoming legislation or otherwise with axes to grind. Honours were lavished on this body, and even relatively undistinguished veterans of the Committee could expect a knighthood (with hereditary honours for the more conspicuous). The integration of these members within the Westminster political elite was otherwise secure, as evidenced by the careers of Sir John Gilmour (MP successively for East Renfrew and Glasgow Pollok and Secretary and Secretary of State for Scotland (1924–1929), Minister of Agriculture (1931–1932), Home Secretary (1932–1935)) and of Walter Elliot (MP successively for Lanark, Kelvingrove, and Scottish Universities, and between 1931 and 1940 successively Financial Secretary to the Treasury, Minister for Agriculture, Secretary of State for Scotland, and Minister of Health). Both Gilmour and Elliot had strong and ongoing links with Ulster Unionism; and a prevailing fear amongst the Scottish Unionist MPs was that Home Rule for Scotland would bring the kind of eclipse and insignificance that Home Rule for Ulster had (in their perception) brought to Northern Ireland's MPs.

Elliot, it is true, also exemplifies some of the tacit limits to this Scottish integration, and some lingering subliminal Scotophobia or Celtic stereotyping within the English backbenches: the curmudgeonly English Conservative MP and diarist, Sir Cuthbert Headlam, tacitly endorsed the value of the 18th-century Scots' investment in elocution when he remarked of Elliot that 'I like him very much as a man, but I dislike listening to him speak—his Scottish (Glasgow) accent is jarring—he speaks far too fast —overflowing with verbosity—and I don't think that he is particularly effective'.[76] Headlam had earlier displayed similarly conflicting emotions in addressing Sir John Gilmour, newly appointed as Home Secretary in 1932: 'although as a patriotic Englishman I deeply resent a Scot being appointed Home Secretary, I am genuinely glad that you are the Scot...should you be wanting an Under Secretary, please think of me...'.[77] Unsurprisingly, Headlam's supplication failed, though he found an Under Secretaryship in the less prestigious Ministry of Transport.

At least two further comments might be made upon the issue of Scottish integration with British parliamentary politics. At a relatively innocuous level, this integration could have an implicit tweeness or condescension: Headlam's comments indicate one of the forms which this might take, but Scots themselves could buy into a certain limited view of Scottishness. For example, much of the surviving communication from Stanley Baldwin in the papers of Sir John Gilmour relates to Gilmour's annual gift to his leader, at Hogmanay, of a haggis.[78] More seriously (again, as hinted by Headlam's banter), the disproportionately strong presence of Scots in government has sometimes demonstrated, not so much the integrity of the union, as its effective limitations. The troubles of Gordon Brown's government, though complex in their origin, certainly gave rise to a degree of scotophobic comment and hostility.

What of the Irish, however? To what extent does this Scottish assimilation, and the intermeshing of Scottish and English politics, contrast with the condition of the Irish in the 19th and early 20th centuries? By the end of the 18th century both the Irish and Scots aristocracy were being bound, by marriage connections, property, and acculturation, within an emergent pan-British landed elite (though, as Julian Hoppit has recently warned, it would be an error to overlook tenacious, if fissiparous, national landed interests in Ireland and Scotland in the century after the Glorious Revolution).[79] In so far as many of the wealthiest magnates at the heart of 19th-century Whiggery and Conservatism possessed landed empires that embraced both England and Ireland (the Devonshires, Lansdownes, Westminsters), then Irish interests of a limited sort were vigorously defended at the most rarified levels of British politics. Some, essentially Irish, members of this pan-British ruling elite fought their way to ministerial politics and to the premiership; two of the three 'Irish' Prime Ministers of the 19th century, Arthur Wellesley, first Duke of Wellington, and Henry Temple, third Viscount Palmerston, were scions of the Ascendancy interest (while the third of this Irish trio, George Canning, was the son of an impoverished gentleman from Garvagh, County Londonderry). In the 20th century Andrew Bonar Law had an Ulster-born father, a Presbyterian minister, and James Callaghan had distant Irish Catholic roots.

But, while it would be wrong to ignore the informal influence of Irish landed interests within British elite politics, it is clear that Irish occupancy of ministerial office (when compared with Scotland, and making due allowance for the declining Irish population) was disproportionately slight. For example, Roland Quinault has made the point that, while the Scottish Secretaryship was generally the preserve of Scotsmen, the equivalent office in the Irish government—the Chief Secretaryship—was almost always held by an Englishman (Sir Arthur Wellesley, Lord Naas, Chichester Fortescue, and James Bryce, Irish-born, but effectively a Scot, were the only exceptions to this rule in the 'long' 19th-century of the union).[80] Indeed, this pattern of appointments to the Irish Office was long-standing, and was rooted in the

18th century: between 1782 and 1800, the years of Irish 'legislative independence', the Chief Secretaries were, bar one, English, and the odd-man-out (Robert Stewart, Lord Castlereagh) was deemed by Lord Cornwallis to be 'so very unlike an Irishman I think he has a clear claim to an exception in his favour'.[81]

Moreover, popular Irish Catholic and national feeling were at a relative disadvantage within the 19th-century British parliament and governments. 'Emancipation' came only in 1829, and only then under relatively restrictive conditions. Irish Catholics were never fully and successfully assimilated within the politics of the union state, though (as Daniel O'Connell's career suggests, and as the next chapter will argue) there were occasional and partly successful, efforts in this direction. But the essentially Protestant nature of the state, combined with the essentially oppositional politics of Irish Catholics in the post-Famine era, meant that few Catholics made it to ministerial office in the 19th or early 20th centuries (Thomas O'Hagan, first Lord O'Hagan, Lord Chancellor of Ireland, and Charles Russell, Lord Russell of Killowen, Attorney General and later Lord Chief Justice, both protégés of Gladstone, were exceptions that illustrated the broad rule). Ironically, the Blair governments (1997–2007) contained a better representation of the Irish Catholic tradition (in the forms of Ruth Kelly, Paul Murphy, and Claire Short) than their predecessors in the heyday of the union: here, as elsewhere, the British state was several steps behind the needs of its Irish Catholic citizens.

By way of contrast, it was not only the case that Scots were better integrated within the structures of union politics than the Irish: in particular, Scots Catholics were better integrated than their Irish counterparts. One critical agency for assimilation was the Labour tradition in Scotland, developing with the creation of the Scottish Labour Party in 1888, and that of the Independent Labour Party in 1893: indeed, the first two leaders of the ILP were the Scots James Keir Hardie (1856–1915) and John Bruce Glasier (1859–1920). Four of the first six leaders of the parliamentary Labour Party (1906) were Scots: Keir Hardie, Arthur Henderson (1863–1935), Ramsay MacDonald (1866–1937), and William Adamson (1863–1936). Although the Liberal Party was the predominant forum for working-class Scots representation until the First World War, Scots Catholics of Irish descent such as John Wheatley (1869–1930) and Patrick Dollan (1881–1963) came to prominence within the ILP and helped to realign their communities away from Liberalism and towards Labour. Wheatley was a founder of the

Catholic Socialist Society in 1906, 'which'—in the view of the ILP agitator and Aberdonian, John Paton, had been (despite the intense suspicions of the Scottish hierarchy) 'a powerful agency in bringing the Catholic vote to Labour': Paton later reported the testimony of 'a simple, unlettered Irish labourer in Lanarkshire', an adherent to the ILP, to the effect 'that we bowed to the [Catholic] Church in all things spiritual, but in matters temporal we are permitted to think for ourselves'.[82] Scottish Catholic support for Labour was rendered more meaningful by the extension of the franchise in 1918; it was focused by 'Red Clydeside', the Forty Hours Strike, and the Glasgow riots of January-February 1919, and was consolidated by popular bitterness at what was perceived as the Liberal party's bloody suppression of Catholic Ireland during the Irish Revolution (1916–1922). The votes of Scots of Irish descent were influential in delivering seats in the West of Scotland, and in ensuring Labour's electoral breakthrough in 1922 (although recent work on Glasgow Labour warns against any exaggerated, still less overly mechanistic, view of Catholic electoral influence): still, Wheatley's role in masterminding Labour's advance in Scotland was recognized by his appointment as Minister for Health in 1924, in the first MacDonald government.[83] Though formally committed to Home Rule until 1958, Labour remained an effective bolster of the union throughout the 20th century; and indeed at the end of the century, as at the beginning, Scots were disproportionately represented within its leadership (in the persons of, for example, Tony Blair, Gordon Brown, Douglas Alexander, Desmond Browne, Alastair Darling, John Reid). As has been said, however, this preponderance has to some extent illustrated not only the strengths, but also the limitations of union.

So, the terms of the Anglo-Scots union facilitated an agreed union between the political elites of the two nations, preserving a range of Scots institutions, apparently bolstering the Scots economy in the mid term (even if the realities were complex), and facilitating Scots access to the British empire, and to British ministerial politics. The predominant definition of Britishness was formulated in the wake of the union, partly around a shared Anglo-Scots Protestantism and a common sense of the French, and Catholic, Other. The Scots participated fully in the invention of this Britishness, and in the imperial and commercial expansion which was its concomitant in the later 18th century. If war, empire, and Protestantism helped to realize the union through the 18th century, then it is worth recalling that war, empire, and Protestantism had made union possible in the first place, in 1707.

But a critical challenge came of course in 1801, when Protestant Britain had to assimilate Catholic Ireland: William Pitt's response to this was, as has been noted, to bind the reimagining of the state to a redefinition of British identity, through linking a British-Irish union with Catholic relief. But the terms of the Acts which came into force in January 1801 offered no immediate 'emancipation', and thus the British state expanded, while the definition of its contingent identity remained the same.[84]

Britishness remained tied to Protestantism throughout much of the 19th century. In Scotland, after the First World War, Labour supplied one structure by which the majority of Scots, and particularly the majority of Scots Catholics, were accommodated within the union state. But in Ireland Labour was taking root at the same time as the consolidation of sectarian and constitutional divisions; and, rather than transcending and binding these divisions, Labour became their victim. In the 19th century there was no compensating political agency or conduit by which Irish Catholics could be propelled towards the centres of power, and fully embraced within the union. Successive Irish Catholic parties at Westminster served to mediate between their constituencies and government; but, while (with time) there was some softening of asperity, ultimately neither these parties nor their electors were ever thoroughly assimilated by the British state. Other agencies and institutions which invigorated Scotland's relationship with the union were certainly relevant to the Irish; but, as will become clear, while these promoted the rude health of the Anglo-Scots union, they merely postponed the demise of its British-Irish successor.

## Official landscapes

So far the longevity of the Anglo-Scots union has been examined, using the terms of the Treaty of 1707 as a starting point. Turning from those explanations for longevity which were partly rooted in the deal negotiated in 1707, from the economic and imperial access which was guaranteed, from the security to the Kirk which was underwritten (if subsequently undermined), it should be stressed that the Anglo-Scots union was bolstered by a range of key social and cultural agencies through the 18th and 19th centuries, as well as by several key institutions of the new British state. Indeed, the economy and empire can only ever really be partial explanations for 18th- and 19th-century Scotland's acceptance of union, in so far as the material benefits of

each enhanced a privileged elite within Scots society, but scarcely percolated down to the badly housed, underpaid, and ill-fed industrial class which
was emerging in the later 18th century. Other contextual explanations have
to be deployed to explain the wide acceptance of union, even amongst
those for whom the immediate material benefits were derisory.

Economic and infrastructural growth in the mid 18th century and after
not only created financial arguments for union: they also bolstered the union
in less direct and more subtle ways. The union was held together, indeed
made viable, by improved transportation and communication (and by
improved surveying and cartography).[85] The free trade guaranteed by union
only made full sense if easy transportation of goods and people were achiev-
able; and the economic (and military) fall-out from union included improved
roads, canals (in the mid and late 18th century), and eventually railways (from
the 1830s onwards). Under the Union of the Crowns James VI and I had
sought to improve communications and post between his two capitals,
London and Edinburgh; but it was only really after the 'incorporating' Union
of 1707 that not only the two capitals, but the two countries, were brought
together by easier communications.[86] The Jacobite threat was initially an
important stimulus; and in 1725 an Irishman, Major General George Wade
(1673-1748), was commissioned to upgrade the road networks in Scotland.
Wade eventually completed some 250 miles of road and forty bridges, bringing much of the central Highlands into closer communication with
Edinburgh and the South. With the collapse of the Jacobite threat after 1746
economic pressures came to provide the major spur towards improved transportation. The Forth and Clyde Canal (1768-1790) in conjunction with the
Union Canal (1818-1822) linked Scotland's two largest cities, Glasgow and
Edinburgh, and permitted easy access between its two principal maritime
trade routes—the Firth of Clyde opening out into the North Atlantic, and
the Firth of Forth spilling into the North Sea. Thomas Telford (1757-1834), a
Scot from (significantly) the Borders, applied engineering skills throughout
Britain, but was particularly active in his homeland: here he devised a grand
plan to further open the Highlands, with the construction of 920 miles of
roadway and the building of the Caledonian Canal along the Great Glen,
linking the north east and western coasts of Scotland. There is indeed a sense
in which the Highlands effectively joined the British state as a consequence
of this intensive engineering activity. There is also, perhaps, a sense in which
Telford, whose work also greatly improved communications between London
and Dublin, can be regarded as one of the great facilitators of union.

The union was also effectively forged with the interlacing of rail networks between Scotland and England. After the opening of Caledonian Railways mainline between Glasgow and London in 1848, it was possible to travel between those two cities in thirteen hours: beginning on 1 March 1848 a daily through train left London Euston at 9 am, arriving in Glasgow at 10 pm. Later that year, with the royal yacht fog-bound in the North Sea, Queen Victoria took the snap decision to travel by train from Montrose to London: 'that event', it has been said, '...may be taken as the moment when the railway became the normal means of long-distance travel in Britain'.[87] In 1860 the collaboration of three rail companies, the North British, the North Eastern, and the Great Northern, in the 'East Coast Joint Stock' initiative created the possibility of an express route connecting Edinburgh and London; and indeed this service was put in place in June 1862, prefiguring the 'Flying Scotsman' trains of the 1870s and afterwards. By 1901 the Scottish unionist historian, R.S. Rait, observed that 'it might in fact be said that the force of steam has accomplished what law has failed to do, and that the real incorporation of Scotland with England dates from the introduction of the railways'.[88]

These express connections, in conjunction with improvements in the postal service (the universal penny post was, famously, established in 1840) were in effect the consummation of James VI and I's halting efforts to realize a vision of an interconnected and intercommunicating Britain.[89] But these connections were also made possible by union—through the accessibility of capital, and through economies of scale. The former Labour Secretary of State for Scotland, Arthur Woodburn, recalled that when, after the First World War, the Minister of Transport, Eric Geddes, proposed a separate and independent railway concern for Scotland, the idea was abandoned in uproar, on account (partly) of the likely hikes in charges.[90]

Easier communications and transportation (and indeed surveying and cartography) simultaneously connected the English and Scots, but also extended the reach and strengthened the grasp of the union state. Improved map-making—William Roy's Military Survey of Scotland (1747–1755) is an important example—consolidated the military and administrative control of the British government. Moreover, Scots in the 18th and 19th centuries increasingly inhabited an environment which was almost always tinctured, and often dominated, by the symbolism and iconography of the union and its institutions. General Wade's roads and bridges were a direct physical manifestation of the power of the state in the furthest reaches of the Highlands;

and the forts that he built or renovated—Fort William, Fort Augustus, and particularly Fort George—simultaneously demonstrated the military strength of the union, while celebrating the Hanoverian monarchy. The acculturation of the Highlands within a British framework was increasingly accomplished after the defeat of the Jacobite cause in 1745–1746; and indeed it has long observed that this taming of the Highlands was so thorough that successive British monarchs in the 19th century could safely embrace aspects of (what had so recently been) its subversive culture—the kilt and tartanry (King George IV), the life of the 'Jacobite' laird (Queen Victoria at Balmoral after 1848). Victoria was also central to the process by which the Highlands were 'tamed' by tourism —the exponential growth of which in the late 19th century and interwar period popularized and validated a particular, romantic, vision of Scotland and Scottishness.[91]

The integration of Scottish highland landscapes within a united monarchy was complemented by the integration of Scottish lowland landscapes within the recreational culture of a unified British political elite. Improvements in the east coast rail service opened up not only the Scottish highlands, but also—closer at hand to London—the Scottish borders, and in particular the golfing landscapes of East Lothian. From the Gosford Estate at Longniddry, owned by the Earl of Wemyss, to the Balfours' Whittingehame estate at North Berwick there stretched out a succession of courses which presented a seemingly irresistible lure to the late Victorian and Edwardian political classes. It is absolutely clear from the archival record that, in the quarter century before the First World War, much business of empire was conducted from the golf links of East Lothian. Golf was, in fact, a cement of union.

Lest this assimilation appear incremental and consensual, it should be remembered that it was achieved after 1745 by military subjugation, and the bloody realization of the potential of Wade's forts and roads—by the widespread killing and expropriation of suspected Jacobites, by a 'burnt earth' strategy designed to break the spirit of Jacobite regions, and by a 'kulturkampf' against aspects of Highland society. The semi-feudal Gaelic communities of the Highlands, and the related clan system, were also being subverted by land clearances beginning in the mid 18th century, when (often) ancient crofting communities were removed to make way for sheep ranches. Against this, it should be remembered that the Highlands were not uniformly Jacobite, that the greatest clan of the territory was Hanoverian in loyalty (the Campbells), and that the Chief of the Clan at the time,

Archibald, third Duke of Argyll and first Earl of Islay, was simultaneously the government's manager in Scotland, and an influence for moderation on its anti-Jacobitism after 1746. Moreover, while their moral dimension is pretty clear-cut, the cultural complexity of the clearances is illustrated well by the fact that they were generally undertaken by anglicized clan leaders (or former leaders) who had now emerged as landlords in their own right, and who were determined to maximize their profits within the wider union economy, but with minimal regard for the attendant human cost. As has been noted, the major aristocratic landowners of Scotland were simultaneously amongst the greatest political and economic beneficiaries of union—and amongst its greatest supporters.[92]

However, the significance of this assimilation, both within its own terms, and in comparison with Ireland, is striking. In the 18th and 19th centuries the Highlands were simultaneously defined as the ultimate locus of Scottishness and effectively (if forcefully) embraced by the union state. By way of contrast, the far west of Ireland, in particular the western islands, were being defined at the same time as the *fons et origo* both of Irish national identity and (with the birth of the Irish National Land League) of the revolution against the union. It is certainly true that, from a particular metropolitan perspective, parts of the Highlands and Islands of Scotland were geographically and imaginatively as far removed from London as the most 'remote' part of the overseas empire: Lord Salisbury likened the Irish to 'Hottentots', but much less well known is the fact that he linked distress in the Outer Hebrides to a similarly (in his terms) derisive colonial analogy (Lord Lothian drily recorded Lord Salisbury's view 'that the [Hebridean] children should be allowed to run about naked, ignorant and as happy as New Guinea natives').[93] But this cynicism was momentary, related to the spread of 'uncivilized' agrarian unrest from Ireland into the Western Highlands. Salisbury notwithstanding, Scottishness was ultimately, and physically, located within the union, while authentic Irishness lay beyond.

The establishment of the union in the 18th and 19th centuries was not only accompanied (and eased by) roads and railways, it was also characterized by the urbanization of Scotland: urban Scotland largely emerged under the shadow of union. Between 1750 and 1800 the proportion of Scots living in towns doubled, while the proportion of English townspeople rose by only a quarter. By 1800 twenty per cent of the population lived in towns of over 5000 inhabitants, a proportion which ranked Scotland as third within the 'league of European urbanization': by 1861 this proportion had virtually doubled (to 39.4 per cent), while by 1901 it had risen to over fifty-seven per cent.[94] In the 1880s more Scots lived in towns than in the countryside. It has been said that, such were the established confines of towns in the early 18th century, a medieval Scot could have navigated himself around his home town if he had found himself transplanted to the time of the union.[95] By the early and mid 19th century the medieval Scot's chances of profound disorientation had risen dramatically, for Scotland's largest cities (Edinburgh, Glasgow, Aberdeen, and Dundee) were enjoying an exponential, and transforming, growth. By 1914 Glasgow's population had topped one million, while Edinburgh now boasted 400,000 inhabitants.

The fashioning of urban Scotland in the 18th and 19th centuries meant that ever larger numbers of Scots were corralled within essentially unionist townscapes—urban spaces where the commemoration or celebration of union was ubiquitous and inescapable. Urban Scots lived, worked, and shopped in streets whose names commemorated the union, the Hanoverian monarchy, or the political leaders of the union state: urban Scots lived in a culture where the memorials and statues celebrated the monarchy, or the heroes of Britain, its wars, and its empire.[96] In the 18th century the subjugation of Jacobitism brought the construction of military barracks which unambiguously embodied the strength and values of the state; but the spread of government at the end of the 19th and into the 20th centuries delivered similar, though more subtle, messages. Otherwise anonymous public buildings might bear a royal cypher, or other evidence of royal patronage: even post boxes, spreading from the late Victorian era, communicated the omnipresence of the union state and its imagery (George Orwell, after all, defined the elements of 'Englishness' as resting in 'solid breakfasts and gloomy Sundays, smoky towns and winding roads, green fields and red pillar boxes').[97]

Edinburgh has provided the clearest and most accessible illustration of the intrusion of the union state into the space inhabited by its citizens. It has been said that James Craig's New Town of Edinburgh (begun in the late 1760s) was a conscious celebration of British patriotism, 'and an assertion of Scotland's and the city's importance in the Union...the very heart of Scotland's capital was now a monument to its parity with England in loyal attachment to the House of Hanover'.[98] The New Town offered (in parallel) Princes Street, George Street, and Queen Street, bisected by Frederick Street and Hanover Street, and flanked by Charlotte Square and St. Andrew's Square (the patriotic connotations of the latter being mitigated by a colossal pillar bearing a statue of the arch-unionist Henry Dundas): all of this was rendered in a classical style which would have been familiar throughout contemporary Britain. Richard Rodger's work on 19th-century Edinburgh tracks a movement away from this austere classicism, the universal architectural idiom of the early union state, towards (in the second quarter of the century and after) a Caledonian reading of the gothic, in the form of the 'Scots baronial' style. The 'baronial' was partly an expression of 'a new confident Scottish nationality'; but it was also clearly (and safely) associated with Sir Walter Scott's unionist romanticism (his home at Abbotsford was an early example of the style), and with the patronage of Queen Victoria and Prince Albert and the rebuilt Balmoral.[99] The suburban Edinburgh fashioned in the 19th century did not celebrate, or evangelize, union as directly as the planners of the New Town; but if the decoration of the tenements sometimes included thistles or saltires, then it also intermingled thistles with English roses, and with polite allusions to the monarchy (just as Craig's New Town had 'Thistle Street' in parallel with 'Rose Street').[100] Moreover, if the New Town of the 1770s had its George Street and its Charlotte Square, then the suburbia of the 1870s offered its Queen's Crescent, its Peel Terrace, and (reflecting a shared British free trade liberalism), its Bright Crescent and Cobden Crescent. If the Georgian New Town had its monuments to William Pitt, George IV, and Henry Dundas, then the late Victorian suburbs had their post boxes, each emblazoned with the royal crown and the cypher of the Queen, and each modestly celebrating as well as realizing union.

Scots baronial was an assertion of patriotism, but within the context of union. It was a style also favoured in the North of Ireland, where architects such as Sir Charles Lanyon provided public buildings and private residences designed in this idiom to the Unionist elite of the province. Belfast Castle, completed by Lanyon's firm in 1870 for the third Marquess of Donegall, dominates the city's northern skyline and is a good example of the adaptation of the style within an Ulster Unionist environment. Equally, Colonel Edward Saunderson (1837–1906), effectively the first leader of Ulster Unionism, plotted the destruction of Charles Stewart Parnell and of Irish nationalism from his Scots baronial mansion, Castle Saunderson, in County Cavan (renovated in this style by Edward Blore in the 1830s).

# Monarchy

If the public space traversed by Scots was dominated by the monarchy, then this partly reflected the central significance of that institution in terms of the nation's relationship with union. The monarchy was one of several critical institutions (including the army and the welfare state) which successfully mediated between the Scots, Scottishness, and the union.

The Scots of the 17th and early 18th century, like the Irish, were monarchists: Scotland in general had not bought into the republican vision of a godly Commonwealth in the 1650s, while the Scottish origins of the Stuart dynasty gave the country an ongoing sense of (not always loving) proprietorship over the monarchy.[101] It is true, however, that the Britishness of the British monarchy in the later 17th century sometimes seemed questionable; and it is also true that, partly in consequence, Scotland's relationship with its (now) largely absentee monarchs grew increasingly attenuated and ambiguous.[102] James VI and I had famously promised to return to his Scottish kingdom every three years, but in the event only struggled back in 1617: Charles I, who succeeded his father in 1625, first managed to travel north for his Scots coronation in 1633 and did not deign to revisit until 1641. Charles II was the last king to be crowned in Scotland, in 1651, vowing never to return; and James VII and II was not even crowned as King of Scots. As Duke of York and Lord High Commissioner, between 1679 and 1681, James had at least held court in Edinburgh; and when he succeeded as king in 1685 it seemed for a fleeting moment that he would successfully restore the Scottish dimension of the united crown. James shrewdly sought to revive the ancient and noble Order of the Thistle in 1687 as a vehicle of policy, and he oversaw the installation at Holyrood of the 'the most significant dynastic paintings of the century', the 111 portraits of his royal ancestors, which had originally been commissioned by Charles II in 1684.[103] But James' Catholicism clearly presented problems; while his deposition lastingly destabilized the British monarchy, particularly in Scotland, where the parallel, Jacobite, claim came to have the greatest purchase.

The Joint Monarchy, with (another) Mary Stuart and William of Orange sharing the united throne of England and Scotland, helped to ease the acceptance of the 'Glorious Revolution' in Scotland, as did the legal guarantee in 1690 of the Kirk's Presbyterian governance. But, despite the historic cultural and economic interconnections between Scotland and the Netherlands, William II and III was ultimately unpopular amongst Scots, blamed for the massacre at Glencoe and for spoiling Scotland's chances of an overseas empire at Darien.

William's sister-in-law and successor, Anne, successfully sought to restore some of the mystique of kingship, was widely respected, and her portrait commonly displayed in Scotland. Anne's clear preference for an incorporating union was of enormous benefit to the success of that cause, and arguably reinvigorated that identification of the monarchy with union first delineated by James VI and I: such was her reputed leverage, it was believed that her public hostility towards the Jacobite opponents of union would have been worth 'more than an army of 10,000' in Scotland.[104] On her death the Hanoverian succession was clearly disputed (but not of course the principle of kingship); and, even then, George I's accession was popular in certain key sections of Scots society, not least within the ranks of the Kirk, to whom he had given his early support. Christopher Whatley has observed that portraits of the King were distributed along the Borders in 1714, to ministers of the Kirk and others, in order to bolster Hanoverian loyalties and dispel Jacobitism.[105]

The Scots of the late 18th century, unlike (increasingly) the Irish, remained monarchists, even if (it has been suggested) Scottish historians still underestimate the significance of popular loyalism.[106] Where American and particularly French republican zeal strongly influenced the United Irish and Catholic Defender movements of the 1790s, and the massive insurgency of 1798, this zeal was proportionately much less influential within Scotland (though the United Scotsmen achieved some support in the western Central Belt).[107] George III, combining 'ritual splendour, an appearance of domesticity and ubiquity', has been seen as central to the evolution of Britishness in Scotland and elsewhere, and central too to the interconnecting of this evolving identity and monarchy.[108] The celebration of the King's birthday enjoyed a 'renaissance' at this time, with increasingly elaborate and complex popular ceremonial.[109] But, while George III eventually won the affections of Scots for his longevity, vulnerability, and professed 'Britishness', and for (however remotely) presiding over a sustained period of economic growth and military endeavour, his personal interest in, or engagement with, Scotland was slight.

It was rather his son, George IV, who was frequently credited with reinventing the relationship between the monarchy and the Scots (though some scholars have been keen to provide wider contexts).[110] George IV's celebrated public visit to Edinburgh in August 1822 was choreographed by Sir Walter Scott, who effectively linked the King with the ancient Scottish monarchy (through the parading of the rediscovered Honours of Scotland), and with Highland dress and culture (the mythic awfulness of the King's flesh-coloured tights, notwithstanding).[111] It is indeed easy to snigger, along with contemporaries, at the campness of the spectacle, or at the distance between reality and pretension (as signified by the tights, or by the hoist necessary to raise the corpulent King onto his luckless horse). But George's single-handed annexation of Scotland's heritage meant that the monarchy could, given a degree of care and sensitivity, act as a bridge between Scottish national identity and the union state: in a sense George became the personification of the 'unionist nationalism' which was to become such a central feature of Scottish political discourse. In any case, the significance of the visit for the national capital is impossible to dispute: George IV is commemorated in Edinburgh, as George III is not. There is no public statue of George III, where Sir Francis Chantry supplied an image of George IV, situated at the junction of Hanover Street and George Street. There is no thoroughfare specifically commemorating George III (George Street, though originally a compliment to George III, evolved as a generic allusion to the Hanoverians): Thomas Hamilton's George IV Bridge, completed in 1829, unambiguously celebrates the First Gentleman of Europe and the 'Chief of Chiefs'.

George IV's brief visit essayed the contours of the relationship which Queen Victoria established with Scotland and bequeathed to the 20th-century British monarchy. If George IV laid claim to the idea of the Highlands, then Victoria took physical possession at Balmoral. If George IV donned the kilt and sporran for a day, then Victoria permanently enshrouded the royal House of Saxe-Coburg-Gotha in tartan. If George IV politely attended a Church of Scotland service at St Giles's on 25 August 1822, then Victoria, Supreme Governor of the Church of England, actively established that complex ecclesiological duality which saw the sovereign of the union as simultaneously Episcopalian and Presbyterian (or rather alternatively Episcopalian and Presbyterian, depending upon geography). Where George IV toyed with the relics of the Stuart monarchy, Victoria emphasised the reality of her Stuart ancestry, and saw herself as embodying or incorporating a final reconciliation of the historic Anglo-Scots antagonism.[112]

Victoria famously relished Scotland and the Scots. She re-established the physical presence of the monarch in Scotland, using Holyrood House as her residence in the national capital after her first visit in 1842. As is well known, in 1852 she and Albert purchased a highland estate at Balmoral in Aberdeenshire, and subsequently lavished attention on a rebuilding programme: aided by the developing rail networks, both within Scotland and between North and South, the annual trip to Balmoral became an established feature of the royal itinerary, and remains so to this day (George IV had had to travel to Scotland by sea). It has been noted that these visits enabled many Scots to view their monarch for themselves; and frequently the halts on the progress north were given permanence through a commemorative plaque or inscription. The Queen's identification with the Stuart kings was often exposed in this way: the restoration of the murdered James III's tomb at Cambuskenneth, Stirling, was memorialized as being by 'Victoria, a descendant'.[113] Similarly, Victoria paid a sightseeing visit to Tantallon Castle in East Lothian in 1878, following in the footsteps of her besieging ancestors, James IV and James V, and left a memorial plaque to commemorate the occasion. She also quietly supported the restoration of other ancient royal edifices, including the 12th-century Chapel of Saint Margaret in Edinburgh Castle.[114] In addition, Victoria identified herself with Gaelic scholarship through subscribing to the campaign to endow the Chair of Celtic at the University of Edinburgh in 1882. She was captivated by the Scottish landscape, and rhapsodized on the beauty and simplicity of Grampian life in her *Leaves from our Journal in the Highlands* (1868) (which appears subsequently to have been one of the influences shaping Margaret Thatcher's equally skewed vision of Scotland).[115] When Albert died in 1861, Victoria famously found solace in the company of a Balmoral gillie John Brown, an intimacy which was allegedly formalized (following the prurient if improbable gossip of scandalized contemporaries) through a covert marriage solemnized by a Presbyterian divine. Victoria certainly came to identify with the Kirk, and took communion at Crathie Church (of Scotland) from 1873 onwards. This religious elision, together with Victoria's skilful emphasis on her Stuart ancestry, was of course highly popular, and helped to tie Scots patriotism both to the crown and to the union. Victoria, paradoxically, turned the anglocentric British monarchy of the Hanoverians into a Scottish monarchy, and thereby reinforced Caledonian loyalties both to the crown and to the union which it headed (see for example illustration C.1).

The relationship between the Irish people and the British crown has been the object of some significant recent scholarship, and will be addressed more fully in the next chapter. It is worth noting here, however, that Victoria's enthusiasm for Ireland was somewhat cooler than for the Scots: equally, this position was broadly reversed under her successor, Albert Edward, the Prince of Wales, and now Edward VII. Edward was (by the standards of his mother) a frequent visitor to Ireland, where he was thought to be sympathetic to Home Rule and to Catholicism, and where he was accordingly well-liked. His philandering reputation was unlikely to appeal to ascetic cultural nationalists, or to the Irish Catholic hierarchy; but the playboy image—his interest in women and horses—presented an accessible vision of monarchy to an Ireland otherwise unpersuaded by the apparent frigidity and aloofness of the English ruling classes. Edward's efforts to charm Ireland were not complemented by any similar exertion in Scotland; and indeed here the new King fell foul of an array of Scottish national sensitivities. Edward's louche image stood in sharp relief to his mother's evident piety and sobriety: Edward, in other words, was not likely to the object of much Calvinist devotion (see illustration C.2).[116]

But even his royal designation was against him in a Scottish context. Repudiating his father to the last, he chose not to employ his first given name, Albert, but to use his second, Edward: Prince Albert Edward, instead of providing the Scots and the English with their first King Albert, determined to offer both the English and the Scots a seventh King Edward. This was offensive to Scottish opinion on a number of levels, and rankled throughout the King's short reign. In the first instance, as Richard Finlay has pointed out, unionist opinion in Scotland at this time was highly sensitive to any creeping anglicization of the union, and in particular any disregard for Scottish history.[117] No king of Scotland had been called Edward, so the proper designation of the new monarch was Edward VII of England and I of Scotland, though (to the affront of patriots in the Young Scots and elsewhere) this formulation was never used.[118] Moreover, aside from the regnal number, Edward's choice of name could scarcely have caused greater offence in Scotland. They, like the Irish, were both historically literate and sensitive; and the new king's chosen name seemed to allude to the first King Edward of England, also known by his sobriquet as 'Hammer of the Scots'.

However, it is worth emphasising that the problem with King Edward I and VII was not universally felt in Scotland, and it was a primarily a difficulty with Edward rather than with kingship. Just as the English working classes (in the argument of Ross McKibbin) expected the monarchy to embody both a moral leadership as well as a political and class neutrality, so the Scots expected the crown to be both moral and (in a sense) above nationality.[119] Moreover, sections of Scots' patriotic opinion were not only intensely suspicious of English predominance within the union, but also jealous of any evidence of legislative favouritism towards the Irish (even if this last seemed, from the Irish nationalist perspective, to be a somewhat remote possibility). On all of these counts Edward failed the Scots.

The subsequent bond between Scotland and the monarchy improved, and in particular because another Prince Albert, George V's second son, who (until 1936) bore the title of Duke of York, married a Scot, Elizabeth Bowes-Lyon of Glamis, the daughter of Claude, fourteenth Earl of Strathmore: in May 1937 Albert and his consort were crowned as King George VI and Queen Elizabeth. The new Queen had a combination of qualities which were well suited to the service of the monarchy whether in Scotland or beyond: Andrew Roberts has emphasised her gift for public relations, and her Christian convictions, while quoting George VI's biographer, Sir John Wheeler-Bennett, who (unpersuaded by the Queen's saccharine manner) detected 'a small drop of arsenic in the centre of that marshmallow'.[120] Elizabeth's own (admittedly distant) connections with the Stuart monarchy served to reinforce the claims of the House of Windsor over the ancient crown of Scotland; and her roots helped to tie the British monarchy more generally to Scotland. Balmoral re-established its importance within the annual peregrinations of the Royal Family at this time. The tangible impact of Elizabeth even on the coinage of the United Kingdom has already been mentioned, with the advent of tens of millions of shilling (five pence) pieces in circulation, all bearing the Scottish royal coat of arms. Her own royal insignia, together with those of her husband, were applied to the facade of the new St Andrew's House at Calton Hill, Edinburgh, an unusual tribute to a queen consort, and undoubtedly a genuflection to her Scottish origins. With the death of George VI in 1952, Elizabeth, now designated as the Queen Mother, sought a Scottish summertime retreat, and acquired the Castle of Mey, the ancestral home of the Earls of Caithness, close to Thurso on the Pentland Firth. This continues to be visited by members of the Royal Family.[121]

Elizabeth II (or, correctly, Elizabeth I of Scotland and II of England) has enjoyed more mixed fortunes with Scottish public opinion—not least because the issue of the regnal number raised its head again when she succeeded to the throne in 1952 (indeed, Scottish Unionist MPs were so concerned about this issue that they petitioned the Postmaster General to omit the royal numeral on Scottish postboxes).[122] Scottish Unionists were also more generally nervous about the presentation of the monarchy in the context of acute national sensitivities: they fretted about the broadcasting of the coronation service to Scottish homes, and they were concerned 'over the fact that the Moderator of the Church of Scotland took no part in the Coronation Service'.[123] Some of these fears were allayed: the Postmaster General reported that there was a stock of 'George VI' postboxes in hand, which would be uncontroversially deployed (George VI of England was also, conveniently, George VI of Scotland); while the Moderator was (modestly) written into the Coronation ceremony by being given some lines, together with the task of presenting the Queen with a Bible.

In the longer term Holyrood House and Balmoral have continued in active usage under Elizabeth. Her consort, Philip, had been given the ducal title of 'Edinburgh' on his marriage in 1947; and was a visible and an energetic Chancellor of the University of Edinburgh between 1953 and his retirement in 2011. The Royal Family has maintained other Scottish educational linkages, with the Prince of Wales attending Gordonstoun School in Moray (1962–1967), and Prince William, the Duke of Cambridge, graduating from the University of St Andrews (in 2005). On the other hand, the monarchy has suffered troughs of unpopularity, with particular difficulties in the protracted aftermath of Diana Princess of Wales' death in August 1997 (which has been seen as a period of resurgence for English nationalism), and a nadir being plumbed in 2002 (when thirty-seven per cent of those polled by a leading Scots newspaper supported the idea of a republic and an elected president, as against thirty per cent supporting the retention of the monarchy).[124] Significantly, a prominent monarchist, Norman St John Stevas, Lord St John of Fawsley, dismissed this evident unpopularity by emphasising the essential Scottishness of the British monarchy, and its descent from the Stuarts—that is to say, by reactivating Victoria's achievement and claims.[125] The importance of the monarchy for Scots (despite pockets of opposition, and occasional low poll ratings) remains such that even the nationalist First Minister for Scotland, Alex Salmond, has been keen to emphasise his support for the institution, and for an ongoing 'union of the crowns'—and indeed 'the constitutional policy of the Scottish National Party... proposes 'Independence in Europe' for Scotland, but with a continuation of the shared British monarchy'.[126]

As in Ireland, so in Scotland the monarchy has been the 'fountainhead' of the honours system; and the complex array of titles and other forms of honorific recognition have been elements in the armoury of union. James VI and I famously lavished knighthoods and other honours on his succession to Elizabeth, his evident intention being to buy favour for the new 'union of the crowns'.[127] He also used the prestigious Order of the Garter 'as an integrative organisation', appointing eight Scots as knights; while (as has been mentioned) his grandson James VII and II revived the Order of the Thistle in 1687.[128] Some mention has been made of the deployment of honours— peerages, promotions in the peerage, and the award of the Order of the Thistle—at the time of the inauguration of union in 1707. But of course honours remained central to the maintenance and politics of union in the 19th and 20th centuries. Successive Scottish ministers recognized their importance in terms of bolstering loyalty; and successive ministers worried about Scotland's purchase within the system. Even a sometime Home Ruler such as Thomas Johnston, while serving as Secretary of State for Scotland, understood the importance of honours to individual Scottish citizens within the union. In a classic expression of unionist nationalism, Johnston was patriotically upset at (what he saw as) the underrepresentation of Scots within the wartime honours system: 'the Secretary of State has to cover Health, Home, Education and Agriculture, and one tenth of the population. But his allocation among the Honours List falls far below this. Very frequently his recommendations are turned down by some committee of senior civil servants'.[129] Even though the honours system has often served to strengthen, or at least to exemplify, the bonds between citizens, the monarchy, and the union, Scottish patriots and nationalists, here as elsewhere in the union, have sometimes sought to express their patriotism by rendering this agency of union more efficient and equitable. Thus, in an apparent paradox, the 'greatest living Scotsman', Sean Connery, was eventually granted a knighthood from Queen Elizabeth in 2000, after protracted suspicions that this honour from the British monarchy had been delayed because of Connery's professed nationalism. In August 2008 Alex Salmond, recognizing the power of these honours and of the monarchy, publicly championed the award of a knighthood for Chris Hoy, the Olympic cyclist.

As in Ireland, so in Scotland influential support for the Unionist cause in the Home Rule era tended to be rewarded: in 1890 Lord Lothian (Secretary for Scotland between 1887 and 1892) argued to Lord Salisbury that the proprietor of the *Scotsman*, J.R. Findlay, should be granted a baronetcy on account of 'the yeoman service [which] has been done by the *Scotsman* to the cause of the union, and how very strongly and efficiently the paper has supported the government': a baronetcy eventually came to the family, but to Findlay's son.[130] The ferocious India merchant, John Muir, was given a baronetcy in 1893, partly because of his service as Lord Provost of Glasgow, but also because he was one of the wealthiest and most influential Liberal Unionists in the West of Scotland at a time when the solidarity of the Unionist alliance was of paramount concern.[131] Similarly, the protracted services of the Cochran-Patrick family of Ayrshire to the Unionist cause were recognized by the award of the KBE to Neil Cochran-Patrick in 1934: Cochran-Patrick's father-in-law had been a Conservative MP for North Ayrshire (1880–1886) and Under Secretary for Scotland (1887–1892), while he himself had twice served as a Unionist parliamentary candidate (for Stirling and Roxburgh), as well as Secretary to the Scottish Unionist Party and convener of Ayrshire County Council.[132]

A related influence and concern was maintaining parity between the honours bestowed upon Englishmen and women and their Scots counterparts: the case was made to Lothian that a Professor Robertson, Dean of the Faculty of Procurators at Glasgow, should be knighted because that honour was enjoyed by both the Presidents of the Incorporated Law Agents of England and Ireland ('surely there is no reason for withholding the honour from Scotland?').[133] Similarly, the eighth Duke of Argyll argued to Lothian that Francis Powell, the President of the Royal Scottish Society of Watercolourists, should be knighted like his two counterparts, the presidents of the related English societies. As Argyll commented, 'there seems to be some feeling about it, and in these days of infectious separatism it is well to satisfy these national aspirations'.[134]

As in Ireland, so in Scotland individual honours were not just about politics and the constitution, but were also a matter of geography and community. Arguments for honours were frequently cast in terms both of the particular services of the individual as well as the wider feeling within the potential honorand's community. Thus, Lord Lothian recommended a knighthood for the efficient but personally awkward Henry Craik, Secretary of the Scottish Education Department, arguing that it would 'meet with universal approval in Scotland' (Craik was eventually given a KCB in 1897).[135] C.J. Pearson (later Solicitor General for Scotland, Lord Advocate, and a judge) was knighted in 1887, an honour which (in Lothian's opinion) 'will give satisfaction to the Church of Scotland', of which communion Pearson was a distinguished member.[136] The 13th Earl of Home sought a knighthood for the Unionist convener of Lanarkshire County Council,

Gavin Hamilton, secure in the knowledge that 'if an honour was bestowed on [...] Hamilton it would be welcomed by people of all opinions in Lanarkshire'.[137]

Compared with Ireland, the number of Scots (even Unionist lawyers) who directly petitioned for honours was few. One of the rare cases which survives amongst the papers of Scottish ministers concerns Matthew Walker, who, as Lord Provost of Glasgow (1923–1926), had reasonable expectations of a knighthood: these expectations looked set to be thwarted in December 1925, and Walker complained at length of the likely injury to his standing ('the seriousness of this to me in my official capacity, in my reputation, and in every other way, I am sure you will realise').[138] However, traces of a more thoroughly unreconstructed attitude towards the honours system remained in Scotland, as a letter from the seventh Duke of Buccleuch reveals. In 1935, shortly before his death, Buccleuch was trying to raise £100,000 to extend and improve the hospital at Dumfries, and he believed that he had located a potential donor: 'I am told there is a man...who will probably give £50,000 if he can get an honour, and you perhaps can tell me how to go about it. Personally I hate the idea and have never had anything to do with a subject like this; but if we can get £50,000 it is worth having and knighthoods are pretty common. What is the tariff for a knighthood or baronetage; perhaps there is no fixed sum, as there was in the time when Lloyd George was Prime Minister?'.[139]

More widely, the monarchy and its symbolism have been omnipresent for Scots. Landscapes and cityscapes were marked by commemorative plaques, statuary, and (at the very least) royal monograms: official buildings and post boxes bore the mark of the sovereign of the United Kingdom. Trains and ships carried the monarch's name, or royal or imperial allusions: the North British Locomotive Company of Glasgow built its 'Jubilee' class for London Midland and Scottish Railways between 1934 and 1936 (commemorating George V's silver jubilee in 1935), while the Clydebank shipbuilders, John Brown, launched the RMS Queen Mary in September 1934 and the RMS Queen Elizabeth in Glasgow in September 1938. The image of the monarch continues to be inescapable even in the home—on banknotes, coins and postage stamps, and on commemorative or celebratory tat (commemorative ceramics, advertising wares). Scottish citizens continue to be granted royal honours, and attend annual investitures at Holyrood House. Scottish soldiers swear allegiance to the monarch, frequently carry her monogram on their kit, and have her image on the campaign medals which they wear. This imagery is of course an insistent reminder of Britishness and Union.

Queen Victoria and Queen Elizabeth, The Queen Mother, each gave the monarchy a decisive Scottish colouring, and captured the loyalties of Scots patriots both to the crown and, secondarily, to the union state which it commanded. Indeed, in a sense, the malleability of the union, though significant, has been outstripped by the capacity of the monarchy for reinvention and survival. One critical way in which the monarchy has been supported rests with the fact that much of the officially endorsed commemorative culture of the United Kingdom focuses exclusively and directly on the crown, and not on the union: royal jubilees, anniversaries, and weddings have been, and are celebrated, but not union. For a time, of course, the success of the monarchy was interconnected with the success of the union, and thus celebration of the crown was, by implication, the celebration of union; but it now seems entirely possible that a reinvented crown will be able to survive the wreckage of the constitutional settlement that it originally sanctioned and indeed for a time embodied.

The future of an 'incorporating' union now seems shaky, while that of the Union of the Crowns seems rather more secure. Queen Victoria may well have ensured that the monarchy could not be salvaged from the debris of the union with Ireland; equally she may well have helped to save Scotland for the House of Windsor.

## Army, navy, and war

Monarchy was of course intimately associated with the armed forces; and these, in particular the Army, have been a critical bulwark of the union for Scots.[140] Between the Restoration and union Scotland possessed its own limited military establishment and a tiny navy; but these were bound to the service of the united monarchy.[141] The accession of William II and III in 1689 brought greater foreign military entanglement for both the Scots and English than had been the case for most of the 17th century (when of course civil, rather than overseas, conflict had been predominant); so in a sense the shared Anglo-Scots experience of war against France long prefigured the creation of a British army in 1707. Moreover, while it would be a mistake to exaggerate the sense of 'Britishness' which was produced by this cooperation, there can be little doubt that English and Scots soldiers were now united by a common endeavour, and shared service to the same monarch.[142] Just as the 'incorporating' union was inducted, as well as bolstered, by the united monarchy of 1603, so 'incorporation' was facilitated and ultimately strengthened by a tradition of Anglo-Scots military cooperation which predated 1707, but which was institutionalized through the Treaty of that year.

The Scottish navy numbered three ships before the Union of 1707; and indeed, since these were unable to offer any serious protection to Scottish trade, Scots commercial interests clearly needed the strength of the Royal Navy. But, if the weakness of the Scottish navy indirectly provided an argument for union, then it also meant that (as opposed to the Army) there was no sustained naval tradition which could feed into the new United Kingdom. Moreover, while recruitment to the Royal Navy was healthy throughout the 18th century, it was no more than proportionate to the Scots' population: there is no evidence (unlike the Army) of any surge of Highland recruitment after the 1745 Rising.[143] And, despite the influence of Dundas, Scotland supplied 1.22 naval officers for every 10,000 of its citizens during the French revolutionary and Napoleonic wars (1793–1815), a proportion almost exactly the same as in England (1.2 officers).[144] Scots certainly came to the fore in the naval struggle against France—in the shape of Charles Middleton, first Lord Barham (1726–1813), Adam Duncan, first Viscount Duncan of Camperdown (1731–1804), George Elphinstone, first Viscount Keith (1746–1823), and Thomas Cochrane, the 10th Earl of Dundonald (1775–1860).[145] But the Scots did not define British naval success, where they soon came to epitomize British and imperial military ferocity and heroism. Nor (given the proportions of Scots), can the Navy be represented as a particularly important mediator between Scotland and the union, while this argument can (and will) be made for the Army.

The creation of the British army, like that of the 'second' British empire in the 18th century, generated professional opportunities which different types of Scot seized with relish. As with the administrative class in the East India Company, so Scots came to exercise a disproportionately great significance within the officer caste of the British Army: by the middle of the 18th century one quarter of army officers were Scotsmen at a time when the population of Scotland was perhaps twelve per cent of that of Britain (there were around 1.26 million people in Scotland, and perhaps 7.5 million in England in the mid 18th century). This proportion remained steady for the rest of the century, though there were naturally variations depending upon the perceived prestige of particular regiments.[146] After the suppression of the 1745 Rising, Scots, Highlanders in particular, came to play a significant part within the British Army: Lord Barrington, later the Secretary at War, declared on the eve of the Seven Years' War in 1751 that 'I am for having always in our army as many Scottish soldiers as possible ... and of all Scottish soldiers I should choose to have and keep in our army as many Highlanders as possible'.[147] This eulogy was subsequently echoed by William Pitt the Elder, addressing the Commons: 'I sought for merit wherever it was to be found. I found it in the mountains of the North ... and a hardy and intrepid race of men. They served with fidelity as they fought with valour, and conquered for you in every part of the world'.[148] It has been remarked that, starting during the Seven Years' War, and accelerating during the American War of Independence, '[Highland] recruitment multiplied to extraordinary levels during the Napoleonic Wars': by this time it is possible that the Highlands were supplying some 74,000 men to the crown forces (excluding the navy) out of a total regional population of 300,000.[149]

Some caution has certainly been urged in interpreting the processes by which highlanders were converted into loyal servants of the Hanoverian monarchy: any crude picture of the regular army supplying an uncomplicated substitute for clanship, or an easy vehicle for Britishness, has been called into question. Recent scholarship has demonstrated that recruitment in the Highlands was energetically pursued by British governments largely uninformed about the collapse of clan society, and by landlords who treated recruitment as a complement to the economic exploitation of their properties: the volunteer units, as distinct from the regular army, effectively replicated the military environment of clanship 'by being particularly sensitive to agrarian needs and accommodating the ultimate priority of farming and the estate economy'.[150] A further complexity or paradox existed in so far as the mythology surrounding the recruitment of clansmen to the British army was being developed at precisely the time that the Highlands were being depopulated through eviction and other forms of clearance.[151]

Having said all this, from at least the mid 18th century Highlanders swiftly acquired a reputation for raw (if reckless) courage which was attested throughout the Peninsular War and at Waterloo (where the Royal North British Dragoons—later renamed the Scots Greys—fought heroically in the 'Union Brigade', a unit which brought together not only the Greys but also the English Royals and the Inniskilling Dragoon Guards): highlanders fought, too, in the Crimea (distinguishing themselves in the 'Heavy Brigade' and elsewhere), and—as recent research has emphasised—in the gamut of imperial conflicts through the 19th century, from the Indian 'Mutiny' (1857–1858) and the Ashantee War (1873–1874) to Dargai on the North West Frontier (1895) and Magersfontein and other battlefields of the South African War (1899–1902). The propagation of this image and reputation was decisively assisted in the mid 19th century by the Glaswegian, Sir Colin Campbell, first Lord Clyde (1792–1863), a hero of the Crimean War and Indian Mutiny, who favoured his Highland Brigade, and who was acutely sensitive to the demands of public relations.[152] Campbell's patronage of journalists and artists was partly self-serving; but he indirectly helped to encourage the popular image of the Highlander as the saviour of Britain and of empire. Elizabeth Thompson, Lady Butler, Catholic and Irish by adoption, was one of the most influential painters of Victorian British military prowess, famed for her celebrations of Highland as well as Irish valour on the battlefield.[153] This was also the age of cheap printing and cheap books; and the fame of Scottish and other military commanders was communicated through popular biographies (Campbell was celebrated in 'lives' by General Shadwell and by the Moray-born war correspondent, Archibald Forbes). Irish-born commanders (Hugh Gough, John Nicholson, Garnet Wolseley) were of course similarly beatified (and indeed, significantly, Gough was memorialized in a two-decker 'life' by one of the leading Scottish unionist intellectuals of the early 20th century, Robert Rait).[154]

Though (as will shortly be shown) there were national rivalries between the Scottish regimental units and their Irish counterparts, a combination of billeting and migration created some significant overlaps between the two national traditions of military service under the crown. This was particularly marked in the mid and late Victorian period with (for example) the 73rd (Perthshire) and 75th (Stirlingshire) regiments, where (it has been calculated) in 1872 the proportions of Irish NCOs and men were twenty-five per cent and thirty-five per cent respectively, while the proportions of Irish officers in the two units in the half century before 1872 were twenty-nine per cent and twenty-four per cent respectively.[155] Underlying these statistics were ongoing religious and political tensions, and indeed Diane Henderson has suggested that the possible 'Fenian leanings' of these two units explain why they were taken over, indeed 'consumed', by 'entirely loyal and primarily Protestant Scottish regiments' (the 42nd and 92nd) in the army reforms of 1881.[156] However, the force of geography and tradition was too strong to extinguish interconnections of this kind. During the First World War, the

6th Battalion, the Royal Highlanders (Black Watch) was distinguished by a very considerable Irish presence. Scots Catholics of Irish descent in the West served in large numbers (proportionately much higher than the figures for Ireland itself) and with distinction in the battalions of the Highland Light Infantry and Royal Scots Fusiliers, while Irish Protestants filtered into a wide array of Scots regiments.[157] The valour of these Scots was unquestioned, and may be illustrated by the example of the several of Irish descent from the West who won the Victorian Cross, or (at a more commonplace and representative level) by the likes of Sergeant John Doyle of the Special Reserve Battalion of the Scots Fusiliers, a Catholic from Tullamore in King's County, Ireland, who migrated to Hamilton in Lanarkshire and, serving in France in 1917, won the Distinguished Conduct Medal 'for conspicuous gallantry and devotion to duty. He maintained his position against very superior numbers of the enemy [and]....was very severely wounded'.[158]

Dorothy Sayers introduced her Galloway novel, *The Five Red Herrings* (1931), through chronicling a row between a Scotsman and an Englishman on the contribution of the Scots to the British Army during the First World War ('Campbell pointed out that all the big administrative posts in London were held by Scotsmen, that England had never succeeded in conquering Scotland, that if Scotland wanted Home Rule, then by God she would take it, that when certain specified English regiments had gone to pieces they had had to send for Scottish officers to control them, and that when any section of the front line had found itself in a tight place, its mind was at once relieved by knowing that the Jocks were on its left').[159] Campbell's rant is instructive in so far as it communicates a mixture of defensive pride both at the Scots' conquest of London, as well as their critical role within the British forces on the Western Front during the Great War (though it should be conceded that Walter Elliot, a twice decorated RAMC officer, and the most distinguished Scottish Unionist of the interwar years, was unpersuaded by Sayers' 'unfathomable' novel).[160] A similar Scottish patriotic pride was evinced by the Revd James Black of Edinburgh: addressing Scottish troops on their way to the Western Front, Black evoked the spectacle of 'a hundred thousand Englishmen at Bannockburn [who] laughed at the puny Scottish army; and yet that little army played with the legions of Edward as the November wind with the autumn leaves'.[161]

Some 688,000 Scots enlisted in the crown forces during the Great War. Scottish voluntary (non-conscript) recruitment to the Army was disproportionately strong (sixty-five per cent of the total as opposed to the English and Welsh figure of fifty-two per cent) and the casualty levels (some 85,000 names are recorded on the Scottish National War Memorial) were also relatively great (though the exact figures and proportions remain, as in Ireland, the subject of some scholarly disputation).[162] Once again, the Highlanders played a prominent and well-publicized role, successfully wooed by recruitment campaigns which emphasised 'an appeal to locality and past loyalties, and [to] a vestigial clan system'.[163] In practice, however, urban Scotland was critical: here there were the legendary 'Pals' Battalions', including the 16th Royal Scots—McCrae's Battalion (named after its founder, the Edinburgh merchant, Sir George McCrae), which famously included a contingent from the Heart of Midlothian Football Club.[164] Scotland also contributed fully to the general staff of the Army, including of course the Commander in Chief, Douglas Haig, first Earl Haig, a scion of the famous whisky distilling clan.

By the time of the Second World War some of the hybrid Scottish-Irish regimental identities had faded, with the waning of migration; though the broad cultural sympathies between the Scots and Irish meant that there remained numerous Irish soldiers in Scots regiments, some achieving great distinction (like Sergeant James Stephenson of the 1st Gordon Highlanders, who won the DCM at El Alamein in 1942, before meeting his death at the hands of a sniper in Normandy in 1944).[165] Stephenson, an Ulster Protestant from Ballykinler, County Down, served with the 51st Highland Division; and he is worth singling out since his individual circumstances serve to highlight some of the complexities of the impact of the Second World War upon Scottish politics and society. The 51st Highland Division was the single most significant vehicle for Scottish, especially highland, military identity during the War, broken at St Valéry, during the retreat to Dunkirk, in 1940, and then, having reformed, fighting across North Africa, Italy, and (in 1944–1945) in Normandy, northern France, and Germany. Scottish martial identity was certainly underpinned by the bloody experiences of the Division, but (equally certainly) not in any simplistic manner. As with Irish failures and losses during the Great War, so the highlanders' debacle at St Valéry was blamed upon the machinations of British politicians. Moreover, the War Office's subsequent decision that the kilt was not suitable for modern warfare provoked further anger within parts of the Division, and invoked memories of the oppression of highland culture in the years after Culloden. But, in reality, as the example of Stephenson suggests, 'it was not possible for the ranks of this famous Division to be populated exclusively, or even mainly, by highlanders'; and it was equally the case that the universal aspects of the experience of the Division, and of other Scots in military service, were probably no less significant than the distinctively Caledonian.[166] Again, therefore, the complexity of Scottish military experience during the Second World War, allied with the complexity of the Scottish military relationship with the Crown, precludes any simplistic characterization of the impact of the War upon political and national identities.

How, then, did this extended tradition of Scots military service, and warfare, influence the union? War in the 18th century and beyond has frequently been seen as one of the great bolsters of British identity and (thus) of the union state.[167] This indeed is a persuasive viewpoint, though (again) any overly reductionist description of the linkage between Scots, the Army, and the union (as indeed of the linkage between the Irish, the crown forces, and union) would also surely be mistaken.[168] The Army, like the monarchy, worked, not to suffocate Scottish national feeling, still less to impose a narrow supranational identity, but rather to contain it within the contexts of an expansive Britishness and union. The operation of this relationship, however, was not always easy.

Despite the British state's cultural assault on the Highlands in the aftermath of the '45 Rising, the Army provided a means by which Highlanders could simultaneously expiate their Jacobitism, while retaining the kilt and other accoutrements of the indigenous culture which were denied to those who spurned King George's Army. These Highland units possessed a strong territorial identity, often had Gaelic language regimental mottos, and were generally separated from their English counterparts by their adherence to Presbyterianism and the Kirk, sometimes indeed the Free Kirk (though there were also concentrations of Episcopalianism and Catholicism in parts of the Highlands). Accommodating this distinctiveness, the Army helped to broker a relationship between the Scottish military tradition and the union state. Moreover, with the accretion of time, battle honours, and heroes, this relationship acquired an independent strength and durability. As has been noted, Scots, particularly Highland, ferocity and valour became legendary; and (with the successful incorporation of Jacobitism by the British state) there was no military counterculture in Scotland. Irish military valour was scarcely less celebrated; but, unlike Scotland, the British state could not claim exclusive rights over the loyalties of Irish fighters (given the untameable legacy—the 'phoenix flame'—of republican insurgency from the 1790s).[169]

But even in Scotland there were some intractable difficulties. Irish and English units (as opposed to Scots) were frequently used to suppress domestic, food and religious, rioting in mid-19th-century Scotland, with (for example) the Irish and Inniskilling Fusiliers being deployed in this way throughout the 1840s: the purpose was to sidestep the possibility of divided loyalties, but the strategy also involved effectively deploying and enflaming rival national loyalties within the United Kingdom.[170] Recent work on the correspondence of Scottish soldiers in the Victorian army also reveals the extent to which national rivalries and sensitivities, far from being eliminated within an homogenous 'British' army, remained alive, and indeed were intrinsic to the politics of military command: Edward Spiers' work highlights Highland dissatisfaction at the praise lavished (by General Wolseley) upon Irish soldiers during the Egyptian and Sudanese campaigns of 1884–1885.[171] National (and class) antagonisms and condescension were not only a feature of 'Tommy Atkins's' lot—they also appear to have been part of the complex background to the suicide in 1903 of Major General Sir Hector MacDonald, a crofter's son from Dingwall, who rose from the ranks to become a hero of the late Victorian empire.[172] Dorothy Sayers' characterization of 'Campbell', while well tinctured with black humour, nevertheless illustrates that, even amidst the carnage of the Western Front, national antagonisms within the union forces could retain a cutting edge.

Moreover, despite the arguments linking Scots' embroilment in 18th-century warfare with British identity, their service in the First and Second World Wars has frequently been linked to the consolidation of Scottish nationalism.[173] The interwar years were certainly ones of Scottish cultural revival, as well as the formulation of modern Scottish nationalist politics: John MacCormick famously created the National Party of Scotland in 1928, which became the main partner in the coalition that created the Scottish National Party in 1934. A minor strain within the formulation of the SNP was provided by the Scottish Party, a ginger group which, originally calling themselves the 'Imperial Unionists', emerged from a split within the Cathcart branch of the Scottish Unionist Party in 1932.[174] These convulsions within Cathcart Unionism, allied with the marked electoral success of the wider party in the period, also in fact illustrate the vitality and complexity of Unionist identity after the Great War. Equally, while the Second World War served to consolidate the nationalism of the Convention (1942) and the Covenant

Association (1951), and to deliver Dr Robert McIntyre's SNP victory at Motherwell in April 1945, it also reaffirmed a Scottish patriotic identity which thrived within the parameters of Unionism. As is well known, Scottish Unionism achieved its electoral apogee in 1955, with fifty-one per cent of the national vote.[175]

If Scots' assimilation within the British Army was constricted both by their own cultural choices, as well as by the preconceptions, sometimes prejudices, of other Britons, then what of the Irish? The complexities of the Irish contribution to the British Army are addressed in the next chapter; but it is striking that irritation at the perceived favouritism shown by the union state towards the Irish should have characterized not only Scots political leaders (as with Lord Rosebery's patriotic resentments of Gladstonian Home Rule), but also the Scottish other ranks of the Army.[176] The union accommodated and negotiated not only historic Anglo-Scottish jealousies, but also resentments separating the Irish and the Scots.

But of course Gladstone, and his military protégé, Wolseley, in addressing popular Irish sensitivities were merely correcting, or compensating for, the past injustices experienced by Irish Catholics within the union state, and indeed its armed forces. Irish Catholics, like Highlanders, had been recruited to the British Army since the 18th century; but while Highlanders, retaining their distinctive identity, were broadly assimilated within a 'British' Army, the postponement of 'emancipation' was probably a critical barrier to the successful assimilation therein of Irish Catholics. The significance of this is underlined by the hugely disproportionate contribution of Irishmen to the British Army, particularly in the early 19th century (it has been pointed out that in 1830, the year after the 'emancipation' act, there were more Irishmen than Englishmen in the Army).[177] So, while the Army accommodated a wide range of Irish national symbols, including the harp and Gaelic mottos or war cries (the 87th (Irish Fusiliers) Regiment's 'faugh-a-ballagh', or 'fág an bealach', is a case in point), it ultimately served a state which was slow to grant Catholic civil liberties, and modify its own confessional embrace.

The British Army mediated between Scots, the monarchy, and the union: it helped to bind some of the Irish some of the time to the monarchy and the union. The Army, on balance, helped to prolong the Union of 1801; but (as with the other bolsters of union) it was a much less efficient mediator for the Irish than for the Scots (though see for example illustration D.1).

# The state

Thus far comment has focused upon the terms of union, the interrelationship between the union, communications and public space, and upon the
ways in which union was propagated through the Army, and by an ever-
more intrusive and visible monarchy. Connecting these themes is a larger
motif, namely the expansion of the British or the union state: David
Marquand, for example, has argued that 'the legitimacy, the authority, and
the efficacy of the British state were on a rising curve from around 1920 to
around 1950'.[178] It is to this 'rising curve' that the last section of this chapter
is devoted.

The expansion of the union state in the 19th, and particularly the 20th
centuries, has at least two interconnected dimensions which are relevant to
the theme of the longevity, or survival, of the union. Both of these dimensions involve a return here, at the end of the chapter, to the issues of finance
and prosperity which were sketched at its beginning. Firstly, the enlarged
state had an expanding tax base from the late 19th century onwards, and
increasing revenues to distribute throughout the United Kingdom: it was
therefore a more significant catalyst for national growth and prosperity than
formerly. The ways in which the tax revenues of the United Kingdom were
to be distributed through its constituent nations could provide discreet marginal advantage to some, and thereby consolidate local arguments for union.
Secondly, a comparatively large, centralized, and powerful state had a greater
capacity to generate official employment as well as to create uniform institutions binding the United Kingdom as a whole. Citizens in Scotland and
Ireland and Northern Ireland would from henceforth be connected more
closely (if not accommodated) within the union state either through work
or benefits. The corollary of these two observations, however, is that any
alteration in the size of the state, or of the employment and benefits which
it purveys, may well have a bearing on the arguments for union. And, as will
be shown, there is in fact an associated paradox—namely that those who
have often been keenest to reduce the dimensions of state employment and
welfarism have often been strongest in their professed unionism.

One critical aspect of the way in which an increasingly dominant British
state addressed the challenge of sustaining the union was through the formulae by which certain identifiable government funds were distributed
between the constituent nations of the United Kingdom. The formula

enunciated by the Unionist Chancellor of the Exchequer, George Joachim Goschen, in his budget of 1888, distributed tax receipts between England and Wales, Scotland and Ireland on the basis of an 80:11:9 division: as Iain McLean has observed, 'the ratio was arbitrary...but it served unionist state-craft for the succeeding eighty years'.[179] Although Scotland's proportion of the UK population, as well as its GDP, fell in the subsequent decades, the Goschen formula remained in place; and indeed, with Irish independence in 1921, the formula was recast to give Scotland not eleven per cent of the public spend, but rather (with the disappearance of the Irish claim on nine per cent) 11/80ths (i.e. 13.75 per cent). Under Stanley Baldwin, public spending in Scotland further exceeded the constraints nominally prescribed by the formula on the grounds that 'political unrest was [not] in the interests of the Union': Goschen had now become 'a device for quiet redistribution'.[180] The Goschen formula, allied with the eloquence of Scottish special plead-ing at the cabinet table in London (which will be discussed further in Chapter 7), provided the basis for an extended form of 'killing Home Rule by kindness': it also helped to provide what would become one of the criti-cal financial arguments in support of the union in the 20th century. With the relegation of arguments based upon a disproportionate share of the riches of empire and industrialization, Goschen effectively substituted an argument for union based upon Scotland's disproportionate share in the riches (such as they were) of the United Kingdom.

With the increasing likelihood of devolution in the late 1970s, the Goschen formula was partly replaced by a new algorithm, the Barnett for-mula, based now upon population: Barnett carved up new forms of United Kingdom expenditure on the basis of population proportions, but permit-ted existing expenditure commitments to continue on the basis of Goschen. Barnett was designed as a short-term mechanism or expedient, though it was recognized that its long-term impact would be to promote the conver-gence of expenditure across the United Kingdom, and to erode the national advantage enjoyed by (in particular) the Scots and Northern Irish. In fact, the overall impact of the mechanisms, given a now static Scottish popula-tion, has been to maintain relatively high levels of funding: the residual aspects of Goschen (allied with some continuing sense of Scotland's needs) continue to deliver well for the Scots, while Barnett applies a fiscal 'squeeze' in those areas where the formula is applied. The danger for proponents of the union, however, is that the marginal advantage which the Scots and Northern Irish continue to enjoy within the fiscal structures of the United

Kingdom will gradually disappear, as the long-term logic of Barnett plays itself out.

Turning from the distribution of cash to the distribution of benefits, from the larger fiscal and macroeconomic issues associated with the state to those of more directly individual concern, one clear expression of the union between England and Scotland (but not wholly between Britain and Ireland) was a shared emergent civil service. The Union of 1707 occurred in the context of relatively small English and Scots states; and the subsequent consolidation of the civil service, particularly in the later 19th and 20th centuries, therefore took place in the context of the union. The Union of 1801, however, left much of the evolving Irish bureaucracy in place; and its subsequent growth (as with so much else connected with the government of Ireland) bore a merely semi-detached relationship with the union.

For Scotland, the massive growth of the civil service in the later 19th century was essentially the growth of the union; and (as in Ireland) this promoted some patriotic disquiet which fed into movements such as the National Association for the Vindication of Scottish Rights (1853) and the Scottish Home Rule Association (1886)—bodies which, as has been noted, were at least partly motivated by anger at the dynamic condition of the union. This growth was certainly impressive. There were 16,000 British civil servants in 1854 (when the Scottish population was 2.89 millions), 100,000 civil servants in 1914 (when the Scots population was 4.76 millions), 424,000 civil servants in 1930 (4.84 millions), and a peak of 750,000 civil servants in 1975 (5.24 millions): that is to say, in the period between 1854 and 1975 the population of Scotland rose by a factor of 1.8, while the number of British civil servants increased by a factor of 46.9. Here, as in empire, were massive employment opportunities for Scots. Moreover, given the growth of administrative devolution to Scotland through the 20th century (the Scottish Office was moved in 1939 from London to St Andrew's House, Edinburgh), it was possible to serve the British state within a set of distinctively Scottish administrative contexts. And, even at the height of the Thatcherite assault on the public service, an astonishing number of Scots did so: in 1988 one third of Scots still worked either in local or central government.[181] A combination of administrative growth and administrative devolution was thus, for a time, a winning combination for union.[182]

But the expansion of the civil service affected many more Scots beyond those who received their weekly pay cheque from the union state: it was related to some of the phenomena already described, such as the intrusion of the union and of its monarchy into the public and private space occupied by the Scottish people. The General Post Office was a particularly ubiquitous and omnipresent component of the state; but, aside from its inescapable physical presence, which has already been briefly discussed, it is important for the present argument in at least three other respects. It was effectively the first nationalized industry, holding monopoly rights over virtually all of the evolving postal and electrical communications systems of the late 19th and early 20th centuries: mail, telegraphs, and telephones. In keeping with these rights, the GPO played a significant role in the emergence of radio and television broadcasting in the United Kingdom, being responsible for the charter of the British Broadcasting Corporation in 1927 (and also being responsible for the collection of license fees for wireless sets (from 1904) and for televisions (from 1946)). It was at the heart of the emerging welfare state, servicing the needs of the new National Insurance scheme (1911), and charged with the local disbursement of the gamut of entitlements, from pensions (1908) to unemployment benefit or 'the dole' (1911), family allowance (1946), and supplementary benefit (1966) (Scots, in comparison with their English and Welsh fellow citizens, were relatively dependent upon the old age pension).[183] Thus the GPO has provided a vital link between Scottish and all other British citizens and the union state, through its propagation of the iconography of union (stamps, postboxes, post offices), and its centrality in peoples' lives (in terms of money and communications). The GPO helped to hold the union together through providing a uniform postal and telegraph systems, and servicing a uniform system of benefits (and some taxes).[184]

The BBC, under the tutelage of the GPO, bolstered the union in a variety of ways. It was of course originally directed by John Reith, a Scot, whose conception of public service broadcasting naturally chimed with bourgeois Presbyterian sensibilities in his native land.[185] But the Corporation also effectively linked the components of the United Kingdom through providing a national news service and a spread of 'regional' programming. It also, originally, sought to unify not just in terms of content, but also in terms of style: the Corporation famously favoured 'received pronounciation', a generic form of middle class English designed to eliminate any damning trace of regional origins. Moreover the BBC for long paid little heed to the Gaelic languages of the constituent parts of the United Kingdom, effectively complementing the monoglot culture encouraged by the national school systems in Scotland and Ireland. The importance of the Corporation

to union is illustrated by the anger which it has inspired amongst nationalists, who (whether in terms of content, language, or accent) have perceived
anglocentricity in its operations.

The GPO and BBC were two great public bodies which were also binding institutions of the union; but the onset of nationalization created other
enterprises with a related, if lesser, impact. The great thrust towards nationalization occurred, of course, under the Attlee government after the Second
World War, building upon wartime industrial mobilization: between 1945
and 1951, the mines (1948), railways (1948), iron and steel production (1951),
were placed under public ownership. There were later nationalization ventures such as that of the British Shipbuilders Corporation in 1977. These
were all industries or services with a marked importance for Scots, particularly given the relative lack of industrial diversification in the 20th century:
mining and steel dominated the industrial landscape of the Central Belt,
while the significance of the railways in terms of the interlinkage of Scotland
and England, and indeed the accessibility of the Highlands, has already been
outlined. If the union had infiltrated public and residential space, then it
now came to dominate the workplace: the National Coal Board, or British
Coal, British Railways, British Gas, linked Scots to the British state and to
the Union as never before. As Walter Elliot, the leading ideologue of interwar Scottish Conservatism, quipped, 'for Scotland, nationalisation means
denationalisation'.[186] But the problem for Elliot's Conservatives was that the
corollary did not hold true: denationalization in fact would come to mean
'deunionization'.

With the rapid retreat of traditional Scottish industries in the interwar
period and in the 1970s, Scots' reliance upon the subventions supplied by
the state was disproportionately great. The creation, particularly in the post-
war years, of a uniform and universal system of health provision, education,
and benefits, was fundamentally about the attainment of social democracy;
but it also implicitly effected the consolidation of union. It is certainly true,
as Morrice McCrae has chronicled, that the National Health Service which
emerged in Scotland under Joseph Westwood, as Secretary of State, was in
some ways distinctive from its English and Welsh counterparts: the Scottish
variant had not only its own legislative nativity (the National Health Service
(Scotland) Act of 1947), but also some different points of origin, in particular the Report of the Cathcart Committee of 1936, and the experience of
the Highlands and Islands Medical Service, formed originally in 1913.[187]
But, as Iain McLean and Alastair McMillan have commented, 'the welfare

state was inherently Unionist…taken in conjunction with the tax system, they therefore represented a double redistribution from rich to poor. They redistributed resources from rich people to poor people. As people live in places, this also implied redistribution from rich places to poor places'.[188] British citizens from the west of Ulster to the North of Scotland, to the South West of England, enjoyed a broadly shared regime of support, administered by a complex and centralized state bureaucracy. The Unionist masters of Northern Ireland were certainly quick to grasp the constitutional implications of welfare reform: though Ulster Unionism was historically associated with Conservatism, the leaders of the movement in the late 1940s understood that (however unpalatable in some respects) importing the welfare state into Northern Ireland meant creating further social barriers between the North and the South of Ireland, and also copperfastening the support of the Protestant working classes for union. In Scotland the heyday of the welfare state was also the heyday of decolonization; and the acquisition of individual support helped to cushion the communal loss of imperial pride. At its height a thriving union removed an economic ceiling for some Scots; but, in the context of imperial decline, a surviving union has supplied them with an economic safety net.

It has sometimes been argued that, given the interconnections, the collapse of empire will precipitate (or, indeed, is precipitating) the collapse of union.[189] But recent scholarship has supplied the evidence for an alternative viewpoint: Paul Ward, in chronicling the lives of eight prominent 20th-century British unionist politicians, has argued that empire was merely tangential to their unionism, while Bernard Porter has downplayed the domestic implications of empire for modern Britain as a whole. Economic vulnerability subverted popular imperialism in Scotland: Walter Elliot observed in 1934 that nobody in Glasgow was interested 'in India. They are interested in what hope, if any, of work there is'.[190] David McCrone has stressed the importance of 'war and welfare' for the survival of the Scots union.[191] Scots also liked the Big State: when polled in 1983, forty-four per cent of British respondents favoured privatization—but the figure in Scotland was only twenty-five per cent.[192] In fact the union was more thoroughly dependent upon the expansion (and retreat) of the union state within the British Isles, than upon the retreat of the union state from empire. The union survived the liquidation of empire: but it is not altogether clear that it will survive the liquidation of the Big State. Here, yet again, Mrs Thatcher, apparently the most thoroughgoing of recent unionist prime ministers, may have inadvertently throttled the object of her constitutional desire.

## Conclusion: crises of expectation

The Anglo-Scots union has been a hardy organism. It has thrived on the strength of a great range of relationships and institutions, spreading its roots and its liabilities widely and intricately. It has, in its time, successfully attached Scottish patriotism to the broader British and union cause. It has provided a framework within which an effective and lasting British identity has emerged. The union has survived individual blows of devastating proportions: epically bloody wars, economic freefall, the dissolution of empire. This survival and longevity is ultimately to be explained by the diversity of its support.

And yet, at the beginning of the millennium, in the context of the first Scottish National Party administrations in Holyrood, the marmoreal permanence of the union was beginning to look weathered. Given all that has been said in this chapter, its concluding arguments are scarcely going to make the mistake of underestimating the durability of the union. But the evident vulnerability of union is also clearly explicable in terms of the preceding analysis.

Predictions of the fall of union based on monocausal explanations carry little weight, because the success of union cannot be explained monocausally. The union survived because of a complex array of forces, relationships, and institutions, and it has been stalling at the beginning of the 21st century partly because these individual forces, relationships, and institutions have all been failing simultaneously. The end of empire has certainly removed one of the motor forces of British identity, and weakened the union accordingly (though not in itself irretrievably). Similarly the end of British global economic ascendancy in the 19th century, and the final collapse of Scotland's Victorian industrial infrastructure in the interwar years, threatened, but did not overturn union. War has long been seen as a foundation of Britishness and union, and served as such in 1914–1918 and 1939–1945; but more recent conflicts, in particular the Iraq War (2003) have tended in fact to underline the chasm between Scottish public opinion and the union state. Indeed, the army, for long a link between Scottish patriotism and the union state, has also effectively served to alienate Scots: the amalgamation or disbanding of historic Scottish regiments from the 1960s has been a severe affront to Scots patriotism. The monarchy, once a key binding agent within the union, now seems at times like a relentless tragicomedy: the younger generation of royals (with the possible and potentially critical exception of the Duke of Cambridge) appear very far removed indeed from the concerns of the Scots and Scotland.

The integration of Scotland within Westminster, and the effective representation of Scots interests in London, for so long a lubricant of union, appeared to falter during the long years of Conservative government under Margaret Thatcher (1979–1990) and John Major (1990–1997). Devolution, installed by the Labour government in 1999, has also critically affected the ways in which Scottish national feeling is mediated within the union: the creation of a Scottish parliament has provided a key focus for patriotism far removed from the British state, while (arguably) overstretching the political and intellectual resources of the Scottish Labour movement, historically one of the great bulwarks of union. The concentration of Scots within the Gordon Brown government was actually therefore a threat to the union, because it denuded Labour benches at Holyrood of unionist talent, and provoked mild (but telling) Scotophobia among some English observers.

The union can, and has been able to, survive the individual failure of any of these forces and institutions; but it is the combination of failures that has caused the crisis of union at the beginning of the 21st century. Moreover, if the integrity of Britishness has been comprehensively challenged in these ways, then it has also been affected by the retreat, since the 1970s, of the British state. The reduction of the number of United Kingdom civil servants, the liquidation of nationalized 'British' industries and services, the logic of 'Barnett', and the paring back of welfare provision, have all been sanctioned by radical conservatives, who have simultaneously professed their devotion to the United Kingdom. In so doing, they may well have helped to break the union in Scotland. But, then, as Wilde famously remarked, 'all men kill the thing they love'.

There is, of course, another possibility. Conservative professions of support for union may have masked, and continue to mask, the love which (at least until lately) 'dare not speak its name': Little Englandism.

# D. The army and union

**Figure D.1.** King George V at Ballater, 1935. Copyright with the National Archives of Scotland AAA01084.

**Figure D.2.** Richard Simkin, 'Grenadier Company of the Royal Tyrone Regiment on guard at Dublin Castle, 1 January 1801, carrying the new Union colour flag for the first time' (1925). Courtesy of the Royal Inniskilling Fusiliers Museum, Enniskillen.

# 6

# The survival of the Irish union, 1800–1921

We are not used to thinking of the British and Irish example as a success... yet the different and equally valid teleology of the Act of Union of 1707 leads to a search for things which were right. The search for problems should not blot out the successes. The most remarkable success of the British and Irish union is that so many parts of it are still there. Conrad Russell, 'Composite Monarchies in Early Modern Europe', *Uniting the Kingdom? The Making of British History* (London, 1995)

Mr Gladstone said, just before the close of his speech, 'Do what you will with your steamers and your electrical telegraph, can you make the [St George's or North] Channel cease to exist, or to be as if it did not exist? These sixty miles of sea may appear but little; but I ask you, what are the twenty miles of sea between England and France?'... In the North of Ireland this language, as reported in the newspapers, was read with blank amazement. W.E. Gladstone, quoted in Thomas MacKnight, *Ulster as It is* (London, 1896), ii, p. 131

A hUachtaráin agus a chairde... Madam President, speaking here in Dublin Castle it is impossible to ignore the weight of history, as it was yesterday when you and I laid wreaths at the Garden of Remembrance ... Of course, the [British-Irish] relationship has not always been straightforward; nor has the record over the centuries been entirely benign. It is a sad and regrettable reality that through history our islands have experienced more than their fair share of heartache, turbulence and loss... To all those who have suffered as a consequence of our troubled past, I extend my sincere thoughts and deep sympathy. With the benefit of historical hindsight, we can all see things which we would wish had been done differently or not at all'. Queen Elizabeth II, Dublin Castle, 18 May 2011

I agree with Arthur [Balfour] who used to say that there were two things in the government of Ireland that he could not abide—the passage and the patronage. Gerald Balfour to Earl Cadogan, 19 September 1898 (House of Lords Record Office, Cadogan Papers, CAD 1398)

## Introduction: the paradox of survival

The constitutional Union of 1800 between Britain and Ireland was an extreme and rushed political formula. From the beginning it was a disappointment. It was conceived partly as a response to republican insurgency in Ireland (in 1798); but its life was characterized by ongoing militant and constitutional assaults. It is sometimes argued that 19th-century Ireland was the laboratory of British imperial statesmanship, with various policies being previewed there and applied elsewhere (for example, in Scotland or in India). If Ireland was indeed a laboratory for British statecraft, then the union came to be regarded by many as a volatile piece of political chemistry—an experiment (unlike partition) not to be repeated or exported.[1]

Louis Cullen, the patriarch of Irish social and economic history, has said that 'the Union has been little studied; its undoing on the other hand has been much debated'.[2] The union has been cast primarily as the grim prologue to Irish independence, or indeed, to the settlement in Northern Ireland which has been evolving since the early 1990s. This emphasis is not confined to popular readings of modern Irish history, but characterizes the wider and scholarly literature on the theme. The political historiography of the British-Irish relationship remains dominated by the Home Rule and revolutionary era; and it is hard to escape the impression that a good deal of Irish history writing still has, as its teleology, the settlements of the early 1920s, when the Irish Free State and Northern Ireland, Irish independence and partition, were each established. The British state in Ireland is generally important in this narrative only in so far as it failed.[3]

This is of course an entirely reasonable emphasis, given the lasting significance of the revolutionary and Ulster Unionist movements. The political historiography of 19th-century Ireland, like that of many other European countries which have struggled against dominant neighbours (including, as has been observed, that of the Scots), is naturally characterized by a concern with the processes of liberation, with the evolution of nationalism and of state-building.

But it is also characterized by an understated or embarrassed or unwritten history of collaboration, compromise, or political inertia. Moreover, the popular as well as scholarly appetite for literature on the hard men and women of Irish revolutionary and loyalist politics has outweighed any concern for accommodationist or centrist themes: while much lip-service is paid to peace-making in modern Ireland, and while (indeed) there has been some criticism of the 'sanitizing' implications of revisionist historiography within Ireland, there is still (for example) no sustained history of consensual politics on the island.[4] For entirely comprehensible reasons, the political historiography of modern Ireland and of the British-Irish relationship is skewed; and it is far from being exceptional in its imbalances and distortions.

But despite the reasonableness and comprehensibility, a paradox has emerged here—that historians have effectively dedicated themselves to explaining the death of a constitutional settlement, the union between Britain and Ireland, which (however debatable the quality or usefulness of its life) has lingered for a remarkable length of time: as Conrad Russell has observed, writing in 1995, 'the most remarkable success of the British and Irish union is that so many parts of it are still there'.[5] The union and its government were widely unpopular, were sometimes actively oppressive or evidently malevolent, and were periodically challenged; but they also survived, and Irish people worked around them, or accommodated themselves to them, or (in the case of the Unionists) became active supporters.[6]

The Union provided a constitutional framework for Ireland for 120 years, and has survived in a truncated form within Northern Ireland since 1920–1921. We know why the union ultimately failed the Irish people, and we have a detailed chronology and pathology of its death. But we still need to explain more directly why it survived for as long as it did. A similar challenge exists within Scottish historiography, as the previous chapter outlines; and indeed here (as in so many other respects) there are similarities between the historiographical contours of the two countries.

## Historiography: corruption and betrayal

The British-Irish union and its mode of passage were focuses of controversy throughout the 19th century, and many of Ireland's later ills were traced back with a crisp historicist logic to this great Fall. The old Irish parliament was, in much 19th-century nationalist exegesis, a prelapsarian golden age.

The Fall was of course defined not just by the loss of a parliamentary Eden, but also by the manner of that loss. In 1801 legislative independence was 'sold' not only for English gold, as had been apparently the case in 1707, but for English and Irish peerages. The Union of 1801, its survival and its management, and ultimately indeed the management of its retreat, owed

much to the controversial application of the British honours system. In fact
the sense of a corrupt bargain was shared both in early Irish and Scots' readings of their respective unions, being enshrined in work such as Lockhart's
*Memoirs* (1714) or (in the case of Ireland) Jonah Barrington's *Rise and Fall of
the Irish Nation* (1833)—with its famously expressive layering of subtitles
'A full Account of the Bribery and Corruption by which the union was
carried: the Family Histories of the Members who voted away the Irish
Parliament: with an extraordinary black List of the Titles, Places and Pensions
which they received for their corrupt Votes'.

Nineteenth- and early twentieth-century Irish nationalists stressed the
consequences of losing the parliament more than their Scots contemporaries. Just as the extent of Irish legislative independence in the years between
1782 and 1800 was frequently elaborated, so the loss of that independence
seemed unreasonably great.[7] Subsequent nationalists emphasised, too, the
baleful legacy of economic dependence and underdevelopment which the
union apparently bequeathed: 'the union and unionist economic policy
were…identified by generations of Irish patriots and nationalists as the
causes of Irish poverty'.[8] Again, there is an obvious comparison to be made
with Scotland, where (while the immediate economic benefits of empire
seemed unclear, and while there are certainly debates about the social spread
of the prosperity generated by the union and by empire) by the middle of
the 18th century the accepted reality of that wealth and enhancement
seemed clear enough. In Ireland, beyond Ulster and the North East, there
was no such acceptance: union did not bring the riches of empire, but rather
(in some early 20th-century readings) the economic shackles of British
colonialism.

The enshrining of these viewpoints owed much to the prevailing popular historical orthodoxies, which were dominated in Ireland (though not
monopolized) by patriotic historians and scholars or by others, like W.E.H.
Lecky, whose historical writing tended to affirm patriotic values, but whose
formal politics were unionist.[9] On the other hand, Scottish historiography
in the late 19th century and early 20th century (the work of Peter Hume
Brown, James Mackinnon, W.L. Mathieson, Robert Rait) tended, however
patriotic and critical, to emphasise the statesmanship embodied in the union,
rather than endorsing any particularly flattering portrayal of the pre-union
Scottish parliament (there was a slighter historical literature, contributed by
the likes of Charles Waddie, in the Home Rule interest).[10] It is well known
that the late 19th-century debate over Irish home rule generated a renewed

interest in Scottish home rule; but it is also the case that the debate over Irish home rule had an historiographical dimension, both in Ireland and Scotland, where a renewed Scots scholarly interest in 1707 was generated— scholarship which (unlike its Irish counterpart) was essentially unionist in sympathy and teleology. A critical point is perhaps that the sense of a corrupt bargain in both national literatures was eventually overshadowed in the Scottish case by the evidence of the good things apparently flowing from union. By 1907 Hume Brown, the Sir William Fraser Professor of Scottish History at the University of Edinburgh, in gathering together a stable of commentators on the centenary of the Anglo-Scots' union, could write that 'all the views expressed converge to one conclusion—that the Union was inevitable, and, at the same time, desirable'.[11]

Of course one key aspect of the British-Irish Union of 1801 was not so much what it did, but rather what it failed to do. Its principal architects, and particularly William Pitt, had conceived the measure as a means of extending and reinforcing the state and— more widely—of consolidating the government of the kingdom and of the empire. But this vision was compromised if the parliamentary union attained in 1801 did not lead to any fuller measure of integration (or, 'incorporation', to use the 'on-message' vocabulary of the time) between the kingdoms. Indeed, it has been said that 'almost by casual default, much of the system of government regarding Ireland [was] left untouched by the union, with the result that it continued to operate as a separate, at times separating, buffer between Britain and Ireland'.[12]

This vision was also spoilt if the new union did not actively seek to incorporate the wider Irish people. British and imperial stability in 1800 required union; and this in turn demanded a measure of civil relief or 'emancipation' for Catholics. The support of leading Catholics for union was crucial, therefore, and it was briefly achieved by 'making it implicitly understood that emancipation would follow union at some point'.[13] As is well known, Catholic hopes of relief were raised, and then dashed with equal speed. The union which was formulated on 1 January 1801 was not (as Pitt had envisioned) between Britain and Ireland, but rather (as the Irish viceroy, Lord Cornwallis feared) an unequal deal between Britain and 'a party in Ireland', the Irish Protestant elite.[14] The failure of emancipation meant that Catholics were not immediately incorporated into the new polity: it also meant that the union would be melded within a popular Irish historiographical reading of English perfidy, linked with the Treaty of Limerick and other examples of Anglo-Saxon treachery and unreliability. Historians widely accept that a significant opportunity to reform the British state in Ireland was wasted in the early 19th century, and in particular with the failure to combine union and emancipation.[15]

So, the British-Irish Union of 1800 was an audacious political stroke which, from the start, was riven with ambiguity and disappointed expectations. The Union of 1800 was designed for British and imperial purposes, and it was sold to the Irish Ascendancy using patronage and arguments which concerned, and sometimes scandalized contemporaries. Building a parliamentary majority for the union meant applying outrageously large sums from the secret service fund, and abandoning any pretence of accountability (to say nothing of legality).[16] The similarities with Scotland, and with unionist practice in 1706, in at least some of these respects are clear.

But, beyond this point, the analogies begin to fracture. The Anglo-Scots union (whatever its failings) was a considered arrangement, building on the dry-run of 1703 (to say nothing of earlier airings of the idea). The British-Irish union was essentially a rushed, perhaps even panicked, response to rebellion and war, though the precedent of 1707 was certainly an important point of reference: 'those who contrived the Union', declared Lord Redesdale in 1806, 'seem to have thought only of carrying that measure without considering how the machine was to work afterwards'.[17] The Anglo-Scots union was framed on the basis of a negotiated treaty (even if modern Scots patriots question the skills of the negotiators, or the equity of the framework within which they conducted their business). The British-Irish union was devised by Pitt and his inner circle, and was essentially imposed upon an initially resistant Irish political elite.

Even more critically, however, the Anglo-Scots union embraced and incorporated Scots Presbyterianism, while the British-Irish union ostensibly betrayed and marginalized Irish Catholics. The Treaty of 1707 constituted a bargain which (at least in the short term) addressed the sensitivities of the majority church, the Kirk: in the summary of James Mackinnon (writing in a highly patriotic but unionist vein in 1896) 'it guaranteed to the Scottish people the Presbyterian creed, worship, discipline and government'.[18] That is to say, it guaranteed to the Scots Kirk rights which were denied in 1801 to Irish Catholics. Irish Catholics felt accordingly deceived and exposed: promised a place in the sun, they were consigned lastingly to the shade of the Irish Protestant Ascendancy and of Westminster.

## Political flexibility and accommodation

Logically, given this complicated nativity, and given its apparent lack of historical legitimacy, the union of Great Britain and Ireland might indeed have been an immediate and complete failure. In fact one of the great paradoxes of modern British and Irish history is that (against the odds) the union provided a lasting, if clearly vitiated, constitutional settlement. The union remained in place for all of Ireland until the ratification of the Anglo-Irish Treaty in 1922. Ulster Unionists have argued that the union enjoyed an afterlife: they have seen the survival of Northern Ireland within the United Kingdom as the last vestige of Pitt's constitutional architecture, and have argued that Northern Ireland's position within the United Kingdom depends still upon the (unrepealed) Act of Union of 1801. This is why the Government of Ireland Act (1920), the measure which partitioned Ireland, was axed in 1998 without serious Unionist complaint: Unionists did not, ultimately, choose to see this as their foundation charter.[19] The Partition Act has gone, but the Act of Union remains in place. How, then, is this survival to be explained?

The longevity of the Scots union is sometimes linked to the 'modernization' of Scots society and politics, with the incomplete or 'illogical' nature of the incorporation of 1707, and with the survival of a distinctive Scottish local and civic culture: Richard Lodge argued that the Scots' union was 'at its origin illogical, and will probably be illogical at the end. It may be well be that this is the secret of its success'.[20] While the embedding of the union in Ireland may (like its Scots equivalent) be viewed as an expression of the 'modernization' of 19th-century Britain, there are also ways in which the union depended partly for its survival on the pre-modern and localized condition of Irish politics at this time. There is some implicit tension in the existing literature over the timing of the development of national politics in Ireland, with attention being paid by scholars such as Tom Bartlett to the development of civil society and the public sphere in late 18th-century Ireland.[21] However, it is also clear that, well into the 19th century, for many Irish people wider political struggles mattered no more than local issues and a passive, or resigned, acceptance of the constitutional status quo. K.T. Hoppen has argued that the focus and structure of popular Irish politics in the middle years of the 19th century was as much the local as the national arena; and that 'limited goals and local priorities' were of at least as great significance for most Irish people at this time as universal causes. In his classic study, *Elections, Politics and Society in Ireland, 1832–1885* (1984), Hoppen observed that 'the more detailed workings of individual political communities were examined [by him] the more striking and important seemed the gap between local realities and the rhetoric of national politics…Irish politics were often profoundly localist in both content and style'.[22]

Again, pursuing Scots' analogies, Graeme Morton (in work which chimes in certain respects with that of Hoppen) has looked at Scotland in the mid 19th century, and argued that—given the contexts of strong local political cultures, and (at this stage) a relatively weak central government—patriotic Scottishness was fully compatible with the union. Morton has sought to demonstrate that 'because of the way civil society was governed in the mid-[19th] century, Scottish nationalism was loyal to the Union of 1707'.[23] A soft form of unionism—what Morton has controversially labelled 'unionist nationalism'—thrived in these conditions. Strong local political cultures and a non-intrusive state helped to support the union, while state growth and intervention gave momentary spurs to devolutionist sympathies. Applying this insight to Ireland, it might be argued that the growth of the British state in late 19th-century Ireland, while partly (that is to say, within certain constrictions) accommodating ever greater numbers of Irish people, also tended to define and sharpen the divide between Irish patriotism and the union.

In Ireland constitutional national endeavours had obviously very great success in recruiting support; but at the same time they had often an ambiguous or pragmatic relationship with the union. It is clear that the British-Irish union survived at least partly because leading national politicians pursued relatively flexible and accommodationist strategies. Again, in broad terms, this should come as no surprise, not least given the intense interrelationship between, and compatibility of, Scots patriotism and the British connection. Moreover, just as it has been argued that late 18th-century Scots were primarily concerned about individual equality within the British state (rather than the co-equality of Scotland and England), so there is a clear sense in which a politician like Daniel O'Connell was seeking the equality of individual Catholics within the United Kingdom state, rather than the co-equality of Ireland and Britain.[24]

O'Connell, the architect of Catholic emancipation in 1829 and the perceived father of Irish constitutional nationalism, devoted the middle section of his career to making the union work for Irish Catholics: his priorities in the 1830s seem quite clear, with a sustained and explicit effort to mould the structure of the union government along more popular and Catholic lines. He famously defined this strategy in 1836, when he claimed (pressing his 'language of prospective loyalism to the limit', as Oliver MacDonagh has remarked) that 'the people of Ireland are ready to become a portion of the Empire...they are ready to become a kind of West Briton if made so in benefits and in justice' or 'Ireland is now ready to amalgamate with the entire empire. We are prepared for full and perpetual conciliation'.[25] In this context, it is worth recalling O'Connell's repeated professions of loyalty to the British monarchy, his welcoming of George IV to Ireland in 1821 (when he crowned the king, otherwise sporting an enormous shamrock rosette, with a laurel wreath), and his avuncular (popular folklore would have knowingly deemed it 'paternal') affection for Queen Victoria.[26] O'Connell's youngest (and last surviving) brother was awarded a baronetcy in 1869. It is also worth recalling the sustained services of the extensive O'Connell clan to the British crown forces in the later 19th century, and particularly to the Royal Navy: there were scions of the family serving in the officer class of the crown forces as late as the Second World War. O'Connell himself was, above all, anxious to demonstrate that Irish loyalists had no monopoly over loyalty.

It ultimately became clear even to O'Connell that Irish Catholics would not quickly transmute into 'kinds of West Briton' in terms of 'benefits and justice': the union in the post-emancipation era did not speedily address Catholic aspirations or fully accommodate Catholic society. But this is very far from saying either that future national politicians wholly gave up on this, O'Connellite, goal, or that the union was a wholly static enterprise, or that it wholly failed to accommodate. And, indeed, it has been recently argued that O'Connell successfully defined the outlines of a lasting relationship between the monarchy and constitutional nationalism.[27]

In fact the strength of the union never lay in any conceptual or institutional rigour (there was arguably, unlike in Scotland, an intellectual deficit)—but rather in its capacity for continual reinvention, and its ability to absorb some political challenge. Scottish historians have sometimes made the same point in relation to the Anglo-Scots union—that 'a key element in the development of the government of Scotland has been the ability of the union to adapt and accommodate nationalist sentiment' and that 'one of the most important characteristics of the Union is its inherent flexibility. It has proved possible to accommodate Scottish distinctiveness throughout its history'.[28] This, in fact, is the essence of Morton's 'unionist nationalism' thesis. But it is also evinced by (for example) the union government's legislative responses to Scottish land agitation, by the creation of the Scots Office in 1885, by the seriousness with which the issue of Scots Home Rule was taken in the 1890s and after, and ultimately by the extent of the administrative devolution granted to the Scots, beginning in the interwar years.[29]

The British-Irish union was, as noted, originally defined by William Pitt in relatively inclusivist terms, was immediately recast as an instrument of Protestant Ascendancy, yet was used tentatively to expand Catholic rights in the 1830s. It has been recently and convincingly argued that at this time, the early years of the repeal agitation, 'the defenders of the union devised many of the basic stratagems that British governments would use to contain Irish nationalism before the establishment of the Irish Free State'—namely a mixture of conciliation, pragmatism, and intermittent coercion: in addressing the subsequent repeal agitation of the 1840s, 'the British ruling class had demonstrated its tactical flexibility and its fundamental resiliency, adapting its means to changing conditions, but never wavering in its determination to preserve the constitutional status quo'.[30] Thereafter, in 1869–1870, the union was substantially overhauled, with the Irish Church Act (through which the Church of Ireland was disestablished, and the United State Church of Britain and Ireland—created under the settlement of 1801—formally dissolved).[31] The union was increasingly 'greened' (to use the label of the late Lawrence McBride) at the end of the 19th century in preparation for Home Rule—that is to say, in terms of the higher civil service and judiciary, though not of the highest levels of the police, slowly repeopled in a manner relatively more accessible to Irish Nationalists.[32] In 1810 the Union remained an instrument of Protestant Ascendancy: by 1910 it may be seen as a mechanism by which successive British governments were undertaking social experiments of a much more daring variety than they would ever have countenanced in England.

Of course this argument cannot be pushed too far. The malleability of the union might reasonably be interpreted as, in part, an expression of the fluid local alliances and encouragement of local division that were in fact the hallmarks of British imperial rule. It is arguable that the British shift from working in partnership with the old Ascendancy interest in the 18th and early 19th centuries to a more direct engagement with the developing elites of Catholic society was in line with wider patterns of colonial government (in, for example, India or Malaya). In the Ireland of the late 19th century, as in the formal colonies, British attention was turning to the patronage and sponsorship of indigenous elites.[33]

Moreover, while a panoramic view of the union reveals some malleability, particular episodes illustrate the abiding potential for ideological rigidity first perceptible with the birth of the union and the 'emancipation' issue. Recent scholarship has characterized the union before emancipation as being vitiated by English overconfidence, ignorance, and incomprehension.[34] Scholars also now routinely emphasise the profound limitations of British relief policy during the Great Famine (1845–1851), as well as the failure of imagination and humanity within Whitehall and Westminster. The severities of liberal economic thought have traditionally been stressed; more recent work, following in the wake of Boyd Hilton, has tended to underline the providentialist outlook of those senior British officials who were characterized by a narrow form of evangelical religious outlook.[35] There is little doubt that this case has power: nor can there be any doubt that perceptions of official neglect or malevolence shaped the militant nationalism of the later 19th century. The polemical and popular historiography of John Mitchel was of course particularly influential in this respect.

Still, the failure of the British government during the Famine years was all the more problematic, because the union could be used as a framework within which fundamental and otherwise unassailable issues such as property rights might be addressed. The union certainly did not preclude types of advanced reform such as the independent arbitration of rent, the legal recognition of effective joint ownership, land purchase, and (ultimately, in 1909) in certain instances compulsory land purchase. Some of these land reforms were adapted and applied to Scotland, with the passage of a Crofters' Act in 1886, the creation of a Crofters' Commission (with similar powers to the Irish Land Commission), and a Congested Districts Board and Board of Agriculture for Scotland (both modelled partly on Irish precursors).[36] Recent scholarship has, it should be said, highlighted some of the parallels uniting Scotland and Ireland, while also pointing to some key distinctions (such as the Scottish crofters' resistance to the attractions of both migration and purchase).[37] However, the different ways in which ostensibly similar policies or agencies were developed in Ireland and Scotland (such as the Congested Districts Board experiment in Ireland (1891) and Scotland (1897)) underlines the larger malleability of union.[38]

This malleability is also evident in the nature of British policy from the late 1860s onwards as Irish national politics attained a greater force and coherence. Though William Gladstone (as Prime Minister) claimed that he was not responding to violence, popular mobilization in support of the

Fenian martyrs and prisoners clearly indirectly helped inspire a succession of far-reaching reforms, or attempted reforms. By 1869 Gladstone was prepared to break the ecclesiastical union of the two kingdoms through the disestablishment of the Irish church: by 1885 he was of course prepared to restore a subordinate Irish parliament in the interests of preserving what he saw as the essence of the union settlement—the supremacy of Westminster, the economic unity and military security of the two islands. Gladstone's efforts towards Home Rule failed in 1886 and in 1893—but this should not detract from the fact that he represented a significant tradition of pragmatic British constitutional thought which was, and has been, prepared to jettison the traditional forms of union in order to preserve a measure of its substance: he also represented (according to recent arguments) a significant tradition of pragmatic constitutional thought which was (and remains) rooted in a reading of Irish history which was profoundly sympathetic to the popular Catholic position.[39] Moreover, Gladstone's commitment to Home Rule, however problematic, helped to encourage an accommodation between Irish nationalism and the United Kingdom parliament which lasted until the eve of the revolution: the mere promise of Home Rule 'domesticated these new forces' in Irish and British politics, and kept constitutional nationalists at Westminster for thirty-five years.[40]

Following on from this, it might be said that Gladstone's vision of the union has had a lasting contemporary relevance. Gladstone, like Tony Blair, invested reform of the union with a strong moral and Providentialist tone. He devised a constitutional proposition which still has an importance—the paradox that the United Kingdom could best be sustained through devolution. He also defined, through Home Rule, a form of 'variable geometry' for the government of the United Kingdom which has been an underpinning principle of the Blair government's constitutional reform. In all of these senses, Gladstone's flexible vision of union seems to have left a greater impact upon contemporary politicians than some at least would care to acknowledge.

## Transportation

But the survival of the British-Irish union was not simply a matter of localism, Nationalist pragmatism, reformism, or political malleability. As in Scotland, so in Ireland, the union was bolstered by cultural and economic structures and mechanisms, and by the armed forces and bureaucratic resources of the British state.

It was served by the achievement of a customs union in 1823, and of a postal union by 1831. The union of the currencies was attained in 1826.[41] The last distinctively Irish coinage before independence was struck in 1823, and thereafter the iconography of the silver and copper in circulation in Ireland was resolutely British. After nearly 300 years the harp (and crown) disappeared from the reverse of Irish copper pennies, halfpennies, and farthings in that year, to be replaced by Britannia and (lurking in the background) symbols of British naval supremacy. The last specifically Irish silver coinage under the union was produced by the Bank of Ireland in 1813, when its final tenpenny tokens were minted bearing the laureated image of King George III on the obverse.

As the Gladstonian epigraph to the chapter suggests, geography was central to the debate on union, and to its perceived chances of survival: the union coincided with, and in fact was aided by, ever swifter modes of transport and communication. It was made possible by the communications revolution beginning with the improvement in the early 19th century of the road network connecting London with Holyhead in Anglesey, the key port for Dublin: Thomas Telford's work on these roads, allied with the development of steamship technology on the Holyhead-Dublin and Liverpool-Dublin crossings eased communication between the two capitals, and between Westminster and Dublin Castle. The first steamship crossings between Liverpool and Dublin were established by George Langtry in 1819, using the 'Waterloo' and 'Belfast': Langtry was also responsible for pioneering the steamship route connecting Liverpool and Belfast.[42]

Similarly the government of the union was aided by the spread of telegraphs and railways after the 1830s, and by telephone linkages by the end of the 19th century (the first cross-channel submarine telephone cable was laid in 1893). Irish republican commentators have pointed out (with some justice) that when the 1916 rebels seized the General Post Office this was partly a very traditional assault on the symbolism of British rule in Ireland; but it also reflected a sensitivity for 20th-century technology—for the GPO was the newly-extended (1905–1914) communications hub, telephone and telegraph, for Dublin, and between Dublin and London.[43]

Improved transport and communication also served as instruments of anglicization in the double sense that they made the export of Irish people through emigration easier, while facilitating the spread of British cultural influence. Irish attention has traditionally focused upon direct British state intervention in cultural questions such as the role of the new National School System (of 1831) in promoting the English language, or the role of the Ordnance Survey (of 1824) in mapping the landscape and establishing place names.[44] But there is an argument for suggesting that British manufacturing dominance, together with improved transport and communications, were at least as important as these direct government initiatives in shaping the British presence in 19th-century Ireland—in promoting the consolidation of the English language, the spread of symbolically British advertising and packaging, and indeed (following the work of John MacKenzie) embedding the message of empire.[45]

It is surely no coincidence, too, that the consolidation of both the Anglo-Scots and the British-Irish unions was occurring in the context of a communications and transport revolution. North Britain and West Britain were conceptually honed in similar ways; and while it was entirely logical that 'the North British Railway' should have terminated at Edinburgh's 'North British Hotel', it was no less fitting that Holyhead-Dublin mail packet should have deposited its passengers at Kingstown and, perhaps, the Royal Marine Hotel, or indeed the Royal St George Yacht Club.

It should be said, in parenthesis, that though railways consolidated the unity of the United Kingdom in certain respects, their strategic potential was also exploited by late 19th-century Irish nationalists (Parnell, for example, acknowledged his debt to trains by admitting that, had the Young Ireland movement been similarly equipped, they would have been able to construct a national organization thirty years ahead of his own)[46] Nor could the rail networks achieve the temporal unity of the Kingdom. Railways were associated with the regularization of timekeeping, with the Great Western Railway adopting and promoting Greenwich Mean Time (GMT) across its burgeoning network as early as 1840. The wider rail and postal networks followed suit in 1847. But the legalization of Greenwich Mean Time was not applied to Ireland until 1916, thirty-six years after the equivalent legislation in Britain, and seventy years after the customary use of GMT in Britain: until 1916 Ireland used Dublin Mean Time. Until the end of the union, the Irish Sea remained not merely a physical but also a temporal or horological barrier: crossing St George's Channel to Ireland before 1916 involved no currency or linguistic conversions, but it did mean turning back one's watch by twenty-five minutes. No such effort was required when crossing the Tweed or Solway.

## Army and navy

Improved transportation facilitated British rule in other, cruder, senses, in so far as it permitted the swifter movement of troops and police. The army was a muscular arm of the British state in 19th-century Ireland. At one level it had an obvious importance in supporting British rule and the Union: the garrison veered between 15,000 and 30,000 in the course of the century, and generally stood at around 25,000 (much larger, proportionately, and more static than in Scotland).[47] In the early part of the 19th century this force was spread across the country in smallish detachments, but a greater concentration was achieved with the construction of a massive garrison at the Curragh in the Irish midlands. Either way, though the army was deployed with comparative rarity, its presence (together with that of the armed Royal Irish Constabulary) may be seen as a much more crude and important bolster to the union than the comparable military and policing establishments in Scotland.[48] Moreover, in addition to direct counter-insurgency action, the army and the RIC were used to enforce the recurrent bouts of special crimes legislation which were a more prevalent feature of Ireland under the union than of Scotland. It is vitally important, in seeking to decipher the survival of union, not to miss the obvious—the inescapable significance of the British garrison, dominating the heart of the island, and thoroughly interconnected, both geographically (to outlying stations at places such as Holywood, County Down, or Clonmel, Tipperary) as well as imaginatively and chronologically—to a bloody history of military subjugation.

At the same time, however, the relationship between the Irish people and the British army was more complicated than this. The army recruited tens of thousands of Irishmen, including (from the time of the Seven Years' War (1756–1763), and perhaps earlier) significant numbers of Catholic Irishmen: as with the Scots, so with the Irish, recruitment escalated during the Revolutionary and Napoleonic wars, when perhaps some 159,000 Irish served (a recent estimate has gone further than this, putting the Irish totals at around 100,000 in 1800, and double this number by 1810).[49] Equally, by 1797, there may have been as many as 40,000 Irishmen serving in the Royal Navy, recruited by posters which sometimes deployed the Irish language (one, professedly more 'conservative', estimate puts the total of Irish in the Royal Navy at around 24,000): moreover, these men appear to have been overwhelmingly loyal to their service during the mutinies at the Nore and

Spithead, with only one fifth of the Irish sailors in the Channel Fleet being regarded as 'disaffected' by their officers.[50]

Edward Spiers has pointed out that in 1830, when the Irish represented less than one third of the total population of the United Kingdom, their proportion in the British army stood at over forty-two per cent: at this time there were in fact more Irish than English in the army. With the Famine, and the associated collapse of the Irish population, this proportion also fell dramatically: but as late as 1900, when separatists were energetically campaigning against recruitment, the Irish proportion of the army (thirteen per cent) was still ahead of the Irish proportion of the United Kingdom population (eleven per cent). The sheer size of Britain's dependence upon Irish (and Irish Catholic) soldiers for much of the 19th century is surely one further explanation for the malleability of union.[51]

However, the full social and political importance of the army to Victorian Ireland is difficult to decipher, and should not be oversimplified. The army was not only a potential agency of oppression, though it was certainly that: it was an institution deeply imbedded in Irish life, with the regimental structure appealing to strong local, county, and provincial identities on the island (as, indeed, in Scotland). Recruitment to the British army in Ireland hinged on a variety of social and economic considerations, rather than on any overt political loyalties: it blossomed in the context of the large and relatively poor population which characterized pre-Famine Ireland. Taking the King or Queen's shilling certainly did not automatically induce loyalism; on the contrary, it seems likely that the absence of full emancipation until 1829 helped to impede Irish soldiers acceptance of, and within, the British state.[52] And there has also of course been an intriguing overlap between service in the British army and revolutionary activism from the 18th century through to the recent 'Troubles'. Revolutionary separatists actively sought to recruit in the ranks of the army from the 1790s through to the time of the Fenian movement, and beyond.

But it has also been argued that 'militarisation was conducive to politicisation'.[53] The very strong recruitment figures suggest that the army was an intimately familiar feature of the lives of many Irish families. This, in turn, is reflected in the relatively wide acceptance which the army retained in Ireland throughout much of the 19th and early 20th centuries. The potential importance of the British army in acclimatizing Irish people to the symbolism, the hierarchies, and perhaps even the strategies of the United Kingdom state was therefore considerable (see for example the romanticized rendering in illustration D.2). The same point holds true for Scotland: though here the role of the army in recruiting Scots to the state, particularly in the aftermath of 1745, has long been recognized, if still debated. It also seems to be the case—and this is a critical distinction—that recruitment to the British Army was much more central to the social structures and economy of the Scottish Highlands in the late 18th and early 19th centuries than it was to contemporary Ireland; and this may point to a shallower, if widespread, rooting of the army in Ireland, in comparison with Scotland.[54]

The liminality of the army in Ireland is well illustrated by the ambiguous responses of constitutional nationalists. Daniel O'Connell offered martial and defiant rhetoric to his repeal movement in the 1840s, and famously (or infamously) blinked first when the British government threatened the military suppression of his planned 'monster' meeting at Clontarf in October 1843; and yet, as has been noted, his family were closely implicated with service in the British army through the Victorian era, and into the Second World War. The Irish Parliamentary Party in the era of Parnell and after maintained a posture of public antagonism towards the crown forces, condemning British imperial militarism in the 1870s and opposing the British campaign in South Africa in 1899. Yet, both in public and in private, attitudes were more complex, in particular after the Asquith government's commitment to Home Rule. Sections of the nationalist press fought hard to carry War Office advertising.[55] John Redmond's commitment to the British war effort, expressed in August and September 1914 within the House of Commons and at Woodenbridge, County Wicklow, is well known, as are the heroic sacrifices of his brother William Redmond and his former colleague, Tom Kettle. Redmond's efforts to negotiate a more honourable and fulfilling role for Irish nationalists within the British army are (in a sense) an extenuation of O'Connellite strategies in the 1830s. But it is less well known that William Redmond, who died at Messines in 1917, was in communication with the Secretary of State for War, J.E.B. Seely, before the outbreak of the Great War, in December 1913, advising on the merits of national cadet forces: Redmond was in the antipodes at the end of 1913, and wrote privately to Seely enthusing over the compulsory cadet service in Australia ('it is a good thing, and makes the boys manly and healthy and trains them into real soldiers').[56]

The army was also intimately connected with the politics of space. The Napoleonic struggle not only militarized a significant proportion of the Irish adult male population, it indirectly served to underline the physical presence and power of the state within Ireland itself. The building of bar-racks and defensive structures—the iconic martello towers—around the Irish coastline served as a lasting reminder of the military power of the union state in Ireland. The construction of the massive Curragh garrison in Kildare later in the 19th century was undertaken probably with the deliber-ate intention of overawing the population in the aftermath of 1848 (much as Fort George at Inverness was erected partly in order to communicate British military might to the Highlands of Scotland after the '45 Rising).[57] The ambiguities of Irish identity which were exposed by service in the Great War were further delineated by the acts of commemoration inaugu-rated in 1919 and afterwards: the great peace parade in Dublin was domi-nated by the institutions and symbolism of the British state (the viceroy, Lord French, presided, and there was a significant display of armoured cars and other weaponry); but the effectiveness of these official claims was now, in the aftermath of the 1916 Rising and the 1918 general election, both theoretically as well as actively contested (there were skirmishes after the parades, and the crowds differentiated between 'acceptable' demobilized and 'unacceptable' regular soldiers).[58] The construction of war memorials in the years after 1919 solidified the contests over commemorative space; and in the event (given that the symbolism and values enshrined by the memorials conflicted with the symbolism and values of the new Irish state), compara-tively few were erected in the South of Ireland.[59] Only in the North East, where there was a perceived continuity between the ideals of the dominant Ulster Unionist movement and those of the war effort, were parades under-taken and memorials constructed in comparatively large numbers. And here, too, by the beginning of the 21st century, the contested nature of the British army, and of its physical presence and domination, was seen with the con-troversies surrounding the homecoming of the Royal Irish Regiment from Afghanistan.

## Monarchy

The army was of course bound to the crown; and the monarchy has tradi-tionally been seen as a pillar of union: as has been discussed, this perception has been occasionally addressed in Scots historiography.[60] The monarchy was clearly of less significance in Ireland than in Scotland—but even here scholars have recognized the survival of Jacobite monarchical feeling within

19th-century Irish patriotism.[61] George IV's coronation tour in 1821–1822, with its shamrockery and tartanry, suggested a possible dual approach on the part of the Hanoverian monarchy towards the susceptibilities of the Celtic nations, but this was not completely followed through; and (certainly so far as Ireland was concerned) served only to raise popular expectations rather than address them. As K. T. Hoppen has remarked of the fall-out from the visit, 'all that happened in Ireland was that the port of Dunleary from which the king departed was renamed Kingstown'.[62]

Queen Victoria did not seek to annex Irish Jacobitism, as she had its Scots variant. There was certainly some development within her attitudes and outlook towards Ireland, away from a relative generosity in the early years of her reign, towards ever more removed and embittered perspectives: the death of her Catholic aunt, Queen Louise of the Belgians, together with her own widowhood in 1861 have been identified as critical turning points.[63] By the second half of her reign it is pretty clear that, while the Queen wore her tartans, lingered at Balmoral, toyed with Presbyterianism, was protected by John Brown and by her highlanders, she had come to see her Irish subjects, particularly with the development of Fenian conspiracy, primarily in threatening terms. There was certainly no Irish equivalent of Balmoral, no Irish version of the *Highlands Journal* (1868), no ready royal donning of Irish clothing or other cultural identification, and (of course) no Hibernian Brown.

Indeed, there was a view that 'Victoria lost Ireland for England', because her antipathy for the island had become palpable, and because (unlike in Scotland) she never yielded to the pressure for an official Irish royal residence.[64] Ministers such as Lord Salisbury (certainly no friend to the Irish) shared this opinion: reflecting on the success of the Duke of York's Jubilee visit to Ireland in August 1897, Salisbury lamented the lack of an Irish 'Sandringham, to remove the impression of a royal boycott of Ireland'.[65] The Duke's visit initiated the last of the several conversations on this theme in Victoria's reign, a discussion closed by the Queen's obduracy on the matter (she shrewdly chose to fight on the issue of money, and specifically the prohibitive cost of an Irish Balmoral).[66] However, the notion of a missed opportunity lingered for long in the official consciousness: in 1972, amidst the wreckage of the Stormont regime and of British-Irish relations, Terence O'Neill recalled that 'when the Irish Republic left the Commonwealth in 1949, Lord Killanin said in the House of Lords that this might not have happened if the Royal Family had had a home in Ireland. I agree'.[67]

On the other hand, the British royal family were periodic visitors to Ireland, and these occasions exposed a vestigial Irish monarchical tradition, and some complex ties between Irish popular opinion and the crown. Queen Victoria herself paid four visits to Ireland (in 1849, 1853, 1861, 1900—a chronology which underlines the development of her sympathies), Edward VII came in 1903, 1904, and 1907 and George V in July 1911, on the eve of the revolution. Here were highly charged and layered occasions which (as the scholars James Murphy and Senia Paseta have been amongst the first to observe) have not fitted well into the hitherto dominant narratives of modern Irish political historiography.[68]

It is certainly difficult to fully decode these royal visits. Irish Unionists, of course, were enthusiastic, as the underutilized correspondence of the Dublin academic and literary Unionist, Edward Dowden, with his brother, John, documents. In March 1885 Dowden and his family were 'looking forward with loyal longing to a visit from the Prince of Wales'.[69] In 1900, during Queen Victoria's last visit, Dowden wrote to his brother, describing a Michael Jackson-style moment, when 'as the Queen's carriage passed, he [Dowden's baby grandson] was let down from an upper window as Cupid with coloured wings and no garments, his hands full of shamrocks and roses which he scattered over the royal carriage'.[70] Aside from testing the limits of taste, these visits also inspired a degree of competitive snobbery amongst the Dublin Unionist middle classes: when Edward VII visited in 1903, Dowden recorded sardonically that 'our neighbour, [John Pentland] Mahaffy, said to me "I must be in College. I have dined half a dozen times with His Majesty, and he will be sure to ask for me". As far as I know, he has not asked yet for Professor Dowden'.[71]

However, the visits were often more generally successful. It is obviously true that in the later years of Victoria's reign the royals faced a low-key but growing level of nationalist animus, focusing on their role as upholders of union and empire: James Loughlin has highlighted the importance of the Prince of Wales's unsuccessful visit of 1871 as a key moment in terms of the faltering of relationships, while both he and James Murphy have identified a turning point in the 1880s, particularly with the highly politicized royal visit of 1885, after which the legitimacy of these events came to be more routinely questioned.[72] In contradistinction to Murphy, Loughlin has posited a date of c.1880 as the effective starting point for the development of the critical 'Famine Queen' mythology—the popular nationalist, particularly separatist, notion that Victoria had mockingly disregarded the victims of the Great Irish Famine during her controversial visit to Ireland in 1849.[73] Victoria's longevity, however, attracted a broad degree of respect across the political spectrum in Ireland, as evidenced by the responses to the Diamond Jubilee of 1897 and the royal visit to Dublin in 1900. Certainly, and predictably, the deeply sentimental reaction of Irish Unionists to Victoria at this time is striking: William Johnston's effusion in his diary on Jubilee Day, 22 June, is indicative ('A Glorious Day..."Glory be to God on High" for the day and its unparalleled splendour. Words would fail me to write it, "God with us"'). But even an intellectually more robust figure such as Edward Carson professed in old age to have been deeply moved by the presence of the Queen at this time (having been introduced to Victoria at a Jubilee garden party, Carson 'went behind one of the great trees and wept').[74]

Both scholars are agreed in accepting that Edward VII, louche but untrammelled by Protestant religious fundamentalism, was broadly popular in Catholic Ireland, though both perhaps underplay the evidence suggesting that Edward's relationship towards Ireland developed in the opposite direction to that of his mother: in the mid 1880s Edward, the ostensible Home Ruler, was confiding to Colonel Saunderson, the Irish Unionists' leader, that he was 'in entire sympathy' with their cause.[75] Suspicions of the king's Catholic sympathies, focused by the debate over the coronation oath in 1902, eventually cooled Unionist ardour somewhat (in 1902 Horace Plunkett despaired of the, apparently representative, Ulster Unionist voter 'who honestly thinks that if a "comma in the King's Oath were changed the foundation of our religious and civil liberties were undermined"!').[76] The alteration of the coronation oath had to wait until Edward VII's death, however. Recent scholarship is strong in characterizing the attitudes of his successor, George V, emphasising (rightly) the complex sympathies of this ever-cautious monarch, and shedding interesting new light on the new King's friendly relationship with John Redmond, and on Redmond's (perhaps) related decision to support the British war effort in 1914. It is certainly quite clear that George V's apparent ambivalence to the Ulster Unionist cause in 1912–1914 caused 'despair' and 'bitterness' within that community, and with its leader, Sir Edward Carson.[77]

But the developing Nationalist animus cut two ways: this anger reflected not only alienation, but also the danger that a relatively popular and politicized monarchy posed for the separatist movement. On the whole these royal visits appear to have reinforced some passive and personal sympathy for the monarchy, while also profoundly dividing Irish nationalism. Leading separatists like Arthur Griffith felt (with some justification) that the visits revealed the extent to which mainstream constitutional nationalism was in danger of being accommodated by the Crown, and within the British connection. But then of course even Griffith at first sought to harness the political usefulness of the crown through his ideas on a dual monarchy for the British Isles, following the Austro-Hungarian model. In December 1926 Kevin O'Higgins, Vice President of the Executive Council of the Irish Free State, disinterred and redeployed the idea of the dual monarchy in making a pitch for the reunification of Ireland.[78] It need hardly be pointed out that the most successful Celtic nationalist of the 21st century, Alex Salmond, has also clearly recognized the challenge and power of monarchy.

The monarchy was also the fountainhead of the honours system in the United Kingdom; and clearly the reward of service through titles, orders, or decorations represented another binding agent within the union (just as they served to bind working class leaders to the British state).[79] A superabundance of honours launched the union in 1801, and (less remarked upon) also sustained it. The establishment of the Order of Saint Patrick in 1783, after the winning of legislative independence, helped to bind senior members of the Irish aristocracy to the British connection at a time when there was a real possibility of drift. Membership of the Order was greatly prized throughout the 19th century, until Irish independence; and indeed there were periodic discussions about its revival after 1921 for the benefit of the luminaries of Northern Ireland, particularly with the profusion of Second World War military commanders who had Ulster connections of one kind or another.[80]

The problem, perhaps, with the honours system was, not that it was unpopular amongst the Irish (many professed nationalists accepted honours from the crown), but rather that it was insufficiently inclusive for the purposes of securing loyalty to the state. The Order of Saint Patrick was designed to address political challenges from within the Ascendancy elite in the late 18th and early 19th centuries, but it did little to meet the needs of those sections of, in particular, Catholic Ireland who were emerging as economically and politically important in late 19th-century Ireland. Unlike India, where the Order of the Indian Empire (founded in 1878, and enlarged in 1887 and 1917) and the Kaisar-I-Hind Medal (awarded in three grades from 1900) were relatively accessible to loyal servants of the Raj, there were no popularly available decorations for the servants of the crown and union in Ireland (aside from the gallantry decorations and campaign medals awarded to soldiers).[81] The creation of the Order of the British Empire in 1917 was designed to meet the wartime need for a relatively demotic honour, and indeed its ubiquity was widely mocked, not least by novelists as diverse as E.F. Benson and Anthony Powell: Mrs Susan Wyse, one of the protagonists in Benson's 'Lucia' novels sports her MBE unfailingly and inappropriately, having received it for 'her services in connection with Tilling hospital...[which were] entirely confined to putting her motor-car at its disposal when she did not want it herself'.[82] But the Order came too late to be of much service as an instrument of the union between Britain and Ireland, though it was widely and effectively deployed for the benefit of supporters of the regime within Northern Ireland after 1921.[83]

It might further be suggested, that though historians have concentrated on the use of titles in smoothing the path to union in 1707 or 1800, there is an equally interesting case to be made for their use in the sustaining of union, the smoothing of the path towards disengagement from union in 1920–1921—or indeed the modification of the union between Britain and Northern Ireland since 1998 (the historian and novelist Ruth Dudley Edwards has referred mockingly to this through her character Rowland Cunningham, who was lavishly rewarded 'for having written a few articles in glowing support of government initiatives on Northern Ireland by being given a peerage for services to peace').[84] It seems clear that (whatever its limitations) the honours system was actively deployed to ease the course of British government both within Ireland and without. For example, during the Plan of Campaign (1886–1891), Arthur Balfour, as Chief Secretary from 1887, actively sought to use the Order of the Bath (third class, civil division) to reward hard-pressed middle-ranking officials—'those who do really energetic work under difficult circumstances'.[85]

More generally, the voracious Irish appetite for title, particularly the peerage, was often seen as worthy of comment, even in the context of the wider passion for ennoblement: Salisbury's private secretary, Schomberg McDonnell, wrote wearily that 'modesty is not a distinguishing characteristic of my countrymen when the peerage hunger seizes on them'; and a close reading of the relevant ministerial papers suggests that a culture of self-promotion and self-application was much more deeply entrenched within Irish, as opposed to Scottish, Unionism.[86] The ambition and brass neck of the Unionist legal community is particularly striking in this respect, a reflection both of the aspirations of the profession, and of the central role played by complaisant Irish lawyers within the workings of the British state in Ireland: an array of correspondence survives from the Home Rule era which documents the persistent demands for title or for high legal office carrying title, with Edward Gibson (later Lord Ashbourne), Peter O'Brien (Lord O'Brien of Kilfenora), James Campbell (Lord Glenavy), and John Atkinson (Lord Atkinson) amongst the most egregious of the many supplicants.[87] Gibson was one of the great survivors of Irish Unionist politics, notorious for his nepotism and for his limpet-like adherence to the Lord Chancellorship of Ireland, to which he had been appointed originally in 1885: successive efforts were made to prise him from this lucrative office, including in 1889, when (having been offered a Lordship of Appeal at £6000 a year) he demanded advancement in the peerage. Balfour was reduced to sarcasm and exasperation: 'it only remains for him to ask for the Garter and a perpetual pension and he will then perhaps feel that his incalculable services to his country have been amply rewarded. The joke is that this man who wants an earldom in order to soothe the bitter pill of receiving £6000 a year had the face to tell me that Lady Ashbourne would have preferred to remain plain (to be sure that she is bound to remain!)—to remain, I say, "plain" Mrs Gibson!'.[88] In fact Ashbourne remained glued to the Unionist shadow cabinet at the time of his death, in 1913. On the other hand, Peter O'Brien's repeated supplication for honours rendered Balfour speechless: forwarding a particularly brazen request from O'Brien for a peerage (he had already received a baronetcy), Balfour wrote to the Irish-born Schomberg MacDonnell, 'I enclose a letter from one of your fellow countrymen. Comment is superfluous'.[89]

In the maelstrom of self-promotion and special pleading, it was not always possible to take a calm and rounded view; and the consequences of error could be serious—affecting even the dignity of the monarchy itself. When, at the peak of the constitutional crisis, in September 1911, the controversial Liberal and Home Rule shipbuilder, Lord Pirrie, was proposed as Lord Lieutenant of Belfast, the Unionist leadership was in uproar: Walter Long, from the Unionist front bench, clearly sought to subvert the process, the outgoing Lord Lieutenant of Belfast (Lord Shaftesbury) was in confusion, and the king's Private Secretary, Lord Stamfordham, was in despair. The issue, ultimately, was the standing of the king: as Stamfordham conceded, 'I quite see … that at this particular moment Pirrie's appointment may evoke much discontent, and possibly affect the King's popularity'.[90] Long, characteristically, offered dry consolation: 'we must make the best of it. if there is an outburst of indignation, I hope the King will not be hurt [as] feelings run high in Belfast just now'.[91]

Fortunately for the stability of the union, and its institutions, such controversies were rare. Indeed, there was a sense in which honours were offered to Ireland and Scotland as much in a representative and crowd-pleasing capacity, as to reward the particular individual; and this provides some indication both of the official mind, as well as of the popular esteem in which the honours system was held, certainly through much of the North of Ireland. Salisbury offered a baronetcy in 1887 on these grounds and in typical style ('Shall I keep this man on his hind legs any longer? I am rather inclined to offer his baronetcy to Ulster as a kind of complimentary present').[92] Equally, when the Attorney General for Ireland, John Atkinson, recommended an Ulsterman for a knighthood in the Jubilee Honours list, it was on the grounds that 'it would be popular among the Protestants of the North'.[93] Honours were of course tied to the issue of regional claims and jealousies, as H.O. Arnold-Forster (the newly elected MP for the marginal West Belfast seat) indicated in making a bid for three honours to the viceroy, Earl Cadogan: 'I may add that Belfast, which has so long been the stronghold of Irish Unionism has certainly not been lavishly treated in the distribution of honours. Indeed, I imagine that fewer honorary distinctions have been conferred upon the leading citizens of Belfast than upon any similar body of men in the United Kingdom'.[94] At the same time John Ross, the MP for Londonderry City, complained to Cadogan that Belfast had been honoured in 1892, but not Derry—and he sought compensating recognition in 1895.[95]

There was also a strong sense in which Unionists, particularly in Ireland, regularly linked their individual claims to the wider condition and fate of the union, and to the morale of their compatriots: in 1895 the Unionist whip, Aretas Akers-Douglas, complained of one petitioner that 'he is one of the 1001 Irish gentlemen who…[base their claims] on the ground "that something done for him would be an encouragement to the other Unionists in Ireland"'.[96] E.T. Herdman, a Tyrone linen magnate, claimed (inevitably) that he did not want an honour (a baronetcy) for himself, but felt that it would help give his (Liberal Unionist) candidature an advantage in the forthcoming elections: 'I believe an honour such as this conferred in this year would assist me immensely in winning back Derry City as it would show the Unionists who have selected me unanimously to contest the seat that I have the favour of the government which would give me a stronger position later on…I am quite satisfied if this course of action be not taken, a large number of Unionists, and especially Liberal Unionists in East Donegal and Derry City will be rather disgusted, and especially so as the Conservatives are rather celebrated in Ireland for dropping their friends and propitiating their enemies'.[97]

Indeed, ultimately, often raw ambition or jealousy dictated the tone of claims or complaints. The Guinness brothers, Arthur and Edward, were prominent businessmen, philanthropists, and statesmen, who quietly bank-rolled much Unionist activity through the Home Rule era, including the militancy of Ulster Unionists in 1912–1914. The Unionist government duly responded with honours, granting Arthur a peerage (as Lord Ardilaun) in 1880, and Edward a baronetcy (1885) on the occasion of the Prince of Wales's (unsuccessful) visit to Ireland: a peerage (as Lord Iveagh) and the Order of Saint Patrick soon followed, in 1891 and 1895. It was this last eleva-tion, which provoked another Irish Unionist stalwart, the second Duke of Abercorn, to complain that the Guinness family, and Iveagh in particular, were being rewarded undeservedly: Abercorn, at the time of writing in 1895, had inherited his family's noble titles, and had been given both the Garter (in 1892) and the Order of the Bath (third class) (1865) by way of personal distinction or recognition.[98] But he did not then, nor did he ever, possess the Order of Saint Patrick.

## The state, official landscapes, and empire

The image and nomenclature of the monarchy were omnipresent signifiers of the British state in Ireland, and intruded into both private and official landscapes. The stamp of monarchy was impressed even within recreational and educational contexts. In 1891 the middle class, disproportionately Protestant players of the Dublin Golf Club, founded by a Scots banker in 1885, loyally petitioned 'Bloody' Balfour, himself a keen golfer, for the use of the 'royal' title (which was duly granted).[99] The hunger of the Dublin golfers for royal sanction was fully matched by their Scots golfing and yachting counterparts. In both countries, too, the monarchy was swift to bless higher education: Ireland had its Royal Irish Academy (1785), Royal College of St Patrick (1795), Queen's Colleges (1845), Royal Irish Academy of Music (1848), Royal University of Ireland (1879), and its Queen's University of Belfast (1908).

Turning to government, the expansion of Victorian bureaucracy meant both that there were ever more Irish people in public employment, and that the physical expression of the state was of increasing importance within everyday life: there is a spatial dimension to the union which has (until lately, at any rate) eluded historians. There is a case for emphasising that the state was intruding ever more into the physical environment of Irish, as indeed Scots, people in the 19th century. Some work has been done on war memorials in British Ireland (by, for example, Nuala Johnson); more research needs to be undertaken on the rich variety of other, Victorian monuments and buildings and street names and their wider significance (though the cultural geographer Yvonne Whelan, through her work on the street names and statuary of 19th-century Dublin, has shown the possibilities).[100] The consolidation of the Royal Irish Constabulary brought with it the erection of police barracks: the battery of land legislation which was passed at the end of the 19th century brought both administrators and official buildings. A major complex of government offices was completed in Merrion Street, Dublin, shortly before the end of the British regime, and inherited by the new Irish authorities: the Irish Taoiseach still works in a building adorned by the monogram of George V. The expansion of the Victorian post office necessitated official buildings and post boxes, all bearing the royal insignia, and brought Irish people into contact with the state in ever more complex ways (sending letters, pensions, national insurance). Iain McLean and Alastair McMillan have rightly described the nascent welfare state, anchored in the post office network, as 'inherently unionist'.[101]

The physical expansion of the British state in Ireland was of course directly linked to increasing bureaucratic control and intrusion into the lives of Irish people. By 1885, in the gendered assessment of Joseph Chamberlain, 'an Irishman at this moment cannot move a step; he cannot lift a finger in any parochial, municipal or educational work without being confronted with, interfered with, controlled by an English official'.[102] More police and civil servants meant that more information was being gathered on the population, and on its social, economic, cultural, and political characteristics. Cultural commentators have of course long stressed the implicitly political and subjugating purposes of much of this bureaucracy in a range of imperial contexts. Thomas Drummond's Irish Railway Commission Report of the late 1830s reflected the perception that Ireland could be mastered and improved through statistical assemblage. The Irish Ordnance Survey (1824) and a succession of investigatory land commissions have parallels with the Great Trigonometrical Survey (1818) or the Geological Survey of India (1851) or in so far as, whatever their ostensible functions, they helped to define and inform British rule.[103] The United Kingdom of Great Britain and Ireland developed alongside advances in cartography and the popular accessibility of map images; and it is possible that the envisioning or the normalizing of the British-Irish union was aided and defined by the increasingly pervasive imagery of cheap maps, provided by (amongst others) the Scottish unionist cartographic dynasty, the Bartholomews.

Irish historians have of course spotted the directly political uses to which this intelligence-gathering might be applied (as, for example, in the use of police and other official data during the interrogation of the nationalist leadership at the Parnellism and Crime Special Commission of the late 1880s).[104] Certainly the centralized and paramilitary structures of policing in Ireland are to be contrasted with the more localized contemporary arrangements in Scotland and England; and these facilitated an elaborate hierarchy of information-gathering from local police stations and districts, where station sergeants reported to district inspectors, who in turn reported to county inspectors, who reported to the RIC Headquarters in Phoenix Park, which in turn reported to Dublin Castle.

On the other hand it was often Irish Catholic officials, policemen and churchmen who were gathering intelligence (as part of what Chris Bayly has deemed the 'global society of knowledge'), and who had been assimilated within this colonial-style administration.[105] Scholarship on the Irish administration in the late 19th and early 20th centuries emphasises that it remained distinctive, that (though relatively politicized and unionist, certainly in terms of its uppermost tiers) it was increasingly able to recruit nationally minded Catholics, and (lastly) that it served as a vehicle for British ideas of government and administration even in the years after independence. It would be quite wrong to overlook the constrictions within which Catholic middle class ambition operated, a point made in the work both of John Hutchinson and of Fergus Campbell—the latter of whom has cogently defined an elite at the highest layer of Irish society which was relatively impervious to Catholic ambition even in the last years of the union.[106] On the other hand, even the polemical work of Barry O'Brien indicated some evidence of movement towards a greater national sympathy within Dublin Castle in the late 19th century[107]; and the notion of a gradually 'greened' Castle administration has been eloquently explored in the work of the late Lawrence MacBride.[108] More recently still, Martin Maguire has argued strikingly (if, perhaps, counter-intuitively) that the Castle regime (before its reform in 1920) was distinctively tailored to Irish conditions, and relied upon 'a large and decentralised corps of non-political experts whose objective was the transformation of Irish society and economy through government action'.[109] Moreover, this was a service which was largely Catholic and nationally minded in the lower grades, and was gradually if slowly opening up at more senior levels to Catholic ambition.

As with the evidence of the army, it would also be quite wrong to posit any crude correlation between administrative service to the union state, and the acceptance of unionism: the familiar example of Michael Collins, hero of the revolution between 1919 and 1921, and a post office clerk between 1906 and 1910, may be sufficient to illustrate this pitfall. And, if (as noted) the constraints to Catholic upward mobility should be recognized, it would also be quite wrong to overlook many of the challenges which nationally minded and/or Catholic civil servants confronted in operating at high levels within the union administration. The well-known example of Sir Antony MacDonnell is relevant here. On the one hand, MacDonnell, a Galway Catholic whose brother had served as an anti-Parnellite MP, serves to illustrate the slow opening of the senior ranks of the service to the majority community: MacDonnell was appointed as Under Secretary for Ireland (that is to say, head of the civil service in Ireland) in 1902, having spent his earlier career within the Indian Civil Service (and, as part of the Bihar group of ICS administrators, applying a sympathetic first-hand knowledge of the Irish tenantry to the challenges of tenurial reform in India).[110] MacDonnell was well connected, and possessed to a degree the patronage of Lords Curzon and Lansdowne, and even that of the king. On the other hand, his uneasy tenure of office highlighted the pressures confronted by a senior Catholic civil servant who was perceived as Home Rule in his sympathies. He was certainly a skilled departmental politician and bruiser; but he also needed to be so. Irish Unionist politicians attacked his work systematically, moving from a succession of official controversies involving alleged clericalism through to the debacle of the devolution scandal, wherein MacDonnell cooperated in producing a proposal for an Irish devolved administration.[111] By November 1904 his position in Ireland was decidedly precarious; and he wrote a *cri de coeur* to St John Brodrick, the Secretary of State for India (and a southern Protestant landowner), protesting that 'my offence is that I am a Roman Catholic with Irish sympathies (kept well, by the way, within Unionist lines). The object of my [Unionist] calumniators is to hound me out of office because of my creed'.[112] There is little reason to question either the sincerity of this distress or the relatively great difficulty at this time of being able to express an Irish (as opposed to Scots) patriotic identity 'within Unionist lines'.

And yet it is striking that, despite the large size of the Irish civil service in the years before independence, and despite the rapidly growing numbers of separatists after the 1916 Rising, only ninety civil servants were investigated at this time for their 'subversive' political sympathies by the Sankey Commission (half of these in fact were in the Post Office). The Irish National Aid Association, formed by Collins to help the survivors of the Rising, assisted some seventy-two civil servants: this was probably the complete list of those civil servants affected. One other (admittedly inconclusive) way of addressing this issue is to look at the numbers who resigned, or who were dismissed, with the coming of the new regime after 1922: Maguire observes that 'by the end of 1925 there were 1851 dismissals or resignations with a further 2139 waiting decision. This represents considerable gaps in a service of just over 6000'.[113] As with elsewhere in the Ireland of the union years, the evidence suggests a widespread, doubtless passive or unenthused, cooperation, even collaboration, with the *ancien regime*. While the celebration of the achievement of the revolution naturally tends to emphasise those who actively defied or betrayed the Castle regime from within, in reality the number of those seeking a quiet life within the structures of union outstripped that of the fighting heroes.

Historians are increasingly interested by the complex and reciprocal nature of the Irish Catholic relationship with the administration of empire—and by the extent to which Irishmen and women (like Antony MacDonnell) were simultaneously subjugated by empire, and also often complicit within its structures.[114] Empire, like the monarchy and army, was a further institution tending to bind Ireland within 'Britishness' and the union. But as with the monarchy and army, empire affected Ireland in similar, if paler and perhaps more complex, ways to Scotland. One way of illuminating these relationships is through the suggestion that the Irish people's ambiguous experience of the Empire was linked to the ambiguous relationship—half colony, half metropole—linking Ireland itself to the empire: equally, the similarities and distinctions in the Scots and Irish experience of union may be linked to the similarities and distinctions in Scotland's and Ireland's interrelationship with empire. Perhaps the central governing distinction in all this is that Scotland, though dominated by its economically and politically more powerful southern neighbour, could not be regarded as an English colony; where, clearly, whatever the complexities of the British-Irish relationship, Ireland's history of military subjugation, expropriation, and plantation placed it on a different, and recognizably colonial, footing.[115]

As has been suggested elsewhere, Ireland's access to the economic and professional possibilities of the 18th-century British empire was less extensive than that enjoyed by the Scots; and the Irish were therefore to some extent playing a game of imperial 'catch-up' within the 19th century. While it would be wrong to exaggerate the social embrace in Scotland of the economic dividends of empire, these were slighter, and both more socially and geographically restricted in Ireland. As a working hypothesis it might be suggested that, while the Irish not only benefited less than the Scots from the economic dividends of imperial exploitation, they also suffered no less than the Scots from the impact of the investment of domestic capital in the development of empire: scattered (but still impressionistic) evidence suggests that Irish landlords selling up under the land purchase acts invested heavily in empire.[116]

Of course the explicitly anti-imperial strain within substantial sections of Irish nationalism (as distinct from Scottish nationalism) is obvious: Irish nationalists consistently defined themselves against the British empire; and recent scholarship has sought to re-emphasise the linkage between anti-imperialism (in particular opposition to British endeavours in Afghanistan and South Africa) and the growth of the Home Rule movement in the 1870s.[117] The historic interconnections between the growth of the Home Rule and separatist movements in Ireland and Indian nationalism, particularly Hindu nationalism, have long been observed.[118] More recently, militant republicans have identified themselves with (apparently) related anti-colonial struggles in Cyprus, South Africa, and Palestine.[119]

Yet, by the end of the 19th century a section of Catholic Ireland had been partly accommodated within the union and empire. Studies of the Catholic elite in the Home Rule era portray a rather conservative community which was only slowly adapting to the inevitability of Home Rule, and which participated wholly in the administration of the union and empire.[120] Irish Catholics were certainly well represented in most sections of the imperial enterprise of the late 19th century, from the army through to the Indian Civil Service.[121] Union and empire worked for Irish Protestants; but they also worked, however tardily and imperfectly, for some Catholics some of the time.

# Conclusion: crises of expectation

The emphasis within the chapter has been on the malleability of the union, as well as on some of the cultural means by which Britishness was insinuated into 19th-century Ireland. One further, critical, aspect of the argument has been that some of the factors, agencies, and institutions which sustained the union in contemporary Scotland operated, albeit in a much weakened manner, in Ireland. It has been argued that these distinctions were grounded partly in the fact that, while Scotland and Ireland shared an experience of union, this joint constitutional condition masked distinctive national experiences not only of England but also of the British Empire.

Of course the longevity of the Irish union is also to be explained in more direct terms—in terms of military and police action. As has been argued, Ireland was permanently garrisoned by British soldiers, and by the armed policemen of the Irish or (after 1867) 'Royal Irish' Constabulary. Ireland was ultimately bound to the union, not only by complex social, cultural, and economic ties, but also by the threat, and sometimes the reality, of force. It was bound by the recurrent use of extra-judicial action, not least in the form of special crimes legislation: throughout the 19th century, in the understated assessment of K.T. Hoppen, 'the maintenance of law and order followed unusual and highly intrusive lines'.[122]

It is also true that, while the union contained the potential to accommodate Catholics, this potential was often realized only with great difficulty. There were vested British and Protestant interests in Irish official and professional life, and in Irish society more widely, which were often difficult to move. This issue expanded in significance, with the growth of the state through the 19th century, and with the concomitant growth of the professions. There were thus critical sections of Catholic Ireland which were not immediately accommodated by the union state, and which sought an outlet for their abilities and ambition within an alternative and separate environment.

Civil society, therefore, functioned very differently in Ireland than in Scotland. Civil society in Ireland, dominated in the 18th century by the Protestant minority, failed in the traumatic circumstances of the 1790s; but it was reinvented in 19th-century Ireland by alienated middle-class Catholics, not as a means of containing their nationalism within the existing order, but rather as a form of counter-state.[123] Ultimately, therefore, unlike Scotland, civil society in Ireland did not serve to defuse nationalism: by the end of the 19th century civil society was increasingly dominated by the cultural and political separatists of the 'Gaelic Revival'. Indeed, John Hutchinson has famously argued that the Revival owed much of its force to the thwarted ambitions of educated lower middle-class Catholics, men and women who aspired to a place in the sun, but who found that it was still occupied by Irish Protestants or by Britons.[124]

The slowness of change often helped to stimulate anger and support for the national cause; but the very fact that reform, however tardy, was within the realms of the possible, meant that some Irish Catholics were disposed to work within the structures of the union for gradual, incremental gains. Ultimately the fundamental problem with the union was not simply that it failed to deliver for Irish Catholics: it was rather that it continually held out the promise of change, and continually either reneged on that promise, or delivered short measure. The history of the union is thus a history of crises of expectation—from Catholic emancipation in 1800, through the Famine in 1845 and after, land reform in the 1880s, structural reform, and ultimately Home Rule. In the end, expectations of legislative independence were created through the Home Rule Act of 1914 which, when crushed, marked the beginning of the end of the British regime in Ireland.

The union worked for a time because it was able to accommodate some key sections of Irish Catholic society at least in a provisional or contractual manner. It also (more obviously) attracted the support of Irish, particularly Ulster, Protestants, who saw it as a guarantee against Catholic cultural and economic supremacy in Ireland. The astonishing economic growth of eastern Ulster, the heartland of Irish Protestantism, was credited to the union settlement. The prosperity of this region permitted, from the mid 1880s, the growth of an organized movement with substantial support in England and Scotland, and dedicated to the preservation of the union: this will be reviewed at length in a subsequent chapter. Certainly, in the end Protestantism and Unionism became synonymous, just as Protestant Unionism was synonymous with the Northern Irish state created out of the wreckage of union in 1921; and though these might seem like predictable outcomes (given the failure of Catholic emancipation in 1800–1801), the union had for a time possessed wider possibilities.

In 1907, on the centenary of the Anglo-Scots union, the Edinburgh historian Richard Lodge complained that 'the history of the relations between England and Scotland is the record of lost opportunities'.[125] Ireland (and

Scotland) have indeed had painful and complex relationships with the union. There is a popular image of union as a kind of detachable superstructure covering Irish society in the 19th century; but in reality the union was pervasive, and impacted upon the physical environment, the market place, and the professional and recreational life of Irish people. We need a social, cultural, and spatial definition of the union which will allow a fuller understanding of the complex relationship between Irish (and Scots) people and their government in the 19th and 20th centuries.

# E. Unionism

**Illustration E.1.** Conservative and Unionist student supporters of George Wyndham as Lord Rector of the University of Edinburgh, 1908. Courtesy of the Wellcome Library, London.

**Illustration E.2.** Ulster Provisional Government, 1912 (postcard image). Private possession.

# PART III

## The survival of the Unions: people, ideas, institutions

# 7

# Scottish unionists and the union, 1707–2007:

## Parties, people, and histories

Nice men with an excessive regard for hierarchy, they presided over a declining party with scant regard for what was happening outside their own playground...they concealed political weaknesses behind portentous titles and procedures. Their speeches were longer and their meals included more courses than their equivalents in England. Douglas Hurd, *Memoirs* (2004 edition), pp. 192, 232

We seem to have problems in Scotland, and the difficulty from my point of view is to get agreement on how to reorganise, and with whom. Margaret Thatcher, 1976 (NLS, Tweedsmuir Papers, Acc. 11884/157: Thatcher to Tweedsmuir, n.d. [1975])

## Introduction: unionism as normative and patriotic politics

The two unions survived because the party structure in the two kingdoms, Ireland and Scotland, provided a critical support. In Scotland, for most of the three hundred years after 1707, a (sometimes grudging) unionism dominated the country's electoral politics and representation at Westminster. As Richard Finlay has observed of 20th century Scotland, 'the sanctity of the union was one of the few issues which commanded a near universal consensus in Scottish political and intellectual circles': Colin Kidd, adapting Michael Billig's 'banal nationalism', has defined a 'banal unionism'—a unionism 'which is so dominant that it does not need to be demonstrative'.[1] Henry Dundas's dominant Tory unionism in the later 18th and early 19th

centuries was superseded after 1832 by the integrationist unionism of
Scottish Whiggery: Conservatism achieved its electoral comeback in
Scotland after 1886 on the strength of the Irish union, and was a major force
in Scottish politics in the second quarter of the 20th century, while Labour
dominated electoral politics for most of the mid and late 20th century partly
through a recurrent demonstration of the value of the Scots union.

In Ireland, parliamentary politics were largely dominated by a tacit unionism between 1801 and the electoral breakthrough of Isaac Butt's Home Rule
movement in 1874. Even with the predominance of Charles Stewart Parnell's
Irish Parliamentary Party in the mid 1880s, there was a well-resourced and
geographically concentrated Unionist movement, active in its propaganda,
organization and deployment, though unionism was no longer the normative or default condition of electoral politics (as it had once occasionally
been, and remained still in Scotland). After the partition of Ireland in 1920,
and the attainment of Irish independence in 1921–1922, Unionism held a
predominant position in the new Northern Ireland for fifty years.

These observations of course require further refinement and elaboration.
There is, for example, an obvious chicken-and-egg dimension: did the survival, or the occasional perceived successes, of the union ensure Unionist
party political influence in each kingdom, or did party support entrench the
success, or survival, of union? The importance of the theme of party can
best be illustrated by underlining its influence at times when the union was
apparently under threat or in decline. In Ireland there can be little doubt
that the rapid development in the 1880s of a formal Unionist movement
critically (perhaps disastrously) delayed the attainment of Home Rule and the
revision of the Act of 1801 (though there is a strong case for arguing that the
success of Irish and Ulster Unionism between 1885 and 1918 destroyed
the possibility of a reformed and revitalized union, and thus bought a
reprieve for the *ancien régime* while guaranteeing its ultimate demise). In
20th century Scotland there also can be little doubt that the commitment
of both the Conservatives and Labour to the union helped to stifle constitutional debate and agitation at a time when it was no longer associated
with great economic advance: the urgent conviction of Labour politicians
like William Ross (Secretary of State for Scotland between 1964–1970 and
1974–1976) that Scottish economic decline could best be managed within
the context of union illustrates the fact that unionism continued to serve as
a useful creed for bad times as well as good. Unionism, whether in its Irish
or Scottish formulations, whether in its Labour or Conservative plumage,

acquired an independent historical and cultural significance; and this meant that it served to bolster the union, even when (as in the Scotland or the Northern Ireland of the 1970s) it appeared to have outlived its utility.

It should again be stressed that the short- or mid-term successes of unionist partisanship may not always have been a long-term asset to the union itself: the tactical victories of Ulster Unionism in the Home Rule era have been mentioned in this respect, but Labour's unionism in the 1960s and 1970s has also been criticized for its short-term salves rather than long-term treatment of Scotland's economic retreat.[2] Nor should the significance of unionism in Scotland and its transient presence in Ireland distract attention from the ongoing strength of national, sometimes anti-union, feeling in both polities. Both the Scots and Irish unions were initially highly unpopular with key sections of the population. The unionist consensus in Scottish and Irish parliamentary politics for part of the 19th century was founded on tiny and disproportionately privileged electorates, and was swiftly demolished in Ireland in the wake of electoral reform (in 1868 and particularly 1884–1885). Irish republicans argue that the survival (indeed thriving) of unionism in Northern Ireland occurred as a result of a corrupt partition scheme, rooted in sectarianism, electoral gerrymandering, and British imperial gamesmanship.

But to highlight these points is also to emphasise the continuing importance of unionist partisanship. Partition was instituted, and a vestigial union thereby preserved, because of the strength of the Unionist party in the North East of Ireland and in Britain. Scottish unionism has survived and thrived not merely in spite of strong national feeling, but *because of* strong national feeling. The great success of Scottish unionism, in whatever party formulation, has been its ability to define itself in the language of nationality. By way of contrast, the Irish and Ulster Unionist parties (despite some hesitant early efforts) never successfully sold the union on the basis of Irish nationality and Irish interests: there were gestures in this direction, but they were neither consistent nor effective. Ulster (as opposed to Irish) Unionists, indeed, tended to define for themselves a distinctive regional history and heritage.[3] Scottish unionism for long encapsulated Scottish values and Scottish heritage: a romanticist vein in Scottish Toryism, popularized by Walter Scott, traced its descent back to Jacobitism.[4] But Unionism in Ireland would quickly be associated in the popular Irish verdict with an alien nationality, alien interests, an alien history, and alien religious convictions.

# Tories

In 1912, in the context of the crisis over Ulster, and the union with Ireland, the Scottish Unionist Party was created as an amalgam of the Scottish Conservative and Liberal Unionist parties; and through this was forged an electoral machine with astonishingly sturdy and complex cultural roots and reach. This was a party which emerged with the largest number of Scottish seats in 1918, 1924, 1931, and 1935, and (famously) won a plurality of the Scottish vote as late as 1955. This was also a party which incorporated influential elements of the great Scottish Whig tradition of unionism, dating back to the inauguration of the union itself; but, remarkably, it also laid claim, like the royal family, to a tradition of romantic, patriotic Toryism, which (now that the Stuarts were no longer an active challenge) was proud of its roots in Jacobite legitimism. The great appeal of Scottish Unionism was anchored partly in the fact that it simultaneously embraced the union and the patriotic forces which, for a time, had sought to undermine it. Since the union was first and foremost about Scotland's interests, there could be little problem with a party which sought to express its Scottishness through its unionism.

The 'unionism' of the new Unionist Party reflected concerns over Home Rule and Irish nationalism, as well as the historic interconnections between the politics of the West of Scotland and those of the North of Ireland. But Scottish Unionism, as formulated in 1912, was not just about the Irish. Given that Scottish Liberalism was now (after 1888) committed to Home Rule for Scotland, and given that the *jeunesse dorée* of the party were enrolled in the nationalist youth movement, Young Scotland, and given, too, the (admittedly increasingly nominal) Home Rule commitments of Labour, the political space now existed for a party which offered a clear commitment, not just on the Irish union, but on the Scots union as well. Of course, within little more than a decade of its creation, the Scottish Unionist Party was wavering in its absolute commitment to both these unions; but this should not distract from the fact that its unionism was multilateral, and not merely Irish or ethnically reactive in its origins.

Some of the streams which coalesced in 1912 should, perhaps, be individually identified. Despite occasional efforts to claim more ancient continuities and lineage, Scottish Conservatism (as elsewhere in Britain) was essentially a creation of the early 19th century, and a product of the old Tory party's efforts to respond to the challenge of an era of continental European revolution and domestic parliamentary reform.[5] The tiny, unreformed Scottish electorate, which had been the basis for the hegemony of the 'despotism' of Henry Dundas and his Tory clan, had been swept away in 1832, inaugurating a half-century of Whig and Liberal predominance in Scotland. By the mid and late 1880s the Liberals were increasingly interested in the idea of a layered Home Rule settlement for both Ireland and Scotland, having previously been identified in both polities with an assimilationist unionism; but the Tories, or (now) Conservatives, remained broadly true to a pragmatic and patriotic unionism, defending Scotland's historic institutions within the framework of the union settlement.

Henry Dundas, whose unwholesome reputation at the hands of Whig historians has been revisited since the early 1990s, is now credited not just with securing Tory electoral predominance in Scotland before 1832, but also in helping to fashion a Tory vision of union, wherein Scotland preserved some at least of its ancient institutions, but also had effective access to government and empire (and, of course, their spoils).[6] Dundas originally took office (as Solicitor General for Scotland, in 1764) in the context of intense English Scotophobia, the still-fresh pain of Jacobite insurgency and its suppression, and amidst the debris of the collapsed (but once all-powerful) Whig and Argathelian supremacy in Scotland. Dundas sprang from the Scottish gentry class, learnt some of his political skills within the distinctive Scottish legal system, and built up a power base inside a distinctively Scottish electoral regime. His lifetime saw a turning point in terms of what A. V. Dicey and Robert Rait described as 'the moral union' between Scotland and England: this event, the realization of a sense of shared political and moral purpose between the two kingdoms, has been variously dated (1784, 1793, and 1815 are contenders), but the fundamental context was perhaps the achievement of a united British enterprise against the challenge of revolutionary and Napoleonic France.[7] In this, Dundas and Scottish Toryism have been held to be crucial. Dundas provided a distinctive Scottish voice within the first rank of British wartime politics, and (while critics saw jobbery and favouritism) he pushed the interests of Scots in a wide range of official and imperial enterprises. Though, as Home Secretary, he prosecuted political dissent with vehemence, he also served to link union with some progressive causes: he was an advocate of Catholic relief, and an opponent of slavery. He endorsed William Pitt's inclusive definition of union with Ireland, rather than the narrowly Protestant version which eventually found its way onto the statute books. Dundas, in sum, defined a Tory unionism which was sensitive to Scottish material and spiritual needs, and to the nation's historical (including its Jacobite) traditions. No individual or vision existed to fulfil a similar function in Ireland (Daniel O'Connell in the 1830s, with his programme of justice for Ireland within the union, is a very inexact parallel); and this critical absence ultimately goes some way to explain the fate of union and empire in each polity.[8]

Toryism and Conservatism had a formidable and a lastingly influential intellectual backing in the first half of the 19th century. Sir Walter Scott, famously, provided a romantic and literary underpinning to the Tory and effectively unionist vision: it has been said that 'adherence to an Anglo-British Whig historiography which stressed the fundamental backwardness of pre-union Scotland meant that he was not capable of using his vast historical knowledge in the service of an accurate and self-confident account of Scottish independence'.[9] Three years after Dundas's death, Scott published *Waverley* (1814), a runaway publishing success, whose eponymous hero worked off his Jacobite sympathies and heritage during the 1745 Rising to find reconciliation within the Hanoverian monarchy and union. Scott's *Rob Roy* (1817) is also notable for its sympathetic treatment of Jacobitism, though this time set against the backdrop of the 1715 Rising: once again, the romance of Jacobitism is celebrated, while Hanover and union are the accepted norms. Scott was, famously, the architect of the cultural and symbolic union of the Hanoverian and Stuart traditions which was achieved in 1822, with George IV's visit to Edinburgh. It should also be observed that Scott's subsequent influence over the British political elite was considerable: Gladstone devoured his novels—and indeed it has been argued recently that Gladstone 'read no works in English (except the Bible) so consistently or completely over such a length of time', and that he shared Scott's patriotic Caledonian unionism.[10] The influence of Scott over Stanley Baldwin is also clear: Baldwin recalled that his parents 'on their wedding journey visited Abbotsford as pilgrims', and that 'the world of the '45, and of the *Lay*, or *Rob Roy* and *Marmion*, of *Guy Mannering* and *The Pirate*, was that in which much of my childhood was lived and had my being'.[11] Baldwin, too, saw Scott (and Maria Edgeworth) as key facilitators of union.[12]

Complementing Walter Scott was a High Tory lawyer and journalist with a related patriotic and unionist vision of British and European history: Sir Archibald Alison. Alison (1792–1867) was trained at the University of

Edinburgh, and served as Sheriff of Lanarkshire; but he was chiefly known both as a contributor to *Blackwood's Magazine*, the Tory riposte to the Whig *Edinburgh Review*, and as the author of a monumental (and monumentally prolix) history of modern Europe.[13] Like Scott, Alison was intensely patriotic, and indeed was attached to the ur-movement of modern Scottish nationalism, the National Association for the Vindication of Scottish Rights (1853) and to the 'symbolic wing of Scottish nationalism' (one of his most ubiquitous photographs shows him proudly clad in tartan trews).[14] But, as is now well known, the National Association was a patriotic critique of inequities or unwelcome innovations within the operation of the union, rather than a campaign for repeal. And Alison, though famed (and indeed satirized) for his great work on modern Europe, was also the author of biographical portraits of the first Duke of Marlborough (1848), a proponent of the Scots union, and of the second Marquis of Londonderry (1861), a key architect of the Irish Union of 1801 (Alison's verdict on the latter was that he had 'laid the only possible foundation for its [Ireland's] future prosperity in an indissoluble union with Great Britain').[15] The National Association may have been a patriotic assertion of Scotland's rights within the union, but (as was more widely the case with Scottish patriotism and nationalism in the late 19th century), it was by no means a cheerleader for Irish nationalism: indeed Scottish assertiveness was partly linked to the disequilibrium created by Westminster's concentration on defusing Irish nationalist discontent. Alison could therefore logically promote Scottish patriotic claims within the union, while simultaneously eulogizing the co-founder of the Act of Union of 1801.

Toryism had thus a distinctive and workable vision of union, and indeed had manufactured a unionism which was compatible with some, at least, of Scotland's Jacobite heritage. However, what the Tories possessed in terms of intellectual ballast, and a capacity to dominate the unreformed electorate, they as yet lacked in numbers and popular electoral support. Part of the paradox of Tory unionism was that, in defining a commitment within the framework of union to Scotland's historic institutions, it was open to the accusation of using history and patriotism as covers for restricting the benefits of union to traditional elites. Moreover, it was also open to the accusation of coping with the challenges of history more effectively than with the problems posed by contemporary politics. Thus, Scots Tories at the beginning of the 19th century remained the 'country party', were opposed to parliamentary reform, and responded only hesitatingly to the new electoral conditions created by the Reform Act of 1832. Indeed, the Act

inaugurated a Whig and Liberal ascendancy within Scottish electoral politics which lasted, in effect, for the rest of the 19th century: this was accompanied by an assimilationist unionism, and then, in the 1880s, by a formal
commitment to Home Rule for Ireland and Scotland. Only with Liberal
division over Home Rule did the Scottish Tories recover an opportunity for
significant electoral advance.

But the Scottish Conservatives of the 1830s, like their Irish counterparts,
were by no means wholly passive: they certainly sought to popularize their
distinctive vision by building up an electoral organization, with a Scottish
Conservative Association (created in May 1835) and an effort in Glasgow
and other cities (as was the case with Irish Conservatives, in Dublin) to
recruit artisan support through Conservative Operatives' Associations.[16] The
Glasgow Conservative Operatives' Association was formed in December
1836, in the aftermath of Sir Robert Peel's successful visit to Glasgow and
election as Lord Rector of the university: its organizing committee started
life as a body charged with the task of drafting a celebratory petition to Peel.
This attracted over 2000 'operatives' signatures, and proclaimed in paternalist style that 'the interests of the working class [were] identified with, and
inseparable from, those of the aristocracy'.[17] The motto of the new
Association was 'Fear God, honour the King, and meddle not with those
who are given to change', while its lengthier 'mission statement' recorded
that it sought 'to maintain...the British Constitution, as established at the
eve of the Revolution in 1688....to defend the interests of the ecclesiastical
and educational establishments of Scotland as an integral part of that
Constitution; and that the Association shall at the same time exert itself to
promote the purity of administration and thereby to increase the efficiency
of the civil, ecclesiastical and educational institutions of the country'.[18]
Images of King William III and Queen Mary ('two valuable portrait prints')
adorned the walls of the Association's reading rooms. But the Association
also drew upon the artisanal coffee house and Presbyterian culture of
Glasgow (meetings alternated between venues such as the Argyle Arcade
Coffee Rooms, Wright's Coffee House, Mr Leckie's Coffee House, and the
session rooms of the Tron and Gaelic churches). Neither Ireland nor anti-
Catholicism were overt or immediate explanations for the emergence of
the Association; but each swiftly became a recurrent preoccupation during
its short life. Support was given in October 1837 for a subscription 'in aid of
the Fund for trying the validity of several of the Irish elections before
Committees of the House of Commons'—this being deemed 'absolutely

necessary as the only method left to the friends of Protestantism in that country of vindicating their rights as citizens against the intimidation of the enemies of the Constitution'.[19] The woes of Ireland provided the theme for a lecture given to the Association in June 1838; while related but wider concerns preoccupied the Association in November 1839, at which time its President 'showed the rapid progress that Popery has made in the legislature and through the Empire at large since the passing of the Roman Catholic Emancipation Bill in 1829'.[20]

But effects of these Conservative organizational reforms were mostly short-lived: the Conservative Operatives' Association dissolved in a welter of recrimination and confusion following the expensive failure of its 'reading room' during the downturn in trade of the early 1840s.[21] More widely, the Scottish party was damaged by the disastrous legacy of Conservative government in London. The schism within the Church of Scotland of 1843, the 'Great Disruption'—'the greatest disaster that Scottish Presbyterianism ever suffered'—was effectively aggravated by Robert Peel's administration, and indeed it may be suspected that, just as a divided Catholicism in Ireland served British ministerial interests at this time, so a fractured Presbyterianism was not wholly unwelcome.[22] In any event, while Catholicism overcame any internal division, and survived to become a key unifying agency in the creation of modern Irish nationalism, and in the Irish challenge to the union, Scottish Presbyterianism remained broken and thus too fragile to provide a confessional foundation for any coherent Scottish nationalism. In the mid term, however, the electoral influence of the break-way, or Free, Church, was thrown towards the Whig and Liberal cause, and Conservatism was for the moment associated with Erastianism, and (still worse) Episcopalianism. Other policies on offer did little to compensate: protectionism, for example, was unwelcome to the influential business classes of the Central Belt and elsewhere.[23]

Thus, despite some efforts in the 1830s, Scottish Conservatism remained 'abnormally weak' for a generation after 1846.[24] Only by the 1860s were the difficult legacies of earlier division (over protectionism, identification with the landed interest and with the pre-1832 *ancien regime*) finally tackled. The explanations for this modest recovery are varied. As in Ireland (where mid-19th-century Toryism was in fact relatively more successful), so in Scotland organizational reform and initiative accompanied extensions of the franchise.[25] Parliamentary reform in 1868 was accompanied by the creation of the first formal party organization to embrace the whole of Scotland, the

National Constitutional Association: the Conservative working classes of Glasgow, always alert to the requirements of discipline and organization (particularly now in the context of Catholic Irish immigration into the city), were organized in 1869 into the strongly Protestant Glasgow Workingmen's Conservative Association.[26] Improved organization brought some electoral dividends, and if the party's advance in 1874 was 'not so total as in England, [then it]...did still turn in, on the surface, a very creditable performance': it possessed some strength in the burghs, while still being blighted in the countryside by its reputation as a landlord party.[27] By 1882 Scottish Conservatism was at last fully affiliated within the structures of the National Union of Conservative Associations, with the creation of a Scottish NUCA structure (replete with eastern and western divisional organizations, based in Edinburgh and Glasgow respectively). Further stimulus was applied at this time to the professionalization of the party's activities (through, for example, the appointment of more full-time electoral agents).[28]

One factor supporting this incremental growth in the 1860s and after, particularly in the urban West of Scotland, was the development of Orangeism, the aggressively Protestant secret society founded in the North of Ireland in 1795. Orangeism in Scotland built partly upon an indigenous tradition of anti-Catholic protest, focused in organizations such as the Protestant Association of the 1770s, which successfully resisted Dundas's efforts to extend the benefits of the Roman Catholic Relief Act of 1778 to Scotland.[29] Elaine McFarland, however, has emphasised the precedents supplied by two other Scottish organizations, the 'Old Revolution Club' and the 'Grand Black Lodge of Scotland', both evidently mid-18th-century in origin, and supplying foundations of Protestant patriotism and invented ritual and mysticism which the Orange Order would subsequently inherit. The Order itself was introduced into Scotland almost certainly by militiamen returning from service in Ireland in countering the 1798 Rising, with its subsequent growth being aided by Irish Protestant immigration into the west of Scotland: the first lodge in Scotland was established in Maybole, Ayrshire, in 1799, 'possibly by a company of the Ayrshire and Wigtownshire Militia returning from service in Ireland'.[30]

As in Ireland, so in Scotland, Orangeism possessed a reputation both for bitter anti-Catholicism, (which alienated Whig reformers), and for plebeian violence (which unsettled Conservative managers). In the first quarter, indeed first half, of the 19th century Tory ministers and law enforcers in both Scotland and Ireland shared a view of Orangeism as an unruly and potentially destabilizing force within society. For example, despite (perhaps because of) his celebration of Lord Castlereagh and union, Archibald Alison, as Sheriff of Lanarkshire, personally led a cavalry force to prevent an illegal Orange march at Airdrie on 12 July 1834, and supervised the arrest and, ultimately, the transportation, of its ringleaders.[31] For Alison, and many Scottish Conservatives at this time, Orangeism was not only a threat to law and order, but essentially an alien threat—an import from Ireland which, whatever the local traditions of anti-Catholicism (which he shared), had essentially little to offer Scottish patriots (Alison's views of popular loyalism are clear from his narrative account of the aftermath of the 1798 Rising in Ireland).[32] Disdainful efforts at this time to provide some elite management of the Order's activities seem to have failed in the face of the infiltration of 'democratic ideals' amongst the Order's working class rank and file.[33]

However, after about 1865 the relative strength and political influence of the Order developed rapidly, even if (in relative terms) it still lagged far behind its sister organization in Ireland. Still, a combination of rapid Irish migration, both Catholic and Protestant, into the West of Scotland in the aftermath of the Great Famine (1845–1851) stimulated nativist reactions which fed into Orangeism (and indeed into other bodies on the fringes of Conservatism such as the West of Scotland Protestant Alliance (1873) and the (rougher) Working Men's Evangelistic Association (1870)).[34] This was also a period when Protestantism appeared to be under challenge, not just in terms of Catholic migration, but also with the proposed disestablishment of the Church of Ireland (in 1869), and the creation of a Scottish Catholic hierarchy in 1878. The urban working classes were now, after the Reform Act of 1868, beginning to enjoy greater enfranchisement, and reform within Scottish Conservative organization, particularly the Glasgow and Edinburgh Conservative Associations (an Edinburgh Conservative Working Men's Association was formed at about this time), was compelled to recognize this reality. McFarland has produced detailed local evidence which suggests that the Orange Order was exercising a significant influence at ward level across Glasgow by the time of the general election of 1880.[35] This accession of Orange support was associated with electoral success: Glasgow elected its first Conservative MP in 1874, and by the 1880s Conservatism had begun to recover a more general prominence in the West of Scotland. The first Orangemen, James Bain, Archibald Campbell (Renfrew) and William Whitelaw (Perth), were elected to the House of Commons for Scottish constituencies in the 1880s and 1890s.[36] By the early Edwardian period a socially more elevated form of Scottish Orangeism was identifiable in the shape of the wealthy brewer, George Younger, MP for Ayr Burghs.[37]

Some mild qualifications to this broad picture should be noted, however. The bond between Orangeism and Conservatism in Glasgow was complemented by 'less impressive and less unilinear [Orange] progress in the Party's directing bodies', and by a strongly contractual and watchful relationship between the two.[38] Moreover a variety of work on local politics in the centre and west of Scotland suggests a more complicated picture of denominational and political loyalties than any easy equation between religion and party provides. Geraldine Vaughan's study of Monklands in the 19th century, and specifically her work on Airdrie in the 1860s, reveals a tradition of Catholic support for Conservative candidates in municipal politics ('this simply seems to confirm that in local elections personal friendship and business relations played a greater role than political beliefs').[39] By way of contrast, Orange outbursts in Airdrie, were really 'quite rare'.[40] Moreover, the work of Foster, Houston, and Madigan on Govan (an area of high Orange concentration) suggests that class, rather than religious, identities were the main (if not the sole) determinants of political behaviour by the last decades of the 19th century.[41] This evidence and argument is confirmed at a macro level—looking at the whole of Scotland across the period 1861–1961—by the research of Eric Kaufmann.[42]

By the end of the 19th century Scottish Conservatism had some patriotic credibility, and was beginning to combine urban working-class support in the West with its traditional landed base: it was identified with Protestantism in the West, and was loosely associated with the Church of Scotland at a time when the Free Church was looking to the Liberals to deliver disestablishment. Scottish Conservatism had eventually adapted to the organizational needs of the reformed electorates of the 19th century. What the party as yet lacked was a single accessible cause which had meaning and clarity throughout Scotland. This came when the Liberal party renounced its historic association with the causes of both Irish and Scots union, adopting Home Rule for Ireland in 1886 and for Scotland in 1888: as Catriona Burness has remarked, 'defence of the Union with Ireland was the political cry that cracked Liberal hegemony in Scotland'.[43] The cause of union, together with an influential minority of Liberals who were unpersuaded by the new policy directions, were now effectively annexed by the Conservatives, who had already (under Disraeli) made a bid for the Palmerstonian legacy of aggressive foreign and imperial policies. The accession of the Liberal dissidents, or

Liberal Unionists, brought great long-term possibilities: but in the short-term came pressure for new policy stands on a range of social and economic questions, as well as challenges to some traditional vested interests within Toryism.

## Unionists, 1886–1920

After the mid 1880s, therefore, Conservatives could appeal to Scotland on the basis of Protestantism, union, and empire, tinctured (thanks to the Liberal Unionists) with a measure of social progressivism. In addition, or perhaps consequently, there is an array of evidence to suggest an intellectual and organizational vitality throughout the movement.

The intellectual underpinning of Irish Unionism in the Home Rule era has been generally overlooked, and (certainly until recently) this was emphatically the case for its Scots counterpart.[44] There were inevitably some connections between the Unionist intellectuals of Ireland and Scotland, as illustrated by the nexus formed by the Dowden brothers—Edward Dowden, Professor of Literature at Trinity College Dublin and illuminatus of the Irish Unionist Alliance, and John Dowden, Bishop of Edinburgh in the Scottish Episcopal Church. Each of the brothers was, in turn, a pivot within a broader network of local Unionist thinkers: Edward was a colleague of Trinity, or Trinity-trained, historians such as Richard Bagwell, C.L. Falkiner, T.D. Ingram, and W.E.H. Lecky, while John (classically trained, and a church historian) maintained contact with S.H. Butcher, H.J. Lawlor, and (through the agency of the Scottish Historical Society) with Peter Hume Brown.[45]

The interlinkages *within* Scottish Unionist thought in the Home Rule era are more difficult to decipher, but some attention should perhaps be directed to key intellectuals such as Sir Robert Rait, Fellow of New College, Oxford, an Aberdonian who later became Principal of the University of Glasgow, and Sir Richard Lodge, Professor of Modern History at the University of Edinburgh (and a Scot by adoption): Rait, famously, was co-author, with A. V. Dicey, of *Thoughts on the Union between England and Scotland* (1920), and Historiographer Royal of Scotland, while Lodge was a prolific lecturer and commentator, an active liberal imperialist, and later unionist (his name regularly cropped up in the deliberations of the Scottish Unionist Association as a potential speaker and lecturer).[46] Rait was also tutor at New College, Oxford, to Philip Kerr, 11th Marquess of Lothian (1882–1940), who was (in turn) part of another circle of pragmatically unionist and impe-rialist Scots associated with the Milnerite Round Table Movement: these also included Frederick Scott Oliver (1864–1934) and John Buchan, first Lord Tweedsmuir (1875–1940) (whom Rait first introduced to Kerr).[47]

In terms of geographical focus, it is striking that several of these Scots unionist intellectuals were anchored, like the leading Scots Baldwinian Tory, Walter Elliot, in (what is now) the Lothian and Borders region, and with a strong sense of the area's bloody history, and of its interconnections with the North of Ireland. Buchan was from Broughton, near Peebles, Lothian was from Dalkeith, and Oliver from Edgerston, near Jedburgh (and a nearish neighbour to Elliot, whom he occasionally visited, and whose home was close to Hawick).[48] It is possible to view this borders network as an intel-lectual complement to, or development from, the minor strain of late Victorian historiographical theorizing, which saw the lowlands of Scotland as a racial and ethnic extension of England—indeed as a locus of Teutonic purity.[49]

In terms of their unionism, these men were all prepared to countenance a form of parliament for Scotland, in the context of a wider 'federalist' reform of the British constitution, and in the interests of preserving the essentials of union as well as consolidating the government of the empire. The most famous statement of this case was perhaps Oliver's *Federalism and Home Rule* (1910), wherein the argument against Gladstonian Home Rule, and in favour of a devolution of power from Westminster to assemblies in Ireland, Scotland, and Wales, was laid out in some detail. Both Oliver and Buchan were (like Elliot) very strongly patriotic Scots.[50]

In general the records of Scottish Conservatism for the period between 1886 and the Great War suggest an active and well-organized enterprise, though there is certainly some evidence for disarray in the years immedi-ately after the election debacle of 1906. The Eastern Division of the NUCA coordinated meetings and finances across the East of Scotland in these years, employing a mixture of national leaders and Irish Unionist MPs as speakers ('failing Sir John Gorst, the Secretary was instructed to apply for Sir Edward Clarke KC MP, and failing him, Colonel Saunderson MP').[51] The Edinburgh Conservative Working Men's Association were relatively successful through-out the period in importing prominent speakers. Speakers from the Irish Unionist Alliance were successfully deployed in the border counties of southern Scotland on the eve of the 1895 general election.[52] Smoking concerts and 'lantern lectures' were in demand (the Division's offering of lantern lectures included 'Egypt', 'the British Empire', 'the Navy', 'Parliament', and 'Fishermen', though there was a request in March 1903 for 'South Africa, to include Joseph Chamberlain's tour'); these provided some light relief from the formal political meetings although speakers such as Saunderson were in demand precisely because they offered an entertaining cocktail of pugnacity and humour.[53] Working men were frequently deployed as speakers in order to connect with the needs of the masses, although they were carefully monitored, and were not always deemed as successful: 'the Secretary reported that a working man speaker had been sent by request to Berwickshire for a series of meetings, but that as his style and matter were unsatisfactory, the meetings had been cancelled'.[54] A Workers' League was created to give form and representation to the Unionist working classes: mimicking the masonic style organization of other aspirational artisan or working class bodies, the League offered membership of 'lodges' and the possibilities of office and status: in 1909–1910 it was judged to be developing 'with considerable success'.[55] Women and Liberal Unionists were cautiously brought into the fold of the formal Conservative organization: a separate Scottish Women's Conservative Association was approved in March 1906, with local bodies being raised almost immediately.[56]

After 1906 there is some evidence of organizational, particularly financial, drift within both Irish and Scottish Unionism. Within each political movement, certainly in the county seats, there was a disproportionately great expectation that the landed classes would supply funds; but, with the political dissolution and reorientation of the late Edwardian period, this expectation was routinely disappointed in Scotland and Ireland.[57] For example, in the comparatively wealthy agricultural constituency of East Lothian it was reported in November 1909 (on the eve of the general election) that 'the many large landowners whose interests are bound with those of the Unionist party are conspicuous by their apathy'.[58] Financial irregularity and conspicuous consumption, rather than elite miserliness, lay at the root of the problems of the Leith Burghs in 1910: the Unionist Association accounts were confused with that of the related social club, and 'the expenses of the club, so far as were ascertainable, were heavier than the circumstances justified'.[59] The balance of social benefits as against subscription cost alarmed the central managers of the Scottish party, with the installation of a telephone causing particular alarm.[60]

The experience of Leith Burghs underlines, however indirectly, that existing assessments fail to capture much of the spirit of middle and lower middle class Scots (or indeed Irish) Unionism at this time. A valuable corrective and insight into this louche and rumbustious world is provided through the records of the Western Conservative Club of Edinburgh, which span the Edwardian era. The Club, located in central Edinburgh, served as a debating forum, library, and networking forum for Edinburgh Unionists: it was a platform, too, for its long-standing Vice Chairman, the rising young lawyer, Robert Horne, who would later serve (in quick succession) as Minister of Labour, President of the Board of Trade, and Chancellor of the Exchequer in Lloyd George's post-war coalition government. Horne, however, was also (in Baldwin's characteristically censorious judgement) the 'Scots cad'; and this (rather than his legal and ministerial grandeur) chimed more closely with the tenor of the Western Club. It was noisy, undisciplined, and badly managed. Like other contemporary and later political clubs, there was a strong emphasis on recreation: billiards, whist (the lifeblood of 20th-century Scottish Unionist society), and dominos were taken seriously, and there were established prizes for the top performers.[61] Newspapers and periodicals were also taken in copious quantities, and old runs were auctioned off for club funds at the end of each year. Whisky was an unusually strong preoccupation (presumably on the principle, endorsed both by Burns and Mrs Thatcher, that 'freedom and whisky gang together'), and there was a recurrent concern over the quality, measure, and price of the spirits provided in the club bar.[62] Whisky, in true temperance narrative style, was in fact the undoing of the club. The Club had a sustained history of drunken rowdiness: the police periodically complained about the noisiness of the merry-making.[63] An unexplained fire at the club in August 1906 was opaquely defined as 'evidence of carelessness'.[64] In May 1911 a member was censured for introducing 'visitors to the club whose conduct in the opinion of the committee was undesirable and preducial [sic] to the interests of the Club'.[65] The contents of the bar, or rather their elusiveness, were an ongoing problem ('the Secretary reported that he had taken stock, and found that all was not in order, there being a shortage which was accounted for by the Clubmaster [the paid manager] in a very unsatisfactory manner').[66] The Club was peculiarly unfortunate in its (rapid) succession of managers, whose various falls from grace were solemnly recorded by the Secretary: in November 1906 the then manager was absent without leave on both days of Musselburgh races, in July 1907 there were accounting problems, in May

1908 there was renewed absence without leave, and in May 1914 there were suspicions concerning the measures of whisky dispensed. By December 1914, with the war raging on the Western Front, the club was deserted, over £10 worth of stock was missing, and the members could not pay the interest on the club's debt. Dissolution swiftly followed.

There is also evidence, however, of a somewhat more 'refined' and disciplined Conservative popular culture in Scotland, driven partly in urban areas by the Primrose League, and encompassing social events of somewhat more salubrious kinds than those organized by the 'Western Club'. The League arrived in Scotland in the autumn of 1885, and from then through to the First World War, it flourished, garnering over 100,000 members in its different grades. The minute book of the Grand Council of the Scottish Primrose League survives for the period between 1904 and 1920, and suggests a broadly thriving enterprise, with a trough in the mid Edwardian period (when of the seventy-three local League associations or 'habitations' on the books, twenty-five were deemed to be either 'in abeyance', 'hopeless', or 'indifferent'), and a peak during the third Home Rule crisis, when much activity (including a 'Help the Ulster Women Scheme' and support for the Women's Covenant) focused on Unionist resistance in the North of Ireland.[67] As Martin Pugh's work underlines, the League placed great emphasis upon title and hierarchy, and the meetings of the Grand Scottish Council were preoccupied with the award of honours (the first and second grades of the League's 'Grand Star', clasps for 'Special Service', 'Banners of Merit', and the 'Champion Banner').[68] It is true that Pugh has warned against overemphasising the popularity of the Primrose League outside of Glasgow and Edinburgh; but in fact in 1920 the last redoubts of the movement (those 'habitations' which most strenuously resisted dissolution) spanned not only Glasgow (the 'Arthur Balfour Habitation') and Edinburgh (the 'Walter Scott Habitation'), but also Fife, Dunbartonshire, and the Solway coast.[69]

Ireland was of course central to the purpose of Scottish Conservatism and Unionism, as Catriona Burness has eloquently established.[70] There were numerous individual Conservative linkages, illustrated most obviously and critically by Arthur Balfour and Andrew Bonar Law—damned by Hanham as 'semi-Scots'—but also by Hugh Thom Barrie, a Scot who was MP for North Londonderry (1906–1922), and Sir William Mitchell-Thomson (Lord Selsdon), the son of a Lord Provost of Edinburgh, who was successively MP for North West Lanark (1906–1910), North Down (1910–1918), and Glasgow

Maryhill (1918–1922).[71] Ian Malcolm, of Poltalloch, Argyll (and after 1930 the seventeenth hereditary chief of the Clan MacCallum), sought, as secretary of the Union Defence League between 1907 and 1910, to reunite British Unionism around opposition to Irish Home Rule: his surviving letters to his friend and patron, Arthur Balfour, reveal a particular interest in the Irish Unionist mission effort within Scotland at this time.[72]

There was also, inevitably, a degree of denominational solidarity between the Church of Scotland and its sister communion, the Presbyterian Church in Ireland. During the Plan of Campaign in Ireland, a Presbyterian minister, Revd J.W. Holms, was boycotted; and the editor of the *Scotsman*, Charles Cooper, was quick to seize upon Holms' plight, and to propose bringing him to Scotland to meet the ministers of Church of Scotland, and of the Free Church.[73] Similarly, during the sittings of the General Assembly of the Church of Scotland in 1913, the Eastern Division Council of the NUCA planned to organize a protest against Home Rule—'to be run by one or more of the Protestant bodies in Ulster which it was hoped might be attended by many of the ministers and elders in Edinburgh at that time'.[74] The Eastern Division Council also decided to translate the Irish Presbyterian Church's appeal against Home Rule into Gaelic, for the consumption of sympathetic Highlanders and the Free Church.[75] But recent research on the Scottish Episcopal Church in the West of Scotland has also emphasised the (hitherto neglected) affinities between Scots Episcopalians and the Church of Ireland—and the extent to which that communion was largely recreated in the 19th century, after the assaults of the 18th century, through the immigration of Irish Protestant Episcopalians.[76]

Emotions ran high over Ulster, even in relatively unperturbable quarters of Scottish Unionism.[77] The otherwise insouciant members of the Western Conservative Club were roused to defiance in February 1914, when they resolved to 'pledge ourselves to assist the loyalists of Ulster in their determined stand against the Government of Ireland being handed over to the enemies of Great Britain without the opinion of the electors being taken at a general election'.[78] Edward Carson rousingly addressed the 'Grand Habitation' of the Scots Primrose League in September 1912; and Ulster Unionism was generally central to the concerns of its Scottish brethren at this time.[79] The Ulster Women's Unionist Council, confident of success, planned to extend its organization to Scotland in November 1912. Though this was a relatively tactless overture (and there were others like it), in general Irish Unionist organizations were regarded as an asset to the Scottish

Unionist enterprise: for example, the intervention of the UAI was thought to have been useful in securing the South Lanarkshire victory for the party in late 1913.[80]

Ireland (and Scotland) were being defined increasingly according to the preconceptions and needs of British tourists; and politics, education, recreation, and leisure were combined and intersected with the development of a 'political' tourism at this time—trips of Scots (and others) to Ulster to see at first-hand the achievements of Unionism and the depredations of Irish Nationalism. The Council of the SUA's Eastern Division granted £250 to subsidize excursions to Ireland in June 1914, although the Party Chairman, Sir Arthur Steel Maitland, 'stipulated that these visits should be of an educative nature and not merely excursions' (and sensibly vetoed the potentially disastrous idea of a trip on 11 July, the eve of the Orangemen's annual festival).[81]

However, there was also some restraint or caution: the flamboyance of Irish Unionism was, generally, better attuned to a Scots than to an English audience, but one Irish outdoor speaker in 1914 overstepped the boundaries of Edinburgh decorum through speechifying in the uniform of the Ulster Volunteer Force ('such action in Scotland at any rate was calculated to bring the Ulster Army and the case against Home Rule into ridicule').[82] And (confirming the scholarly insights of W.S. Rodner) it should be stressed that not every Scottish Unionist gave an unqualified support to Ulster Unionist militancy.[83] For example, the British Covenant in Support of Ulster was (it was calculated) signed by 102,000 people in the West of Scotland by the spring of 1914, but not all were swayed by the emotions of the moment: addressing the Committee of the Western Division of the NUCA, 'the Hon. F. Elliott desired more information on the [British Covenant], with regard particularly to passive resistance, and he urged before coming to any decision in the matter they should know exactly how far they were committing themselves in signing, and in asking others to sign'.[84] There was also a discreetly held view among certain Scots Tories that devolution for Scotland was desirable; and, accordingly, men such as Alexander Bruce, Lord Balfour of Burleigh, were 'afraid of finding myself committed to opposing things for Ireland, when I would take them for my own country, and would [thus] be in an impossible situation so far as Scotland is concerned'.[85] Complementing this was the lingering elite view, as expressed by Balfour of Burleigh, that the Ulster Orangemen were not desirable political company: 'I am anxious not to be connected with what I hope I may describe without offence as the extreme "Orange" position', Balfour informed a doubtless apoplectic Walter Long in February 1907.[86]

What, indeed, of Scottish Home Rule at this time? As in the 1880s, so in 1914, the campaign for Irish Home Rule stimulated some interest in Scotland on the question of a devolved parliament. But there was in general little public passion; and the Scottish Unionist Party took a very leisurely approach to the question. The Committee of the Western Division of the SUA thought, for example, that 'the question did not interest the electors very much, but it was felt that as a parliament for Scotland was now part of the official Liberal programme, some information should be prepared for the use of candidates and others'.[87] The Eastern Division of the SUA held a discussion on 'objections to Home Rule All Round' in January 1914, and organized a subcommittee to report on the issue ('as a question of present political importance').[88] But, certainly for Scottish Unionists, Home Rule for Scotland was thoroughly overshadowed by the mounting crisis in Ulster.

It is true that this relatively vibrant platform did not overturn Liberal dominance in Scotland in the 1885–1918 era, and indeed it would be a profound mistake to ignore some of the more negative features of the movement at this time: it was undermined by the divisions created through tariff reform (much of the progress sustained by Conservatives between 1886 and 1900 was undone at the general election of 1906, when the combined Unionist tally of seats was only ten out of the seventy available).[89] However, the defeat of Scottish Unionism in 1906 (as was the case with Ulster Unionism) produced an immediate and extensive reawakening and professionalization of constituency organization.[90] And if Liberalism's dominance remained, then its hegemony was certainly challenged in these years. In 1895 the Unionists secured thirty-one of Scotland's seats, and in 1900 they briefly emerged as the dominant force in Scottish politics, with thirty-six seats to the Liberals' thirty-four. Moreover, as has been outlined, Ulster provided a critical galvanizing stimulus between 1910 and 1914, as all of the surviving Scottish Unionist records demonstrate.[91] By December 1918, with tariff reform forgotten, and working on the basis of some constituency redistribution and universal male suffrage, the Unionists gained twenty-eight of the seventy-one Scottish seats available. They were now poised both to exploit the wartime divisions within Liberalism by making a bid for the middle class vote, and to challenge Labour for a section of Protestant working class support.

# Liberal Unionists

Scottish Unionism derived its strength not merely from its Tory roots, but also from the accession of strength delivered in 1886 by Liberal Unionism. This in turn was anchored in a tradition of Whig unionism which dated back to the inauguration of the treaty itself, in 1707. For these Whigs of the 18th and 19th centuries, the union was a great and necessary and, indeed, inevitable reform. England provided an inescapable model of progress; and the union could facilitate the improvement and modernization of Scotland through easing the acceptance of English forms of political and economic intercourse. It has been provocatively said that, for the Whig tradition, 'Scotland's heritage amounted to little more than archaic uncouthness, with even its virtues preserved at the cost of extreme political backwardness'.[92]

Certainly one example of 'archaic uncouthness' was the unreformed electoral system, wherein forty-five MPs representing the burghs and counties of Scotland and a population of around 2.25 millions were returned by 3255 voters.[93] This was swept away by the Scottish Reform Act of 1832, which has been criticized for pursuing 'abstract rationalism' at the expense of 'continuity in Scottish history': the new order preserved property right while extending the franchise, but was based upon the imposition of a uniform English electoral regime on the Scots. In a sense, this would be a hallmark of Whig government in the 19th century: the elevation of an assimilationist unionism, founded often on fair and sensible principles, but regardless of the distinctiveness of Scottish institutions. With the reform of the ancient Scottish electorate, and with the fragmentation of the Kirk in the 'Great Disruption' of 1843, Scotland no longer possessed 'a single institution which could represent the character, the conscience, the soul of the nation, and no touchstone for the process of social and political renewal that was bound to continue'.[94]

Just as Scottish Toryism provided a popular fictional and historical bolster to unionism, assimilating a romantic Jacobite patriotism within the framework of union, so Scottish Whig historians of the Enlightenment era provided a narrative of shared Britishness and union. Whig historians in the 18th and early 19th centuries—scholars such as William Robertson (1721–1793), the Principal of the University of Edinburgh, and author of a *History of Scotland* (1759) or Thomas Babington Macaulay (1800–1859)–effectively undermined any autonomous reading of Scottish history, by positing a vision of Scottish history and identity which was moving inexorably towards union and Britishness. Colin Kidd has argued that this Whig historiography, particularly that of the 18th century, not only forefronted and bolstered union, it also effectively subverted the subsequent development in the 19th century of the kinds of romantic historiography which complemented nationalist movements elsewhere in Europe.[95] The predominance of Whig historiography, in this reading, is one of the explanations underlying the unionist nature of much Scottish patriotism in the 19th century, as well as the lack of a unified cultural nationalism in Scotland. This is certainly a critical distinction between Scotland in the age of Enlightenment and Ireland. Though there was a Whig reading of Irish history, the highly contested and politicized nature of late 18th- and early 19th-century Irish historiography simultaneously precluded any single predominant narrative, as well as permitting the widespread deployment of a popular (Catholic) historical vision and sensibility. This not only denied the validity of Whig historicism, it also supplied an alternative reading of the Irish past, which challenged the existing political and social order, and thus supplied the intellectual fuel for a nationalist challenge. There was no Hibernian equivalent of what Kidd has identified as 'the dissolution of Scottish historical confidence in the nineteenth century'.[96] Scottish Whigs gave union a popular history and legitimacy: Irish Whigs were not able to replicate this achievement.

The central focus both of Whig historical narratives as well as Whig and Liberal government policy in the mid and late 19th century was on a full integration of Scotland within the United Kingdom; but ministerial policy in Scotland was as much characterized by benign neglect as by proactive interference. From at least the 1830s, with the creation of the O'Connellite grouping in the House of Commons, Irish concerns were seen as occupying a disproportionate amount of British parliamentary time and effort, a development which culminated in the overwhelming dominance of Irish issues in the early and mid 1880s. But of course the reason for such sustained Whig and Liberal attention on Ireland from the 1830s onwards was that the union was a more recent, less settled, and more contentious relationship for the Irish than for the Scots. Union for Ireland was not just an issue of national relationships, but was explosively entangled with religion division and disputed property right. Scots Presbyterians were no lovers of the established Church of England; but they were bound into union and empire by a shared Protestantism. Though disestablishment of the Church of Scotland became a priority for the Free Church, and was considered by Gladstone, the Kirk did not occupy the same controversial position in Scots society as did the Church of Ireland for the Irish. Moreover, while Irish landowner-ship was tied up with bitterly contested religious and historical controver-sies, disputes over Scottish land were generally between co-religionists and compatriots. In sum, Irish land and religion dominated the concerns of Whig governments in the 1850s and 1860s in a way that Scots land and religion (whatever their problems) did not.

One obvious further binding agent between Whig ministers in London and party politics in Scotland was that, just as Whiggery and Liberalism commanded government in the middle years of the 19th century, so they were electorally dominant north of the border. Scotland, therefore, was (in electoral terms, at any rate) fully in tune with the drift of Whig government policy. In Ireland, however, the distance between Whig government and the Irish popular political mood could hardly have been more completely unbridgeable. While (as has been noted in the previous chapter) there was some complicated affinity between the Melbourne government and O'Connellite politics in the late 1830s, with a Scots Whig, Thomas Drummond, as a reforming head of the Irish civil service (and subsequent hero to Irish nationalists), this relationship was broken under the Russell government of 1846–1852.[97] Lord John Russell, though a proponent of Catholic emancipation and the friend of the Irish patriot poet, Thomas Moore, was in office during the Great Irish Famine, when over one million people died from hunger or disease; and he and his Whig administration were lastingly blamed for their apparent inactivity and heartlessness. Whiggery, which was (for much of the 19th century) the normative condi-tion of Scottish politics, came to be reviled in Ireland as the ideological complement to British mass murder. Whiggery, thus, served as a binding agent of union in Scotland, while acting as a constitutional solvent in Ireland.

William Gladstone's accession to the premiership in 1868 did not funda-mentally alter Scotland's relationship with Whig or (now) Liberal govern-ment. There was certainly a Scottish Whig presence in government, commanded by the intellectually formidable George Campbell, 8th Duke of Argyll, who served as Secretary of State for India. Gladstone, whose fam-ily origins were Scottish, was also broadly sympathetic to Scotland's con-cerns, and allotted more parliamentary time for Scottish debates; but sympathy did not translate into much action, and until the 1880s he contin-ued to work along assimilationist and centralizing lines.[98] There had been no separate Secretary for Scotland since 1746, with Scottish business being transacted mostly through the Home Office: Gladstone at first refused pressure to recreate the Scottish Secretaryship (this would have to wait until a Tory reform in 1885), nor would he at first even assent to a more modest proposal for a dedicated Scottish Under Secretary at the Home Office. He also swept aside a motion for the creation of a House of Commons Select Committee on Scottish affairs, opining in 1872 that 'the grievances of Scotland are not more real to Scottish members than the grievances of England are to English members'.[99] Though consideration was being given to the problems of church establishment and land in Ireland (through disestablishment in 1869 and a modest land reform in 1870), no such legislative action was undertaken in Scotland. Gladstonian Liberalism, therefore, while fully capable of addressing some generic challenges within the United Kingdom (such as parliamentary reform), offered a unionism which in neither a legislative nor intellectual sense fully recognized Scottish patriotic sensitivities or Scottish distinctiveness.

In opposition, Gladstone inevitably showed rather more interest in Scotland than this, most famously through the Midlothian campaigns of 1879–1880. But here, as elsewhere, it has been fairly said that what was on offer was 'high moral inspiration rather than practical improvements': John Buchan certainly thought that Gladstone provided Scottish Liberalism with a vacuous superiority—'an aura of earnest morality so that its platforms were also pulpits and its harangues had the weight of sermons'.[100] Gladstone's providentialist outlook, his high moral tone, his principled censoriousness, all played well in Calvinist Edinburgh, and more widely in Scotland; and Gladstone at least recognized the common Scottish perception of inequity in proclaiming (at Dalkeith, Midlothian, in 1879) that 'I will consent to give to Ireland no principle, nothing that is not upon equal terms offered to Scotland and to the different portions of the United Kingdom'.[101] But this generous avowal ran contrary to those political realities, of which he was generally a master: Ireland had been offered the principle of disestablishment, and would shortly (in 1881, after Gladstone had formed his second administration) be offered the principle of dual land ownership. Neither of these was on immediate offer for all of Scotland, nor was Gladstone ever interested in Scottish Home Rule in the same way that he was persuaded by its Irish variant. Scotland simply represented (at least in terms of surface realities) much less of a challenge to British government and the unity of the United Kingdom than did Ireland: Scottish politics were broadly integrated within a wider British canvas, while Scottish religion was so broken by internal schism as to present a relatively weak political threat (though it is true that Free Church support for disestablishment caused problems within Liberalism). In Ireland, however, the coalition between a unified Catholicism, land agitation, and nationalism, was a much more dangerous problem, which demanded more time and attention than could be applied to Scotland. It is indeed possible that Gladstone's increasingly great and public identification with Ireland—and Wales—should be seen as a deliberate complement, or counterweight, to the monarchy's embrace, from the 1850s onwards, of a version of Scottish highland tradition.

By the early and mid 1880s Gladstone's vision of union was beginning to flag in Scotland. In essence Gladstonian 'unionism' was concerned with the salvaging or adaptation of existing institutions, even if this meant radical surgery and the amputation of diseased extremities which were threatening the whole constitutional organism. If Scottish Whiggery was tied in with the union and with the interests of the existing landed elite, then the surgical strategies which Gladstone felt compelled to pursue in Ireland posed some difficult challenges. For some Scottish Whigs, the specific nature of Gladstone's land reforms in Ireland were unacceptable, positing too great a challenge to the existing property order, not just in Ireland but potentially in Scotland as well. The Duke of Argyll was an early emigrant from the government and from Liberalism, resigning from his office as Lord Privy Seal in May 1881 over the issue of the Irish land bill of that year. Second, the amount of time which Irish matters were consuming at Westminster was a matter of wide Scottish Liberal concern, and reinforced the notion that the government of the United Kingdom was not being pursued along equitable lines. Third, the ultimate means by which Gladstone sought to address Irish unrest (and, incidentally, the problem of Ireland's dominance of the parliamentary timetable) was Home Rule, an initiative which raised as many questions as it proposed to answer. Gladstone's great conversion to Home Rule, announced in December 1885, certainly (in its original formulation) looked set to subcontract Irish business to a Dublin assembly, as well as substantially exclude the infinitely loquacious representatives of Ireland from Westminster; but of course in freeing up the timetable for the consideration of Scottish and other business, Gladstone was apparently favouring one Celtic nationalism over another, and rewarding political dissent rather than political acquiescence. The launch of Gladstone's Irish Home Rule Bill in April 1886 drove Scottish Liberals in at least three directions: some Whig landowners like Rosebery, right-of-centre luminaries like Haldane, and a few radicals, remained within the Gladstonian fold, masking their antipathies and (in the case of Rosebery and Haldane) waiting for the moment to advertise a more imperialist Liberalism.[102] Other Liberals turned to the advocacy of a separate settlement for Scotland, participating in the creation of the Scottish Home Rule Association (1886), and in the conversion of the Scottish Liberal Association to the idea of Scots Home Rule (1888). But still others dealt with the paradoxes of Gladstonian Liberalism through taking the route that a trickle of moderate Whigs had traversed since the 1830s—towards Conservatism.

At the general election of July 1886, following the defeat of the Home Rule Bill at its second reading in the House of Commons, seventeen former Gladstonians were elected as Liberal Unionists in Scotland.[103] This number dipped to eleven in 1892, but broadly remained static until tariff reform temporarily broke Unionism in Scotland at the general elections of 1906 and 1910. The notion that the Liberal split in Scotland (as in the House of Commons) was essentially a parting of 'left' and 'right' has been closely scrutinized and challenged.[104] Scottish Liberal Unionism was a socially and regionally complex phenomenon, embracing landed Whiggery throughout Scotland, as well as urban Whigs in the west of the country: there was an admixture of radicals, influenced by a variety of motives, including (perhaps) Joseph Chamberlain's lead, disillusion with Gladstone's linking of Home Rule with an apparent bailout for Irish landlordism (in the form of land purchase), and disillusion, too, with his hesitant stand on disestablishment. Rejection of Gladstone did not, of course, mean at this stage any automatic marriage with Conservatism. More generally, Liberal Unionism was fired by the close interconnections between, in particular, the West of Scotland and the North of Ireland: ties of trade, capital, and technological exchange bound Glasgow and Belfast, while the movement of people was facilitated by easy and cheap ferry boats across the North Channel and the Firth of Clyde (a snapshot study of the regional origins of Irish immigrants for the years 1876–1881 suggests that the four most Protestant counties of Ireland were supplying the majority).[105] Presbyterianism was central to the political and commercial cultures of both the North East of Ireland and Scotland.[106] There was also a shared Liberal Unionist political community bridging the North Channel: for example, Archibald Cameron Corbett, the radical Unionist MP for Glasgow Tradeston between 1886 and his reversion to Liberalism in 1908, was a brother of Thomas Lorimer Corbett, the temperance-minded Liberal Unionist MP for North Down (1900–1910). Thomas Wallace Russell, MP for South Tyrone (1885–1910), and the leading Irish radical Unionist of the era, was the son of a Fife crofter. The Belfast-born mathematician and physicist, William Thomson, Lord Kelvin, was President of the West of Scotland Liberal Unionist Association between 1886 and 1892.

The relationship between Scottish Conservatives and Liberal Unionists, like their counterparts in the North of Ireland, was never easy, and indeed was fraught from the beginning with jealousies and resentments concerning the representation of seats, to say nothing of larger policy issues.[107] In both Scotland and the North of Ireland Liberal Unionism acted as a defensive junior partner in the alliance, often (in the short-term) diverting political energies into in-fighting within the Unionist family. But in the long-term the accession of these Gladstonian dissidents brought critical strengths to Scottish, and wider, Unionism: in particular, the reforming pressure of Liberal Unionists on issues such as land helped to create a more socially responsive and progressive Unionism—a more viable Unionism—than would have been the case, had Conservativism had sole proprietorial rights over the cause of union.[108] While it would be wrong to discount the longer tradition of progressive Toryism, and to overestimate the influence of Liberal Unionism, particularly after 1895, it is unquestionably the case that concern for the integrity of the Unionist alliance was a powerful motivating force in the evolution of Conservative reformism in the decade after 1886.[109] In Glasgow, unionism emerged as a powerful collectivist and interventionist force—'a reconstructed form of ethical Liberalism': detente between Conservatives and Liberals in the city was facilitated by (for example) Lord Kelvin's Imperial Union Club ('an outstanding example of the kind of harmony that ought to prevail amongst all good Unionists and...one of the most important political forces in the West of Scotland').[110] More widely the success of unionism, even allowing for the setbacks induced by tariff reform, represented in effect the end of Scotland's long decades of one-party politics, and the beginnings of a more competitive party environment. Uniting with their Conservative allies in 1912, Liberal Unionists were unsure whether they were commemorating 'a birth, a marriage or a funeral'; but in a sense their relationship with Conservatism was educational rather than sacramental, for they taught Scottish Tories how to address an electorate beyond the Protestants of Glasgow or the landed proprietors of the New Club.[111]

# Unionists, 1920–1970

In 1955 the Scottish Unionist party, famously, won 50.5 per cent of the popular vote. The Unionists were a major force in Scottish politics through most of the second and third quarters of the 20th century, achieving electoral lift-off in 1924 (in the context of a fatally fractured Liberalism), with thirty-six of Scotland's seventy-one parliamentary seats, while retaining twenty-two seats as late as the advent of Margaret Thatcher in 1979. In 1931 the party captured forty-eight of the Scottish seats, and in the early and mid 1950s, together with its National Liberal allies, it was still seriously threatening Labour for electoral predominance in Scotland.

An obvious interpretative challenge arises in seeking to explain this electoral success (certainly relative to Conservatism's performance in the 19th, and indeed the early 21st centuries).[112] The Unionists' bid for the middle class vote was assisted by the collapse of the Liberals in the 1920s, who were divided over both the Coalition Government, and later by support for the Labour administrations of 1924 and 1929–1931. The general election of 1924 saw the Liberals largely concentrated in the Highlands and Islands, and it has been rightly said that 'the eclipse of the party which had been so dominant...since 1832 was now complete, and Scottish politics took on a new complexion'.[113]

However, the Unionists' success was not only brought by Liberal implosion, for they also worked energetically for votes: they sustained a comparatively high level of organizational efficiency and were adept at appealing to those newly enfranchised under the 1918 and 1928 Representation of the People Acts—women and young people generally. The mobilization of these two critical electoral groupings has been described as 'the two masterstrokes of Unionist organisation'.[114] Women's sections of the movement were developed, as were a range of educational and social activities specifically targeting women: women organizers were appointed for the first time in 1918–1919.[115] In July 1923 the SUA decided against any separate women's association, and in favour of 'absolute equality' within the one body.[116] Provision was made for 'oratorical classes' for women speakers.[117] The first Unionist woman to be appointed as a government minister was the MP for West Perthshire, Katharine Atholl—subsequently 'the Red Duchess', who was Parliamentary Secretary to the Board of Education between 1924 and 1929.[118] The Unionist MP for Dundee (1931–1945), Florence Gertrude Horsbrugh, graduated from the staff of the SUA to serve as Parliamentary

Secretary to the Ministry of Health (1939–1945), and later as Secretary of State for Education in Churchill's last cabinet (1951–1954): Horsbrugh also achieved fame as the first woman to move the Address in reply to the King's Speech (in November 1936).[119] Chips Channon thought her 'extremely likeable and able'; and even the curmudgeonly Cuthbert Headlam, hard to impress in such matters, thought Horsbrugh 'much more able' than her Secretary of State for Health, Ernest Brown.[120] By 1954, admittedly, some of this sheen had dulled, and Harold Macmillan had decided that '"Auntie Flo", as Miss Horsbrugh is irreverently called, is also a very poor politician'.[121]

Young voters, or those on the cusp of acquiring the vote, were offered the Junior Imperial League, which had 20,000 members by the late 1920s, while a later generation of children and teenagers were enrolled in the Young Unionists, or Young Britons.[122] The Junior Imperialists were active in the interwar years, organizing essay prizes ('Imperial Union: how can it best be promoted?'), missionary jaunts to the terra incognita of East Stirling's mines, and 'Children's Nights' ('to counteract…the propaganda carried on by the Socialists among the children'): they were rebranded in June 1946 as the 'Scottish Junior Unionists'.[123] The Young Unionists held their inaugural meeting at Edinburgh in April 1933, a somewhat high-minded affair, whereat discussions were held on Anglo-Russian trade relations and the World Economic Conference, with small groups on 'currency stabilisation', the 'removal of trade barriers', and the 'raising of price levels' (a moderate concession to levity was offered in the form of trips to Craigmillar Castle, and to Edinburgh Central Fire Station)[124]

Whether in appealing to women or young people, the Unionists were adept at packaging their message in attractive and winning ways. The (still somewhat underestimated) social and popular cultural dimension to Scottish (and indeed contemporary Ulster) Unionism was critical to the electoral success of the party.[125] Scottish (and Ulster) Unionists used the press and film, distributing copious quantities of propaganda sheets, and commissioning touring cinema vans. This was the era when the tobacco companies used cigarette cards as a marketing device; and the importance of these as a collecting fad, particularly for the working classes and the young, was such that they (or 'something similar to cigarette cards') were actively considered as a means of disseminating political propaganda.[126] Indeed tobacco supplies one crisp illustration of the cross-currents of interwar Scottish Unionism: in the late 1930s the tobacco blender, Gales of Dundas Street, Glasgow, successfully marketed their 'Dr White's Glasgow Presbyterian Mixture'—'as smoked by the Rt. Hon. Stanley Baldwin', replete with an illustration of St Mungo Cathedral, and Baldwin's endorsement ('My thoughts grow in the aroma of that particular tobacco') (see illustration B.3).

The overt interconnection between Orangeism and Unionism was waning much earlier in Scotland than in Northern Ireland (from around 1922), though a generalized association between the Party and Orange Protestantism remained (and at least six Orange MPs were returned for Scottish constituencies in the interwar years, including a Secretary of State, Sir John Gilmour); other, much less contentious, forms of social organization and recreational activity were more than compensating for the Order's relegation, which also paved the way for a more ecumenical appeal.[127] There was a plethora of summer schools, easter schools, and organizers' conferences at this time.[128] As well as lecture courses and conferences, Union and empire were also upheld by kitchen and garden meetings, fetes and bazaars, whist and bridge drives, and golf and tennis competitions.[129] Youth were recruited to the Unionist movement, not merely through the formal structures already described, but also (as in Ireland) through highly organized, socially conservative, and (often) Church-related bodies such as the Boys' Brigade. It is noticeable, for example, that Alec Douglas-Home's training for Conservative parliamentary politics involved a variety of local engagement, including Burns' Clubs, literary societies, the yeomanry, but—above all—the Boys' Brigade, where he was president of the West of Scotland District (1934–1939), at a time when his father (the 13th Earl of Home) was national president. Douglas-Home's fellow Scottish Unionist parliamentarian, the Marquess of Douglas (East Renfrew, 1930–1940), later the 14th Duke of Hamilton, served as Treasurer of the Boys' Brigade between 1938 and 1963, when he was appointed to its presidency.[130]

There are certainly dangers in being overly sanguine or reductionist about the state of interwar Unionism. The Irish settlement of December 1921 had created some division within the Party, particularly (but not exclusively) in the West (and unlike Liverpool, there was no charismatic Boss Salvidge to impose discipline and unity).[131] For example, in January 1922, at a meeting of the Central Committee of the SUA, the Irish policy of the coalition government was indeed formally approved, but not before Sir Alexander Sprot (MP for East Fife between 1918 and 1922, and for North Lanarkshire between 1924 and 1929) and Admiral Thomas Adair (MP for Shettleston between 1918 and 1922) had sought support for a rival resolution deploring 'the action of the government in departing from the provisions of the 'Better Government of Ireland Act', so recently passed into law, and in surrendering to the murder gang of Sinn Feinn [sic] thereby setting up in Southern Ireland a potential danger to the security of Great Britain and at the same time causing bitterness in Ulster with reference to the question of the boundaries'.[132] Moreover, with the relegation of Irish politics in Britain after 1921–1922, Scots Unionists lost a rallying call; and though Ireland in some senses may have been a damaging diversion for the Unionists, Baldwinian Toryism held a somewhat less 'primordial' or visceral appeal.

It was also the case that by the early 1930s all was not well at local level, partly because of the wider economic conditions of the era. The tradition of free spending and indebted local Conservative associations, which was clear from the 1830s, with the Glasgow Conservative Operatives' Association, and represented by the Western Conservative Club and the Leith Unionists in the Edwardian era, was sustained into the 1930s by the likes of Govan and Bridgeton Unionist associations (both of which were deemed to be 'in serious financial difficulties' in March 1930).[133]

In addition, there were clear limits to the usefulness and efficiency of much local activity, and some of the problems which would characterize the party in the post-war era were already evident in the 1920s and 1930s. The leading Scottish Unionist activist, P.J. Blair, privately admitted that, for all the electoral success and public confidence, 'one sometimes has the feeling that the party in Scotland is not quite what it should be. Perhaps the ideal is a little high. People who should take an interest do not; people who do seem to carry weight in it are really 'light horsemen', and hot air and futility sometimes prevail'.[134] There were reported tensions or 'lack of cooperation' between the youth wing of the Party and the 'senior' Unionist Associations.[135] The practicality of some of the political education was also open to question, and organizers occasionally found it difficult to attract sufficient numbers to make summer schools viable ('Mr Benton said that he did not think lectures on economics were much good to speakers to go and talk on practical politics').[136] There was also a recurrent, perhaps growing, danger that the medium and message of party activity would be confused: members of the Executive Committee of Glasgow UA complained in January 1932 that there was a 'need to see that a proper balance is held between social activities and political activities. Whist drives and other social functions are necessary... but still more important is it to carry on propaganda work'.[137] All of these issues—the balance between social and political activity, a lack of practical political focus, lack of synergy between the youth and mainstream movements, and money—are relevant in understanding the later retreat of Unionism.

One typically genteel Unionist stratagem of the interwar years was the garden fete; and one striking example of this was held 'under the auspices' of the Lanark and North Lanark Unionist Associations at Douglas Castle on 27 August 1927, and boasted Stanley Baldwin as the principal speaker, flanked by Sir Alexander Sprot and his fellow MP for Lanark, Stephen Mitchell, as well as a printed souvenir history of 'Douglas and the Douglas Family', specially produced for the fete by a local luminary, C.C. Riach, and by the *Hamilton Advertiser*.[138] Riach's history of Douglas serves to shift the analytical focus away from the electoral strategies of interwar Unionism towards a brief discussion of some of its intellectual content at this time, as it illustrates the particular mixture of Scottish patriotism and Britishness which was actively, and successfully, promoted by the Unionist party throughout the second and third quarters of the 20th century: it also serves to introduce the ideas of Walter Elliot, who began his distinguished political career as MP for this area (1918–1923).

Riach's description of the Douglas Castle demesne unblushingly combined—within the one paragraph—lyrical descriptions of the 'Doom Tree' ('on which seven Englishmen were hanged at one time') as well as 'a chestnut tree planted by King Edward on his visit on October 1906'.[139] The contribution of the Douglases to Scotland's independence was celebrated ('loyal supporters of their sovereign and the mainstay of Scottish independence'), and the particular association of the family with Robert Bruce ('Sir James was the heroic comrade and faithful subject of Bruce. To their united achievements Bruce owed his crown, and Scotland its independence').[140] A sub-text of the narrative, however, is the inconsistency and capriciousness of the Stuart monarchs. The achievement of the Reformation and sacrifices of the Covenanters (whose heartland was of course in the South West of Scotland) are directly lauded.[141]

Riach's little volume exemplifies one of the two central Unionist approaches to Scottish history and the challenge of reconciling union and patriotism. One of the intellectual and political legacies of Whiggery was an assimilationist unionism, which tended to play down the distinctiveness of Scotland's history and traditions, and (in policy terms) to enfold Scotland within the embrace of the United Kingdom state: in this reading Scotland was, adapting Margaret Thatcher's dictum, 'as British as Finchley', and indeed

Mrs Thatcher herself pursued essentially integrationist strategies when Prime Minister (1979–1990). Paradoxically, an integrationist or assimilationist unionism has also been a major influence within the Labour party, which (without being particularly responsive to Scottish cultural distinctiveness) has sought to demonstrate that a centralized British state can be made to work for Scottish needs. However, there has also been a strongly patriotic strain within Scottish Conservatism and Unionism, which (while it has been criticized by some scholars for its apparent superficiality or opportunism) was extremely effective as an electoral and administrative weapon.[142]

Thankfully, from the point of view of its own well-being, Scottish Unionism did not have to rely solely upon the intellectual luminosity generated by C.C. Riach or the *Hamilton Advertiser*. Interwar Scots Unionism was a relatively high-voltage affair, with several leaders of the movement contributing studies which had an illumination and influence beyond the local. The significant Unionist thinker, A.N. (Noel) Skelton (MP successively for Perth and the Scottish Universities in the interwar years and Under Secretary of State for Scotland between 1931 and his death from cancer in 1935) defined (if he did not devise) the tempting idea of a 'property-owning democracy', a notion further elaborated in his highly influential *Constructive Conservatism* (1924). Skelton appears to have been well informed on recent Irish history, and to have drawn partly on the success of Irish land purchase in formulating his thoughts.[143] He also gave voice to the prevailing Conservative fear (which underpinned the Scottish and wider programme of political education) that the educated working classes would be prey to the lures of the Socialist ('who comes disguised as an educator and teacher') unless the Conservatives sought to sell their own message with greater vigour and clarity.[144] Profit-sharing in industry, cooperation in agriculture, and—drawing upon older, Edwardian, Tory responses to the challenges of progressive politics—tariff reform and use of 'the referendum' were the nostra by which Skelton proposed to rescue Scotland, and Britain, from socialism. Skelton influenced a generation of younger Tory MPs in the 1920s—the 'YMCAs', who were themselves both disproportionately Scottish in their make-up (Robert Boothby, Walter Elliot), and also determined to codify their political values and principles in published manifestos.[145]

A more sweeping revision of the faith was elaborated at length by a young Unionist journalist and economist from Abertay, James A.A. Porteous, in *The New Unionism* of 1935. Porteous sought to build upon both Skelton's diagnoses, as well as Baldwinian one-nation rhetoric, and to frame each within a corporatist social and industrial structure, involving national commissions or councils for each of the main industries: 'the name Unionism must stand for the creed of national unity between all classes and sections of the people, a new unity in government...Unionism should also be given a special significance in the narrower sphere of economics and industry'.[146] But the carefully framed appeal evidently failed, to judge by the rejection slips among Porteous's papers from Conservative journal editors, and the small print-run of his magnum opus.[147] And Porteous himself, disappointed and impecunious, moved towards nationalist politics, holding office as Honorary Secretary, and (after 1950) as economic advisor, to the Covenant movement. Later still, in the late 1960s, Porteous graduated to the SNP.[148]

Others underpinned a Scottish version of Baldwinian unity, while giving succour to the nationalist project. One of the most frequently cited court cases in the history of Scottish nationalism is MacCormick v. HM Lord Advocate of 1953, in which John MacCormick and Ian Hamilton sought to contest the relevance of Queen Elizabeth II's regnal number within Scotland (where there had been no previous Queen Elizabeth).[149] The case was dismissed on appeal, but it was made famous by the Lord President's opinion that 'the principle of unlimited sovereignty of Parliament is a distinctively English principle, and has no counterpart in Scottish constitutional law'— an opinion which has been held to have implications for the validity and prospects of the 1707 Treaty of Union. However, much more attention has focused on the judgement than on the political and intellectual background of the judge, the Lord President of the Court of Session, Lord Cooper of Culross. Thomas Mackay Cooper was a Baldwinian, who ran as Unionist candidate for Banffshire in 1931, and was returned as Unionist member for Edinburgh West in 1935: he was raised to the judiciary in 1941. Like Porteous, Cooper favoured 'that word "Unionism". It's a better title than the old name "Conservative". For it suggests to the mind three of the ideals which are central and vital to Unionist party policy—union and fellowship between employer and employed, union and goodwill between class and class within the community; union and cooperation between the old country and the Dominions beyond the seas'.[150] He argued in the 1930s for a proactive, an 'applied Unionism'. But Cooper was also a patriot, deeply proud of the distinctive Scottish legal tradition, and interested in its (and wider Scottish) history. He was a founder of Stair, the Scottish Legal History Society, and active within the Scottish Historical Society. He turned down a Lordship of

Appeal in 1953 because he did not wish to leave Edinburgh; and it is significant that those trying to persuade him to move thought it best to couch their arguments in strongly Scottish terms, claiming to be 'thinking only of Scottish patriotic interests'.[151] The future Lord Advocate and judge, Gordon Stott, who (as a QC) handled numerous marital and divorce cases, commented on Cooper's legal patriotism in 1957, saying that 'if Cooper were alive [he had died in 1955] and head of the Scottish judiciary, he would have made short shrift of any argument that a decree of an English court could be an impediment to marriage in Scotland'.[152]

This vision of 'unionism' as embodying more than arid constitutionalism survived into the post-war era. It remained a defining feature of the political creed of one of the more successful Scottish Unionists of the third quarter of the 20th century, Priscilla Buchan, Baroness Tweedsmuir (MP for South Aberdeen between 1946 and 1966, Under Secretary of State for Scotland (1962–1964), Minister of State for Scotland (1970–1972) and Minister of State at the Foreign Office (1972–1974)).[153] Buchan (then Priscilla Grant) launched her political career in March 1945 with a speech delivered to the Scottish Unionist Association at St Andrews' Hall, Glasgow, wherein she summarized much of her colleagues' thinking in the interwar years: 'as Unionists we have pledged ourselves to attain great objects. Perhaps the foundation of them all is our belief in a union of all classes in a true democracy. A democracy that is based on family life and the rights of property'.[154] The sentiments hit home: the speech was widely lauded, and Buchan's career was launched.[155]

Scottish Unionism may indeed, as its critics alleged, have been opportunistic, pragmatic, and slippery; but there is certainly much evidence, both private and published, to suggest a deep-seated concern for the sentiment, symbols, and culture of Scottishness in this period. In private debate Noel Skelton rehearsed an argument which had been familiar in principle to patriotic Irish Unionists before the First World War—'he thought that it was degrading to talk of placing Scotland in the position of a Dominion. Scotsmen are all nationalists, we have our laws and customs and kingdom and it would be a retrograde step to quit the Union'.[156] During the same debate (within the Scottish Unionist Members' Committee at Westminster), J.S.C. Reid (Unionist MP for Stirling and Falkirk, later Lord Reid) argued that the Unionists 'should have a clear-cut policy of a constructive character to put forward to appeal to the sentiment of the Scottish nation ... he thought it might be wise to stress our individuality as a Unionist party in Scotland apart from the Conservative party'.[157] Amongst these Unionist parliamentarians perhaps the most pronounced cultural 'nationalist' was Major Duncan McCallum (Unionist MP for Argyll between 1940 and 1958), who was a proponent of Gaelic broadcasting, and who was also resentful of English members' interference in exclusively Scottish parliamentary debates.[158]

Robert Boothby (MP for East Aberdeen, between 1924 and 1958) was a no less patriotic Unionist, though his fame (or notoriety) now perhaps rests not so much with his lyrical attachment to Aberdeenshire and Scotland as with his rather more tangible attachments to Dorothy Macmillan and Ronnie Kray. Certainly amongst the most impressively passionate passages of his first essay in autobiography, *I Fight to Live* (1947), was an indictment of the 'betrayal', by successive British governments, of the Scottish agricultural and fishing industries, as well as of the more general neglect of Scotland: 'every year the encroachments of the Whitehall octopus increase, and greater power is transferred to London . . . The English had better take care! Their combination with the Scotch has for so long been so felicitous that they are inclined to take it for granted. The truth is that they can no longer do without them. At the same time, there are limits beyond which the lamentable process described above cannot be allowed to continue. For my part, I am content to say, with Burns: "O Scotia! My dear, my native soil!"'.[159] This sense of the 'denationalization' of Scotland was becoming (as will become clear) a favoured trope within Scottish Unionism in the later 1940s; but Boothby's emotion and precision suggest that he was going beyond partisan norms and rhetoric in articulating a vision for Scottish Unionism.

There were certainly 'insubstantial, cosmetic and ugly' aspects to this vision: Unionists occasionally pursued a nativist or exclusivist line, and (unlike Labour, which 'avoided any particular religious association') they never wholly threw off their Protestant associations.[160] On the one hand, the formal association between Glasgow Unionists and the Orange Order had been terminated in January 1922 (by the Orangemen, protesting at the Anglo-Irish Treaty); and by the late 1920s Glaswegian Tories, led by Sir Lewis Shedden, were plotting about ways in which 'trusted Conservative Roman Catholics' might be used to suborn the vote of their co-religionists.[161] Alexander Ratcliffe's Scottish Protestant League, not the Unionists, were the most aggressive and successful contenders for the populist, sectarian vote in the West of Scotland at this time (and inspiring a Catholic counter-mobilization).[162] On the other hand, Unionist candidates sometimes enjoyed Protestant League and Orange support in western constituencies, a fact carefully observed by the main Catholic organ, the *Glasgow Observer*.[163] Moreover, at an individual level, Walter Elliot, perhaps the most distinguished and successful Scottish Unionist of the interwar years (an era scarred by calls for the repatriation of the Irish from Scotland), littered his private correspondence and commentaries on the arcana of Glasgow politics with a casual but strikingly persistent sectarianism ('Compton Mackenzie and the Papists have won Glasgow Rectorial'; juvenile delinquency in Glasgow was caused by 'religious training'—'if one reckons Papistry as religion').[164]

Irish immigration into interwar Scotland, a subject on which the Church of Scotland notoriously expounded a hard-line viewpoint, evidently did not generate much wider concern within the Unionist hierarchy, if the copious surviving evidence of their committee and organizational work is a guide; but the IRA's 'S-Plan' (its campaign in Britain of 1939–1940, which was partly organized by a Scot of Irish origins) invoked expressions of rage from the residually Orange sections of the Central Committee of the SUA: in July 1939 the Glasgow Orangeman and councillor, Sir Charles Cleland (who was the father-in-law of Dawson Bates, the chauvinistic Unionist Minister of Home Affairs for Northern Ireland) told the Central Committee that the issue of Irish immigration 'was a serious one in the West of Scotland, as those immigrants had the vote after a very short residence, and moreover, being of a low type for the most part, came in numbers upon Public Assistance. Their voting power in Glasgow was over 25 per cent, and he considered that they should not have the power of voting [until] after residence of some such period as seven years. He did not consider that the Bill now under consideration in Parliament giving power to round up persons suspected of being implicated in the IRA outrages touched the matter at all'.[165] However, while one other member of the Committee, Ian Clark Hutchison (who had had a rough handling as Unionist candidate for Maryhill in 1935, before moving to represent the tranquil suburbia of Edinburgh West in 1941) expressed concern, Cleland alone pursued the issue with any energy or venom.[166]

Moreover, Scottish Unionists were also making common cause both before and after the war with right-wing Catholic activists on the theme of opposition to communism. Indeed, Scottish Unionists, backed sometimes by the residual Scottish Catholic landed classes, were well represented on the pro-Franco, and sometimes pro-German and anti-semitic wing of British Conservatism in the 1930s. This is perhaps best illustrated by the famous West Perthshire by-election of December 1938, where the sitting MP, Katharine, Duchess of Atholl, faced particular opposition for her Spanish republican stand from landed Catholic Unionists, as well as fellow Scottish Unionist MPs such as Captain Archibald Maule Ramsay (MP for Peebles, 1931–1945), Sir Thomas Moore (Ayr Burghs, 1925–1964), and the Catholic convert Sir John McEwen (Berwick and Haddington, 1931–1945): Ramsay founded the United Christian Front in 1937 (which Alec Douglas-Home joined) and the Right Club in 1939, and was strongly influenced in his ferocious anti-Semitism by the work of Father Denis Fahey, the Tipperary priest who led Maria Duce.[167] More general evidence of aristocratic Unionism's sympathies is supplied by Lord Walter Montagu-Douglas-Scott, Earl of Dalkeith (M.P. for Roxburgh and Selkirk between 1923 and 1935, when he succeeded as 8th Duke of Buccleuch): Dalkeith reported to Cuthbert Headlam in 1942 that 'he is much annoyed because he is accused of being a Fascist—for no other reason than because like a good many other people he thought that this war might have been avoided had we been a little less foolish with Germany in the years after the last war'.[168] Dalkeith's brother, Lord William Montagu-Douglas-Scott (MP for for Roxburgh and Selkirk between 1935 and 1950) was a founding member of Oswald Mosley's January Club in 1934. Perhaps one explanation for the failure of Fascism to find roots in interwar Scotland was the capacity of the existing party structure to accommodate some at least of its sympathizers.[169]

After the war Scottish Unionist MPs, petitioned by the Catholic Truth Society, lodged a protest against the state visit to the United Kingdom of President Tito of Yugoslavia (who had imprisoned the controversial Archbishop of Zagreb, Aloysius Stepinac, after what many Catholics believed was a show trial).[170] While the picture, then, is complicated, there are some grounds for believing that sectarian and ethnic chemistry of Scottish Unionist prejudice changed and waned in the early 20th century from being a primarily Protestant religious formulation into a primarily ethnic or national compound, wherein Protestants and Catholics were unified against other perceived enemies on the eve of the Second World War. This would certainly chime with assessments of other forms of nativist exclusivism and prejudice at this time.[171]

There may indeed have been a sense in which Unionist patriotism was dangerously nostalgic—a rhetorical device through which contemporary needs for radical change might sometimes be masked or defused. On the other hand, change there was—and change which, whatever the spin of presentation, reflected a particular and sincere expression of Scottish patriotism: Unionists offered a vision of an unsullied United Kingdom, which was nevertheless often compatible with a social progressivism, a distinctive Scottish historical sensibility, and the effective devolution of *some* Scottish business to Edinburgh. Walter Elliot (Under Secretary at the Scottish Office in 1923 and between 1924 and 1929, and later Secretary of State) was, as noted, not above making some sectarian or nativist jibes; but otherwise (or, perhaps, therefore) he best exemplifies the complex socially and historically engaged traditions within Scottish Unionism in the interwar period.[172] He was a proponent of free milk for schoolchildren (1927), the expansion and modernization of hospitals and housing in Scotland (including the steel-framed 'Weir homes'), and of Scottish local government reform. Elliot also favoured 'administrative devolution', cooperating with his Secretary of State, Sir John Gilmour (1924–1929) towards this end. As Secretary of State himself (1936–1938), he returned to the administrative and housing problems, creating the Scottish (Special Areas) Housing Association, which had delivered 26,400 new homes by 1938. In 1937, in the context of George VI's coronation tour, he planned a grand ball at Holyrood in imitation of that hosted by Prince Charles Edward Stuart in 1745.[173] In 1938 he was involved with the organization of the great Empire Exhibition at Glasgow, where George VI again made an appearance. These occasions exemplified Elliot's combination of an intense Scottish patriotism together with a wider definition of union and empire.[174]

Elliot had thus an unusually strong sense of the past, and combined Scotland's medieval heroes, Jacobitism, and empire within his historical framework. He celebrated Bruce and Bannockburn, not because he wanted Scottish independence, but rather because Scotland's heroes and medieval achievement had made possible Scottish dignity and autonomy within the beneficent context of union ('How thankful we should be to our forefathers who fought Bannockburn (and indeed who held the border)!'; 'we remember and exalt ourselves about Bannockburn, which was when we first stood in the line against England').[175] In the interwar years, the period of his ministerial ascendancy, he projected a broader (if counter-intuitive) reading of unionist nationalism from the circumstances of his personal political success: the true 'Scottish Scot' wanted to take on and dominate London politics and culture, while the 'Anglo-Scot' cowered in the bastion of a rhetorical nationalism.

The increasing ambiguities of Elliot's patriotism from the late 1930s onwards are captured in a letter written to Blanche Dugdale in 1937, when he intimated that he was simultaneously frustrated at being confined to the Scottish Office, and was plotting radical structural reform: 'I am revolving in my mind the continuation of the Kingdom of Scotland. Neville [Chamberlain] will yet find it dangerous to intern me here [as Secretary of State]. I will break up the United Kingdom'.[176] By the early 1940s, in the context of war and of his humiliatingly precipitate exit from British cabinet politics, he was confiding to Blanche Dugdale that 'sometimes I am tempted to become a Home Ruler': 'the Home Rule Parliament [...] seems to me more and more coming over the horizon, owing to the growing divergence of our two countries'.[177] In the immediate post-war period, he remained privately tempted by the possibility of aligning himself with Scottish nationalism, and indeed contributed to the 'nationalistic' Unionist party prospectus, *Scottish Control of Scottish Affairs* (1949), as part of the campaign to attack Labour's centralizing thrusts.[178] But Elliot was also convinced that (for the moment) the English were needed to mediate and mitigate the tensions within Scottish society, created by 'the introduction of a subject people (the Irish)': 'it may be that the tolerant English are still needed as a midwife to this travail'. Moreover, the depth of 'this travail' was further illustrated by the fact that 'not a single member of the Scots upper or middle classes has yet ever stood, far less been returned, as a candidate in favour of the party [Labour] which polls far more than half the nation's votes'. This was, indeed, 'a sinister fact'.[179]

As can be seen, Elliot thought with unusual frequency about Ireland, and to some degree tailored his view of the Irish according to his own Scottish sympathies and prejudices. His pronounced lowland identity has been recognized; but less conspicuous was his genial suspicion of highlanders, and the extent to which he equated the cultural divisions within Scotland with those in Ireland.[180] He thought that the British had countered the Easter Rising in 1916 with 'dignity and restraint', but he was also a supporter of the Treaty of 1921, and appalled by the deaths of Griffith and Collins in August 1922.[181] He was a partitionist, and advocated that expedient in Cyprus on the basis of what he saw as its success in Ireland: 'partition is a Good Thing, not a Bad Thing. Catholics and Protestants are not the same thing, and pretending makes it worse'.[182] Ireland was an immediate source of reference for the hatred between Romanians and Magyars, and even between Northern and Southern French.[183] Ireland was also relevant to Palestine, a common subject in Elliot's letters to Dugdale (who was a passionate Zionist): as with Cyprus, Palestine looked like a needy recipient of the British blessing of partition (and, as with Cyprus) there were—to Elliot's mind —analogies with Irish politics.[184] He was angrily (but equally breathtakingly) flippant in denouncing Irish neutrality in 1940: 'I think, however, that we shall need to conquer Southern Ireland during its [the war's] course, just to have somewhere to live in. We could deport the Southern Irish—now that they are reduced in numbers by 20 years of resolute and 20 more years of irresolute government, that should not be impossible'.[185]

Elliot himself never publicly embraced Home Rule, but (as shown) he enjoyed occasional, if transient, temptation: his fellow Scottish Unionist MPs were sometimes even more pragmatic or circumspect or contingent in their approach to Home Rule than Elliot himself—and certainly much more so than the Ulster Unionists of the pre-1920 era. In 1928 Elliot feared that Baldwin's dying Unionist administration would introduce Scottish Home Rule 'as a last throw'; and indeed he had some evidence to hand that the former Chancellor and veteran Scottish Unionist, Sir Robert Horne, was 'getting panicky' on the subject.[186] In the context of economic recession in the late 1920s and early 1930s, nationalism gained ground; and in 1932 Scottish Unionist MPs shrank from accepting the (one might have been forgiven for thinking) fundamental proposition that 'we as Scottish Unionist members are definitely opposed to the establishment of a separate parliament in Scotland': on this occasion Horne (who was chairing the meeting, and whose 'panic' clearly had not subsided from 1928) 'advised that we should postpone the decision, and answer all questioners that we must first consult with all our colleagues'.[187] Out of this (doubtless partly strategic) hesitation and electoral anxiety sprang some of the subsequent advocacy of administrative devolution.

However, 'administrative devolution' (as with so many other unionist initiatives applied in Scotland—including, perhaps, Noel Skelton's 'constructive conservatism') had also partly originated in an Irish context, as a means by which British Conservatives and Unionists might mediate between their own convictions, the needs of the United Kingdom state, and the demands of mainstream Irish nationalism: successive unionist Chief Secretaries for Ireland, such as Gerald Balfour (1895–1900) and George Wyndham (1900–1905), had effectively created new areas of Irish administration (as in 1899, when a new Irish Department of Agriculture and Technical Instruction was launched), while some (Wyndham and his Liberal successor, James Bryce) had toyed with the notion of devolving greater administrative authority from London to Dublin (Wyndham also served, significantly, as

Lord Rector of the University of Edinburgh between 1908 and 1911—see illustration E.1).[188] In Scotland 'administrative devolution' was associated with the creation, under the first Salisbury government, of the Scottish Office, the expansion of its powers under the formidable Arthur Balfour (Secretary for Scotland, 1886–1887), and the elevation of its minister to the rank of 'Secretary of State' in 1926.[189] This was followed, in 1928, by a reorganization of the different and originally asymmetrical boards which had developed as the Scottish Office expanded its powers: by 1939 these had been fully integrated within the Scottish Office, and within the structures of the civil service.[190] In October 1932 Skelton, as Under Secretary for Scotland, was suggesting to his parliamentary colleagues that 'there might be a just complaint in that the Scottish Office, comprising all the work of the Home Office in Scotland, is concentrated in London. This might be moved to Edinburgh with suitable accommodation erected there for the Secretary of State to transact his business'.[191] Under Sir Godfrey Collins (Secretary of State, 1932–1936) and Walter Elliot, his successor, reform along these lines was pursued by means of a Committee of Enquiry, headed by Sir John Gilmour. In 1937 Gilmour reported to Elliot, his former Under Secretary, and recommended the further concentration and regularization of the Scottish administration in Edinburgh: though most of the movement of people and functions was within Edinburgh, rather than from London to Edinburgh, the building of St Andrew's House on Calton Hill (an impressive Caledonian take on art deco) served as a striking physical manifestation of the concentration of administrative authority in the heart of the nation's capital city.[192]

In Ireland 'administrative devolution' created two broad areas of difficulty which were never fully resolved under the union. First, if 'devolution' was (amongst other matters) a means of dividing nationalists, then it also served to divide unionists.[193] Second, though the administrative reach of Dublin Castle was extended in the last years of the union, and though greater numbers of Catholic nationalists were recruited to the civil service in Ireland, the Castle remained a relatively complex, unsystematic, and unreformed enterprise, which was also uniformly associated with British, indeed English, rule in Ireland.[194] In this last sense, perhaps, lessons had been learnt from Ireland: the 'devolution' of powers to Edinburgh was vigorously presented in Scottish patriotic terms, while the creation of a new purpose-built administrative headquarters (unburdened by any associations with the jackboot of English rule) also served as a focus for patriotic pride. Moreover, 'administrative devolution' in Scotland was as much about regularization and efficiency as it was about the transfer of powers: in Ireland the Castle was a by-word, not just for English oppression, but for bureaucratic miasma, and a similarly comprehensive reform had to wait until 1920, by which time the union was already moribund.

However, another corollary of 'administrative devolution' in Ireland had been that it served to excite divisions within the unionist family; and here the experience of Ireland foreshadowed, but certainly did not inform, the experience of Scots unionists, particularly in the second half of the 20th century. George Wyndham's record as a reforming Chief Secretary culminated in quiet negotiations between the head of the Irish administration, Sir Antony MacDonnell, and various interested parties on the possibility of administrative devolution for Ireland. These conversations were almost certainly conducted with Wyndham's knowledge (though he denied this), and caused a furore on the unionist benches of the House of Commons, where there was no preparation for this initiative, and where 'devolution' was regarded as a synonym for 'home rule'.[195] In the same way, Scottish Unionists were divided over devolution when it was discussed at a special conference in November 1949, and divided, too, over Winston Churchill's ambiguous remarks on Scotland's relationship with Westminster, delivered at the Usher Hall, Edinburgh, in 1950.[196]

The Irish experience was, in fact, relevant both to the Scottish Unionists' embrace of administrative devolution, as well as to their discreet consideration of legislative devolution. Labour's policies of nationalization in the years after 1945 reopened the question of the relationship between 'centre' and 'periphery' for both the Scots and Northern Irish; and indeed the experience of Northern Ireland was scrutinized carefully at this time (1949) by Scottish Unionists (and others) with a view to its usefulness as an exemplar.[197] Here, again, however, the attitude of the party was highly cautious. Instead of pursuing distinctive and high risk strategies of this kind, Scottish Unionism in the 1950s effectively adapted some of Labour's statist policies for its own ends, and in particular in the area of public housing and new towns. From Churchill's accession in 1951 until Heath's resignation in 1974 between 25,000 and 40,000 homes were being constructed annually, the overwhelming majority being in the public sector, and this has been identified as a key element in Scottish Unionism's electoral success.[198] For much of the 1950s a disjointed mixture of opposition to 'socialism', the effective development of the public sector, and a vocally patriotic rhetoric served Scottish Unionism well. In fact much the same political chemistry, suitably adapted for local conditions, also served the Ulster Unionism of the 1950s.

However, the challenges of Scottish devolution did not disappear in the frenzy of public housing development. More difficulties and divisions— reminiscent of those pertaining in the late 1940s—were caused by Edward Heath's Declaration of Perth in May 1968, when Heath (influenced both by the Scottish Unionists' meagre twenty seats in the 1966 general election as well as Winifred Ewing's victory for the SNP at Hamilton in November 1967) supported the idea of an elected Scottish chamber which, in coopera- tion with Westminster, would participate in the legislative process.[199] Heath's line was (predictably) confirmed by the musings of a party commission, headed by the ever-compliant Sir Alec Douglas-Home, and its report on 'Scotland's Government' (March 1970). Though Heath's initiative was also riven with ambiguity, it was designed (with the mounting SNP threat in mind) to look like a major policy departure; and it had been delivered (like his other constitutional about-turn, over the survival of Stormont) with minimal consultation ('without any consultation that I could discern', recorded Ian Lang), and with typical bullishness.[200] Scottish Conservatism (the party had dropped its 'Unionist' appellation in 1965) was left disori- ented and divided (Lord Hailsham subsequently described the affair as a 'fiasco'), a state compounded by the fact that, in office, and confronted with major problems with the economy, Europe, and Northern Ireland, Heath no longer treated Scotland as a pressing issue.[201] Only in May 1973, when the party specifically rejected any effort to move on the issue of a Scottish assembly, was some clarity finally attained.[202]

By this time, however, there was clear evidence of organizational sclero- sis. The electoral failures of the early 1960s had (in time-honoured fashion) been blamed partly on the party's machinery; and this had in turn precipi- tated a major overhaul in 1964–1965, when the two great divisional machines of Scottish Unionism—the Eastern and the Western—were amalgamated into a single Scottish Conservative and Unionist Association. Amongst many other casualties of this reform was the forty year old Glasgow Unionist Association, which was replaced by the Glasgow Regional Council of the SCUA. But there is evidence of more fundamental disquiet and difficulty within the party records of this time. Heath's Perth initiative was indeed launched on an unprepared party, and caused deep resentment in (for example) the new Glasgow Regional Council: Heath, as leader, was absolved from blame, but—again in time-honoured fashion—the royal advisers were vigorously condemned ('the whole thing had been mishandled at Central Office').[203] This complaint was followed by a forthright condemnation of 'the proposal to create a Scottish Assembly'.[204]

But, if anything, these divisions over policy amplified some more worrying realities within the Unionist organization, certainly in the West. It is sometimes said that the problem with post-war Unionism was that it remained disproportionately and narrowly aristocratic; but there is some archival and other evidence to suggest that the party's problems arose not so much from the narrowness of the Big House as from the preoccupations of the suburban villa.[205] Here the media of politics, developed with such assiduity in the interwar years, appear to have become more important than the message. For example, Uddingston Unionist Association (South Lanarkshire) in the 1960s sustained some of the traditional social pursuits of the party—whist drives, dinner dances, Christmas draws, and raffles—with some mild concessions to the 'swinging sixties' in the form of wine and cheese parties and coffee mornings.[206] But, though the Association was prepared to dine or dance for the cause, it was not prepared to talk politics: if (in Terence O'Neill's quip) the Ulster Unionist leader, Lord Brookeborough, liked to relax away from a desk which did not exist, then the Unionists of Uddingston sought diversion from political business which was left untouched. A proposal in January 1961 to start or join a political discussion group caused consternation, and 'after consideration the [Uddingston] Committee decided not to take part in either, saying that this type of meeting would be of more value to the Young Unionists'.[207] In fact the Young Unionist movement seems to have been no less atrophied than the mainstream organization; and certainly in the nearby Scotstoun Unionist Association the Young Unionist movement was in near complete abeyance by the mid 1960s. The Honorary President of the Scotstoun Association, Sir James Hutcheson, addressed the body in February 1966; and his speech, which might have been lifted from a 'That Was the Week That Was' sketch, also highlighted some of the developing problems within Western Unionism: 'Being deep in industrial affairs, Sir James said he knows [sic] what is happening at the present time. Much of the false thinking in our midst arise from communist and socialist doctrines and it is with industrial action that the communists hope eventually to bring this country to communist rule....Sir James stated that socialist doctrines of equality leads to envy, and jealousy leads to crime; and nowadays crime does seem to pay. [He] considers the government policy as benefiting the criminals, and in fighting socialism the Conservatives would also be helping to improve the moral standards of the country'.[208] Moreover, if candid, this was a comparatively rare expression of the grass-roots convictions of the Association (it 'was enthusiastically received by everyone present'), which (like its counterpart in Uddingston) was otherwise relatively unburdened by political thought or argument. It is striking, for example, that neither in Scotstoun, Uddingston, nor at the level of the Glasgow Regional Council, was much interest devoted to the evolving crisis in Northern Ireland in the late 1960s (even though the complex sectarian frontiers and relationships of the West bore some semblance and relevance to those in Ulster). The single issue which moved these western Unionists into (very occasional) debate was the looming presence of the European Economic Community in the early 1970s.

A similar state of affairs appears to have prevailed in Central Ayrshire in the 1960s, when the youthful Ian Lang (subsequently a Conservative Secretary of State for Scotland (1990–1995) and President of the Board of Trade (1995–1997)) was first seeking election as a Unionist. Lang records that he subsisted on 'whist drives, coffee mornings, brains trusts and the like' while he nursed his constituency, and that the advice provided by his local chairman was, when speaking, to offer 'nothing too political'. A badly judged speech to the whist-playing Unionists of Kilbirnie produced a withering response: 'in the silence that followed, echoing round that large hall, several farmers' wives gave me a look of blank incomprehension, while others started to shuffle and deal out the cards'.[209]

It is also striking that, where once the Unionist organizations—certainly at metropolitan level—were systematically well connected with the leading figures within United Kingdom politics, this link was now growing more tenuous. It is true that, in January 1970, the chairman of the Glasgow Regional Council, proudly announced that a lunch had been arranged for the visiting Shadow Education Secretary, Mrs Margaret Thatcher ('it would be held in the Ca'doro Restaurant...after discussion it was agreed that lunch would consist of tomato soup, cold meat and salad and apple pie à la mode'). But, in the event, the apple pie 'à la mode' went unserved: Mrs Thatcher decided that, with the dissolution of parliament in May, the Conservatives of Glasgow were not an electoral priority.[210] This, indeed, was a portent of things to come.[211]

# Thatcherite unionism

Edward Heath's ambiguous devolutionist sympathies formed little part of Margaret Thatcher's approach to the challenge of governing Scotland. Thatcher, of course, was a convinced unionist, albeit of a highly anglocentric quality: although originally interested in devolution, she had led opposition to the Labour government's plans for devolved assemblies in Scotland and Wales, and was delighted when these were effectively rejected in plebiscites in March 1979.[212] Moreover, Thatcher's alternative unionist vision played relatively well at the general election of 1979, when the Scottish Conservatives garnered 31.3 per cent of the poll (as opposed to the 24.7 per cent recorded at the general election of October 1974). And in the first years of the Thatcher government, with 'Gentleman' George Younger as Secretary of State (1979–1986), some of the full brunt of the new Conservative government's monetarist policies bypassed Scotland: the insolvent steelmill at Ravenscraig, Lanarkshire, was given a temporary reprieve, money was spent on infrastructure such as new roads, and the Scottish Development Agency and Scottish New Town Corporations were also given longer extensions of life than their English counterparts.[213] David Torrance has suggested that Younger strove to translate the asperities of Thatcherism into Scots in three broad ways: by seeking compromises or mitigation over closures and privatization, by seeking to protect the relatively high levels of public spending in Scotland, and (not least) by emollient presentation.[214] This honeymoon was short-lived, however.

The problem with Thatcher's unionism was not lack of sympathy for Scotland (or, in the Irish context, for 'Ulster'): indeed, given her identification with supposed Calvinist values, and her party's appropriation of some of the economic legacies of the Scottish Enlightenment, there was evidence that the Prime Minister identified warmly with a particular vision of Scotland, however limited or flawed: as her biographer, John Campbell, noted, 'she fancied she had a special affinity with the Scots, whom she imagined as thrifty, enterprising and inventing, a mixture of Adam Smith, George Stephenson and David Livingstone, hardy pioneers who had made the industrial revolution and built the British Empire'.[215] Indeed, a recent study has emphasised not only Thatcher's indebtedness to Adam Smith, as mediated through several key academics at St Andrews University, but also the indirect influence of Noel Skelton: an Edinburgh-born Latin teacher at Grantham appears to have been a likely additional communicator of

'Victorian values'.[216] The problem was rather that (unlike the tradition of unionist nationalism which Heath inherited and sustained) Thatcher's unionism was of a Whig and assimilationist variety; and she had no real understanding of the importance of Scottish national sensitivities and symbols. In truth, she had no real knowledge of Scotland, or of Northern Ireland, where she also vigorously maintained the union; but, unlike Northern Ireland, where she was bombarded with advice on the need for radical constitutional action, and where the oddness of the place (as judged even from Finchley) was ultimately unmistakeable, her knowledge of Scotland was largely filtered through anglicized Scots politicians and businessmen (such as Sir James Goold, the Scottish Party Chairman—'nice man but knew f★★k all about politics'), whose cultural separation from England seemed slight, and who effectively masked critical areas of national distinctiveness.[217] Malcolm Rifkind (Secretary of State, 1986–1990) bluntly summarized one aspect of this cultural gap when he remarked that 'the problem that Margaret had was she was a woman; an English woman and a bossy English woman'.[218]

However, the single most significant blow to Scottish unionists originated, not with Mrs Thatcher herself, her gender, or bossiness, or from a brute insensitivity to Scottish needs, but rather from some of the 'wetter' members of her cabinet, and (at least in part) from a desire to bolster rather than subvert unionism. The political and fiscal challenge was that a massive rise in local government rates was due to coincide with a general election, in 1987; and several ministers, including Younger and Ken Clarke, looked to a wholesale reform of local taxation in order to fend off electoral crisis (and also to produce a more equitable and efficient means of raising revenue). Younger died in 2003, and there is a possibility that he has now been made the fall guy of the ensuing debacle by the surviving ministerial veterans of the era; but the evidence available at present clearly suggests that he actively wanted to trailblaze rating reform in Scotland, and did so in the face of expert advice and criticism from the likes of the Chancellor, Nigel Lawson.[219] The Abolition of Domestic Rates (Scotland) Bill duly passed into law in May 1987, and became operative as the Council Charge, or—colloquially— the Poll Tax, in April 1989—but this in spite of continuing scepticism from Thatcher and senior ministers, who believed that they were 'doing Younger, and his successor, a favour'.[220] In fact the 'successor', Malcolm Rifkind, had to manage the near-annihilation of Scottish Conservatism at the general election of 1987 (when the party was reduced to ten members, a depth not plumbed since 1910)—precisely the kind of meltdown which the Poll Tax had been partly designed to avert.

The problem was that the Council Charge seemed like an additional, as opposed to an alternative burden: its popular label, 'the Poll Tax', had overtones of a medieval regression, and—above all—it was launched first, and experimentally, in Scotland. Moreover, this was being implemented by a government in command of the English electorate, but with no real democratic mandate in Scotland: as the journalist Allan Little has observed, 'when the Poll Tax bills appeared on Scottish doormats, it brought the democratic deficit—and the urgency of the constitutional question—plopping into every home'.[221] What had been designed as a means of defusing rates increases, and of saving the union cause, had evidently become instead a reinvention of medieval English overlordship within Scotland.

Scottish Conservatism, and unionism, never recovered from this debacle. Other Thatcherite actions certainly have had a contributory role in the parliamentary annihilation of the party in Scotland by 1997. In general Thatcherism undermined Scotland's traditional and antiquated reliance on heavy industry, in the short-term an extremely painful and socially disruptive proceeding. The bitterness generated by the Miners' Strike of 1984–1985 and its aftermath badly affected Scotland, where the Polmaise colliery at Stirling was one of those initially targeted by the National Coal Board for accelerated closure.[222] Ravenscraig, a potent symbol of Scotland's industrial inheritance (though itself of relatively recent creation), was effectively doomed with the privatization of the British Steel Corporation in 1988, and closed in 1992.[223] The recession of the early and mid 1980s hit Scotland with much greater severity than the rest of the United Kingdom, full-time employment levels sinking to sixty-four per cent in Scotland in 1985 (as compared with sixty-nine per cent in the United Kingdom as a whole). The Conservative government's campaigns of privatization were sorely felt in Scotland, where (as was discussed in a previous chapter) the popularity of state ownership was disproportionately stronger than elsewhere in the United Kingdom. Related to this, the introduction of Compulsory Competitive Tendering into the Scots National Health Service and Scottish local government in 1988–1989 was disproportionately threatening in a country where (as was discussed in a previous chapter) so many (one third) were employed by central or local government.[224]

Labour was not working, Scotland was not working, the union was not working: Thatcherism, and (by extension) unionism, in the short-term, appeared to offer Scotland neither prosperity nor even the comfort of national symbols and rhetoric. Indeed, paradoxically, the case against Thatcherite unionism—that it was centralized, ideological, and authoritarian—had been foreshadowed by the kinds of attack that an earlier generation of Scots unionist (such as Walter Elliot) had made against the centralizing, ideological, and authoritarian policies of post-war Labour. This was one measure of the political and intellectual strains which Mrs Thatcher's vision of union had imposed upon unionism in Scotland.

Under John Major, successive ministers (Ian Lang, Michael Forsyth) returned to a unionism sensitive towards national symbols (saving Rosyth Naval Dock Yard, returning the Stone of Scone), and located within the traditions of administrative devolution: a detailed strategy along these lines was laid out in Lang's White Paper, *Scotland and the Union—A Partnership for Good*, published in 1993. But, as Lang himself said, 'in truth it was already too late. It was a package which, if implemented thirty or forty years earlier, might have done the trick'.[225]

## Labour's unionism

It should be stressed immediately that the Labour party, though traditionally associated with support for Home Rule, had by the time of the Second World War, quietly relegated any practical interest in its immediate application to Scotland. The British Labour leadership was strongly infiltrated by Scots; and the party's accession to power in 1924 (and 1929 and 1945), together with mounting levels of unemployment, persuaded many Scots socialists that Home Rule, however emotionally satisfying as a concept, was for practical purposes redundant: John Taylor, Secretary of Scottish Labour Party in the 1940s, articulated a widespread view in declaring that 'I myself ceased to desire self-government as soon as we secured a Socialist Government for Britain'.[226] The importance of the accession of Labour to state power in this process of conversion was underlined by the fact that Labour governments were generally dependent upon the support of Scots and Welsh MPs: indeed, as Iain McLean has observed, 'most left-wing governments since 1886 have held a minority of seats in England'.[227]

It is true that the Independent Labour Party maintained its Home Rule faith within the wider Labour family, but its relative significance was waning, and particularly after the decision to leave the mainstream Labour party in 1931. The Scottish Trades Union Congress supported the amalgamation of Scots and English unions 'on industrial lines', and had abandoned its commitment to Home Rule in 1932, turning instead to administrative devolution.[228] Scottish nationalism appeared, in the interwar period (and indeed afterwards) to be a marginal phenomenon, tainted by a bourgeois romantic conservatism (as evidenced, for example, by the split within the Unionists of Glasgow Cathcart, who broke with their party in 1932 to form the Scottish Party, later one of the planks of the Scottish Nationalist Party). In the context of Scotland's economic free fall in the interwar years, Joseph Vissarionavich Stalin appeared to offer a more useful model than Charles Edward Stuart: for most of its Scottish supporters, the future of Labour appeared to be increasingly tied to the achievement of a centralized British socialist state.

Without overtly identifying itself as such, Scottish Labour in the 20th century functioned effectively as a unionist party—and, arguably, indeed a more successful unionist party than the Conservatives. The Scottish Labour Party was founded by Keir Hardie in 1888, and was affiliated to the Independent Labour Party in 1893: a separate Scottish Trades Union Congress followed in 1897. Labour's electoral breakthrough in Scotland came in 1922, when 29 MPs were returned, many of whom came from the radical Clydeside ILP tradition. This electoral consolidation continued throughout the 1920s, and was only checked in the 1930s by the party's divisions over the National Government: after the war, between 1945 and 1966, the lowest share of the vote achieved by Labour was 46.2 per cent.[229] Rising trade union membership (numbers doubled during the Great War), massive unemployment in Scotland in the interwar years, controversies in the early 1920s over rack-renting, all fed into the electoral momentum behind the Labour Party. Already by 1925 sixty per cent of Scottish trade unionists belonged to British unions, and even those within Scottish unions were often bound within British federations, and into British negotiating structures.[230] Essentially, the politics of Great Britain (as opposed to the United Kingdom) in the early and mid 20th centuries were dominated by class rather than region; and this effectively meant that a party such as Labour, elaborating a class-based message throughout Britain, served as a force for union.

An additional factor behind the party's rise in Scotland was that it was increasingly able to attract those who had been previously divided over the union with Ireland. The compromises in British politics which had driven the Anglo-Irish war and produced the Irish settlement of 1921 had strained 'traditional' party allegiances in Scotland, and this had delivered some rea-lignments which strengthened the position of Labour. The Orange Order, alienated by the Unionist party's 'surrender to Fenianism' in 1921, pursued a more isolated track after 1922, supporting militant Protestant candidates who ate into the vote of mainstream Unionism.[231] This indirectly strength-ened Labour; but it has also been suggested that Labour independently 'began to attract the votes of working class Orangemen'.[232] However, the support of Irish Catholics for the main Home Rule party in Britain, the Liberals, had been lost at the same time: the bloody pursuit by the crown forces of revolutionary insurgency in Ireland between 1919 and 1921 had been authorized by a coalitionist Liberal Prime Minister, David Lloyd George, and by coalitionist Liberal Chief Secretaries for Ireland, such as the Canadian Hamar Greenwood. Paradoxically, therefore, Labour was able to benefit not only from Orange disillusion with Unionism, but also (and more significantly) from the disillusion felt by Irish Catholic migrants and their families at Lloyd Georgian Liberalism.

It would doubtless be wrong to exaggerate Labour's powers of political ecumenism, and there is evidence of some only partly decommissioned Orange and Green bitterness within the party even in the last decades of the 20th century: for example, John Smith, a future leader of the British Labour party, combined Gaitskellite and Orange sympathies as a student debater in the Glasgow University Union in the late 1950s, while at the end of his life he tried to deal with divisions in Scottish Labour arising from complex, partly sectarian, disputes over the allocation of resources by Monklands council in the 1990s.[233] But it is nevertheless the case that Labour came to function as a unionist party while being able to overcome some of the reli-gious divisions which bedevilled Scottish society. One of the critical unsung achievements of Scottish Labour was that, virtually uniquely, it created a largely secular unionism—a unionism which largely transcended the reli-gious origins of 'Britishness', and the religious polarization which had accompanied the birth of Unionism in Ireland, and been exploited by British Unionists.

Some of the elisions and tensions within the development of Scottish Labour are clearly evident in the thought and career of Thomas Johnston, widely regarded as one of the party's greatest ornaments in the 20th century as well as the greatest Secretary of State for Scotland from any party tradi-tion.[234] Johnston certainly illustrates the ambiguous attitude prevailing

within the Party towards Home Rule. For many within the Labour movement, like Johnston, Home Rule was a lasting, emotional commitment,
which tended (however) to be displaced by the realities of political power
and the requirements of major social and economic change. For Johnston,
economic recovery was a more urgent priority than Home Rule: he professed himself 'uneasy lest we should get political power without first
having...an adequate economy to administer'.[235] But there was an ambiguity in this assessment, for (like the constructive unionists in Ireland) he
simultaneously believed that economic strength would dispel nationalist
pressure: 'the real bellows which blow the fires of Scots nationalism are not
the symbols upon the coinage, but the absence of adequate supplies of it'.[236]

Johnston's Home Rule sympathies were bound in with his sense of
Labour tradition, and his deep sense of Scottish history and place: he declared
revealingly that he 'had always put Scottish Home Rule on my election
programmes—as Keir Hardie did upon his'.[237] Like the Tory Walter Elliot,
who rhapsodized about the Borders, Johnston celebrated his own local
roots, producing various works of Scottish history, including a study of his
home town, Kirkintilloch in Dunbartonshire (Elliot and Johnston also
cooperated in launching the Saltire Society, a cultural nationalist body, in
1935). This intense patriotism fed originally into support for Home Rule:
Johnston seconded two Home Rule proposals in the 1920s, the first in May
1924, during the brief Labour administration, and the second (for dominion
Home Rule) in 1927. He helped to found the Scottish Self Government
Committee in 1936. However, Johnston's historical sensibility was indeed
often very local in its focus, and was certainly far removed from the romantic paternalist notions of a patriotic and socially unified Scotland: he had
already dispelled any suspicion of Jacobite nostalgia when he published his
views of the Scottish aristocracy in a blistering (and much reprinted) pamphlet, *Our Scottish Noble Families*, (1909).

And there were countervailing pressures in Johnston's political formation. In 1922, as MP for West Stirling, Johnston helped to found the
Commonwealth Labour Group. His claim for Home Rule was in the context of Commonwealth and empire—in the context of apparently successful imperial settlements in South Africa (in 1910) and Ireland (1922), and
with the empire apparently at its apex. Home Rule also made sense, for
Johnston, as for Milnerite federalists, in terms of the pressure of imperial
business at Westminster.[238] Moreover, Johnston and others from the Clydeside
Independent Labour tradition favoured imperial preference, believing that

the bulk purchase of foodstuffs within the empire would benefit the Scots and British working classes. Like Elliot, Johnston saw the British empire as a great force for good, and (given the strong Labour presence in dominions such as Australia) he saw the weakening of empire as potentially dangerous to the future of British socialism. As Paul Ward has commented, 'Labour, it was clear, was not immune to the claims of imperial Scotland. Indeed, Empire moved close to the centre of the thought of Scottish (though not British) Socialism in the 1920s'.[239] Upending the arguments of Tom Nairn on empire and union, the political scientist Michael Keating has argued that empire in fact validated Labour's moderate nationalism in the mid 20th century: 'in the case of the Labour movement, it was the very existence of the Empire which made it possible to be nationalist without being separatist'.[240]

Moreover, Johnston, as with many others in the Scottish Labour tradition, increasingly came to see that (given the electoral strength of Labour) the British state could function as an effective vehicle for social and economic reform. Johnston was Under Secretary in the Scottish Office between 1929 and 1931; and the experience of economic crisis, together with his admiration for the nationalization project in Canada, confirmed his belief that only a strong British state, dominated by Labour, could deliver the fundamental reforms—particularly in the field of social ownership—which were required to rescue Scotland and the rest of the United Kingdom.[241] However, he remained clear that, while the weight of the British state was required to achieve root and branch change, the prioritization and local implementation of change could best be achieved in Scotland by the decentralization of power to the Scots. Like many others within the British Labour movement, he visited Russia, and was impressed by the apparent effectiveness of centralized economic planning: centralized planning, of course, implied a strong centralized state. He was a product of his times, however, and no revolutionary: just as Walter Elliot translated Baldwinian one-nation Toryism for a Scots audience, so Johnston offered a Scots reading of Ramsay MacDonald's incremental and constitutional socialism.[242]

As Secretary of State for Scotland between 1941 and 1945, Johnston effectively demonstrated the benefits of a powerful Scots voice at the heart of a strong and centralized British state: Johnston, the nominal Home Ruler, was in fact a progenitor of the distinctive Labourite unionism which prevailed in Scotland through most of the second half of the 20th century—a unionism which was conditioned by a strong Labour presence at Westminster, and by the willingness of the British state to accept Scottish special pleading. Johnston defined his own role as effectively that of the state's strong man in Scotland: while historians now tend to warn against such self-serving definitions and valuations, certainly at the time Churchill jokingly referred to him as 'the king of Scotland'.[243] The 'king' necessarily had advisors: Johnston, echoing the national nature of British wartime politics, brought together a council of (by definition mostly Conservative) former Secretaries of State for Scotland to act as an advisory body, and this met on sixteen occasions during his tenure of office. Johnston was also keen to hone the diversity of Scottish opinion, through this Council of State, and through the Scottish Office, into a unified political weapon, which would then be deployed to bludgeon his cabinet colleagues in London. As part of this mobilization of Scottish opinion, Scotland's MPs were brought together for occasional meetings, gathering first at St Andrew's House in Edinburgh in October 1941 to meet the departmental heads of the Scottish Office.[244] Out of Johnston's energetic planning came the Hydro-Electric Development (Scotland) Bill (1943), the Scottish Council on Industry, and a precursor to the universal hospital provision of the National Health Service, piloted in the underused Civil Defence hospitals of the Clyde Valley.[245] Johnston sought the devolution of certain powers to Edinburgh, but also aimed to retain these within the constraints of the Scottish Office, one of the agencies of the British state: he also fought some of the centralizing ambitions of the state, while seeking to deploy its strength to Scottish advantage. In other words, as Michael Fry has drily remarked, his 'true accomplishment was to make Scotland the biggest pressure group in Britain'.[246]

One leitmotif which resonates throughout Johnston's papers, autobiography, and indeed the Scots Labour tradition more widely, was that a sentimental—angry or lachrymose—nationalism was no substitute for economic advance. He argued that 'there was a form of Scots nationalism which lost itself in Jacobite mists. Drunk men on Saturday nights sang beerily of Bonnie Prince Charlie 'Will ye no come back again?' although the last thing anybody wanted was a restoration of Stuart feudalism, with all its rags, squalor, famines and blood feuds, which had so cursed the country in the days of the hereditary jurisdictions... Scotland's hope lay not in heraldic restoration but in social ownership of soil, industry and finance, and there was one political route and one only to social ownership—it was through the British Labour Party'.[247] Economic improvement—and economic control—were essential precursors to moderate Home Rule: in March 1945 he opined that 'for my own part I welcome any advance whatever towards self government. But for years past I have been convinced that while the political forms were being discussed it was essential we should get economic control'; in March 1949 he asserted that 'if there is to be a Scottish parliament, it must inherit something more than a poorhouse or a graveyard'.[248]

Johnston retained an interest in the possibility of a Scottish assembly, but (unsurprisingly) he also championed the continuing existence of a powerful Secretary of State for Scotland, as an advocate for the nation's interests at the heart of the British state. Like moderate Irish patriots in the 20th century, he deployed separatism as a lever through which to advance national interests: he used the Council of State to cajole British high political opinion, but he also evoked the recent memory of the Irish revolution as a threat. He recognized that (certainly in terms of the Covenant movement of the late 1940s) 'there is [at present] little Sinn Feinery (sic), but there is considerable support for a parliament on something like Ulster lines'.[249] But if British ministers did not accede to his particular definition of Scotland's national interests, he was certainly keen to point out that there was an alternative ('a sort of Sinn Fein movement') waiting in the wings.[250] The Irish national leader, John Redmond, had tried to bend the British state to Irish purposes, and had failed, with devastating consequences for the British-Irish relationship; Johnston was keen to remind British opinion of this, and to underline that he was not about to play Redmond to the SNP's Sinn Féin.

Johnston's immediate Labour successors (Joseph Westwood, Arthur Woodburn, and Hector McNeil) were less effective in defending Scotland's interests against the centralizing tendencies of the British state; and this reflected, not only the relative paucity of their skills, but also the solidity of their unionism (Woodburn in particular was an unrelenting critic of the nationalists), and the strengthening centripetal forces of the state. In the late 1940s Clement Attlee's Labour government launched the NHS, the Scottish element of which was created through the National Health Service (Scotland) Act of 1947. The pursuit of social ownership, with the nationalization of electricity generation and Cable and Wireless Limited in 1946, the coal mines in 1947, the creation of the British Transport Authority and the nationalization of the railways in 1948, and iron and steel production in 1949, all dramatically enhanced the extent and power of the British state. The importance of coal mining, and of iron and steel production within Scotland meant that it was one of the components of the United Kingdom which was most directly and comprehensively affected by this sweeping state intervention. Equally, the size and spread of Scotland, and the large number of relatively remote communities, meant that railways arguably possessed a disproportionately large significance here: certainly the nationalization of rail was a critical event for Scots. In a sense, therefore, it might be said that no sooner had Johnston curtailed the impact of the centralized state in Scotland, than the powers of the state were redefined and enhanced. Under Attlee Labour was inferentially, but effectively, unionist: supportive of Unionists in Northern Ireland (through the Ireland Act of 1949), the government also created a uniform system of health care, and linked this to state ownership and the centralized management of key services and industries across the entire United Kingdom.[251] 'Nationalisation', Walter Elliot complained in a famous quip, 'meant denationalisation'.[252] 'Nationalization' also meant a period of constitutional destabilization as the Scots and Northern Irish responded to the challenge of an enhanced British state.

And, though there was occasional transient interest in the exploration of devolution, on the whole this definition of unionism was upheld by Labour throughout the 1950s and 1960s. Certainly, the dominant figure of the 1960s within Scottish Labour, Willie Ross (Secretary of State between 1964 and 1970, and again between 1974 and 1976), was able to combine an intense cultural nationalism with a conviction that the union state was delivering for Scotland and for the working classes. His effectiveness in working the British state for the benefit of Scots has been described as an 'achievement second only to [Thomas] Johnston's'.[253] In the context of a fashion for regional economic planning, Ross won a Highland and Islands Development Board in 1965, presenting this achievement to parliament essentially as an act of historical reparation.[254] At the same time a Scottish Economic Council was created, chaired by Ross himself: this fed into the National Economic Plan for the United Kingdom, within which the whole of Scotland, bar Edinburgh, was specially designated as a development area. Ross also sponsored the reform of social work provision within the gamut of Scottish local authorities: the Social Work (Scotland) Act brought together and regularized the provision of social and educational services under a central department within each local government area. These innovations were followed by a new and separate Scottish Transport Group, a Scottish Countryside Commission, and a General Teaching Council for Scotland. Once again, as with Johnston, a formidable Labour Secretary of State was protecting Scottish distinctiveness, creating new Scottish institutions, and defending the whole in the language of cultural nationalism. Like Johnston, Ross was expressing a political agenda in the vocabulary of patriotism, but within the grammatical framework of union.

If Johnston had a long-term, but often passive, interest in Scottish Home Rule, then Ross was essentially a political, indeed a constructive, Unionist, who (only very late in the day) discovered a pragmatic interest in devolution. The economic crises of the later 1960s and early 1970s suggested that centralized state planning was not in fact working; and they were accompanied by a renaissance within Scottish nationalism, a development epitomized by the return of Winifred Ewing as the SNP member for Hamilton in October 1967, and by the thirty per cent poll won by the SNP at the local government elections in May 1968. Ross was up for a fight, but using the political and constitutional weapons which he believed he had delivered for Scotland. Like Dicey and the 'constructive unionists' of the late 19th century, or (indeed) like reforming Ulster Unionists such as Terence O'Neill in the 1960s, Ross believed that nationalism was susceptible to economic improvement; and thus the more that he gained for Scotland, and the better Scotland's economic circumstances and prospects, the weaker the arguments for nationalism became.[255] In essence, if some Irish unionists had sought to 'kill Home Rule by kindness', then Ross was seeking to 'kill independence by kindness' (though his strikingly vituperative eloquence distinguished him from the emollient gentility of O'Neill or—in the late 19th century—George Wyndham, or the tongue-tied Horace Plunkett). The creation of a Scottish Development Agency in 1975, and the location of the British National Oil Corporation in Glasgow, and the British Offshore Supplies Office in Aberdeen, carried faint echoes of strategies pursued in Ireland three quarters of century earlier. But 'constructive unionism', whether in its Scottish or Irish formulations, was open to the same charge—that it was essentially reductionist in its analysis. Fearghal Cochrane has remarked of Terence O'Neill that he dealt with Irish nationalism as 'a kind of behavioural problem', susceptible to economic therapy.[256] Richard Crossman felt, similarly, that Ross 'was determined to treat nationalism as a mere emotional attitude which can be cured by economic policies alone'.[257]

Indeed, Ross's cabinet colleagues, demonstrating (ironically) the extent to which a malleable and creative unionism could deliver for Scotland, sought to undercut the SNP in more substantial ways than Ross envisioned. In 1968 Harold Wilson sought to buy some time with which to monitor the SNP challenge by creating a Royal Commission on the Constitution, chaired originally by Lord Crowther, and then (in March 1972, after

Crowther's death) by Lord Kilbrandon. The Commission reported in October 1973, in the turbulent final months of Edward Heath's government; and it was left to Wilson (who was returned to power in February 1974) to respond to its recommendations. In the context of the apparently chaotic condition of the union government in the early 1970s, and particularly after 1972, the SNP had consolidated rapidly, gaining 7 seats and twenty-two per cent of the vote in February 1974 and 11 seats and thirty per cent of the vote at the October 1974 general election ('it's not the seven SNP firsts I'm worried about', observed Michael Foot after February, 'it's the 13 seconds').[258] As with the Gladstonian conversion to Home Rule in the 1880s, political and electoral realities played a considerable role in Wilson's conversion to devolution, and Wilson (like Gladstone) remained committed to an idea of union. As with the Liberals in the mid 1880s, so with Labour in the mid 1970s, devolution threatened to be internally divisive; but Wilson was aided by Ross's ascendancy over Scottish Labour, and by his pragmatism. The way forward was still difficult, however: the party's proposals were published as a White Paper, *Our Changing Democracy: Devolution to Scotland and Wales*, in November 1975, and this in turn formed the basis for the Scotland and Wales Bill of 1976, which fell to a new Labour Secretary of State, Bruce Millan, to defend (Ross, out of favour with James Callaghan, had left the cabinet when Wilson retired in March 1976). But the complexities of this measure, in particular the complicated counter-weighting of central and devolved authorities, proved an overly fertile source of parliamentary contention; and the measure was effectively mothballed in February 1977. A second attempt, the Scotland Bill (1977), proved (in parliamentary terms, at least) relatively more successful, separating the Scots from the Welsh case, and proposing a referendum and the prospect of a devolved parliament. However, it was seriously weakened by the Cunningham Amendment (which decreed that, for the Act to operate, forty per cent of the total electorate had to be supportive), while the Grimond Amendment looked forward to the exclusion of Orkney and Shetland from a future Scottish legislature. In the event, Cunningham alone did for devolution: in the referendum of 1 March 1979 1.253 million Scots voted for devolution, 51.6 per cent of the poll, but—crucially—'only' 32.85 per cent of the total electorate.[259]

The referendum of 1979 demonstrated that a majority of those Scots voting favoured devolution: but it also revealed that the union retained formidable support, with 1.23 million voters (48.5 per cent of the electorate) repudiating the opportunity to reacquire a Scots parliament.[260] These are particularly striking figures, given that there was a strong argument for suggesting that—given the contexts of massive industrial unrest, significant inflation, the generally catastrophic condition of the national finances, the apparent radicalization of Welsh nationalism, republican insurgency in Northern Ireland—the union was not in fact working. The emotional pull of union for Scots in the late 1970s should not, then, be underestimated. By extension, the success of Labour in promoting a distinctively Scottish interest within a centralized union state should be acknowledged: Labour's malleable and constructive unionism must surely be regarded as one of the key bolsters of the United Kingdom in the 20th century.

By way of contrast the deracinated and centralized unionism effectively promoted by Margaret Thatcher between 1979 and 1990 proved to be a much less subtle agency for union.[261] Though the long-term decline of Conservatism and Unionism in Scotland is frequently stressed, it should not be forgotten that in 1979 the Conservatives retained 31.4 per cent of the Scottish vote and twenty-two seats: by 1987, with Mrs Thatcher still in power, this had sunk to 24 per cent of the vote and ten seats, and by 1997 to 17.5 per cent of the vote and no seats. One other, key, perspective on Scottish voters' response to Thatcherite unionism is provided by the new referendum on devolution, held in September 1997, immediately after Labour's election victory: in this 74.3 per cent of those Scots who voted desired the restoration of a Scottish parliament (as mentioned, the figure in 1979 had been 51.6 per cent). In the context of a gradually improving British economy, growing employment, the prospect of a settlement in Northern Ireland, the union did indeed appear now to be working (as opposed to the conditions of 1979). But, critically, the union did not appear to be working for Scotland.

There are good grounds for supposing that the relative longevity of the union in Ireland may be illuminated by the periodic pragmatism and malleability of unionist government, both Liberal and Conservative. Equally, there are clear grounds for supposing that apparently ideological government (such as that provided by the Russellite Whigs) proved to be both murderously painful to the Irish and profoundly detrimental to the relationship between them and the British government. These were lessons that Scottish Labour, and certainly leaders like Thomas Johnston or William Ross, appeared to have taken on board. But it was Mrs Thatcher, unionist by instinct rather than historical grounding, who inadvertently revisited the errors of the 19th century.

# Conclusion: Whigs and Constructive Unionists

This book is ultimately concerned, not with unionist party politics, but rather with the politics, culture, and impact of unionism in Scotland and Ireland. However, the survival of the Scots union clearly owed much to the party structure of Scotland, and of the British state. The Scottish Unionist party was deeply rooted in the political and intellectual history of Scotland, and brought together a Tory legacy of romantic nationalism with a Whig tradition of assimilation. The party thrived in the context of a politics still heavily infiltrated and conditioned by religious faith.

Labour in Scotland was originally supportive of Home Rule, but had migrated towards unionism by the interwar years. Where the Unionist Party's appeal was partly based, at least in the era of Irish Home Rule, upon religion, Labour cultivated the politics of class. This, combined with its economistic social diagnoses, its centralist prescriptions, and its disproportionate contribution to the formation and leadership of the British Labour movement, effectively made for unionism—or at best for a rigorously unsentimental, pragmatic, and materialist patriotism.

But, in defining the successes of the two parties, their weaknesses also become apparent. The Unionist Party in Scotland was, like its counterpart in the sectarianized politics of late 19th-century Ireland, founded partly upon religion; and though Scottish Unionism eventually distanced itself from the more extreme expressions of denominational anger in a way that Ulster Unionism did not, still the association survived. Scottish Unionism, in brief, was in danger of replicating the limitations of its Ulster counterpart, by building electoral success upon a specifically sectarian appeal. Moreover, Scottish Unionism was also plagued with some of the wider intellectual tensions inside British Conservatism: the history of British Conservatism in the 20th century was (inter alia) a history of tension between Whig assimilationists and Tory patriots, between doctrinaire economic neo-liberals, and paternalist one-nation romantics. Scottish unionism thrived by cultivating Scottish institutions, administrative devolution, and making patriotic appeals within the wider framework of union. But Mrs Thatcher represented an alternative unionism; and moreover it was a unionism which was simultaneously proactive and radical—and without electoral mandate in Scotland. What therefore emerged in Scotland between 1979 and 1997, during the Conservative years in power, was a political situation not dissimilar to that prevailing in Ireland in the last forty or so years of the union, when the Irish (Nationalist) Parliamentary Party was overwhelmingly dominant: taxation without (effective) representation.

Labour's advantages were also circumscribed. Class politics were essentially unionist politics; and Labour's appeal to class effectively created a unionism in Scotland which transcended the endemic religious rivalries of the West. But, in the end, if Mrs Thatcher replicated the mistakes of a *dirigiste* Whiggery in mid-19th-century Ireland, then the Labour leadership may have replicated the mistakes of constructive unionism in the late 19th century: Scottish, like Irish, nationalism has indeed proved to be more than 'a mere emotional attitude which can be cured by economic policies alone'. And Tony Blair, who has been compared with William Gladstone, may yet be seen to have realized the dire predictions that late 19th-century Unionists made for Gladstonian Home Rule. For them, Home Rule was not a bolster to the union, but rather the first step—indeed 'a leap in the dark'—towards Irish independence.[262] It remains to be seen whether devolution is the first step towards a revitalized Scots union—or the prelude to liberation.

# 8

# Irish unionists and the union, 1801–2007

## Parties, people, and histories

It is a delusion to suppose that a desire for Imperial Supremacy with Home Rule is a law of the being of the Irish Protestant. If I were a young man, and Home Rule were carried, I'd join Sinn Fein, and advocate separation and a republic, with all the power that I possess [but] not out of a sense of pique, or a sense of wrong, or a feeling of having been deserted or betrayed—that's the English delusion…John Lord Atkinson to Walter Long, 28 Mar. 1908 (BL, Long Papers, Add Ms.62413)

The real truth is that you in Belfast are far too sensitive. Even you, who are largely in touch with imperial affairs and with English political society, the moment you go back to Belfast become parochialised…F.E. Smith, Earl of Birkenhead, to Lord Londonderry, 26 April 1927 (PRONI Londonderry Papers, D.3099/2/2/117).

A union state without unionism can survive a long time. But not perhaps for ever. Iain McLean and Alastair McMillan, *State of the Union: Unionism and the Alternatives in the United Kingdom since 1707* (Oxford, 2005), p. 256

## Introduction

In both Scotland and Ireland the union and unionism were sustained and defended through successful party political institutions. In both the condition of unionism at the beginning of the new millennium does not suggest any particularly strong or complex political or ideological heritage; but in both appearances belie realities. If (as scholars now recognize) Scottish unionism was forged out of a particular indigenous reading of the nation's historical origins and evolution, and out of a particular assessment of its economic needs and aspirations—if it was more than grudging support for the treaties of 1707—then Irish unionism, too, was more than a pragmatic or artificial coalition assembled to support the legislation of 1800.[1]

Scottish and Irish unionism owed much to the Conservative parties of the two nations, which in turn drew upon strong local patriotic and loyalist cultures. As has been seen, Scottish unionism melded an emasculated Jacobitism with an Enlightenment tradition celebrating Scotland's role and contribution within the British state: 20th-century Scottish unionism uneasily combined an integrationist Whiggery, rooted in the Enlightenment, with a nostalgic patriotic Toryism. For its part, Irish unionism, as a party and as an ideology, inherited many of the complexities and contradictions of 18th-century Irish Whiggery and patriotism, as well as the exclusivity of 19th-century Protestant loyalism and Conservatism.[2] Just as Irish republicanism would be simultaneously defined by local sectarian frontiers as well as universal human ideals, so Irish unionism would come to be defined both as a crude instrument of Ascendancy and of sectarian defensiveness as well as (certainly in the estimation of its defenders) a vehicle for Enlightenment values and a metropolitan vision.[3]

The union and unionism became central, inescapable (if also deeply contested) features of Irish politics and society in the 19th century. As has been suggested in an earlier chapter, Ireland (like Scotland) was successfully infiltrated by the British state and British culture—and indeed, just as Scottish historians commonly link the development of Scots national institutions in the 19th century to the condition and intrusiveness of the union, so no assessment of the revival or creation of Celtic political and cultural institutions in the late 19th century is possible without an appreciation of the challenge posed by the union to Irish distinctiveness. In the constricted electoral circumstances of the 19th century, where the practice of politics remained bound to the possession of property, unionism thrived. For much of the first three quarters of the century, Irish electoral politics were dominated by parties, Conservative and Liberal, which were united by a shared commitment to union. Each of these traditions, but in particular the Conservative, fed into the creation of an organized unionist movement between 1884 and 1886. Drawing upon a formidable range of social, financial, and cultural resources, this movement (though representing perhaps only thirty per cent of the Irish people) successfully delayed the implementation of any form of Home Rule until 1920–1921; and it has so far prevented the attainment of the historic nationalist goal of a united and autonomous Irish state.[4] Whether the Unionist movement, in achieving this delay, effectively scuppered an historic reconciliation between Irish nationalism and the British state is open to counterfactual debate.

## Protestants, patriots, loyalists

The mid 1880s saw the creation of an organized and formal Irish Unionism. Just as the forging of a Scottish Unionist party in 1912 brought together within the one structure a formidable range of traditions and resources, so in Ireland in 1885–1886 unionism brought together several broad and deep streams within the political life of the island. Irish unionism was a confluence or a node: it was a religious, geographical, economic, and party political intermingling. Irish unionism brought together different traditions of Protestant, drawing in particular upon unifying proto-evangelical and loyalist subcultures from the 18th century; but it also appealed for a time to a small minority of propertied Catholics, those who had been enfolded by schooling or profession within the union and empire, or whose economic standing depended upon the stability of the British state (Liberalism was, as will be shown, an important factor in this embrace). Irish unionism was also, originally, an all-Ireland phenomenon, with perhaps 250,000 adherents outside the six counties of what would become Northern Ireland in 1920: a scattered and (allowing for the Big House strain) predominantly urban, indeed metropolitan, and Anglican and propertied unionism characterized the south and west, while the North was simultaneously more industrial, more rural, and more Presbyterian in character. Liberals and Conservatives, Presbyterians and Anglicans, once mutually antagonistic, came to cooperate in the context of the looming threat from Parnellite Home Rule. An Irish Unionist Parliamentary Party, a forum for loyalists of all party traditions, was created in 1885–1886; unionist missionary organizations—the Irish Loyal and Patriotic Union, the Loyal Irish Union—were created in Dublin and Belfast at the same time and united enthusiasts of all party creeds. Electoral cooperation between the parties at the local, constituency, level slowly took shape, though (as in Scotland) tensions and jealousies survived until (and beyond) the formal merger of Conservatism and Liberal Unionism.[5]

However, the rapidity of this unionist organization and coalescence in the mid 1880s was not simply a consequence of the enormity of the—Gladstonian and Parnellite—political threat, though it was certainly partly that. Unionism was created with speed and efficiency because it built upon existing institutions and ideologies and half-formed alliances. Much, therefore, of the groundwork for Unionist mobilization had been prefabricated in an earlier age. In particular, the success of Unionism in the mid 1880s rested upon the adaptability and strength of the Conservative tradition on the island. Unionism survived the crisis of the mid 1880s because (within certain clear parameters) its Conservative parent had responded successfully to the political challenges posed over fifty years of development (what K.T. Hoppen has described as 'the characteristic tendency of Irish Toryism to make the best of a bad job').[6]

The 1790s were critical years in terms of the formulation of the institutions and culture of Irish, as of Scots, loyalism. The 1830s were critical years in terms of the invention of modern Conservatism and unionism in Ireland, as in Scotland and the rest of the United Kingdom. In part, this reflected the need for fresh institutions to address the practical challenges of the new, reformed, British politics. Certainly in Ireland the imminent threat of reform stimulated the creation of the Irish Protestant Conservative Society (1831), designed to bolster local electoral registration and to raise funds through a 'Protestant rent' (an obvious borrowing from the earlier Catholic Association).[7] This was followed by the foundation of the Belfast Conservative Society in 1835 and, in 1836, of the Dublin Metropolitan Conservative Society, a body which had significant intellectual ballast in the form of Isaac Butt and other Trinity College Dublin heavyweights.[8] But while the Metropolitan Society reflected some of the emphases and inclusivity of Robert Peel's new 'Conservatism' and of his Tamworth Manifesto, there were of course specifically Irish contexts and inflections.

The emergent Irish Conservatism reflected not only Peelite initiatives in Britain, but also the seismic shifts in local politics created by Daniel O'Connell, Catholic Emancipation, and Repeal. The creation of a self-confident, assertive, and historically informed Catholic politics in the 1820s served both as an exemplar and as a warning to Irish Protestants. In part, the mobilization of emancipationists through the Catholic and New Catholic Associations provided a model for their Protestant opponents; and the Brunswick Club movement of the later 1820s and, then, the several Conservative initiatives of the 1830s duly copied some of the features of successful Catholic organization, including the use of parish organization and clergy.

But the challenge of O'Connellite politics was critical, not just in terms of indirectly inspiring Conservative reorganization, but also through precipitating some more fundamental movement within Irish Protestant politics. Wider ideological shifts in Irish society from an emphasis on the 'ancient constitution' and 'limited kingship' and rights of conquest towards individual rights and liberties involved a supersession of traditional patriotism. Irish patriots had always been intensely divided over the issue of political rights for Irish Catholics; and these divisions helped ultimately to propel some towards unionism. J.R. Hill has made the case for understanding the national importance of patriotism within Dublin civic politics; and she has depicted a politics defined by support for the 'ancient constitution', constitutional balance, and Protestant libertarianism.[9] But these were, indeed, a politics characterized by Protestantism, and by the effective absence, through much of the 18th century, of any serious Catholic challenge: they were the politics of the *ancien régime*—'aristocratic, corporatist and confessional'.[10] They were utterly incompatible with the popular bourgeois Catholicism mobilized by O'Connell, even though by the 1830s he was championing the restoration of an Irish parliament, the historic focus of Dublin Protestant patriot affections and economic need. O'Connell's envisioned parliament and politics were in fact far removed from those of *ancien régime* patriotism; and thus Dublin Protestants carried their patriot inheritance into the emergent unionism.

This transition was facilitated by the evolving condition of Protestant spirituality in Ireland. Evangelicalism, with its emphases on personal salvation through faith, and on religious witness, had been imported into Irish Protestantism from England and from continental Europe in the mid 18th century; but it rapidly gained ground in Ireland in the first half of the 19th century.[11] The Revolution in France and O'Connell's 'velvet' revolution with Catholic emancipation stimulated this development of Irish evangelical Protestantism; for each, in their way, fundamentally challenged the existing political and religious order in Ireland. Thus, the 1820s saw the 'Second Reformation', an evangelical counter-attack on Catholic mobilization, designed to secure religious conversion and reawakening throughout Ireland, but beginning with the impoverished Catholic cottiers of south Ulster and Connacht.[12] This effective reinvention of Irish Protestantism was occurring simultaneously with the reorganization of Conservatism as well as the first effective challenge—O'Connellite repeal—to the union settlement of 1801. Several of the lay architects of the 'Second Reformation' in the 'frontier' counties of Ulster, including John Maxwell, fifth Lord Farnham, combined a patronage for the religiously motivated 'Reformation Societies' with support for the precursors of Tory mobilization, the Brunswick Clubs.[13] Leading evangelical Protestants in Dublin, such as the Revd Tresham Dames Gregg (nicknamed 'Thrash-em' on account of his bracing approach to theological debate) easily incorporated a commitment to Conservative electoral mobilization within their religious strategies: Gregg was simultaneously a prolific evangelical polemicist, a founder of the Dublin Protestant Operatives' Association, and an Orange and Tory sympathizer.[14]

The challenge of O'Connell, and the opportunities created by a buoyant evangelicalism, also helped to shape other emerging features of the new Conservative politics of the 1830s. It was said that 'during the first quarter of the present [19th] century, nine-tenths of the Presbyterians of Ireland were Whigs'.[15] The foremost Presbyterian divine of the age was Henry Cooke, who (though a moderate emancipationist in the 1820s) had been an opponent of the legislation of 1829, and was rooted in the 'Old Light', or Calvinist and theologically conservative, traditions of his Church. He was, perhaps, the leading Presbyterian evangelical of the mid 19th century. In the new—emancipated and reformed—circumstances of the 1830s Cooke shifted from the traditional Whiggery of his communion, and aligned himself behind the new Conservatism and in sympathy with the Established Church. He interpreted O'Connell's assaults on the Established Church as being part of a wider campaign against Irish Protestantism; similarly, he viewed the Whigs, newly (in 1834) allied with the 'Liberator', as instruments of O'Connell's strategic designs. But, as he famously argued to a mass meeting at Hillsborough, County Down, in 1834, he was not selling out to Toryism or the ascendancy of the Established Church: 'whilst I reject alike the name of Whig or Tory, I decidedly avow myself a Conservative...amongst the principles of a Conservative are these: to protect no abuse that can be proved; to resist reckless innovation, not rational reform; to sacrifice no honest interest to hungry clamour; to yield no principle to time-serving expediency; to stand by religion in opposition to every form of infidelity'.[16] Just as O'Connell sought to define a unified Catholic historical identity, Cooke sought (despite the denominational tensions between Presbyterianism and Anglicanism) to proclaim its Protestant equivalent: for Cooke, O'Connell was James II, and 1689 was being replayed in 1834, with Presbyterians and members of the Church of Ireland 'uniting in a similar defence within the walls of Derry, or at the passes of Enniskillen'.[17]

But, significantly, Cooke, a graduate of the University of Glasgow, also looked to Scotland in terms of historical validation and identity: some of his best friends were now Anglicans, although the Church of Scotland was his spiritual home, and its travails retained a profound importance for a wider Irish Presbyterian identity and sense of victimhood. Standing alongside the Established Church within a Conservative union demanded some rethinking, but it certainly did not mean any diplomatic amnesia: 'Presbyterians, I speak to you. The days are gone by when, in Ireland, Wentworth unleashed his bloodhounds on the track of your fathers; when Laud, papist at heart, forged chains at once for their consciences and their liberties. The days are gone by when a Lauderdale plotted, and, upon the mountains of Scotland, a Dundee executed the purposes of a bloody and heartless tyranny'.[18] The message was clear: the Established Church, its predecessors, agents, and allies, had indeed done bloody deeds, but they were no longer the principal threat to Irish Presbyterianism. This now came from O'Connell; and Peelite Conservatism could provide the means by which Irish Protestants would rediscover the unity which had saved them in 1689.

Evangelical religion was not simply a useful cement through which Presbyterians would be bound to Conservatism: it was also an essential component of the leadership and culture of mid-19th-century Irish Conservatism (and ultimately thereby of Irish Unionism). Belfast and Ulster, particularly the outer, or 'frontier' counties, were hotbeds of evangelical conviction; but even the South, and in particular Dublin, was not immune to its attractions. The extended Guinness family combined brewing, Conservatism and evangelical religion in the 19th century: Sir Arthur Guinness (1768–1855), for example, was a contributor to the Waldensian church in Italy in the 1850s.[19] Trinity College Dublin was a particular hotbed of the evangelical faith in the second quarter of the 19th century; and this influence was transmitted to a generation of Irish Conservative leader. Setting aside great Victorian Tory clans such as the Hamiltons (dukes of Abercorn) and Stewarts (marquesses of Londonderry), the dominant figures in mid-century Conservatism, certainly bourgeois Conservatism, were a community of evangelical lawyers, including Sir Joseph Napier (1804–1882), James Whiteside (Napier's brother-in-law) (1804–1876), and Hugh McCalmont Cairns (later first Earl Cairns) (1809–1885).[20] Each was educated at Trinity College Dublin, and each held high political or judicial office: Napier was Lord Chancellor of Ireland (1857–1858), Whiteside served as Lord Chief Justice of Ireland (1866–1876), and Cairns was Lord Chancellor of England (1868 and 1874–1880). Whiteside was one of a handful of bright young Tories identified by the 14th Earl of Derby as the party's emerging leadership cadre: Cairns was advanced and admired even by patrons (such as Disraeli) who found his intense religiosity incomprehensible (for Disraeli, Cairns was privately 'Moody and Sankey').[21] Indeed, each of the three law-yers was strongly evangelical in his principles: each was a strict sabbatarian. 'Holy Joe' Napier invested much energy in the Church Missionary Society and the Young Men's Christian Society, lecturing frequently to these bodies, while Cairns began each day with an hour and half's study of the Bible, and was a patron of the rescue work of another prominent Irish evangelical, Dr Thomas Barnardo.[22] All three lawyers were convinced opponents of the disestablishment of their mother church, the Church of Ireland. As will become clear, opposition to disestablishment provided a training ground and dry-run for the campaign against Home Rule; but both movements rested partly upon evangelical foundations which had been laid down much earlier, in the 1820s and 1830s.[23]

While intellectual leadership was provided by the evangelical and other Tories, particularly the lawyers, emanating from Trinity, recent scholarship has also made the case for the contribution of a liberal conservative mercan-tile and professional community within Belfast in the first half of the 19th century. The focuses of this included the wealthy Tennent and Emerson clans, with (for example) James Emerson Tennent, Conservative MP for Belfast and (later) Lisburn, a prolific author, who identified with a range of 'advanced' causes, such as Greek nationalism.[24] The wider significance of this literate and outward-looking conservatism may still be open to debate (there is the possibility that the hunt for a generous Belfast conservatism in the era of the 'Second Reformation' may be a genealogical quest for a Trimbleite unionism *avant la lettre*); but at the very least it represented a minor Britannic and metropolitan strain within the party, which was car-ried over (certainly in a vestigial manner) into Irish and Ulster Unionism.

Aside from (or connected with) evangelicalism, the Orange Order sup-plied an additional medium through which forms of Protestant association and solidarity could be built in Ireland (and between Ireland and Scotland), and through which the different cultures of late 18th-century loyalism could be melded within 19th-century unionism: unionism ultimately drew strength from the forms of loyalism which were being defined in the era of the Revolutionary and Napoleonic Wars, of which the most important in Ireland was the Protestant loyalism that underpinned Orangeism.[25] As is well known, Orangeism grew largely from Protestant combinations in south Ulster, with its nativity being dated to a fall-out from a sectarian clash in North Armagh, the Battle of the Diamond, in September 1795. The Orange Order was exclusively Protestant and modelled on freemasonry (which also supplied an organizational template to the United Irishmen): it was committed to the achievement of the 'Glorious Revolution', and to the cult of its protagonist, William III, and devoted in practice to the ascendancy of the Protestant interest in Ireland. With the militarization of Ireland in the late 1790s, the crown forces served as an effective means by which the Order and its principles were spread throughout Protestant Ireland and beyond, into Scotland and the North West of England: by the 1820s there were perhaps 100,000 members of the Order in Ireland and in Scotland. Again, as is well known, the Order was not at first wholly in favour the abolition of the Protestant parliament in Dublin; but, in the context of Catholic mobilization, it swiftly realigned itself behind the union. Moreover, though the Order was a useful prop to the Ascendancy class, it was also occasionally associated with violence and uncouthness (it was proscribed in 1825 and, reformed, went into voluntary dissolution in 1836); and thus the social and political leadership of Tory Ireland (as of Tory Scotland) had good reason to be ambivalent. The Order was also relatively less popular with Presbyterians than with members of the Established Church, though it certainly should not be assumed that Presbyterians universally withheld their support.[26]

With these significant caveats, it is still clear that the Order functioned from the beginning as a binding agent within Irish Protestantism, amongst the Irish Protestant diaspora in Britain and North America, and between Irish Protestants and British sympathizers: Allan Blackstock has suggested that already by 1797 a militarized Orangeism had become the predominant (though certainly not the only) form of loyalist expression in Ireland.[27] Its numbers, as discussed, are one measure of its significance in this respect, as was an extraordinarily diverse and complex associated popular culture (in particular Orange tracts, ballads, and poetry).[28] The Order had, for a time, royal patronage (in the shape of the Dukes of York and Cumberland, brothers to King George IV); and indeed in the mid 1830s it was (wrongly) viewed as a tool for Cumberland's alleged ambitions over the crown. The Order had other forms of polite sanction: it had from the beginning the patronage of south Ulster gentry such as Colonel William Blacker; and in 1845, when it was reconstituted, a Fermanagh landowner, the third Earl of Enniskillen, agreed to act as the Grand Master. The Order also attracted some middle class and intellectual backing: Castle lawyers such as William Saurin (Attorney General of Ireland between 1807 and 1822) and Thomas Lefroy (beloved of Jane Austen, Prime Serjeant, and later—between 1852 and 1866—Lord Chief Justice of Ireland) combined family roots in continental European Protestant refugee culture with an aggressive Orange Toryism. Isaac Butt and other Trinity College luminaries were either enrolled within the Order or were sympathizers. Orangeism and evangelicalism were separate, but often related phenomena: Tresham Dames Gregg, the evangelical cleric and patron of popular Dublin Protestant mobilization, was an Orange sympathizer, and (amongst his many other literary effusions) published *Protestant Ascendancy Vindicated* in 1840.

However, perhaps the most significant electoral exponent of an evangelical Orange Toryism was the impecunious landowner, journalist, and novelist, William Johnston of Ballykilbeg.[29] Johnston's eccentricity and epic improvidence are such that it is tempting to view him as an isolated, or even comedic, phenomenon. He first stood for parliament in February 1857, when his effort to win Downpatrick for Conservatism garnered one vote (in a total poll of 130). His heroic status by the late 1860s and his successful defiance of the Belfast Conservative establishment at that time appear to underline his uniqueness. Johnston (after an unsuccessful excursion into newspaper proprietorship) gained national celebrity through flouting the controversial Party Processions Act: in July 1867 he led an illegal Orange march between Newtownards and Bangor in North Down, an act of defiance which won him two months' detention in Downpatrick Gaol. His subsequent beatification within Orangeism allowed him to take on the Belfast Conservative establishment at the general election of 1868, when he and his Liberal ally humiliated their two Tory opponents (no less figures than the society architect Sir Charles Lanyon and John Mulholland, greatest of the linen barons). Though Johnston was soon reconciled within the Irish Conservative party (he was too hard up to maintain any resistance), his defiance was widely celebrated in Protestant popular culture: ballads and poetry proclaimed his fame, while his bearded and patriarchal features adorned plates and cups and scarves. This heroic cult clearly prefigured that which was generated around Sir Edward Carson in 1912–1914.[30]

But Johnston, distinctive and defiant in several respects, also epitomizes much of 19th-century Irish Conservatism. He clearly embodied the landed tradition of Orange sponsorship, which had been so central to the foundation and restoration of the Order; but he also represented a type of Trinity educated lawyer and evangelical, so that (whatever his intellectual confusion and gaucheness) he stood at one end of a spectrum which included Napier, Whiteside, and Cairns. His enthusiasms and fads, fully documented within an extensive diary, illustrate much of the powerful interlocking components of Victorian unionist popular culture: Orangeism and evangelical religion, certainly, but also other related forms of association or political activism (such as temperance, educational self-improvement, and women's suffrage).[31] Moreover, Johnston's swift rehabilitation within mainstream Conservatism underlines the capacity of that very formidable tradition to address and absorb many types of dissent. The party had powerful intellectual, financial, and patronage resources at its disposal; but in the event, it required nothing more elevated than an inspectorship of fisheries to persuade Johnston to surrender his parliamentary seat and to bring him into line.[32]

## Tories

Drawing on these different cultural strands, Irish Conservatism survived the challenge of Catholic mobilization, and indeed thrived. As with Scots Conservatism in Glasgow and the West, so Irish Conservatism was well-placed to channel popular urban reactions to Catholic growth and activism. However, Scots Conservative success in rural constituencies was much less marked than that achieved by their Irish counterparts, who had relatively strong roots in the landscape of the North of Ireland: Irish landlordism, and by extension Conservatism, benefited from a mild consolidation in the aftermath of the Great Famine, while Conservatism was also well-anchored amongst the Protestant labouring classes. Both Scots and Irish Conservatives benefited, too, from an accession of Orange strength; but this was proportionately more significant for the Irish, who were also drawing upon a coalescent Protestantism (as opposed to the Scots, where the Kirk was, after the 'Great Disruption' of 1843, in a more than usually complete state of schism). Where Scottish Conservatism was overshadowed by the dominant Liberal tradition for much of the century (remaining 'abnormally weak'), Irish Conservatives enjoyed consistent success, being the single largest party in Ireland at the general elections of 1835, 1841, and 1859; in 1859, boosted by Independent support, and possibly by evangelical religious revival, they peaked with a majority of Irish seats (55 out of the 105 available).[33] Only in the context of a wider franchise and a more coherent Home Rule and farmer challenge did the Irish Conservative standing falter: these factors reduced the number of Conservative seats by roughly one half from their average in the 1832–1885 era to between 16 and 22 in the years between 1885 and 1918.

Like its Scottish counterpart, the Irish Conservative party responded to the challenge of electoral reform through reorganization and relaunch, but the Irish were first in creating a national coordinating body: the Central Conservative Society of Ireland was founded in 1850, in the aftermath of the critical Irish Franchise Act, and antedated its Scottish equivalent by over thirty years.[34] The Central Conservative Society not only foreshadowed the creation of the Scottish National Union of Conservative Associations (in 1882), it also anticipated the emergence of a distinctive Irish Unionism in the mid 1880s: one of the Society's patrons, Joseph Napier, stressed 'the importance of having our Irish Party kept together', and indeed this was its principal purpose and achievement.[35] The Society, like Unionism, was also strongly infiltrated by members of the Orange Order.[36] Specifically northern bodies were created in the shape of the Ulster Constitutional Union (1880) and the Ulster Constitutional Club (1883). Two key local apparatchiks—John Bates and Edward Shirley Finnegan—dominated Conservative organizational effort in Belfast and eastern Ulster from the 1830s through to the Home Rule era.[37]

Like the Scottish Conservatives, though in a rather more modest manner, these Irish Conservatives drew some strength from their good contacts with the London leadership in the mid 19th century (it is in fact reasonably clear that one of the mainstays of Scottish unionism in the 19th and 20th centuries was the strength of its integration within British high politics). The Irish were less well integrated than the Scots, but not without resource— and by no means as marginal to leadership politics as some interpretations of Victorian politics once suggested.[38] In June 1859, speaking to a meeting of 193 Conservative MPs, the outgoing Prime Minister, Lord Derby, identified six parliamentary colleagues as future leaders of the party: Hugh Cairns, James Whiteside, Gathorne-Hardy, William Vesey Fitzgerald, Richard Hely-Hutchinson, fourth Earl of Donoughmore, and Henry Herbert, fourth Earl of Carnarvon.[39] Of these six young hopefuls, four were Irish: Cairns (as has been noted) served as Solicitor General (1858–1859), Attorney General (1866), and Lord Chancellor of England (1866 and 1874–1880), Whiteside served as Lord Chief Justice of Ireland (1866–1876), Donoughmore, who died in 1866 at the age of forty-three, was Paymaster General and President of the Board of Trade (1858–1859), and Fitzgerald was Under Secretary of Foreign Affairs (1858–1859) and Governor of Bombay (1866–1872). In addition to these rising stars, there were more established luminaries such as the Hamilton family (Marquesses, and—after 1868—Dukes of Abercorn): James Hamilton, first Duke of Abercorn, served as Viceroy of Ireland (1866–1868, 1874–1876), and linked the worlds of Irish and Scottish Conservatism, Disraelian ministerial politics, the royal court, and freemasonry. Of Hamilton's six surviving sons, five served as Members of Parliament, and one—Lord George Hamilton—had a lengthy career as a Conservative cabinet minister under Salisbury and Arthur Balfour: both sons and daughters married strategically, creating a network of sympathy across the British aristocracy.[40] Other aristocrats were important, though inevitably less prolific and well-connected. Richard Southwell Bourke, the sixth Earl of Mayo, who (as Lord Naas) was an oft-serving Chief Secretary for Ireland (1852, 1858–1859, 1866–1868), before being elevated to the viceroyalty of India, where he met his death at the hand of an assassin in 1872 (his celebrant and biographer, William Wilson Hunter, was a Scots member of the Indian Civil Service).[41] Colonel Thomas Edward Taylor (whose grandfather was the fourth Earl of Bective and uncle the first Marquis of Headfort), was MP for County Dublin for over forty years (1841–1883), and held the strategically vital role of Conservative Chief Whip (1859–1868 and 1873–1874) before serving as Chancellor of the Duchy of Lancaster (1874–1880). Naas's and Taylor's position at Westminster, the favour they enjoyed from Derby and Disraeli, stemmed in large part from their marked success in organizing and managing the Conservative party in Ireland in the middle decades of the 19th century.[42]

Irish Conservatives shared a view of union with their mid-century Scottish counterparts. Just as Scots Conservatives (and others) emphasised that the Union of 1707 was an international treaty, so, too, Irish Conservatives of the period defined the Union of 1801 in similar terms. In the 1850s and 1860s Irish Conservatives, highlighting their patriot ancestry, referred back to the ancient constitution and traditions of the kingdom of Ireland: in 1853 the Conservative *Dublin Daily Express* remarked that it had been forgotten that before the union Ireland had been 'an ancient kingdom…[with] her own army, her own treasury, her own fiscal arrangements, and peculiar system of taxation'.[43] Joseph Napier and James Whiteside (the latter of whom wrote at length on the 'life and death of the Irish parliament') were keen advocates of the idea, familiar enough within mid-19th-century Scottish political discourse, that union was a treaty and a contract, any aspect of which (if dishonoured) might bring the voiding of the whole.[44] Napier argued in 1864 that the union was 'an international treaty in its very nature permanent, because on each side there was the giving up of the separate and independent existence of a state, a legislature and a national church'.[45] The corollary of this deeply entrenched view was of course that Irish Conservatives, like their Scottish counterparts, reserved the right to revisit or even to reject the union if it was tweaked or otherwise redefined by any British government.

All of these speculations were of course tied up with the question of the Church of Ireland establishment, which was coming to the fore in the 1860s, and was a natural development of the tithe and church endowment questions of the 1830s, and the rise of a separatist nationalism. Proponents of the union such as Napier and Whiteside were also prominent lay members of the Church of Ireland, and enthusiastic defenders of the Church establishment. One key purpose in defining the union as 'an international treaty' was not only to prevent any tampering with this 'treaty', but also, specifically, to discourage any infringement of the rights of the United Church of Britain and Ireland, as confirmed by the union itself. Disestablishment had of course a Scottish (and Welsh) dimension; and indeed the issue served the Conservative cause in both Ireland and Scotland in so far as it provided a rallying call and inspiration for Conservatives, while serving to divide their opponents. Scottish Conservatives benefited from the support of those within the Kirk and the Free Church who were either unsettled by the possibility that Gladstone might abruptly declare for disestablishment, or by his evident procrastination and hedging on the issue.

For both Ireland and Scotland disestablishment was, both fundamentally and indirectly, about union. For both Ireland and Scotland, the rights and status of the national churches were effectively tied up with the union establishment. In each country the question of disestablishment was linked, therefore, to the politics of union. Indeed, the ferocious battle over the Irish Church in 1868–1869 has been seen as a precursor to the Home Rule crisis, because disestablishment was an amendment of the terms of union; and also because disestablishment brought to the fore individuals, attitudes, and alliances, which would be soon redeployed, in 1885–1886.[46] In a sense, therefore, the crisis of the Irish union was first precipitated, not in 1885, but rather in 1868—not when Gladstone first proclaimed that the Act of 1801 stood in the way of a true British-Irish union, but rather when he first published his conclusion that 'the true interests of religion were in conflict with establish-ment'.[47] Fortunately for the Conservatives, Gladstone's devastating insights into the location of Truth in public affairs were not always accessible to lesser mortals: there remained enough 'stupid men' in the United Kingdom to preserve his opponents' electoral fortunes.[48]

# Whigs

The political confluence which created Irish Unionism in the mid 1880s also owed much to its Liberal tributary. Like its Scottish and wider British counterparts, Irish Liberalism had both Whig and radical strains, and a vari-egated ancestry: all looked back to a history of support for the 'Glorious Revolution' of 1688, limited monarchy, cautious reform, and parliamentary sovereignty. Whiggery was associated with union, the Hanoverian succes-sion, and the varieties of Protestantism: Scottish Whiggery was associated with an integrationist unionism, and with an idealized North Britain. Irish Whiggery in the 18th century was Protestant and patriotic, 'enlightened', aristocratic, and loyal. Great Whig magnates such as James Caulfeild, first Earl of Charlemont (1728–1799), corresponded with Montesquieu, upheld classical and enlightened values in art and architecture, and pursued a patri-otic agenda in politics. Enlightenment also frequently implied hostility towards the Catholic Church, however; and Whigs such as Charlemont eas-ily combined the historic religious presumptions of Irish Protestantism with ostensibly 'enlightened' political ideals: Charlemont, for example, in com-mon with other Whig patriots, was an opponent of Catholic emancipation in the 1780s. Equally, a Whig country gentleman such as Francis Saunderson, member for Cavan in the Irish House of Commons (1788–1800), struck a variety of patriotic postures, while opposing both emancipation (in 1795) and union (in 1800).[49]

Although Irish historians periodically fret over the interpretative chal-lenge posed by Presbyterian unionism—seeking explanations for the rapid transition of Presbyterian sympathies from reformist Whiggery and indeed republicanism in the 1790s to conservative unionism in the 19th century—in fact this problem is part of a wider, and less frequently examined issue. The Whig landed leadership of the late 18th century was patriotic and often anti-unionist; Whig families reeled back from the radical separatism of the insurgents in 1798, though even here isolated scions of great Whig clans provided some political and military leadership (the classic example being Lord Edward Fitzgerald, the fifth son of the first Duke of Leinster). And, yet, by the end of the 19th century Irish Whigs had generally taken their intellectual and political heritage into Unionism.

The Irish Whig tradition was sustained in the 19th-century House of Commons by landowning clans such as the Achesons (earls of Belmore), the Caulfeilds (earls of Charlemont), Chichesters (marquesses of Donegall), Hills (marquesses of Downshire), and Saundersons. Most of these clans migrated to a unionist Liberalism, and thence to either Liberal Unionism or full-blooded Conservatism. James Caulfeild, first Earl of Charlemont, was a patriot and an opponent of union; James Caulfeild, eighth Viscount Charlemont, served as a Unionist minister in James Craig's partitionist government of Northern Ireland. Where Francis Saunderson had been a leader of patriotic and reformist opinion in the Irish House of Commons in the 1790s, and an opponent of union, his grandson, Edward Saunderson, was a leader of conservative unionism in the United Kingdom House of Commons of the 1890s.[50] For many of these clans epiphanies appear to have been reached in the 1820s and again in the 1870s, when the challenge of popular Catholic mobilization forced some fundamental political reassessments. Again, the Saundersons may be taken as an illustration: Francis Saunderson's son, Alexander, was Whig MP for Cavan (1826–1831), and (on the basis of his rare parliamentary interventions) both a very nervous convert to Catholic emancipation, and a strong advocate of the disfranchisement of the forty shilling freeholders. His son, Edward, sat as a Liberal MP for Cavan between 1865 and 1874, before migrating towards a defensive Orangeism and Conservatism during the Land War: Edward's metamorphosis was completed by his election as a Conservative MP for North Armagh, the birthplace of the Orange Order, in 1885. Edward Saunderson and other former Whigs brought to Unionism after 1885–1886 a family tradition of aristocratic parliamentarianism, cautious reform, concern for property right, together with a clear strain of anti-Catholicism.[51]

But, in addition to the aristocratic and landed heritage within Whiggery, an urban variant of the tradition also thrived in Belfast. The capitalist class within early 19th-century Belfast was largely Whig, and rooted disproportionately in the textile industries.[52] The identification of Home Rule with moderate protectionism emphatically did not chime with the interests of this class, who often combined (in a characteristic mid-Victorian formulation) non-conformist, Liberal, and free trade convictions. Of course, not all of these magnates were Presbyterian or Liberal: some enormously wealthy linen clans such as the Ewarts or Mulhollands were already, by the 1870s, Conservative, while Peter Gibbon has argued that the ship owners of the city were generally Conservative from the 1850s onwards.[53] But, even allowing for this drift towards Conservatism, and for the Conservatives' electoral ascendancy (from the 1850s), there remained a significant tradition of free trade Liberalism within the Presbyterian (and dissenting) business community (sustained by a 'nexus of interrelated Whig families' such as the Andrews, Barbours, Duffins, Dunvilles, Herdmans, Richardsons, and Sinclairs).[54] Taking their lead from John Bright, this business elite carried their free trade convictions, and the commercial clout of their industry, into organized Unionism.

Landed and Belfast Whiggery were not the only forms of Liberal bequest to Unionism, however. If some landed Whigs were being swiftly compelled towards Conservatism and Unionism by the perceived pressure of popular Catholic activism, then other, more bourgeois and radical, forms of Irish Liberal initially identified different sources of political challenge. In addition, the aftermath of the Famine was characterized by a resurgence of landlordism, aided by a new class of incoming landlord, the actions of the land courts, and the ending of the old semi-feudal relationships binding landlord and tenant. Government legislation on the land question encouraged landlords to take a more legalistic view of their social and economic obligations, and this contributed to a cooling of agrarian relations even before the dramatic downturn of the later 1870s. By the 1860s there was a widespread suspicion that landlords were determined to destroy the customary rights of tenant farmers in the North of Ireland (the 'Ulster Custom').[55] This (in the event, temporary) landlord efflorescence fed into the electoral consolidation of Irish Conservatism, the party tradition which identified most unequivocally with the rights of Irish property.

This landed and Conservative growth provided a spur to Liberal party organization in Ireland, and also created an opportunity for electoral gain. On 4 August 1865 the Ulster Liberal Society was established (in the Royal Hotel, Belfast), to be followed by the Ulster Reform Club.[56] But, more important even than these organizational initiatives, was the realization that the otherwise formidable edifice of landed and Protestant Conservatism did not accommodate the needs of the influential farmer interest, particularly in Ulster. This permitted Irish Liberals to draw upon their traditions of radical agrarian reform—traditions most conspicuously represented by the radical landed MP for Dundalk (1835–1837) and Rochdale (1842–1852), William Sharman Crawford. The Liberals successfully underscored a commitment to tenant right at the general elections of 1868 (when they won 66 out of the 103 seats) and 1874 (when their successful appeal to Ulster farmers staved off electoral annihilation by the Home Rulers).[57] The particular success of this appeal to Ulster farmers was highlighted by the fact that, outside the Northern province, their party performed abysmally at the elections of 1874 and 1880.[58]

But, while this strain within Irish Liberalism deserves emphasis, it is important not to exaggerate its importance, or to invest the era before the Home Rule crisis with the wishful thinking of a later ecumenism. While it is possible to read the history of the 1870s as evidence of the creative potential remaining within Ulster politics, and indeed as evidence for the enormity of the shifts which came in 1885–1886, the last hurrah of Ulster Liberalism concealed some more mundane realities. It is true that, by appealing to the farmer interest, Liberals succeeded in uniting Catholics and Presbyterians behind a reform agenda, and that this, ostensibly ecumenical, alliance brought electoral success in 1874 and 1880, on the eve of the open sectarianization of the early and mid 1880s.[59] But, as K.T. Hoppen has observed, 'the most obvious feature of Liberal activity in Ulster was its dependence upon Presbyterian leadership and Catholic numbers'; and Presbyterian enthusiasm for Gladstone in 1874 and 1880 owed as much to the Grand Old Man's choleric thoughts on the Vatican Decrees as to his determination to root out the crimes of Ascendancy.[60] Moreover, Northern Catholic support for Liberalism in 1880 depended largely upon the fact that only two Home Rulers had sufficient temerity to stand for election in Ulster (both in County Cavan). Presbyterian Liberals were opponents of Anglican Ascendancy, but they were also opponents of Rome; while Ulster Catholics had, as yet, nowhere else to go, save for Liberalism.

Little wonder, then, that the glorious, but thinly rooted flowers of Ulster Liberalism wilted so dramatically in the early and mid 1880s. In a sense, shifting analogies, Ulster Liberalism was an alliance founded, not upon any historic reconciliation or empathy, but rather upon pragmatism and the appeal of a single issue. When that issue, tenant right, was satisfactorily addressed (through Gladstone's Land Act of 1881), then the alliance faltered; and indeed there was a certain irony here, in so far as the legislation owed much to the effort expended by Ulster Liberal MPs, who were thereby in a sense undercutting their own electoral support.[61] The material needs of

Presbyterian farmers were satisfied by this legislation; while the spiritual needs of their Catholic counterparts were satisfactorily addressed by the developing Nationalist political assault on Ulster. In sum, Ulster Liberalism stalled when (after 1881) Presbyterians felt once again that the Catholic threat to their consciences was greater than the threat posed by the Ascendancy to their livelihood: it stalled when Catholics found alternative structures wherein they could lead themselves.

Irish Liberals were mostly shocked by Gladstone's conversion to Home Rule, for (in the words of the editor of the *Northern Whig*), they looked upon 'any proposal to repeal the Act of Union, or to tamper with it, as not a Liberal policy at all, but retrogressive, dangerous, incredible and impossible'.[62] Gladstone, in other words, was challenging the fundamentals of Irish Liberal self-definition. On 30 April 1886, in the context of the introduction of the first Home Rule Bill, a large gathering of Liberals met in the Ulster Hall to declare their opposition; and shortly afterwards the Ulster Liberal Unionist Committee was formed, soon to be renamed the Ulster Liberal Unionist Association. From these developments it was abundantly clear that the 'vast majority of the leading Liberals in Ulster opposed the Home Rule Bill'.[63] There had already been quiet and preliminary cooperation in 1885; but the general election of July 1886 revealed a wholesale (and, in the event, lasting) electoral alliance between Irish Conservative and Liberal Unionists.

Liberals shaped unionism, both in terms of general acceptance of the union in mid-Victorian Ireland, as well as the formal movement of 1885–1886. Irish Liberalism, like Labour in 20th-century Scotland, was one critical means by which some Catholics were (at least temporarily and partly) reconciled to the union state. Ulster Liberalism may have been broadly 'presbyterian in leadership and Catholic in numbers', but it still served as a conduit by which able middle class Catholics could gain access to some social mobility and senior office. It would be wrong to exaggerate this function; but, just as Irish Conservatism served the ends of evangelical Protestant lawyers, so Liberalism brought judicial office and peerages to Catholic lawyers such as Thomas O'Hagan (MP for Tralee between 1863 and 1865, and subsequently Lord Chancellor of Ireland) and Charles Russell (MP for Dundalk between 1880 and 1885, and later Lord Chief Justice of England).[64] Liberal Unionism inherited some of this capacity to serve Catholic needs; and, while the overwhelming majority plumped for Home Rule, Liberal Unionism functioned briefly as a means by which a few Catholics were carried into the wider Unionist movement after 1886. For example, the three Catholic Unionist MPs of the Home Rule era—William Kenny (St Stephen's Green, 1892–1898), Michael Morris (Galway, 1900–1901), and D.S. Henry (Londonderry South, 1916–1921)—were all either Liberal Unionists, or had strong family roots in Liberalism.

But the Liberal bequest was complex; for it offered not only this small Catholic accession to Unionism, but also Whig legacies of patriotism, concern for property and aristocracy, cautious reformism, and support for the religious and political achievements of the 'Revolution' of 1688. In addition Liberalism brought a radical strain, focusing on the immediate needs and aspirations of tenant farmers as well as (to a lesser extent) the living and working conditions of the urban working classes. Much of this was far removed from the precepts of Orange Conservatism; and (as with Scottish Unionism) the effort to reconcile Conservative and Liberal traditions within the one broad enterprise sometimes seemed overwhelming. There was certainly an unremitting danger that the new alliance would cling to the lowest common (sectarian) denominators of the two traditions; there was also a very real danger that the effort of maintaining the alliance would emerge as a political end in itself. But, on the whole, while its legacy was certainly mixed, Liberalism brought to Unionism a breadth and social concern that might otherwise have been diminished or lacking. In the end, though, it could not free the movement from the shackles of religious chauvinism and fear.

## Political cultures

The elaborate organizational carapace of formal Unionism in the mid 1880s was supported not only by this diverse and complex party heritage, but also by a rich popular and high culture. In part, this was influenced by the ascendancy in parts of Ireland and of Irish society, particularly in the North, of British commercial and imperial culture (and indeed this broad issue has already been broached in Chapter 6). But there was certainly much more to Irish unionism than the presence and direct influence of the union state.

In a general sense, it was possible to grow up in the North of Ireland at the end of the 19th century in an environment where schooling and work, recreation and leisure, religious worship and environment were all influenced by the values upheld within the British state. Youth organizations such as the Boys' Brigade, imported from Scotland into Belfast by the evangelical William McVicker in 1890, or Baden-Powell's Scouting Movement, with its strong imperial resonances, which had arrived in Belfast by 1909, provided a training not merely for life, but also for Unionism. The Orange Order organized youth lodges from the 1880s onwards. Public schooling was conducted in the English language, using texts where the history and geography of the empire featured largely, and where the classroom might be overshadowed by the ubiquitous pink-splattered map of the World. The workplace might well be located within the expanding public service; alternatively in a city such as Belfast, the dependence of most businesses upon the British or imperial connection would be made clear by the political activity of owners and managers.[65] Trade union membership in Victorian and Edwardian Ulster generally connected workers to their comrades in Britain. Place names and public space were disproportionately Unionist: a Belfast worker might journey to the shipyards of the Queen's Island, traversing Victoria Square and the Albert Bridge, and passing the Spencer Dock (named after the eponymous Earl, and Lord Lieutenant): he might later spend his wages in the shops of the main thoroughfare, Royal Avenue, or take a drink in the Crown Bar, or (venturing a mile or so further), the Hatfield Arms, by Salisbury Street.[66] Voluntary associations, such as the Young Men's Christian Association, were clearly conditioned by the impact of union and empire: their reading materials and entertainments reflected these two critical influences. Church life, equally, was often inseparable from these political influences: while some Church of Ireland and Presbyterian ministers were either Home Rulers, or fought to keep the church community as a politically neutral space, in reality much of the spiritual life of Ulster Protestants was Unionist, at least in undertone.[67] The liturgy of the Church of Ireland was sprinkled with loyal references to the monarchy, as were the pew Bibles: funerary monuments, and aging military standards, in Anglican and other Protestant churches, testified to British imperial exploits on the battlefield and elsewhere.

The intense interlinkages of the aristocracy continued to bind the upper echelons of Irish society with Britain and to unionism, as recent work has affirmed. The formal political influence of Irish Unionists peers and landed gentlemen within the United Kingdom parliament has long been recognized (not least through the pioneering scholarship of Patrick Buckland).[68] Equally, the consolidation of a pan-British aristocracy 'in the last quarter of the 18th century and the first quarter of the 19th century' has been traced through the work of Linda Colley.[69] The integration of an individual clan such as the Londonderrys has been observed through the research of Diane Urquhart.[70] But the full extent of the engagement by Northern aristocratic clans such as the Abercorns, Annesleys, Belmores, Caledons, Enniskillens, Ernes, Londonderrys, and Rossmores with metropolitan society has not yet been fully grasped. These were families who, in the era of Home Rule, lived a life of privileged transhumance, shifting from Irish pastures to the ostensibly more elevated feeding grounds of the imperial capital. The marriage patterns, leisure activities, dress and social codes, and artistic tastes of these Irish clans meant that they were enfolded within a broadly homogeneous United Kingdom social and political elite. Judged whether by the shape and print of their calling cards, their choice of dress or schools, their military and racing enthusiasms, or by their close observance of an agreed social calendar, these were British aristocrats. The corollary of this, of course, was than any weakening of their status in Ireland implied a weakening of the overall condition of the United Kingdom.

In addition, it might be said that the intellectual condition of Unionism in the early 20th century fed into the strength of the party and movement in Ireland. The success of Edwardian Unionism in the North of Ireland was linked, not just to the diversity of its political heritage and cultural underpinnings, but also to the strength of its command over intellectuals. As in Scotland, so in Ireland, Unionism flourished within the press, literature, and the academy (though the intellectual hegemony of unionism in Scotland was more obviously robust than in Ireland). Unionism was not yet wholly seen in terms of party or sectarian ascendancy: this perspective would gain focus after fifty years of one-party rule by the Unionist bourgeoisie and residual gentry in Northern Ireland. But in the second half of the 19th century, it was still possible to interpret union in Burkean terms—that is, as a guarantee, rather than a negation, of individual freedom. Liberal Unionism was therefore a morally and politically less challenging option for (in particular) Protestant intellectuals and scholars than would subsequently be the case in the aftermath of the Stormont years.

The main Liberal Unionist organ in the North was the *Northern Whig*, and its editors demonstrated intellectual distinction, not just in their copy, but more widely: Thomas MacKnight (1866–1891), J.R. Fisher (1891–1913), and W.S. Armour, successive editors, all published substantial books on historical and political themes (though Armour was eventually lost to the union).[71] Irish Unionist proprietors and editors featured prominently elsewhere: Alfred and Harold Harmsworth (Lord Northcliffe and Lord Rothermere), the greatest journalistic forces of the age, owed something of their British nationalism and imperialism to family roots in Protestant Ireland (although they were also unsettled by the potentially catastrophic militancy of the Ulster Unionist campaign in 1912–1914).[72] Lesser figures still made significant contributions: The Dungannon-born W.F. Monypenny, Disraeli's biographer, was a respected journalist on *The Times*, and used its columns (and his position as the paper's Special Correspondent in Ireland) to promote a 'two nations' view of the political conflict in Ulster (his reports were later, posthumously, collected in a volume, *The Two Irish Nations*).[73]

The Unionist presence in other realms of literature was significant. Fiction, the novel, and unionism were intertwined in the 19th century in ways which were appreciated by contemporary Unionists, and sanctioned by them. As is well known, the conflict over union in 1800 was fought using a fusillade of pamphlets, which in turn relied upon 'an armoury of fictional methods and techniques'.[74] Equally, it has been observed that the novel was 'a genre adopted by Irish authors under the very shadow of the union'.[75] The work of Maria Edgeworth and Sydney Owenson, Lady Morgan, though often highly responsive towards its Irish Catholic subjects, and (in the case of Owenson) bleak in its assessment of the fall-out from union, can nevertheless (or, perhaps, consequently) be read within what Seamus Deane has famously referred to as 'the pathology of literary unionism': both authors have been seen as offering a form of complement to political or statutory unionism, in so far as their work was seen as a means of 'relating one cultural tradition to another'.[76] The literary critic, Mary Jean Corbett, has suggested that 'marriage-and-family plots by Edgeworth and Owenson...represent the narrative consequences of union as a matter of legitimating inequality in gendered terms'.[77] Certainly Edgeworth, who grew more conservative with age, was championed by the doyen of Scottish Toryism and literary unionism, Sir Walter Scott: as no less a literary critic than Stanley Baldwin observed, Scott 'regarded her as the interpreter of Ireland, and as one who by her writings had helped to make more easy the passage of Union'.[78] Owenson found supporters (and a husband) within the Abercorn household, a stronghold of Irish Toryism, and won plaudits from the very architects of union, Lord Castlereagh and William Pitt.[79]

Complementing the literature characterized by an implicit or subliminal unionism, was fiction produced by those who frankly embraced political unionism. Among the many careers of the Orange hero William Johnston was that of novelist: Johnston produced *Nightshade* in 1857, where a world peopled by Bible-burning Catholic priests, trimming Anglo-Catholics ('I don't think it is very honourable to be a papist, and call one's self a Protestant'), oleaginous tractarians ('Mr Tractate'), and covert and oppressive Jesuits was presented to its readers.[80] Like many other conservative unionists at this time, the Siege of Derry and the Battle of the Boyne were important cultural reference points; and indeed these supplied a central focus for Johnston's *Under which King?* (1873) (as well as for work by Charlotte Elizabeth Tonna, Cecil Frances Alexander, Lord Ernest Hamilton, and others).[81] The plays and novels of St John Ervine (though originally a cultural nationalist) increasingly reflected his concern to capture the speech patterns and cadences of his fellow Northerners, their personalities and environments; and a novel such as *Mrs Martin's Man* (1914) was part of a wider genre of 'Ulster' literature which effectively complemented the partitionist thrusts of formal Unionism.[82]

But Unionist politics also had a diverse scholarly grounding, particularly in Trinity College Dublin, which elected two (invariably Unionist) MPs, and Queen's University Belfast. Historians and classicists were particularly notable for their identification with unionism, both in terms of their scholarly work and their political profession. By the Edwardian era a large number of (in particular Trinity) historians advanced unionist claims and interpretations: Richard Bagwell, F.E. Ball, C.L. Falkiner, T.D. Ingram, W.E.H. Lecky, W.A. Phillips (Bagwell was active in the Irish Unionist Alliance, Ball was Irish Secretary of the Unionist Joint Committee in the 1890s, Falkiner was a Unionist parliamentary candidate, while Lecky sat as a Liberal Unionist MP for Trinity).[83] Other scholars with historical or antiquarian passions such as Edward Dowden (Yeats' bête noire and a distinguished historian of English literature), Sir Samuel Ferguson, or Standish O' Grady combined scholarship and unionism (Dowden, again, was a stalwart of the Irish Unionist Alliance). Some of the greatest scientists and medical doctors of the age professed the unionist faith: the Belfast-born William Thomson, Lord Kelvin, Professor of Natural Philosophy at Glasgow, was an active Liberal Unionist in the west of Scotland, while Sir William Whitla, author of the best-selling *Elements of Pharmacy* (1882) and *A Dictionary of Treatment* (1892), served as a Unionist member of the Irish Convention (1917–1918) and Unionist M.P. for Queen's University Belfast (1918–1923).

Classics and unionism tended to go hand-in-hand, though it certainly should not be supposed that there was any automatic complementarity:

R.M. Henry (Professor of Latin at Queen's University Belfast) and (later) E.R. Dodds (Regius Professor of Greek at Oxford) were both Northern Protestants, and were both convinced Irish separatists, while (turning to Scotland) two of the most distinguished Nationalists of the late 19th and 20th centuries were Professors of Greek, John Stuart Blackie and Douglas Young. Still, it was perhaps amongst the classicists that the greatest concentration of Irish unionist sympathy was to be found within the academy: John Bagnell Bury (the Monaghan-born Regius Professor of Greek at Trinity College Dublin, and of Modern History at Cambridge), Samuel Henry Butcher (the Kerry-born Professor of Greek at Edinburgh and afterwards Conservative MP for Cambridge University), Samuel Dill (Fellow of Corpus Christi, Oxford, and Professor of Greek at Queen's College Belfast, 'quietly unionist', and related by marriage to James Craig's Minister for Home Affairs, Dawson Bates), Richard Jebb (Professor of Greek at Glasgow and Cambridge, and Conservative MP for Cambridge University), and John Pentland Mahaffy (Provost of Trinity College Dublin). Bury's and Dill's abiding interest in late antiquity (the latter was the author of *Roman Society in the Last Century of the Western Empire* (1898) and *Roman Society in Gaul in the Merovingian Age* (1926)) was shared by other Irish Protestants, and perhaps reflected some subliminal sense that the experience of the Western Empire had—however tenuously—resonances with the decline of an embattled aristocratic, imperial, and 'pagan' culture in Ireland.[84] Each of these men, with the exception of Dill (who was a Northerner), were from southern Irish Unionist and minor gentry backgrounds.

## Unionists

The organized Unionism of the Home Rule era drew upon these various strains within popular and high culture, within Irish Conservativism and Whiggery, and inherited many of their characteristics. Unionism combined the support of much of the industrial and landed capital on the island, and subsumed a popular Protestantism, bound by Orangeism, loyalism, and evangelical conviction. In addition Unionism drew strength both from the consolidation and expansion of the British state, as well as from a tradition of Irish patriotism and anti-Catholicism. Unionism was simultaneously an expression of perceived Enlightenment, economic ascendancy, and sectarian defensiveness.

These, then, were some of the roots of the movement which flourished between 1885 and 1921, and which (in a truncated form) has survived within Northern Ireland since the establishment of partition in 1920: these were the roots of the movement which successfully thwarted Home Rule, and the ideal of a unified, autonomous Ireland. The party political origins of the movement help to explain this longevity; but many other aspects of the movement's early organization, development, and appeal are also relevant in any effort to illuminate its traction and success.

Paradoxically, given the strength of the Conservative inheritance, and the formerly close relationship between British and Irish parties, a semi-autonomous Irish Unionist organization was precipitated in the context of British Tory betrayal in 1884–1885. The occasion of the apparent treachery was the parliamentary reform (1884) and constituency redistribution (1885) of those years; and, as Sir Stafford Northcote remarked (with some insouciance), the British Conservative leadership had 'forgotten Ulster' in the negotiations to establish the details of the third reform measure.[85] But, if British Tories 'forgot Ulster', then Ulster loyalists did not readily forget Tory betrayal, particularly in the context of the developing electoral challenge from Parnellite Home Rule. By January 1885 a semi-independent Irish Unionist Parliamentary Party (or 'Ulster Party') had emerged at Westminster, to be followed by local organizational initiatives such as the Loyal Irish Union and the Irish Loyal and Patriotic Union (each formed in August 1885).

This autonomy had its immediate roots in the politics of reform, but (as has been observed) there was also a longer history of Irish Conservative distinctiveness. In part this reflected the condition of other national Conservative parties within the United Kingdom; and there were certainly some broad parallels between the development of Irish and Scottish Conservatism (with shared bursts of activity in the 1830s, late 1860s, and early 1880s, all in the context of reform). But one measure of the distinction between the two, and of the paradoxical condition of Irish unionist politics, was that, while Ireland and its union conditioned some of the fundamental contours of British politics between 1885 and 1920, Irish Unionism remained distinct and semi-detached—despite the exasperation of senior ministers on the issue.[86] Scotland certainly had its separate Conservative institutions; but those in Ireland and (eventually) in Ulster were more elaborate and independent, and were more often revisited and extended. For example, the challenge of Home Rule in 1886 and 1893 brought comprehensive Irish Unionist organizational activity, and the creation of (aside from the bodies already named) the Ulster Defence Union (1886), the Irish Unionist Alliance (1891), the Unionist Convention League (1892), and the Templetown Unionist Clubs movement (from 1893). The reality of internal, popular unionist, dissent, and the renewed threat of devolution and Home Rule, brought a root-and-branch and localist reorganization of Ulster Unionism in 1904–1905, in the shape of the Ulster Unionist Council. This in turn provided an essential platform for the highly distinctive and particularist Ulster Unionist reaction against the third Home Rule Bill, in 1912–1914.

The fundamental drift within Irish Unionist politics, unlike in Scotland, was towards a regional concentration and predominance. In Scotland it was possible to identify strongholds of (in particular) Conservative Unionism, such as in Glasgow and Lanarkshire, and in the Borders: and it is indeed arguable that, whether intellectually, imaginatively, or in terms of electoral strength, the Scottish Borders have been insufficiently recognized as a powerhouse of Unionism in the modern United Kingdom. But this is very different from saying that any one Scots region achieved an ascendancy within the national Unionist party in the way that was the case for Ulster and Ireland.

The explanations for this 'ulsterization' of Irish Unionism are manifold, and are well-established. Home Rule coincided with a major democratic thrust in British politics, with the achievement of the secret ballot (1872), the curtailment of corrupt electoral practices (1883), and the reform and redistribution measures of 1884–1885: politics retained a vestigial aristocratic presence and exclusivity, but they were more than ever about popular mobilization. In Ireland, given the sectarian and political demographics, popular Unionist mobilization could only be achieved in the North.

Moreover, while there were some urban concentrations, the fatal strength of southern Unionism lay in its disproportionate command over the landed classes. A formal, urban unionism certainly survived in Dublin City, where a thin network of Anglican parishes and Orange lodges upheld the faith: work on working-class and lower middle-class Dublin Protestantism in the era of Home Rule and the revolution unveils a still largely forgotten world of railwaymen, brewery workers, and low-grade clerks and civil servants— the world from which Sean O'Casey (railwayman and then lowly employee of Eason's & Co) and his brother (a British soldier) were sprung.[87] In the prosperous Protestant townships of South County Dublin a more deeply entrenched Unionism thrived into the era of the Revolution, as the records of Kingstown Unionist Club, and the election of successive Unionist MPs for South County Dublin demonstrate. Other pockets of Unionism and Protestantism existed in the suburbs as well as the more exclusive parts of central Dublin (Pembroke, Rathmines, St Stephen's Green). But, in general, this was a financially and socially vulnerable Unionism—a Unionism precariously dependent upon the patronage of a handful of Protestant business magnates (such as Edward Cecil Guinness, Lord Iveagh, or Andrew Jameson, or the Dockrells). Also critical to its survival were Nationalist tolerance and the protection of the British state in Ireland. With the gradual exhaustion of the former, and the collapse of the latter, Dublin Unionism speedily dissolved, giving rise to Nationalist expectations that the 'false consciousness' of Northern Unionists would be similarly transitory.

In fact the strength of the South, even in the heyday of union, rested with the landed classes and their financial and political influence over the island as a whole. They were not only wealthy, but also comparatively well-organized: they had their own, powerful lobbying organization, the Irish Landowners' Convention, dominated by old Ascendancy magnates such as the Beresfords, marquesses of Waterford.[88] The wealth of great landed clans fed into the representative organizations of southern Unionism (the Irish Loyal and Patriotic Union, the Irish Unionist Alliance), and from thence (in the 1880s and 1890s) into Ulster Unionist election campaigns.[89] Southern landlords were disproportionately well represented in the House of Lords and indeed in the House of Commons.[90] But these landed foundations for the southern Unionist edifice were almost as precarious as those supporting urban unionism in the South. Land was, relatively, a declining asset in the late 19th century, and nowhere in Europe at this time was the decline more precipitate than in Ireland, where the moral and legal title of the existing landlord class was subjected to a ferocious assault by the farming interest. Successive land legislation defined the tenants' legal title—their right to 'free sale', 'fair rent', and 'freedom from eviction'—and ultimately created the financial mechanisms by which they could buy their holdings outright. Land purchase, as it was called, was the principle underlying legislation in 1885, 1887, and—most famously—in 1903, when the Chief Secretary, George Wyndham, created the most expensive and successful of the purchase measures. The incremental effect of this legislation was to consolidate farmers' legal rights at the expense of their landlords, to curtail landlord freedom to arbitrarily fix rent levels, and in the end to encourage landlords to sell up. Complementing this economic retreat was a political and physical retreat. Selling landlords retired, both physically and imaginatively, behind the walls of their demesnes, or to Dublin or England. The Irish landed presence in the House of Commons retreated, to be replaced by a bourgeois, professional and commercial, caste, more completely rooted in the North of Ireland. This process touched Scotland, where the Irish purchase (and Congested Districts) legislation provided a template for measures affecting parts of the western Highlands and Islands; but its economic, geographical, and social impact was comparatively slight.

Ulsterization was also related to the fissiparous condition of southern Unionism. Southern Unionism numbered at most perhaps 250,000 adherents in the Home Rule era; but this relatively small community contained all conditions and classes. The remnants of the evangelical and Orange working class and artisan Conservatism, which had been championed by the likes of Tresham Gregg, existed alongside the metropolitan sophisticates of Trinity College and the law courts. There was evidence of a small-scale and propertied Catholic unionism.[91] There were early symptoms of a politically suicidal bloody-mindedness, as in 1891, when Cork Unionists ran a parliamentary candidate against the urgent advice of Arthur Balfour in Dublin Castle ('as regards the Cork election, I am in despair at the stupidity of our people'; 'the loyalists are, in my opinion, making perfect idiots of themselves over the Cork election, and I am as nearly as possible in despair')— or in 1900 when the self-regarding Sir Horace Plunkett and the hungrily ambitious James Campbell were each defeated for Dublin constituencies through the abstention of dissident Unionists from the poll.[92] These divisions multiplied with the pressures of radical separatism, so that the main representative body of southern Unionism, the Irish Unionist Alliance, split in 1919, with the schismatics led by the Earl of Midleton into a new organization, the Anti-Partition League. Midleton, like Plunkett (and indeed many others within the culture of an embattled Unionism) was blessed with an unshakeable confidence in his own political intelligence; and he subsequently broke with the dissidents whom he had originally led. In this way, southern Unionism, already socially and financially reduced through the retreat of landlordism, lost whatever residual punch it might have delivered during the crucial early years of the independent Irish state.

All of this cast into sharper relief the distinctiveness and influence of Ulster Unionism. As the most gifted southern Protestant writers sought to express their political and cultural aspirations within the Irish literary revival, and indeed sometimes within advanced separatism, so many Northern Protestant writers and historians (building upon the regional economic success story) elaborated a literature and a history with particular Ulster thrusts and resonance. One strain within this apologetic literature (evident, for example, in the work of Lord Ernest Hamilton) presented a racialized analysis of the plantation tradition, linked by ethnicity to Britain: this chimed with contemporary Anglo-Saxonist readings of English history, as well as a 'Teutonized' Scottish historiography which emphasised the shared racial heritage of the lowlands with England.[93] As southern landlordism and Unionism retreated, so Belfast business and Ulster Unionism blossomed: the social and political regression of southern landlordism gained pace in the Edwardian period, at precisely the moment when Belfast business and its unionist captains reached their apogee—when the Harland and Wolff yards and the associated White Star Shipping Line achieved an ascendancy within their respective spheres: the launch and fate of the Titanic in 1911–1912, emblematic of a universal hubris, can also be held to represent the high-water mark of the vaulting ambition and self-confidence of the Belfast Unionist bourgeoisie (the designer of the vessel, Thomas Andrews, was the son of a wealthy Unionist mill-owner, and the brother of John Andrews, Unionist Prime Minister of Northern Ireland (1940–1943), and was himself 'a firm Unionist, being convinced that Home Rule would spell financial ruin to Ireland').[94]

Complementing these cultural and economic developments in the North, was the elaboration of a separate party structure. As has been mentioned, Ulster Unionism was thoroughly reorganized in 1904–1905, with the creation of the Ulster Unionist Council and (as in contemporary Scotland) the revitalization of local electoral machinery. By 1910–1911 this local organizational machine, allied with a more middle-class leadership, was pushing Ulster Unionism not only towards a more particularist strategy, but also towards greater militancy. These thrusts were also encouraged by the condition of British politics, where a combination of Liberal electoral ascendancy and the cerebral but bloodless leadership supplied by Arthur Balfour to the Conservatives, meant that Ulster Unionists appeared to be increasingly dependent upon their own local political resources. This was confirmed by the passage of the Liberal's Parliament Act in 1911, when one of the key obstacles to Home Rule—the House of Lords' veto—was converted into a mere suspensory power. Already by 1910 Unionists were importing small quantities of weapons into Ulster and adopting military formations: after 1911 this militarization accelerated towards civil conflagration.

The military capacity of Ulster Unionism delayed and subverted Home Rule, and (whatever the deep moral challenges) clearly may be regarded as a source of short-term advantage which had no parallel in Scotland (or, rather, since the Ulster militants had a presence in Glasgow, only the weakest of parallels).[95] The outlines of Ulster Unionist militancy in 1912–1914 are familiar enough, though the central interpretative problems posed by this militancy still remain contentious: were the Unionists serious in their apparent determination to go to war, and (in counterfactual terms) could they have been successful in resisting the might of a British state intent on enforcing Home Rule? The creation of the Ulster Volunteer Force during the winter of 1912–1913 certainly created a strong military capacity, for (at its peak, in 1914) perhaps 90,000 to 100,000 oath-bound Ulster Unionists were recruited within its ranks. The UVF was heavily influenced by the British army, both in terms of its regimental structure and its use of ex-servicemen: it was also equipped with a nursing corps, motorcyclists, telegraphists, and other advanced forms of communication, and a special forces unit. It had organized support outside Ulster, in various areas of Irish Protestant settlement in Britain, including Glasgow, where (as noted) there is evidence of a UVF unit in operation. Also, Leith, the port of Edinburgh, was used as one of the key entrepôts through which weapons were brought into Britain for the use of the Volunteers. There were several importations of weapons, undertaken with the knowledge and cooperation of leading Conservative politicians, and culminating in the Larne gunrunning of 24–25 April 1914, when perhaps 25,000 rifles were landed: this was achieved, with the foreknowledge of the Conservative front bencher and leadership candidate, Walter Long, and almost certainly with that of the leader himself, the Scotsman Andrew Bonar Law.[96] The UVF also appears to have had good sources of intelligence emanating (on occasion) from sources close to the Asquith government itself.

The strength of Ulster Unionist militancy lay, not only in its support within the Conservative elite, and in areas of traditional sympathy (such as the West of Scotland), but also more generally within popular British Conservatism. British organizations such as the Union Defence League, founded by Walter Long in 1907, or the British League for the Support of Ulster, founded by Lord Willoughby de Broke, a redoubtable 'ditcher' peer, in March 1913, focused money and support for the Ulster militants: Long's

UDL seems to have been the key conduit through which money for the gunrunners was channelled. The British League was the means by which the British Covenant of support for Ulster was organized, in March 1913: this document, based upon the Ulster Solemn League and Covenant of September 1912, was launched by an array of British luminaries, including Scots such as Lord Balfour of Burleigh, the economist William Cunningham, Lord Lovat, and John Stirling-Maxwell. Dan Jackson's work on the Unionist campaign tours of 1912–1914, from Liverpool (September 1912), Gateshead, Glasgow, Inverness, to Hyde Park, has dissected the elaborate rhetoric and organization of these events, with their skilful use of large public buildings, arc-light technology, scarcely concealed sectarian appeals, and manipulation of the press.[97] The most famous of these meetings was of course that held at Blenheim on 27 July 1912, when Bonar Law endorsed the most extreme forms of Ulster Unionist resistance.

This threatened resistance was also expressed within, and bolstered by, popular and high culture. British supporters were useful in this respect, with (in particular) the laureate of empire, Kipling, versifying on behalf of his Ulster Unionist allies: his 'Ulster 1912' carried a superscription from the book of Isaiah, and concluded with the ominous line—'If England drives us forth, We shall not fall alone'. Sir Edward Elgar, whose music was inflected with some of the prevailing anxiety of the late Edwardian climacteric, was one of the lead signatories of the British Covenant (and, as one of several prominent Catholic supporters—along with the likes of the 14th Lord Lovat, the 15th Duke of Norfolk, Lord Edmund Talbot—particularly useful to those worried by the sectarian overtones of Ulster Unionism). Another pillar of the Edwardian musical establishment in Britain, the Dublin-born Sir Charles Villiers Stanford, wrote Unionist letters to *The Times*, signed the Covenant, questioned hapless candidates for the Royal College of Music about their stand on 'Home Rule' ('and what d'ye think of Home Rule, me bhoy?'), and banned productions of his opera, 'Shamus O'Brien', during the crisis for fear that its romantic Irishness would inadvertently give succour to the enemy's cause.[98]

Stanford's breezy interrogations illustrate the ways in which unionist fury percolated into every corner of the British cultural establishment. Indeed the experience of C.S. Lewis further illustrates that the third Home Rule crisis influenced the outlook even of an emergent elite: as a Belfast schoolboy Lewis was already writing essays on the threat of Home Rule. In fact there is little real surprise in this, given the extent to which Home Rule and militant Unionism were all-encompassing themes in Irish and British society. In Ireland the seriousness of Unionist conviction was reflected in the hero cult surrounding the leader, Edward Carson, and in the ways in which Unionist popular opinion was mobilized in support of the militants' strategies. As in Britain, so in Ireland mass demonstrations focused and intensified militant feeling (the most famous of these being the mass meetings which launched the Ulster Solemn League and Covenant on 28 September 1912). Those (just under half a million men and women) who signed the Covenant were presented with a parchment copy of the document, which in many instances was framed and displayed: just under half of the 237,000 men who signed the Covenant joined the Ulster Volunteer Force, and were given a lapel badge and armband, and subsequently more elaborate adornment and uniform. Carson, too, was energetically marketed: his lantern-jawed image adorned china ware (produced by the Paragon Company), and Staffordshire crockery. He featured in high culture—in the work of the artists of *Vanity Fair*, or in the (somewhat less friendly) caricatures of Max Beerbohm.[99] He was represented on badges and buttons, fund-raising stamps, and (in epic numbers) on postcards. He was endlessly photographed, and filmed by pressmen.[100]

Militant Unionism, its leadership, and symbolism were therefore pervasive (see for example illustration E.2). It is clear that this all-embracing propaganda was a critical element of the militants' campaign, and that leaders like Carson knew the importance of a persuasive ferocity. It is also clear that Carson and some others within the leadership (like the sixth Marquess of Londonderry) talked the talk of insurgency, but held back from action, and counselled caution. The Ulster Volunteer Force has generally been seen as a brake upon militancy, in so far as it channelled the furies of Unionism within a disciplined and hierarchical environment. On the other hand, the gamble implicit in the Ulster Unionist strategy was that Asquith and the Liberal government would acquiesce before the pent-up aggression of the Volunteers spewed into sectarian or other forms of outrage; and by the summer of 1914 the odds on this gamble appeared to be narrowing perilously as Asquith obfuscated and played for time. Damned for indecision, it is just possible that there was strategic method in the apparent madness of Asquith's procrastination.[101]

The achievement of Unionists in 1912–1914 was not so much that they created an alternative state; it was rather that they succeeded in commodifying their political case, so that (by the summer of 1914) the images and messages of their militancy were virtually inescapable throughout British and Irish society. However, one measure of Asquith's success was that, despite this cultural spread, indeed hegemony, the Unionists did not wholly succeed in thwarting the passage of Home Rule onto the statute books of the British parliament: this was achieved in September 1914. Nor did these militants create the partition issue, since this had been privately mooted within British high politics from the moment that Home Rule was accepted by part of the British political elite. All that had been achieved, by the summer of 1914, was that Asquith's Liberal government, in company with reluctant Irish Nationalists, had accepted that some form of exclusion from Home Rule might be granted to some of the counties of the North. It would take the real militancy and bloodshed of the Western Front, as opposed to the virtual wars of the Ulster countryside, to translate this acceptance into something approaching practical politics.

With both Scotland and Ireland, the First World War acted to re-enforce national identities, though in the Scots case national sentiment remained largely curtailed within the frameworks of union and of cultural politics. In Ireland, the experience of war appears to have radicalized and trained a generation of separatist who subsequently served with the IRA in the War of Independence and Civil War. In the North of Ireland, mass participation in the Great War coincided with, and advanced, a stronger Unionist sense of Ulster's distinctiveness. This was partly the point of the mythology surrounding the actions of the main Unionist fighting force on the Western Front, the 36th Ulster Division: on 1 July 1916, at the start of the epically bloody Somme offensive, (following the official narrative by Cyril Falls) the Division successfully stormed the German Front Line, where (with over 5000 casualties sustained) they were stranded in a maelstrom of killing owing to the failure of other British units and of the high command.[102] In essence, the Somme offensive served as a metaphor for the wider Ulster Unionist condition and self-perception: in this particular reading the Ulstermen had done their duty, but in the end had fought and died on their own. Moreover, the (in fact far from complete) overlap between the Ulster Division and the Ulster Volunteer Force meant that the Division's purpose and actions were equated with those of the pre-war Unionist militants. The badges, uniforms, gallantry certificates, and (after the war) commemorative histories all emphasised the 'Ulsterness' of the Division, which (however inexactly) was equated with its Unionism. The Division's memorial at Thiepval reiterated this point: this was a copy of Helen's Tower, the gothic folly which overlooked the UVF's training ground at Clandeboye, the County Down estate of the leading Liberal Unionist, Lord Dufferin, and it was inaugurated by Sir Henry Wilson, former Chief of the Imperial General Staff and Ulster Unionist MP for North Down. The narrative of the war was therefore woven into the wider history of Ulster Unionist struggle and political identity; and these were phenomena which were taking on an increasingly particularist hue.

The idea of separating out the counties of the North with the greatest concentrations of Protestant and Unionist population had been publicly mooted from June 1912, and by 1914 the principle of exclusion had begun to achieve a form of consensus, although deep disagreements remained over the physical and temporal extent of any practical scheme. In March 1914 it was fleetingly proposed that the six north-eastern counties of Ulster should be excluded temporarily but en bloc; and this idea was resurrected in the aftermath of the Easter Rising, in May 1916, when it briefly (but deceivingly) appeared to have won the agreement of both Unionists and Nationalists. However, the notion of six-county partition reappeared in 1919–1920, when it was given a federalist inflection; and it was thus a two-parliament, two-polity Ireland which emerged in the legislative cladding supplied by the Government of Ireland Act. The celebrants of 'Ulster' had won a form of homeland, even if the newly minted 'Northern Ireland' (the name had been mooted at least as early as July 1916) did not do justice to the intensity of their historical and political vision. Moreover, 'Ulster' came at a cost: over half a million dissatisfied and vulnerable Nationalists were trapped within the new Unionist polity, while Ulster Unionism had effectively cast off one third of its provincial identity (three Ulster counties were excluded from 'Northern Ireland'), as well as the whole of 'southern' Unionism.

The impact of this new polity on Irish Unionism is (naturally enough) frequently underplayed, given the history of alienation and injustice experienced by Northern Nationalists. The strength of Edwardian Unionism had rested in its standing as an opposition creed, backed by landed and industrial capital, and boasting a formidable geographical, cultural, and intellectual diversity. In their apparent moment of victory, Unionists in fact demonstrated the extent to which they had dissipated these former assets. Unionism was now reduced to a north-eastern, and pre-eminently bourgeois, core, with the complex cultures of southern landed unionism now dismissed and isolated. Equally, the bastion of Trinity College, with its heritage of an academic and literary unionism, was largely set aside, even though its law-yers (most obviously Carson himself) had hitherto been a mainstay of the Ulster Unionist leadership. The plantation creed—the celebration of the achievement and travails of the Ulster colonists—now became the wholly inadequate governing theme—or, rather, colonial nationalist ideology—of Northern Ireland, rather than merely a balancing counterpoint to the motifs of Catholic Gaeldom and Irish Irelandism. In sum, just as it was once alleged of the Scottish National Party in office at Holyrood that they 'don't believe they're a government. They are a campaign', so Unionists had difficulty making the same leap in faith and belief in 1921.[103]

A more unified and homogeneous Unionism looked out from its six-county bawn; but it was intellectually and culturally diminished. And the movement's very homogeneity—its more complete identification with the economic interests of the northern industrial and commercial elite—rendered it more vulnerable than ever.


## 'Northern' Irish


How, and with what success, did Ulster Unionism contribute to the survival of the union after 1920? The most important aspect of this challenge involves revisiting Unionism's comprehensive failure regarding the Catholic and Nationalist population of Northern Ireland. In Scotland, the Labour Party came to function as a conduit through which Catholics of Irish descent, par-ticularly in the West, were tacitly recruited to the politics of the Union (although it should also be underlined that Labour retained a nominal commitment to Scottish Home Rule in the 1920s and after, and that there now appears to be a comparatively high level of support amongst Catholics for devolution and even independence).[104] Scottish Conservatism and Unionism retained con-nections with the Orange Order, but also embraced a tame Jacobitism and patriotism which were evidently accessible to some Scots Catholics. The Ulster Unionist government of Northern Ireland exercised none of this appeal, and (while it would be wrong to make assumptions about the negotiability of identity) it never really sought so to do. It defined itself (despite the size and influence of the Northern Catholic minority) as the Protestant complement to what it saw as the Catholic and Gaelic Irish state, centred on Dublin; and (as a later Ulster Unionist leader, David Trimble, would famously concede), 'Ulster Unionists...built a solid house, but it was a cold house for Catholics'.[105]

Both Ulster Unionism and Irish Nationalism were in fact partly ethnic mobilizations, originally based upon (at the very least) radically different readings of Irishness, and different cultural and religious emphases: there is also an inconclusive argument for seeing Ulster Unionism as unequivocally an expression of British nationality.[106] The two Irish polities created in 1921–1922, the Irish Free State and Northern Ireland, were born out of civil war; and, particularly in the Northern case, the civil war had strong ethnic overtones, given that (certainly after 1922) the crown forces were primarily Protestant and Unionist, and the republican insurgents primarily Catholic. The association of Protestantism and Unionism with the new Northern state was therefore inescapable; and this was reinforced both by the ongoing institutional connection between Unionism and the exclusively Protestant Orange Order and by the elaboration of an 'Ulster' political identity in the 1920s and 1930s, accessible only to Protestants and partitionists.[107] Ulster Unionists saw a disjunction between Catholic and state interests (again, in Trimble's assessment, 'although they [Northern Nationalists] had a roof over their heads, they seemed to us as if they meant to burn the house down'). But these political perceptions were formed, and thrived, in a state where Catholics (and, broadly, Nationalists) were one third of the population, and growing in strength. While there were isolated and desultory earlier efforts (by, for example, Sir Clarence Graham), it was only really under David Trimble's leadership (1995–2005) that a coherent attempt was made to open Unionism to Catholic sympathizers. In Scotland, by contrast, patriotic identity, as well as the nation's party structures were not (despite some threats and challenges and setbacks) ethnically or religiously exclusive.

One expression of this ethnic mobilization rests with the abiding concern within the Ulster Unionist party for solidarity, and its relative success in this respect until the early 1970s. The precarious nature of the Unionist majority in many areas of Northern Ireland, combined with a critical heritage of division in the Edwardian era over denominational, class, and land questions, meant that successive Unionist leaders were willing to sacrifice any ecumenical gesture to the exigencies of political unity. The movement's leaders did not make any serious effort to accommodate Catholic opinion (at least until the late 1960s, when popular Catholic mobilization was in full spate): but they did, however, continually fret about striking a balance between maintaining civilized relations with Westminster and responding to the fissiparous and sometimes angrily defensive nature of their political base (navigating 'the constraints that the Unionist regime increasingly operated under as a devolved regime within the UK, and the more ethnically autistic expectations of many of its supporters').[108] These expectations focused on a wide range of issues, including (as has been mentioned) employment and housing, and also the educational and health reforms of the Attlee government; but from the 1940s onwards one key emphasis was upon the right to parade through areas where the local nationalist population had become, or always had been, hostile to perceived Orange triumphalism.[109] It is true that when (after 1968) massive civil unrest forced Westminster to attend to the problems of Northern Ireland, the Ulster Unionist party was speedily compelled to strike a new balance between local and metropolitan pressures, and to resist 'ethnic autism': in 1970—71 this brought the fracturing of the Party, and the creation of Ian Paisley's Democratic Unionists. It is also the case that David Trimble's defence of the Belfast Agreement between 1998 and 2005 risked sacrificing local concerns and unity for wider gains and principles. But both these episodes involved rapid and disorienting responses to largely external challenges by leaders (Faulkner, Trimble) who were anchored in the populist traditions of their party: both were exceptions which illustrated the abiding preoccupation with unity in the movement.

It was not just that the Unionists were culpably introspective, however: political violence for long negated the likelihood of political accommodation. The IRA's bloody effort to overturn the Northern Irish state in 1921–1922 was complemented by violence pursued by the crown forces and loyalist terror gangs against Northern Catholics. The apparently unflagging tradition of republican insurgency (represented by campaigns conducted during the Second World War and between 1956 and 1962) also tended to heighten Ulster Unionist defensiveness and reaction. The bloody complexities of this violence were also distilled into particular episodes, or martyr cults, or (indeed, in some cases) mythologies. Anti-Catholic violence in the early 1920s was grimly epitomized by the murder of the McMahon Family in March 1922, apparently by the crown forces; anti-Protestant or Unionist violence in the same era was symbolized by the murders at Altnaveigh, County Down, in June 1922, orchestrated apparently at the hands of the leading republican and future Irish minister, Frank Aiken.[110] Nationalists accused Unionists of engaging in pogroms; Unionists accused Nationalists of (in effect) ethnic cleansing. Nationalists sought to identify Unionism with fascism; Unionists recoiled from what they saw as republicanism's entanglement with National Socialism. In Scotland, however, while a significant contribution was made to the 1916 Rising (by Edinburgh's James Connolly) and the revolution (by, for example, a Scottish brigade of the IRA, and Margaret Skinnider from Coatbridge) Irish republican activism went into steep decline after the mid 1920s, and political violence generally did not intrude into the processes of assimilation (though the IRA's 'S-Plan'—their campaign strategy of 1939—was partly devised by Seamus O'Donovan, a Scot of Irish extraction, and an alumnus of the prestigious Catholic school, St Aloysius's Academy in Glasgow).[111] In the absence of sustained violence, there could be no martyrs, no memories, and no myths.

Northern Ireland's depressed industrial economy also tended to precipitate and heighten sectarian competition. This rendered the Unionist state politically vulnerable, both in terms of its relationship with Britain (which held the purse strings, certainly in the interwar years) as well as in terms of social unrest (evident in particular in the context of the depression of the early 1930s). The slow failure of key Northern industries such as textiles and shipbuilding, the absence of those 'new' and compensating industries which restored economic life to the midlands and south of England, had a variety of critical political dimensions. First, these failures represented the retreat of those local capitalists who had created Belfast industry (and Belfast Unionism) in the mid and late 19th century: shipbuilding and linen manufacturing dynasties originally critical to both commerce and Unionism were now superseded (just as the great Unionist landowning clans had been partly overturned by falling land values, land agitation, and legislation in early 20th century). But the failure of the traditional industries put increasing pressure on public employment, particularly within the area of local government, as well as on the dispensation of various forms of welfare entitlement, including public housing. Unionism's control of the state, allied with its relative political insecurity through much of Northern Ireland, led to electoral abuse and religious or political discrimination in the fields of employment and housing; and indeed there is some evidence to suggest that these abuses became worse, or at any rate more pressing, in the post-war era (just as the growth of the British state in late 19th-century Ireland brought sectarian resentments and rivalries into sharper relief). Thus the parlous condition of the Northern economy for much of the fifty-year history of the devolved parliament (1921–1971) meant that Ulster Unionism functioned effectively as a patronage machine for the needs of its supporters. In Scotland, however, the shared experience of industrial failure fed (at least in terms of overt expression), not into the politics of faith, but rather into the politics of class: Labour has served to mediate both Catholic and Protestant working-class interests, and to address particular denominational concerns (most famously in 1918 with the agreed public funding of Catholic schooling). This is clearly not to deny that Scotland in the 20th century has had histories of sectarian competition and discrimination (there is a weighty literature on these themes, particularly in relation to their footballing manifestations): it is to suggest, however, that this history has not fully coincided with the nation's party political structures, as was the case in Northern Ireland.[112] If, as in Northern Ireland, Scottish parties, at local government and above, have served the troughs of patronage to their supporters, then the key (and valuable) distinction has been that the questing snouts have not emanated exclusively from Protestant sties.

The continuing ethnic imperatives of Ulster Unionism owed much to the cultural significance of the 'frontier' within the mentality and structure of the movement. As has been indicated, frontiers also mattered with Scottish Unionism, both in terms of the complex sectarian borderlands within Glasgow and Lanarkshire, and (in particular) the territorial border (of sorts) between Scotland and England: Orange Conservatism was important in late 19th-century urban Conservatism, while a romantic Scots patriotism was cultivated amongst border Tories and Conservatives, from Walter Scott, through to Frederick Scott Oliver and Walter Elliot. The 'frontier', in southern Ulster, between predominantly Protestant and predominantly Catholic Ireland, had produced networks of embattled landlords as well as popular sectarian bonding which had, in turn, fed significantly into organized Unionism in the mid 1880s. The vulnerability of border unionists after 1921 emerges in recent scholarship more thoroughly than ever as a key determinant of the direction of wider Unionist strategy.[113] Their position, for example, was a vital consideration in the Unionist party's failure to reform the local government franchise after the Second World War, and to bring it into line with both the parliamentary franchise and British local government practice (as established in 1948). Extending the local government vote beyond the community of ratepayers would have weakened Unionism's already tenuous hold on local government authorities west of the Bann, and transferred control over to Nationalists. The price of appeasing border Unionists' fears and defensiveness was high: Nationalists were effectively robbed of votes and local government control (and patronage) in the west of Ulster, while in the east 'tens of thousands of working-class Protestants, including many members of the Unionist party' were also disenfranchised.

Moreover, as Patterson and Kaufmann argue, 'this core concern of border Unionism ensured that the one issue that might have forestalled the civil rights movement, and the subsequent crisis of the Unionist state, was not addressed until it was too late'.[114] Paradoxically, however, the relatively great pressures experienced by border Unionists during the 'Long War' appear to have rendered them disproportionately more enthusiastic for the Belfast Agreement: so border Unionists underwent a rapid political transition similar to that experienced by southern Unionists in the years before independence and partition, graduating swiftly from fundamentalism and exclusivism towards a panicked consensuality.

This heightened Unionist sensitivity to local pressures reflected the large, and perhaps too large, degree of autonomy which the movement possessed from any wider responsibility or higher authority. Labour and Conservatism in Scotland, while possessing strong local identities, were also direct offshoots of the main parties of the British state; and, as such, they were subject to a range of opportunities as well as disciplines which the indigenous parties within the devolved politics of Northern Ireland, in particular Unionism, did not experience. As earlier chapters have made clear, the two Scottish parties contributed extensively to their respective front benches, with Scottish Labour in particular exercising a significant influence over the fortunes of the British party, and over the government of Scotland, throughout the 20th century. Whether the nature of this influence was beneficial in the long-term is debatable, and there is a case to be made (and indeed has been made) for the embedding of a Scots culture of dependence on the welfare of the United Kingdom state.[115] But the controversial effects of Scots influence are to be distinguished from the incontestable nature and reality of that influence. With Ulster Unionism, however, while the party had a clear institutional relationship with Conservatism until 1974 (and a vestigial relationship until 1985), its Ulster-focused politics meant that it played little serious role within front-bench politics at Westminster (the only Ulster Unionists to attain cabinet rank between 1920 and 1972 were Ronald McNeill, representing a Kent constituency, and a peer, the seventh Marquess of Londonderry). Indeed, the party was largely left unattended by successive British governments until the rise of the movement for Catholic civil rights in the mid 1960s and after, when its controversial record in office forced itself onto the agenda of Westminster.

Ulster Unionism had begun a process of reorienting its political focus away from Westminster and into the North of Ireland long before the formal establishment of partition and a devolved government and parliament in 1920–1921; and the corollary of this was a relative decline in the significance of the 'Imperial Parliament' within the culture of the party and movement.[116] Twelve (later eighteen) representatives from Northern Ireland, mostly Unionist, sat in each parliament throughout the 20th century: the Ulster Unionists continued the tradition, begun in 1885, of meeting as a separate grouping, with sessional officers (a chairman and secretary) and relevant agenda.[117] For a time after the establishment of the devolved parliament in 1921, the quality of this Unionist representation remained reasonably high, with able and articulate lawyers such as Sir Malcolm Macnaghten (later a High Court judge) maintaining good links with the Conservative front bench. But this situation subsequently weakened, and by the 1940s and 1950s (despite ongoing efforts at reform) the overall quality of the 'Ulster Party' at Westminster was low, and the relationship between it and the devolved parliament often unclear or inefficiently managed: successive generations of Ulster Unionist rediscovered the need for 'liaison' between Westminster and Stormont, sketched action plans, encountered personal or structural impediments, and gave up. There were also periodic complaints, stemming originally in the Edwardian period, of the detached nature of Irish and Ulster Unionist parliamentary representation, though in fact this accusation was also levied at Scottish Unionist members.[118]

In general, too, the Ulster grouping at Westminster (despite the acquisition of a formal constitution and ongoing sessional meetings) did not present any coherent or systematic case to their parliamentary colleagues (in February 1949 the leading Scottish Unionist MP, Sir Thomas Moore, thought 'the Ulster MPs had no influence at Westminster').[119] There seems to have been little systematic cooperation with other parliamentary groupings (such as the Scottish Unionists), with whom they might have been expected to have had an affinity: an SUMC minute of 17 May 1949 which documents the Ulster Unionists discreetly networking with a prominent Scottish colleague, Walter Elliot, is the exception which demonstrates the wider rule of poor communications ('Mr Elliot told the Committee that he had been informed from Northern Irish sources that the absence of a speech from a Scottish Unionist member had been noted. If possible it was desirable that a Member should speak on the Ulster pledge during the [Ireland Bill] Third Reading debate').[120] Walter Elliot, active and prominent, and drawing upon his wide ministerial contacts, appears to have had unusually close relations with Ulster Unionists. But, to judge by the period between

1932 and 1967, when there is good evidence on the Scottish side, Ulster and Scottish Unionists at Westminster only formally met once, on 25 July 1950, when Sir Hugh O'Neill (Antrim) and Sir Ronald Ross (Londonderry) explained the constitution of Northern Ireland to the Scots (arguing that while 'the Ulster model had worked well and to Ulster's advantage', its application to Scotland would be more problematic on account of 'the tendency towards further separation' and the threat posed by the 'socialist element in Glasgow').[121]

The records of the Ulster Party at Westminster appear to have been destroyed in a bomb explosion; but the extensive related and surviving evidence within various MPs' and official papers strongly suggests that there was little to destroy. By way of contrast, the Scottish Unionist Members' Committee, formed in 1932, met virtually every week when the Commons was in session, and regularly attracted around twenty MPs as well as the presence of cabinet ministers: the extensive records of the Committee indicate a highly serious and regulated approach to the demands of Westminster. But, then, Westminster was the apex of Scottish Unionist ambition, where it was merely a sideshow for Ulster Unionists (save those few with English social and economic ambitions); and indeed there is every indication (in terms of the overall distribution of Scottish political talent) that Westminster remains the lodestar for the Scottish unionist parties, while Holyrood (for the moment, at any rate) holds attractions primarily for first class Scottish Nationalists.

Linked with the problems of Unionist representation at Westminster was the wider paradox that one of Ulster Unionism's key problems arose from the devolved parliament, the institution which apparently defined its success. Created in 1921, the Northern Ireland parliament and government became the central institutions of Ulster Unionist power within the partition state, responsible for administering the limited authority which Westminster had ceded through the Government of Ireland Act. Stormont became an emblem of despair for Northern Nationalists; it also proved, at best, a very mixed blessing even for those who were supposed to be the beneficiaries. Unionists, representing a community of less than one million people, were obliged, alongside their Northern Nationalist compatriots, to thinly distribute their available political talent from the lowest reaches of local government—the local and district councils—through the two chambers of the local parliament, at Stormont, to the houses of parliament at Westminster. In practice, the available talent (such as it was) tended to coalesce within Stormont, where ministerial office and other perquisites were not only relatively accessible (for Unionists), but also relatively well-rewarded (in 1936 Nicholas Mansergh calculated that twenty-seven per cent of Stormont MPs received official salaries, compared with eight per cent of their Westminster counterparts): moreover, a Stormont cabinet minister cut a more imposing because more meaningful figure within Northern Ireland (the only arena that mattered for much of Unionist political culture) than a minister from London.[122] The relatively small base of the Party, and its cliquish and nepotistic operations, may have had a reflection in the relatively poor calibre of leadership (for example, the Scottish judge, Lord Stott, a Labour sympathizer, deemed Terence O'Neill 'to be a pathetic figure, like a drunk man who had reached the melancholy stage').[123]

In practice, too, Stormont did not function as a multiparty democratic forum, but rather as a one-party political assembly, elected after 1929 on a winner-takes-all basis (Marc Mulholland has made the point that Unionist control of the parliament was so strong that gerrymandering or other malpractice was superfluous); so the parliament not only stretched and diverted Unionist political resources, it also institutionalized the relative powerlessness of Nationalists, and enflamed a sense of political suppression which exploded in the mid 1960s through movements such as the Campaign for Social Justice and the Northern Ireland Civil Rights' Association.[124] Stormont effectively liberated Westminster from the compromises, diversions, and entanglements of Ulster politics; while it also purged the 'Imperial Parliament' of a strong and effective Unionist presence. For much of the half century of its existence, Stormont served the short-term and local purposes of a Unionist elite; but the price of this parliamentary gravy train was the derailing of the union (and often Unionists) from British politics.

There have been other structural anomalies or difficulties within Ulster Unionism. After the Second World War the number of party members was relatively constricted: as with the Orange Order, so with the Unionist Party, scholars are now arguing that the numbers of members were generally much slighter than inflated claims (by, for example, John Harbinson, writing in 1973) have suggested.[125] They depict a party which was organizationally weak in Belfast and in much of eastern Ulster, but which (like the Orange Order) was relatively better organized in the west and south of the Province (hence, partly, the disproportionate influence exercised by these areas in the Party's policies): related to its weakness in Belfast was the fact that the party was losing its working-class membership in the post-war period.[126]

A further long-term challenge rested with the Party organization, which had been designed in 1905 to translate power from an overweening parliamentary party and to distribute it amongst the growing number of 'stakeholders' in the Edwardian unionist movement. This inevitably made for party democracy and inclusivity, but hampered decisive or dynamic leadership. The party's constitution was a particular problem for reforming leaders from the 1960s onwards, such as Terence O'Neill, Brian Faulkner, and David Trimble; but it also (ironically) made the task of competing with Ian Paisley's Democratic Unionist Party ('which is far more disciplined, centralised and hierarchical') relatively difficult. In part, as scholars such as Christopher Farrington have observed, these structural distinctions help to explain why Ulster Unionism has been superseded by Democratic Unionism; on the other hand, the same distinctions (Farrington argues) may also ensure 'more hope for the longevity of any deal that [the Democratic Unionists] strike'.[127]

Yet, accepting the significance of all of these structural limitations and failures, Ulster Unionism has still helped to preserve an embattled and contested form of union between 1921 and the present day. Having outlined the case for Ulster Unionism's weakness in its central purpose and function, the maintenance of the union, it remains the case that a form of union is still in place and that, however controversially or inadequately, the movement is partly responsible for this survival. Thus the second, and final part of this section of the chapter, briefly explores Ulster Unionism's achievement in this respect.

At a basic level, Unionism and the union have survived partly because the movement has exercised a form of state power in Northern Ireland for fifty of the ninety years covered by partition; during the remaining period Unionism has (contrary to the emphases within the literature) enjoyed some assimilation within British high politics. If Unionists governed Northern Ireland narrowly, selfishly, and unimaginatively, then they still governed: if the Unionist bourgeoisie has used the Northern Irish state as effectively its own resource, then it has still been a resource at their disposal for most of the period under consideration.

Unionism (again, despite its reputation) has also had friends within British politics and the British establishment. James Craig and Stanley Baldwin had served their apprenticeship together on the Unionist backbenches in the later Edwardian era, and maintained close relation throughout the 1920s and 1930s. Basil Brooke (Prime Minister of Northern Ireland

between 1943 and 1963), whatever his failings of political vision or imagination, was clubbable and affable, and was able to sustain excellent working relationships both with Attlee's Labour government as well as the
Conservatism of the 1950s: Brooke was on particularly good terms with
Herbert Morrison (Deputy Prime Minister and Leader of the Commons),
and this relationship helped to smooth the preparations for the Labour
government's controversial Ireland Act (the terms of which were regularly
previewed at Stormont). Equally, however, Brooke was on good terms
with the Churchillian Conservatives: his uncle was Churchill's Chief of
the Imperial General Staff, Lord Alanbrooke, and he himself (like many of
the Tory grandees) was a decorated veteran of the Great War. At Westminster
Brooke's Unionists were relatively well-placed: in 1959, shortly after
Harold Macmillan assumed the British premiership, he appointed Samuel
Knox Cunningham (MP for South Antrim, and a member of an old and
monied Ulster Unionist clan) as his Parliamentary Private Secretary, and
thus to a strategically critical position within the Commons.

There were admittedly downsides to these relationships. Within the
broadly friendly and supportive connection between the two parties, there
were recurrent (if low-key) examples of friction or disappointment: in the
1950s and early 1960s Catholic Conservatives, such as Councillor
J.S. Doherty of Morpeth, or Councillor Guy Collis of Leicester, were occasionally offended by the sectarian dimension to Ulster Unionism, while Sir
Anthony Nutting, Conservative MP for Melton, memorably summarized
his view of Ulster Unionist parliamentarians that 'as a smug, offensive
and mediocre collection of bible-basing hypocrites they would be hard to
beat'.[128] On the other hand, the generally strong relationship between
Conservatism and Unionism in the 1950s in fact underpinned great difficulties for the latter, when Harold Wilson and Labour were returned to
power in October 1964 with a majority of six (at a time when there were
twelve Ulster Unionists). Moreover, the Ulster Unionists (reflecting perhaps
the intimacy and conventions of local political culture) tended to place too
great a faith in their personal connections at times when these conflicted
with wider principles and interests: Brian Faulkner and Edward Heath had
good relations of long standing, dating back to their parliamentary service
as, respectively, Unionist and Conservative chief whips; but this may have
allowed Heath (otherwise sensitive to Unionist concerns) to wrong-foot
Faulkner in March 1972 over the prorogation of Stormont. Equally, James
Molyneaux's strong parliamentary networks did not provide adequate

warning of the secretive negotiations which produced the Anglo-Irish (or Hillsborough) Agreement of 1985.

Opposition to the Anglo-Irish Agreement culminated in a mass rally at Belfast City Hall on 23 November 1985, the setting for numerous of the great demonstrations of Ulster Unionist sentiment from the signing of the Ulster Solemn League and Covenant in September 1912 onwards. State power meant effectively that Unionists controlled the public space and cer-emonial of the Northern Ireland polity; and the physical presence of Unionism must be regarded as simultaneously a reflection of its strength and ubiquity, and a bolster. Restricted official finances meant that there was no rash of public works in the aftermath of the creation of the Unionist state in 1921: moreover overly elaborate and expensive plans, such as the original designs for the Stormont parliament buildings, had to be scaled down in the light of economic downturn. However, a simplified Stormont was finally opened in 1932, and complemented by a massive court complex in central Belfast, completed in 1933: in that same year a substantial double-decker bridge was opened at Derry, and named after the incumbent Unionist Prime Minister, Lord Craigavon. Merrifield's statue of Lord Carson at Stormont is often used as an illustration of Unionist iconography in this period; but in fact the overt and direct celebration of Unionist leadership was relatively sparse. Craigavon was again commemorated (controversially) in the name of the new town designed to link Lurgan and Portadown in North Armagh; but generally references and allusions of this kind were rare—certainly in contrast to a Scottish city like Edinburgh, which was in effect an architectural obeisance to union. The link with Britain was cele-brated, or at any rate symbolized, not so much in terms of the formal cele-bration of Unionist heroes, as in the commemoration of war-time service, or other, more discreet, means. The creation of the Royal Ulster Constabulary brought a programme of building work, which placed police 'barracks' (in fact modest domestic-looking buildings, constructed to a uniform design, and all bearing the official harp-and-crown design) in virtually every town and village in Northern Ireland. War memorials dominated many town centres in the interwar years: the battlefields of the Great War and the Ulster-born generals of World War II were commemorated widely in the street names of East Belfast.

Admittedly some of these physical expressions of Unionist predominance were either offensive or counterproductive (such as the naming of 'Craigavon' new town), and focused opposition to the union state. Some Unionist public ceremonial (the deeply contested marches of the Orange Order in places such as Longstone, County Down, in the 1950s, or Drumcree, County Armagh, in the 1990s) were clearly designed without regard for wider communal needs, and brought offence to Nationalists, and damage to Unionism rather than consolidation. Indeed, in general Orange marches (despite recent marketing efforts of the 'Orangefest' variety) have been divisive and counterproductive, viewed by most Nationalists in terms of triumphalism and territorial claim rather than legitimate cultural tradition. This has also clearly applied to military occasions such as the Home Coming Parade (from Afghanistan) of the Royal Irish Regiment in Belfast in November 2008, the object of much republican opposition. On the other hand, the great military commemorations of victory in 1919 and 1945 were implicitly unionist occasions, but attracted widespread participation and acceptance. Moreover, the succession of royal visits to Northern Ireland, though exploited by Unionists in partisan ways, and energetically repudiated by republicans, also appear to have been relatively complex and ambiguous occasions. Certainly, as was explored in Chapter 6, the link between Irish nationalism and the British monarchy has been complex and layered.[129]

Ulster Unionism, though constrained both structurally as well as ideologically, has continued to draw upon other complex social and cultural resources. Ex-service associations served as informal fora for unionist sociability in the interwar years and after. Many of the institutions which bolstered late 19th-century Unionism survived and thrived well into the era of partition: the Orange Order, for example, has served as an important binding agent, particularly in the south and west of Ulster, although scholars have noted a falling off both in the numbers and social standing of the membership through the last thirty years of the 20th century (membership of the Order being incompatible with new forms of mobility and sociability).[130] Work by Diane Urquhart and Rachel Ward, amongst others, indicates the rich variety of institutions which existed to incorporate women within organized Unionism.[131] The childrens' organizations which were created in the late Victorian and Edwardian eras (the Boys' Brigade, the Church Lads' Brigade, the Boy Scouts), and which served effectively as adjuncts to Unionism, survived through the 20th century.

Schools and universities sustained Ulster unionism after 1921: the history books supplied by the Ministry of Education to Northern Ireland's direct grant schools, such as D. A. Chart's *History of Northern Ireland* (1927) provided a partitionist history for the new state.[132] Popular historians such as Lord

Ernest Hamilton continued to celebrate the plantation tradition into the 1920s (Hamilton, *The Irish Rebellion of 1641: With a History of the Events Which Led Up to It and Succeeded It* (1920), *Tales of the Troubles* (1925)). Hamilton's efforts were complemented within the academy by Cyril Falls, Chichele Professor of the History of War at Oxford University, and son of a prominent Unionist election agent in County Fermanagh: Falls produced accounts of *The 36th Ulster Division* (1922), *The Birth of Ulster* (1936), *Elizabeth's Irish Wars* (1950), and of the Elizabethan general, *Mountjoy* (1955) (he also, revealingly, celebrated the life and work of *Rudyard Kipling* (1915)). Other university historians such as John W. Blake of Queen's Belfast celebrated, with the help of a government commission, *Northern Ireland in the Second World War* (1956). Hugh Shearman, who completed a Ph.D. at Trinity College Dublin on the disestablishment of the Irish Church, was commissioned by the Northern Ireland government to write a commemorative volume for the fiftieth anniversary of the state, *Northern Ireland, 1921–71* (1971). Queen's University, the only university in Northern Ireland until the creation of the New University of Ulster at Coleraine in 1968, was closely associated with the Unionist state: its chancellor between 1923 and 1949 was the seventh Marquess of Londonderry, Minister for Education in James Craig's government, who was succeeded by Viscount Alanbrooke, who was (as has been mentioned) the uncle of the incumbent Unionist Prime Minister, Viscount Brookeborough. In 1940 Douglas Savory graduated from service as Professor of French at Queen's to representing the university's parliamentary seat at Westminster in the Unionist interest (and indeed he later served both as secretary and chairman of the Ulster Unionists in the House of Commons).

Unionism (despite its unflattering reputation in this and other respects) has also occasionally demonstrated evidence of intellectual engagement, even flexibility. It would be useless to pretend that this has uniformly been the case, however; but the very wide array of Unionist polemic in the Home Rule era and afterwards testifies to the importance of historical and constitutional ideas within the Unionist case. The two greatest constitutional lawyers of the day, Dicey and Sir William Anson, were Irish Unionist sympathizers; and each, particularly Dicey, was in (controversially) close contact with the Unionist leadership during the Home Rule crisis.[133] A.L. Lowell, Professor of Government at Harvard, supplied Unionists with a critique of the third Home Rule Bill.[134] After partition successive Ulster Unionist governments received support from friendly academics for specific purposes—such as Thomas Wilson, Professor of Economics at Glasgow, who edited *Ulster under Home Rule* (1955), and co-authored the report, *Economic Development in Northern Ireland* (1965): Wilson also occasionally offered advice sympathetic to Ulster Unionism to Edward Heath.[135] Novelists in the interwar period and after, whether of a popular (Freeman Wills Crofts) or more cerebral (Forrest Reid) variety, produced relatively benign depictions of Northern Ireland and its institutions: Crofts, one of the most prominent detective novelists of the era, provided essentially sympathetic portrayals of the partition state, and the Royal Ulster Constabulary in works such as *Sir John Magill's Last Journey* (1930) and *Fatal Venture* (1939). But it is difficult to think of any intellectual ferment similar to that of the Home Rule era, before the advent of David Trimble to frontline Unionist politics in the 1980s. This is one definition of the introversion and of the fragile and dangerous confidence of Unionist political culture for much of the Stormont years.

Linked with this is the suggestion that Unionism and Orangeism may have recently taken an intellectual 'turn' of sorts. Here the two critical epiphanies were supplied by the Anglo-Irish Agreement of 1985 and the disputed Orange marches at Drumcree, County Armagh, between 1995 and 1998. The apparent failure of a rejectionist strategy both before and certainly after the Agreement of 1985 was a setback for the James Molyneaux's Ulster Unionist party and for its excessive caution; and it created space for some alternative visions of unionism and loyalism. Some of these were supplied by the loyalist paramilitaries, who embarked upon a bloody offensive in the late 1980s and early 1990s; but there was also a significant cultural turn within the movements from the mid 1980s onwards. Trimble, then a law lecturer at Queen's University, was a major influence, particularly in terms of the Ulster Society ('for the promotion of Ulster-British heritage and culture'), founded in June 1985, just before the publication of the Anglo-Irish Agreement. Christopher Farrington has identified Arthur Aughey of the University of Ulster as a further critical figure, in so far as Aughey's investigation of the Unionist campaign against the Agreement, and his delineation of a more thoroughly positive and civic vision of the union, were very widely influential within the disoriented unionism of the late 1980s and after.[136] In a sense, the period witnessed the birth not just of the 'new' unionism, but of an intellectually engaged unionism, as evidenced both by key figures like Trimble and Aughey (and, in Christopher Farrington's listing, Paul (Lord) Bew, Esmond Birnie, Ruth Dudley Edwards, Graham

Gudgin, Steven King, Gordon Lucy, Dermott Nesbitt, Patrick Roche, Peter Weir) and also by the 'higher number of young graduates who were prominent in writing for Unionist publications and working for Unionist politicians'.[137]

However, there was also a darker, and militant, side to Unionism's defence of the union. The history of British government in 19th-century Ireland tended to suggest a dangerous equation between political violence and reform (the Fenian Rising of 1867 was succeeded by disestablishment and land reform, the Land War of 1879–1881 was succeeded by the great Land Act of 1881 and Arrears Act of 1882, to say nothing of the Gladstonian conversion to Home Rule in 1885). Ulster Unionists and British Conservatives helped to bring the United Kingdom close to civil war in 1912–1914, and stalled the promulgation of Home Rule in what the political scientist Iain McLean has defined as a 'coup d'état'.[138] The Ulster Volunteer Force was recreated in 1919, and seems to have underpinned a variety of loyalist vigilante and terror groups (such as the 'Imperial Guards') in the blood-strewn Belfast of the early 1920s: here the IRA faced both the forces of the crown as well as loyalist paramilitarism, though sometimes the distinction was hard to perceive (as with the McMahon murders, where the killers wore police uniforms, and probably were policemen).[139] In the later 20th century Unionist paramilitarism tended to benefit less from the sponsorship of constitutional Unionism (though there were some exceptions) than from its confusion and defeat: the brand name 'UVF' was reinvented in loyalist West Belfast in 1966 against the background of Terence O'Neill's tentative ecumenism, and of the first cracks within mainstream Unionism; and an explosion of paramilitarism accompanied the retreat and meltdown within constitutional Unionism in the early 1970s, culminating in the creation of the Ulster Defence Association ('the Wombles', named for their furry parkas rather than their cuteness) and the associated Ulster Freedom Fighters in 1971. The humiliating failure of constitutional Unionism in 1985, over the Anglo-Irish Agreement, led to a reinvigoration of the memory of militant resistance to the third Home Rule Bill within Unionist culture; and there was an accompanying explosion of loyalism paramilitarism and an effort (mimicking the Larne gunrunning of April 1914) to smuggle (South African) weapons into Northern Ireland in 1987.[140] The effort to recapture the spirit and strategies of 1914 was underlined by the association of some leading Unionist politicians with a new militant organization, Ulster Resistance, and with some of the older loyalist paramilitary bodies within Northern

Ireland. The prelude to the first paramilitary ceasefires of 1994 was characterized by a furious blood-letting which saw loyalist paramilitaries kill more people than their republican enemies for the first time in the history of the 'Long War'.

If the vestigial union of the 21st century owes something to the intellectual reinvention of constitutional unionism in the 1990s and after, then it also rests partly upon the peace of exhaustion. If Ulster Unionism in the 21st century was about Trimbleite intellectualism, or Paisleyite religious fundamentalism, then it was also about the bling culture and bloody machismo of loyalist paramilitarism and clubland.

## Conclusion: the two Unionisms

The interconnections and parallels between Scottish and Irish Unionism are striking and significant. Each was bound to the other by family and institutional connections, and by ties of trade and commerce: the two Unionisms shared some personnel, some structures (such as Orangeism), and a wide range of cultural and economic affinities. Each owed much to their frontiers, whether in terms of the Scottish borders or the south and west of Ulster. Each was rooted in a complex and interlinked political ancestry; and each produced a lush and lavish social and cultural efflorescence.

But in the end it was the distinctions which ruled. Irish Unionism and Irish Nationalism quickly became associated with apparently complementary ethnic identities, while Scottish politics drew on a broadly shared sense of Scottish patriotism. Devolution in Northern Ireland between 1920 and 1972 created an autonomous and ethnically defensive Unionism—a Unionism which, in many respects, was both culturally and financially asphyxiated. But in Scotland, Unionism became more closely enmeshed within a metropolitan political culture; and, though originally tinctured with some of the religious passions of Ulster, Scottish unionism soon largely shed the confessional politics of Glasgow and Lanark. Ulster Unionism for long defined itself against an array of exclusivist reference points (the Ulster Plantation, evangelical Protestantism), and was thus never able to break out of an electoral ghetto. The central achievement of Scottish Unionism was that it defined a faith which ultimately contained little overt ethnic baggage, and which could be transmitted to other quarters of the political spectrum: ultimately Scottish unionism transcended Scottish Unionism.

The two Unionisms, Scottish and Irish, were for long bound in a symbiotic relationship. But devolution in Northern Ireland produced an introverted and sometimes arrogant Unionist political culture, while, for its part, Scottish Unionism outgrew the connection with its Irish and Ulster sibling. Small wonder, then, that, despite the history, and despite vestigial loyalist passions, Scotland offered little to an embattled and fragmented Ulster Unionism in the desperate years of the Long War.

# PART IV

## Reflections on the Unions

# 9

# Conclusion: North Britain, West Britain

There is no need to press the moral of a forgotten chapter in history. What is worth notice, because it has some bearing on the solution of existing problems, is that Scotch history before, at, and since the Union shows, not that just policy produces one effect in Ireland and another in Scotland, but that in each country justice and injustice produce each of them its natural fruits. A.V. Dicey, 'The Two Acts of Union: A Contrast', *Fortnightly Review*, 30, 176 (August, 1881)

A most beautiful creature; admirable in its contexture; agreeable in its figure; squared like a most exquisite piece of architecture, both for ornament, strength and usefulness. They would have seen in it a complete circle, all lines of which were drawn from and depended upon one general centre—the public good; a mighty arch, every stone of which mutually contributed not to its private support only, but to the strength of the whole. Daniel Defoe on the Scottish Union, *History of the Union between England and Scotland* (1799 edition), p.59

The Irish, like the Highlanders, are capable of being at one and the same time the loyalest and most generous of friends and the bitterest and most treacherous enemies. From 20 years of experience of a business branch in Dublin, I know that one can always evoke the former response *provided one treats them as equals*. It was that lesson it took us 800 years to learn. David James MP, Report of Irish Visit, October 1972 (Robin Chichester-Clark Papers, CCLK 3/39)

## The spiritual union

The concept of union, certainly the Scots union, was, from the beginning, linked with religious and imperial ambition and vision: the practice of union, in and after 1707 and 1801, was bound with a range of more earthy, material, and pragmatic concerns. The concept of union was born at the same time as the consolidation of the reformation in England and Scotland, and was contemporary with the first envisioning (and indeed mention) of a

'British Empire'. The first unionists, in the 16th century, tied their idea of an Anglo-Scots union to the spread of reformed religion; while James VI and I, that most energetic unionist of the early 17th century, envisioned his uni-fied crown and kingdom along the lines foreshadowed by Constantine the Great, the unifier of empire and patron of an imperial orthodox Christianity. For James, union was intertwined with the language of empire and of faith: the union was defined in the vocabulary of empire, and it was promoted using biblical imagery and quotation and through engaging the mysteries of kingship. Faith and empire would remain central to the conceptualization of the United Kingdom of Great Britain, and later of Ireland.

Much of this early conceptualization in fact was a failure; and the impli-cations for the survival of the union enterprise were potentially dire. Elizabethan and Jacobean Englishmen, secure in the faith that 'God was English', and that England was providentially blessed, were not persuaded by Scottish calls for politico-religious union, and in particular by a union which might be designed to further Presbyterian spiritual ambition. Equally, while shared imperial notions might have bolstered the call for union, in reality the elusiveness of the concept of a 'British Empire' meant that this linkage did not automatically occur. At root, the English of the 17th century, always likely to be the predominant partners in any union alliance, wanted an English king, an English empire and an English church ('that any new British institutions would be essentially English in character; and that Scotland would not be an equal but in many respects a subordinate partner in the union').[1] The Scots, cut off by the reformed faith from many of their former continental European linkages, and financially and militarily strait-ened, were more vulnerable; but they believed for a time that they could supply a united monarchy and Presbyterianism to the union, while gaining an empire. By 1607–1608 the effort to provide a wider political and spiritual vision had failed; but 'the ramshackle union lurched on, satisfying neither ideologically nor practically'.[2]

In this early formulation can be seen much of the subsequent limitation and development of the union. Certainly for some union would retain an evangelizing spiritual and imperial dimension as late as the 19th and 20th centuries. Already in 1801, with the inauguration of the Irish union, the fic-tion of a shared and unifying national communion was maintained through the formulation of the United Church of England and Ireland (in the face of the majority Catholic presence on the island).[3] But religious and imperial faith did not then, or ever would, gain widespread practical acceptance as an ideology of union; and subsequent contingent influences would partly take their place (even Orange Protestants in Ireland were not initially persuaded that union served any meaningful religious interest, still less as an instrument of Providence). The practice of union, for both Scotland and Ireland, was characterized, not by any widely accepted sense of spiritual or imperial unity or mission (except among a zealous few), but rather by military and economic pressures and the negotiation of national sensitivities. As Colin Kidd has said of Britain on the eve of the Scots union, it 'remained an uninspiringly underimagined community. Contemporary constructions of British nationhood lacked a compelling ethnic or historical vision. Instead of a hegemonic British identity, there remained the existing national traditions and a few areas which permitted a degree of common identification'.[4] The same point might be made with even greater force for the 'British Isles' on the eve of the Irish union: the United Kingdom was 'an uninspiringly underimagined community', but (unlike Britain and Britishness, which enjoyed some subsequent evolution) it has remained underimagined ever since. In the end union, in 1707 and 1801, made sense (or not) in terms of the immediate circumstances of the time, and as a practical negotiation, but little else. In other words, union largely lacked 'the vision thing'.

Having said all that, it is worth noting that there was a much stronger tradition of representing the Scots union as providentially inspired, as compared with the Irish union. James VI and I drew upon this tradition, while melding it within his related vision of divinely sanctioned absolutism: God had ordained union, and the divinely ordained crown would be the instrument of union.[5] By the end of the 17th century union was seen–by Daniel Defoe at any rate–as an essential part of a grand scheme 'of general peace amongst the Protestant interests of Europe'.[6] For the Irish, however, union was broached either in the context of bloody conquest, or as a military, political, or economic expedient. With the success of the Scots union clear for all to see in the 19th century ('the Union of England and Scotland was one of the events most clearly fore-ordained by a benignant fate'), providentialist readings of the union recovered some credibility.[7] But reading God into the Union of 1801 was a much tougher call for the Irish, and even Irish unionists. The most that might be (and was indeed) said by 19th-century unionists was that, while God had clearly blessed the Scots through the union, he had created opportunities for the restructuring of Irish society, and for a closer union, in the wake of the Great Famine.[8]

One continuing measure of the general lack of unionist vision, spiritual or otherwise, is to be found in the absence of any widespread popular commemorative culture surrounding the two unions. Even though the popular celebration of royal coronations and anniversaries was well established in the 17th and 18th centuries ('by the late 17th century the king's birthday had become one of the few recognized symbols of unity and loyalty to the monarchy throughout Britain', according to Keith Brown), and even though Scots and English annually remembered the demise of the Scotophobe Guy Fawkes, while Irish Protestants annually commemorated the blood-letting of 1641 and the Williamite victories of 1690–1691, little popular attention or enthusiasm was directly invested in the anniversaries of union.[9] There is certainly evidence of elite interest. The passage of the Anglo-Scots union was accompanied by some official commemoration: the event was, for example, marked by a series of official medals, designed by the Royal Mint engraver, John Croker. Equally, the passage of the British-Irish union in 1801 was discreetly commemorated by the striking of an official medal, designed by C.H. Küchler, and proclaiming (in a tag worthy of James VI and I) 'junguntur opes firmatur imperium' (their resources are united, the empire is strengthened) (see illustration B.2). Expensive jewellery bearing the conjoined emblems of the three kingdoms was manufactured in the years after the Irish union and adorned high-ranking unionist women.[10] But, despite the existence of a vibrant 'cultural loyalism' in Ireland in the late 18th and early 19th centuries ('tracts, ballads and poems specifically addressed to a plebeian audience confirm the empowering potential of loyalism'), there was as yet no similarly vibrant 'cultural unionism'.[11]

The centenary of 1707 passed with little comment, and was in any event overshadowed throughout the new United Kingdom by King George III's Golden Jubilee in 1809–1810: the ultra-loyalist lawyer, John Giffard, commanded the organization of the celebration in Dublin, which was characterized by dinners, placards, transparencies, and ribbons.[12] Cork and other loyalists found the time and resource to celebrate the centenary of the establishment of the House of Hanover on the throne of Britain, in 1814, but not the centenary of the establishment of Great Britain itself. The centenary of the British-Irish union fell during the South African War, when popular loyalist and separatist sympathies were otherwise diverted, and when popular loyalism had been spent through the Diamond Jubilee of Queen Victoria (1897), and her visit to Ireland in 1900. It is true that a range of largely sympathetic historical comment on the Irish union and its architects was produced in the years before the First World War; but the stimulus here was the third Home Rule crisis rather than any centenary celebration or reflection. By way of contrast, the bicentenary of the Scots union fell at the high tide of its popularity; and while there was certainly little by way of popular eruption, Scottish historians such as Peter Hume Brown (*The Union of 1707: A Survey of Events* (1907), *The Legislative Union of England and Scotland* (1914)), Alexander MacRae (*Scotland, from the Treaty of Union with England to the Present Time* (1908)), and W.L. Mathieson (*Scotland and the Union, 1695–1747* (1905)) did take the opportunity to reflect upon the achievements of the previous two centuries. The 250th anniversary of the Scots union, which fell in 1957, two years after the electoral high-water mark of Scottish Unionism, was drily noted in the press, but emphatically not in any jingoistic sense: 'the 250th anniversary', a sober Matthew Moulton commented in the *Scotsman*, 'is hardly an occasion for putting out flags, or for burning the Treaty of Union, but for thinking how far Scotland can continue to live with it without losing her identity'.[13] Equally, the tercentenary of the Scots union coincided with disillusion over the Iraq War, the consolidation of SNP support, and generated modest official recognition: a commemorative two pound coin was struck in 2007, a successor to James VI and I's 'British' coinage, with the ambiguous reverse image of a jigsaw of national symbols, together with the singularly low-key edge inscription 'United into One Kingdom' (the Jacobean propagandists had produced much more resonant, biblically based, sloganeering).[14]

However, all this was crudely emotional compared with the commemoration of the bicentenary of the Irish union, which fell in 2000–2001: as with the centenary, other events conspired to defuse whatever limited enthusiasm for commemoration may have been in place. The institutions created by the Good Friday Agreement were fresh and vulnerable, the thirty year conflict in Northern Ireland was a close and bitter memory; and there was, accordingly, little official or popular, even popular unionist, appetite for flag-waving.[15]

There was no popular commemoration, partly because (except perhaps amongst some Ulster Unionists) there was so little sentimental or spiritual investment in union. From the beginning, union appealed primarily (the Elizabethan and Jacobean ideologues notwithstanding) to a sense of individual, sectional, or national advantage, and not generally to any higher ideal. The problem, paradoxically, with the union was that it depended largely upon rational, or supposedly rational, calculation: it had often little to counter competing ideological claims based upon history or a more thoroughly elaborated rival national sentiment. One obvious expression of this failing was that the nationalist ideology which was the supposed complement to the United Kingdom–Britishness–by definition primarily embraced only one of the two main islands which, from 1800 to 1921, constituted the United Kingdom. Moreover, 'Britishness' was to a large extent formulated before the Irish union: in this regard Linda Colley has laid stress upon the impact of both the Seven Years War and the American War of Independence, arguing that the latter promoted a 'far more consciously and officially constructed [British] patriotism which stressed attachment to the monarchy, the importance of empire, the value of military and naval achievement, and the desirability of strong, stable government by a virtuous, able and authentically British elite'.[16] But of course not only were the Irish not part of this–not 'in on the ground floor' of this Britishness–the American War of Independence stimulated a separate and parallel Irish patriotism which expressed itself in calls for greater trading and legislative autonomy. Moreover, this 'officially constructed' British patriotism did not incorporate the aspirations and identity of Irish Catholics (and, arguably, it did not even fully chime with the historical identity of much of Irish Protestantism). Moreover, while a homogenizing Britishness evidently appealed to some Whiggish Scots in the 18th century, by the 19th century British identity was contingent upon the recognition and respect accorded to a range of Scottish patriotic sensitivities. Britishness, in other words, did not meet the ideological needs of the constitutional unit which it came to complement. The result was what A. V. Dicey described as 'the delayed moral unification of the United Kingdom'.[17]

This, as it might be termed, emotional or spiritual deficit with the union had other ramifications. Union as a concept had indeed originally been linked to the spread of the reformed faith; and while notions of an imperial Presbyterianism or a uniform Episcopalianism receded in the 17th century, it was still inescapably true that union and reformation had a linkage, albeit (with the passage of time) one of increasing tenuousness. But a central problem with the union was not just that the concept was tied to the reformation; the fundamental problem was that the bond was unsuccessful, and–moreover–that different later efforts to bind religion emotionally and structurally within the institutions of the union state were by and large failures. As has been said, the idea of creating a uniform Presbyterian or Episcopal empire of the spirit to coincide with the new 'British Empire' failed. But William Pitt's effort to launch the Irish Union with the 'libera-tion' of Ireland's Catholic population was also swiftly scuppered, while William Gladstone's further steps towards a multi-faith definition of the union (through the disestablishment of the Irish Church in 1869) seemed to be too reactive and too late to achieve any meaningful impact. Irish Catholic disillusionment, and the community's search for some form of revised con-stitutional relationship with Britain, not only directly undermined the union; they also helped to stimulate a defensive Protestant Unionism, which came to interpret the union as a necessary weapon for the protection of a range of material and religious interests. This, however, was very far from the notion of union as a great spiritual enterprise, as briefly envisioned by the ideologues of the Jacobean era.

## The material union

If the visions of union largely failed to inspire, then what was left was an appeal to self-interest–national, sectional, and individual. In the event both the unions of 1707 and 1801 were shaped by English policy needs in the context of turbulent and unruly Scots and Irish parliaments, by Scots and Irish chal-lenges to the monarchy, and by the pressures of international conflict: the details of both union settlements were shaped by the interests of local political elites in Scotland and Ireland, whether financial or political. Both unions shored up existing propertied establishments, even if (as with the Irish case) the original intention had been to enact a much more radical political reform. Linked with this, both unions generated an interpretative literature which emphasised the themes of corruption and venality on the part of the two nation's political classes. In the event, the Irish union of 1801, influenced by its Scots predecessor, served to maintain the landed elite, at least in the mid term: the ascendancy's parliament was gone, but the interest still dominated Irish parliamentary representation. The limited scope of union meant that much of Ireland's *ancien régime*, together with its ascendancy masters, remained firmly in place for the time being. Only slowly, in the aftermath of Catholic eman-cipation, was this situation significantly corrected.

Related to this point was the fact that neither union was (at least legally) a wholly integrative or 'incorporating' enterprise: each, instead, was piecemeal, the result of political compromise and contingency. Not only were the unions far removed from any coherent visionary impulse, they also reflected the need to cobble together a constitutional settlement speedily and in the teeth of opposition from significant vested interests. In 1707 the Scottish and English parliaments were unified, but the heritable jurisdictions of Scotland, powerful burgh, judicial, university, and church interests remained largely in place: in Ireland, the parliaments were united, but the Irish peerage, judiciary, the Castle bureaucracy, and other ascendancy interests remained untouched. In essence, the two unions chimed with the developing pattern of English or British colonial government throughout the 19th-century empire—establishing order, and sometimes pursuing radical reform, on the strength of having recruited or co-opted influential local interests. The much-used notion of hybridity is relevant here, with the emergence or consolidation of sections of Scottish and Irish government and society which were clearly now, after the unions, Anglo-Scottish or Anglo-Irish (or 'British'), while vast hinterlands remained, if not untouched, then much less affected by the acculturation of the metropolitan power. It seems clear that the survival of a range of distinctive Scottish institutions helped to acclimatize Scots patriotism to the union, since it was thereby possible to express patriotic sentiments and identity within the structures of union.[18] But, by way of contrast, the survival of distinctive Irish institutions after 1801 helped to undermine union in so far as these demonstrated the limited embrace of the settlement. The survival of a separate Scottish judiciary (for example) proclaimed the integrity and autonomy of Scottish law: the survival of an Irish judiciary and legal establishment proclaimed instead the abiding power of the ascendancy interest. A semi-complete union with emancipation (where an Irish Catholic identity might have been expressed within distinctive institutions, but also within the framework of union), or—possibly—a fully fledged union with emancipation, might each have been better 'fit for purpose' than the measure of 1801, framed as it was with the sensibilities and sensitivities of ascendancy Ireland chiefly in view.

But if the contexts for the two unions were strikingly similar, then the implications and fall-out from each was sharply different. Both unions were passed against the backdrop of international warfare; and both were passed in the context of English military threat and supremacy. Both Scotland and Ireland had experienced the recent reality of English conquest combined with an enforced union (this in the Cromwellian era). For both, therefore, union was tainted by the notions of external compulsion and subjugation. But, for the Scots, though the reality of English military supremacy was hard to escape, and though there were rumours of troop deployments at the time of union, no military threat ever materialized. For the Irish, however, union was passed in the immediate aftermath of a ferocious civil war, with at least 30,000 deaths, and perhaps 100,000 taking the field from both sides: an English general (Cornwallis) was now, after 1798, lord lieutenant, and the predominance of English arms indisputable. Union was passed in Ireland, not just with the illegal application of secret service funding, but with the glint of military steel in the background. The union was sustained in Ireland, not only through the steel of a large garrison, but also with the aid of a large and militarized police force, wielding both firearms as well as (periodically) special crimes legislation.

In terms of the historical literature, the notion of corruption remained a dominant trope within popular interpretations of the Union of 1801, and was a politically useful tool for nationalists when the maintenance of the union was under discussion in 1886 and after. More generally, the controversial deployment of honours in 1799–1801 (and long after) for services to the cause of union, eventually helped to further undermine the standing and integrity of the Irish landed aristocracy by the time, the late 19th century, that landlordism was under a more general political and legal assault. But in Scotland, however, though the 'sordid' origins of many noble titles continued to rankle democrats such as Thomas Johnston in the early 20th century, in general the notion of a 'union peerage' did not carry any of the negative connotations which were applied in Ireland. Already by the mid 18th century a Whig historiography had emerged which, building upon a shared sense of British national and ethnic origins, provided an intellectual rationale and apology for union. Taken in the round, and allowing for some Jacobite sentimentality and Home Rule polemic, the historiography of Scotland was predominantly a unionist enterprise until well into the 20th century.

The Scots union may no longer have encompassed a grand Presbyterian project for a new British empire, but the rights of the Kirk in Scotland were guaranteed nonetheless. As has been repeatedly noted, this was not the case for the Catholic Church in Ireland in 1800: and the implications of this distinction have been recognized here (as elsewhere in the literature on union) as bleak. On the other hand, this is very far from saying that the relationship between the union state and Irish Catholicism was foredoomed to failure. On the contrary, the mutual usefulness of Catholicism and the union state was such that—even though there were periodic ministerial retreats towards a defensive Protestantism—in practice a form of symbiotic relationship emerged and survived. As Sir George Errington, the British representative at the Vatican, opined in 1880: 'the British Empire extends over the whole world. In the Indies, in America, everywhere it finds itself in rapport with the Church and her works, and the interests of civilisation and religion require that the understanding between the two powers should also be as cordial as possible'.[19] According to the historian Oliver Rafferty, a wide array of Catholic bishops believed in the providential nature of the union state and of its empire. Certainly, as is well known, the Vatican periodically chastised the leaders of late 19th-century Irish nationalism (over the Land League, the Parnell Tribute, and the Plan of Campaign). Ten Irish bishops spoke on fourteen different occasions in support of the British war effort between 1914 and 1918: the Church's attitude towards the 1916 Rising was initially decidedly cool. It remains undoubtedly true that the British failure to grant emancipation in 1800, and their ongoing resistance to the Catholic campaign until 1829, were highly damaging to the long-term prospects of the union. But, as Rafferty has rightly argued, 'even with this what is most striking is not Irish Catholic disgruntlement with the union and empire, but rather the relative degree of support exhibited by Irish Catholics for both institutions'.[20] This, again, was one measure of the opportunity bungled in 1801.

The same caution has to be deployed when approaching the issue of economic fall-out from the unions. Both Scotland and Ireland enjoyed no immediate economic benefits from their respective unions. But, for the Scots, the economic blessings of union eventually came, though only after a wait; while, for the Irish, the blessings came—but only to the north-eastern part of the island. Again, the timing of union benefited the Scots, as opposed to the Irish. Scots historians now emphasise the embryonic strengths of aspects of the national economy in the 17th century, in particular the spread of international trading connections. This nascent trading network, allied with the raw materials of the Central Belt, and the economic union affected in 1707 (Britain was 'the largest free trade zone in Europe'), meant that Scotland was well placed to contribute to, and benefit from the British 'industrial revolution' of the 18th century.[21] In the Irish case the comparatively high level of political disturbance in the late 17th century (the 'Glorious Revolution', after all, was effectively and bloodily fought out in Ireland), the comparative lack of imperial trading linkages and industrial raw materials, and the effective exclusion from the British free trade zone inaugurated in 1707, all meant that the country was marginal to British industrial growth. It would certainly be wrong to overlook the importance of economic growth in Ireland after the 1740s, and with it the growth not just of the agricultural sector, but also of towns, and of small industrial concerns linked to the agrarian economy (such as brewing and textiles). But at root Ireland was a bystander to the British Industrial Revolution, and to the prosperity which it generated. This partly meant that in the 18th century, and even after 1801, Ireland also remained marginal to the union, because (while linked in so many other respects) it was distant from some of the essential definitions of the enterprise. Or perhaps, more accurately, the Irish were distant from the pre-eminent definition of union (which emphasised *inter alia* economic modernization, imperial enterprise, and shared Protestantism), while failing to persuade the British political elite of the merits of any alternative revision.

This semi-detachment, or perhaps, again, 'liminality', is also evident in Ireland's relationship with empire. As noted, Ireland's trading connections with empire were slow to develop in the 18th century, and thus (taken in the round) Irish participation in the 'first' British empire was less significant than that of the Scots (who exercised a disproportionate influence in many territories, including India and North America). But, if the search for a revised union was one of the great themes of 19th-century British-Irish relations, then one aspect of this was played out within the confines of the 'second' empire. Irish Catholic migration within the empire, Irish Catholic participation in the colonial civil service and judiciary, Irish Catholic participation in the policing of empire, were also relatively significant phenomena in the mid and late 19th century. The role of the Irish and English Catholic Church within empire was important, whether in terms of supplying clergy to established or growing Catholic communities, supplying missionaries, or (more generally) as stabilizing and conservative forces. The significance and success of Catholicism, in particular Irish Catholicism, within the 19th-century empire enhanced the chances of longevity for the British-Irish union, since so many Irish Catholics were caught up within the 'British' imperial project. But Irish Catholicism's engagement with empire was contingent upon a degree of official encouragement and flexibility which was not always evident within the structures of the United Kingdom; and thus Irish Catholicism's engagement with union did not live up to the potential which was clearly evident elsewhere. The chances for union were real enough, but were ultimately dependent upon its adaptability and reform.

Empire, in short, serves as a metaphor for the broader condition of the two unions. It worked for the Scots, who were in 'on the ground floor' in

the 18th century, producing significant professional and business opportunities. In some, less extravagant, ways it indicated the possibilities for Irish
Catholics within a Britannic constitutional framework. But these were contingent upon a revision of the union which created greater scope for social
mobility and national expression at home. And while the union was sufficiently malleable to survive for 120 years, ultimately this revision only began
to take place when it was too late, and Irish nationalism (in contradistinction to its Scots counterpart) had been refined along more aggressive and
exclusive lines.

## The longevity of union

The evidence of the spiritual, economic, and imperial dimensions to union
on the whole illustrates the broader contours of the distinction between the
Scots and Irish experiences. The elaboration of the British state presented a
range of institutions and social and political relationships which helped to
bind Scotland and Ireland within the embrace of the union. But while institutions such as the monarchy or the crown forces had a shared impact and
importance, the distinctive origins of the union in 1801– the peculiar nature
of its relationship with British identity–partly meant that this impact and
importance played out in distinctive ways in Ireland.

The two unions were created by legislation, but they were realized by
improved transportation and communication, rendered marmoreal and celebrated in (particularly) urban space, and sustained by the spiritual and
material bonds forged through the monarchy, the crown forces, and (more
generally) the expanding British state. Support for the survival of each union
was organized within formal political movements, which were (by no means
unfailing or unfailingly effective) bulwarks of the constitutional settlements.
The Scottish and Irish unions were each sustained by these varying structures, institutions, and relationships; but (as with the origins of the two
unions), so the chemistry of survival and longevity varied greatly between
the two countries.

The development of steam technology, and its application to shipping
and rail transportation certainly facilitated the government of union in the
19th and 20th centuries; but rail was also critical to the spread of a coherent
and disciplined Irish nationalism in the last quarter of the 19th century. The
cityscapes of both Ireland and Scotland bore the iconography and imagery

of union; but these were much more contested phenomena in Ireland, where an alternative set of historic and national reference points were speedily defined in the course of the 19th century. However, both in Ireland and Scotland the unions had an inescapable physical manifestation in the form of government buildings, police and army barracks, and even–at a more intimate and unthreatening level–postboxes. The centrality and intimacy of union in Scotland, however, was illustrated in a number of ways, not least by the use of the symbols of union in domestic architecture.[22] Much public space was therefore 'unionist' in both countries; and little wonder that the campaign to reject union in Ireland should have partly taken the form of an effort to rename offending counties, streets, and towns, to remove the iconography of union from public buildings, and to repaint the postboxes of the British Post Office in the emerald green colours of the Irish nation.

The Irish and Scots have had complex and similar relationships with various of the institutions related to the union state, and in particular the monarchy and the forces of the crown. Despite the development of an Irish republican tradition after 1791, monarchical sympathies were deeply embedded within the Catholic and Gaelic traditions in Ireland; and there is plenty of evidence for the period up to the 1880s to suggest that the monarchy might have served as a reconciling force between Catholic Ireland and a reformed union state. There is indeed some evidence to suggest that the monarchy retained the sympathetic interest of many Irish people until the eve of the Great War. All this is broadly in line with the Scots relationship with the monarchy. But the British monarchy, Supreme Governors of that *via media*, the Church of England, were able for much of the 19th century and after to accommodate the Calvinism of the Kirk, where they were evidently not able to accommodate the Roman Catholicism of the majority of Irish people. There were no natural antipathies: Irish Catholics responded eagerly to any evidence of royal goodwill from the late 18th century onwards, and were keen to register public expressions of loyalty as a means of strengthening the case for the removal of the remaining legal disabilities. But the monarchy was, fundamentally, too deeply rooted in the English reformation, as affirmed by the 'Glorious Revolution', to fully address the needs of its Catholic subjects in Ireland: it was also too closely aligned with the aspirations, interests, and enthusiasms of the Ascendancy in Ireland. It has been accepted here (and, of course, elsewhere) that the great missed opportunity of union was the failure of George III to embrace Catholic emancipation in

1800; but in truth the history of the 19th-century relationship between the union state and the Irish is a succession of missed opportunities to accommodate Catholic sensitivities. On the whole the modern monarchy has only adapted when its own immediate survival, as opposed to that of the wider constitutional settlement, has been at stake: it has outlived the original British-Irish union, and there is every indication (particularly given the present constitution of the Scottish National Party) that it will now survive that between England and Scotland.

The crown forces served to bind Scots to the cause of monarchy and union from at least the time of the War of the Spanish Succession. Irish Catholics were tacitly recruited to the British Army from at least the time of the Seven Years' War. Both the Scots and the Irish served in disproportionately strong numbers in the Army during the French Revolutionary and Napoleonic Wars. Both the Scots and the Irish were distinctive and disproportionate presences in the Victorian army (as late as the South African War of 1899 the Irish were overrepresented in the British Army). With Ireland supposedly on the cusp of Home Rule during the Great War, conscription was not applied; and the Irish involvement with the War was relatively slighter than that of the Scots, or indeed as compared with most of the great conflicts of the preceding century. But a strong Irish tradition of engagement with the British Army continued during the War of Independence, and survived the establishment of the Free State in 1921–1922.

For both the Scots and the Irish service in the Army was not, of course, primarily about political or national loyalties (in so far as motivations can be reconstructed); it was about earning a living, the opportunity to escape grinding local poverty, and to travel, when long-distance travel was still generally the preserve of the wealthy. The structure of the army, which was built upon county units, appealed to passionate regional identities. For the Irish the Army represented, again, a kind of liminality–a cultural frontier between an indigenous fighting tradition, strong local identities, and the union state: the Army helped to achieve a loose bond between Irish people and the Crown, softening some national asperities, although regimental and service loyalties and identities were certainly of much greater significance than any crude Unionist acculturation. For the Scots, too, the Army served as a means of embracing and engaging a variety of indigenous fighting traditions, most obviously that of the Highlands (which had been a hotbed of Jacobite insurgency): for the Scots, too, local identities were helpfully

reflected and augmented in the regimental structures of the Army. The differences between Scots and Irish in the 19th century lay in the fact that Irish
nationalism was able to provide an alternative focus for patriotic military
duty, through the Confederation of 1848 and its offspring, the Irish
Republican Brotherhood of 1858: moreover the cult of Scottish military
heroism within the Victorian Army was much more highly developed than
its Irish counterpart. The panoply of Scottish military dress—bonnets, tartans,
kilts—was also much more thoroughly elaborated than its Irish counterpart,
although the Irish certainly had their harps and Gaelic battle cries. In general, however, the Victorian Army celebrated a distinctive Scottish national
fighting tradition more effectively than its Irish equivalent.

The First World War reinforced both Scottish and Irish national identities
and loyalties. But by the end of the War this consolidation had very different
implications for the two neighbours. Irish sacrifice in the War had taken
place within the context of ongoing disputes over Irish self-government
and about the ways in which Irishmen would be organized, and Irishness
represented, within the Army. The 1916 Rising had been a cogent reminder
of the alternative Irish military tradition. The Irishness reinforced in the
trenches often fed into republican activism, and a minority of veterans took
their military skills into the ranks of the Irish Republican Army after 1919.
Scottish sacrifice, disproportionately great, took place within a relatively
stable constitutional and military framework: Scottish Home Rule was an
issue, but not pressing; while Scotland's position, and that of Scottishness,
within the Army was valued and secure. Scottish national identity was consolidated amidst the carnage of War; but this remained an identity which
could still be articulated within a union framework. The Scottish sacrifice
was commemorated in a National War Memorial at Edinburgh Castle, using
the iconography of union and monarchy. Scottish veterans were demobilized, not into the ranks of a Caledonian guerrilla movement, but (as often
as not) into the ranks of the unemployed. Though modern Scottish nationalism was born in the interwar era, Scottish unionism was also significantly
enhanced, just as it enjoyed a 'last hurrah' of electoral success in the years
after the Second World War.

In both Ireland and Scotland the embrace of the union state was growing
in the 19th and 20th centuries; but only Scotland, significantly, experienced
the full growth of those great binding agents of the United Kingdom,
nationalization and welfarism. The union state expanded significantly from
the late 19th century onwards, with an enlarged bureaucracy, and ever

greater pressures towards interference, regularity, and uniformity in the lives of citizens. One critical aspect of this was welfarism, building up from the legislative experiments of Asquith's government in the field of old age pensions, national insurance, and support for the unemployed. The second great advance of course came with the legislation of the Attlee government, and in particular with the creation of the National Health Service. If one of the binding agents of union was a bigger state, then one critical aspect of this was a uniform system of welfare support applied throughout the United Kingdom, and in effect involving the sponsorship of the richer areas of the union for those with fewer resources and greater poverty. There seems little doubt that this provision helped to ameliorate a range of political and economic difficulties, and to bolster the union: in Northern Ireland for example the Ulster Unionist Party (which was ideologically wary of interventionist welfare support) accepted the gamut of 'socialist' welfare provision partly in order to ensure continuing working class Protestant loyalty to the union and partition settlements. The reforms of the Asquith government came too late to exercise a powerful influence within the debate for Irish independence; and the absence of a welfare state in Ireland to match that of the British has been seen as a significant augmentation for partition, even with those who might otherwise have been disposed to support a unitary Irish state. In Scotland, industrial and imperial decline might have been thought to represent powerful arguments for constitutional change; but the provision of public housing and welfare support has been a factor in limiting electoral support for independence. Scotland, too, came to be bound by union in ways which did not touch Ireland before 1921, or even Northern Ireland: the drive towards nationalization in the post-war years had a particularly significant impact upon large sections of the Scottish industrial economy, including coal, steel, rail transportation, and energy production. By the Labour heyday of the 1960s major sections of the Scottish economy were owned and managed by the British state, which was therefore the employer of disproportionately large numbers of the Scottish people.

Successive British governments effectively bolstered union through the formulae by which tax revenues were distributed to the nations of the Kingdom. Successive governments sought to 'kill Home Rule by kindness' in both Ireland and Scotland, and one means by which this end was ultimately pursued rested with the Goschen formula of 1888. In Ireland Goschen underpinned the strategies of constructive unionism through which Conservative-led administrations sought to ameliorate social conditions, and more specifically to disconnect agrarian grievance from the nationalist movement.[23] Irish Home Rule was not in fact killed by kindness, partly because Goschen came too late in the history of the union to be politically useful, and partly because the sense of fiscal grievance in Ireland was too long-standing and too well-documented to be easily dispelled (Goschen was in fact rapidly succeeded, in the mid 1890s, by a bitter dispute between Irish politicians of all parties and the British state over the inequitable financial relations between Ireland and Great Britain).[24] However, though Goschen may not have saved the union between Britain and Ireland, the notion of using fiscal structures to bolster the union survived. Northern Ireland stood beyond the Goschen formula, but the finances of devolution rapidly became dependent upon the largesse of the union state, and on the willingness of British ministers to subsidize British standards of education and welfare within a devolved polity which could not otherwise afford them. And in Scotland, in the context of industrial decline and imperial disengagement, Goschen for long gave critical validation to the economic arguments in support of union.

Through welfarism and nationalization, through its use of the Goschen and Barnett funding formulae, through its reliance upon Scottish (and Welsh) MPs, the Labour Party developed into a powerful advocate of union. In both Scotland and Ireland numerous party organizations and structures upheld the union, and were bound (at least superficially) by many similarities. Scottish and Irish Unionism were in close and consistent communication in the Home Rule era, and were characterized by sometimes similar challenges and opportunities. For each the alliance between Conservatism and Liberal Unionism produced complex internal tensions, and for each the catastrophe of the Liberal success in 1906 stimulated significant local revival and reorganization. Each had a religious—Protestant and Orange—dimension to its electoral appeal. Each reflected and represented a wider and complex political culture. The establishment of partition, and with it the mutation of Ulster Unionism into a party of permanent government, meant that some of its similarities and connections with Scottish Unionism ceased to have the same significance as formerly. Ulster and Scottish Unionism have declined for different reasons and with different chronologies and different results: the Ulster Unionist Party held up well in the polls until the political turmoil of the early 1970s, and in particular the prorogation of Stormont in 1972, after which division and disorientation characterized the wider Unionist electorate. Scottish Unionism, however, reached a high point in the mid 1950s, after which (according to the taxonomy of David Seawright) a distinctive combination of factors—the leftward movement of the Scots electorate, a misjudged party reorganization and rebranding (as Conservatives) in 1965, and the loss of key aspects of party identity—all fed into its electoral demise.[25] One aspect of this decline was the increasingly attenuated connection between Scottish Unionism and its Ulster partner organization. But, in fact, a study of the records of the Party suggests that a loss of interest in Ireland was merely symptomatic of a wider intellectual disengagement, wherein the social activities of the local party were an end rather than a means, and where insensitive initiatives were imposed from England. There is a sense in which Unionism in Scotland in the 1960s was being stifled both by a locally cultivated epidemic of whist parties and by well-meaning outside interference and condescension.

But in particular ways mid-20th century Scotland resembled the party scene in mid-19th century Ireland, rather than in mid-20th century Ulster. In both places and times unionism was, broadly, the default position of national politics, and was a shared presumption across a broad swathe of the party spectrum: unionism, in other words, was much more than 'Unionism'. As has been argued, Labour, with its nationalization and welfare projects, was a much more powerful, certainly a more radical, unionist voice in Scottish politics than Scottish 'Unionism'. In Ireland, with the emergence of an aggressive and well-organized Home Rule movement in the 1870s and 1880s the effectively unionist consensus of Irish electoral politics was permanently overturned. In the Scotland of the 21st century, the electoral eclipse of the great party of union, Labour, at the Holyrood elections of 2007 and 2011, together with the continuing marginalization of the Scottish Conservatives and the successes of the SNP government, suggests that the effectively unionist consensus of Scottish politics has now been permanently overturned.


# Decline (and fall?)

The history of Ireland, Scotland, and union has been intertwined since at least the negotiations of 1706, and arguably for much longer—from the time that James VI and I's vision of British union and civilization was given tangible form in the Plantation of Ulster of 1609. Ireland and Scotland shared in the bloody Cromwellian experience of enforced parliamentary union; and the Irish political elite were jealously interested in the negotiations which produced the agreed

Union of 1707. This Scots union provided a template for the Irish Union of 1801. Through Home Rule and land legislation in the 1880s, Ireland provided a model for the revision of the union which was relevant to both the Irish and Scots. Defence of the Irish union was a shared priority within both Scots and Irish politics until 1921. The Stormont model of devolution provided an inspiration for Scottish nationalists in the Covenant movement after the Second World War. The debates over a federal constitution which raged in the decade before 1920, and which helped to produce partition and devolution in Northern Ireland, have also been relevant to both Scotland and Northern Ireland in the constitutional revisions of the late 1990s.[26] And yet, despite this symbiosis, no systematic effort has been made until now to compare the origins and experience of union in Ireland and Scotland, still less to use any such comparison to inform a discussion of contemporary history and politics.

The survival of the Scottish union since 1707 has illuminated (perhaps in dangerous ways) the condition of the relationship between Britain and Ireland: it illuminates the survival of the British-Irish union between 1801 and 1921. The (from the perspective of 1799) success of the Scottish union was a significant encouragement to the architects of the union with Ireland; indeed it is possible that the apparent completeness of this success may have blinded the unionists of 1799 into too great a reliance upon the Scottish precedent and too great a disregard for the specific challenges of the Irish case. As it was, while much of the wider context for the two unions was strikingly similar, and while there were similarities in the political arts deployed to ensure the passage of the two measures, in fact there were several ways in which the measure of 1801 was damagingly distinctive. Unlike the Scots Treaty of Union, the Irish measure was not the product of formal negotiation between two sovereign powers—it was an imposition by a sovereign over an effectively dependent kingdom; and the associated religious settlement was not 'fit for purpose'—if one of the purposes of union is defined as accommodating the spiritual and political aspirations of as many people as possible within the embrace of the settlement. The Scots union envisioned a variable religious geometry for Great Britain, while the Irish union incorporated the minority Church of Ireland into a uniform ecclesiastical establishment spanning the entire United Kingdom. Much of the subsequent history of union may be explained through these peculiarities of the Irish settlement.

How and why did the unions survive? Little of the literature on the United Kingdom is concerned to explain the longevity of the union set-

tlements, and little effort has been expended to discover whether the survival of the Scots union helps to illuminate the survival of its British-Irish
counterpart in the 19th century and beyond. For the Scots, the union was
sufficiently capacious and flexible to allow the flourishing of distinctive
Scottish institutions and patriotic sentiments. The institutions of union, or
those associated with union—parliament, the monarchy, the armed forces,
empire, and—later—welfarism—proved receptive and useful to the Scots,
and therefore served as buttresses to the union state. However, it is rarely
understood that most of these institutions were also relevant to the Irish in
the 19th century, and to some extent help to explain why the union
remained in place for 120 years in defiance of developing national sentiment and armed rebellion. For the Irish, the union was an inefficient but
by no means broken machine for reform and advancement: it permitted
the survival of a range of distinctive Irish institutions, although the problem was that for most of the 19th century these remained under the control of the Ascendancy interest, and thus did not function (as in Scotland)
as a means of reconciling the national sentiments of the majority population to the union state. Moreover, the very malleability of the Irish union
tended to encourage political expectations throughout the 19th century
which were often (as in the case of emancipation or Home Rule) partly or
wholly disappointed. For the Irish parliament, the monarchy, armed forces,
and empire were relevant to the survival of union in so far as each of these
complex institutions accommodated at least some Irish Catholics for some
of the time. Parliament provided a focus for a propertied political class,
whose economic interests frequently spanned the entire United Kingdom.
W.C. Lubenow has said of Gladstonian Home Rule that it succeeded in
accommodating Irish nationalism within a United Kingdom parliament
for thirty years.[27] The responsiveness of the monarchy to Irish Catholic
needs and sensitivities varied considerably; but on the whole the monarchy,
even a Protestant monarchy, held some appeal for Irish Catholics, although
there were certainly numerous missed opportunities for goodwill and reconciliation.[28] The empire created freedoms and opportunities for Catholic
middle-class ambition which were not available in an Ireland where
Ascendancy influence was still significant; although for some (like Antony
MacDonnell) the experience of imperial service only served to underline
the constrictions of union.

Why, then, did the unions fail? The Irish union failed because it could
neither permanently accommodate nor defuse a distinctive Irish national

sentiment. The institutions of union provided a partial and intermittent accommodation to Irish Catholic conviction and ambition; but the compromises demanded by the reconciliation of a Protestant monarchy, the vested interests of the Ascendancy, and the claims and rights of the Irish Catholic people, certainly stimulated some imaginative political action, but ultimately proved overwhelming. The obstacles to the success of union were overwhelming; but it still took the universal conflagration of 1914–1918 to bring down the 120-year-old edifice.

The pathology of Scottish failure appears to be somewhat different. The Scots union has survived thus far because it has, in fact, been able to contain and represent much Scottish national feeling. The institutions of union have provided a solid receptacle for Scots conviction and ambition; and the compromises demanded by the reconciliation of an Anglican monarchy, the vested interests of Scottish society, and the claims and rights of the Scottish people have proved manageable within the structures of union. Moreover, though seers who foretell the death of union are inclined to focus upon single issues such as empire or economic retreat, in reality the union (whatever its wider justice) has proved simultaneously flexible and sturdy— supported by a wide range of ostensibly solid institutions and relationships.

The Irish union, maimed from the start, limped to its death in the killing fields of the Great War. The Scots union has survived war, the death of empire and of British economic ascendancy. It has been upheld until now by a sympathetic and broadly popular monarchy, armed forces which are respectful towards Scottish national sensibilities and traditions, a welfare state which has provided for the victims of Scottish industrial decline, and a parliament in London which has simultaneously provided a forum for Scottish political ambition and relatively generous support (if not always imaginative leadership) for the Scottish people.

The threat to the Scots union at present lies not with a single conflagration (such as befell the Irish union with the Great War), but rather with the simultaneous failure of all of the props upon which it rests. The empire and industrial prosperity have indeed gone; but the embarrassing travails of monarchy, bitter conflicts over unpopular wars and regimental amalgamation and disbandment, the denationalization of state assets and industries, and the slow erosion both of a uniform national regime of welfare provision and of a beneficial fiscal funding formula are all taking their toll. As the Unionists of the Home Rule era predicted for Ireland, devolution has proved to be a starting point for Scottish national aspirations rather than a one-off settlement. As the unionist constitutional architects of the 1990s were unable to predict, devolution has proved to be a vehicle for the SNP, rather than a constraint.

One of the great props to the union settlement in the 20th century has been the effective unionist consensus binding the Scots Labour and Conservative parties. Another has been the capacity of Westminster to provide a platform for Scottish politicians. One of the great *threats* to the settlement in the early 21st century is now the effective free market consensus binding the two unionist parties. Another is the failure of a union government led by Scots to persuade the English people of its capacity to govern. With friends like these, the union clearly has no need of its nationalist enemies.

# *Endnotes*

CHAPTER I

1. C.Sanford Terry (ed.), *De Unione Regnorum Britanniae Tractatus by Sir Thomas Craig* (Edinburgh, 1909); Keith Brown, *Kingdom or Province? Scotland and the Regal Union 1603–1715* (London, 1992), p.78.
2. Daniel Szechi, *George Lockhart of Carnwath, 1681–1731: A Study in Jacobitism* (Edinburgh, 2002), pp.173–4.
3. Brown, *Kingdom or Province*, pp.79–80; Colin Kidd, *Union and Unionisms: Political Thought in Scotland, 1500–2000* (Cambridge, 2008), pp.42ff., 62.
4. Brown, *Kingdom or Province*, p.136.
5. P.H. Scott, *Andrew Fletcher and the Treaty of Union* (Edinburgh, 1992), pp.149–50.
6. Brian Levack, *The Formation of the British State: England, Scotland and the Union, 1603–1707* (Oxford, 1987), p.145.
7. See, e.g. Linda Colley, *Britons: Forging the Nation, 1707–1837* (New Haven, 1992).
8. Maurice Lee, *The 'Inevitable' Union and Other Essays on Modern Scotland* (Edinburgh, 2003), p.1.
9. A.T.Q. Stewart, *The Narrow Ground: Aspects of Ulster History, 1609–1969* (London, 1977), p.16. Personal knowledge.
10. Bruce Galloway, *The Union of England and Scotland, 1603–1608* (Edinburgh, 1986), p.61; Iain McLean and Alastair McMillan, *State of the Union: Unionism and the Alternatives to the United Kingdom* (Oxford, 2005), p.15.
11. See Colin Kidd, *Subverting Scotland's Past: Scottish Whig Historians and the Creation of an Anglo-British Identity, 1689–1830* (Cambridge, 1993).
12. Donald MacCartney, 'The Writing of History in Ireland, 1800–30', *Irish Historical Studies*, x, 40 (Sept. 1957), pp.352, 356–7.
13. Daniel Defoe, *The History of the Union between England and Scotland* (Dublin, 1799) [London, 1709], pp.21, 60.
14. Ebenezer Marshal, *History of the Union of Scotland and England* (Edinburgh, 1799), p.5.
15. NLS, Melville Papers, Ms.1051, f.5: John Bruce to Henry Dundas, 18. Aug. 1799.
16. John Bruce, *Report on the Events and Circumstances which produced the Union of the Kingdoms of England and Scotland* (London, 1799), pp.12, 184, 402.

17. See David Wilkinson, 'How did they pass the Union? Secret Service Expenditure', *History*, 82, 266 (April, 1997), pp.223–51; Douglas Kanter, *The Making of British Unionism, 1740–1848: Politics, Government and the Making of the Anglo-Irish Constitutional Relationship* (Dublin, 2009), p.79.

18. Discussed in H.J.Hanham, *Scottish Nationalism* (London, 1969), pp.86–90.

19. W.E. Gladstone, *Special Aspects of the Irish Question* (London, 1892), pp.136–86.

20. See Earl of Rosebery, *Pitt: Twelve English Statesmen* (London, 1891); Lord Ashbourne, *Pitt: Some Chapters of His Life and Times* (London, 1898).

21. British Library, Walter Long Papers, Add.Ms. 62409: MacNeill to Long, n.d.

22. Alexander MacRae, *Scotland, from the Treaty of Union with England to the Present Time* (London, 1908), p.1.

23. Peter Hume Brown, *The Legislative Union of England and Scotland* (Oxford, 1914), p.v.

24. Matthew Moulton, 'Anniversary of the Union', *Scotsman*, 22 April 1957.

25. John Robertson (ed.), *A Union for Empire: Political Thought and the Union of 1707* (Cambridge, 1995), p.xv.

26. See T.C. Smout, *Scottish Trade on the Eve of the Union* (Edinburgh, 1963); Rosalind Mitchison, *Lordship to Patronage: Scotland, 1603–1745* (Edinburgh, 1990).

27. P.W.J. Riley, *The Union of England with Scotland* (Manchester, 1978).

28. William Ferguson, *Scotland's Relations with England: A Survey to 1707* (Edinburgh, 1977).

29. See Ned Landsman, 'The Legacy of British Union for the North American Colonies: Provincial Elites and the Problem of Imperial Union' in John Robertson (ed.), *A Union for Empire: Political Thought and the Union of 1707* (Cambridge, 1995); J.G.A. Pocock, 'Empire, State and Confederation: The War of Independence as a Crisis in Multiple Monarchy' in John Robertson (ed.), *A Union for Empire: Political Thought and the Union of 1707* (Cambridge, 1995).

30. See T.M. Devine (ed.), *Scotland and the Union, 1707–2007* (Edinburgh, 2008); Michael Fry, *The Union: England, Scotland and the Treaty of 1707* (Edinburgh, 2007); Allan Macinnes, *Union and Empire: The Making of the United Kingdom in 1707* (Cambridge, 2007); Andrew MacKillop and Micheál Ó Siochrú (eds), *Forging the State: European State Formation and the Anglo-Scottish Union of 1707* (Dundee, 2008); P.H. Scott, *The Union of 1707: Why and How* (Edinburgh, 2006); Jeffrey Stephen, *Scottish Presbyterians and the Act of Union, 1707* (Edinburgh, 2007); Christopher Whatley, *The Scots and the Union* (Edinburgh, 2006).

31. See Keith Brown and Roland J. Tanner (eds), *The History of the Scottish Parliament 1: Parliament and Politics in Scotland, 1235–1560* (Edinburgh, 2004); Allan Macinnes, *Union and Empire: The Making of the United Kingdom in 1707* (Cambridge, 2007); Andrew MacKillop and Micheál Ó Siochrú (eds), *Forging the State: European State Formation and the Anglo-Scottish Union of 1707* (Dundee, 2008).

32. Ciarán Brady, '"Constructive and Instrumental": The Dilemma of Ireland's First "New Historians"', in Ciarán Brady (ed.), *Interpreting Irish History: The*

*Debate on Historical Revisionism, 1938–1994* (Dublin, 1994), pp.25–6; Ferguson, *Scotland's Relations with England*, p.181.

33. Brendan Bradshaw, 'Nationalism and Historical Scholarship in Modern Ireland', *Irish Historical Studies*, xxvi, 104 (November 1989), p. 341.

34. For the themes of class and sectarianism, see e.g. Michael Rosie, *The Sectarian Myth in Scotland: of Bitter Memory and Bigotry* (Basingstoke, 2004); Michael Rosie, 'Protestant Action and the Edinburgh Irish' in Martin Mitchell (ed.), *New Perspectives on the Irish in Scotland* (Edinburgh, 2008); Eric Kaufmann, 'The Orange Order in Scotland since 1860: A Social Analysis' in Martin Mitchell (ed.), *New Perspectives on the Irish in Scotland* (Edinburgh, 2008), p.159. Michael Keating, *The Independence of Scotland*, (Oxford, 2009), pp. 9–10.

35. http://www.scotland.gov.uk/News/This-Week/Speeches/First-Minister/dublin

36. *The Guardian*, 15 October 2009. There are twelve allusions to Parnell in David Torrance, *Salmond: Against the Odds* (Edinburgh, 2011): early in his career Salmond read R. Barry O'Brien's *Life of Charles Stewart Parnell*, 2 vols (London, 1898).

37. Kanter, *Making of British Unionism*, p.106.

38. Conrad Russell, 'Composite Monarchies in Early Modern Europe', in Alexander Grant and Keith Stringer (eds), *Uniting the Kingdom? The Making of British History* (London, 1995), p.134.

39. A.V. Dicey, 'The Two Acts of Union: A Contrast', *Fortnightly Review*, 30, 176 (Aug. 1881), p.168. This may have been inspired by J.A. Froude's comparison of the English conquests of Wales, Scotland and Ireland in his *The English in Ireland*, 3 vols [London, 1872-4], revised edition (London, 1881), I, pp.7–15.

40. Ibid., p.176.

41. Ibid., p.169.

42. Ibid., p.168.

43. Gladstone, *Special Aspects*, p.103.

44. Ibid., p.216.

45. Ibid., p.101. Kidd, *Union and Unionisms*, pp.161–3. See also John Hill Burton, *A History of the Reign of Queen Anne*, 3 vols (Edinburgh, 1880).

46. Gladstone, *Special Aspects*, p.101.

47. Duke of Argyll, *Irish Nationalism: An Appeal to History* (London, 1893), pp.49–50.

48. Kidd, *Union and Unionisms*, p.161.

49. See e.g. Charles Withers, *Urban Highlanders: Highland-Lowland Migration and Urban Gaelic Culture, 1700–1900* (East Linton, 1998).

50. Thomas Johnston, *Our Scots Noble Families* (Glasgow, 1909); Thomas Johnston, *History of the Working Classes in Scotland* (Glasgow, 1929).

51. See Sean Connolly, *Religion, Law and Power: The Making of Protestant Ireland, 1660–1760* (Oxford, 1992).

52. Patrick McNally, *Parties, Patriots and Undertakers: Parliamentary Politics in Early Hanoverian Ireland* (Dublin, 1997), p.31.

53. Earl of Dunraven, *The Outlook in Ireland: The Case for Devolution and Conciliation* (Dublin, 1907), pp.177–91.

54. Justin McCarthy, *The Reign of Queen Anne* (London, 1905 edition [1902]), pp.141–2.

55. Mathieson, *Scotland and the Union*, p.175.

56. Ron Weir, 'The Scottish and Irish Unions: The Victorian View in Perspective', in S.J. Connolly (ed.), *Kingdoms United? Great Britain and Ireland since 1500: Integration and Diversity* (Dublin, 1999), p.57.

57. Ibid., p.57. Compare McNally, *Parties, Patriots and Undertakers*, p.206.

58. Weir, 'Scottish and Irish Unions', p.59.

59. William Law Mathieson, *Scotland and the Union, 1695–1747* (Glasgow, 1905), p.178.

60. Levack, *Formation of the British State*, p.222; John Morrill in Alexander Grant and Keith Stringer (eds), *Uniting the Kingdom?*, p.172.

61. Russell, 'Composite Monarchies', pp.134–5.

62. Weir, 'Scottish and Irish Unions', pp.63, 65.

63. Graham Walker, *Intimate Strangers: Political and Cultural Interaction between Scotland and Ulster in Modern Times* (Edinburgh, 1995), Máirtin Ó Catháin, *Irish Republicanism in Scotland, 1858–1916: Fenians in Exile* (Dublin, 2007), are exceptions.

64. James Handley, *The Irish in Scotland, 1798–1845* (Cork, 1945); James Handley, *The Irish in Modern Scotland* (Cork, 1947); Louis Cullen and T.C. Smout (eds), *Comparative Aspects of Scottish and Irish Economic and Social History* (Edinburgh, 1977); T.M. Devine and David Dickson (eds), *Ireland and Scotland, 1600–1850: Parallels and Contrasts in Economic and Social Development* (Edinburgh, 1983); R.A. Morris and Liam Kennedy (eds), *Ireland and Scotland: Order and Disorder, 1600–2000* (Edinburgh, 2007); Martin J. Mitchell (ed.), *New Perspectives on the Irish in Scotland* (Edinburgh, 2008).

65. Julian Hoppit, *Parliaments, Nations and Identities in Britain and Ireland, 1660–1850* (Manchester, 2003), pp.15–47.

66. Kanter, *Making of British Unionism*, is a recent exception.

67. Correlli Barnett, *The Audit of War: The Illusion and Reality of Britain as a Great Nation* (London, 1986); Richard English and Michael Kenny (eds), *Rethinking British Decline* (London, 1999).

68. Michael Hechter, *Internal Colonialism: The Celtic Fringe in British National Development, 1536–1966* (London, 1975); Paul Ward, *Unionism in the United Kingdom, 1918–74* (London, 2005), p.9. Compare Walker, *Intimate Strangers* and Duncan Tanner, Chris Williams, Will Griffith, and Andrew Edwards (eds), *Debating Nationhood and Government in Britain, 1885–1939: Perspectives from the 'Four Nations'* (Manchester, 2007).

69. Hechter, *Internal Colonialism*, p.11.

70. Kanter, *Making of British Unionism*, pp.12–13.

71. Reginald Coupland, *Welsh and Scottish Nationalism: A Study* (London, 1954); Christopher Harvie, *Scotland and Nationalism: Scottish Society and Politics, 1707–1994*, second edition (London, 1994).

72. Gordon Donaldson, *Scotland's History: Approaches and Reflections* (Edinburgh, 1995) pp.118–35. For a critique of Donaldson as 'the last of the line' see Kidd, *Union and Unionisms*, pp.170–2.

73. Richard Pares, 'A Quarter Millennium of Anglo-Scottish Union', *History*, xxxix (1954), p.98.

74. David McCrone, *Understanding Scotland: The Sociology of a Stateless Nation* (London, 1992); David McCrone, 'W(h)ither the Union? Anglo-Scottish Relations in the 21st Century' in William L. Miller (ed.), *Anglo-Scottish Relations From 1900 to Devolution and Beyond* (Oxford. 2005).

75. See Iain McLean, 'Financing the Union: Goschen, Barnett and Beyond' in Miller (ed), *Anglo-Scottish Relations*; Keating, *Independence of Scotland*, pp. 17–44.

76. T.M. Devine (ed.), *Conflict and Stability in Scottish Society, 1700–1850: Proceedings of the Scottish Historical Studies Seminar, University of Strathclyde, 1988–89* (Edinburgh, 1990), pp.1–30, 51–63, 83–105.

77. Geoffrey Crossick, *An Artisan Elite in Victorian Society: Kentish Town, 1840–80* (London, 1978); R.Q. Gray, *The Labour Aristocracy in Victorian Edinburgh* (Oxford, 1976); Brian Harrison, *Peaceable Kingdom* (Oxford, 1982), pp. 309–77.

78. Ross McKibbin, *The Ideologies of Class: Social Relations in Britain, 1880–1950* (Oxford, 1990), pp.1–41.

79. Ibid., p.24.

80. Ibid., p.25.

81. Graeme Morton, *Unionist Nationalism: Governing Urban Scotland, 1830–60* (East Linton, 1999). See also James Livesey, *Civil Society and Empire: Ireland and Scotland in the Eighteenth Century Atlantic World* (New Haven, 2009).

82. Hechter, *Internal Colonialism*, p.166.

83. For example, Donaldson, *Scotland's History*.

84. For example, Norman Davies, *The Isles: A History* (London, 1999); Hugh Kearney, *The British Isles: A History of Four Nations* (Cambridge, 1989).

85. Coupland, *Welsh and Scottish Nationalism*.

86. Julian Hoppit, *A Land of Liberty? England, 1689–1727* (Oxford, 2000), p.243.

87. Brendan Bradshaw, 'The Tudor Reformation and Revolution in Wales and Ireland: The Origins of the British Problem' in Brendan Bradshaw and John Morrill (eds), *The British Problem, 1534–1707: State Formation in the Atlantic Archipelago* (London, 1996), pp.66–88; Ciarán Brady, 'Comparable histories? Tudor Reform in Ireland and Wales' in Steven Ellis and Sarah Barber (eds), *Conquest and Union: Fashioning a British State* (Harlow, 1995), pp.64–86; http://www.ahrc. ac.uk/ Funded Research/ Case Studies/ Pages/ irelandwalesresearchnetwork)

88. Though see Walker, *Intimate Strangers*.

89. Compare David Seawright, *An Important Matter of Principle: The Decline of the Scottish Conservative and Unionist Party* (Ashgate, 1999).

CHAPTER 2

1. William Ferguson, *Scotland's Relations with England: A Survey to 1707* (Edinburgh, 1977); Richard Pares, 'A Quarter Millennium of Anglo-Scottish Union', *History*, xxxix (1954), pp.84–5.

2. Charles Sanford Terry (ed.), *The Cromwellian Union: Papers relating to the Negotiations of an Incorporating Union between England and Scotland, 1651–52* (Edinburgh, 1902); T.C. Barnard, *Cromwellian Ireland* (Oxford, 1975); Frances Dow, *Cromwellian Scotland, 1651–1660* (Edinburgh, 1979); R. Scott Spurlock, *Cromwell and Scotland: Conquest and Religion* (Edinburgh, 2007).

3. Colin Kidd, *Union and Unionisms: Political Thought in Scotland, 1500–2000* (Cambridge, 2008), pp.81–133.

4. John R Young, 'The Scottish Parliament and the Covenanting Tradition: The Emergence of a Scottish Commons' in John R. Young (ed.), *Celtic Dimensions of the British Civil Wars* (Edinburgh, 1997), p.164.

5. Keith Brown and Roland J. Tanner (eds), *The History of the Scottish Parliament 1: Parliament and Politics in Scotland, 1235–1560* (Edinburgh, 2004), pp.3, 8; Robert Rait, *The Parliaments of Scotland* (Glasgow, 1924), pp.3, 127n.

6. Brown and Tanner (eds), *Scottish Parliament*, pp.10–11; Rait, *Parliaments*, p.19; Michael Penman, *David II* (Edinburgh, 2005)

7. Brown and Tanner (eds), *Scottish Parliament*, p.12.

8. Brian Farrell (ed.), *The Irish Parliamentary Tradition* (Dublin, 1973), p.43.

9. A.V. Dicey and Robert S. Rait, *Thoughts on the Union between England and Scotland* (London, 1920), pp.23, 345.

10. John R Young, *The Scottish Parliament 1639–61: A Political and Constitutional Analysis* (Edinburgh, 1996); Brown and Tanners (eds), *Scottish Parliament*; Keith Brown and Alastair J. Mann (eds), *The History of the Scottish Parliament 2: Parliament and Politics in Scotland, 1567–1707* (Edinburgh, 2005).

11. Farrell (ed.), *Irish Parliamentary Tradition*, pp.69–70; James Kelly, *Poynings' Law and the Making of Law in Ireland: Monitoring the Constitution* (Dublin, 2007)

12. Farrell (ed.), *Irish Parliamentary Tradition*, p.78; Brendan Bradshaw, *The Irish Constitutional Revolution of the Sixteenth Century* (Cambridge, 1979).

13. Brown and Tanner (eds), *Scottish Parliament*, pp.22, 159.

14. Roger Mason (ed.), *Scots and Britons: Scottish Political Thought and the Union of 1603* (Cambridge, 1994), p.161; Brown and Tanner (eds), *Scottish Parliament*, p.23.

15. Brown and Tanner (eds), *Scottish Parliament*, pp.14, 19.

16. Ibid., pp.34, 101–37.

17. Jenny Wormald (ed.), *Scotland: A History* (Oxford, 2005), p.158.

18. Brown and Tanner (eds), *Scottish Parliament*, pp.37, 52, 138–62.

19. Rait, *Parliament*, pp.95–101; Young, *Scottish Parliament*; Young (ed.), *Celtic Dimensions*, pp.164–181; Edith Thomson, *The Parliament of Scotland, 1690–1702* (Oxford, 1929), pp.1–3.

20. Aidan Clarke, 'Patrick Darcy and the Constitutional Relationship between Ireland and Britain', in Jane Ohlmeyer (ed.), *Political Thought in Seventeenth Century Ireland: Kingdom or Colony?* (Cambridge, 2000), p.35.

21. Farrell (ed.), *Irish Parliamentary Tradition*, p.115; Thomas Bartlett, *Ireland* (Cambridge, 2010), p.122.

22. C.P. Meehan, *The Confederation of Kilkenny*, new edition (Dublin, 1905); Thomas Davis, *The Patriot Parliament of 1689: With Its Statutes, Votes and Proceedings*, third edition (London, 1893).

23. Daniel Szechi, *George Lockhart of Carnwath, 1681–1731: A Study in Jacobitism* (Edinburgh, 2002), pp.46–7.

24. Charles Sanford Terry, *The Scottish Parliament: Its Constitution and Procedure, 1603–1707* (Glasgow, 1905), pp.103–20; Brown and Tanner (eds), *Scottish Parliament*, p.28.

25. Brown and Tanner (eds), *Scottish Parliament*, p.28.

26. *Ibid.* pp.28–9.

27. Reviewed in Kelly, *Poynings' Law*.

28. David Hayton, 'The Beginnings of the "Undertaker System"', in Thomas Bartlett and David Hayton (eds), *Penal Era and Golden Age: Essays in Irish History, 1690–1800* (Belfast, 1979), pp.32–54; Patrick McNally, *Parties, Patriots and Undertakers: Parliamentary Politics in Early Hanoverian Ireland* (Dublin, 1997), pp.118–47; Eoin Magennis, *The Irish Political System, 1740–65: The Golden Age of the Undertakers* (Dublin, 2000), pp.17ff.

29. Thomas Bartlett, 'The Townshend Viceroyalty, 1767–72', in Bartlett and Hayton (eds), *Penal Era and Golden Age*, pp.88–112; Magennis, *Irish Political System*, pp.195–7.

30. Bradshaw, *Irish Constitutional Revolution*.

31. John Morrill, 'Three Kingdoms and One Commonwealth: The Enigma of Mid-Seventeenth Century Britain and Ireland', in Alexander Grant and Keith Stringer (eds), *Uniting the Kingdom? The Making of British History* (London, 1995), p.172.

32. Ciarán Brady, *The Chief Governors: The Rise and Fall of Reform Government in Tudor Ireland, 1536–88* (Cambridge, 1994); Thomas Bartlett, *Ireland* (Cambridge, 2010), pp.80–2.

33. Kidd, *Union and Unionisms*, p.44.

34. Roger Mason (ed.), *Scots and Britons: Scottish Political Thought and the Union of 1603* (Cambridge, 1994), pp.161–86.

35. See William Ferguson, *Scotland's Relations with England: A Survey to 1707* (Edinburgh, 1977).

36. Bruce Galloway, *The Union of England and Scotland, 1603–1608* (Edinburgh, 1986), p.74.

37. Galloway, *Union*, p.166; Wormald (ed.), *Scotland: A History*, p.164; Andrew Nicholls, *The Jacobean Union: A Reconsideration of British Civil Policies under the Early Stuarts* (Westport, 1999).

38. Conrad Russell, 'Composite Monarchies in Early Modern Europe' in Grant and Stringer (eds), *Uniting the Kingdoms*, p.139; Brian Levack, *The Formation of the British State: England, Scotland and the Union, 1603–1707* (Oxford, 1987), pp.60–1.

39. Quoted e.g. in Ferguson, *Scotland's Relations*, p.100; David Daiches, *Scotland and the Union* (London, 1977), p.15.

40. Galloway, *Union*, p.60; Daiches, *Scotland and the Union*, p.17; Jenny Wormald, 'The Union of 1603' in Mason (ed.), *Scots and Britons*, p.37.

41. Jenny Wormald, 'The Union of 1603' in Roger Mason (ed.), *Scots and Britons: Scottish Political Thought and the Union of 1603* (Cambridge, 1994), pp.19–20.

42. Keith Brown, 'The Vanishing Emperor: British Kingship and its Decline, 1603–1707' in Mason (ed.), *Scots and Britons*, p.61.

43. Ibid., p.82.

44. Nicholas Canny, *Making Ireland British, 1580–1650* (Oxford, 2001), p.195; John McCavitt, *The Flight of the Earls* (Dublin, 2002).

45. Canny, *Making Ireland British*, p.198.

46. Christopher Whatley, *The Scots and the Union* (Edinburgh, 2006), p.85.

47. Jane Ohlmeyer, 'Introduction: For God, King or Country? Political Thought and Culture in Seventeenth Century Ireland', in Jane Ohlmeyer (ed.), *Political Thought in Seventeenth Century Ireland: Kingdom or Colony?* (Cambridge, 2000), pp.15–16, 196–7.

48. Galloway, *Union*, p.17. See also Maurice Lee, *Government by Pen: Scotland under James VI and I* (Urbana, Ill., 1980).

49. Ferguson, *Scotland's Relations*, p.107.

50. Galloway, *Union*, p.170.

51. Russell, 'Composite Monarchies', p.146.

52. Ibid., p.145.

53. Morrill, 'Three kingdoms', in Grant and Stringer (eds), *Uniting the Kingdom?*, p.173.

54. See Colin Kidd, *Union and Unionisms: Political Thought in Scotland, 1500–2000* (Cambridge, 2008).

55. Alvin Jackson, *Home Rule: An Irish History, 1800–2000*, paperback edition (London, 2004), pp.373–82; Levack, *Formation of the British State*; G.W.T. Omond, *The Early History of the Scottish Union Question*, bicentenary edition (London, 1906).

56. Ferguson, *Scotland's Relations*, p.133; Maurice Lee, 'Scotland, the Union, and the Idea of a "General Crisis"' in Mason (ed.), *Scots and Britons*, p.53.

57. John Robertson (ed.), *A Union for Empire: Political Thought and the Union of 1707* (Cambridge, 1995), p.xix. See, however, Allan Macinnes, *Union and Empire: The Making of the United Kingdom in 1707* (Cambridge, 2007), pp.80–5; Omond, *Early History*, pp.122–47.

58. Levack, *Formation of the British State*, p.151.

59. Kidd, *Union and Unionisms*, p.61.

60. Sarah Barber, 'Scotland and Ireland under the Commonwealth: A Question of Loyalty' in Steven Ellis and Sarah Barber (eds), *Conquest and Union: Fashioning a British State, 1485–1725* (Harlow, 1995), p.219.

61. R. Scott Spurlock, *Cromwell and Scotland*, p.199.

62. Canny, *Making Ireland British*, p.552.

63. See Micheál Ó Siochrú, *God's Executioner: Oliver Cromwell and the Conquest of Ireland* (London, 2008).

64. Patrick Little, *Lord Broghill and the Cromwellian Union with Ireland and Scotland* (London, 2004), p.122.

65. Dow, *Cromwellian Scotland*.

66. Daiches, *Scotland and the Union*, p.30; Spurlock, *Cromwell*, p.199.

67. Maurice Lee, *The 'Inevitable' Union and Other Essays on Modern Scotland* (Edinburgh, 2003), p.11; Little, *Broghill*, pp.91–123.

68. Colin Kidd, 'Scotland and the Three Unions', in T.C. Smout (ed.), *Anglo-Scottish Relations from 1603 to 1900* (Oxford, 2005), p.184.

69. James Black, *Around the Guns: Sundays in Camp* (Edinburgh, n.d. [1916]), p.22. I am grateful to Owen Dudley Edwards for the point about Carlyle.

70. e.g. Ferguson, *Scotland's Relations*, p.138.

71. Quoted in Daiches, *Scotland and the Union*, p.31.

72. Sir John Clerk of Penicuik, *History of the Union of Scotland and England* (edited and translated by Douglas Duncan) (Edinburgh, 1993), p.79.

73. Patrick Little, 'The First Unionists? Irish Protestant Attitudes to Union with England, 1653–59', *Irish Historical Studies*, 31, 125 (May, 2000); Patrick Little, *Lord Broghill and the Cromwellian Union with Ireland and Scotland* (London, 2004), pp.238–9.

74. T.C. Barnard, 'The Uses of 23 October 1641 and Irish Protestant Celebrations', *English Historical Review*, 106, 421 (1991); Canny, *Making Ireland British*, p.575.

75. Christopher Whatley, *The Scots and the Union*, p.5; see also P.W.J. Riley, *The Union of England and Scotland* (Manchester, 1978).

76. P.W.J. Riley, *King William and the Scottish Politicians* (Edinburgh, 1979), pp.48–53; P.H. Scott, *Andrew Fletcher and the Treaty of Union* (Edinburgh, 1992), pp.44ff.

77. Ferguson, *Scotland's Relations*, p.171; Scott, *Andrew Fletcher*, pp.44–6, 103. For a recent discussion of Fletcher's complex outlook see Kidd, *Union and Unionisms*, pp.70–2.

78. Riley, *King William*, p.52.

79. *Ibid.* p.53; Clerk, *History of the Union*, p.81.

80. Clerk, *History of the Union*, p.81.

81. James I McGuire, 'The Irish Parliament of 1692', in Bartlett and Hayton (eds), *Penal Era and Golden Age*, pp.1–31; Hayton, 'Undertaker System', in Bartlett and Hayton (eds), *Penal Era and Golden Age*, pp 32–54.

82. William Molyneux, *The Case of Ireland being bound by Acts of Parliament in England Stated* [Dublin, 1698], edited and introduced by J.G. Simms (Dublin, 1977), p.84.

83. J.R. Hill, 'Ireland without Union: Molyneux and his Legacy' in John Robertson (ed.), *A Union for Empire: Political Thought and the Union of 1707* (Cambridge, 1995), p.287; Macinnes, *Union and Empire*, p.128.

84. Macinnes, *Union and Empire*, p.130.

85. Quoted in Ferguson, *Scotland's Relations*, p.199.

86. See e.g. Anon ['Thistledown'/Charles Waddie], *The Treaty of Union between Scotland and England with an Historical Introduction* (Edinburgh, 1883); Charles Waddie, *How Scotland Lost Her Parliament, and What Came of it* (Edinburgh, 1891).

87. W.E.H. Lecky, *Historical and Political Essays* (London, 1908), p.75.

88. A.V. Dicey, 'The Two Acts of Union: A Contrast', *Fortnightly Review*, 30, 176 (Aug. 1881), p.177; cf. S.J. Connolly, 'Varieties of Britishness: Ireland, Scotland and Wales in the Hanoverian State', in Alexander Grant and Keith Stringer (eds), *Uniting the Kingdom?*, p.196.

89. Ferguson, *Scotland's Relations*, p.188.

90. Macinnes, *Union and Empire*, p.271.

91. Wormald, *Scotland: A History*, p.168.

## CHAPTER 3

1. William Law Mathieson, 'The Scottish and the Irish Union' in P. Hume Brown (ed.), *The Union of 1707: A Survey of Events* (Glasgow, 1907), p.175.

2. Patrick Little, *Lord Broghill and the Cromwellian Union with Ireland and Scotland* (London, 2004).

3. Christopher Whatley, *The Scots and the Union* (Edinburgh, 2006), p.125.

4. William Ferguson, *Scotland's Relations with England: A Survey to 1707* (Edinburgh, 1977), pp.153–4, 180–2, referring to T.C. Smout, *Scottish Trade on the Eve of the Union* (Edinburgh, 1963).

5. e.g. in fact Smout, *Scottish Trade*, p.278.

6. e.g. T.M. Devine, *The Tobacco Lords: A Study of the Tobacco Merchants of Glasgow and their Trading Activities, 1740–90* (Edinburgh, 1975); T.M. Devine, *The Scottish Nation, 1700–2000* (London, 1999), p.52.

7. Devine, *Scottish Nation*, p.53.

8. See Karen Cullen, *Famine in Scotland: The 'Ill Years' of the 1690s* (Edinburgh, 2010); Philipp Robinson Rossner, *Scottish Trade in the Wake of Union, 1700–1760* (Stuttgart, 2008).

9. cf. T.M. Devine, *The Great Highland Famine: Hunger, Emigration and the Scottish Highlands in the Nineteenth Century* (Edinburgh, 1988); Cullen, *Famine in Scotland*.

10. James Mackinnon, *The Union of England with Scotland* (London, 1896), p.19.

11. Douglas Watt, *Price of Scotland: Darien, Union and the Wealth of Nations* (Edinburgh, 2007), pp.24–5; see also G.P. Insh, *Scottish Colonial Schemes, 1620–1686* (Glasgow, 1922).

12. Ferguson, *Scotland's Relations*, p.177.

13. Devine, *Scottish Nation*, p.52.

14. Watt, *Price of Scotland*, p.24.

15. *Ibid.* pp.97, 109–10; Whatley, *Scots and the Union*, p.169.

16. Watt, *Price of Scotland*, pp.136–7.

17. *Ibid.* pp.114, 105–16.

18. *Ibid.* p.271.

19. *Ibid.* pp.155–6.

20. e.g. Watt, *Price of Scotland*, pp.xviii, 251–4.

21. Whatley, *Scots and the Union*, p.166.

22. Rosalind Mitchison, *Lordship to Patronage: Scotland, 1603–1745* (Edinburgh, 1990 edition), p.125.

23. See Iain McLean and Alistair McMillan, *State of the Union: Unionism and the Alternatives in the United Kingdom since 1707* (Oxford, 2005).

24. Brian Levack, *The Formation of the British State, 1603–1707* (Oxford, 1987), p.221.

25. Ferguson, *Scotland's Relations*, p.199.

26. Levack, *Formation of the British State*, pp.216, 220.

27. Whatley, *Scots and the Union*, p.87.

28. *Ibid.* p.235; Ferguson, *Scotland's Relations*, p.250; Daniel Szechi (ed.), *Letters of George Lockhart of Carnwath, 1698–1732* (Edinburgh, 1989).

29. *Ibid.* pp.32–4.

30. See Andrew MacKillop, *More Fruitful than the Soil: Army, Empire and the Scottish Highlands, 1715–1815* (Edinburgh, 2000).

31. Quoted in Sir John Clerk of Penicuik, *History of the Union of Scotland and England* (edited and translated by Douglas Duncan) (Edinburgh, 1993), p.115.

32. Whatley, *Scots and the Union*, p.230.

33. Clerk of Penicuik, *History of the Union*, p.186.

34. See Alvin Jackson, *Home Rule: An Irish History, 1800–2000*, paperback edition (London, 2004), pp.123–64.

35. Smout, *Scottish Trade*, p.260.

36. Ferguson, *Scotland's Relations*, p.245.

37. Smout, *Scottish Trade*, p.260.

38. cf. Allan Macinnes, *Union and Empire: The Making of the United Kingdom in 1707* (Cambridge, 2007), p.272; Watt, *Price of Scotland*, p.236. For a summary of the contrary case see Paul Henderson Scott, *Andrew Fletcher and the Treaty of Union* (Edinburgh, 1992), pp.148–50.

39. Ferguson, *Scotland's Relations*, p.199. See P.W.J. Riley, *The Union of England and Scotland* (Manchester, 1978).

40. Riley, *Union*, p.8.

41. Charles Sanford Terry, *The Scottish Parliament: Its Constitution and Procedure, 1603–1707* (Glasgow, 1905), pp.103–20.

42. William Law Mathieson, *Scotland and the Union, 1695–1747* (Glasgow, 1905), p.157; William Law Mathieson, 'The Scottish and the Irish Union' in P.Hume Brown (ed.), *The Union of 1707*, p.176.

43. Daniel Szechi, *George Lockhart of Carnwath, 1681–1731: A Study in Jacobitism* (Edinburgh, 2002), pp.87–9.

44. Riley, *Union*, p.8.

45. Macinnes, *Union and Empire*, pp.67–94. See also Allan Macinnes, 'Union failed, union accomplished: the Irish union of 1703 and the Scottish union of 1707', Daire Keogh and Kevin Whelan (eds), *Acts of Union: The Causes, Contexts and Consequences of the Act of Union* (Dublin, 2001).

46. Douglas Kanter, *The Making of British Unionism, 1740–1848: Politics, Government and the Anglo-Irish Constitutional Relationship* (Dublin, 2009), pp.24–5.

47. Kanter, *Making of British Unionism*, p.35.

48. James Kelly, 'The Origins of the Act of Union: An Examination of Unionist Opinion in Britain and Ireland, 1650–1800', *Irish Historical Studies*, 25 (1987); James Kelly, 'The Act of Union: Its Origins and Background' in Daire Keogh and Kevin Whelan (eds), *Acts of Union*, pp.56–7.

49. Cormac Ó Gráda, *Ireland: A New Economic History, 1789–1939* (Oxford, 1994), pp.43–4.

50. Quoted in Michael Fry, *The Dundas Despotism*, paperback edition (Edinburgh, 2004), p.64.

51. See e.g. Daniel Mansergh, *Grattan's Failure: Parliamentary Opposition and the People in Ireland, 1779–1800* (Dublin 2005).

52. Kelly, 'Act of Union', p.58.

53. Kanter, *Making of British Unionism*, pp.50–8.

54. Kelly, 'Act of Union', p.59.

55. Stephen Small, *Political Thought in Ireland, 1776–1798: Republicanism, Patriotism and Radicalism* (Oxford, 2002), p.46.

56. Ó Gráda, *Ireland: A New Economic History*, p.6.

57. *Ibid.* p.273.

58. Quoted in O Grada, *Ireland: A New Economic History*, p.4.

59. See David W Miller (ed.), *Peep O'Day Boys and Defenders: Selected Documents on the County Armagh Disturbances, 1784–1796* (Belfast, 1990).

60. See Thomas Bartlett, 'An End to Moral Economy: The Militia Riots of 1793', *Past & Present*, 99 (May 1983); Thomas Bartlett, *The Fall and Rise of the Irish Nation: The Catholic Question, 1690–1830* (Dublin, 1992).

61. Smout, *Scottish Trade*, p.278.

62. Ó Gráda, *Ireland: A New Economic History*, pp.307–8.

63. See George O'Brien, *The Economic History of Ireland in the Eighteenth Century* (Dublin, 1918); George O'Brien, *The Economic History of Ireland from the Union to the Famine* (Dublin, 1921).

64. See Macinnes, *Union and Empire*.

65. Thomas Bartlett, 'Defence, Counter-Insurgency and Rebellion: Ireland, 1793–1803' in Thomas Bartlett and Keith Jeffery (eds), *A Military History of Ireland* (Cambridge, 1996), p.248.

66. Quoted in Fry, *Dundas Despotism*, p.170. See also Elaine McFarland, *Ireland and Scotland in the Age of Revolution* (Edinburgh, 1994) for an overview of these linkages.

67. See Nancy Curtin, *The United Irishmen: Popular Politics in Ulster and Dublin, 1791–98* (Oxford, 1994).

68. Bartlett, 'Defence, Counter-Insurgency and Rebellion', p.247.

69. Quoted in Gillian O'Brien, 'Camden and the move towards union, 1795–1798', Daire Keogh and Kevin Whelan (eds), *Acts of Union*, p.119.

70. O'Brien, 'Camden and the move towards union', p.121.

71. Earl of Dunraven, *The Finances of Ireland before the Union and After: An Historical Study* (London, 1912), p.43.

72. Whatley, *Scots and the Union*, p.58.

73. Fry, *Dundas Despotism*, p.70.

74. Bartlett, 'Defence, Counter-Insurgency and Rebellion', p.247.

75. See Whatley, *Scots and the Union*.

76. James Kelly, *Henry Flood: Patriots and Politics in Eighteenth Century Ireland* (Dublin, 1998)

77. Kelly, 'Act of Union', p.60.

78. Fry, *Dundas Despotism*, p.178.

79. Quoted in Bartlett, 'Defence, Counter-Insurgency and Rebellion', p.253.

80. Kelly, 'Act of Union', p.62; cf. Small, *Political Thought in Ireland*, p.210.

81. Kelly, Act of Union', p.63.

82. Mathieson, *Scotland and the Union*, p.157; Mathieson, 'The Scottish and the Irish Union', p.176.

83. Small, *Political Thought in Ireland*, p.210.

84. Quoted in Kelly, 'Act of Union', p.62. See also P.W.J. Riley, *King William and the Scottish Politicians* (Edinburgh, 1979).

85. cf. Mansergh, *Grattan's Failure*, pp.4–5.

86. cf. Szechi (ed.), *Letters of George Lockhart*, p.19, where Lockhart deploys the same analogy regarding one of the architects of the 1707 Union, the second Duke of Argyll.

## CHAPTER 4

1. Stephen Small, *Political Thought in Ireland, 1776–1798: Republicanism, Patriotism and Radicalism* (Oxford, 2002), p.46.

2. Peter Hume Brown (ed.), *Letters Relating to Scotland in the Reign of Queen Anne by James Ogilvy, First Earl of Seafield and Others* (Edinburgh, 1915), p.87.

3. Hume Brown (ed.), *Letters Relating to Scotland*, p.101; Iain McLean and Alastair McMillan, *State of the Union: Unionism and the Alternatives in the United Kingdom since 1707* (Oxford, 2005), p.27.

4. See e.g. McLean and McMillan, *State of the Union*, pp.14–15.

5. Daniel Szechi, *George Lockhart of Carnwath, 1681–1731: A Study in Jacobitism* (Edinburgh, 2002), p.60.

6. Sir John Clerk of Penicuik, *History of the Union of Scotland and England* (edited and translated by Douglas Duncan) (Edinburgh, 1993), p.5.

7. Hume Brown (ed.), *Letters Relating to Scotland*, pp.45–6; Ferguson, *Scotland's Relations with England: A Survey to 1707* (Edinburgh, 1977), p.226.

8. Hume Brown (ed.), *Letters Relating to Scotland*, p.96, n.1.

9. See McLean and McMillan, *State of the Union* , pp.58–9.

10. See Matthew Glozier, 'The Earl of Melfort, the Court Catholic Party, and the Foundation of the Order of the Thistle, 1687', *Scottish Historical Review*, 79, 2 (October, 2000) for an earlier, Catholic, revival of the Order.

11. Hume Brown (ed.), *Letters Relating to Scotland*, pp.180–1

12. Quoted in Ferguson, *Scotland's Relations*, p.248.

13. Christopher Whatley, *The Scots and the Union* (Edinburgh, 2006), p.302.

14. Patrick Geoghegan, *The Irish Act of Union: A Study in High Politics, 1798–1801* (Dublin, 1999), p.120.

15. McLean and McMillan, *State of the Union*, p.30.

16. Quoted in Ferguson, *Scotland's Relations*, p.248.

17. Whatley, *Scots and the Union*, p.268.

18. McLean and McMillan, *State of the Union*, p.43.

19. Ferguson, *Scotland's Relations*, p.201; Allan Macinnes, *Union and Empire: The Making of the United Kingdom in 1707* (Cambridge, 2007), p.95.

20. Daniel Szechi (ed.), *Letters of George Lockhart of Carnwath, 1698–1732* (Edinburgh, 1989), p.31.

21. McLean and McMillan, *State of the Union*, p.45. See also Philipp Robinson Rossner, *Scottish Trade in the Wake of Union, 1700–1760* (Stuttgart, 2008).

22. Whatley, *Scots and the Union*, p.330.

23. Szechi (ed.), *Letters of George Lockhart*, p.33; Macinnes, *Union and Empire*, p.282. Compare Douglas Watt, *Price of Scotland: Darien, Union and the Wealth of Nations* (Edinburgh, 2007), p.221.

24. Macinnes, *Union and Empire*, p.320.

25. *Ibid.* p.320.

26. Ferguson, *Scotland's Relations*, p.188.

27. Alvin Jackson, *Ireland 1798–1998: War, Peace and Beyond*, second edition (Oxford, 2010), p.262.

28. Szechi (ed.), *Letters of George Lockhart*, p.31.

29. Ferguson, *Scotland's Relations*, p.235.

30. Macinnes, *Union and Empire*, p.320; Whatley, *Scots and the Union*, p.331; Watt, *Price of Scotland*, p.240.

31. Whatley, *Scots and the Union*, p.330.

32. McLean and McMillan, *State of the Union*, p.33.

33. Hume Brown (ed.), *Letters Relating to Scotland*, p.96.

34. William Law Mathieson, *Scotland and the Union, 1695–1747* (Glasgow, 1905), p.155.

35. Charles Ross, *Correspondence of Charles, First Marquess of Cornwallis*, three vols (London, 1859), ii, p.440; Sir Archibald Alison, *Lives of Lord Castlereagh and Sir Charles Stewart, Second and Third Marquesses of Londonderry. With Annals of Contemporary Events in Which They Bore a Part. From the Original Papers of the Family*, three vols (Edinburgh, 1861), i, p.83; Small, *Political Thought*, p.210.

36. G.C. Bolton, *The Passing of the Irish Act of Union: A Study in Parliamentary Politics* (Oxford, 1966), p.186.

37. e.g. Jonah Barrington, *The Rise and Fall of the Irish Nation: A Full Account of the Bribery and Corruption by which the Union was Carried* (Dublin, 1833).

38. See J.G. Swift MacNeill, *Titled Corruption: The Sordid Origins of some Irish Peerages* (London, 1894).

39. Geoghegan, *Irish Act of Union*, p.56.

40. See e.g. A.M. Sullivan, *The Story of Ireland* (Dublin, 1867) and the commentary by R.F. Foster, *The Irish Story: Telling Tales and Making it Up in Ireland* (London, 2001).

41. W.E.H. Lecky, *History of Ireland in the Eighteenth Century*, five vols (London, 1892), v, p.289.

42. James Mackinnon, *The Union of England and Scotland* (London, 1896); G.W.T. Omond, *The Early History of the Scottish Union Question*, [Edinburgh, 1897] bicentenary edition (Edinburgh, 1906); Robert S. Rait, *An Outline of the Relations between England and Scotland (500–1707)* (London, 1901); William Law Mathieson, *Scotland and the Union, 1695–1747* (Glasgow, 1905); Peter Hume Brown (ed.), *The Union of 1707: A Survey of Events* (Glasgow, 1907); Peter Hume Brown, *The Legislative Union of England and Scotland* (Oxford, 1914).

43. Hume Brown, *Legislative Union*, pp.126–7; cf Paul Henderson Scott, *Andrew Fletcher and the Treaty of Union* (Edinburgh, 1992), pp.vi–vii.

44. Mathieson, *Scotland and the Union*, p.157.

45. Thomas Dunbar Ingram, *History of the Legislative Union of Great Britain and Ireland* (London, 1887); Thomas Dunbar Ingram, *A Critical Examination of Irish History*, two volumes, [London, 1900] reissue (London, 1904); Caesar Litton Falkiner, *Essays in Irish History and Biography, Mainly of the Eighteenth Century* (London, 1902); John Roche Ardill, *The Closing of the Irish Parliament* (Dublin, 1907); Joseph R. Fisher, *The End of the Irish Parliament* (London, 1911). See the summary in Alvin Jackson, 'Unionist History' in Ciarán Brady (ed.), *Interpreting Irish History: The Debate on Historical Revisionism, 1938–1994* (Dublin, 1994).

46. See James Loughlin, *Gladstone, Home Rule and the Ulster Question, 1882–93* (Dublin, 1986).

47. Quoted in Michael Fry, *The Dundas Despotism*, paperback edition (Edinburgh, 2004), p.236.

48. Quoted in Fry, *Dundas Despotism*, p.177.

49. Geoghegan, *Irish Act of Union*, p.114

50. Anne Kavanaugh, *John Fitz Gibbon, Earl of Clare: A Study of Personality and Politics* (Dublin, 1997), p.356.

51. McLean and McMillan, *State of the Union*, pp.59–60.

52. Geoghegan, *Irish Act of Union*, p.106; Bolton, *Passing of the Irish Act of Union*, p.102.

53. Bolton, *Passing of the Irish Act of Union*, p.34.

54. *Ibid.* p.100.

55. *Ibid.* p.171.

56. *Ibid.* pp.205–6.

57. *Ibid.* p.205.

58. cf. Douglas Watt, *The Price of Scotland: Darien, Union and the Wealth of Nations* (Edinburgh, 2007), p.221.

59. See David Wilkinson, 'How did they pass the Union? Secret service expenditure', *History*, 82, 266 (April, 1997), pp.223–51.

60. See e.g. William John Fitzpatrick, *The Secret Service under Pitt* (London, 1892).

61. Geoghegan, *Irish Act of Union*, p.87; Wilkinson, 'How did they pass the Union?'.

62. Geoghegan, *Irish Act of Union*, p.105.

63. *Ibid.* p.140.

64. *Ibid.* p.87.

65. *Ibid.* pp.137–8.

66. James Kelly, 'The Failure of Opposition' in Michael Brown, Patrick Geoghegan, James Kelly (eds), *The Irish Act of Union: Bicentennial Essays* (Dublin, 2003), p.116.

67. *Ibid.* p.121.

68. *Ibid.* p.127.

69. Julian Hoppit (ed.), *Parliaments, Nations and Identities in Britain and Ireland, 1660–1850* (Manchester, 2003), p.15.

70. Bolton, *Passing of the Irish Act of Union*, p.162.

71. Ferguson, *Scotland's Relations*, p.138.

72. Hoppit (ed.), *Parliaments, Nations and Identities*, p.39.

73. William Law Mathieson, 'The Scottish and the Irish Union' in P. Hume Brown (ed.), *The Union of 1707: A Survey of Events* (Glasgow, 1907), p.181.

74. Hume Brown (ed.), *Letters Relating to Scotland*, p.101n; Szechi (ed.), *Letters of George Lockhart*, p.23.

75. See Jeffrey Stephen, *Scottish Presbyterians and the Act of Union, 1707* (Edinburgh, 2007).

76. Oliver Rafferty, *The Catholic Church and the Protestant State: Nineteenth Century Realities* (Dublin, 2008), p.53, emphasises some of the distance between the Catholic hierarchy, relatively phlegmatic on the question of Union-cum-emancipation, and popular Catholic opinion.

77. For a sustained comparison of the national churches, see Stewart J. Brown, *The National Churches of England, Ireland and Scotland, 1801–46* (Oxford, 2001).

78. Danny Mansergh, *Grattan's Failure: Parliamentary Opposition and the People in Ireland, 1779–1800* (Dublin 2005), pp.254–5.

79. cf. Macinnes, *Union and Empire*.

80. See Graeme Morton, *Unionist Nationalism: Governing Urban Scotland, 1830–60* (East Linton, 1999).

81. See Fergus Campbell, *The Irish Establishment, 1879–1914* (Oxford, 2009).

82. Hoppit (ed.), *Parliaments, Nations and Identities*, pp.26–7; R.B. McDowell, *The Irish Administration, 1801–1914* (London, 1964).

83. Hoppit (ed.), *Parliaments, Nations and Identities*, p.27.

84. Peter Gray, ' "Ireland's Last Fetter Struck Off" ': The Lord Lieutenancy Debate, 1800–67' in Terrence McDonough (ed.), *Was Ireland a Colony? Economics, Politics and Culture in Nineteenth Century Ireland* (Dublin, 2005), pp.87–101.

85. R. Barry O'Brien, *Dublin Castle and the Irish People* [London, 1909] second edition (London, 1912), p.6.

86. R.B. McDowell, *The Irish Administration, 1801–1914* (London, 1964), pp.52ff; Gray, ' "Ireland's Last Fetter Struck Off" ', p.99.

87. Justin McCarthy, *The Reign of Queen Anne* [London, 1902] (London, 1905 edition), p.141.

88. Brian Girvin, *From Union to Union: Nationalism, Democracy and Religion in Ireland—Act of Union to EU* (Dublin, 2002), p.141.

## CHAPTER 5

1. Christopher Whatley, *Scottish Society, 1707–1830: Beyond Jacobitism towards Industrialisation* (Edinburgh, 2000), p.192.

2. T.M. Devine (ed.), *Conflict and Stability in Scottish Society, 1700–1850: Proceedings of the Scottish Historical Studies Seminar, University of Strathclyde, 1988–89* (Edinburgh, 1990), pp.6–7; Whatley, *Scottish Society*, p.54. Philipp Robinson Rossner, *Scottish Trade in the Wake of Union, 1700–1760* (Stuttgart, 2008).

3. Whatley, *Scottish Society*, pp.142–74; Devine (ed.), *Conflict and Stability*.

4. Alexander Murdoch, *The People Above: Politics and Administration in Mid-Eighteenth Century Scotland* (Edinburgh, 1980), pp.31–2.

5. T.M. Devine, 'Scottish Elites and the Indian Empire, 1700–1815', in T.C. Smout (ed.), *Anglo-Scottish Relations, 1603–1900* (Oxford, 2005), p.227.

6. Murdoch, *The People Above*, p.32.

7. Christopher Whatley, *The Scots and the Union* (Edinburgh, 2006), p.342. See also Daniel Szechi, *Jacobitism and Tory Politics, 1710–14* (Edinburgh, 1984); Daniel Szechi, *The Jacobites: Britain and Europe, 1688–1788* (Manchester, 1994)

8. Ian Lang, *Blue Remembered Years: A Political Memoir* (London, 2002), p.114. An example of Ulster Unionist obeisance towards Jacobitism may be found in the essay of the former MP and last Lord Chancellor of Ireland, Sir John Ross, on 'Lord George Murray and the "Forty-Five" ' in his *Essays and Addresses* (London, 1930), pp.31–53.

9. Daniel Szechi, *George Lockhart of Carnwath, 1681–1731:* (Edinburgh, 2002), p.115; Daniel Szechi, *1715: The Great Jacobite Rebellion* (Edinburgh, 2006).

10. Peter Hume Brown (ed.), *Letters Relating to Scotland in the Reign of Queen Anne by James Ogilvy, First Earl of Seafield and Others* (Edinburgh, 1915), pp.1–110.

11. See Sir John Clerk of Penicuik, *History of the Union of Scotland and England* (edited and translated by Douglas Duncan) (Edinburgh, 1993).

12. Hume Brown (ed.), *Letters Relating to Scotland*, pp.75–7.

13. Michael Fry, *The Union: England, Scotland and the Treaty of 1707* (Edinburgh, 2006); Iain McLean and Alastair McMillan, *State of the Union: Unionism and the Alternatives in the United Kingdom since 1707* (Oxford, 2005); Allan Macinnes, *Union and Empire: The Making of the United Kingdom in 1707* (Cambridge, 2007); Christopher Whatley, *Bought and Sold for English Gold: Explaining the Union of 1707*, second edition (Edinburgh, 2001); Whatley, *The Scots and the Union*; T.M. Devine (ed.), *Scotland and the Union, 1707–2007* (Edinburgh, 2008); Andrew Mackillop and Micheál Ó Siochrú (eds), *Forging the State: European State Formation and the Anglo-Scottish Union of 1707* (Dundee, 2008).

14. P.W.J. Riley, *The Union of England and Scotland* (Manchester, 1978); P.W.J. Riley, *King William and the Scottish Politicians* (Edinburgh, 1979); William Ferguson, *Scotland's Relations with England: A Survey to 1707* (Edinburgh, 1977).

15. James Mackinnon, *The Union of England and Scotland* (London, 1896); G.W.T. Omond, *The Early History of the Union Question* [Edinburgh, 1897], bicentenary edition (Edinburgh, 1906); Robert Rait, *An Outline of the Relations between England and Scotland (500–1707)* (London, 1901); William Law Mathieson, *Scotland and the Union, 1695–1747* (Glasgow, 1905); Peter Hume Brown (ed.), *The Union of 1707: A Survey of Events* (Glasgow, 1907); Peter Hume Brown, *The Legislative Union of England and Scotland* (Oxford, 1914); A.V. Dicey and R.S. Rait, *Thoughts on the Union between England and Scotland* (London, 1920).

16. Fry, *Union*; Paul Henderson Scott, *Andrew Fletcher and the Treaty of Union* (Edinburgh, 1992); Paul Henderson Scott, *The Boasted Advantages: The Consequences of the Union of 1707* (Edinburgh, 1999); Paul Henderson Scott, *The Union of 1707: Why and How* (Edinburgh, 2006); Macinnes, *Union and Empire*.

17. Colin Kidd, *Union and Unionisms: Political Thought in Scotland, 1500–2000* (Cambridge, 2008), pp.151–72.

18. e.g., Christopher Harvie, *Scotland and Nationalism: Scottish Society and Politics, 1707–1994*, second edition (London, 1994), pp.34–78.

19. Michael Fry, *Patronage and Principle: A Political History of Modern Scotland* (Aberdeen, 1988), p.201.

20. Richard Finlay, 'Scotland and the Monarchy in the Twentieth Century' in William Miller (ed.), *Anglo-Scottish Relations from 1900 to Devolution and Beyond* (Oxford, 2005), pp.19–20; Colin Kidd, 'Scotland and the Three Unions', in T.C. Smout (ed.), *Anglo-Scottish Relations from 1603 to 1900* (Oxford, 2005), p.176. Cf. Michael Keating, *The Independence of Scotland* (Oxford, 2009), pp.17–78.

21. See Jeffrey Stephen, *Scottish Presbyterians and the Act of Union, 1707* (Edinburgh, 2007).

22. Hume Brown (ed.), *Letters Relating to Scotland*, p.174; Daniel Szechi (ed.), *Letters of George Lockhart of Carnwath, 1698–1732* (Edinburgh, 1989), pp.22–3; Whatley, *Scots and the Union*, pp.323, 349.

23. cf Devine (ed.), *Conflict and Stability*, pp.83–105.

24. Mackinnon, *Union*, p.501.

25. Callum Brown, *Religion and Society in Scotland since 1707* (Edinburgh, 1997), p.189. See also of course Linda Colley, *Britons: Forging the Nation, 1707–1837* (New Haven, 1992).

26. Oliver Rafferty, *The Catholic Church and the Protestant State: Nineteenth Century Realities* (Dublin, 2008), pp.35–53, 142–76. See also Oliver Rafferty, *The Church, the State and the Fenian Threat, 1861–75* (London, 1999).

27. Thomas Bartlett, *The Fall and Rise of the Irish Nation: The Catholic Question, 1690–1830* (Dublin, 1992), p.294.

28. See e.g. T.M. Devine, *The Tobacco Lords: A Study of the Tobacco Merchants of Glasgow and their Trading Activities, 1740–90* (Edinburgh, 1975).

29. Devine, *Scottish Nation*, p.55.

30. G.P. Dyer, *The Proposed Coinage of King Edward VIII* (London, 1972), p.14.

31. National Library of Scotland, Thomas Johnston Papers, Acc.5862/8: 'Tribute to Bannockburn'.

32. Reginald Coupland, *Welsh and Scottish Nationalism: A Study* (London, 1954), p.246; H.J. Hanham, *Scottish Nationalism* (London, 1969), p.35; Thomas Somerville, *My Own Life and Times, 1741–1814* (Edinburgh, 1861), pp.56–7.

33. Gordon Donaldson, *Scotland's History: Approaches and Reflections* (Edinburgh, 1995), p.130.

34. Colley, *Britons*, p.132. Keating, *Independence of Scotland*, pp.24–26.

35. T.M. Devine, 'Scottish Elites and the Indian Empire, 1700–1815', pp.220–1.

36. Quoted in Brian Lavery, *Shield of Empire: The Royal Navy and Scotland* (Edinburgh, 2007), p.83.

37. Colley, *Britons*, p.128.

38. T.M. Devine (ed.), *Scotland and the Union*, p.104.

39. Colley, *Britons*, pp.128, 131.

40. e.g. Douglas Hamilton, *Scotland, the Caribbean and the Atlantic World, 1750–1820* (Manchester, 2005); John M. MacKenzie with Nigel Dalziel, *The Scots in South Africa: Ethnicity, Gender, Identity and Race, 1772–1914* (Manchester, 2007).

41. Hamilton, *Scotland, the Caribbean and the Atlantic World*, pp.222–3.

42. Mackenzie, *Scots in South Africa*, p.274; though compare C.H. Lee, *Scotland and the United Kingdom: The Economy and the Union in the Twentieth Century*, (Manchester, 1995), p.47, for the later disproportionate outflow of capital.

43. S.J. Connolly, 'Varieties of Britishness: Ireland, Scotland and Wales in the Hanoverian State', in Alexander Grant and Keith Stringer (eds), *Uniting the Kingdom? The Making of British History* (London, 1995), p.194.

44. Thomas Bartlett, 'Ireland, Empire and Union, 1690–1801', in Kevin Kenny (ed.), *Ireland and the British Empire* (Oxford, 2004), p.67.

45. *Ibid.* p.63.

46. Bartlett, 'Ireland, Empire and Union', p.67. See also Thomas Truxes, *Irish-American Trade, 1660–1783* (Cambridge, 1988).

47. Bartlett, 'Ireland, Empire and Union', pp.61–89.

48. *Ibid.* p.68.

49. R.A. Houston and Ian Whyte (eds), *Scottish Society, 1500–1800* (Cambridge, 1989), pp.242–23.

50. e.g. Tom Nairn, *The Break Up of Britain: Crisis and Neo-Nationalism* (London, 1977).

51. Ewen Cameron, 'The Politics of Union in an Age of Unionism', in T.M.Devine (ed.), *Scotland and the Union, 1707–2007* (Edinburgh, 2008), p.48.

52. Richard Lodge, 'The English Stand-Point (II)', in P. Hume Brown (ed.), *The Union of 1707: A Survey of Events* (Glasgow, 1907), p.173; though cf. Julian Hoppit (ed.), *Parliaments, Nations and Identities in Britain and Ireland, 1660–1850* (Manchester, 2003), p.40.

53. See Murdoch, *People Above*, pp.29–30.

54. Lodge, 'English Stand-Point', in Hume Brown (ed.), *Union of 1707*, pp.173–4.

55. James Livesey, *Civil Society and Empire: Ireland and Scotland in the Eighteenth Century Atlantic World* (New Haven, 2009), pp.23, 215; Colin Kidd, 'Scotland and the Three Unions', p.186.

56. Graeme Morton, *Unionist Nationalism: Governing Urban Scotland, 1830–60* (East Linton, 1999), p.190.

57. *Ibid.* pp.202–4.

58. *Ibid.*

59. cf Fergus Campbell, *The Irish Establishment, 1879–1914* (Oxford, 2009).

60. Murdoch, *People Above*, p.27.

61. See Eoin Magennis, *The Irish Political System, 1740–65: The Golden Age of the Undertakers* (Dublin, 2000).

62. See e.g. Thomas Bartlett, 'The Townshend Viceroyalty, 1767–72' in Thomas Bartlett and David Hayton (eds), *Penal Era and Golden Age: Essays in Irish History, 1690–1800* (Belfast, 1979).

63. Murdoch, *People Above*, p.132.

64. See John Wilson of Thornly, *The Political State of Scotland* (London, 1831), p.48.

65. Colley, *Britons*, p.126.

66. Colley, *Britons*, p.206.

67. Colley, *Britons*, pp.121–2.

68. See R.F. Foster, *Paddy and Mr Punch: Connections in Irish and English History* (London, 1993).

69. Colley, *Britons*, pp.121–3; L.P. Curtis, *Apes and Angels: The Irishman in Victorian Caricature* (Newton Abbot, 1971); see also Foster, *Paddy and Mr Punch*.

70. I.G.C. Hutchison, 'Anglo-Scottish Political Relations in the Nineteenth Century, *c.*1815–1914' in T.C. Smout (ed), *Anglo-Scottish Relations from 1603 to 1900* (Oxford, 2005), p.247.

71. R.E. Quinault, 'Scots on Top: Tartan Power at Westminster, 1707–2007', *History Today* (July, 2007). For Baldwin's Scottish romanticism see e.g. Stanley Baldwin, *Our Inheritance: Speeches and Addresses* (London, 1928), pp.37–43; Stanley Baldwin, *This Torch of Freedom: Speeches and Addresses* (London, 1935), pp.155–72.

72. National Archives of Scotland, Gilmour Mss, GD.383/43/38, 122: Hendry to Gilmour, 29 September 1932; Moore to Gilmour, 8 October 1932.

73. Quinault, 'Scots on Top'.

74. See e.g. K.O. Morgan, *Wales in British Politics, 1868–1922* (Cardiff, 1963).

75. See Bodleian Library, Conservative Party Archive, SUMC 2/1 ff.: Minutes of the Scottish Unionist Members' Committee.

76. Stuart Ball (ed.), *Parliament and Politics in the Age of Churchill and Attlee: The Headlam Diaries, 1935–41* (London, 1999), p.590.

77. Gilmour Mss, GD.383/43/63: Headlam to Gilmour, 29 September 1932.

78. Gilmour Mss, GD.383/51/10: Baldwin to Gilmour, 3 January 1934.

79. Hoppit (ed.), *Parliaments, Nations and Identities*, pp.97–8.

80. See Quinault, 'Scots on Top'; R. Barry O'Brien, *Dublin Castle and the Irish People*, second edition (London, 1912), p.6.

81. Edith Mary Johnston, *Great Britain and Ireland, 1760–1800: A Study in Political Administration* (Edinburgh, 1963), p.44; Charles Ross, *Correspondence of Charles, First Marquess of Cornwallis*, three volumes (London, 1859), ii, p.441.

82. John Paton, *Proletarian Pilgrimage: An Autobiography* (London, 1935), p.148; John Paton, *Left Turn! The Autobiography of John Paton* (London, 1936), pp.186–7. See also E.W. McFarland, *John Ferguson, 1832–1906: Irish Issues in Scottish Politics* (East Linton, 2003).

83. James J. Smyth, *Labour in Glasgow: Socialism, Suffrage, Sectarianism* (East Linton, 2000), pp.125–54; Ian Wood, *John Wheatley* (Manchester, 1990).

84. cf. K. Theodore Hoppen, 'An Incorporating Union: British Politicians and Ireland, 1800–30', *English Historical Review*, cxxiii, 501 (April 2008), p.341.

85. Gordon Donaldson, *Scotland's History: Approaches and Reflections* (Edinburgh, 1995), p.130.

86. Bruce Galloway, *The Union of England and Scotland, 1603–1608* (Edinburgh, 1986), p.17.

87. P.J.G. Ransom, *Iron Road: The Railway in Scotland* (Edinburgh, 2007), p.61.

88. R.S. Rait, *Outline of the Relations between England and Scotland, 500–1707* (London, 1901), p.194.

89. cf. Galloway, *Union*, p.17.

90. *Evening News*, 5 February 1952. Cf. Michael Keating and David Bleiman, *Labour and Scottish Nationalism* (London, 1979), p.89.

91. See Katherine Haldane Grenier, *Tourism and Identity in Scotland, 1770–1914: Creating Caledonia* (Aldershot, 2005).

92. cf. Devine, *Conflict and Stability*, pp.54–6.

93. National Archives of Scotland, Lothian Papers, GD.40/16, f.151: Lothian to Balfour, 21 March 1888 (copy).

94. Devine, *Conflict and Stability*, p.4.

95. Michael Lynch (ed.), *The Oxford Companion to Scottish History* (Oxford, 2001), p.618.

96. Donaldson, *Scotland's History*, p.133.

97. Peter Davison, *Orwell's England: The Road to Wigan Pier in the Context of Essays, Reviews, Letters and Poems* (London, 2001), p.252.

98. Colley, *Britons*, p.123.

99. Richard Rodger, *The Transformation of Edinburgh: Land, Property and Trust in the Nineteenth Century* (Cambridge, 2001), p.474.

100. Rodger, *Transformation of Edinburgh*, p.468.

101. Maurice Lee, 'Scotland, the Union, and the Idea of a "General Crisis"' in Roger Mason (ed.), *Scots and Britons: Scottish Political Thought and the Union of 1603* (Cambridge, 1994), p.53.

102. Keith Brown, 'The Vanishing Emperor: British Kingship and its Decline, 1603–1707' in Roger Mason (ed.), *Scottish Political Thought and the Union of 1603* (Cambridge, 1994), p.87.

103. *Ibid.* p.81. See also Matthew Glozier, 'The Earl of Melfort, the Court Catholic Party, and the Foundation of the Order of the Thistle, 1687', *Scottish Historical Review*, 79, 2 (October, 2000).

104. Quoted in Whatley, *Scots and the Union*, p.88.

105. *Ibid.* pp.349–50.

106. Whatley, *Scottish Society*, p.305. The shape and chronology of Irish Catholic monarchical feeling—the extent of the hinterland behind the notion of 'Ní saoirse go Seoirse' ('No freedom without [King] George')—remains unclear.

107. See Elaine McFarland, *Ireland and Scotland in the Age of Revolution: Planting the Green Bough* (Edinburgh, 1994).

108. Colley, *Britons*, p.236; Brown, 'Vanishing Emperor', p.62.

109. Whatley, *Scottish Society*, p.305.

110. Richard Finlay, 'Scotland and the Monarchy in the Twentieth Century' in William Miller (ed.), *Anglo-Scottish Relations from 1900 to Devolution and Beyond* (Oxford, 2005), p.21.

111. See John Prebble, *The King's Jaunt: George IV in Scotland* (London, 1988).

112. Finlay, 'Scotland and the Monarchy', p.22.

113. *Ibid.* p.22.

114. Lucy Menzies (et al.), *St Margaret, Queen of Scotland and Her Chapel*, revised edition (Edinburgh, 2007), p.6.

115. David Torrance, *We in Scotland: Thatcherism in a Cold Climate* (Edinburgh, 2009), p.42.

116. See, inter alia, James Loughlin, *The British Monarchy and Ireland: 1800 to the Present* (Cambridge, 2007); James H. *Abject Loyalty: Nationalism and Monarchy in Ireland During the Reign of Queen Victoria* (Washington, 2001); Senia Paseta, 'Nationalist Responses to Two Royal Visits to Ireland, 1900 and 1903', *Irish Historical Studies*, 31, 124 (November 1999). Compare the view of Edward VII and I outlined here with that of Mr Henchy in James Joyce, 'Ivy Day in the Committee Room', *Dubliners* [London, 1914], World's Classics edition (Oxford, 2000), p.102.

117. Finlay, 'Scotland and the Monarchy', pp.25–35.

118. Mark Stuart, *John Smith: A Life* (London, 2005), p.48

119. Ross McKibbin, *The Ideologies of Class: Social Relations in Britain, 1880–1950* (Oxford, 1990), pp.17–18.

120. Andrew Roberts, *Eminent Churchillians* (London, 1994), p.9.

121. William Shawcross, *Queen Elizabeth, The Queen Mother: The Official Biography* (London, 2009), pp.669–70, 790–7.

122. Bodleian Library, Conservative Party Archives, SUMC 2/6: Minutes of the Scottish Unionist Members' Committee, 9 December 1952.

123. Conservative Party Archives, SUMC 2/6: Minutes of the Scottish Unionist Members' Committee, 28 October 1952.

124. Neal Ascherson, 'Future of an Unloved Union' in T.M. Devine (ed.), *Scotland and the Union*, p.231.

125. *Scotland on Sunday*, 29 December 2002.

126. *Daily Telegraph*, 19 April 2007; Neil MacCormick, 'New Unions for Old' in William L. Miller (ed.), *Anglo-Scottish Relations From 1900 to Devolution and Beyond* (Oxford, 2005), p.249.

127. Galloway, *Union*, p.15.

128. Brown, 'Vanishing Emperor', p.71.

129. National Library of Scotland, Thomas Johnston Mss., Acc.5862/8: 'Patronage Notes', *c.*1943.

130. National Archives of Scotland, Lothian Papers, GD.40/16, f.122: Lothian to Salisbury, 3 April 1890 (copy).

131. Lothian Papers, GD.40/16/60, f.185: Simpson to McDonnell, 11 May 1892 (copy).

132. Gilmour Papers, GD.383/51/1: Hunter-Weston to Gilmour, 1 January 1934.

133. Lothian Papers, GD.40/16/33, f.61: Lord Provost [?] to Dalrymple, 13 August 1887.

134. Lothian Papers, GD.40/16/61: Argyll to Lothian, 10 October 1889.

135. Lothian Papers, GD.40/16/60, f.237: Lothian to Salisbury, 15 August 1892 (copy).

136. Lothian Papers, GD.40/16/58, f.83: Lothian to Pearson, 8 August 1887 (copy).

137. Gilmour Papers, GD.383/41/36: Home to Gilmour, 14 September 1932.

138. Gilmour Papers, GD.383/21/8: Montgomery to Gilmour, 22 December 1925.

139. Gilmour Papers, GD.383/53/1: Buccleuch to Gilmour, 9 January 1935.

140. cf. Donaldson, *Scotland's History*, pp.129–35.

141. Diane Henderson, *Highland Soldier, 1820–1920* (Edinburgh, 1989), p.2.

142. Whatley, *Scots and the Union*, p.88.

143. Lavery, *Shield of Empire*, p.81.

144. *Ibid* p.87.

145. *Ibid*. p.91.

146. Paul Langford, 'South Britons and North Britons, 1707–1820', in T.C. Smout (ed.), *Anglo-Scottish Relations from 1603 to 1900* (Oxford, 2005), p.162.

147. Quoted in Colley, *Britons*, p.120.

148. Quoted in Colley, *Britons*, p.103.

149. Devine, *Scottish Nation*, pp.184–5; Henderson, *Highland Soldier*, p.5.

150. Andrew Mackillop, *More Fruitful than the Soil: Army, Empire and the Scottish Highlands, 1715–1815* (Edinburgh, 2000), pp.129, 233; Henderson, *Highland Soldier*, pp.6–7.

151. Ewen Cameron, *Impaled Upon a Thistle: Scotland since 1880* (Edinburgh, 2010), p.103

152. Edward Spiers, *The Scottish Soldier and Empire, 1854–1902* (Edinburgh, 2006), p.13.

153. See Paul Usherwood and Jenny Spencer Smith, *Lady Butler, Battle Artist, 1846–1933* (London, 1987).

154. Robert S Rait, *The Life and Campaigns of Hugh, First Viscount Gough*, two vols (London, 1903).

155. Henderson, *Highland Soldier*, pp.39, 91.

156. *Ibid*. pp.217–18.

157. See Elaine McFarland, '"How the Irish Paid their Debt": Irish Catholics in Scotland and Voluntary Enlistment, August 1914—July 1915', *Scottish Historical Review*, 82, 2 (October, 2003).

158. *London Gazette*, 26 July 1917.

159. Dorothy L Sayers, *Five Red Herrings* [London, 1931], New English Library Edition (London, 2003), p.9.

160. National Library of Scotland, Walter Elliot Papers, Acc.12198/6: Elliot to Dugdale, 14 April 1936.

161. James Black, *Around the Guns: Sundays in Camp* (Edinburgh, n.d. [1916]), p.58.

162. Summarized in Cameron, *Impaled upon a Thistle*, pp.121–2.

163. Catriona MacDonald and Elaine McFarland (eds), *Scotland and the Great War* (Edinburgh, 1999), p.97.

164. MacDonald and McFarland (eds), *Scotland and the Great War*, p.103. See also J. Alexander, *McCrae's Battalion: The Story of the 16th Royal Scots* (Edinburgh, 2003).

165. *London Gazette*, 14 January 1943.

166. See Jeremy A. Crang, 'The Second World War', in Jeremy Crang, Edward Spiers, and Matthew Strickland (eds), *Military History of Scotland* (Edinburgh, forthcoming).

167. See Colley, *Britons*.

168. cf. Mackillop, *More Fruitful than the Soil*, pp.204–33.

169. See Desmond Ryan, *The Phoenix Flame: A Study of Fenianism and John Devoy* (London, 1937).

170. Henderson, *Highland Soldier*, p.219.

171. Spiers, *Scottish Soldier and Empire*, pp.6, 74–6.

172. See Trevor Royle, *Fighting Mac: The Downfall of Major General Sir Hector MacDonald* (Edinburgh, 2003).

173. I.G.C. Hutchison, 'The Impact of the First World War on Scottish Politics', MacDonald and MacFarland (eds), *Scotland and the Great War*, p.55.

174. *Daily Record*, 9 September 1932.

175. Cameron, *Impaled Upon a Thistle*, pp.273, 275.

176. Spiers, *Scottish Soldier and Empire*, pp.74–6.

177. Edward Spiers, 'Army Organisation and Society in Nineteenth Century Ireland' in Thomas Bartlett and Keith Jeffery (eds), *A Military History of Ireland* (Cambridge, 1996), p.336.

178. David Marquand, 'How united is the modern United Kingdom?' in Alexander Grant and Keith Stringer (eds), *Uniting the Kingdom? The Making of British History* (London, 1995), p.279. See also Paul Ward, *Unionism in the United Kingdom, 1918–74* (London, 2005), p.3.

179. Iain McLean, 'Financing the Union: Goschen, Barnett and Beyond' in William L. Miller (ed.), *Anglo-Scottish Relations from 1900 to Devolution and Beyond* (Oxford, 2005), p.82.

180. *Ibid.* p.83.

181. David Torrance, *We in Scotland: Thatcherism in a Cold Climate* (Edinburgh, 2009), p.167.

182. See C.H. Lee, *Scotland and the United Kingdom: The Economy and the Union in the Twentieth Century* (Manchester, 1995).

183. Cameron, *Impaled upon a Thistle*, p.94.

184. See Martin Daunton, *Royal Mail: The Post Office since 1840* (London, 1985).

185. Ian McIntyre, *The Expense of Glory: A Life of John Reith* (London, 1992); Keating, *Independence of Scotland*, p.28.

186. Michael Fry, *Patronage and Principle: A Political History of Modern Scotland* (Aberdeen, 1988), p.193.

187. Morrice McCrae, *The National Health Service in Scotland: Origins and Ideals, 1900–50* (Edinburgh, 2003), pp.1–29, 38–41.

188. Iain McLean and Alastair McMillan, *State of the Union: Unionism and the Alternatives in the United Kingdom since 1707* (Oxford, 2005), p.157. Keating, *Independence of Scotland*, pp.53–55.

189. Nairn, *Break Up of Britain*, pp.69–71, 368.

190. Bernard Porter, *The Absent Minded Imperialists: Empire, Society and Culture in Britain* (Oxford, 2004); Ward, *Unionism in the United Kingdom*, p.186. Elliot Papers, Acc.12198/4: Elliot to Dugdale, 17 Nov. 1934.

191. David McCrone, 'W(h)ither the Union? Anglo-Scottish Relations in the 21st Century' in Miller (ed.), *Anglo-Scottish Relations From 1900 to Devolution*, p.207.

192. Quoted in Torrance, *We in Scotland*, p.130.

## CHAPTER 6

1. e.g. Rev Thomas Johnstone, *Ulstermen: Their Fight for Fortune, Faith and Freedom* (Belfast, 1914), p.90.
2. Louis Cullen, 'Alliances and Misalliances in the Politics of the Union', *Transactions of the Royal Historical Society*, 6th series, vol.10 (2000), p.221.
3. Though cf. Brian Girvin, *From Union to Union: Nationalism, Democracy and Religion in Ireland—Act of Union to EU* (Dublin, 2002), pp.1–28 ('Why the Irish did not become British!').
4. Brendan Bradshaw, 'Nationalism and Historical Scholarship in Modern Ireland', *Irish Historical Studies*, xxvi, 104 (November 1989); cf. Alvin Jackson, *Home Rule: An Irish History, 1800–2000*, paperback edition (London, 2004), especially pp.376–7.
5. Conrad Russell, 'Composite Monarchies in Early Modern Europe', in Alexander Grant and Keith Stringer (eds), *Uniting the Kingdoms: The Making of British History* (London, 1995), p.135.
6. Fergus Campbell, *The Irish Establishment, 1879–1914* (Oxford, 2009), p.312n.
7. e.g. Stephen Gwynn, *The Student's History of Ireland* (London, 1925), p.223.
8. e.g. George O'Brien, *The Economic History of Ireland from the Union to the Famine* (Dublin, 1921). Douglas Kanter, *The Making of British Unionism, 1740–1848: Politics, Government and the Anglo-Irish Constitutional Relationship* (Dublin, 2009), p.154.
9. See Donal McCartney, *W.E.H. Lecky: Historian and Politician, 1838–1903* (Dublin, 1994).
10. H.J. Hanham, *Scottish Nationalism* (London, 1969), pp.86–90.
11. Peter Hume Brown, 'Introduction', in Peter Hume Brown (ed.), *The Union of 1707: A Survey of Events* (Glasgow, 1907), p.1.
12. K. Theodore Hoppen, 'An Incorporating Union: British Politicians and Ireland, 1800–30', *English Historical Review*, cxxiii, 501 (April 2008), p.350.
13. Patrick Geoghegan, *The Irish Act of Union: A Study in High Politics, 1798–1801* (Dublin, 1999), p.119. See also Oliver Rafferty, *The Catholic Church and the Protestant State: Nineteenth Century Irish Realities* (Dublin, 2008), pp.35–53.
14. Charles Ross, *Correspondence of Charles, First Marquess of Cornwallis*, three vols (London, 1859), ii, pp.414–15.
15. See, most recently, Campbell, *Irish Establishment*, p.312.
16. Geoghegan, *Irish Act of Union*, p.87.
17. Quoted in Hoppen, 'An Incorporating Union', p.331.
18. James Mackinnon, *The Union of England and Scotland: A Study of International History* (London, 1896), p.303.
19. Thomas Hennessey, *The Northern Ireland Peace Process: Ending the Troubles?* (Dublin, 2000), pp.140–2.
20. Richard Lodge, 'The English Stand-Point (II)', in Hume Brown (ed.), *Union of 1707*, p.173.
21. See Thomas Bartlett, *The Fall and Rise of the Irish Nation: The Catholic Question, 1690–1830* (Dublin, 1992).

22. K.Theodore Hoppen, *Elections, Politics and Society in Ireland, 1832–1885* (Oxford, 1984), pp.vii–viii.

23. Graeme Morton, *Unionist Nationalism: Governing Urban Scotland, 1830–60* (East Linton, 1999), p.10.

24. cf. Colin Kidd, 'Scotland and the Three Unions', in T.C. Smout (ed.), *Anglo-Scottish Relations from 1603 to 1900* (Oxford, 2005), p.186.

25. Oliver MacDonagh, *O'Connell:The Life of Daniel O'Connell, 1775–1847* (London, 1991), p.418.

26. Hoppen, 'An Incorporating Union', p.345.

27. James Loughlin, *The British Monarchy and Ireland: 1800 to the Present* (Cambridge, 2007), p.54.

28. Ewen Cameron, 'The Politics of Union in an Age of Unionism', in T.M. Devine (ed.), *Scotland and the Union, 1707–2007* (Edinburgh, 2008), p.130.

29. See John Gibson, *The Thistle and the Crown: A History of the Scottish Office* (Edinburgh, 1985); James Mitchell, *Governing Scotland: The Invention of Administrative Devolution* (London, 2003).

30. Kanter, *Making of British Unionism*, pp.206–7, 318.

31. See Stewart J Brown, *The National Churches of England, Ireland and Scotland, 1801–46* (Oxford, 2001).

32. Lawrence McBride, *The Greening of Dublin Castle:The Transforming of Bureaucratic and Judicial Personnel in Dublin Castle in Ireland, 1892–1922* (Washington, 1991): though see also the note of caution sounded by Campbell, *Irish Establishment*, p.303.

33. Alvin Jackson, 'Ireland, the Union and the Empire, 1800–1960', in Kevin Kenny (ed.), *Ireland and the British Empire*, paperback edition (Oxford, 2006), pp.130–1.

34. Hoppen, 'An Incorporating Union', p.345.

35. e.g. Boyd Hilton, *The Age of Atonement: The Influence of Evangelicalism on Social and Economic Thought, 1795–1865* (Oxford, 1992); Peter Gray, *Famine, Land and Politics: British Government and Irish Society, 1843–50* (Dublin, 1999); Christine Kinealy, *'This Great Calamity':The Irish Famine, 1845–52* (Dublin, 1994).

36. e.g. Ewen Cameron, *Land for the People?: Government and the Scottish Highlands, 1880–1925* (East Linton, 1996);Andrew Newby, *Ireland, Radicalism and the Scottish Highlands, 1870–1912* (Edinburgh, 2006).

37. Cameron, *Land for the People*, pp.5, 199.

38. *Ibid.* pp.100–1.

39. See John Paul McCarthy, 'Gladstone's Irish Questions, 1830–86: An Historical Approach', (University of Oxford Unpublished D. Phil thesis, 2010).

40. W.C. Lubenow, *Parliamentary Politics and the Home Rule Crisis:The British House of Commons in 1886* (Oxford, 1986), pp.323–4.

41. See e.g. R.B. McDowell, *The Irish Administration, 1801–1914* (London, 1964).

42. Malcolm McRonald, *The Irish Boats:Volume 1 Liverpool to Dublin* (Stroud, 2005), p.17.

43. Peter Beresford Ellis, 'Easter 1916', *Irish Democrat*, 6 April 2006.

44. See e.g. John Andrews, *A Paper Landscape: The Ordnance Survey in Nineteenth Century Ireland* (Oxford, 1975); Stiofán Ó Cadhla, *Civilising Ireland: Ordnance Survey, 1824–42: Ethnography, Cartography, Translation* (Dublin 2006).

45. See e.g. John MacKenzie (ed.), *Imperialism and Popular Culture* (Manchester, 1986).

46. William O'Brien, *Recollections* (London, 1905), p.347; Jackson, *Home Rule*, p.26.

47. See Elizabeth Muenger, *The British Military Dilemma in Ireland: Occupation Politics, 1886–1914* (Dublin, 1991); Diana Henderson, *Highland Soldier, 1820–1920* (Edinburgh, 1989).

48. See e.g. T.M. Devine (ed.), *Conflict and Stability in Scottish Society, 1700–1850: Proceedings of the Scottish Historical Studies Seminar, University of Strathclyde, 1988–89* (Edinburgh, 1990), p.53.

49. Ian McBride, *Eighteenth Century Ireland: The Isle of Slaves* (Dublin, 2009), p.353.

50. *Ibid.* p.353.

51. Edward Spiers, 'Army Organisation and Society in Nineteenth Century Ireland' in Thomas Bartlett and Keith Jeffery (eds), *A Military History of Ireland* (Cambridge, 1996), pp.336, 340; J.E. Cookson, *The British Armed Nation, 1793–1815* (Oxford, 1997), pp.180–1.

52. See Bartlett, *Fall and Rise of the Irish Nation*; Cookson, *British Armed Nation*, pp.176–7.

53. Thomas Bartlett, 'Defence, Counter-Insurgency and Rebellion: Ireland, 1793–1803' in Thomas Bartlett and Keith Jeffery (eds), *A Military History of Ireland* (Cambridge, 1996), p.247.

54. See especially Andrew Mackillop, *More Fruitful than the Soil: Army, Empire and the Scottish Highlands, 1715–1815* (Edinburgh, 2000). Cookson, *British Armed Nation*, p.154.

55. Nuffield College, Oxford, Mottistone Papers, Ms.22, f.62: R.W. Brade [?] to Seely, 24 January 1914.

56. Mottistone Papers, Ms.22, f.72: William Redmond to Seely, 28 December 1913.

57. Muenger, *British Military Dilemma*, pp.2–4; Cookson, *The British Armed Nation*, pp.155–6.

58. Nuala Johnson, *Ireland, the Great War, and the Geography of Remembrance* (Cambridge, 2007), pp.63–9.

59. *Ibid.* pp.80–111.

60. e.g. Richard Finlay, 'Queen Victoria and the Cult of Scottish Monarchy' in E.J. Cowan and R.J. Finlay (eds), *Scottish History: The Power of the Past* (Edinburgh, 2002); Richard Finlay, 'Scotland and the Monarchy in the Twentieth Century' in William Miller (ed.), *Anglo-Scottish Relations from 1900 to Devolution and Beyond* (Oxford, 2005).

61. See e.g. Tom Garvin, *Nationalist Revolutionaries in Ireland, 1858–1928* (Oxford, 1987).

62. Sean Connolly, 'Varieties of Britishness: Ireland, Scotland and Wales in the Hanoverian State', in Alexander Grant and Keith Stringer (eds), *Uniting the*

*Kingdom? The Making of British History* (London, 1995), p.206; Hoppen, 'An Incorporating Union', p.345.

63. Loughlin, *British Monarchy and Ireland*, pp.80, 200.

64. James H. Murphy, *Abject Loyalty: Nationalism and Monarchy in Ireland During the Reign of Queen Victoria* (Washington, 2001), p.293.

65. House of Lords Record Office, Cadogan Papers, CAD.1185: Salisbury to Cadogan, 7 September 1895.

66. Cadogan Papers, CAD.1242: Cadogan to Prince of Wales, 15 November 1897 (copy).

67. Terence O'Neill, *The Autobiography of Terence O'Neill* (London, 1972), p.4.

68. Murphy, *Abject Loyalty*; Senia Paseta, 'Nationalist Responses to Two Royal Visits to Ireland, 1900 and 1903', *Irish Historical Studies*, 31, 124 (November 1999).

69. National Library of Scotland, John Dowden Papers, dep.171/7: Edward Dowden to John Dowden, 29 March 1885.

70. John Dowden Papers, dep.171/7: Edward Dowden to John Dowden, 12 April 1900.

71. John Dowden Paper, dep.171/7: Edward Dowden to John Dowden, 24 July 1903.

72. Murphy, *Abject Loyalty*, pp.241–2; Loughlin, *British Monarchy and Ireland*, pp.146, 192.

73. Loughlin, *British Monarchy and Ireland*, p.192.

74. PRONI, William Johnston Diary, D.880/2/49: 22 June 1897; Edward Marjoribanks and Ian Colvin, *Life of Lord Carson*, 3 vols (London, 1932–6), i, p.282.

75. William Johnston Diary, D.880/2/39: 11 March 1887.

76. PRONI, Pack Beresford Papers, D.664/D/355/B: Plunkett to Dunbar Buller, 2 August 1902.

77. Loughlin, *British Monarchy and Ireland*, p.295; PRONI, Theresa, Marchioness of Londonderry Papers, D.2846/1/1/86, 88: Carson to Theresa Londonderry, 27 March 1912, 13 August 1912.

78. PRONI, Cabinet Papers, CAB.9Z/8: Amery to Craig, 11 Dec. 1926; Craig to Amery, 16 Dec. 1926. Craig appears to have been more emphatically negative than Carson, with whom O'Higgins first raised the idea.

79. Ross McKibbin, *The Ideologies of Class: Social Relations in Britain, 1880–1950* (Oxford, 1990), pp.19–20.

80. Peter Galloway, *The Most Illustrious Order: The Order of Saint Patrick and Its Knights* (London, 1999).

81. David Cannadine, *Ornamentalism: How the British saw their Empire* (London, 2001), pp.88–90.

82. E.F. Benson, *Lucia Rising* (London, 1991), p.246.

83. e.g. Churchill College, Cambridge, Robin Chichester Clark Papers, CCLK 1/5, 1/8: R.J.Moore to Chichester Clark, 22 June 1960; Jack Sayers to Chichester Clark, 30 December 1968.

84. Ruth Dudley Edwards, *Murdering Americans* (Bristol, 2007), p.104.

85. British Library, Arthur Balfour Papers, Add.49828, f.525: Balfour to MacDonnell, 28 December 1889 (copy).

86. Balfour Papers, Add.49690, f.39: MacDonnell to Balfour, 1 November 1898.

87. National Archives of Scotland, Gerald Balfour Papers, TD.83/133/112/10, 24, 25, 26, 28: John Atkinson to Balfour, 14 January 1900, 30 November 1905, 26 November 1905, 5 December 1905 3 Dec. 1905.

88. Hatfield House, Salisbury Papers, Balfour Correspondence, f.296: Balfour to Salisbury, 16 November 1889.

89. Salisbury Papers, Balfour Correspondence, f.267: Balfour to MacDonnell, 14 June 1898.

90. British Library, Walter Long Papers, Add.Ms.62405, f.18: Stamfordham to Long, 25 September 1911.

91. Long Papers, Add.Ms.62405, f.19: Long to Stamfordham, 27 September 1911 (copy).

92. Kent Record Office, Akers-Douglas Papers, U.564/C18/21: Salisbury to Akers-Douglas, 7 March 1887.

93. Cadogan Papers, CAD.1111/1: Atkinson to Cadogan, 2 June 1897.

94. Cadogan Papers, CAD.691: Arnold-Forster to Cadogan, 27 July 1895.

95. Cadogan Papers, CAD.705: Ross to Cadogan, 8 August 1895.

96. Akers-Douglas Papers, CLp.4/321: Akers-Douglas to Cadogan, 27 August 1895.

97. Cadogan Papers, CAD.1113: Herdman to Cadogan, 3 June 1897.

98. Cadogan Papers, CAD.753: Abercorn to Cadogan, 18 November 1895.

99. Arthur Balfour Papers, Add. 49829, f.937: Balfour to Matthews, 7 May 1891.

100. Alvin Jackson, 'Ireland, the Union and the Empire, 1800–1960', in Kevin Kenny (ed.), *Ireland and the British Empire*, pp.129–30; Keith Jeffery (ed.), *An Irish Empire? Aspects of Ireland and the British Empire* (Manchester, 1996), pp.107–43, 154–5; Johnson, *Ireland, the Great War and the Geography of Remembrance*; Yvonne Whelan, *Reinventing Modern Dublin: Streetscape, Iconography and the Politics of Identity* (Dublin, 2003).

101. Iain McLean and Alastair McMillan, *State of the Union: Unionism and the Alternatives in the United Kingdom since 1707* (Oxford, 2005), p.157.

102. Quoted in George Peel, *The Reign of Sir Edward Carson* (London, 1914), p.180.

103. See e.g. Stiofán Ó Cadhla, *Civilising Ireland*.

104. Margaret O'Callaghan, 'New Ways of Looking at the State Apparatus and State Archive in Nineteenth Century Ireland: 'Curiosities from that Phonetic Museum'—Royal Irish Constabulary Reports and Their Political Uses', *Proceedings of the Royal Irish Academy*, 104c (2004), p.124.

105. Chris Bayly, 'Ireland, India and the Empire, 1780–1914', *Transactions of the Royal Historical Society*, sixth series, 10 (Cambridge, 2000), p.382.

106. John Hutchinson, *The Dynamics of Cultural Nationalism: The Gaelic Revival and the Creation of the Irish Nation State* (London, 1987); Fergus Campbell, *The Irish Establishment*.

107. R. Barry O'Brien, *Dublin Castle and the Irish People*, second edition (London, 1912), pp.10–12.

108. See Lawrence McBride, *The Greening of Dublin Castle*.

109. See Martin Maguire, *The Civil Service and the Revolution in Ireland, 1912–1938: Shaking the Blood-Stained Hand of Mr Collins* (Manchester, 2008).

110. Scott Cook, *Imperial Affinities: Nineteenth Century Analogies and Exchanges between India and Ireland* (New Delhi, 1993), pp.88–94.

111. See Alvin Jackson, *The Ulster Party: Irish Unionists in the House of Commons, 1884–1911* (Oxford, 1989), pp.244–53.

112. Wiltshire Record Office, Walter Long Papers, 947/68: MacDonnell to Brodrick, 4 November 1904 (copy).

113. Maguire, *Civil Service and the Revolution in Ireland*.

114. e.g. Jeffery (ed.), *An Irish Empire?*; Kenny, *Ireland and the British Empire*. For an example of an Irish critic of colonial administration from within the service see Barry Crosbie, '"L'enfant terrible of the ICS": C.J. O'Donnell and the British Administration of Bengal, 1872–82' in Robert Blyth and Keith Jeffery (eds), *The British Empire and its Contested Pasts: Historical Studies XXVI* (Dublin, 2009), pp.115–34.

115. Kenny (ed.), *Ireland and the British Empire*, pp.123–53.

116. e.g. Alvin Jackson, *Colonel Edward Saunderson: Land and Loyalty in Victorian Ireland* (Oxford, 1995), p.208.

117. See Paul Townend, 'Between Two Worlds: Irish Nationalists and Imperial Crisis, 1878–80', *Past & Present* (February, 2007).

118. See Cook, *Imperial Affinities*; Kate O'Malley, *Ireland, India and Empire: Indo-Irish Radical Connections, 1919–64* (Manchester, 2008); Jennifer Regan-Lefebvre, *Cosmopolitan Nationalism in the Victorian Empire: Ireland, India and the Politics of Alfred Webb* (Cambridge, 2009).

119. See Helen O'Shea, 'Irish Interventions with Empire: The Cyprus Emergency, 1955–59', (University of Edinburgh unpublished Ph.D. thesis, 2009).

120. See Senia Paseta, *Before the Revolution: Nationalism, Social Change and Ireland's Catholic Elite, 1879–1922* (Cork, 1999).

121. Cook, *Imperial Affinities*. Oliver Rafferty underlines the utility of empire to the Catholic hierarchy in Ireland: 'The Catholic Church, Ireland and the British Empire, 1800–1921', Historical Research, 84, 224 (May 2011).

122. Hoppen, 'An Incorporating Union', p.349.

123. Compare James Livesey, *Civil Society and Empire: Ireland and Scotland in the Eighteenth Century Atlantic World* (New Haven, 2009), pp.198ff.

124. Hutchinson, *Dynamics of Cultural Nationalism*; cf. Jackson, 'Ireland, the Union and the Empire', p.136.

125. Richard Lodge, 'The English Stand-Point (I)', in Peter Hume Brown (ed.), *The Union of 1707*, p.160.

## CHAPTER 7

1. Richard Finlay, *A Partnership for Good? Scottish Politics and the Union since 1800* (Edinburgh, 1997), p.102; Colin Kidd, *Union and Unionisms: Political Thought in Scotland, 1500–2000* (Cambridge, 2008), pp.25ff.

2. Michael Fry, *Patronage and Principle: A Political History of Modern Scotland* (Aberdeen, 1988), p.239.

3. e.g. Lord Ernest Hamilton, *The Soul of Ulster* (London, 1917)

4. See e.g. Gerald Warner, *The Scottish Tory Party: A History* (London, 1988), pp.5–15.

5. cf. Warner, *Scottish Tory Party*, pp.126–7.

6. See Michael Fry, *The Dundas Despotism* (Edinburgh, 2004 edition).

7. A.V. Dicey and Robert S. Rait, *Thoughts on the Union between England and Scotland* (London, 1920), p.313.

8. Fry, *Dundas Despotism*, p.309.

9. Michael Michie, *An Enlightenment Tory in Victorian Scotland: The Career of Sir Archibald Alison* (Edinburgh, 1997), p.189; see also Colin Kidd, *Subverting Scotland's Past: Scottish Whig Historians and the Creation of an Anglo-British Identity, 1689–1830* (Cambridge, 1993).

10. Ruth Clayton Windscheffel, 'Gladstone and Scott: Family, Identity and Nation', *Scottish Historical Review*, vol. 86 (April, 2007), p.69.

11. Stanley Baldwin, *This Torch of Freedom: Speeches and Addresses* (London, 1935) pp.156–7.

12. *Ibid.* pp.166–7.

13. Archibald Alison, *History of Europe from the Commencement of the French Revolution in 1789 to the Restoration of the Bourbons in 1815*, 10 vols, second edition (Edinburgh, 1835–43). See also Sir Archibald Alison, *Lives of Lord Castlereagh and Sir Charles Stewart, Second and Third Marquesses of Londonderry. With Annals of Contemporary Events in Which They Bore a Part. From the Original Papers of the Family*, three vols (Edinburgh, 1861); Sir Archibald Alison (Lady Alison ed.), *Some Account of My Life and Writings: An Autobiography*, two vols (Edinburgh, 1883).

14. Michael Michie, *An Enlightenment Tory in Victorian Scotland*, p.195; I.G.C Hutchison, *A Political History of Scotland, 1832–1924: Parties, Elections and Issues* (Edinburgh, 1986), p.92.

15. Alison, *Castlereagh*, ii, p.139.

16. Michael Fry, *Patronage and Principle*, p.34; Hutchison, *A Political History of Scotland*, pp.8, 11; J.R. Hill, *From Patriots to Unionists: Dublin Civic Politics and Irish Protestant Patriotism, 1660–1840* (Oxford, 1997).

17. National Library of Scotland, Scottish Conservative and Unionist Papers, Acc.10424/65: Glasgow Operatives' Association Minute Book, 23 December 1886.

18. Scottish Conservative and Unionist Papers, Acc.10424/65: Glasgow Operatives' Association Minute Book, 10 February 1837.

19. Scottish Conservative and Unionist Papers, Acc.10424/65: Glasgow Operatives' Association Minute Book, 3 October 1837.

20. Scottish Conservative and Unionist Papers, Acc.10424/65: Glasgow Operatives' Association Minute Book, 6 November 1839.

21. Scottish Conservative and Unionist Papers, Acc.10424/65: Glasgow Operatives' Association Minute Book, 28 April 1843.

22. Fry, *Patronage and Principle*, p.51; Donal Kerr, *Peel, Priests and Politics: Sir Robert Peel's Administration and the Roman Catholic Church in Ireland, 1841–46* (Oxford, 1982).

23. Hutchison, *Political History of Scotland*, p.91.

24. *Ibid.* p.59.

25. See Andrew Shields, *The Irish Conservative Party, 1852–68: Land, Politics and Religion* (Dublin, 2006).

26. Catriona Burness, *'Strange Associations': The Irish Question and the Making of Scottish Unionism, 1886–1918* (East Linton, 2003), pp.18–19; Fry, *Patronage and Principle*, pp.80, 89.

27. Hutchison, *Political History of Scotland*, p.103; Ewen Cameron, *Impaled Upon a Thistle: Scotland since 1880* (Edinburgh, 2010), p.74.

28. Hutchison, *Political History of Scotland*, p.113.

29. Burness, *Strange Association*, p.14; Elaine McFarland, *Protestants First: Orangeism in 19th Century Scotland* (Edinburgh, 1990), p.47.

30. Elaine McFarland, *Ireland and Scotland in the Age of Revolution: Planting the Green Bough* (Edinburgh, 1994), p.210.

31. Michie, *Enlightenment Tory*, pp.70, 170–1; McFarland, *Protestants First*, p.54.

32. Alison, *Lives of Lord Castlereagh*, i, pp.40–1.

33. McFarland, *Protestants First*, p.61.

34. Burness, *Strange Association*, p.9.

35. *Ibid.* p.13; McFarland, *Protestants First*, pp.165, 208.

36. Eric Kaufmann, 'The Orange Order in Scotland since 1860: A Social Analysis' in Martin Mitchell (ed.), *New Perspectives on the Irish in Scotland* (Edinburgh, 2008), p.188.

37. PRONI, Wallace Papers, D.1889/6/6: Craig to Wallace, 5 December 1906. Younger was the only Scottish MP identified by Craig as a member of the Orange Order.

38. McFarland, *Protestants First*, pp.165, 208.

39. Geraldine Vaughan, 'Shaping the Scottish Past: Irish Migrants and Local Politics in the Monklands in the Second Half of the Nineteenth Century' in Martin Mitchell (ed.), *New Perspectives on the Irish in Scotland* (Edinburgh, 2008), p.109.

40. Vaughan, 'Shaping the Scottish Past', p.111.

41. John Foster, Muir Houston, and Chris Madigan, 'Sectarianism, Segregation and Politics on Clydeside in the later Nineteenth Century' in Martin Mitchell (ed.), *New Perspectives on the Irish in Scotland* (Edinburgh, 2008), p.95.

42. Kaufmann, 'Orange Order in Scotland', p.189.

43. Burness, *Strange Associations*, p.215.

44. cf. Colin Kidd, *Union and Unionisms: Political Thought in Scotland, 1500–2000* (Cambridge, 2008). Tom Dunne, 'La trahison des clercs: British Intellectuals and the first Home Rule Crisis', *Irish Historical Studies*, xxiii, no. 90 (Nov. 1982).

45. National Library of Scotland, John Dowden Papers, dep.171/17: Butcher to Dowden, 20 March 1903, 24 August 1903; Hume Brown to Dowden, 24 August 1903, 23 July 1907, 10 January 1908; H.J. Lawlor to Dowden, 16 October 1908.

46. NLS, Scottish Conservative and Unionist Papers, Acc.10424/45: 5 June 1913, 24 March 1920.

47. J.R.M. Butler, *Lord Lothian (Philip Kerr), 1882–1940* (London, 1960), pp.6, 11.

48. Paul Ward, *Unionism in the United Kingdom, 1918–74* (London, 2005), pp.25–6. See also NLS, Walter Elliot Papers, Acc.12198/3: Elliot to Dugdale, 28 June 1926; Acc.12247/11: Elliot to Dugdale, 26 August 1927, 2 October 1928.

49. Kidd, *Union and Unionisms*, pp.161–9.

50. Stephen Gwynn (ed.), *The Anvil of War: Letters of F.S. Oliver to His Brother* (London, 1936), p.26. See also Jonathan Parry, 'From the 39 Articles to the 39 Steps: Reflections on the Thought of John Buchan', in Michael Bentley (ed.), *Public and Private Doctrine: Essays in British History Presented to Maurice Cowling* (Cambridge, 2002).

51. Scottish Conservative and Unionist Papers, Acc.10424/39: 21 February 1894.

52. Scottish Conservative and Unionist Papers, Acc.10424/39: 6 February 1895.

53. Alvin Jackson, *Colonel Edward Saunderson: Land and Loyalty in Victorian Ireland* (Oxford, 1995), pp.102–4. See also Scottish Conservative and Unionist Papers, Acc.10424/42: 25 March 1903.

54. Scottish Conservative and Unionist Papers, Acc.10424/42: 24 June 1903.

55. Scottish Conservative and Unionist Papers, Acc.10424/42: Report of the Eastern Divisional Council, NUCA Scotland, 1909–10.

56. Scottish Conservative and Unionist Papers, Acc.10424/42: 25 March 1906.

57. cf. Alvin Jackson, *The Ulster Party: Irish Unionists in the House of Commons, 1884–1911* (Oxford, 1989), p.205.

58. Scottish Conservative and Unionist Papers, Acc.10424/42: 19 November 1909.

59. Scottish Conservative and Unionist Papers, Acc.10424/42: 25 May 1910.

60. Scottish Conservative and Unionist Papers, Acc.10424/42: 25 May 1910.

61. Scottish Conservative and Unionist Papers, Acc.11368/34: 11 July 1906.

62. Scottish Conservative and Unionist Papers, Acc.11368/34: 13 November 1907, 14 October 1908. See also David Torrance, *We in Scotland: Thatcherism in a Cold Climate* (Edinburgh, 2009), p.140.

63. Scottish Conservative and Unionist Papers, Acc.11368/34: 10 October 1906, 6–9 May 1907.

64. Scottish Conservative and Unionist Papers, Acc.11368/34: 6 August 1906.

65. Scottish Conservative and Unionist Papers, Acc.11368/34: 10 May 1911.

66. Scottish Conservative and Unionist Papers, Acc.11368/34: 12 July 1907.

67. Scottish Conservative and Unionist Papers, Acc.10424/2: 19 January, 1905 16 December , 1913, 20 January 1914.

68. Scottish Conservative and Unionist Papers, Acc.10424/2: 21 November 1905. See also Martin Pugh, *The Tories and the People, 1880–1935* (Oxford, 1985).

69. Burness, *Strange Associations*, p.82; Hutchison, *Political History of Scotland*, p.198; Pugh, *Tories and the People 1880–1935*, pp.128–33. See also Scottish Conservative and Unionist Papers, Acc.10424/2: 2 February 1920.

70. See Burness, *Strange Associations* and Daniel Jackson, *Popular Opposition to Irish Home Rule in Edwardian Britain* (Liverpool, 2009), pp.113–19, 147–51, 184. cf. Cameron, *Impaled upon a Thistle*, p.100.

71. Hanham, *Scottish Nationalism*, p.103. See also R.J.Q. Adams, *Bonar Law* (London, 1999); Catherine Shannon, *Arthur J Balfour and Ireland, 1874–1922* (Washington, 1988).

72. Arthur Balfour Papers, Add.Ms.49859, ff.205, 207: Malcolm to Balfour, 2 December 1907, 15 December 1907.

73. Bodleian Library Oxford, Selborne Papers, v.26, f.57: Cooper to Wolmer, 7 October 1890.

74. Scottish Conservative and Unionist Papers, Acc.10424/42: 24 November 1912.

75. Scottish Conservative and Unionist Papers, Acc.10424/45: 30 April 1914.

76. See Ian Meredith, 'Irish Migrants in the Scottish Episcopal Church in the Nineteenth Century' in Martin Mitchell (ed.), *New Perspectives on the Irish in Scotland* (Edinburgh, 2008).

77. cf. Cameron, *Impaled upon a Thistle*, p.100.

78. Scottish Conservative and Unionist Papers, Acc.11368/34: 6 February 1914.

79. Burness, *Strange Associations*; Scottish Conservative and Unionist Papers, Acc.10424/2: 1 October 1912.

80. Scottish Conservative and Unionist Papers, Acc.10424/28: 17 December 1913.

81. Scottish Conservative and Unionist Papers, Acc.10424/43: 24 June 1914; Acc.10424/45: 27 May 1914.

82. Scottish Conservative and Unionist Papers, Acc.101424/45: 24 June 1914.

83. See W.S Rodner, 'Covenanters, Leaguers, Moderates: British Support for Ulster, 1913–14', *Eire-Ireland*, 17, 3 (1982).

84. Scottish Conservative and Unionist Papers, Acc.10424/28: 18 March 1914.

85. British Library, Walter Long Papers, Add.Ms.62411, f.70: Balfour of Burleigh to Long, 2 February 1907.

86. British Library, Walter Long Papers, Add.Ms.62411, f.67: Balfour of Burleigh to Long, 23 January 1907. On the other hand, intimate contact existed between leading Orange and Unionist figures in the North of Ireland and West of Scotland: see e.g. PRONI, Wallace Papers, D.1889/1/2/3: Wallace to J. Rice, 17 March 1911.

87. Scottish Conservative and Unionist Papers, Acc.10424/28: 18 March 1914.

88. Scottish Conservative and Unionist Papers, Acc.10424/43: 28 January 1914.

89. Alan Sykes, *Tariff Reform in British Politics, 1903–13* (Oxford, 1979).

90. See Jackson, *Ulster Party,* and Hutchison, *Political History of Scotland,* p.222.

91. Cf. Cameron, *Impaled Upon a Thistle,* p.100.

92. Fry, *Patronage and Principle,* p.203.

93. See John Wilson of Thornly, *The Political State of Scotland* (London, 1831), pp.i–ii.

94. Fry, *Patronage and Principle,* p.52.

95. See Colin Kidd, *Subverting Scotland's Past: Scottish Whig Historians and the Creation of an Anglo-British Identity, 1689–1830* (Cambridge, 1993).

96. *Ibid.* p.7.

97. R. Barry O'Brien, *Dublin Castle and the Irish People,* second edition (London, 1912).

98. Windscheffel, 'Gladstone and Scott', pp.69–95.

99. Fry, *Patronage and Principle,* p.83.

100. Fry, *Patronage and Principle,* pp.93, 130. See Jonathan Parry, 'From the 39 Articles to the 39 Steps: Reflections on the Thought of John Buchan'.

101. Fry, *Patronage and Principle,* p.92.

102. Hutchison, *Political History of Scotland,* p.162.

103. cf. Burness, *Strange Associations,* p.68.

104. *Ibid.* p.47; Fry, *Patronage and Principle,* p.103. See also W.C. Lubenow, *Parliamentary Politics and the Home Rule Crisis: The British House of Commons in 1886* (Oxford, 1986).

105. Quoted in Burness, *Strange Associations,* p.10.

106. Hutchison, *Political History of Scotland,* pp.154–5, 162ff.

107. cf. Jackson, *Ulster Party,* pp.214–15.

108. cf. Burness, *Strange Associations,* pp.70, 217.

109. *Ibid.* p.70.

110. Bodleian Library, J.S. Sandars Papers, c.761, ff.111, 134: Secretary to Balfour, 23 September 1910; Scott Dickson to Balfour, 27 September 1910. See Fry, *Patronage and Principle,* p.110.

111. Burness, *Strange Associations,* p.213; Harry Cockburn, *A History of the New Club, Edinburgh, 1787–1837* (Edinburgh, 1938).

112. cf. David Seawright, *An Important Matter of Principle: The Decline of the Scottish Conservative and Unionist Party* (Ashgate, 1999).

113. Hutchison, *Political History of Scotland,* p.328.

114. *Ibid.* p.76.

115. Scottish Conservative and Unionist Papers, Acc.10424/43: 25 June 1919.

116. Scottish Conservative and Unionist Papers, Acc.10424/43: 27 July 1923.

117. Scottish Conservative and Unionist Papers, Acc.10424/45: 9 October 1923.

118. Sheila Hetherington, *Katharine Atholl, 1874–1960* (Aberdeen, 1990), pp.98–118.

119. Robert Rhodes James (ed.), *Chips: The Diaries of Sir Henry Channon* (London, 1967), p.75; Jean Mann, *Woman in Parliament* (London, 1962), p.24. Douglas Haig was also impressed, crediting Edinburgh's 'changed attitude' towards

Poppy Day to Horsbrugh: Churchill College, Horsbrugh Papers, HSBR 6/7: Haig to Horsbrugh, 15 Nov. 1926.

120. Stuart Ball (ed.), *Parliament and Politics in the Age of Churchill and Attlee: The Headlam Diaries, 1935–41* (London, 1999), p.263.

121. Peter Catterall (ed.), *The Macmillan Diaries: The Cabinet Years, 1950–57* (London, 2003), p.296; Catriona Burness, ' "Count Up to Twenty One": Scottish Women in Formal Politics, 1918–90' in Esther Breitenbach and Pat Thane (eds), *Women and Citizenship in Britain and Ireland in the 20th Century* (London, 2010).

122. Scottish Conservative and Unionist Papers, Acc.10424/43: 5 July 1933. See also Hutchison, *Political History of Scotland*, pp.316–17; I.G.C. Hutchison, 'Scottish Unionism between the Two World Wars' in Catriona M.M. MacDonald (ed.), *Unionist Scotland, 1800–1997* (Edinburgh, 1998), p.78.

123. Scottish Conservative and Unionist Papers, Acc.10424/28: 3 May 1922; Acc.10424/64: 7 June 1946.

124. Scottish Conservative and Unionist Papers, Acc.10424/43: 5 July 1933.

125. Scottish Conservative and Unionist Papers, Acc.10424/45: 28 March 1923.

126. Scottish Conservative and Unionist Papers, Acc.10424/45: 24 June 1925.

127. Gilmour Papers, GD.383/43/103: Mills to Gilmour, 3 October 1932. See also Eric Kaufmann, 'The Orange Order in Scotland since 1860: A Social Analysis' in Martin Mitchell (ed.), *New Perspectives on the Irish in Scotland* (Edinburgh, 2008), p.188.

128. Scottish Conservative and Unionist Papers, Acc.10424/43: 27 April 1923, 17 July 1925, 26 October 1927, 25 March 1931.

129. Hutchison, 'Scottish Unionism', pp.77–8.

130. Kenneth Young, *Sir Alec Douglas-Home* (London, 1970), p.26n; D.R. Thorpe, *Alec Douglas-Home* (London, 1996), p.37. See also NLS, Walter Elliot Papers, Acc.12198/7: Elliot to Dugdale, 1/5/[1937] (where Elliot as Secretary of State for Scotland reviewed 10,000 members of the Boys' Brigade, and 'felt that Mussolini…had nothing whatever on me').

131. Stanley Salvidge, *Salvidge of Liverpool* (London, 1934); Philip Waller, *Democracy and Sectarianism: A Political and Social History of Liverpool, 1868–1939* (Liverpool, 1981). See also e.g. Scottish Conservative and Unionist Papers, Acc.10428/8: 7 December 1921.

132. Scottish Conservative and Unionist Papers, Acc.10424/63: 19 January 1922.

133. Scottish Conservative and Unionist Papers, Acc.11368/11: 25 March 1930.

134. Gilmour Papers, GD.383/62/7: Blair to Gilmour, 14 July 1935.

135. Scottish Conservative and Unionist Papers, Acc.10424/43: 24 October 1934.

136. Scottish Conservative and Unionist Papers, Acc.10424/43: 17 July 1925.

137. Scottish Conservative and Unionist Papers, Acc.11368/11: 11 January 1932.

138. C.C. Riach, *Douglas and the Douglas Family* (Hamilton, 1927), p.12.

139. *Ibid.* p.12.

140. *Ibid.* pp.21–2, 26.

141. *Ibid.* pp.34–6.

142. James Mitchell, *Conservatives and the Union: A Study of Conservative Party Attitudes to Scotland* (Edinburgh, 1990), pp.48–50.

143. See A.N. Skelton, *Constructive Conservatism* (Edinburgh, 1924); David Torrance, *Noel Skelton and the Property-Owning Democracy* (London, 2010), pp.40, 252n.

144. Torrance, *Skelton*, p.232.

145. Robert Boothby et al., *Industry and the State: A Conservative View* (London, 1927); Walter Elliot, *Toryism and the Twentieth Century* (London, 1927).

146. National Library of Scotland James Porteous Papers, Acc.7505/1: 'The Future of the Conservative and Unionist Party'.

147. Porteous Papers, Acc.7505/1: Colebourn, *National Review*, to Porteous, 13 March 1936; Editor, *English Review*, to Porteous, n.d.

148. Porteous Papers, Acc.7505/1: J.M.MacCormick to Porteous, 27 December 1949.

149. e.g. Iain McLean and Alastair McMillan, *State of the Union: Unionism and the Alternatives in the United Kingdom since 1707* (Oxford, 2005), pp.247–8.

150. *Banffshire Journal*, 9 December 1930.

151. National Library of Scotland, Thomas Cooper, Lord Cooper of Culross, Papers, Acc.6188/6: James Stuart to Cooper, 27 November 1952.

152. Gordon Stott, *QC's Diary, 1954–1960* (Edinburgh, 1998), p.153; Kidd, *Union and Unionisms*, pp.116ff, 202.

153. Paul Ward, *Unionism in the United Kingdom*, pp.57–71.

154. National Library of Scotland, Priscilla Tweedsmuir Papers, Acc.11884/157: speech notes, 21 March 1945.

155. Priscilla Tweedsmuir Papers, Acc.11884/157: P.J.Blair to Grant, 22 March 1945.

156. Bodleian Library, Oxford, Scottish Unionist Members' Committee, SUMC 2/1: 19 October 1932.

157. Scottish Unionist Members' Committee, SUMC 2/1: 19 October 1932.

158. Scottish Unionist Members' Committee, 2/3: 20 July 1943, 9 May 1944, 5 December 1944.

159. Robert Boothby, *I Fight to Live* (London, 1947), pp.55–6.

160. Fry, *Patronage and Principle*, p.140; Mitchell, *Conservatives and the Union*, p.50.

161. Scottish Conservative and Unionist Papers, Acc.10424/8: Beckett to Shedden, 23 February 1929.

162. Walter Elliot Papers, Acc.12198/4: Elliot to Dugdale, 12 November 1934.

163. See e.g. *Glasgow Observer*, 23 February 1929, 24 October 1931.

164. Walter Elliot Papers, Acc.12267/11: Elliot to Dugdale, 25 October 1931. See also Walter Elliot Papers, Acc.12267/16: Elliot to Dugdale, 30 December 1943.

165. Scottish Conservative and Unionist Papers, Acc.10424/64: 26 July 1939.

166. Gilmour Papers, GD.383/64/3: Clark Hutchison to Gilmour, 10 November 1935, referring to the 'Irishness' of the district.

167. Hetherington, *Katharine Atholl*, pp.176, 187, 192; Kenneth Young, *Sir Alec Douglas-Home* (London, 1970), p.43. See also Richard Griffiths, *Patriotism*

*Perverted: Captain Ramsay, the Right Club and British Anti-Semitism, 1939–40* (London, 1998).

168. Ball (ed.), *Parliament and Politics*, p.307.

169. Cameron, *Impaled upon a Thistle*, p.152.

170. Scottish Unionist Members' Committee, SUMC 2/6: 25 November 1952.

171. e.g. Michael Rosie, 'Protestant Action and the Edinburgh Irish' in Martin Mitchell (ed.), *New Perspectives on the Irish in Scotland* (Edinburgh, 2008), pp.145–8.

172. See Walter Elliot Papers. Also: David Torrance, *The Scottish Secretaries* (Edinburgh, 2006), pp.135–45; Paul Ward, *Unionism in the United Kingdom, 1918–74* (London, 2005), pp.21–40.

173. Walter Elliot Papers, Acc.12198/7: Elliot to Dugdale, 8 July 1937.

174. Ward, *Unionism in the United Kingdom*, p.25.

175. Walter Elliot Papers, Acc.12198/8: Elliot to Dugdale, 24 August 1938. See also Walter Elliot Papers, Acc.12198/10: Elliot to Dugdale, 24 September 1940.

176. Walter Elliot Papers, Acc.12198/7: Elliot to Dugdale, 29 December 1937.

177. Walter Elliot Papers, Acc.12267/16: Elliot to Dugdale, 22, 25 June 1943.

178. David Torrance, *We in Scotland: Thatcherism in a Cold Climate* (Edinburgh, 2009), p.14.

179. Walter Elliot Papers, Acc.12267/19: Elliot to Dugdale, 9 September 1946.

180. Walter Elliot Papers, Acc.12198/7: Elliot to Dugdale, 9 July 1937.

181. Walter Elliot Papers, Acc.12198/1: Elliot to Dugdale, 31 August 1922. See also Walter Elliot Papers, Acc.12198/6: Elliot to Dugdale, 27 August 1936.

182. Walter Elliot Papers, Acc.12267/6: Elliot to Dugdale, 4 May 1943.

183. Walter Elliot Papers, Acc.12267/16: Elliot to Dugdale, 4, 14 August 1943.

184. Walter Elliot Papers, Acc.12267/18: Elliot to Dugdale, 24 August 1945.

185. Walter Elliot Papers, Acc.12198/10: Elliot to Dugdale, 19 November 1940.

186. Walter Elliot Papers, Acc.12247/11: Elliot to Dugdale, 21 December 1928.

187. Scottish Unionist Members' Committee Papers, SUMC 2/1: 19 October 1932.

188. Alvin Jackson, *The Ulster Party: Irish Unionists in the House of Commons, 1884–1911* (Oxford, 1989), pp.114–95. Compare Mitchell, *Conservatives and the Union*, p.24.

189. Mitchell, *Conservatives and the Union*, p.22.

190. *Ibid.* pp.22–3.

191. Scottish Unionist Members' Committee Papers, SUMC 2/1: 19 October 1932.

192. Mitchell, *Conservatives and the Union*, p.25. Gilmour Papers, GD.383/68/9, 14: Elliot to Gilmour, 4 November 1936, 14 September 1936.

193. Compare Andrew Gailey, *Ireland and the Death of Kindness: The Experience of Constructive Unionism, 1890–1905* (Cork, 1987).

194. See Lawrence McBride, *The Greening of Dublin Castle: The Transforming of Bureaucratic and Judicial Personnel in Dublin Castle in Ireland, 1892–1922* (Washington, 1991); Fergus Campbell, *The Irish Establishment, 1879–1914* (Oxford, 2009).

195. See Jackson, *Ulster Party*, pp.253–66.

196. Scottish Unionist Members' Committee Papers, SUMC 2/1: 15 February 1949.

197. See e.g. Graham Walker, *A History of the Ulster Unionist Party: Protest, Pragmatism and Pessimism* (Manchester, 2004).

198. Cameron, *Impaled upon a Thistle*, p.220.

199. See Mitchell, *Conservatives and the Union*, pp.55–7; Lindsay Paterson, *A Diverse Assembly: The Debate on a Scottish Parliament* (Edinburgh 1998), pp.26–30.

200. Lang, *Blue Remembered Years*, p.167.

201. D.R. Thorpe, *Alec Douglas-Home* (London, 1996), pp.399–400; Torrance, *We in Scotland*, p.16.

202. Mitchell, *Conservatives and the Union*, p.65.

203. Scottish Conservative and Unionist Papers, Acc.11368/17: 16 September 1968.

204. Scottish Conservative and Unionist Papers, Acc.11368/17: 23 November 1968.

205. Michael Keating and David Bleiman, *Labour and Scottish Nationalism* (London, 1979), p.150.

206. See e.g. Scottish Conservative and Unionist Papers, Acc.11368/55 (Uddingston Unionist Association Papers).

207. Scottish Conservative and Unionist Papers, Acc.11368/55: 11 January 1961. Terence O'Neill, *The Autobiography* (London, 1972), p.40.

208. Scottish Conservative and Unionist Papers, Acc.11368/69: 11 February 1966.

209. Lang, *Blue Remembered Years*, p.37.

210. Scottish Conservative and Unionist Papers, Acc.11368/17: 18 May 1970.

211. Compare, though, Torrance, *We in Scotland*, pp.6–7, 41, for Thatcher's private social visits to Scotland.

212. Torrance, *We in Scotland*, p.31.

213. *Ibid.* p.177. See also David Torrance, *George Younger: A Life Well Lived* (Edinburgh, 2008).

214. David Torrance, *The Scottish Secretaries* (Edinburgh, 2006), pp.298–9; Torrance, *We in Scotland*, pp.45ff.

215. John Campbell, *Margaret Thatcher, Volume Two: The Iron Lady* (London, 2003), p.397.

216. See Skelton, *Constructive Conservatism*; Torrance, *We in Scotland*, pp.26, 42, 131; David Torrance, *Noel Skelton and the Property-Owning Democracy* (London, 2010), pp.214–17.

217. Torrance, *We in Scotland*, pp.xxiii, 144, 154.

218. Quoted in Torrance, *Scottish Secretaries*, p.314. See also Lang, Blue *Remembered Years*, pp.68–9.

219. Torrance, *We in Scotland*, p.149. See also Nigel Lawson, *The View from No.11: Memoirs of a Tory Radical* (London, 1991), p.580.

220. Torrance, *Scottish Secretaries*, p.307. See also Lang, *Blue Remembered Years*, pp.96–7.

221. Quoted in Torrance, *We in Scotland*, p.221.

222. Torrance, *We in Scotland*, p.126.

223. Lang, *Blue Remembered Years*, p.70.

224. Torrance, *We in Scotland*, p.167. See Chapter 5.

225. Lang, *Blue Remembered Years*, pp.203, 206.

226. Murray Pittock, *Scottish Nationality* (Basingstoke, 2001), p.112; Vernon Bogdanor, *Devolution in the United Kingdom* (Oxford, 2001), p.138.

227. Iain McLean, 'Financing the Union: Goschen, Barnett and Beyond' in William L. Miller (ed.), *Anglo-Scottish Relations from 1900 to Devolution and Beyond* (Oxford, 2005), p.84.

228. Keating and Bleiman, *Labour and Scottish Nationalism*, p.91.

229. Ward, *Unionism in the United Kingdom*, p.41.

230. Keating and Bleiman, *Labour and Scottish Nationalism*, p.94.

231. James J. Smyth, *Labour in Glasgow: Socialism, Suffrage, Sectarianism* (East Linton, 2000); James J. Smyth, 'Resisting Labour: Unionists, Liberals and Moderates in Glasgow between the Wars', *Historical Journal*, 46 (2003).

232. Hutchison, *Political History of Scotland*, p.288.

233. Mark Stuart, *John Smith: A Life* (London, 2005), pp.23, 350–63.

234. See Graham Walker, *Thomas Johnston* (Manchester, 1988); Ward, *Unionism in the United Kingdom*, pp.41–56.

235. Thomas Johnston, *Memories* (London, 1952), p.66.

236. Johnston, *Memories*, p.64

237. *Ibid.* p.66.

238. *Ibid.* p.66.

239. Ward, *Unionism in the United Kingdom*, p.49.

240. Keating and Bleiman, *Labour and Scottish Nationalism*, p.113.

241. Johnston, *Memories*, p.90.

242. cf. Ward, *Unionism in the United Kingdom*, p.56.

243. T.M. Devine, *The Scottish Nation, 1700–2000* (London, 1999), p.552. See also Cameron, *Impaled upon a Thistle*, p.189.

244. Torrance, *Scottish Secretaries*, p.163.

245. Johnston, *Memories*, p.152.

246. Fry, *Patronage and Principle*, p.239.

247. National Library of Scotland, Thomas Johnston Papers, Acc.5862/8: 'Tribute to Bannockburn' (draft).

248. *Sunday Times*, 25 March 1945; *Daily Mail*, 28 December 1949.

249. *Sunday Times*, 25 March 1945.

250. Bogdanor, *Devolution,* pp.112–13.

251. See Alvin Jackson, *Home Rule: An Irish History, 1800–2000*, paperback edition (London, 2004), p.254.

252. See e.g. Bogdanor, *Devolution*, p.139.

253. Fry, *Patronage and Principle*, p.229.

254. Quoted in Torrance, *Scottish Secretaries*, p.252.

255. See A.V. Dicey, 'The Two Acts of Union: A Contrast', *Fortnightly Review*, 30, 176 (Aug. 1881).

256. Fergal Cochrane, *Unionist Politics and the Politics of Unionism since the Anglo-Irish Agreement* (Cork, 1997), p.148.

257. Richard Crossman, *The Diaries of a Cabinet Minister: Volume III: Secretary of State for Social Services, 1968–70* (London, 1977), p.106.

258. Torrance, *Scottish Secretaries*, p.262.

259. Bogdanor, *Devolution*, p.190.

260. *Ibid.* p.190; Fry, *Patronage and Principle*, p.250.

261. cf. Torrance, *We in Scotland*.

262. See A.V. Dicey, *A Leap in the Dark: A Criticism of the Principles of Home Rule, As Illustrated by the Bill of 1893* (London, 1911).

## CHAPTER 8

1. See e.g. Colin Kidd, *Union and Unionisms: Political Thought in Scotland, 1500–2000* (Cambridge, 2008).

2. See Allan Blackstock, *Loyalism in Ireland, 1789–1829* (London, 2007); J.R. Hill, 'Ireland without Union: Molyneux and his Legacy' in John Robertson (ed.), *A Union for Empire: Political Thought and the Union of 1707* (Cambridge, 1995); J.R. Hill, *From Patriots to Unionists: Dublin Civic Politics and Irish Protestant Patriotism, 1660–1840* (Oxford, 1997).

3. See e.g. J.T. Ball, *Historical Review of the Legislative Systems Operative in Ireland, 1172–1800* (London, 1889), p.159.

4. e.g. Douglas Kanter, *The Making of British Unionism, 1740–1848: Politics, Government and the Anglo-Irish Constitutional Relationship* (Dublin, 2009), p.12.

5. Alvin Jackson, *The Ulster Party: Irish Unionists in the House of Commons, 1884–1911* (Oxford, 1989), pp.214–16.

6. K.T. Hoppen, *Elections, Politics and Society in Ireland, 1832–1885* (Oxford, 1984), p.278.

7. *Ibid.* p.280. Cf. Ian D'Alton, *Protestant Society and Politics in Cork, 1812–44* (Cork, 1980), pp.226–7.

8. Hill, *Patriots to Unionists*, p.371n.

9. *Ibid.* p.385.

10. *Ibid.* p.388.

11. See e.g. David Hempton and Myrtle Hill, *Evangelical Protestantism in Ulster Society, 1740–1890* (London, 1992), pp.86–94.

12. See Desmond Bowen, *The Protestant Crusade in Ireland, 1800–1870: A Study of Protestant-Catholic Relations between the Act of Union and Disestablishment* (Dublin, 1978); Irene Whelan, *The Bible War in Ireland: The 'Second Reformation' and the Polarisation of Protestant-Catholic Relations, 1800–40* (Chicago, 2005).

13. Stewart J. Brown, *The National Churches of England, Ireland and Scotland, 1801–46* (Oxford, 2001), p.141.

14. *Ibid.* p.126; Hill, *Patriots to Unionists*. See also Paul Connell, 'Evangelicalism, the Church of Ireland, and Anti-Catholicism in the Life and

Thought of the Rev Tresham Dames Gregg (1800–81)' (National University of Ireland Maynooth unpublished Ph.D. thesis, 2007).

15. James Porter, *Life and Times of Henry Cooke DD, LLD* (Belfast, 1875 edition), p.224. See also Finlay Holmes, *Henry Cooke* (Belfast, 1981).

16. Porter, *Henry Cooke*, pp.224–5.

17. *Ibid.* p.233.

18. *Ibid.* p.236.

19. Danilo Raponi, 'British Protestants, the Roman Question, and the Formation of Italian National Identity, 1861–75' (University of Cambridge Ph.D. thesis, 2009), p.92.

20. See Anon [Catherine Marsh], *Brief Memories of Hugh McCalmont, First Earl Cairns* (London, 1885); A.C. Ewald, *The Life of Sir Joseph Napier, Bart., Ex-Lord Chancellor of Ireland, From His Correspondence* (London, 1887); James Whiteside, *Essays and Lectures: Historical and Literary* (Dublin, 1868); James Whiteside, *Early Sketches of Eminent Persons* (Dublin, 1870).

21. Alfred Gathorne-Hardy, *Gathorne Hardy, First Earl of Cranbrook: A Memoir with Extracts from his Correspondence*, two vols (London, 1910), i, p.134. Compare Thomas Macknight, *Ulster As It is: Or Twenty Eight Years' Experience as an Irish Editor*, 2 vols (London, 1896), i, pp.26–9.

22. Anon., *McCalmont*, pp.9, 46–7, 90.

23. See D.C. Savage, 'The Irish Unionists, 1867–86', *Eire-Ireland*, 2 (1967).

24. See John Bew, *The Glory of being Britons: Civic Unionism in Nineteenth Century Belfast* (Dublin, 2008).

25. See the arguments of Blackstock, *Loyalism in Ireland*.

26. Hereward Senior, Hereward, *Orangeism in Ireland and Britain, 1795–1836* (London, 1966).

27. Blackstock, *Loyalism in Ireland*, p.129.

28. *Ibid.* pp.270–1.

29. See Aiken McClelland, *William Johnston of Ballykilbeg* (Belfast, 1990).

30. Alvin Jackson, 'Unionist Myths, 1912–85', *Past & Present*, 136 (August 1992); R.F. Foster and Alvin Jackson, '"Men for all Seasons"?: Carson, Parnell, and the Limits of Heroism in Modern Ireland', in *European History Quarterly*, 39, 3 (July 2009), p. 425.

31. See PRONI, William Johnston Diary, D.989; Jackson, *Ulster Party*, p.111.

32. Brian Walker, *Ulster Politics: The Formative Years, 1868–86* (Belfast, 1989), p.122.

33. Hutchison, *Political History of Scotland, 1832–1924: Parties, Elections and Issues* (Edinburgh, 1986), p.59.

34. Hoppen, *Elections, Politics and Society*, p.284.

35. *Ibid.* pp.284–5.

36. *Ibid.* p.286.

37. *Ibid.* p.289. See also Walker, *Ulster Politics*, pp.140–2.

38. Compare A.B. Cooke and John Vincent, *The Governing Passion: Cabinet Government and Party Politics in Britain, 1885–6* (Brighton, 1974). See also Chapter 5.

39. Gathorne-Hardy, *Cranbrook*, i, pp.134, 137.

40. Walker, *Ulster Politics*, p.3.

41. See William Wilson Hunter, *A Life of the Earl of Mayo, Fourth Viceroy of India*, two vols (London, 1876).

42. Hoppen, *Elections, Politics and Society*, pp.293–9.

43. Quoted in Andrew Shields, *The Irish Conservative Party, 1852–68: Land, Politics and Religion* (Dublin, 2006), p.211.

44. James Whiteside (ed.), *Essays and Lectures: Historical and Literary* (Dublin, 1868), pp.2–206.

45. Quoted in Shields, *Irish Conservative Party*, p.163.

46. See P.M.H. Bell, *Disestablishment in Ireland and Wales* (London, 1969); Savage, 'Irish Unionists'.

47. *Ibid.* p.79.

48. Quoted in *Ibid.* p.80.

49. See Alvin Jackson, *Colonel Edward Saunderson: Land and Loyalty in Victorian Ireland* (Oxford, 1995), pp.20–2.

50. *Ibid.* pp.19–23.

51. *Ibid.* pp.243–8.

52. Peter Gibbon, *The Origins of Ulster Unionism: The Formation of Popular Protestant Politics and Ideology in Nineteenth Century Ireland* (Manchester, 1975), p.105.

53. *Ibid.* p.106.

54. *Ibid.* p.106.

55. Frank Thompson, *The End of Liberal Ulster: Land Agitation and Land Reform, 1868–86* (Belfast, 2001), p.302.

56. Hoppen, *Elections, Politics and Society*, p.270.

57. Thompson, *End of Liberal Ulster*, p.5 and chapter six; Walker, *Ulster Politics*, p.116.

58. Hoppen, *Elections, Politics and Society*, p.274.

59. Compare Walker, *Ulster Politics*.

60. Hoppen, *Elections, Politics and Society*, p.265.

61. e.g. Charlotte Fell Smith, *James Nicholson Richardson of Bessbrook* (London, 1925), pp.68–9.

62. MacKnight, *Ulster as It is*, i, p.170.

63. Walker, *Ulster Politics*, p.236.

64. For biographical treatments, see R. Barry O'Brien, *The Life of Lord Russell of Killowen* (London, 1902); A.D. McDonnell, *The Life of Sir Denis Henry: Catholic Unionist* (Belfast, 2000).

65. cf. Gibbon, *Origins of Ulster Unionism*.

66. Macknight, *Ulster as It is*, i, p.263.

67. See Alvin Jackson, 'Unionist Politics and Protestant Society in Edwardian Ireland', *Historical Journal*, xxxiii, 4 (1990). cf. W.S. Armour, *Armour of Ballymoney* (London, 1934); J.R.B. McMinn, *Against the Tide: J.B. Armour, Irish Presbyterian Minister and Home Ruler* (Belfast, 1985). See also Harry Waddell, *John Waddell* (Belfast, 1949), pp.43–4.

68. See Patrick Buckland, *Irish Unionism I: The Anglo-Irish and the New Ireland, 1885–1922* (Dublin, 1972); Patrick Buckland, *Irish Unionism II: Ulster Unionism and the Origins of Northern Ireland, 1886–1922* (Dublin, 1973).

69. Linda Colley, *Britons: Forging the Nation, 1707–1837* (New Haven, 1992), p.193.

70. Diane Urquhart, *The Ladies of Londonderry: Women and Political Patronage* (London, 2007).

71. See Macknight, *Ulster As It is*; J.R. Fisher, *The End of the Irish Parliament* (London, 1911); Armour, *Armour of Ballymoney*; W.S. Armour, *Facing the Irish Question* (London, 1935); W.S. Armour, *Ulster, Ireland, Britain: A Forgotten Trust* (London, 1938).

72. D.G. Boyce, 'Alfred Harmsworth, First Viscount Northcliffe', *New Oxford Dictionary of National Biography* (Oxford, 2004).

73. W.F. Monypenny, *The Two Irish Nations: An Essay on Irish Home Rule* (London, 1913)

74. Claire Connolly, 'Completing the Union: The Irish Novel and the Moment of Union' in Michael Brown, Patrick Geoghegan, and James Kelly (eds), *The Irish Act of Union, 1800: Bicentennial Essays* (Dublin, 2003), p.162.

75. Joep Leersen, *Remembrance and Imagination: Patterns in the Literary and Historical Representation of Ireland in the Nineteenth Century* (Cork, 1996), pp.38–9.

76. Connolly, 'Completing the Union', p.160; W.J. MacCormack, 'Maria Edgeworth', *New Oxford Dictionary of National Biography* (Oxford, 2004).

77. Mary Jean Corbett, *Allegories of Union in Irish and English Writing* (Cambridge, 2000), p.12.

78. Stanley Baldwin, *This Torch of Freedom: Speeches and Addresses* (London, 1935), p.166.

79. Connolly, 'Completing the Union', p.164.

80. William Johnston, *Nightshade: A Novel* (London, 1857), p.295.

81. For a discussion of the Siege theme see Ian McBride, *The Siege of Derry in Ulster Protestant Mythology* (Dublin, 1997).

82. John Wilson Foster, *Forces and Themes in Ulster Fiction* (Dublin, 1974), pp.130–9.

83. British Library, Arthur Balfour Papers, Add.Ms.49849, f.53: Ball to Middleton, 9 July 1891.

84. See e.g. Peter Brown, *Augustine of Hippo: A Biography* (London, 1969); E.R. Dodd, *Missing Persons: An Autobiography* (Oxford, 1977). John Pentland Mahaffy, *Greek Life and Thought: From the Age of Alexander to the Roman Conquest* (London, 1887) offered a variety of anachronistic aspersions on modern democracy. I am grateful to Owen Dudley Edwards for this point. On a more general and qualifying note, A.V. Dicey thought that Oxford university signatories for the British Covenant were 'less satisfactory than you might have expected. My reason for this conclusion is that I do not see anything like the number of university men as protestors whom I know to be Unionist': Bodleian Library, Milner Papers, dep.41/40: Dicey to Milner, 6 March 1914.

85. Jackson, *Ulster Party*, pp.25ff.

86. Balfour Papers, Add.Ms.49773, f.99: Balfour to Chamberlain, 29 February 1896 (copy).

87. Martin Maguire, 'The Organisation and Activism of Dublin's Protestant Working Class, 1883–1935', *Irish Historical Studies*, 29, 113 (1994). For an insight into Unionist behaviour in Dublin local politics see James Joyce, 'Ivy Day in the Committee Room', *Dubliners* [London, 1914], World's Classics edition (Oxford, 2000), pp.91–105. See also PRONI, Kingstown and District Unionist Club Minutes, 1911-14, D.950/1/147: minute for 31 Jan. 1912, referring to the 'Kingstown and Blackrock Protestant Temperance Band'. The minute for 20 Oct. 1913 carries a petition from 'we the Unionist workingmen of Kingstown' concerning inadequate representation on the urban district council.

88. See Adam Pole, 'Landlord Responses to the Irish Land War, 1879–82' (University of Dublin unpublished Ph.D. thesis, 2006).

89. See Jackson, *Ulster Party*, pp.198–211.

90. Buckland, *Anglo-Irish and the New Ireland*; Jackson, *Ulster Party*, pp.55–7, 154.

91. See John Biggs-Davison and George Chowdharay-Best, *The Cross of Saint Patrick: The Catholic Unionist Tradition in Ireland* (Bourne End, 1984).

92. Arthur Balfour Papers, Add.Ms.49830, ff.321, 428: Balfour to MacDonnell, 29 October 1891; Balfour to Goschen, n.d. [12 Dec.1891].

93. Colin Kidd, *Union and Unionisms*, pp.157–69.

94. See Shan Bullock, *Thomas Andrews: Shipbuilder* (Dublin, 1912) p.50.

95. See Timothy Bowman, *Carson's Army: The Ulster Volunteer Force, 1910–22* (Manchester, 2008); Daniel Jackson, *Popular Opposition to Irish Home Rule in Edwardian Britain* (Liverpool, 2009), p.184.

96. Alvin Jackson, *Home Rule: An Irish History, 1800–2000*, paperback edition (London, 2004), pp.154–5.

97. See Jackson, *Popular Opposition to Irish Home Rule*, pp.66–99 for Carson's visit to Liverpool in September 1912.

98. See e.g. Jeremy Dibble, *Charles Villiers Stanford: Man and Musician* (Oxford, 2002).

99. See e.g. Max Beerbohm, *Fifty Caricatures* (London, 1913), p.10.

100. Alvin Jackson, 'Unionist Myths, 1912–85', *Past & Present*, 136 (August 1992); Foster and Jackson, '"Men for all Seasons"?', pp.423–33. See also PRONI, Edward Carson Papers, D.1507/1/1934/15: William Gillespie to Carson, 6 Mar. 1934 (where Carson's permission is sought to use a portrait for the skin of an Orange drum).

101. Jackson, *Home Rule*, pp.152–3.

102. See Cyril Falls, *The History of the Thirty Sixth (Ulster) Division* (Belfast, 1922), pp.57, 61–2.

103. *Scotland on Sunday*, 1 February 2009. For the name 'Northern Ireland' see e.g. House of Lords Record Office, Herbert Samuel Papers, A/41/19: Edward Carson to Samuel, 21 July 1916 ('I do not imagine there will be any objection to calling them [the six counties] 'Northern Ireland').

104. Máirtín Ó Catháin, 'A Winnowing Spirit' in Martin Mitchell (ed.), *New Perspectives on The Irish in Scotland* (Edinburgh, 2008), p.123; T.M. Devine, 'The End of Disadvantage? The Descendants of Irish Catholic Immigrants in Modern Scotland since 1945' in Martin Mitchell (ed.), *New Perspectives on The Irish in Scotland* (Edinburgh, 2008), p.206.

105. Dean Godson, *Himself Alone: David Trimble and the Ordeal of Unionism*, paperback edition (London, 2005), p.402.

106. See e.g. James Loughlin, *Ulster Unionism and British National Identity since 1885* (London, 1995).

107. See Gillian V. McIntosh, *The Force of Culture: Unionist Identities in Twentieth Century Ireland* (Cork, 1999).

108. Henry Patterson and Eric Kaufmann, *Unionism and Orangeism in Northern Ireland since 1945* (Manchester, 2007), p.15.

109. See Henry Patterson, 'Party versus Order: Ulster Unionism and the Flags and Emblems Act', *Contemporary British History*, 13, 4 (1999).

110. Timothy Wilson, '"The most terrible assassination that has yet stained the name of Belfast": The McMahon Murders in Context', *Irish Historical Studies*, xxxvii, 145 (Sept.2010).

111. Ó Catháin, 'Winnowing Spirit', p.129.

112. See e.g. T.M. Devine (ed.), *Scotland's Shame? Bigotry and Sectarianism in Modern Scotland* (Edinburgh, 2000).

113. In e.g. Patterson and Kaufmann, *Unionism and Orangeism*, pp.44–56.

114. *Ibid.* p.57.

115. See the arguments of Richard Finlay, 'Politics and State Intervention in Scotland, 1918–97' in Catriona MacDonald (ed.), *Unionist Scotland, 1800–1997* (Edinburgh, 1998); see also Fry, *Patronage and Principle*.

116. Jackson, *Ulster Party*, pp.322–6.

117. See Alvin Jackson, '"Tame Tory Hacks"? The Ulster Party at Westminster, 1922–72', *Historical Journal*, 54, 2 (June, 2011).

118. National Library of Scotland, Scottish Conservative and Unionist Papers, Acc.10424/63: 4 November 1921.

119. Bodleian Library, Oxford, Scottish Unionist Members' Committee Papers, SUMC 2/4: 15 February 1949.

120. Scottish Unionist Members' Committee Papers, SUMC 2/4: 17 May 1949.

121. Scottish Unionist Members' Committee Papers, SUMC, 2/5: 25 July 1950.

122. Nicholas Mansergh, *The Government of Northern Ireland: A Study in Devolution* (London, 1936), pp.176, 179.

123. Gordon Stott, *Judge's Diary, 1967–73* (Edinburgh, 1995), p.86. For the political culture which propelled O'Neill to political leadership see Alvin Jackson, *Home Rule: An Irish History*, paperback edition (London, 2004), pp.271–86.

124. Marc Mulholland, *The Longest War: Northern Ireland's Troubled History* (Oxford, 2002), pp.41–5.

125. John Harbinson, *The Ulster Unionist Party, 1882–1873: Its Development and Organisation* (Belfast, 1973); Patterson and Kaufmann, *Unionism and Orangeism*.

126. Patterson and Kaufmann, *Unionism and Orangeism*, p.5.

127. Christopher Farrington, *Ulster Unionism and the Peace Process in Northern Ireland* (Basingstoke, 2006), p.186.

128. Alistair Horne, *Harold Macmillan, 1957–1986: Volume II of the Official Biography* (London, 1989), p.493. For the relationship between Basil Brooke, his government, and Clement Attlee's Labour administration see: PRONI, CAB 9B/267/6: Attlee to Brooke, 21 March 1949. See also: CAB 9B/267/3: Brooke to Attlee, Morrison, Chuter Ede et al., 3 June 1949; Morrison to Brooke, 15 June 1949 ('My dear Basil, If I may say so, I shall always have the most friendly feelings for your part of the United Kingdom'). For an excellent assessment of Brooke, see PRONI, G.B. Newe Papers, D.3687/1/7/8: Newe to Butler, 3 Sept. 1973. Bodleian Library, Conservative Central Office Papers, CCO 1/8/617: Nutting to Buchan Hepburn, 30 Oct.1950; Collis to Central Office, 25 Nov.1950. CCO 2/6/23: Collis to Central Office, 29 Jan.1964.

129. See the studies by James Murphy, *Abject Loyalty: Nationalism and Monarchy in Ireland During the Reign of Queen Victoria* (Washington, 2001) and by James Loughlin, *The British Monarchy and Ireland: 1800 to the Present* (Cambridge, 2007).

130. See Eric Kaufmann, *The Orange Order: A Contemporary Northern Irish History* (Oxford, 2007), p.310.

131. Diane Urquhart, *Women in Ulster Politics, 1890–1940: A History Not Yet Told* (Dublin, 2000); Diane Urquhart, *The Ladies of Londonderry: Women and Political Patronage* (London, 2007); Rachel Ward, *Women, Unionism and Loyalism in Northern Ireland: From Teamakers to Political Actors* (Dublin, 2006).

132. D.A. Chart, *A History of Northern Ireland* (Belfast, 1927).

133. British Library, Walter Long Papers, Add.Ms.62416, f.102: Anson to Long, 18 December 1913. See also Long Papers, Add.Ms.62406: correspondence between Long and Dicey. Anson, though, was not keen to sign the British Covenant: Bodleian Library, Milner Papers, Ms.Eng.Hist.c689, f.25: Anson to Amery, 20 Feb. 1914.

134. British Library, Arthur Balfour Papers, Add.Ms.49792, f.75: Lowell to Plunkett, 3 July 1912 (copy).

135. Churchill College Cambridge, Robert Chichester Clark Papers, CCLK 1/1, 3/4: Wilson to Chichester Clark, 30 March 1955; Wilson to Chichester Clark, 6 July 1967.

136. Arthur Aughey, *Under Siege: Ulster Unionism and the Anglo-Irish Agreement* (Belfast, 1989).

137. Farrington, *Ulster Unionism and the Peace Process*, pp.17–19.

138. In Iain McLean, 'The 1909 Budget and the Destruction of the Unwritten British Constitution', History and Policy Papers (November, 2009), www.historyandpolicy.org/papers/policy-paper-94.html. See Iain McLean and

Alastair McMillan, *State of the Union:Unionism and the Alternatives in the United Kingdom since 1707* (Oxford, 2005). See also Timothy Bowman, *Carson's Army: The Ulster Volunteer Force, 1910–22* (Manchester, 2008).

139. Wilson, 'The most terrible assassination'. For the shadowy 'Imperial Guards' see e.g. PRONI, Cabinet Papers, CAB.9Z/1/1: R.Boyd (Honorary Secretary), 'Resolution of Ulster Imperial Guards', 4 Feb.1922 ('that we, representing 30,000 loyalists of the industrial workers of the City of Belfast view with alarm the results of the negotiations... conducted by Sir James Craig. We warn him and the members of his cabinet that we will stand solidly behind the men of the Border Counties...').

140. Jackson, 'Unionist Myths'.


## CHAPTER 9

1. Brian Levack, *The Formation of the British State: England, Scotland and the Union, 1603–1707* (Oxford, 1987), p.30.

2. Jenny Wormald, 'The Union of 1603' in Roger Mason (ed.), *Scots and Britons: Scottish Political Thought and the Union of 1603* (Cambridge, 1994), p.36.

3. See Stewart Brown, *The National Churches of England, Ireland and Scotland, 1801–46* (Oxford, 2001).

4. Colin Kidd, *Subverting Scotland's Past: Scottish Whig Historians and the Creation of an Anglo-British Identity, 1689–1830* (Cambridge, 1993), pp.336–6; Levack, *Formation of the British State*, pp.212–13.

5. Bruce Galloway, *The Union of England and Scotland, 1603–1608* (Edinburgh, 1986), p.33.

6. See Daniel Defoe, *The History of the Union between England and Scotland* [London, 1709] (Dublin, 1799), p.2.

7. Robert S. Rait, *An Outline of the Relations between England and Scotland (500–1707)* (London, 1901), p.146; cf Levack, *Formation of the British State*, pp.214–15.

8. See Christine Kinealy, *'This Great Calamity': The Irish Famine, 1845–52* (Dublin, 1994); Peter Gray, *Famine, Land and Politics: British Government and Irish Society, 1843–50* (Dublin, 1999).

9. Allan Blackstock, *Loyalism in Ireland, 1789–1829* (London, 2007), pp.28–9; Keith Brown, 'The Vanishing Emperor: British Kingship and its Decline, 1603–1707' in Roger Mason (ed.), *Scottish Political Thought and the Union of 1603* (Cambridge, 1994), p.69.

10. See e.g. Christie's Auction no.5383, Lot 144 (7 Oct.2008). See also Diana Scarisbrick, *Ancestral Jewels* (London, 1989), p.77.

11. Blackstock, *Loyalism in Ireland*, pp.270–1.

12. *Ibid.* pp.150–1. Michael Keating, *The Independence of Scotland*, (Oxford 2009), p.17.

13. *Scotsman*, 27 April 1957.

14. e.g. Brown, 'Vanishing Emperor', p.79.

15. Alvin Jackson, 'The Irish Act of Union, 1801–2001', *History Today* (January 2001).

16. Linda Colley, *Britons: Forging the Nation, 1707–1837* (New Haven, 1992), p.145.

17. A.V. Dicey, *A Fool's Paradise* (London, 1913), p.ix.

18. See e.g. Levack, *Formation of the British State*, p.222, for a somewhat different reading.

19. National Archives, Granville Mss, FO.362: Errington to Granville, 20 December 1880 (quoted in Oliver Rafferty, 'The Catholic Church, Ireland and the British Empire, 1800–1921', *Historical Research*, 84, 224 (May, 2011), p.309).

20. See e.g. Rafferty, 'Catholic Church', p.308.

21. Levack, *Formation of the British State*, p.138.

22. See e.g. Richard Rodger, *The Transformation of Edinburgh: Land, Property and Trust in the Nineteenth Century* (Cambridge, 2001).

23. Andrew Gailey, *Ireland and the Death of Kindness: The Experience of Constructive Unionism, 1890–1905* (Cork, 1987).

24. Alvin Jackson, *The Ulster Party: Irish Unionists in the House of Commons, 1884–1911* (Oxford, 1989), pp.152–3. See also Thomas Lough, *England's Wealth; Ireland's Poverty* (London, 1897 edition); Alice E. Murray, *A History of the Financial and Commercial Relations between England and Ireland from the Time of the Restoration* (London, 1903), pp.394–421.

25. See David Seawright, *An Important Matter of Principle: The Decline of the Scottish Conservative and Unionist Party* (Ashgate, 1999), pp.195–206.

26. See Alvin Jackson, *Home Rule: An Irish History, 1800–2000*, paperback edition (London, 2004).

27. See W.C. Lubenow, *Parliamentary Politics and the Home Rule Crisis: The British House of Commons in 1886* (Oxford, 1986), pp.323–4.

28. See James Murphy, *Abject Loyalty: Nationalism and Monarchy in Ireland During the Reign of Queen Victoria* (Washington, 2001); James Loughlin, *The British Monarchy and Ireland: 1800 to the Present* (Cambridge, 2007).

# Bibliography

MANUSCRIPT SOURCES

**Bodleian Library, Oxford**
Antony MacDonnell (1st Lord MacDonnell of Swinford) Papers.
Alfred Milner (1st Viscount Milner) Papers.
National Union of Conservative and Unionist Associations Papers (Scottish Unionist Members' Committee).
William Waldegrave Palmer (2nd Earl of Selborne) Papers.
J.S. Sandars Papers.

**British Library, London**
Arthur Balfour (1st Earl Balfour) Papers.
Walter Long (1st Viscount Long) Papers.

**Cambridge University Library**
Stanley Baldwin (1st Earl Baldwin of Bewdley) Papers.

**Centre for Kentish Studies, Maidstone (Kent Archives Office)**
Aretas Akers-Douglas (1st Viscount Chilston) Papers (consulted by arrangement in the Bodleian, Oxford).

**Churchill College, Cambridge**
Sir William Bull Papers.
Robin Chichester Clark Papers.
David Maxwell Fyfe (1st Earl of Kilmuir) Papers.
Florence Gertrude Horsbrugh (Baroness Horsburgh) Papers.

**Hatfield House**
Robert Gascoyne-Cecil (3rd Marquess of Salisbury) Papers.

**House of Lords Record Office, London**
George Henry Cadogan (5th Earl Cadogan) Papers.
Edward Gibson (1st Lord Ashbourne) Papers.
Andrew Bonar Law Papers.
Herbert Samuel (1st Viscount Samuel) Papers.

## National Archives (United Kingdom)
St John Brodrick (1ˢᵗ Earl of Midleton) Papers.
Cabinet Office Papers.
Home Office Papers.

## National Archives of Scotland
Arthur Balfour (1st Earl Balfour) Papers.
Gerald Balfour (2nd Earl Balfour) Papers.
Sir John Clerk of Penicuik Papers.
Sir John Gilmour Papers.
Philip Kerr (11th Marquis of Lothian) Papers.
Schomberg Henry Kerr (9th Marquis of Lothian) Papers.
Arthur Steel-Maitland Papers.

## National Library of Scotland (NLS)
Robert Boothby (Lord Boothby) Papers.
John Buchan (1st Lord Tweedsmuir) Papers.
Priscilla Buchan (Lady Tweedsmuir) Papers.
Campbell (Argyll) Papers.
Cardross Unionist Association.
Central Ayrshire Unionist Association Papers.
Thomas Mackay Cooper (Lord Cooper of Culross) Papers.
Darien Papers.
John Dowden Papers.
Dunbarton Conservative and Unionist Association Papers.
Dundas (Melville) Papers.
Walter Elliot Papers.
Andrew Fletcher of Saltoun Papers
Richard Haldane (1st Viscount Haldane of Cloan) Papers.
Robert Stevenson Horne (1st Viscount Horne of Slamannan) Papers.
Thomas Johnston Papers.
F.S. Oliver Papers.
James A.A. Porteous Papers.
Archibald Primrose (5th Earl of Rosebery) Papers.
Scottish Conservative and Unionist Association Papers.
Arthur Woodburn Papers.

## Newcastle University Library
Sir George Trevelyan Papers.

## Nuffield College, Oxford
J.A. Pease (Lord Gainford) Papers.
J.E.B. Seely (Lord Mottistone) Papers.

## Public Record Office of Northern Ireland (PRONI)
Pack Beresford Papers.
Edward Carson (Lord Carson of Duncairn) Papers.

H.D. Gribben Papers.
William Johnston Diaries.
Kingstown and District Unionist Club Papers.
Ronald McNeill (Lord Cushendun) Papers.
G.B. Newe Papers.
Charles Vane-Tempest-Stewart (7th Marquess of Londonderry) Papers.
Theresa Vane-Tempest-Stewart, Marchioness of Londonderry, Papers.
Ulster Unionist Council Papers.
Colonel Robert H. Wallace Papers.

**Wiltshire Record Office, Trowbridge**
Walter Long (1st Viscount Long) Papers.


PRINTED PRIMARY SOURCES

Anon [A Friend to Both Countries], *The Utility of an Union between Great Britain and Ireland Considered* (London, 1788).

Anon ['Thistledown'/Charles Waddie], *The Treaty of Union between Scotland and England with an Historical Introduction* (Edinburgh, 1883).

Anon [Catherine Marsh], *Brief Memories of Hugh McCalmont, First Earl Cairns* (London, 1885).

Anon, *The Union of 1707 Viewed Financially* (Edinburgh, 1887).

Anon, *Scotland and Home Rule* (Edinburgh, 1888).

Adam, Charles Elphinstone (ed.), *View of the Political State of Scotland in the Last Century* (Edinburgh, 1887).

Alison, Sir Archibald, *History of Europe from the Commencement of the French Revolution in 1789 to the Restoration of the Bourbons in 1815*, 10 vols, second edition (Edinburgh, 1835–43).

——, *Lives of Lord Castlereagh and Sir Charles Stewart, Second and Third Marquesses of Londonderry. With Annals of Contemporary Events in Which They Bore a Part. From the Original Papers of the Family*, three vols (Edinburgh, 1861).

Alison, Sir Archibald (Lady Alison ed.), *Some Account of My Life and Writings: An Autobiography*, two vols (Edinburgh, 1883).

Ardill, John Roche, *The Closing of the Irish Parliament* (Dublin, 1907).

Argyll, Duke of, *Irish Nationalism: An Appeal to History* (London, 1893).

Argyll, Duke of, *Autobiography and Memoirs*, two volumes (London, 1906).

Armour, W.S., *Armour of Ballymoney* (London, 1934).

——, *Facing the Irish Question* (London, 1935).

——, *Ulster, Ireland, Britain: A Forgotten Trust* (London, 1938).

Ashbourne, Lord, *Pitt: Some Chapters of his Life and Times* (London, 1898).

Baldwin, Stanley, *Our Inheritance: Speeches and Addresses* (London, 1928).

——, *This Torch of Freedom: Speeches and Addresses* (London, 1935).

Balfour, Lady Frances, *A Memoir of Lord Balfour of Burleigh, KT* (London, [1924])

Ball, J.T., *Historical Review of the Legislative Systems Operative in Ireland, 1172–1800* (London, 1889).

Ball, Stuart (ed.), *Parliament and Politics in the Age of Churchill and Attlee: The Headlam Diaries, 1935–41* (London, 1999).

Barrington, Jonah, *Historic Anecdotes and Secret Memoirs of the Legislative Union* (1810).

——, *The Rise and Fall of the Irish Nation: A Full Account of the Bribery and Corruption by which the Union was Carried* (Dublin, 1833).

Beerbohm, Max, *Fifty Caricatures* (London, 1913).

Benson, E.F., *Lucia Rising* (London, 1991).

Black, James, *Around the Guns: Sundays in Camp* (Edinburgh, n.d. [1916]).

Blackie, J.S., *The Union of 1707 and its Results: A Plea for Scottish Home Rule* (Glasgow, 1892).

Boothby, Robert et al., *Industry and the State: A Conservative View* (London, 1927).

Boothby, Robert, *I Fight to Live: An Autobiography* (London, 1947).

Brash, J.L. (ed.), *Papers on Scottish Electoral Politics, 1832–54* (Edinburgh, 1974).

Bruce, John, *Report on the Events and Circumstances which produced the Union of the Kingdoms of England and Scotland* (London, 1799).

Bryce, James, *Two Centuries of Irish History, 1691—1870* (London, 1888).

Bullock, Shan, *Thomas Andrews: Shipbuilder* (Dublin, 1912).

Burton, John Hill, *The History of Scotland from the Revolution to the Extinction of the Last Jacobite Insurrection*, two vols (London, 1870).

——, *A History of the Reign of Queen Anne*, three vols (Edinburgh, 1880)

Callaghan, James, *Time and Chance* (London, 1987).

Cambray, Philip, *Irish Affairs and the Home Rule Question* (London, 1911).

Campbell, Duncan, *Records of Clan Campbell in the Service of the Honourable East India Company, 1600–1858* (London, 1925).

Carlyle, Thomas, *On Heroes and Hero Worship and the Heroic in History* (London, 1841).

——, *Oliver Cromwell's Letters and Speeches: With Elucidations*, 3 vols (London, 1845).

Catterall, Peter (ed.), *The Macmillan Diaries: The Cabinet Years, 1950–57* (London, 2003).

Chart, D.A., *A History of Northern Ireland* (Belfast, 1927).

Childers, Lt Col Spencer, *The Life and Correspondence of the Rt Hon Hugh C.E. Childers, 1827–96*, two vols (London, 1901).

Clare, Earl of, *The Speech of the Rt. Hon. John, Earl of Clare, Lord High Chancellor of Ireland, in the House of Lords of Ireland, on a Motion made by Him on February 10th 1800* (Dublin and London, 1886).

Clerk of Penicuik, Sir John, *History of the Union of Scotland and England* (edited and translated by Douglas Duncan) (Edinburgh, 1993).

Cockburn, Harry, *A History of the New Club, Edinburgh, 1787–1837* (Edinburgh, 1938).

Cockburn, Henry, *Letters Chiefly Concerned With the Affairs of Scotland From Henry Cockburn* (London, 1874).

Coote, Colin, *Editorial: The Memoirs of Colin R. Coote* (London, 1965).

Corkey, William, *The McCann Mixed Marriage Case* (Edinburgh, 1911).

Craig, Thomas, *De Unione Regnorum Britanniae Tractatus* (edited and translated by C.S. Terry) (Edinburgh, 1909).

Crossman, Richard, *The Diaries of a Cabinet Minister: Volume III: Secretary of State for Social Services, 1968–70* (London, 1977).

Dalyell, Tom, *Devolution: The End of Britain?* (London, 1977).

Davidson, J. Morrison, *The Book of Erin: Or Ireland's Story Told to the New Democracy* (London, n.d.).

——, *Scotia Rediviva: Home Rule for Scotland* (London, n.d.).

——, *Scotland for the Scots* (London, 1902).

Davis, Thomas, *The Patriot Parliament of 1689: With Its Statutes, Votes and Proceedings*, third edition (London, 1893).

de Lolme, Jean Louis, *An Essay Containing a Few Strictures on the Union of Scotland with England and on the Present Situation of Ireland. Being an Introduction to Defoe's History of the Union* (London, 1787).

Defoe, Daniel, *The History of the Union between England and Scotland* [London, 1709] (Dublin, 1799).

Dicey, A.V., 'The Two Acts of Union: A Contrast', *Fortnightly Review*, 30, 176 (Aug. 1881).

——, *England's Case Against Home Rule* (London, 1887).

——, *A Leap in the Dark: A Criticism of the Principles of Home Rule, As Illustrated by the Bill of 1893* (London, 1911).

——, *A Fool's Paradise* (London, 1913).

——, and R.S. Rait, *Thoughts on the Union between England and Scotland* (London, 1920).

Dodd, E.R., *Missing Persons: An Autobiography* (Oxford, 1977).

Dunraven, Earl of, *The Outlook in Ireland: The Case for Devolution and Conciliation* (Dublin, 1907).

——, *The Legacy of Past Years: A Study of Irish History* (London, 1911).

——, *The Finances of Ireland Before the Union and After* (London, 1912).

Edwards, Owen Dudley, *A Claim of Right for Scotland* (Edinburgh, 1989).

Edwards, Ruth Dudley, *Murdering Americans* (Bristol, 2007).

Elliot, Walter, *Toryism and the Twentieth Century* (London, 1927).

Ewald, A.C., *The Life of Sir Joseph Napier, Bart., Ex-Lord Chancellor of Ireland, From His Correspondence* (London, 1887).

Falkiner, Caesar Litton, *Essays in Irish History and Biography, Mainly of the Eighteenth Century* (London, 1902).

Falls, Cyril, *The History of the Thirty Sixth (Ulster) Division* (Belfast, 1922).

Fisher, Joseph R., *The End of the Irish Parliament* (London, 1911).

Fitzpatrick, William John, *The Secret Service under Pitt* (London, 1892).

Forbes, Archibald, *Colin Campbell, Lord Clyde* (London, 1895).

Fraser, Major General Sir Thomas, *The Military Danger of Home Rule* (London, 1913).

Froude, James Anthony, *The English in Ireland in the Eighteenth Century* 3 vols [London, 1872–4] revised edition (London, 1881).

Galloway, Bruce, and Brian Levack (eds), *The Jacobean Union: Six Tracts of 1604* (Edinburgh, 1985).

Gardiner, Grace (ed.), *The Lectures, Letters and Essays of the Right Hon. Sir Joseph Napier, Bart* (London, 1888).

Gathorne-Hardy, Alfred, *Gathorne Hardy, First Earl of Cranbrook: A Memoir with Extracts from his Correspondence*, two vols (London, 1910).

Gladstone, William Ewart, *Remarks on the Royal Supremacy, as it is defined by Reason, History and the Constitution* (London, 1850).

——, *Special Aspects of the Irish Question: A Series of Reflections in and since 1886* (London, 1892).

Gray, John (ed.), *Memoirs of the Life of Sir John Clerk of Penicuik* (Edinburgh, 1892)

Gwynn, Stephen, *The Student's History of Ireland* (London, 1925).

—— (ed.), *The Anvil of War: Letters of F.S. Oliver to His Brother* (London, 1936).

Hamilton, Lord Ernest, *The Soul of Ulster* (London, 1917).

——, *The Irish Rebellion of 1641: With a History of the Events Which Led Up to It and Succeeded It* (London, 1920).

——, *Tales of the Troubles* (London, 1925).

Healey, Denis, *The Time of My Life* (London, 1989).

Hume Brown, Peter (ed.), *The Union of 1707: A Survey of Events* (Glasgow, 1907).

——, *The Legislative Union of England and Scotland* (Oxford, 1914).

——, (ed.), *Letters Relating to Scotland in the Reign of Queen Anne by James Ogilvy, First Earl of Seafield and Others* (Edinburgh, 1915).

——, *Surveys of Scottish History* (Glasgow, 1919).

Hunter, William Wilson, *A Life of the Earl of Mayo, Fourth Viceroy of India*, two vols (London, 1876).

Hurd, Douglas, *Memoirs* (London, 2003).

Ingram, Thomas Dunbar, *History of the Legislative Union of Great Britain and Ireland* (London, 1887).

——, *A Critical Examination of Irish History*, two volumes, reissue [London, 1900] (London, 1904).

Insh, G.P., *Scottish Colonial Schemes, 1620–1686* (Glasgow, 1922).

——, *The Company of Scotland Trading to Africa and the Indies* (Glasgow, 1932).

James, Robert Rhodes (ed.), *Chips: The Diaries of Sir Henry Channon* (London, 1967).

Jefferson, Herbert, *Viscount Pirrie of Belfast* (Belfast, n.d.).

Johnston, Thomas, *Our Scots Noble Families* (Glasgow, 1909).

——, *History of the Working Classes in Scotland* (Glasgow, 1929).

——, *Memories* (London, 1952).

Johnston, William, *Nightshade: A Novel* (London, 1857).

Johnstone, Revd Thomas, *Ulstermen: Their Fight for Fortune, Faith and Freedom* (Belfast, 1914).

Jones, Thomas A., *The Union of England and Wales* (London, 1937).

Joyce, James, 'Ivy Day in the Committee Room', *Dubliners* [London, 1914], World's Classics edition (Oxford, 2000).

Kiernan, T.J., *History of the Financial Administration of Ireland to 1817* (London, 1930).

Kilmuir, Earl of, *The Memoirs of the Earl of Kilmuir: Political Adventure* (London, 1967).

Laing, Malcolm, *History of Scotland from the Union of the Crowns on the Accession of King James VI to the Throne of England to the Union of the Kingdoms in the Reign of Queen Anne*, four vols (London, 1802).

——, *The History and Life of King James the Sixth* (London, 1804).

Lang, Ian, *Blue Remembered Years: A Political Memoir* (London, 2002).

Lang, William, *The Case for Union* (Dundee, 1912).

Lawson, Nigel, *The View from No. 11: Memoirs of a Tory Radical* (London, 1991).

Lecky, W.E.H., *History of Ireland in the Eighteenth Century*, five vols (London, 1892).

——, *Historical and Political Essays* (London, 1908).

Locker Lampson, Geoffrey, *A Consideration of the State of Ireland in the Nineteenth Century* (London, 1907).

Lockhart, George, *The Lockhart Papers: Containing Memoirs and Commentaries Upon the Affairs of Scotland from 1702 to 1715* (London, 1822).

Lodge, Margaret, *Sir Richard Lodge: A Biography* (Edinburgh, 1946).

Lough, Thomas, *England's Wealth; Ireland's Poverty* (London, 1897 edition).

McCarthy, Justin, *Ireland since the Union: Sketches of Irish History from 1798–1886* (London, 1887).

——, *The Reign of Queen Anne* (London, 1905 edition [1902]).

MacCormick, J.M., *The Flag in the Wind: The Story of the National Movement in Scotland* (Edinburgh, 1955).

McGinnis, P.J., and A.H. Williamson (eds), *The British Union: A Critical Edition and Translation of David Hume's De Unione Insulae Britannicae* (Aldershot, 2002).

MacKenzie, B.D., *Home Rule for Scotland: Why Should Scotland Wait?* (Edinburgh, 1890).

MacKenzie, W.C., *The Races of Ireland and Scotland* (Paisley, n.d. [1913]).

——, *The Life and Times of John Maitland, Duke of Lauderdale (1616–82)* (London, 1923).

Mackinnon, James, *The Union of England and Scotland: A Study of International History* (London, 1896).

MacKnight, Thomas, *Ulster as It is: Or Twenty Eight Years' Experience as an Irish Editor*, two vols (London, 1896).

McLeish, Henry, *Scotland First: Truth and Consequences* (Edinburgh, 2004).

McMinn, J.R.B., *Against the Tide: J.B.Armour, Irish Presbyterian Minister and Home Ruler* (Belfast, 1985).

MacNeill, J.G. Swift, *How the Union was carried* (London, 1887).

——, *Titled Corruption: The Sordid Origins of some Irish Peerages* (London, 1894).

——, *The Irish Parliament: What it was and what it did* (London, 1912).

MacRae, Alexander, *Scotland, from the Treaty of Union with England to the Present Time* (London, 1908).

Mahaffy, John Pentland, *Greek Life and Thought: From the Age of Alexander to the Roman Conquest* (London, 1887).

Major (Mair), John, *A History of Greater Britain As Well England as Scotland* (edited and translated by Archibald Constable) (Edinburgh, 1892).

Major, John, *The Autobiography* (London, 1999).

Mann, Jean, *Woman in Parliament* (London, 1962).

Mansergh, Nicholas, *The Government of Northern Ireland: A Study in Devolution* (London, 1936).

Marjoribanks, Edward and Ian Colvin, *Life of Lord Carson*, three vols (London, 1932–6).

Marshal, Ebenezer, *A History of the Union of Scotland and England* (Edinburgh, 1799).

Marshall, H.E., *Our Island Story* (London, 1905).

Mathieson, William Law, *Scotland and the Union, 1695–1747* (Glasgow, 1905).

——, 'The Scottish and the Irish Union' in P. Hume Brown (ed.), *The Union of 1707: A Survey of Events* (Glasgow, 1907).

Maxwell, Henry, *An Essay Upon an Union of Ireland with England* (London, 1703).

Meehan, C.P., *The Confederation of Kilkenny*, new edition (Dublin, 1905).

Mitchell, William, *Home Rule for Scotland and Imperial Federation* (Edinburgh, 1892).

——, *Is Scotland to be Sold Again?: Home Rule for Scotland* (Edinburgh, 1893).

Molyneux, William, *The Case of Ireland being bound by Acts of Parliament in England Stated* [Dublin, 1698], edited and introduced by J.G. Simms (Dublin, 1977).

Monypenny, W.F., *The Two Irish Nations: An Essay on Home Rule* (London, 1913).

Murray, Alice E, *A History of the Financial and Commercial Relations between England and Ireland from the Time of the Restoration* (London, 1903).

Murray of Stanhope, Alexander, *The True Interest of Great Britain, Ireland and our Plantations: Or a Proposal for making such an Union between Great Britain and Ireland and all our Plantations as that already made between Scotland and England* (London, 1740).

Musgrave, Richard, *Memoirs of the Different Rebellions in Ireland* (1801).

O'Brien, George, *The Economic History of Ireland in the Eighteenth Century* (Dublin, 1918).

——, *The Economic History of Ireland from the Union to the Famine* (Dublin, 1921).

O'Brien, R. Barry, *The Life of Charles Stewart Parnell*, 2 vols (London, 1898).

——, *The Life of Lord Russell of Killowen* (London, 1902).

——, *Dublin Castle and the Irish People*, [London, 1909] second edition (London, 1912).

O'Brien, William, *Recollections* (London, 1905).

O'Connor, Sir James, *History of Ireland 1798–1924*, 2 vols (London, 1926).

O'Neill, Terence, *The Autobiography of Terence O'Neill* (London, 1972).

Oliver, Frederick Scott [Pacificus], *Federalism and Home Rule* (London, 1910).

Omond, G.W.T., *The Early History of the Scottish Union Question* [Edinburgh, 1897], bicentenary edition (Edinburgh, 1906).

Paton, John, *Proletarian Pilgrimage: An Autobiography* (London, 1935).

——, *Left Turn! The Autobiography of John Paton* (London, 1936).

Peel, George, *The Reign of Sir Edward Carson* (London, 1914).

Plowden, Francis, *An Historical Review of the State of Ireland* (1805–1806).

——, *The History of Ireland from its Union with Great Britain* (1811).

Porteous, James A.A., *The New Unionism* (London, 1935).

Porter, James, *Life and Times of Henry Cooke DD, LLD* (Belfast, 1875 edition).

Pryde, George, *The Treaty of Union of Scotland and England 1707* (London, 1950).

Rait, Robert, *An Outline of the Relations between England and Scotland (500–1707)* (London, 1901).

——, *The Life and Campaigns of Hugh, First Viscount Gough*, two vols (London, 1903).

——, *The Story of an Irish Property* (Oxford, 1908).

——, *The Parliaments of Scotland* (Glasgow, 1924).

Ramsay, Robert, *Ringside Seats: An Insider's View of the Crisis in Northern Ireland* (Dublin, 2009).

Riach, C.C., *Douglas and the Douglas Family* (Hamilton, 1927).

Rosebery, Earl of, *Pitt: Twelve English Statesmen* (London, 1891).

Ross, Charles, *Correspondence of Charles, First Marquess of Cornwallis*, three vols (London, 1859).

Ross, Sir John, *Essays and Addresses* (London, 1930).

Ryan, Desmond, *The Phoenix Flame: A Study of Fenianism and John Devoy* (London, 1937).

Salvidge, Stanley, *Salvidge of Liverpool* (London, 1934).

Samuels, Arthur Warren, *Home Rule Finance: An Examination of the Financial Bearings of the Government of Ireland Bill, 1912* (Dublin, 1912).

Sayers, Dorothy, *Five Red Herrings* [London, 1931] (New English Library Edition, 2003).

Skelton, A.N, *Constructive Conservatism* (Edinburgh, 1924).

Smith, Charlotte Fell, *James Nicholson Richardson of Bessbrook* (London, 1925).

Smith, R.J., *Ireland's Renaissance* (Dublin, 1903).

Somerville, Thomas, *My Own Life and Times, 1741–1814* (Edinburgh, 1861).

Stott, Gordon, *Lord Advocate's Diary, 1961–66* (Edinburgh, 1991).

——, *Judge's Diary, 1967–73* (Edinburgh, 1995).

——, *QC's Diary, 1954–1960* (Edinburgh, 1998).

Stuart, James, *Viscount Stuart of Findhorn, Within the Fringe: An Autobiography* (London, 1967).

Sullivan, A.M., *The Story of Ireland* (Dublin, 1867).

——, *New Ireland: Political Sketches and Personal Reminiscences of Thirty Years of Irish Public Life*, two vols (London, 1877).

Szechi, Daniel (ed.), *Letters of George Lockhart of Carnwath, 1698–1732* (Edinburgh, 1989).

Taaffe, Denis, *An Impartial History of Ireland from the Period of the English Invasion to the Present Time*, 4 vols (Dublin, 1809–11).

Terry, Charles Sanford (ed.), *The Cromwellian Union: Papers relating to the Negotiations of an Incorporating Union between England and Scotland, 1651–52* (Edinburgh, 1902).

——, *The Scottish Parliament: Its Constitution and Procedure, 1603–1707* (Glasgow, 1905).

—— (ed.), *De Unione Regnorum Britanniae Tractatus by Sir Thomas Craig* (Edinburgh, 1909).

——, *The Jacobites and the Union: Being a Narrative of the Movements of 1708, 1715 and 1719* (Cambridge, 1922).

Waddell, Harry, *John Waddell* (Belfast, 1949).

Waddie, Charles, *The Treaty of Union* (Edinburgh, 1883).

——, *How Scotland Lost Her Parliament, and What Came of it* (Edinburgh, 1891).

——, *The Federation of Greater Britain* (Edinburgh, 1895).

——, *The Bicentenary of the Union of the Scottish and English Parliaments: A Brief Historical Account of How it Affected the Welfare of Scotland* (Edinburgh, 1907).

Whiteside, James, *Essays and Lectures: Historical and Literary* (Dublin, 1868).

——, *Early Sketches of Eminent Persons* (Dublin, 1870).

Wilson of Thornly, John, *The Political State of Scotland* (London, 1831).


SECONDARY SOURCES

Adams, R.J.Q., *Bonar Law* (London, 1999).

Akroyd, Robert John, 'Lord Rosebery and Scottish Nationalism, 1868–1896', (University of Edinburgh Unpublished Ph.D. thesis, 1996).

Alexander, J., *McCrae's Battalion: The Story of the 16th Royal Scots* (Edinburgh, 2003).

Alexander, W., *Chasing the Tartan Tiger: Lessons from a Celtic Cousin* (Edinburgh, 2003).

Allan, Stuart, and Allan Carswell, *The Thin Red Line: War, Empire and Visions of Scotland* (Edinburgh, n.d.).

Andrews, J.H., *A Paper Landscape: The Ordnance Survey in Nineteenth Century Ireland* (Oxford, 1975).

Armstrong, Robert, 'Ireland's Puritan Revolution? The Emergence of Ulster Presbyterianism Reconsidered', *English Historical Review*, 121, 493 (September, 2006).

Ascherson, Neal, *Stone Voices: The Search for Scotland* (London, 2002).

——, 'Future of an Unloved Union' in T.M. Devine (ed.), *Scotland and the Union, 1707–2007* (Edinburgh, 2008).

Ash, M., *The Strange Death of Scottish History* (Edinburgh, 1980).

Aughey, Arthur, *Under Siege: Ulster Unionism and the Anglo-Irish Agreement* (Belfast, 1989).

——, *Nationalism, Devolution and the Challenge to the United Kingdom State* (London, 2001).

Bagwell, Philip, *The Transport Revolution from 1770* (London, 1974).

Ball, S.R., 'The Politics of Appeasement: The Fall of the Duchess of Atholl and the Kinross and West Perth By-Election, December 1938', *Scottish Historical Review*, 69 (1990).

Ball, Stuart, and Ian Holliday (eds), *Mass Conservatism: The Conservatives and the Public since the 1880s* (London, 2002).

Barber, Sarah, 'Scotland and Ireland under the Commonwealth: A Question of Loyalty' in Steven Ellis and Sarah Barber (eds), *Conquest and Union: Fashioning a British State, 1485–1725* (Harlow, 1995).

Barczweski, Stephanie, *Myth and National Identity in Nineteenth Century Britain: The Legends of King Arthur and Robin Hood* (Oxford, 2000).

Barnard, T.C., *Cromwellian Ireland* (Oxford, 1975).

——, 'The Uses of 23 October 1641 and Irish Protestant Celebrations', *English Historical Review*, 106, 421 (1991).

Barnett, Correlli, *The Audit of War: The Illusion and Reality of Britain as a Great Nation* (London, 1986).

Barr, Colin, ' "Imperium in Imperio": Irish Episcopal Imperialism in the Nineteenth Century', *English Historical Review*, 123, 502 (June, 2008).

Bartlett, Thomas, 'The Townshend Viceroyalty, 1767–72' in Thomas Bartlett and David Hayton (eds), *Penal Era and Golden Age: Essays in Irish History, 1690–1800* (Belfast, 1979).

——, 'An End to Moral Economy: The Militia Riots of 1793', *Past & Present*, 99 (May 1983).

——, *The Fall and Rise of the Irish Nation: The Catholic Question, 1690–1830* (Dublin, 1992).

——, 'Defence, Counter-Insurgency and Rebellion: Ireland, 1793–1803' in Thomas Bartlett and Keith Jeffery (eds), *A Military History of Ireland* (Cambridge, 1996).

——, *Acts of Union: An Inaugural Lecture delivered at University College Dublin on 24 February 2000* (Dublin, 2000).

——, 'Ireland, Empire and Union, 1690–1801', in Kevin Kenny (ed.), *Ireland and the British Empire* (Oxford, 2004).

——, *Ireland* (Cambridge, 2010).

——, and David Hayton (eds), *Penal Era and Golden Age: Essays in Irish History, 1690–1800* (Belfast, 1979).

—— and Keith Jeffery (eds), *A Military History of Ireland* (Cambridge, 1996).

Barton, Brian, 'Relations between Westminster and Stormont during the Attlee Premiership', *Irish Political Studies*, 7 (1992).

Bayly, C.A., *Empire and Information: Intelligence Gathering and Social Communication in India, 1780–1870* (Cambridge, 1996).

Bayly, C.A., 'Ireland, India and the Empire, 1780–1914', *Transactions of the Royal Historical Society*, sixth series, 10 (Cambridge, 2000).

Bebbington, David W., 'Religion and National Feeling in Nineteenth Century Wales and Scotland', *Studies in Church History*, 18 (1982).

——, *William Ewart Gladstone: Faith and Politics in Victorian Britain* (Grand Rapids, 1993).

——, *The Mind of Gladstone: Religion, Homer and Politics* (Oxford, 2004).

Bell, P.M.H., *Disestablishment in Ireland and Wales* (London, 1969).

Bew, John, *The Glory of being Britons: Civic Unionism in Nineteenth Century Belfast* (Dublin, 2008).

Bew, Paul (Lord), *Ireland: The Politics of Enmity, 1789–2006* (Oxford, 2007).

Biagini, Eugenio, *British Democracy and Irish Nationalism, 1876–1906* (Cambridge, 2007).

Bielenberg, Andy (ed.), *The Irish Diaspora* (London, 2000).

——, 'The Irish Distilling Industry under the Union', in David Dickson and Cormac Ó Gráda (eds), *Refiguring Ireland: Essays in Honour of L.M. Cullen* (Dublin, 2003).

—— and Frank Geary, 'Growth in Manufacturing Output in Ireland between the Union and the Famine: Some Evidence', *Explorations in Economic History*, 43 (2006).

Biggs-Davison, John, and George Chowdharay-Best, *The Cross of Saint Patrick: The Catholic Unionist Tradition in Ireland* (Bourne End, 1984).

Black, Lawrence, 'The Lost World of Young Conservatism', *Historical Journal*, 51, 4 (December, 2008).

Blackstock, Allan, *Loyalism in Ireland, 1789–1829* (London, 2007).

Blyth, Robert, and Keith Jeffery (eds), *The British Empire and its Contested Pasts: Historical Studies XXVI* (Dublin, 2009).

Bobotis, A, 'Rival Maternities: Maud Gonne, Queen Victoria and the Reign of the Political Mother', *Victorian Studies*, 49, no. 1 (Fall, 2006).

Bogdanor, Vernon, *Devolution in the United Kingdom* (Oxford, 2001).

Bolton, G.C., *The Passing of the Irish Act of Union: A Study in Parliamentary Politics* (Oxford, 1966).

Bowen, Desmond, *The Protestant Crusade in Ireland, 1800–1870: A Study of Protestant-Catholic Relations between the Act of Union and Disestablishment* (Dublin, 1978).

——, and Jean Bowen, *Heroic Option: The Irish in the British Army* (London, 2005).

Bowie, Karin, 'Public Opinion, Popular Politics and the Union of 1707', *Scottish Historical Review*, 82, 2 (October, 2003).

——, *Scottish Public Opinion and the Anglo-Scottish Union, 1699–1707* (London, 2007).

Bowman, Timothy, 'The Ulster Volunteer Force and the Formation of the 36th (Ulster) Division', *Irish Historical Studies*, 33, 128 (November, 2001).

——, *Carson's Army: The Ulster Volunteer Force, 1910–22* (Manchester, 2008).

Boyce, D. George, 'Alfred Harmsworth, First Viscount Northcliffe', *New Oxford Dictionary of National Biography* (Oxford, 2004).

——, Robert Eccleshall, and Vincent Geoghegan (eds), *Political Thought in Ireland since the Seventeenth Century* (London, 1993).

Bradshaw, Brendan, *The Irish Constitutional Revolution of the Sixteenth Century* (Cambridge, 1979).

——, 'Nationalism and Historical Scholarship in Modern Ireland', *Irish Historical Studies*, xxvi, 104 (November 1989).

——, 'The Tudor Reformation and Revolution in Wales and Ireland: The Origins of the British Problem' in Brendan Bradshaw and John Morrill (eds), *The British Problem, 1534–1707: State Formation in the Atlantic Archipelago* (London, 1996).

Bradshaw, Brendan, and John Morrill (eds), *The British Problem, 1534–1707: State Formation in the Atlantic Archipelago* (London, 1996).

——, and Peter Roberts (eds), *British Consciousness and Identity: The Making of Britain, 1533–1707* (Cambridge, 1998).

Brady, Ciarán, *The Chief Governors: The Rise and Fall of Reform Government in Tudor Ireland, 1536–1588* (Cambridge, 1994).

—— (ed.), *Interpreting Irish History: The Debate on Historical Revisionism, 1938–1994* (Dublin, 1994).

——, 'Comparable histories? Tudor Reform in Ireland and Wales' in Steven Ellis and Sarah Barber (eds), *Conquest and Union: Fashioning a British State* (Harlow, 1995).

——, and Jane Ohlmeyer (eds), *British Interventions in Early Modern Ireland* (Cambridge, 2005).

Brennan, Niamh, 'A Political Minefield: Southern Loyalists, the Irish Grants Committee and the British Government, 1922–31', *Irish Historical Studies*, 30, 119 (May, 1997).

Brewer, John, with Gareth Higgins, *Anti-Catholicism in Northern Ireland, 1600–1998: The Mote and the Beam* (Basingstoke, 1998).

Brotherstone, Terry, Anna Clarke, and Kevin Whelan (eds), *These Fissured Isles: Ireland, Scotland and British History, 1798–1848* (Edinburgh, 2005).

Brown, Callum, *Religion and Society in Scotland since 1707* (Edinburgh, 1997).

Brown, Keith, *Kingdom or Province? Scotland and the Regal Union, 1603–1715* (London, 1992).

——, 'The Vanishing Emperor: British Kingship and its Decline, 1603–1707' in Roger Mason (ed.), *Scots and Britons: Scottish Political Thought and the Union of 1603* (Cambridge, 1994).

——, and Roland J. Tanner (eds), *The History of the Scottish Parliament 1: Parliament and Politics in Scotland, 1235–1560* (Edinburgh, 2004).

——, and Alastair J. Mann (eds), *The History of the Scottish Parliament 2: Parliament and Politics in Scotland, 1567–1707* (Edinburgh, 2005).

——, and Alan MacDonald, *The History of the Scottish Parliament, 1286–1707, 3: A Thematic History* (Edinburgh, 2009).

Brown, Michael, Patrick Geoghegan, and James Kelly (eds), *The Irish Act of Union, 1800: Bicentennial Essays* (Dublin, 2003).

Brown, Peter, *Augustine of Hippo: A Biography* (London, 1969).

Brown, Stewart J., '"Outside the Covenant": The Scottish Presbyterian Churches and Irish Immigration, 1922–1938', *Innes Review*, 42, 1 (1991).

——, *The National Churches of England, Ireland and Scotland, 1801–46* (Oxford, 2001).

Brown, Terence, *Northern Voices: Poets from Ulster* (Dublin, 1974).

Bruce, Steve, *No Pope of Rome: Militant Protestantism in Modern Scotland* (Edinburgh, 1985).

Bryant, Christopher, *The Nations of Britain* (Oxford, 2006).

Buckland, Patrick, *Irish Unionism I: The Anglo-Irish and the New Ireland, 1885–1922* (Dublin, 1972).

——, *Irish Unionism II: Ulster Unionism and the Origins of Northern Ireland, 1886–1922* (Dublin, 1973).

Burgess, Glenn, 'Scottish or British? Politics and Political Thought in Scotland, *c*.1500–1707', *Historical Journal*, 41, 2 (June, 1998).

Burness, Catriona, *'Strange Associations': The Irish Question and the Making of Scottish Unionism, 1886–1918* (East Linton, 2003).

——, '"Count Up to Twenty One": Scottish Women in Formal Politics, 1918–90' in Esther Breitenbach and Pat Thane (eds), *Women and Citizenship in Britain and Ireland in the 20th Century* (London, 2010).

Butler, J.R.M., *Lord Lothian (Philip Kerr), 1882–1940* (London, 1960).

Cameron, Ewen, *Land for the People?: Government and the Scottish Highlands, 1880–1925* (East Linton, 1996).

——, 'Communication or Separation? Reactions to Irish Land Agitation and Legislation in the Highlands of Scotland, *c*.1870–1910', *English Historical Review*, cxx, 487 (June 2005).

——, 'The Politics of Union in an Age of Unionism', in T.M. Devine (ed.), *Scotland and the Union, 1707–2007* (Edinburgh, 2008).

——, *Impaled Upon a Thistle: Scotland since 1880* (Edinburgh, 2010).

Campbell, Fergus, 'Who Ruled Ireland? The Irish Administration, 1879–1914', *Historical Journal*, 50, 3, (September, 2007).

——, *The Irish Establishment, 1879–1914* (Oxford, 2009).

Campbell, John, *Margaret Thatcher, Volume One: The Grocer's Daughter* (London, 2000).

——, *Margaret Thatcher, Volume Two: The Iron Lady* (London, 2003).

Campbell, R.H., *The Rise and Fall of Scottish Industry, 1707–1939* (Edinburgh, 1980).

Cannadine, David, *The Decline and Fall of the British Aristocracy* (New Haven, 1990).

——, *Ornamentalism: How the British saw their Empire* (London, 2001).

Canny, Nicholas, *Making Ireland British, 1580–1650* (Oxford, 2001).

Carter, Ian, *Railways and Culture in Britain: The Epitome of Modernity* (Manchester, 2001).

Clark, J.C.D., 'Protestantism, Nationalism and National Identity, 1660–1832', *Historical Journal*, 43, 1 (March, 2000).

Claydon, Tony, and Ian McBride (eds), *Protestantism and National Identity in Britain and Ireland, c.1650–1850* (Cambridge, 1998).

Cochrane, Fergal, *Unionist Politics and the Politics of Unionism since the Anglo-Irish Agreement* (Cork, 1997).

Colley, Linda, *Britons: Forging the Nation, 1707–1837* (New Haven, 1992).

Comerford, R.V., *Ireland: Inventing the Nation* (London, 2003).

Connell, Paul, 'Evangelicalism, the Church of Ireland, and Anti-Catholicism in the Life and Thought of the Rev Tresham Dames Gregg (1800–81)' (National University of Ireland Maynooth Unpublished Ph.D. thesis, 2007).

Connolly, Claire, 'Writing the Union' in Daire Keogh and Kevin Whelan (eds), *Acts of Union: The Causes, Contexts and Consequences of the Act of Union* (Dublin, 2001).

——, 'Completing the Union: The Irish Novel and the Moment of Union' in Michael Brown, Patrick Geoghegan and James Kelly (eds), *The Irish Act of Union, 1800: Bicentennial Essays* (Dublin, 2003).

Connolly, S.J., *Religion, Law and Power: The Making of Protestant Ireland, 1660–1760* (Oxford, 1992).

——, 'Varieties of Britishness: Ireland, Scotland and Wales in the Hanoverian State', in Alexander Grant and Keith Stringer (eds), *Uniting the Kingdom? The Making of British History* (London, 1995).

—— (ed.), *Kingdoms United? Great Britain and Ireland since 1800: Integration and Diversity* (Dublin, 1999).

——, *Contested Island: Ireland, 1460–1630* (Oxford, 2007).

——, *Divided Kingdom: Ireland, 1630–1800* (Oxford, 2008).

——, R.A. Houston, and R.J. Morris (eds), *Conflict, Identity and Economic Development: Ireland and Scotland, 1600–1939* (Preston, 1995).

Constable, Philip, 'Scottish Missionaries, "Protestant Hinduism", and the Scottish Sense of Empire in Nineteenth and Early Twentieth Century India', *Scottish Historical Review*, 86, 2 (October, 2007).

Conway, Stephen, 'War and National Identity in the Mid-Eighteenth Century British Isles', *English Historical Review*, 116, 468 (2001).

Cook, Scott, 'The Irish Raj: Social Origins and Careers of Irishmen in the Indian Civil Service, 1855–1919', *Journal of Social History*, 20 (Spring, 1987).

——, *Imperial Affinities: Nineteenth Century Analogies and Exchanges between India and Ireland* (New Delhi, 1993).

Cooke, A.B., and John Vincent, *The Governing Passion: Cabinet Government and Party Politics in Britain, 1885–6* (Brighton, 1974).

Cookson, J.E., *The British Armed Nation, 1793–1815* (Oxford, 1997).

——, 'The Edinburgh and Glasgow Duke of Wellington Statues: Early 19th Century Unionist Nationalism as a Tory Project', 83, 1 *Scottish Historical Review* (April, 2004).

Coote, Colin, *A Companion of Honour: The Story of Walter Elliot* (London, 1965).

Corbett, Mary Jean, *Allegories of Union in Irish and English Writing* (Cambridge, 2000).

Coupland, Reginald, *Welsh and Scottish Nationalism: A Study* (London, 1954).

Cowan, E.J., and R.J. Finlay (eds), *Scottish History: The Power of the Past* (Edinburgh, 2002).

Cragoe, Matthew, *Culture, Politics and National Identity in Wales, 1832–86* (Oxford, 2004).

——, ' "We like local patriotism": The Conservative Party and the Discourse of Decentralisation, 1947–51', *English Historical Review*, 122, 498 (September, 2007).

Crang, Jeremy A., 'The Second World War', in Jeremy Crang, Edward Spiers, and Matthew Strickland (eds), *Military History of Scotland* (Edinburgh, forthcoming).

Crosbie, Barry, " 'L'Enfant Terrible of the ICS": C.J. O'Donnell and the British Administration of Bengal, 1872–82' in Robert Blyth and Keith Jeffery (eds), *The British Empire and its Contested Pasts: Historical Studies XXVI* (Dublin, 2009).

——, 'Ireland, Colonial Science and the Geographical Construction of British Rule in India, c.1820–70', *Historical Journal*, 52, 4 (2009).

——, *Irish Imperial Networks: Migration, Social Communication and Exchange in Nineteenth Century India* (Cambridge, forthcoming).

Crossick, Geoffrey, *An Artisan Elite in Victorian Society: Kentish Town, 1840–80* (London, 1978).

Cullen, Karen, *Famine in Scotland: The 'Ill Years' of the 1690s* (Edinburgh, 2010).

Cullen, Louis, 'Alliances and Misalliances in the Politics of the Union', *Transactions of the Royal Historical Society*, 6th series, vol. 10 (2000).

——, and T.C. Smout (eds), *Comparative Aspects of Scottish and Irish Economic and Social History* (Edinburgh, 1977).

Cullen, Stephen, 'The Fasces and the Saltire: The Failure of the British Union of Fascists in Scotland, 1932–40', *Scottish Historical Review*, 87, 2 (October, 2008).

Curtin, Nancy, *The United Irishmen: Popular Politics in Ulster and Dublin, 1791–98* (Oxford, 1994).

Curtis, L.P., *Apes and Angels: The Irishman in Victorian Caricature* (Newton Abbot, 1971).

D'Alton, Ian, *Protestant Society and Politics in Cork, 1812–44* (Cork, 1980).

——, *The Paradox of Scottish Culture: The Eighteenth Century Experience* (Oxford, 1964).

Daiches, David, *Scotland and the Union* (London, 1977).

Daunton, Martin, *Royal Mail: The Post Office since 1840* (London, 1985).

Davidson, Neil, *The Origins of Scottish Nationhood* (London, 2000).

Davies, Norman, *The Isles: A History* (London, 1999).

Davis, Leith, *Acts of Union: Scotland and the Literary Negotiation of the British Nation, 1707–1830* (Stanford, 1998).

Davison, Peter, *Orwell's England: The Road to Wigan Pier in the Context of Essays, Reviews, Letters and Poems* (London, 2001).

De Groot, G.J., *Liberal Crusader: The Life of Sir Archibald Sinclair* (London, 1993).

Denman, Terence, 'The Catholic Irish Soldier in the First World War: The "Racial Environment"', *Irish Historical Studies*, 27, 108 (November, 1991).

——, ' "The Red Livery of Shame": The Campaign against Army Recruitment in Ireland, 1899–1914', *Irish Historical Studies*, 29, 114 (November, 1994).

Devine, T.M., *The Tobacco Lords: A Study of the Tobacco Merchants of Glasgow and their Trading Activities, 1740–90* (Edinburgh, 1975).

——, *The Great Highland Famine: Hunger, Emigration and the Scottish Highlands in the Nineteenth Century* (Edinburgh, 1988).

—— (ed.), *Conflict and Stability in Scottish Society, 1700–1850: Proceedings of the Scottish Historical Studies Seminar, University of Strathclyde, 1988–89* (Edinburgh, 1990).

—— (ed.), *Irish Immigrants and Scottish Society in the Nineteenth and Twentieth Centuries: Proceedings of the Scottish Historical Studies Seminar, University of Strathclyde, 1989–90* (Edinburgh, 1991).

—— (ed.), *Scottish Elites: Proceedings of the Scottish Historical Studies Seminar, University of Strathclyde, 1991–2* (Edinburgh, 1994).

——, *The Scottish Nation, 1700–2000* (London, 1999).

—— (ed.), *Scotland's Shame? Bigotry and Sectarianism in Modern Scotland* (Edinburgh, 2000).

——, *Scotland's Empire, 1600–1815* (London, 2003).

——, 'Scottish Elites and the Indian Empire, 1700–1815', in T.C. Smout (ed.), *Anglo-Scottish Relations, 1603–1900* (Oxford, 2005).

——, 'The Break-Up of Britain? Scotland and the End of Empire', *Transactions of the Royal Historical Society*, sixth series, 16 (2006).

——, 'In Bed with an Elephant: Three Hundred Years of the Anglo-Scots Union', *Scottish Affairs*, 57 (Autumn, 2006).

—— (ed.), *Scotland and the Union, 1707–2007* (Edinburgh, 2008).

——, 'The End of Disadvantage? The Descendants of Irish Catholic Immigrants in Modern Scotland since 1945' in Martin Mitchell (ed.), *New Perspectives on The Irish in Scotland* (Edinburgh, 2008).

——, and David Dickson (eds), *Ireland and Scotland, 1600–1850: Parallels and Contrasts in Economic and Social Development* (Edinburgh, 1983).

——, and J.F. McMillan (eds), *Celebrating Columba: Irish-Scottish Connections, 597–1997* (Edinburgh, 1997).

Dewey, Clive, 'Celtic Agrarian Legislation and the Celtic Revival: Historicist Implications of Gladstone's Irish and Scottish Land Acts, 1870–86', *Past & Present*, 64 (1974).

Dibble, Jeremy, *Charles Villiers Stanford: Man and Musician* (Oxford, 2002).

Dodghson, Robert, *From Chiefs to Landlords: Social and Economic Change in the Western Highlands and Islands, 1493–1820* (Edinburgh, 1998).

Doherty, Gabriel, 'National Identity and the Study of Irish History', *English Historical Review*, III, 441 (1996).

Donaldson, Gordon, *The Scots Overseas* (London, 1966).

——, *Scotland's History: Approaches and Reflections* (Edinburgh, 1995).

Donnachie, Ian, Christopher Harvie, and Ian Wood (eds), *Forward! Labour Politics in Scotland, 1888–1988* (Edinburgh, 1989).

Donohue, Laura, 'Regulating Northern Ireland: The Special Powers Acts, 1922–72', *Historical Journal*, 41, 4 (December, 1998).

Dow, Frances, *Cromwellian Scotland, 1651–1660* (Edinburgh, 1979).

Dunne, Tom, 'La trahison des clercs: British Intellectuals and the First Home Rule Crisis', Irish Historical Studies, xxiii, no. 90 (Nov. 1982).

Dunne, Tom (ed.), *James Barry, 1741–1806: The Great Historical Painter* (Cork, 2005).

——, and William Pressly (eds), *James Barry, 1741–1806: History Painter* (London, 2010).

Du Toit, Alexander, '"Unionist Nationalism" in the Eighteenth Century: William Robertson and James Anderson (1662–1728)', *Scottish Historical Review*, 85, 2 (October, 2006).

Dyer, G.P., *The Proposed Coinage of King Edward VIII* (London, 1972).

Dyer, Michael, *Capable Citizens and Improvident Democrats: The Scottish Electoral System, 1884–1929* (Aberdeen, 1996).

——, '"A Nationalist in the Churchillian Sense": John MacCormick and the Paisley By-Election of 18 February 1948: Home Rule and the Crisis in Scottish Liberalism', *Parliamentary History*, 22, 3 (October, 2003).

Edwards, Owen Dudley, *Macauley* (London, 1988).

——, *A Claim of Right for Scotland* (Edinburgh, 1989).

——, Gwynfor Evans, Ioan Rhys, and Hugh MacDiarmaid (eds), *Celtic Nationalism* (London, 1968).

Ellis, Peter Beresford, 'Easter 1916', *Irish Democrat*, 6 April 2006.

Ellis, Steven, *Tudor Frontiers and Noble Power: The Making of the British State* (Oxford, 1995).

——, and Sarah Barber (eds), *Conquest & Union: Fashioning a British State, 1485–1725* (Harlow, 1995).

English, Jim, 'Empire Day in Britain, 1904–58', *Historical Journal*, 46, 1 (March, 2006).

English, Richard, *Irish Freedom: The History of Nationalism in Ireland* (London, 2006).

——, and Michael Kenny (eds), *Rethinking British Decline* (London, 1999).

Evans, A., and J. Gough (eds), *The Impact of the Railway on Society in Britain* (Aldershot, 2003).

Farrell, Brian (ed.), *The Irish Parliamentary Tradition* (Dublin, 1973).

Farrington, Christopher, *Ulster Unionism and the Peace Process in Northern Ireland* (Basingstoke, 2006).

Federowich, Kent, 'The Problems of Disbandment: The Royal Irish Constabulary and Imperial Migration, 1919–29', *Irish Historical Studies*, 30, 117 (May, 1996).

Ferguson, Frank, and James McConnell (eds), *Ireland and Scotland in the Nineteenth Century* (Dublin, 2009).

Ferguson, William, 'The Making of the Treaty of Union, 1707', *Scottish Historical Review*, 43 (1964).

——, *Scotland: 1689 to the Present* (Edinburgh, 1968).

Ferguson, William, 'Imperial Crowns: A Neglected Facet of the Background to the Treaty of 1707', *Scottish Historical Review*, 53 (1974).

——, *Scotland's Relations with England: A Survey to 1707* (Edinburgh, 1977).

——, *The Identity of the Scottish Nation: An Historic Quest* (Edinburgh, 1998).

Finlay, Richard, 'Nationalism, Race, Religion and the Irish Question in Inter-War Scotland', Innes Review, 42 (1991).

——, 'Pressure Group or Political Party?: The Nationalist Impact on Scottish Politics, 1928–45', *Twentieth Century British History*, 3 (1992).

——, '"For or Against?": Scottish Nationalists and the British Empire, 1919–39', *Scottish Historical Review*, 71 (1992).

——, *Independent and Free: Scottish Politics and the Origins of the Scottish National Party, 1918–45* (Edinburgh, 1994).

——, 'National Identity in Crisis: Politicians, Intellectuals and the "End of Scotland"', 1920–39', *History*, 79 (1994).

——, 'Scottish Conservatism and Unionism since 1918' in Martin Francis and Ina Zweiniger-Bargielowska (eds), *The Conservatives and British Society* (Cardiff, 1996).

——, *A Partnership for Good? Scottish Politics and the Union since 1800* (Edinburgh, 1997).

——, 'The Rise and Fall of Popular Imperialism in Scotland, 1850–1950', *Scottish Geographical Magazine*, 113, 1 (1997).

——, 'Politics and State Intervention in Scotland, 1918–97' in Catriona MacDonald (ed.), *Unionist Scotland, 1800–1997* (Edinburgh, 1998).

——, 'Caledonia or North Britain? Scottish Identity in the 18th Century' in D. Brown, R.J. Finlay, and M. Lynch (eds), *Image and Identity: The Making and Remaking of Scotland through the Ages* (Edinburgh, 1998).

——, 'New Britain, New Scotland, New History?: The Impact of Devolution on the Development of Scottish Historiography', *Journal of Contemporary History*, 36 (2001).

——, 'Queen Victoria and the Cult of Scottish Monarchy' in E.J. Cowan and R.J. Finlay (eds), *Scottish History: The Power of the Past* (Edinburgh, 2002).

——, *Modern Scotland, 1914–2000* (London, 2004).

——, 'Scotland and the Monarchy in the Twentieth Century' in William Miller (ed.), *Anglo-Scottish Relations from 1900 to Devolution and Beyond* (Oxford, 2005).

Fitzpatrick, David, 'The Orange Order and the Border', *Irish Historical Studies*, 33, 129 (May, 2002).

Foley, Tadhg, and Maureen O'Connor (eds), *Ireland and India: Colonies, Culture and Empire* (Dublin, 2006).

Ford, Trowbridge, *Albert Venn Dicey: The Man and His Times* (Chichester, 1985)

Foster, John, Muir Houston, and Chris Madigan, 'Sectarianism, Segregation and Politics on Clydeside in the later Nineteenth Century' in Martin Mitchell (ed.), *New Perspectives on the Irish in Scotland* (Edinburgh, 2008).

Foster, John Wilson, *Forces and Themes in Ulster Fiction* (Dublin, 1974).

Foster, R.F., *Paddy and Mr Punch: Connections in Irish and English History* (London, 1993).

Foster, R.F., *The Irish Story: Telling Tales and Making it Up in Ireland* (London, 2001).

——, and Alvin Jackson, 'Parnell and Carson' in *European History Quarterly*, 39, 3 (July 2009).

Fry, Michael, *Patronage and Principle: A Political History of Modern Scotland* (Aberdeen, 1988).

——, *The Scottish Empire* (Edinburgh, 2001).

——, *The Dundas Despotism* (Edinburgh, 2004 edition).

——, *The Union: England, Scotland and the Treaty of 1707* (Edinburgh, 2007).

Gailey, Andrew, *Ireland and the Death of Kindness: The Experience of Constructive Unionism, 1890–1905* (Cork, 1987).

——, 'King Carson: An Essay on the Invention of Political Leadership', *Irish Historical Studies*, 30, 117 (May, 1996).

Galbraith, Russell, 'Without Quarter: A Biography of Tom Johnston, the "Uncrowned King of Scotland"' (Edinburgh, 1995).

Gallagher, Tom, 'Protestant Extremism in Urban Scotland, 1930–39: Its Growth and Contraction', *Scottish Historical Review*, 64, 2 (1985).

——, *Glasgow, The Uneasy Peace: Religious Tension in Modern Scotland, 1919–1914* (Manchester, 1987).

——, *Edinburgh Divided: John Cormack and No Popery in the 1930s* (Edinburgh, 1987).

——, and Graham Walker (eds), *Sermons and Battle Hymns: Protestant Popular Culture in Modern Scotland* (Edinburgh, 1990).

Galloway, Bruce, *The Union of England and Scotland, 1603–1608* (Edinburgh, 1986).

——, and Brian Levack (eds), *The Jacobean Union: Six Tracts of 1604* (Edinburgh, 1985).

Galloway, Peter, *The Most Illustrious Order: The Order of Saint Patrick and Its Knights* (London, 1999).

Garnham, Neal, 'Riot Acts, Popular Protest and Protestant Mentalities in Eighteenth Century Ireland', *Historical Journal*, 46, 2 (June, 2006).

Garvin, Tom, *Nationalist Revolutionaries in Ireland, 1858–1928* (Oxford, 1987).

Geoghegan, Patrick, *The Irish Act of Union: A Study in High Politics, 1798–1801* (Dublin, 1999).

——, 'The Irish House of Commons, 1799–1800' in Michael Brown, Patrick Geoghegan and James Kelly (eds), *The Irish Act of Union: Bicentennial Essays* (Dublin, 2001).

Gibbon, Peter, *The Origins of Ulster Unionism: The Formation of Popular Protestant Politics and Ideology in Nineteenth Century Ireland* (Manchester, 1975).

Gibson, John, *The Thistle and the Crown: A History of the Scottish Office* (Edinburgh, 1985).

Gillespie, Raymond, *Colonial Ulster: The Settlement of East Ulster, 1600–41* (Cork, 1986).

Gilley, Sheridan, 'Catholics and Socialists in Glasgow, 1906–12' in K. Lunn (ed.), *Hosts, Immigrants and Minorities: Historical Responses to Newcomers in British Society, 1870–1914* (Folkestone, 1980).

——, 'Catholics and Socialists in Scotland, 1900–30" in Roger Swift and Sheridan Gilley (eds), *The Irish in Britain* (London, 1989).

Girvin, Brian, *From Union to Union: Nationalism, Democracy and Religion in Ireland— Act of Union to EU* (Dublin, 2002).

Glozier, Matthew, 'The Earl of Melfort, the Court Catholic Party, and the Foundation of the Order of the Thistle, 1687', *Scottish Historical Review*, 79, 2 (October, 2000).

Godson, Dean, *Himself Alone: David Trimble and the Ordeal of Unionism* (London, 2005).

Goodare, Julian, *The Government of Scotland, 1560–1625* (Oxford, 2004).

Grant, Alexander, and Keith Stringer (eds), *Uniting the Kingdom? The Making of British History* (London, 1995).

Gray, Peter, *Famine, Land and Politics: British Government and Irish Society, 1843–50* (Dublin, 1999).

—— (ed.), *Victoria's Ireland: Irishness and Britishness, 1837–1901* (Dublin, 2004).

—— (ed.), '"Ireland's Last Fetter Struck Off"': The Lord Lieutenancy Debate, 1800–67' in Terrence McDonough (ed.), *Was Ireland a Colony? Economics, Politics and Culture in Nineteenth Century Ireland* (Dublin, 2005).

Gray, R.Q., *The Labour Aristocracy in Victorian Edinburgh* (Oxford, 1976).

Green, E.H.H., *The Crisis of Conservatism: The Politics, Economics and Ideology of the British Conservative Party, 1880–1914* (London, 1995).

——, *Ideologies of Conservatism: Conservative Political Ideas in the Twentieth Century* (Oxford, 2002).

Greer, Alan, 'Sir James Craig and the Construction of Parliament Buildings at Stormont', *Irish Historical Studies*, 31, 123 (May, 1999).

Grenier, Katherine Haldane, *Tourism and Identity in Scotland, 1770–1914: Creating Caledonia* (Aldershot, 2005).

Griffiths, Richard, *Patriotism Perverted: Captain Ramsay, the Right Club and British Anti-Semitism, 1939–40* (London, 1998).

Hadfield, Andrew, 'Briton and Scythian: Tudor Representations of Irish Origins', *Irish Historical Studies*, 28, 112 (November, 1993).

Hamer, D.L., *Liberal Politics in the Age of Gladstone and Rosebery* (Oxford, 1972).

Hamilton, Douglas, *Scotland, the Caribbean and the Atlantic World, 1750–1820* (Manchester, 2005).

Handley, James, *The Irish in Scotland, 1798–1845* (Cork, 1945).

——, *The Irish in Modern Scotland* (Cork, 1947).

Hanham, H.J., 'The Sale of Honours in Victorian England', *Victorian Studies*, 3, 3 (March 1960).

——, *Scottish Nationalism* (London, 1969).

——, 'Religion and Nationality in the Mid-Victorian Army' in M.R.D. Foot (ed.), *War and Society: Historical Essays in Honour and Memory of J.R. Western, 1928–71* (London, 1973).

Harbinson, John, *The Ulster Unionist Party, 1882–1973: Its Development and Organisation* (Belfast, 1973).

Hardie, Frank, *The Political Influence of the British Monarchy, 1868–1952* (London, 1970).

Harris, Bob, and Christopher Whatley, '"To solemnize His Majesty's Birthday": New Perspectives on Loyalism in George II's Britain', *History*, 83 (July, 1998).

Harrison, Brian, *Peaceable Kingdom* (Oxford, 1982).

——, *The Transformation of British Politics, 1860–1995* (Oxford, 1996).

——, *Seeking a Role: The United Kingdom, 1951–70* (Oxford, 2009).

——, *Finding a Role: The United Kingdom, 1970–90* (Oxford, 2010).

Hart, Peter, '"Operations Abroad": The IRA in Britain, 1919–23', *English Historical Review*, 115, 460 (2000).

Harvie, Christopher, *No Gods and Precious Few Heroes: Scotland 1914–80* (Edinburgh, 1981).

——, *Scotland and Nationalism: Scottish Society and Politics, 1707–1994*, second edition (London, 1994).

——, 'The Moment of British Nationalism, 1939–70', *Political Quarterly* 71 (2000).

——, *A Floating Commonwealth: Politics, Culture and Technology on Britain's Atlantic Coast, 1860–1930* (Oxford, 2008).

Hassan, Gerry (ed.), *The Scottish Labour Party: History, Institutions and Ideas* (Edinburgh, 2004).

Hechter, Michael, *Internal Colonialism: The Celtic Fringe in British National Development, 1536–1966* (London, 1975).

Hempton, David, and Myrtle Hill, *Evangelical Protestantism in Ulster Society, 1740–1890* (London, 1992).

Henderson, Diana, *Highland Soldier, 1820–1920* (Edinburgh, 1989).

Hennessey, Thomas, *The Northern Ireland Peace Process: Ending the Troubles?* (Dublin, 2000).

Hepburn, A.C., *A Past Apart: Studies in the History of Catholic Belfast, 1850–1950* (Belfast, 1996).

——, *Catholic Belfast and Nationalist Ireland in the Era of Joe Devlin, 1871–1934* (Oxford, 2008).

Hetherington, Sheila, *Katharine Atholl, 1874–1960* (Aberdeen, 1990).

Hill, J.R., 'Ireland without Union: Molyneux and his Legacy' in John Robertson (ed.), *A Union for Empire: Political Thought and the Union of 1707* (Cambridge, 1995).

——, *From Patriots to Unionists: Dublin Civic Politics and Irish Protestant Patriotism, 1660–1840* (Oxford, 1997).

Hilton, Boyd, *The Age of Atonement: The Influence of Evangelicalism on Social and Economic Thought, 1795–1865* (Oxford, 1992).

Holmes, Andrew, 'Presbyterian Religion, Historiography and Ulster Scots Identity, c1800–1914', *Historical Journal*, 52, 3 (September 2009).

Holmes, Finlay, *Henry Cooke* (Belfast, 1981).

Hopkinson, Michael, 'The Craig-Collins Pacts of 1922: Two Attempted Reforms of the Northern Ireland Government', *Irish Historical Studies*, 27, 106 (November, 1990).

Hoppen, K. Theodore, *Elections, Politics and Society in Ireland, 1832–1885* (Oxford, 1984).

——, 'Grammars of Electoral Violence in Nineteenth Century England and Ireland', *English Historical Review*, 109, 432 (1994).

——, 'An Incorporating Union: British Politicians and Ireland, 1800–30', *English Historical Review*, cxxiii, 501 (April 2008).

Hoppit, Julian, *A Land of Liberty? England, 1689–1727* (Oxford, 2000).

—— (ed.), *Parliaments, Nations and Identities in Britain and Ireland, 1660–1850* (Manchester, 2003).

Horne, Alistair, *Harold Macmillan, 1957–1986: Volume II of the Official Biography* (London, 1989).

Houston, R.A., and Ian Whyte (eds), *Scottish Society, 1500–1800* (Cambridge, 1989).

Howe, Stephen, *Ireland and Empire: Colonial Legacies in Irish History and Culture* (Oxford, 2000).

Hutchison, I.G.C., *A Political History of Scotland, 1832–1924: Parties, Elections and Issues* (Edinburgh, 1986).

——, 'Scottish Unionism between the Two World Wars' in Catriona M.M. MacDonald (ed.), *Unionist Scotland, 1800–1997* (Edinburgh, 1998).

——, 'The Impact of the First World War on Scottish Politics', Catriona MacDonald and E.W. MacFarland (eds), *Scotland and the Great War* (East Linton, 1999).

——, *Scottish Politics in the Twentieth Century* (Basingstoke, 2000).

——, 'Anglo-Scottish Political Relations in the Nineteenth Century, c.1815–1914' in T.C. Smout (ed.), *Anglo-Scottish Relations from 1603 to 1900* (Oxford, 2005).

Hutchinson, John, *The Dynamics of Cultural Nationalism: The Gaelic Revival and the Creation of the Irish Nation State* (London, 1987).

Jackson, Alvin, *The Ulster Party: Irish Unionists in the House of Commons, 1884–1911* (Oxford, 1989).

——, 'Unionist Politics and Protestant Society in Edwardian Ireland', *Historical Journal*, 33, no. 4 (1990).

——, 'Unionist Myths, 1912–85', *Past & Present*, 136 (August 1992).

——, 'Unionist History' in Ciaran Brady (ed.), *Interpreting Irish History: The Debate on Historical Revisionism, 1938–1994* (Dublin, 1994).

——, *Colonel Edward Saunderson: Land and Loyalty in Victorian Ireland* (Oxford, 1995).

——, 'The Irish Act of Union, 1801–2001', *History Today*, 51, no. 1 (January 2001).

——, *Home Rule: An Irish History, 1800–2000*, paperback edition (London, 2004).

——, 'Ireland, the Union and the Empire, 1800–1960', in Kevin Kenny (ed.), *Ireland and the British Empire*, paperback edition (Oxford, 2006).

——, *Ireland 1798–1998: War, Peace and Beyond*, second edition (Oxford, 2010).

——, '"Tame Tory Hacks"? The Ulster Party at Westminster, 1922–72', *Historical Journal*, 54, 2 (June, 2011).

Jackson, Daniel, *Popular Opposition to Irish Home Rule in Edwardian Britain* (Liverpool, 2009).

Jalland, Patricia, 'United Kingdom Devolution, 1910–14: Political Panacea or Tactical Diversion', *English Historical Review* 94 (1979).

Jalland, Patricia, *The Liberals and Ireland: The Ulster Question in British Politics to 1914* (London, 1980).

James, F.G., *Ireland in the Empire, 1688–1770: A History of Ireland from the Williamite Wars to the Eve of the American Revolution* (Cambridge, Mass., 1973).

James, Robert Rhodes, *Bob Boothby: A Portrait* (London, 1991).

Jarvis, David, 'British Conservatism and Class Politics in the 1920s', *English Historical Review*, III, 440 (1996).

Jeffery, Keith (ed.), *An Irish Empire? Aspects of Ireland and the British Empire* (Manchester, 1996).

——, *Ireland and the Great War* (Cambridge, 2000).

Jenkins, Brian, *Era of Emancipation: British Government in Ireland, 1812–30* (Montreal, 1988).

Jenkins, T.A., 'The Funding of the Liberal Unionist Party and the Honours System', *English Historical Review*, 105, 417 (1990).

Jenkinson, Jacqueline, *Scotland's Health, 1919–48* (Oxford, 2003).

Johnson, Nuala, *Ireland, the Great War, and the Geography of Remembrance* (Cambridge, 2007).

Johnston, Edith Mary, *Great Britain and Ireland, 1760–1800: A Study in Political Administration* (Edinburgh, 1963).

Johnston-Liik, Edith Mary (ed.), *History of the Irish Parliament, 1692–1800*, 6 vols (Belfast, 2002)

Jones, Barry, and Michael Keating, *Labour and the British State* (Oxford, 1985).

Jones, W. Douglas, 'The Bold Adventurers: A Quantitative Analysis of the Darien Subscription List (1696)', *Journal of Scottish Historical Studies*, 21, 1 (May, 2001).

Jupp, Peter, *The Governing of Britain, 1688–1848: The Executive, Parliament and the People* (London, 2006).

Kanter, Douglas, *The Making of British Unionism, 1740–1848: Politics, Government and the Anglo-Irish Constitutional Relationship* (Dublin, 2009).

Kaufmann, Eric, *The Orange Order: A Contemporary Northern Irish History* (Oxford, 2007).

——, 'The Orange Order in Scotland since 1860: A Social Analysis' in Martin Mitchell (ed.), *New Perspectives on the Irish in Scotland* (Edinburgh, 2008).

Kavanaugh, Anne, *John FitzGibbon, Earl of Clare: A Study of Personality and Politics* (Dublin, 1997).

Kearney, Hugh, *The British Isles: A History of Four Nations* (Cambridge, 1989).

Keating, Michael, *The Independence of Scotland: Self-Government and the Shifting Politics of Union* (Oxford, 2009).

——, and David Bleiman, *Labour and Scottish Nationalism* (London, 1979).

Kelly, James, 'The Origins of the Act of Union: An Examination of Unionist Opinion in Britain and Ireland, 1650–1800', *Irish Historical Studies*, 25 (1987).

——, *Prelude to Union: Anglo-Irish Politics in the 1780s* (Cork, 1992).

——, *Henry Flood: Patriots and Politics in Eighteenth Century Ireland* (Dublin, 1998).

——, 'The Historiography of the Act of Union' in Michael Brown, Patrick Geoghegan, James Kelly (eds), *The Irish Act of Union: Bicentennial Essays* (Dublin, 2001).

——, 'The Failure of Opposition' in Michael Brown, Patrick Geoghegan, James Kelly (eds), *The Irish Act of Union: Bicentennial Essays* (Dublin, 2001).

——, 'The Act of Union: Its Origins and Background' in Daire Keogh and Kevin Whelan (eds), *Acts of Union: The Causes, Contexts and Consequences of the Act of Union* (Dublin, 2001).

——, *Poynings' Law and the Making of Law in Ireland: Monitoring the Constitution* (Dublin, 2007).

——, *Sir Richard Musgrave: Ultra-Protestant Ideologue* (Dublin, 2009).

Kelly, Matthew, 'Dublin Fenianism in the 1880s: "The Irish Culture of the Future?"', *Historical Journal*, 43, 2 (June, 2000).

Kelly, Paul, 'British and Irish Politics in 1785', *English Historical Review*, 90, 356 (July, 1975).

Kelly, William, and John Young (eds), *Ulster and Scotland, 1600–2000: History, Language and Identity* (Dublin, 2004).

——, and John Young (eds), *Scotland and the Ulster Plantation: Explorations in the British Settlement of Stuart Ireland* (Dublin, 2009).

Kendle, John, *Ireland and the Federal Solution: The Debate over the United Kingdom Constitution, 1870–1921* (Montreal, 1989).

——, *Federal Britain: A History* (London, 1997).

Kendrick, S., and David McCrone, 'Politics in a Cold Climate: The Conservative Decline in Scotland', *Political Studies*, 37 (1989).

Kennedy, Thomas C, 'Troubled Tories: Dissent and Confusion Concerning the Party's Ulster Policy, 1910–14', *Journal of British Studies*, 46, 3 (July, 2007).

Kenny, Kevin (ed.), *Ireland and the British Empire*, paperback edition (Oxford, 2006).

Keogh, Daire, and Kevin Whelan (eds), *Acts of Union: The Causes, Contexts, and Consequences of the Act of Union* (Dublin, 2001).

Kerr, Donal, *Peel, Priests and Politics: Sir Robert Peel's Administration and the Roman Catholic Church in Ireland, 1841–46* (Oxford, 1982).

——, *A Nation of Beggars? Priests, People and Politics in Famine Ireland, 1846–52* (Oxford, 1994).

Kidd, Colin, *Subverting Scotland's Past: Scottish Whig Historians and the Creation of an Anglo-British Identity, 1689–1830* (Cambridge, 1993).

——, 'Gaelic Antiquity and National Identity in Enlightenment Ireland and Scotland', *English Historical Review*, 109, 434 (November, 1994).

——, *British Identities before Nationalism: Ethnicity and Nationhood in the Atlantic World, 1600–1800* (Cambridge, 1999).

——, 'Conditional Britons: The Scots Covenanting Tradition and the Eighteenth Century British State', *English Historical Review*, 117, 474 (2002).

——, 'Race, Empire and the Limits of Nineteenth Century Scottish Nationhood', *Historical Journal*, 46, 3 (2003).

——, 'Scotland and the Three Unions', in T.C. Smout (ed.), *Anglo-Scottish Relations from 1603 to 1900* (Oxford, 2005).

Kidd, Colin, *Union and Unionisms: Political Thought in Scotland, 1500–2000* (Cambridge, 2008).

Kinealy, Christine, *'This Great Calamity': The Irish Famine, 1845–52* (Dublin, 1994).

——, *A Disunited Kingdom? England, Ireland, Scotland and Wales, 1800–1949* (Cambridge, 1999).

Kirk, James (ed.), *The Scottish Churches and the Union Parliament, 1707–1999* (Edinburgh, 2001).

Landsman, Ned, 'The Legacy of British Union for the North American Colonies: Provincial Elites and the Problem of Imperial Union' in John Robertson (ed.), *A Union for Empire: Political Thought and the Union of 1707* (Cambridge, 1995).

Langford, Paul, 'South Britons and North Britons, 1707–1820', in T.C. Smout (ed.), *Anglo-Scottish Relations from 1603 to 1900* (Oxford, 2005).

Lant, Jeffrey, *Insubstantial Pageant: Ceremony and Confusion at Queen Victoria's Court* (London, 1980).

Lavery, Brian, *Shield of Empire: The Royal Navy and Scotland* (Edinburgh, 2007).

Lavin, Deborah, *From Empire to International Commonwealth: A Biography of Lionel Curtis* (Oxford, 1995).

Lawrence, Jon, 'Class and Gender in the Making of Urban Toryism, 1880–1914', *English Historical Review*, 108, 428 (1993).

Lee, C.H., *Scotland and the United Kingdom: The Economy and the Union in the Twentieth Century* (Manchester, 1995).

Lee, Maurice, *Government by Pen: Scotland under James VI and I* (Urbana, Ill., 1980).

——, 'Scotland, the Union, and the Idea of a "General Crisis"' in Roger Mason (ed.), *Scots and Britons: Scottish Political Thought and the Union of 1603* (Cambridge, 1994).

——, *The 'Inevitable' Union and Other Essays on Modern Scotland* (Edinburgh, 2003).

Leersen, Joep, *Remembrance and Imagination: Patterns in the Literary and Historical Representation of Ireland in the Nineteenth Century* (Cork, 1996).

Lenman, Bruce, *An Economic History of Modern Scotland, 1660–1976* (London, 1977).

Levack, Brian, *The Formation of the British State: England, Scotland and the Union, 1603–1707* (Oxford, 1987).

Little, Patrick, 'The First Unionists? Irish Protestant Attitudes to Union with England, 1653–59', *Irish Historical Studies*, 31, 125 (May, 2000).

——, *Lord Broghill and the Cromwellian Union with Ireland and Scotland* (London, 2004).

Livesey, James, 'Acts of Union and Disunion: Ireland in Atlantic and European Contexts' in Daire Keogh and Kevin Whelan (eds), *Acts of Union: The Causes, Contexts, and Consequences of the Act of Union* (Dublin, 2001).

——, *Civil Society and Empire: Ireland and Scotland in the Eighteenth Century Atlantic World* (New Haven, 2009).

Loughlin, James, *Gladstone, Home Rule and the Ulster Question, 1882–1893* (Dublin, 1986).

——, *Ulster Unionism and British National Identity since 1885* (London, 1995).

——, *The British Monarchy and Ireland: 1800 to the Present* (Cambridge, 2007).

Lowe, W.J., 'The Constabulary Agitation of 1882', *Irish Historical Studies*, 31, 121 (May, 1998).

Lownie, Andrew, *John Buchan: Presbyterian Cavalier* (London, 1995).

Lubenow, W.C., *Parliamentary Politics and the Home Rule Crisis: The British House of Commons in 1886* (Oxford, 1986).

Lynch, Michael, *Scotland: A New History* (London, 1991).

—— (ed.), *Scotland 1850–1979: Society, Politics and the Union* (London, 1993).

—— (ed.), *The Oxford Companion to Scottish History* (Oxford, 2001).

McBride, Ian, *The Siege of Derry in Ulster Protestant Mythology* (Dublin, 1997).

——, *Eighteenth Century Ireland: The Isle of Slaves* (Dublin, 2009).

McBride, Lawrence, *The Greening of Dublin Castle: The Transforming of Bureaucratic and Judicial Personnel in Dublin Castle in Ireland, 1892–1922* (Washington, 1991).

McCaffrey, John, 'The Origins of Liberal Unionism in the West of Scotland', *Scottish Historical Review*, 50 (1971).

McCahill, Michael, and Ellis Archer Wasson, 'The New Peerage: Recruitment to the House of Lords, 1704–1847', *Historical Journal*, 46, 1 (March, 2003).

McCarthy, John Paul, 'Gladstone's Irish Questions, 1830–86: An Historical Approach', (University of Oxford Unpublished D. Phil thesis, 2010).

McCartney, Donal, 'The Writing of History in Ireland, 1800–1830', *Irish Historical Studies*, x, 40 (Sept. 1957).

——, *W.E.H. Lecky: Historian and Politician, 1838–1903* (Dublin, 1994)

McCavitt, John, *The Flight of the Earls* (Dublin, 2002).

McClelland, Aiken, *William Johnston of Ballykilbeg* (Belfast, 1990).

MacCormack, W.J., *The Pamphlet Debate on the Union between Great Britain and Ireland, 1797–1800* (Dublin, 1996).

——, 'Maria Edgeworth', *New Oxford Dictionary of National Biography* (Oxford, 2004).

MacCormick, Neil, 'New Unions for Old' in William L. Miller (ed.), *Anglo-Scottish Relations From 1900 to Devolution and Beyond* (Oxford, 2005).

McCrae, Morrice, *The National Health Service in Scotland: Origins and Ideals, 1900–50* (Edinburgh, 2003).

McCrone, David, *Understanding Scotland: The Sociology of a Stateless Nation* (London, 1992).

——, 'W(h)ither the Union? Anglo-Scottish Relations in the 21st Century' in William L. Miller (ed.), *Anglo-Scottish Relations From 1900 to Devolution and Beyond* (Oxford, 2005).

MacDonagh, Oliver, *O'Connell: The Life of Daniel O'Connell, 1775–1847* (London, 1991).

MacDonald, Alan, 'James VI and I, the Church of Scotland and Ecclesiastical Convergence', *Historical Journal*, 48, 4 (December, 2005).

MacDonald, Alan, R.J. Tanner, A.J. Mann, and Keith Brown (eds), *The History of the Scottish Parliament: Parliament and Politics in Scotland, 1567–1707* (Edinburgh, 2005).

MacDonald, Catriona (ed.), *Unionist Scotland, 1800–1997* (Edinburgh, 1998).

——, *The Radical Thread: Political Change in Scotland. Paisley Politics, 1885–1924* (East Linton, 2000).

——, and Elaine McFarland (eds), *Scotland and the Great War* (Edinburgh, 1999).

MacDonald, Fiona, *Mission to the Gaels: Reformation and Counter-Reformation in Ulster and the Highlands and Islands of Scotland, 1560–1760* (Edinburgh, 2006).

McDonnell, A.D., *The Life of Sir Denis Henry: Catholic Unionist* (Belfast, 2000).

McDonough, Terrence (ed.), *Was Ireland a Colony? Economics, Politics and Culture in Nineteenth Century Ireland* (Dublin, 2005).

MacDougall, Norman, *Scotland and War, AD 79–1918* (Edinburgh, 1991).

McDowell, R.B., *The Irish Administration, 1801–1914* (London, 1964).

McFarland, Elaine W., *Protestants First: Orangeism in 19th Century Scotland* (Edinburgh, 1990).

——, *Ireland and Scotland in the Age of Revolution: Planting the Green Bough* (Edinburgh, 1994).

——, *John Ferguson, 1832–1906: Irish Issues in Scottish Politics* (East Linton, 2003).

——, '"How the Irish Paid their Debt': Irish Catholics in Scotland and Voluntary Enlistment, August 1914–July 1915', *Scottish Historical Review*, 82, 2 (October, 2003).

McGrath, Charles Ivar, *The Making of the Eighteenth Century Irish Constitution: Government, Parliament and the Revenue, 1692–1714* (Dublin, 2000).

——, 'English Ministers, Irish Politicians and the Making of a Parliamentary Settlement in Ireland, 1692–5', *English Historical Review*, 119, 482 (2004).

McIlvanney, Liam, and Ray Ryan (eds), *Ireland and Scotland: Culture and Society, 1700–2000* (Dublin, 2005).

Macinnes, Allan, 'Union failed, union accomplished: the Irish union of 1703 and the Scottish union of 1707', Daire Keogh and Kevin Whelan (eds), *Acts of Union: The*

*Causes, Contexts and Consequences of the Act of Union* (Dublin, 2001).

——, *The British Revolution, 1629–60* (Basingstoke, 2005).

——, *Union and Empire: The Making of the United Kingdom in 1707* (Cambridge, 2007).

——, and Jane Ohlmeyer (eds) *The Stuart Kingdoms in the Seventeenth Century: Awkward Neighbours* (Dublin, 2002).

MacIntosh, Gillian, *The Scottish Parliament under Charles II, 1660–85* (Edinburgh, 2007).

McIntosh, Gillian V., *The Force of Culture: Unionist Identities in Twentieth Century Ireland* (Cork, 1999).

——, 'Symbolic Mirrors: Commemorations of Edward Carson in the 1930s', *Irish Historical Studies*, 32, 125 (May, 2000).

McIntyre, Ian, *The Expense of Glory: A Life of John Reith* (London, 1992).

McKay, Collins, *The Duke of Queensberry and the Union of Scotland and England: James Douglas and the Act of Union of 1707* (Youngtown, 2008).

MacKenzie, John M. (ed.), *Imperialism and Popular Culture* (Manchester, 1986).

——, 'Essay and Reflection: On Scotland and the Empire', *International History Review*, xv, 4 (1993).

——, 'Empire and National Identities: The Case of Scotland', *Transactions of the Royal Historical Society*, 6th series, viii (1998).

——, with Nigel Dalziel, *The Scots in South Africa: Ethnicity, Gender, Identity and Race, 1772–1914* (Manchester, 2007).

McKibbin, Ross, *The Evolution of the Labour Party, 1906–14* (Oxford, 1974).

——, *The Ideologies of Class: Social Relations in Britain, 1880–1950* (Oxford, 1990).

MacKillop, Andrew, *More Fruitful than the Soil: Army, Empire and the Scottish Highlands, 1715–1815* (Edinburgh, 2000).

——, 'The Political Culture of the Scottish Highlands from Culloden to Waterloo', *Historical Journal*, 46, 3 (September, 2003).

——, and Micheál Ó Siochrú (eds), *Forging the State: European State Formation and the Anglo-Scottish Union of 1707* (Dundee, 2008).

McKinstry, Leo, *Rosebery: Statesman in Turmoil* (London, 2005).

McLean, Iain, *The Legend of Red Clydeside* (Edinburgh, 1983).

——, 'Financing the Union: Goschen, Barnett and Beyond' in William L. Miller (ed.), *Anglo-Scottish Relations from 1900 to Devolution and Beyond* (Oxford, 2005).

——, *What's wrong with the British Constitution?* (Oxford, 2009).

——, and Alistair McMillan, *State of the Union: Unionism and the Alternatives in the United Kingdom since 1707* (Oxford, 2005).

McNally, Patrick, *Parties, Patriots and Undertakers: Parliamentary Politics in Early Hanoverian Ireland* (Dublin, 1997).

McNamee, Colm, *The Wars of the Bruces: Scotland, England and Ireland, 1306–28* (East Linton, 1998).

McRonald, Malcolm, *The Irish Boats: Volume 1 Liverpool to Dublin* (Stroud, 2005).

Magennis, Eoin, *The Irish Political System, 1740–65: The Golden Age of the Undertakers* (Dublin, 2000).

Maguire, Martin, 'The Organisation and Activism of Dublin's Protestant Working Class, 1883–1935', *Irish Historical Studies*, 29, 113 (1994).

——, *The Civil Service and the Revolution in Ireland, 1912–1938: 'Shaking the Blood-Stained Hand of Mr Collins* (Manchester, 2008).

Maitles, H., 'Blackshirts Across the Border: The British Union of Fascists in Scotland', *Scottish Historical Review*, 82 (2003).

Mandler, Peter, *The English National Character: The History of An Idea From Edmund Burke to Tony Blair* (New Haven, 2006).

Mansergh, Danny, *Grattan's Failure: Parliamentary Opposition and the People in Ireland, 1779–1800* (Dublin 2005).

Marquand, David, 'How united is the modern United Kingdom?' in Alexander Grant and Keith Stringer (eds), *Uniting the Kingdom? The Making of British History* (London, 1995).

Marshall, Tristan, *Theatre and Empire: Great Britain on the London Stages under James VI and I* (Manchester, 2000).

Mason, Roger (ed.), *Scotland and England, 1286–1815* (Edinburgh, 1987).

——, *Scots and Britons: Scottish Political Thought and the Union of 1603* (Cambridge, 1994).

Meikle, Maureen, *A British Frontier?: Lairds and Gentlemen in the Eastern Borders, 1540–1603* (East Linton, 2003).

Menzies, Lucy, et al., *St Margaret, Queen of Scotland and Her Chapel*, revised edition (Edinburgh, 2007).

Meredith, Ian, 'Irish Migrants in the Scottish Episcopal Church in the Nineteenth Century' in Martin Mitchell (ed.), *New Perspectives on the Irish in Scotland* (Edinburgh, 2008).

Michie, Michael, *An Enlightenment Tory in Victorian Scotland: The Career of Sir Archibald Alison* (Edinburgh, 1997).

Millar, Gordon, 'The Conservative Split in the Scottish Counties, 1846–57', *Scottish Historical Review*, 80, 2 (October 2001).

Miller, David (ed.), *Peep O'Day Boys and Defenders: Selected Documents on the County Armagh Disturbances, 1784–1796* (Belfast, 1990).

Miller, William L., *The End of British Politics? Scottish and English Political Behaviour in the Seventies* (Oxford, 1981).

—— (ed.), *Anglo-Scottish Relations from 1900 to Devolution and Beyond* (Oxford, 2005).

Mitchell, James, *Conservatives and the Union: A Study of Conservative Party Attitudes to Scotland* (Edinburgh, 1990).

——, *Governing Scotland: The Invention of Administrative Devolution* (London, 2003).

——, 'Undignified and Inefficient: Financial Relations between London and Stormont', *Contemporary British History*, 20, 1 (March, 2006).

——, *Devolution in the UK* (Manchester, 2009).

Mitchell, Martin, *The Irish in the West of Scotland* (Edinburgh, 1998).

—— (ed.), *New Perspectives on the Irish in Scotland* (Edinburgh, 2008).

Mitchison, Rosalind, *Lordship to Patronage: Scotland, 1603–1745* (Edinburgh, 1990 edition).

Morgan, Hiram, 'An Unwelcome Heritage: Ireland's Role in British Empire Building', *History of European Ideas*, 19 (July, 1994).

—— (ed.), *Political Ideology in Ireland, 1541–1641* (Dublin, 2000).

Mori, Jennifer, 'Languages of Loyalism: Patriotism, Nationhood and the State in the 1790s', *English Historical Review*, 118, 475 (2003).

Morgan, Kenneth O., *Wales in British Politics, 1868–1922* (Cardiff, 1963).

Morrill, John, 'Three Kingdoms and One Commonwealth: The Enigma of Mid-Seventeenth Century Britain and Ireland' in Alexander Grant and Keith Stringer (eds), *Uniting the Kingdom? The Making of British History* (London, 1995).

Morris, R.A., and Liam Kennedy (eds), *Ireland and Scotland: Order and Disorder, 1600–2000* (Edinburgh, 2007).

Morton, Graeme, *Unionist Nationalism: Governing Urban Scotland, 1830–60* (East Linton, 1999).

——, 'The First Home Rule Movement in Scotland, 1886–1918' in H.T. Dickinson and Michael Lynch (eds), *The Challenge to Westminster: Sovereignty, Devolution and Independence* (East Linton, 2000).

Moulton, Matthew, 'Anniversary of the Union', *Scotsman*, 22 April 1957.

Muenger, Elizabeth, *The British Military Dilemma in Ireland: Occupation Politics, 1886–1914* (Dublin, 1991).

Mulholland, Marc, *Northern Ireland at the Cross Roads: Ulster Unionism in the O'Neill Years, 1963–69* (London, 2000).

——, *The Longest War: Northern Ireland's Troubled History* (Oxford, 2002).

——, ' "The Best and Most Forward Looking" in Ulster Unionism: The Unionist Society (est.1942)', *Irish Historical Studies*, 33, 129 (May, 2002).

Murdoch, Alexander, *The People Above: Politics and Administration in Mid-Eighteenth Century Scotland* (Edinburgh, 1980).

—— (ed.), *The Scottish Nation: Identity and History. Essays in Honour of William Ferguson* (Edinburgh, 2007).

Murphy, James H, *Abject Loyalty: Nationalism and Monarchy in Ireland During the Reign of Queen Victoria* (Washington, 2001).

Murray, Douglas, *Rebuilding the Kirk: Presbyterian Reunion in Scotland, 1909–29* (Edinburgh, 2000).

Nairn, Tom, *The Break Up of Britain: Crisis and Neo-Nationalism* (London, 1977).

——, *The Enchanted Glass: Britain and its Monarchy* (London, 1988).

Nash, R.C., 'Irish Atlantic Trade in the Seventeenth and Eighteenth Centuries', *William & Mary Quarterly*, Third Series, xliii (July 1985).

Nenadic, Stana, 'The Impact of the Military Profession on Highland Gentry Families, 1730–1830', *Scottish Historical Review*, 85, 1 (April, 2006).

Neville, C.J., *Violence, Custom and Law: The Anglo-Scottish Borderlands in the Later Middle Ages* (Edinburgh, 1998).

Newby, Andrew, 'Edward McHugh, the National Land League of Great Britain and the "Crofters' War", 1879–82', *Scottish Historical Review*, 82, 1 (April, 2003).

——, *Ireland, Radicalism and the Scottish Highlands, 1870–1912* (Edinburgh, 2006).

Nicholls, Andrew, *The Jacobean Union: A Reconsideration of British Civil Policies under the Early Stuarts* (Westport, 1999).

Noonan, Kathleen, ' "The Cruell Pressure of an Enraged, Barbarous People": Irish and English Identity in Seventeenth Century Policy and Propaganda', *Historical Journal*, 41, 1 (January, 1998).

O'Brien, Gillian, 'Camden and the move towards union, 1795–1798', Daire Keogh and Kevin Whelan (eds), *Acts of Union: The Causes, Contexts and Consequences of the Act of Union* (Dublin, 2001).

Ó Cadhla, Stiofán, *Civilising Ireland: Ordnance Survey, 1824–42: Ethnography, Cartography, Translation* (Dublin 2006).

O'Callaghan, Margaret, *British High Politics and a Nationalist Ireland: Criminality and the Law under Forster and Balfour* (Cork, 1994).

O'Callaghan, Margaret, 'New Ways of Looking at the State Apparatus and State Archive in Nineteenth Century Ireland: 'Curiosities from that Phonetic Museum'—Royal Irish Constabulary Reports and Their Political Uses', *Proceedings of the Royal Irish Academy*, 104c (2004).

Ó Catháin, Máirtín, *Irish Republicanism in Scotland, 1858–1916: Fenians in Exile* (Dublin, 2007).

——, 'A Winnowing Spirit' in Martin Mitchell (ed.), *New Perspectives on The Irish in Scotland* (Edinburgh, 2008).

O'Connell, Sean, *The Car and British Society: Class, Gender and Motoring, 1869–1939* (Manchester, 1998).

O'Connor, Gary, *Sean O'Casey: A Life* (London, 1988).

O'Day, Alan, 'Ireland and Scotland: The Quest for Devolved Political Institutions, 1867–1914' in R.J. Morris and Liam Kennedy (eds), *Ireland and Scotland: Order and Disorder, 1600–2000* (Edinburgh, 2005).

Ó Gráda, Cormac, *Ireland: A New Economic History, 1789–1939* (Oxford, 1994).

——, '"The Greatest Blessing of All": The Old Age Pension in Ireland', *Past & Present*, 175, 1 (May, 2002).

Ó hAnnracháin, Tadhg, 'Conflicting Loyalties, Conflicted Rebels: Political and Religious Allegiance among the Confederate Catholics of Ireland', *English Historical Review*, 119, 483 (December, 2004).

Ohlmeyer, Jane (ed.), *Political Thought in Seventeenth Century Ireland: Kingdom or Colony?* (Cambridge, 2000).

O'Malley, Kate, *Ireland, India and Empire: Indo-Irish Radical Connections, 1919–64* (Manchester, 2008).

O'Shea, Helen, 'Irish Interaction with Empire: The Cyprus Emergency, 1955–59', (University of Edinburgh Unpublished Ph.D. thesis, 2010).

Ó Siochrú, Micheál, *God's Executioner: Oliver Cromwell and the Conquest of Ireland* (London, 2008).

Palmer, Stanley, *Police and Protest in England and Ireland, 1780–1850* (Cambridge, 1988).

Pares, Richard, 'A Quarter Millennium of Anglo-Scottish Union', *History*, xxxix (1954).

Parry, Jonathan, 'From the 39 Articles to the 39 Steps: Reflections on the Thought of John Buchan', in Michael Bentley (ed.), *Public and Private Doctrine: Essays in British History Presented to Maurice Cowling* (Cambridge, 2002).

Paseta, Senia, 'Nationalist Responses to Two Royal Visits to Ireland, 1900 and 1903', *Irish Historical Studies*, 31, 124 (November 1999).

——, *Before the Revolution: Nationalism, Social Change and Ireland's Catholic Elite, 1879–1922* (Cork, 1999).

Paterson, Lindsay, *A Diverse Assembly: The Debate on a Scottish Parliament* (Edinburgh 1998).

Paterson, Raymond Campbell, *King Lauderdale, The Corruption of Power: The Life of John Maitland, Second Earl and Only Duke of Lauderdale* (Edinburgh, 2007).

Patterson, Henry, *Class Conflict and Sectarianism: The Protestant Working Class and the Belfast Labour Movement, 1868–1920* (Belfast, 1980).

——, 'Party versus Order: Ulster Unionism and the Flags and Emblems Act', *Contemporary British History*, 13, 4 (1999).

——, 'Brian Maginess and the Limits of Liberal Unionism', *Irish Review*, 25 (1999–2000).

——, 'In the Land of King Canute: the Influence of Border Unionism on Ulster Unionist Politics, 1945–63', *Contemporary British History*, 20, 4 (2006).

——, and Eric Kaufmann, *Unionism and Orangeism in Northern Ireland since 1945* (Manchester, 2007).

Penman, Michael, *David II* (Edinburgh, 2005).

Pentland, Gordon, 'Scotland and the Creation of a National Reform Movement, 1830–32', *Historical Journal*, 48, 4 (December, 2005).

Perkin, Harold, *The Age of the Railway* (London, 1970).

Peters, Marie, 'Early Hanoverian Consciousness: Empire or Europe?', *English Historical Review*, 122, 497 (June 2007).

Phillipson, Nicholas, 'Scottish Public Opinion and the Union in the Age of the Association' in N.T. Phillipson and Rosalind Mitchison (eds), *Scotland in the Age of Improvement* (Edinburgh, 1970).

——, *The Scottish Whigs and the Reform of the Court of Session, 1785–1830* (Edinburgh, 1990).

——, *Adam Smith: An Enlightened Life* (London, 2010).

Pittock, Murray, *Celtic Identity and the British Image* (Manchester, 1999).

——, *Scottish Nationality* (Basingstoke, 2001).

Pocock, J.G.A., 'Empire, State and Confederation: The War of Independence as a Crisis in Multiple Monarchy' in John Robertson (ed.), *A Union for Empire: Political Thought and the Union of 1707* (Cambridge, 1995).

Pole, Adam, 'Landlord Responses to the Irish Land War, 1879–82' (University of Dublin Unpublished Ph.D. thesis, 2006).

Porter, Andrew (ed.), *Oxford History of the British Empire, Volume III: The Nineteenth Century* (Oxford, 1999).

Porter, Bernard, *The Absent Minded Imperialists: Empire, Society and Culture in Britain* (Oxford, 2004).

Potter, Simon, 'Richard Jebb, John Ewart and the Round Table, 1898–1926', *English Historical Review*, 122, 495 (February, 2007).

Powell, David, *Nationhood and Identity: The British State since 1800* (London, 2002).

Powell, Martyn, 'The Reform of the Undertaker System: Anglo-Irish Politics, 1750–67', *Irish Historical Studies*, 31, 121 (May, 1998).

Prebble, John, *The King's Jaunt: George IV in Scotland* (London, 1988).

Pressly, William, *The Life and Art of James Barry* (New Haven and London, 1981).

Pugh, Martin, *The Tories and the People, 1880–1935* (Oxford, 1985).

Quinault, Roland, 'Scots on Top: Tartan Power at Westminster, 1707–2007', *History Today*, 57, no. 7 (July, 2007).

Rae, T.I. (ed.), *The Union of 1707: Its Impact on Scotland* (Glasgow and London, 1974).

Rafferty, Oliver, *The Church, the State and the Fenian Threat, 1861–75* (London, 1999).

——, *The Catholic Church and the Protestant State: Nineteenth Century Irish Realities* (Dublin, 2008).

——, 'The Catholic Church, Ireland and the British Empire, 1800–1921', *Historical Research*, 84, 224 (May, 2011).

Ransom, P.J.G., *Iron Road: The Railway in Scotland* (Edinburgh, 2007).

Raponi, Danilo, 'British Protestants, the Roman Question, and the Formation of Italian National Identity, 1861–75' (University of Cambridge Ph.D. thesis, 2009).

Rees, William, *The Union of England and Wales* (Cardiff, 1948).

Regan-Lefebvre, Jennifer, *Cosmopolitan Nationalism in the Victorian Empire: Ireland, India and the Politics of Alfred Webb* (Cambridge, 2009).

Richards, Judith, 'The English Accession of James VI: "National" Identity, Gender and the Personal Monarchy of England', *English Historical Review*, 117, 472, (2002)

Richards, Peter, *Patronage in British Government* (London, 1963).

Richardson, H.G., and G.O. Sayles, *The Irish Parliament in the Middle Ages* (Philadelphia, 1952).

Ridden, Jennifer, 'Britishness as an imperial and diasporic identity: Irish elite perspectives, *c.*1820s–1870s' in Peter Gray (ed.), *Victoria's Ireland? Irishness and Britishness, 1837–1901* (Dublin, 2004).

Riedi, Eliza, 'Women, Gender and the Promotion of Empire: the Victoria League, 1901–14', *Historical Journal*, 45, 3 (September, 2002).

Riley, P.W.J., *The English Ministers and Scotland, 1707–27* (London, 1964).

——, *The Union of England and Scotland* (Manchester, 1978).

——, *King William and the Scottish Politicians* (Edinburgh, 1979).

Robbins, Keith, *Great Britain: Identities, Institutions and the Idea of Britishness* (Harlow, 1998).

Robbins, Michael, *The Railway Age* (Manchester, 1998).

Roberts, Andrew, *Eminent Churchillians* (London, 1994).

Roberts, Matthew, 'Villa Toryism and Popular Conservatism in Leeds, 1885–1902', *Historical Journal*, 46, 1 (March, 2006).

Robertson, C.J.A., *The Origins of the Scottish Railway System, 1722–1844* (Edinburgh, 1983).

Robertson, John (ed.), *A Union for Empire: Political Thought and the Union of 1707* (Cambridge, 1995).

Rodger, Richard, *The Transformation of Edinburgh: Land, Property and Trust in the Nineteenth Century* (Cambridge, 2001).

Rodner, W.S., 'Covenanters, Leaguers, Moderates: British Support for Ulster, 1913–14', *Eire-Ireland*, 17, 3 (1982).

Rosie, Michael, *The Sectarian Myth in Scotland: of Bitter Memory and Bigotry* (Basingstoke, 2004).

——, 'Protestant Action and the Edinburgh Irish' in Martin Mitchell (ed.), *New Perspectives on the Irish in Scotland* (Edinburgh, 2008).

Rossner, Philipp Robinson, *Scottish Trade in the Wake of Union, 1700–1760* (Stuttgart, 2008).

Royle, Trevor, *Fighting Mac: The Downfall of Major General Sir Hector MacDonald* (Edinburgh, 2003).

——, *The Flowers of the Forest: Scotland and the Great War* (Edinburgh, 2007).

Russell, Conrad, 'Composite Monarchies in Early Modern Europe', in Alexander Grant and Keith Stringer (eds), *Uniting the Kingdom? The Making of British History* (London, 1995).

Ryan, Ray, *Ireland and Scotland: Literature and Culture, State and Nation, 1966–2000* (Oxford, 2002).

Savage, D.C., 'Scottish Politics, 1885–6', *Scottish Historical Review*, xl (1961).

——, 'The Origins of the Ulster Unionist Party, 1885–6', *Irish Historical Studies*, xii, 47 (March 1961).

——, 'The Irish Unionists, 1867–86', *Eire-Ireland*, 2 (1967).

Scarisbrick, Diana, *Ancestral Jewels* (London, 1989).

Scott, David, 'The "Northern Gentlemen", the Parliamentary Independents, and Anglo-Scottish Relations in the Long Parliament', *Historical Journal*, 42, 2 (June, 1999).

——, 'The Barwis Affair: Political Allegiance and the Scots during the British Civil Wars', *English Historical Review*, 115, 463 (2000).

Scott, Paul Henderson, *1707: The Union of Scotland and England* (Edinburgh, 1979).

——, *Andrew Fletcher and the Treaty of Union* (Edinburgh, 1992).

——, *The Boasted Advantages: The Consequences of the Union of 1707* (Edinburgh, 1999).

——, *The Union of 1707: Why and How* (Edinburgh, 2006).

Seawright, David, *An Important Matter of Principle: The Decline of the Scottish Conservative and Unionist Party* (Ashgate, 1999).

Senior, Hereward, *Orangeism in Ireland and Britain, 1795–1836* (London, 1966).

Shannon, Catherine, *Arthur J Balfour and Ireland, 1874–1922* (Washington, 1988).

Shaw, Dougal, 'Thomas Wentworth and Monarchical Ritual in Early Modern Ireland', *Historical Journal*, 49, 2 (June, 2006).

Shaw, John Stuart, *The Management of Scottish Society, 1707–64: Power, Nobles, Lawyers, Edinburgh Agents and English Influences* (Edinburgh, 1983).

——, *The Political History of Eighteenth Century Scotland* (Basingstoke, 1999).

Shawcross, William, *Queen Elizabeth, The Queen Mother: The Official Biography* (London, 2009).

Shields, Andrew, *The Irish Conservative Party, 1852–68: Land, Politics and Religion* (Dublin, 2006).

Small, Stephen, *Political Thought in Ireland, 1776–1798: Republicanism, Patriotism and Radicalism* (Oxford, 2002).

Smith, Anthony D., *Chosen Peoples: Sacred Sources of National Identity* (Oxford, 2003).

Smith, Jeremy, *The Tories and Ireland, 1910–14: Conservative Party Politics and the Home Rule Crisis* (Dublin, 2002).

——, ' "Ever Reliable Friends"? The Conservative Party and Ulster Unionism in the Twentieth Century', *English Historical Review*, 121, 490 (February, 2006).

Smout, T.C., *Scottish Trade on the Eve of the Union* (Edinburgh, 1963).

—— (ed.), *Anglo-Scottish Relations from 1603 to 1900* (Oxford, 2005).

Smyth, James J., *Labour in Glasgow: Socialism, Suffrage, Sectarianism* (East Linton, 2000).

Smyth, James J, 'Resisting Labour: Unionists, Liberals and Moderates in Glasgow between the Wars', *Historical Journal*, 46 (2003).

Smyth, Jim (ed.), *Revolution, Counter-revolution and Union: Ireland in the 1790s* (Cambridge, 2000).

——, *The Making of the United Kingdom, 1660–1800* (London, 2001).

Spence, Joseph, 'The Philosophy of Irish Toryism, 1833–52: A Study of Reactions to Liberal Reformism in Ireland in the Generation between the First Reform Act and the Famine', (University of London Unpublished Ph.D. thesis, 1990).

——, 'Isaac Butt, Nationality and Irish Toryism, 1833–52', *Bullán*, 2 (1995).

——, 'Isaac Butt, Irish Nationality and the Conditional Defence of the Union, 1833–70' in D.G Boyce and Alan O'Day (eds), *Defenders of the Union: A Survey of British and Irish Unionism since 1800* (London, 2001).

Spiers, Edward, 'Army Organisation and Society in Nineteenth Century Ireland' in Thomas Bartlett and Keith Jeffery (eds), *A Military History of Ireland* (Cambridge, 1996).

——, *The Victorian Soldier in Africa* (Manchester, 2004).

——, *The Scottish Soldier and Empire, 1854–1902* (Edinburgh, 2006).

Spurlock, R. Scott, *Cromwell and Scotland: Conquest and Religion* (Edinburgh, 2007).

Stewart, B (ed.), *Hearts and Minds: Irish Culture and Society under the Union* (Monaco, 2002).

Stephen, Jeffrey, *Scottish Presbyterians and the Act of Union, 1707* (Edinburgh, 2007).

Stewart, A.T.Q., *The Narrow Ground: Aspects of Ulster, 1609–1969* (London, 1977).

Stewart, J., 'The National Health Service in Scotland, 1947–74: Scottish or British?', *Historical Research*, 76, 193 (2003).

Stuart, Mark, *John Smith: A Life* (London, 2005).

Sykes, Alan, *Tariff Reform in British Politics, 1903–13* (Oxford, 1979).

——, 'Radical Conservatism and the Working Classes in Edwardian England: The Case of the Workers Defence Union', *English Historical Review*, 113, 454 (1998).

Szechi, Daniel, *Jacobitism and Tory Politics, 1710–14* (Edinburgh, 1984).

——, *The Jacobites: Britain and Europe, 1688–1788* (Manchester, 1994).

——, *George Lockhart of Carnwath, 1681–1731: A Study in Jacobitism* (Edinburgh, 2002).

——, *1715: The Great Jacobite Rebellion* (Edinburgh, 2006).

Tanner, Duncan, Chris Williams, Will Griffith, and Andrew Edwards (eds), *Debating Nationhood and Government in Britain, 1885–1939: Perspectives from the 'Four Nations'* (Manchester, 2007).

Tanner, Roland, 'The Lords of the Articles before 1540: A Reassessment', *Scottish Historical Review*, 79, 2 (October, 2000).

Thompson, Frank, *The End of Liberal Ulster: Land Agitation and Land Reform, 1868–86* (Belfast, 2001).

Thomson, Edith, *The Parliament of Scotland, 1690–1702* (Oxford, 1929).

Thornley, David, 'The Irish Conservatives and Home Rule, 1869–73', *Irish Historical Studies*, 11 (1959).

——, *Isaac Butt and Home Rule* (London, 1964).

Thorpe, D.R., *Alec Douglas-Home* (London, 1996).

Torrance, David, *The Scottish Secretaries* (Edinburgh, 2006).

——, *George Younger: A Life Well Lived* (Edinburgh, 2008).

——, *We in Scotland: Thatcherism in a Cold Climate* (Edinburgh, 2009).

——, *Noel Skelton and the Property-Owning Democracy* (London, 2010).

——, *Salmond: Against the Odds* (Edinburgh, 2011).

Townend, Graham, 'Rendering the Union more complete: The Squadrone Volante and the Abolition of the Scottish Privy Council', *Parliamentary History*, 28, 1 (February, 2009).

Townend, Paul, 'Between Two Worlds: Irish Nationalists and Imperial Crisis, 1878–80', *Past & Present*, 194 (February, 2007).

Truxes, Thomas, *Irish-American Trade, 1660–1783* (Cambridge, 1988).

Tyrrell, Alex, 'The Queen's "Little Trip": The Royal Visit to Scotland in 1842', *Scottish Historical Review*, 82, 1 (April, 2003).

Urquhart, Diane, *Women in Ulster Politics, 1890–1940: A History Not Yet Told* (Dublin, 2000).

——, *The Ladies of Londonderry: Women and Political Patronage* (London, 2007).

Urwin, D.K., 'The Development of Conservative Party Organisation in Scotland until 1912', *Scottish Historical Review*, xliv (1965).

Usherwood, Paul, and Jenny Spencer Smith, *Lady Butler, Battle Artist, 1846–1933* (London, 1987).

Vaughan, Geraldine, 'Shaping the Scottish Past: Irish Migrants and Local Politics in the Monklands in the Second Half of the Nineteenth Century' in Martin Mitchell (ed.), *New Perspectives on the Irish in Scotland* (Edinburgh, 2008).

Vaughan, W.E. (ed.), *A New History of Ireland Volume 5: Ireland under the Union I, 1801–1870* (Oxford, 1989).

—— (ed.), *A New History of Ireland Volume 6: Ireland under the Union II, 1870–1921* (Oxford, 1996).

Velychenko, Stephen, 'Empire Loyalism and Minority Nationalism in Great Britain and Imperial Russia, 1707–1914', *Comparative Studies in Society and History*, 39 (1997).

Vincent, J.R., 'Gladstone and Ireland', *Proceedings of the British Academy*, 62 (1977).

Walker, Brian, *Ulster Politics: The Formative Years, 1868–86* (Belfast, 1989).

Walker, Graham, *Thomas Johnston* (Manchester, 1988).

——, *Intimate Strangers: Political and Cultural Interaction between Scotland and Ulster in Modern Times* (Edinburgh, 1995).

Walker, Graham, *A History of the Ulster Unionist Party: Protest, Pragmatism and Pessimism* (Manchester, 2004).

Walker, John, *The Queen Has Been Pleased: The British Honours System at Work* (London, 1986).

Wallace, Stuart, *John Stuart Blackie: Scottish Scholar and Patriot* (Edinburgh, 2006).

Waller, Philip, *Democracy and Sectarianism: A Political and Social History of Liverpool, 1868–1939* (Liverpool, 1981).

Walton, John, *The British Seaside: Holidays and Resorts in the Twentieth Century* (Manchester, 2000).

Ward, J.T., *The First Century: A History of Scottish Tory Organisation, 1882–1982* (Edinburgh, 1982).

Ward, Paul, *Britishness since 1870* (London, 2004).

——, *Unionism in the United Kingdom, 1918–74* (London, 2005).

Ward, Rachel, *Women, Unionism and Loyalism in Northern Ireland: From Teamakers to Political Actors* (Dublin, 2006).

Warner, Gerald, *The Scottish Tory Party: A History* (London, 1988).

——, 'Disraeli, the Conservative Party and the Government of Ireland, 1868–81', *Parliamentary History*, 18 (1999).

Warren, Alan, 'Disraeli, the Conservatives and the National Church, 1837–81', *Parliamentary History*, 19 (2000).

Watt, Douglas, *Price of Scotland: Darien, Union and the Wealth of Nations* (Edinburgh, 2007).

Weight, Richard, *Patriots: National Identity in Britain, 1940–2000* (Basingstoke, 2003).

Weir, Ron, 'The Scottish and Irish Unions: The Victorian View in Perspective', in S.J. Connolly (ed.), *Kingdoms United? Great Britain and Ireland since 1500: Integration and Diversity* (Dublin, 1999).

Whatley, Christopher, *Scottish Society, 1707–1830: Beyond Jacobitism towards Industrialisation* (Edinburgh, 2000).

——, *Bought and Sold for English Gold: Explaining the Union of 1707*, second edition (Edinburgh, 2001).

——, *The Scots and the Union* (Edinburgh, 2006).

——, and Derek Patrick, 'Contesting Interpretations of the Union of 1707: The Abuse and Use of George Lockhart of Carnwath's Memoirs', *Journal of Scottish Historical Studies* 27, 1 (May, 2007).

—— et al, 'Supplementary Issue: The Union of 1707', *Scottish Historical Review*, 87 (October, 2008).

Wheatley, Michael, 'John Redmond and Federalism in 1910', *Irish Historical Studies*, 32, 127 (May, 2001).

Whelan, Irene, *The Bible War in Ireland: The 'Second Reformation' and the Polarisation of Protestant-Catholic Relations, 1800–40* (Chicago, 2005).

Whelan, Kevin (ed.), *These Fissured Isles: Ireland, Scotland and British History, 1798–1848* (Edinburgh, 2008).

Whelan, Yvonne, *Reinventing Modern Dublin: Streetscape, Iconography and the Politics of Identity* (Dublin, 2003).

Wilkinson, David, 'How did they pass the Union? Secret Service Expenditure', *History*, 82, 266 (April, 1997).

Williamson, Arthur, *Scottish National Consciousness in the Age of James VI* (Edinburgh, 1979).

——, 'Union with England Traditional, Union with England Radical: Sir James Hope and the Mid-Seventeenth Century British State', *English Historical Review*, 110, 436 (1995).

Wilson, Timothy, ' "The most terrible assassination that has yet stained the name of Belfast": The McMahon Murders in Context', *Irish Historical Studies*, xxxvii, 145 (Sept. 2010).

Windscheffel, Alex, *Popular Conservatism in Imperial London, 1868–1906* (London, 2007).

Windscheffel, Ruth Clayton, 'Gladstone and Scott: Family, Identity and Nation', *Scottish Historical Review*, vol.86 (April, 2007).

Withers, Charles, *Urban Highlanders: Highland-Lowland Migration and Urban Gaelic Culture, 1700–1900* (East Linton, 1998).

——, *Geography, Science and National Identity: Scotland since 1520* (Cambridge, 2001).

Wood, Ian, *John Wheatley* (Manchester, 1990).

——, *Crimes of Loyalty: A History of the UDA* (Edinburgh, 2006).

Wormald, Jenny, *Court, Kirk and Community: Scotland, 1470–1625* (Edinburgh, 1991).

——, 'The Creation of Britain: Multiple Kingdoms or Core and Colonies', *Transactions of the Royal Historical Society*, sixth series, vol. 2 (1992).

——, 'The Union of 1603' in Roger Mason (ed.), *Scots and Britons: Scottish Political Thought and the Union of 1603* (Cambridge, 1994).

—— (ed.), *Scotland: A History* (Oxford, 2005).

—— (ed.), *The Seventeenth Century: 1603–1688* (Oxford, 2008).

Young, John R., *The Scottish Parliament 1639–61: A Political and Constitutional Analysis* (Edinburgh, 1996).

——, *Celtic Dimensions of the British Civil Wars* (Edinburgh, 1997).

Young, Kenneth, *Sir Alec Douglas-Home* (London, 1970).

# Index

Bold numbers denote reference to illustrations.